UPSC
Civil Services Preliminary Examination

Practice Questions & Mock Tests

General Studies
Paper I

for UPSC Civil Services Preliminary Examination

G K Publications (P) Ltd

Title   : Practice Questions and Mock Tests: General Studies Paper I
                 UPSC Civil Services Preliminary Examination

Language   : English

Editor's Name : Kannath Prakash

Copyright ©   : 2021 CLIP

Typeset & Published by :

Career Launcher Infrastructure (P) Ltd.

A-45, Mohan Cooperative Industrial Area, Near Mohan Estate Metro Station, New Delhi - 110044

Marketed by :

G.K. Publications (P) Ltd.

Plot No. 9A, Sector-27A, Mathura Road, Faridabad, Haryana-121003

ISBN   : **978-93-91061-54-8**

Word to the Reader

The General Studies Paper I of the UPSC Civil Services Preliminary Examination is a challenging paper for the aspirants. The questions asked are rarely direct and more often than not, is application based. Therefore, mere rote learning of facts will not help. Also, in recent years, questions are based more on current affairs, government schemes and latest developments in economy, polity and science and technology.

Towards the end of the preparation, it is practice that makes the difference.

This book is a collection of high quality questions based on the difficulty level and standard asked in the preliminary examination.

Divided into two parts, Part I of the book is a collection of practice of practice questions, while Part II comprises mock tests.

A thorough perusal of these two Parts will enable the aspirant to have a feel of the latest questions and thereby reinforce their preparation.

Answer key is accompanied by `Explanatory Note' that will complete the information on the question.

We are confident that this book will be of immense help to aspirants in their preparation.

We wish all aspirants the best in their endeavours.

The Publishers

Contents

PART I - PRACTICE QUESTIONS

Practice Questions Set – 1
General Studies Paper I

1. Consider the following statements about International Transport Forum (ITF)
    1. It is an intergovernmental organisation with 60 member countries.
    2. India is a founder member of ITF
    3. The ITF also maintains the International Road Traffic and Accident Database (IRTAD)

   Which of the statements given above is/are correct?

   (a) 1 and 3 only   (b) 2 and 3 only

   (c) 1 and 2 and 3   (d) 2 only

2. An initiative 'YUKTI 2.0 has been launched to help systematically assimilate technologies having commercial potential and information related to incubated start-ups in higher education institutions by which of the following ministries/organisations?

   (a) Ministry of Science and Technology

   (b) Council of Scientific and Industrial Research

   (c) The National Informatics Centre

   (d) Ministry of Human Resource and Development

3. Consider the following statements about Ambubachi Mela of Kamakhya temple
    1. The Kamakhya temple is one of 51 Shakti Peethas
    2. It is an important shrine in the Hindu tradition of Shaktism

   Which of the statements given above is/are correct?

   (a) 1 only   (b) 2 only

   (c) Both 1 and 2   (d) Neither 1 nor 2

4. Favipiravir is now the first oral COVID-19 treatment approved in India

   With reference to it consider the following statements about Favipiravir
    1. It is an antiviral medication that was developed in Japan
    2. Favipiravir can't be used in COVID-19 patients with co-morbid conditions

   Which of the statements given above is/are correct?

   (a) 1 only   (b) 2 only

   (c) Both 1 and 2   (d) Neither 1 nor 2

5. Consider the following statements about Ashadhi Beej
    1. It is a Kutchi New Year celebrated by the Kutch people
    2. It is a small festival to predict the monsoon.
    3. Ashadhi-beej is celebrated only in the region of Kutch

   Which of the statements given above is/are correct?

   (a) 3 only   (b) 2 and 3 only

   (c) 1 and 2 only   (d) 2 only

6. Consider the following statements about YUKTI and YUKTI 2.0
    1. Both these initiatives have been launched by the department of Science and Technology
    2. YUKTI 2.0 is not an extension of earlier version of YUKTI as its objective is to identify ideas relevant in COVID pandemic.

   Which of the statements given above is/are correct?

   (a) 1 only   (b) 2 only

   (c) Both 1 and 2   (d) Neither 1 nor 2

7. A Unique Scheme called Play little, Study little has been launched by which of the following state governments?

   (a) Tripura government

   (b) Tamil Nadu government

   (c) Assam government

   (d) Goa government

8. Consider the following statements about Kamakhya temple
    1. The structure of temple is a hybrid indigenous style called as Nilachal type
    2. Nilachal is a style of Hindu temple architecture in Odisha
    3. This style became popular across India under the Ahom kingdom.

   Which of the statements given above is/are correct?

   (a) 1 only   (b) 2 and 3 only

   (c) 1 and 2 and 3   (d) 2 only

9. Senkaku Islands is a group of uninhabited islands in the East China Sea

   It is a disputed territory between which of the following countries?

   (a) China - Japan

   (b) China - Vietnam

   (c) China - Philippines

   (d) None of the above

10. Bharat Skills Learning platform is a e-learning portal under the aegis of which of the following organisations/ministries?

    (a) Directorate General of Training (DGT)

    (b) Department of Science and Technology(DST)

    (c) Ministry of Labour

    (d) Ministry of Human Resource and Development (HRD)

11. Manodarpan initiatives have been launched recently by which of the following organisations?

    (a) Ministry of Culture

    (b) Ministry of Health and Family Welfare

    (c) HRD Ministry

    (d) Ministry of Tourism

12. Consider the following statements about the Hope Probe

    1. The Hope Probe blasted off from Japan's Tanegashima Space Center

    2. It is the first MARS mission of The Japan Aerospace Exploration Agency (JAXA)

    3. It will not land on the planet, but instead orbit it for a whole Martian year

    Which of the statements given above is/are incorrect?

    (a) 1 and 2 only

    (b) 2 only

    (c) 1, 2 and 3

    (d) 1and 3 only

13. Consider the following statements about the New Consumer Protection Act 2019

    1. Consumers can file complaints from anywhere

    2. Consumers need to hire lawyer to represent their cases.

    3. On misleading advertisements there is fine for manufacturers but no jail term

    Which of the statements given above is/are correct?

    (a) 1 only

    (b) 2 and 3 only

    (c) 1, 2 and 3

    (d) 1and 3 only

14. Consider the following statements about Retrofit of Air-conditioning to improve Indoor Air Quality for Safety and Efficiency (RAISE)

    1. It has been launched by the Ministry of Environment, Forest and Climate Change

    2. The initiative will alleviate the issue of bad air quality in households across the nation and pioneer ways to make them healthier and greener.

    Which of the statements given above is/are correct?

    (a) 1 only

    (b) 2 only

    (c) Both 1 and 2

    (d) Neither 1 nor 2

15. Consider the following statements about MAITREE

    1. It is a joint naval exercise between India and US

    2. Japan and Australia also participated as an observer in the recent MAITREE exercise

    Which of the statements given above is/are incorrect?

    (a) 1 only

    (b) 2 only

    (c) Both 1 and 2

    (d) Neither 1 nor 2

16. Consider the following statements about P7 Heavy Drop System

    1. It is developed indigenously by DRDO

    2. It has been inducted in the Air Force.

    Which of the statements given above is/are correct?

    (a) 1 only

    (b) 2 only

    (c) Both 1 and 2

    (d) Neither 1 nor 2

17. Consider the following statements about Corosure

    1. It has been launched by the Human Resource Development (HRD) Ministry

    2. It is RT-PCR based COVID19 diagnostic kit

    3. It has been developed by Indian School of Science (ISC)

    Which of the statements given above is/are incorrect?

    (a) 1 and 2 only

    (b) 3 only

    (c) 1, 2 and 3

    (d) 1and 3 only

18. Consider the following statements about recently launched India Energy Modeling Forum

    1. Ministry of Power will initially coordinate the activities of the forum

    2. The forum will provide a platform to examine important energy and environmental related issues

    Which of the statements given above is/are correct?

    (a) 1 only   (b) 2 only

    (c) Both 1 and 2   (d) Neither 1 nor 2

19. Consider the following statements about Pneumococcal Polysaccharide Conjugate Vaccine

    1. It is country's first fully indigenously developed vaccine against pneumonia

    2. The vaccine will be used for active immunisation against invasive disease and pneumonia caused by 'Streptococcus pneumonia' among adults.

    Which of the statements given above is/are correct?

    (a) 1 only   (b) 2 only

    (c) Both 1 and 2   (d) Neither 1 nor 2

20. Recently we heard about Kohala project, Karot Hydropower station and Azad Pattan hydel power project in news

    These three projects are going to be constructed on which of the following rivers?

    (a) Jhelum   (b) Chenab

    (c) Sutlej   (d) Brahmaputra

21. Consider the following statements about NISHTHA programme

    1. It is a National Initiative for School Heads' and Teachers' Holistic Advancement at the elementary stage

    2. It is a flagship programme of MHRD to improve learning outcomes.

    3. The first on-line NISHTHA programme has been launched recently in all the States/UTs of India

    Which of the statements given above is/are correct?

    (a) 1 and 2 only   (b) 3 only

    (c) 1, 2 and 3   (d) 1and 3 only

22. Consider the following statements about The Economic and Social Council (ECOSOC)

    1. It one of the six main organs of the United Nations.

    2. Non-governmental organizations have been granted consultative status to the Council

    Which of the statements given above is/are correct?

    (a) 1 only   (b) 2 only

    (c) Both 1 and 2   (d) Neither 1 nor 2

23. Consider the following statements about Animal Husbandry Infrastructure Development Fund

    1. There won't be any contribution by the beneficiaries to avail the Fund

    2. 100% loan to be made available by scheduled banks.

    3. Government of India will provide 3% interest subvention to eligible beneficiaries.

    Which of the statements given above is/are incorrect?

    (a) 1 and 2 only   (b) 3 only

    (c) 1, 2 and 3   (d) 1 only

24. Recently ZyCoV-D has initiated Phase I/ II clinical trials in healthy subjects, making it the first indigenously developed vaccine for COVID-19

    With reference to it consider the following statements about ZyCoV-D

    1. It is a plasmid DNA vaccine

    2. It is developed by Zydus and fully funded by the Department of Biotechnology

    Which of the statements given above is/are correct?

    (a) 1 only   (b) 2 only

    (c) Both 1 and 2   (d) Neither 1 nor 2

25. Consider the following statements about PRASHAD Scheme

    1. The objective is integrated development of all the pilgrimage and heritage destinations of India

    2. The scheme aimed at infrastructure development

    3. It was launched by the Ministry of Culture in the year 2014-15

    Which of the statements given above is/are correct?

    (a) 1 and 2 only   (b) 3 only

    (c) 1, 2 and 3   (d) 2 only

26. Consider the following statements about the Decarbonising Transport in Emerging Economies (DTEE) projects

    1. It is an initiative under the International Transport Forum

    2. India, Argentina, Azerbaijan, and Morocco are current participants of DTEE projects

    Which of the statements given above is/are correct?

    (a) 1 only   (b) 2 only

    (c) Both 1 and 2   (d) Neither 1 nor 2

27. Consider the following statements about Organisation for Economic Co-operation and Development (OECD)

    1. OECD is an intergovernmental economic organisation

2. It was founded in 1961 to stimulate economic progress and world trade.

3. India is not a member of OECD

Which of the statements given above is/are correct?

(a) 1 and 3 only   (b) 2 and 3 only

(c) 1 and 2 and 3   (d) 2 only

28. Consider the following statements about FICCI

1. It is a non-government, not-for-profit organisation

2. FICCI draws its membership from the corporate sector, both private and public sector

3. It is the first port of call for Indian industry, policy makers and the international business community

Which of the statements given above is/are correct?

(a) 1 and 3 only   (b) 3 only

(c) 1 and 2 and 3   (d) 2 only

29. Consider the following statements about Golden Langurs

1. It is an endangered species of monkey

2. It is found only in Assam and parts of Bhutan

Which of the statements given above is/are correct?

(a) 1 only   (b) 2 only

(c) Both 1 and 2   (d) Neither 1 nor 2

30. Consider the following statements about Decarbonising Transport in India project

1. This program has been launched by NITI Aayog in collaboration with International Transport Forum (ITF)

2. This project will design a common transport emissions assessment framework for all the emerging economies

Which of the statements given above is/are correct?

(a) 1 only   (b) 2 only

(c) Both 1 and 2   (d) Neither 1 nor 2

31. Consider the following statements about Skills Build online learning platform

1. It has been developed by the Ministry of Human Resource Development in partnership with the Ministry of Skill Development and Entrepreneurship

2. The Skills Build online learning platform is available to Indian and Foreigner students through Bharatskills e - learning platform of MHRD

Which of the statements given above is/are correct?

(a) 1 only   (b) 2 only

(c) Both 1 and 2   (d) Neither 1 nor 2

32. Consider the following statements about Dairy Infrastructure Development Fund (DIDF)

1. DIDF was announced under NABARD over a period of 3 years in the Union Budget of 2017-18.

2. The Scheme will be implemented only in a few selected states of India

Which of the statements given above is/are correct?

(a) 1 only   (b) 2 only

(c) Both 1 and 2   (d) Neither 1 nor 2

33. A behaviour change campaign called Navigating the New Normal has been launched by which of the following organisations?

(a) NITI Aayog

(b) Ministry of Health and Family Welfare

(c) Environment Ministry

(d) World Health Organisation

34. Consider the following statements about the Society of Indian Defence Manufacturers (SIDM).

1. SIDM is a not-for-profit association

2. It is the apex body of the Indian defence industry.

3. It works closely with the government

Which of the statements given above is/are correct?

(a) 1 only   (b) 2 and 3 only

(c) 1 and 2 and 3   (d) 3 only

35. Consider the following statements about the eBlood Services Mobile App

1. It has been developed by the Health & Family Welfare Ministry

2. This app makes it easy for those in need to request for blood units at various blood banks

Which of the statements given above is/are correct?

(a) 1 only   (b) 2 only

(c) Both 1 and 2   (d) Neither 1 nor 2

36. Plasma bank has been set up by the Delhi government for coronavirus patients. With reference to it consider the following statements about Plasma therapy

1. The plasma of recovered COVID-19 patients contains antigen thereby fighting infection and helping critically ill patients recover

2. The plasma therapy, is still at trial stage and yet to be approved by the ICMR

Which of the statements given above is/are incorrect?

(a) 1 only   (b) 2 only

(c) Both 1 and 2   (d) Neither 1 nor 2

37. Consider the following statements about Tribes India e-Mart

1. It is a specialised e-marketplace only for the tribals

2. The Ministry of Social Justice and Empowerment will train these tribals and help them get registered

3. It will function under the Union Tribal Affairs Ministry.

Which of the statements given above is/are correct?

(a) 1 and 2 only   (b) 2 only

(c) 1 and 3only   (d) 3 only

38. A new web portal for issue of No Objection Certificate (NOC) for power projects and Research Survey Exploration Exploitation (RSEE) activities in the Indian Territorial Waters (TW) and Exclusive Economic Zone (EEZ) has been launched by which of the following Organisations/Ministries?

(a) Ministry of Defence

(b) Ministry of Shipping

(c) Directorate General of Hydrocarbons

(d) None of the above

39. Consider the following statements about United Nations Convention on the Law of the Sea (UNCLOS)

1. UNCLOS divides marine areas into five main zones

2. All areas extending up to 12 nautical miles from a country's coastline are its Exclusive Economic Zone (EEZ)

Which of the statements given above is/are correct?

(a) 1 only   (b) 2 only

(c) Both 1 and 2   (d) Neither 1 nor 2

40. Consider the following statements about Strengthening Teaching-Learning and Results for States Program (STARS)

1. This project aims to improve the quality and governance of school education in six States only.

2. The Program has been approved by Asian Development Bank

3. It will be implemented through the Samagra Shiksha Abhiyan

Which of the statements given above is/are correct?

(a) 1 and 2 only   (b) 3 only

(c) 1 and 3only   (d) 1 only

41. Consider the following statements about Directorate General of Training (DGT)

1. It is an joint initiative of Ministry of trade and Commerce and Ministry of Electronics and Information Technology

2. It is responsible for implementing long and short term institutional training to the nation's youth

3. Skills like Artificial Intelligence (AI), Big Data, 3D - Technology, Cloud Computing and Cyber Security also comes under the aegis of DGT

Which of the statements given above is/are correct?

(a) 1 only   (b) 2 and 3 only

(c) 1 and 2 and 3   (d) 3 only

42. Recently Fugaku supercomputer claimed the top spot. The Supercomputer Fugaku belongs to which of the following countries?

(a) South Korea   (b) Japan

(c) China   (d) United States

43. Consider the following statements about the recently approved Animal Husbandry Infrastructure Development Fund

1. The fund is not a part of the Rs 20 lakh crore stimulus package that was announced by the government last month

2. The eligible beneficiaries would have to contribute minimum 50% money and the balance 50% would be the loan component to be made available by scheduled banks.

Which of the statements given above is/are correct?

(a) 1 only   (b) 2 only

(c) Both 1 and 2   (d) Neither 1 nor 2

44. Consider the following statements about Credit Guarantee Scheme for Sub-ordinate Debt (CGSSD)

1. This scheme extends support to the promoters of all the operational MSMEs

2. The maximum tenure for repayment will be 10 years

Which of the statements given above is/are correct?

(a) 1 only   (b) 2 only

(c) Both 1 and 2   (d) Neither 1 nor 2

45. Consider the following statements about the Credit Guarantee Fund Trust for MSEs (CGTMSE).

1. It has been set up by the consortium of Scheduled Commercial banks (SCB)
2. Both the existing and the new enterprises are eligible to be covered under the scheme.
3. Credit Guarantee Fund Trust for Micro and Small Enterprises (CGTMSE) has been set up to operationalize Credit Guarantee Scheme (CGS)

Which of the statements given above is/are correct?

(a) 1 only   (b) 2 and 3 only
(c) 1 and 2 and 3   (d) 3 only

46. Recently the Indian Navy has inducted an advanced anti-torpedo decoy system called 'Maareech'

With reference to it consider the following statements about Maareech

1. It is capable of being fired from all frontline warships.
2. It has been designed and developed indigenously by the Defence Research and Development Organization (DRDO)
3. It is capable of detecting, locating and neutralizing incoming torpedo.

Which of the statements given above is/are incorrect?

(a) 1 only   (b) 2 and 3 only
(c) 1, 2 and 3   (d) None of the above

47. The Defence Conclave 2020 has been organised by which of the following organisations

(a) Jointly organised by Confederation of Indian Industry (CII) and Defence Research and Development Organisation (DRDO)
(b) Defence Research and Development Organisation (DRDO)
(c) Jointly Organised by Confederation of Indian Industry (CII) and Society of Indian Defence Manufacturers (SIDM)
(d) Ministry of Defence

48. Consider the following statements about Indian National Space promotion and Authorization Centre (IN-SPACE)

1. IN-SPACE will also performs the role of a regulator
2. Its Board will comprise members from the private industry, academia and government of India
3. It will be a separate vertical within the Defence Research and Development Organisation (DRDO)

Which of the statements given above is/are correct?

(a) 1 and 3 only   (b) 2 and 3 only
(c) 1 and 2 only   (d) 3 only

49. Consider the following statements about the Khadi and Village Industries Commission (KVIC)

1. It is a statutory body
2. It is an apex organisation under the Ministry of Rural Development

Which of the statements given above is/are correct?

(a) 1 only   (b) 2 only
(c) Both 1 and 2   (d) Neither 1 nor 2

50. Consider the following statements about the recently launched behaviour change campaign called 'Navigating the New Normal'

1. The web portal will be a repository of strategies and collaterals to practise Covid-safe behaviours
2. It aims to provide open-source access to anyone
3. It has been developed in consultation with the ICMR

Which of the statements given above is/are correct?

(a) 1 only   (b) 2 and 3 only
(c) 1 and 2 only   (d) 3 only

51. Consider the following statements about anti-torpedo decoy system (ATDS)

1. Torpedoes are self propelled weapon with a warhead and can be used only under the water surface
2. India hasn't operationalised any anti-torpedo decoy system (ATDS)
3. ATDS can detect and divert the under-water torpedo attacks on ships and submarines.

Which of the statements given above is/are correct?

(a) 1 only   (b) 2 and 3 only
(c) 1, 2 and 3only   (d) 3 only

52. Consider the following statements about Nasha Mukt Bharat : Annual Action Plan (2020-21)

1. The action plan has been e-launched by the Narcotics Control Bureau (NCB)
2. The action plan will be implemented across all the districts of India in a phase manner

3. It will be combining efforts of Narcotics Bureau, Outreach/Awareness by Social Justice and Treatment through the Health Dept.

Which of the statements given above is/are incorrect?

(a) 1 and 2 only   (b) 2 and 3 only

(c) 1, 2 and 3only   (d) 3 only

53. Consider the following statements about AatmaNirbhar Uttar Pradesh Rojgar Abhiyan

1. It will cover all the districts of Uttar Pradesh

2. It will be undertaken as part of the Centre's Garib Kalyan Rojgar Abhiyan

Which of the statements given above is/are correct?

(a) 1 only   (b) 2 only

(c) Both 1 and 2   (d) Neither 1 nor 2

54. Consider the following statements about the recently inaugurated Quick Interchange Service (QIS)

1. It is a battery swapping facility for electric vehicles

2. It has been launched by the Ministry of Heavy Industries and Public Enterprises under its FAME initiative

Which of the statements given above is/are correct?

(a) 1 only

(b) 2 only

(c) Both 1 and 2

(d) Neither 1 nor 2

55. Consider the following statements about New Space India Limited (NSIL)

1. It is a Central Public Sector Enterprise

2. It is under the administrative control of Department of Space (DOS)

3. Its objective is to scale up both public and private participation in Indian space programmes.

Which of the statements given above is/are correct?

(a) 1 and 2 only   (b) 2 and 3 only

(c) 1, 2 and 3only   (d) 3 only

56. The webinar 'TRIFED Goes Digital' and "Be Vocal for Local' #GoTribal was organised recently by which of the following organisations?

(a) Minister of Tribal Affairs

(b) Ministry of Trade and Commerce

(c) NITI Aayog

(d) Ministry of Rural Development

57. Consider the following statements about Government e-Market Place (GeM)

1. GeM is a completely paperless, cashless and system driven e-market place

2. It is a portal for making procurement by the government officers of both Centre and States

Which of the statements given above is/are correct?

(a) 1 only   (b) 2 only

(c) Both 1 and 2   (d) Neither 1 nor 2

58. Consider the following statements about VanDhan Yojana

1. The Ministry of Tribal Affairs is the nodal agency for this scheme at both central and State level

2. It is a 100% central government funded scheme

3. The objective is to open Van Dhan Vikas Kendras (VDVKs) in predominantly forested tribal villages.

Which of the statements given above is/are correct?

(a) 1 and 2 only   (b) 2 only

(c) 1, 2 and 3only   (d) 1 and 3 only

59. Consider the following statements about Cooperative Banking

1. Co-operative banks are registered under the States Cooperative Societies Act.

2. They don't come under the regulatory ambit of Banking Regulations Act, 1949

Which of the statements given above is/are correct?

(a) 1 only   (b) 2 only

(c) Both 1 and 2   (d) Neither 1 nor 2

60. Consider the following statements about the Directorate General of Supplies and Disposals (DGS&D)

1. It is an erstwhile procurement arm of the central government

2. It has been closed by the Ministry of Commerce

3. Government e-Market Place hosted by Directorate General of Supplies and Disposals (DGS&D)

Which of the statements given above is/are correct?

(a) 1 and 2 only

(b) 2 and 3 only

(c) 1, 2 and 3 only

(d) 3 only

61. The 49th Governing Council Meeting of National Productivity Council (NPC), was held recently

With reference to it consider the following statements about the National Productivity Council (NPC)

1. The GC Meeting of NPC has been conducted every year and it is chaired by the Commerce & Industry Minister

2. It is an autonomous body under Department for Promotion of Industry & Internal Trade (DPIIT)

3. NPC undertakes research in the area of productivity

Which of the statements given above is/are correct?

(a) 1 and 2 only   (b) 2 only

(c) 2 and 3only   (d) 1 and 3 only

62. Consider the following statements about the Cairns Group

1. It is an interest group of 20 agricultural exporting countries including India

2. It seeks to liberalize global trade in agricultural produce.

3. Its members aim to abolish export subsidies and trade-distorting green box of WTO

Which of the statements given above is/are correct?

(a) 1 and 2 only   (b) 2 only

(c) 2 and 3only   (d) 3 only

63. Project PLATINA, the world's largest convalescent plasma therapy trial cum treatment of severe COVID-19 patients has been inaugurated by which of the following states?

(a) Maharashtra   (b) Delhi

(c) Chennai   (d) Uttar Pradesh

64. Consider the following statements about Ottawa Group

1. Canada is leading efforts on United Nations reform through the Ottawa Group

2. India is an active participant of Ottawa group

Which of the statements given above is/are correct?

(a) 1 only   (b) 2 only

(c) Both 1 and 2   (d) Neither 1 nor 2

65. Consider the following statements about Asian Productivity Organisation (APO)

1. National Productivity Council is not a constituent of the Tokyo-based Asian Productivity Organisation (APO)

2. APO is an intergovernmental organization established in 1961 to increase productivity in the Asia-Pacific region

Which of the statements given above is/are correct?

(a) 1 only   (b) 2 only

(c) Both 1 and 2   (d) Neither 1 nor 2

66. Consider the following statements about Samagra Shiksha Abhiyan (SSA)

1. It is an overarching programme for the school education sector extending from pre-school to class 12.

2. It subsumes the three Schemes of Sarva Shiksha Abhiyan (SSA), Rashtriya Madhyamik Shiksha Abhiyan (RMSA) and Teacher Education (TE).

Which of the statements given above is/are correct?

(a) 1 only   (b) 2 only

(c) Both 1 and 2   (d) Neither 1 nor 2

67. Recently a new award called P. (C) Mahalanobis National Award has been constituted by which of the following ministries?

(a) The Department for Promotion of Industry and Internal Trade (DPIIT)

(b) The Ministry of Statistics and Programme Implementation (MoSPI)

(c) Ministry of Home Affairs

(d) None of the above

68. The new process of Classification and Registration of Micro, Small and Medium Enterprises (MSME) has been started from 1st July, 2020.

With reference to it consider the following statements?

1. An MSME in the country will now be known as Udyam

2. No documents or proof are required to be uploaded for registering an MSME

3. Udyam Registration has also been fully integrated with the IT and GST systems.

Which of the statements given above is/are correct?

(a) 1 and 2 only   (b) 3 only

(c) 1, 2 and 3   (d) 1 only

69. Consider the following statements about CogX 2020

1. CogX is one of the world's largest events on e-governance, held annually in London

2. MyGov Corona Helpdesk bagged two awards at the recently held CogX 2020

Which of the statements given above is/are correct?

(a) 1 only   (b) 2 only

(c) Both 1 and 2   (d) Neither 1 nor 2

70. Consider the following statements

    1. The first edition of the Fisheries and Aquaculture Newsletter "MATSYA SAMPADA" has been published recently by NITI Aayog

    2. The Pradhan Mantri MatsyaSampada Yojana (PMMSY) will be implemented over a period of 5 years in all the Coastal States/Union Territories.

    3. The PMMSY will be implemented as a Central Sector Scheme

Which of the statements given above is/are correct?

(a) 1 and 2 only   (b) 2 only

(c) 1 and 3only   (d) None of the above

71. Consider the about the new classification of MSME

    1. A unit with Rs 50 crore of investment and Rs 250 crore of turnover will fall under the 'medium' enterprise category

    2. A new composite formula of classification for manufacturing and services units has been notified

    3. The new definition of MSMEs is based on the MSMED Act, 2006 and now it is different for manufacturing and services units.

Which of the statements given above is/are correct?

(a) 1 and 2 only   (b) 3 only

(c) 1, 2 and 3   (d) 1 only

72. Consider the following statements about One Nation One Ration Card

    1. Ration card portability is aimed at providing intra-state as well as inter-state portability of ration cards.

    2. The Integrated Management of Public Distribution System (IM-PDS) portal and Annavitran portal both are associated with One Nation One Ration Card Scheme

    3. The Annavitran portal enables a migrant worker or his family to avail the benefits of PDS outside their district in any states

Which of the statements given above is/are correct?

(a) 1 and 2 only

(b) 1 and 3 only

(c) 1, 2 and 3

(d) 2 only

73. Consider the following statement about the world's first-ever online (B)S(c) Degree in Programming and Data Science

    1. The Program has been offered by all India Council of Technical Education (AICTE)

    2. This programme is open to anyone who has completed graduation

Which of the statements given above is/are correct?

(a) 1 only   (b) 2 only

(c) Both 1 and 2   (d) Neither 1 nor 2

74. To provide a single platform for research internships, capacity building programs, and workshops across the country, a new scheme called 'Accelerate Vigyan' (AV) has been launched by which of the following organisations?

(a) India School of Science

(b) The Science and Engineering Research Board (SERB)

(c) Department of Biotechnology

(d) Council of Scientific and Industrial Research(CSIR)

75. Consider the following statements about the National Board of Examinations

    1. It comes under the ambit of the National Eligibility cum Entrance Test

    2. The Board was registered as an Autonomous Organization under Ministry of Human Resource and Development

Which of the statements given above is/are incorrect?

(a) 1 only   (b) 2 only

(c) Both 1 and 2   (d) Neither 1 nor 2

76. The Science and Engineering Research Board (SERB) has launched a new scheme called 'Accelerate Vigyan' (AV).

With reference to it consider the following statements about Accelerate Vigyan (AV).

    1. A new component ABHYAAS programme has been created under AV which further divides into 'SAYONJIKA' and 'SANGOSHTI'.

    2. SAYONJIKA is an open-ended program to catalogue the capacity building activities in science and technology supported only by the department of Science and Technology

    3. SANGOSHTI is a pre-existing program of SER(B)

Which of the statements given above is/are correct?

(a) 1 and 2 only   (b) 3 only

(c) 1, 2 and 3   (d) 1 only

77. Recently a report called 'towards a Clean Energy Economy' has been released by which of the following Ministries/Organisations?

(a) The Ministry of Environment, Forest and Climate Change

(b) International Monetary Fund

(c) NITI Aayog

(d) UNFCC

78. Consider the following statements about Emergency Credit Line Guarantee Scheme (ECLGS)

1. It has been introduced by RBI

2. Banks from the Public Sector only can sanction loans under ECLGS

Which of the statements given above is/are correct?

(a) 1 only   (b) 2 only

(c) Both 1 and 2   (d) Neither 1 nor 2

79. Consider the following statements about the Diplomates of National Board (DNB) programme

1. It is as an Autonomous Organization under Ministry of Health and Family Welfare

2. It has been conducting undergraduate and Postgraduate Medical Examinations

Which of the statements given above is/are correct?

(a) 1 only   (b) 2 only

(c) Both 1 and 2   (d) Neither 1 nor 2

80. Consider the following statements about ABHYAAS programme of the Science and Engineering Research Board (SERB)

1. It is an attempt to boost Research and Development in the country by enabling and grooming potential UG /PG level students

2. It will be achieved through two of its subcomponents / programs, namely 'KARYASHALA' (Research Internships) and 'VRITIKA' (High End Workshops).

Which of the statements given above is/are incorrect?

(a) 1 only

(b) 2 only

(c) Both 1 and 2

(d) Neither 1 nor 2

81. Consider the following statements about the fellowship Programme for International Students (FPIS) of National Board of Examinations (NBE)

1. The International Fellowship Programme organised every year for the International Students under the ambit of Ministry of Human Resource development

2. It is being launched for International Students from all countries including SAARC Nations, through common Fellowship Entrance Test

Which of the statements given above is/are correct?

(a) 1 only   (b) 2 only

(c) Both 1 and 2   (d) Neither 1 nor 2

82. Consider the following statements about recently launched Drug Discovery Hackathon

1. It is a joint initiative of Ministry of Health and Family Welfare and World Health Organisation's Solidarity trail

2. It is a national initiative for supporting drug discovery process

3. Professionals and researchers from anywhere in the world can participate.

Which of the statements given above is/are correct?

(a) 1 and 2 only   (b) 3 only

(c) 2 and 3 only   (d) 1 only

83. Consider the following statements about PM Formalization of Micro Food Processing Enterprises scheme

1. PM FME is a centrally sponsored scheme

2. The only objective is to provide financial support for upgradation of existing micro food processing enterprises

3. The PM FME Scheme will not have any Sunset clause

Which of the statements given above is/are correct?

(a) 1 and 2 only   (b) 3 only

(c) 2 and 3 only   (d) 1 only

84. Consider the following statements about Operation Greens Scheme

1. It is being implemented by the Ministry of Food Processing Industries (MoFPI)

2. The scheme has been extended to all perishable fruits and vegetables

3. Any other fruit/vegetable can be added in future on the basis of recommendation by Ministry of Ministry of Food Processing Industries (MoFPI)

Which of the statements given above is/are correct?

(a) 1 and 2 only   (b) 1 and 3 only

(c) 2 only   (d) 1, 2 and 3

85. In a new research, scientists have identified a "recently emerged" strain of influenza virus G4 swine flu that is infecting pigs and that has the potential of triggering a pandemic in which of the following countries?

(a) Afghanistan   (b) Kazakhstan

(c) South Korea   (d) China

86. Consider the following statements about National Mission for Clean Ganga (NMCG)

1. NMCG is the implementation wing of National Ganga Council

2. National Ganga Council has replaced National Ganga River Basin Authority (NGRBA)

3. The Ministry of Water Resources, River Development and Ganga Rejuvenation is the chairman of NGC

Which of the statements given above is/are correct?

(a) 1 and 2 only   (b) 2 only

(c) 1, 2 and 3   (d) 3 only

87. Consider the following statements about Fit Hai to Hit Hai India program

1. The program will be organized under the Fit India campaign.

2. It has been launched jointly by Human Resource Development Ministry and Ministry of Sports and Youth Affairs

Which of the statements given above is/are correct?

(a) 1 only   (b) 2 only

(c) Both 1 and 2   (d) Neither 1 nor 2

88. A new category of awards titled 'Prerak Dauur Samman' introduced by which of the following Ministries?

(a) The Ministry of Housing & Urban Affairs

(b) The Ministry of Human Resource and Development

(c) Ministry of Culture

(d) Department for Promotion of Industry & Internal Trade.

89. The President of India, inaugurated the Asadha Poornima celebrations being observed as Dhamma Chakra Day .

With reference to it consider the following statements

1. It being organized by the International Buddhist Confederation (IBC) in partnership with Ministry of Culture

2. The day marks Buddha's first teaching after attaining Enlightenment to the first five ascetic disciples

Which of the statements given above is/are correct?

(a) 1 only   (b) 2 only

(c) Both 1 and 2   (d) Neither 1 nor 2

90. Recently Hul Divas has been observed by which of the following states?

(a) Jharkhand

(b) Chhattisgarh

(c) Telangana

(d) Odisha

91. Consider the following statements about Aatmanirbhar Bharat App Innovation Challenge

1. It has been launched jointly by the Ministry of Human Resource and Development and The Ministry of Electronics and Information Technology

2. This challenge will run to promote the existing Apps only

Which of the statements given above is/are incorrect?

(a) 1 only   (b) 2 only

(c) Both 1 and 2   (d) Neither 1 nor 2

92. Consider the following statements about the Central Drugs Standard Control Organisation (CDSCO)

1. It comes under the department of Pharmaceuticals under the Ministry of Chemicals and Fertilizers

2. It is the National Regulatory Authority (NRA) of India.

3. Under the Drugs and Cosmetics Act, CDSCO is responsible for approval of Drugs and Conduct of Clinical Trials

Which of the statements given above is/are correct?

(a) 1 and 2 only   (b) 2 and 3only

(c) 1, 2 and 3   (d) 3 only

93. Consider the following statements about National Atlas and Thematic Mapping Organization (NATMO)

1. It functions as a subordinate department under the Department of Science & Technology, Ministry of Science & Technology

2. It is the sole authority for depicting National framework data in the form of thematic maps and atlases

Which of the statements given above is/are correct?

(a) 1 only   (b) 2 only

(c) Both 1 and 2   (d) Neither 1 nor 2

94. Recently, Prime Minister Narendra Modi performed Sindhu Darshan puja at Nimu, the forward brigade place in which of the following states/UT.

(a) Jammu and Kashmir

(b) Ladakh

(c) Himachal Pradesh

(d) None of the above

95. Consider the following statements about the recently launched app called Elyments

1. India's first official social media super app.

2. The app has been built by the Ministry of Electronics and Information Technology

Which of the statements given above is/are correct?

(a) 1 only   (b) 2 only

(c) Both 1 and 2   (d) Neither 1 nor 2

96. The first National Atlas of India in Hindi popularly known as Bharat: Rashtriya Atlas was published in 1957 by which of the following organisations/ministries?

(a) The Ministry of Statistics and Programme Implementation

(b) National Atlas and Thematic Mapping Organization

(c) Survey of India

(d) Ministry of External affairs

97. Consider the following statements about Directorate General of Quality Assurance (DGQA)

1. DGQA comes under Deptt. of Defence Production , Ministry of Defence.

2. It provides Quality Assurance (QA) cover for the entire range of Arms, Ammunitions and Stores supplied to Armed Forces.

Which of the statements given above is/are incorrect?

(a) 1 only   (b) 2 only

(c) Both 1 and 2   (d) Neither 1 nor 2

98. Consider the following statements about the Global Environment Facility (GEF)

1. GEF funds are available to developing countries only

2. The GEF Trust Fund (contributions by donors) administered by UNEP

3. The World Bank serves as the GEF Trustee

Which of the statements given above is/are correct?

(a) 1 and 2 only   (b) 2 and 3only

(c) 1, 2 and 3   (d) 3 only

99. A special winter-grade diesel that remains unfrozen up to minus 33 degree Celsius has been launched by which of the following organisations?

(a) The Ministry of Petroleum and Natural Gas

(b) Petroleum Conservation Research Association

(c) World Energy Forum

(d) None of the above

100. Recently we heard about Sakteng Wildlife Sanctuary which emerged as a disputed territory between which of the following Nations

(a) India - China   (b) India - Nepal

(c) China-Nepal   (d) None of the above

101. Consider the following statements about the Representation of the People Act, 1951

1. It is an act of Parliament of India

2. The Act was enacted by the parliament under Article 327 of Indian Constitution before the first general election.

Which of the statements given above is/are correct?

(a) 1 only   (b) 2 only

(c) Both 1 and 2   (d) Neither 1 nor 2

102. Consider the following statements

1. Every pathogen has specific molecular structures called as antigen.

2. Both the pathogen and antibodies produced by the human immune cells

3. Our immune system hasten thousand types of antibodies and antigens

Which of the statements given above is/are correct?

(a) 1 and 2 only   (b) 2 and 3only

(c) 1, 2 and 3   (d) 1 only

103. The The Global Environment Facility (GEF) serves as financial mechanism for which of the following conventions

1. Convention on Biological Diversity (CBD)

2. United Nations Environment Program (UNEP)

3. United Nations Convention to Combat Desertification (UNCCD)

4. Stockholm Convention on Persistent Organic Pollutants (POPs)

5. Montreal Protocol

Choose the correct one from the options given below

(a) 1 and 5 only   (b) 2 3 and 4 only

(c) 1 3 and 4 only   (d) All of the above

104. Consider the following statements about World Bank's MSME Emergency Response Programme

1. This project will support the Government in providing targeted guarantees to incentivize MSMEs directly to sustain them through the crisis

2. The World Bank Group, excluding its private sector arm - the International Finance Corporation (IFC), will support the government's initiatives to protect the MSME sector

Which of the statements given above is/are correct?

(a) 1 only   (b) 2 only

(c) Both 1 and 2   (d) Neither 1 nor 2

105. Consider the following statements about Kawasaki disease

1. Kawasaki typically affects children aged under five.

2. WHO termed this new illness "multisystem inflammatory disorder".

Which of the statements given above is/are correct?

(a) 1 only   (b) 2 only

(c) Both 1 and 2   (d) Neither 1 nor 2

106. Consider the following statements about the Agriculture Infrastructure Fund

1. It will provide a short term debt financing facilityfor investment in viable projects for post-harvest management Infrastructure

2. All loans under this financing facility will have interest subvention of 3% per annum

3. A centralised National level Monitoring Committees will be set up to ensure real-time monitoring and effective feed-back across all the states and districts

Which of the statements given above is/are incorrect?

(a) 1 and 2 only   (b) 2 only

(c) 1, 2 and 3   (d) 1and 3 only

107. Consider the following statements about Affordable Rental Housing Complexes (AHRCs)

1. It is a sub-scheme under Pradhan Mantri Awas Yojana - Urban (PMAY - U)

2. The government funded housing in the cities and villages will be converted into Affordable Rental Housing Complexes under PPP (public-private partnership) mode

Which of the statements given above is/are correct?

(a) 1 only   (b) 2 only

(c) Both 1 and 2   (d) Neither 1 nor 2

108. The Road Transport and Highways Ministry has prepared a blueprint for implementing the scheme of cashless treatment of motor accident victims.

With reference to it consider the following statements about the Scheme

1. The Scheme has been implemented by the Ministry of Road Transport and Highways

2. The scheme to provide compulsory insurance cover to all road users in the country.

Which of the statements given above is/are correct?

(a) 1 only   (b) 2 only

(c) Both 1 and 2   (d) Neither 1 nor 2

109. Consider the following statements about recently released 34th Global Real Estate Transparency Index

1. India has registered one of the largest improvements globally and regionally

2. Global Real Estate Transparency Index is a biennial India published by the World Bank

Which of the statements given above is/are correct?

(a) 1 only   (b) 2 only

(c) Both 1 and 2   (d) Neither 1 nor 2

110. Consider the following statements about National Health Authority (NHA)

1. It is an attached office of the Ministry of Health and Family Welfare with full functional autonomy

2. NHA has been set-up to implement Ayushman Bharat Pradhan Mantri Jan Arogya Yojan(a)

Which of the statements given above is/are correct?

(a) 1 only
(b) 2 only
(c) Both 1 and 2
(d) Neither 1 nor 2

111. The state government has decided to upgrade the DehingPatkai wildlife sanctuary into a national park

Dehing Patkai wildlife sanctuary is situated in which of the following states?

(a) Assam
(b) Arunachal Pradesh
(c) Kerala
(d) Manipur

112. Consider the following statements

1. Wildlife sanctuaries conserve the genetic diversity of the plants, animals birds, etc

2. The Biosphere Reserve provides protection to the entire set of the ecosystem

Which of the statements given above is/are correct?

(a) 1 only
(b) 2 only
(c) Both 1 and 2
(d) Neither 1 nor 2

113. Consider the following statements about the bubonic plague.

1. It is spread mostly by rodents.

2. Human to human transmission of bubonic plague has been ruled out completely

Which of the statements given above is/are correct?

(a) 1 only
(b) 2 only
(c) Both 1 and 2
(d) Neither 1 nor 2

114. Consider the following statements about National Board for Wildlife (NBWL)

1. It is a Statutory Organization

2. It is constituted under the Wildlife Protection Act, 1972.

3. It advises the Central and State Governments on framing policies and measures for conservation of wildlife in the country.

4. It is chaired by the Prime Minister

Which of the statements given above is/are correct?

(a) 1 and 2 only
(b) 2 and 4 only
(c) 1, 2 and 4 only
(d) All of the above

115. Which of the following Nations Parks is/ are situated in the state Assam?

1. Dibru-Saikhowa National Park.

2. Kaziranga National Park.

3. Manas National Park.

4. Nameri National Park.

5. Orang National Park.

Choose the correct one from the options given below

(a) 1 and 5 only
(b) 2 3 and 4 only
(c) 1 3 and 4 only
(d) All of the above

116. Consider the following statements about National Mission for Manuscripts (NMM).

1. It was launched in February 2003 by the Government of India, under the Ministry of HRD

2. Its objectives of the mission is to publish rare and unpublished manuscripts

Which of the statements given above is/are correct?

(a) 1 only
(b) 2 only
(c) Both 1 and 2
(d) Neither 1 nor 2

117. Consider the following statements about Rewa Solar Project

1. The Solar Park was developed by the Solar Energy Corporation of India (SECI), a Central Public Sector Undertaking along with World Bank

2. The Rewa Solar Project was the first solar project in the country to break the grid parity barrier.

3. It is the first renewable energy project to supply to an institutional customer outside the State

Which of the statements given above is/are correct?

(a) 1 and 2 only
(b) 2 and 3 only
(c) 1 and 3 only
(d) All of the above

118. Consider the following statements about Solar Energy Corporation of India ltd

1. It is an autonomous body and doesn't come under the administrative control of the Ministry of New and Renewable Energy (MNRE)

2. Solar Energy Corporation of India (SECI) has been renamed as the Renewable Energy Corporation of India (RECI).

3. SECI is a not-for-profit company under Section-25 of the Companies Act 1956.

Which of the statements given above is/are correct?

(a) 2 only
(b) 2 and 3 only
(c) 1 and 3 only
(d) All of the above

119. The Indian Space Research and Research Organisation (ISRO) gets ready to launch Amazonia -1 satellite next month onboard PSLV.

Amazonia -1 satellite belongs to which of the following nations?

(a) Brazil   (b) Argentina

(c) Peru   (d) Colombia

120. Consider the following statements about Project Mongolian Kanjur

1. The Project has been taken by the Ministry of Culture

2. The complete volumes of Mongolian Kanjur reprinted under the National Mission for Manuscripts (NMM) has been handed over to Mongolia

Which of the statements given above is/are correct?

(a) 1 only   (b) 2 only

(c) Both 1 and 2   (d) Neither 1 nor 2

121. Often we heard about Projects like Arunank, Beacon, Brahmank, Chetak, Sampark, Setuk, Sewak, Shivalik, Swastik etc. in the news

These projects are operated under which of the following Ministries/organisations?

(a) National Highway Authority of India

(b) Border Road Organisation

(c) Ircon International Limited

(d) None of the above

122. Consider the following statements about India Global Week 2020

1. It is a virtual conference being organised recently in the New Delhi

2. The forum focused on India's trade and foreign investment prospects.

Which of the statements given above is/are correct?

(a) 1 only   (b) 2 only

(c) Both 1 and 2   (d) Neither 1 nor 2

123. Consider the following statements about Aatamanirbhar Skilled Employee Employer Mapping

1. It has been launched by the Ministry of Labour & Employment

2. ASEEM will bridge the demand supply gap in skilled and unskilled workforce market

3. ASEEM will provide employers a platform to assess the availability of workforce and formulate their hiring plans

Which of the statements given above is/are correct?

(a) 3 only   (b) 2 and 3 only

(c) 1 and 3 only   (d) All of the above

124. Cycles4Change Challenge initiatives has been launched recently by which of the following organisations

(a) The Ministry of Youth Affairs and Sports

(b) Ministry of Human Resource and Development

(c) Ministry of Environment, Forest and Climate Change

(d) Ministry of Housing and Urban Affairs.

125. Consider the following statements about Fish Cryobanks

1. It will facilitate all time availability of fish of desired species to fish farmers.

2. This would be the first time in the world when "Fish Cryobank" will be establishedby the National Fisheries Development Board (NFDB).

Which of the statements given above is/are correct?

(a) 1 only   (b) 2 only

(c) Both 1 and 2   (d) Neither 1 nor 2

126. Recently a virtual workshop with Central Ministries/Departments in furtherance of the Government of India's decision to monitor the performance of 29 select Global Indices to drive reforms and growth in the country was organised by which of the following organisations?

(a) United Nation Development Programme

(b) World Bank

(c) NITI Aayog

(d) Ministry of External Affairs

127. Consider the following statements about ATL App Development Module

1. It is a free online app development course exclusively for school students across the country.

2. The course has been jointly developed by NITI Aayog's AIM and the Ministry of Electronics and Information Technology

Which of the statements given above is/are correct?

(a) 1 only

(b) 2 only

(c) Both 1 and 2

(d) Neither 1 nor 2

128. Consider the following statements about Generation Unlimited

1. It is a new UNESCO-led global partnership
2. It aims to ensure that every young person age 10-24 is in some form of school, learning, or age-appropriate employment by 2030.

Which of the statements given above is/are correct?

(a) 1 only   (b) 2 only
(c) Both 1 and 2   (d) Neither 1 nor 2

129. Recently M-STrIPES app, CaTRAT software and the Extract Compare programs were in news as these features have been used extensively in which of the following programs?

(a) Tiger Census   (b) Elephant Census
(c) Rhino Census   (d) None of the above

130. Consider the following statements

1. In Atal Tinkering Labs students of class 6th to 12th acquire problem-solving mindset across schools in Indi(a)
2. Atal Innovative Mission is the Government of India's flagship initiative to promote a culture of innovation and entrepreneurship in the country.

Which of the statements given above is/are correct?

(a) 1 only   (b) 2 only
(c) Both 1 and 2   (d) Neither 1 nor 2

131. Recently a virtual workshop with Central Ministries/Departments in furtherance of the Government of India's decision to monitor the performance of 29 select Global Indices to drive reforms and growth in the country was organised by which of the following organisations?

(a) United Nations Development Program
(b) World Bank
(c) NITI Aayog
(d) Ministry of External Affairs

132. Consider the following statements about ATL App Development Module

1. It is a free online app development course exclusively for school students across the country.
2. The course has been jointly developed by NITI Aayog's AIM and the Ministry of Electronics and Information Technology

Which of the statements given above is/are correct?

(a) 1 only   (b) 2 only
(c) Both 1 and 2   (d) Neither 1 nor 2

133. Consider the following statements about Generation Unlimited

1. It is a new UNESCO-led global partnership
2. It aims to ensure that every young person age 10-24 is in some form of school, learning, or age-appropriate employment by 2030.

Which of the statements given above is/are correct?

(a) 1 only   (b) 2 only
(c) Both 1 and 2   (d) Neither 1 nor 2

134. Recently M-STrIPES app, CaTRAT software and the Extract Compare programs were in news as these features have been used extensively in which of the following programs?

(a) Tiger Census   (b) Elephant Census
(c) Rhino Census   (d) None of the above

135. Consider the following statements

1. In Atal Tinkering Labs students of class 6th to 12th acquire problem-solving mindset across schools in India.
2. Atal Innovative Mission is the Government of India's flagship initiative to promote a culture of innovation and entrepreneurship in the country.

Which of the statements given above is/are correct?

(a) 1 only   (b) 2 only
(c) Both 1 and 2   (d) Neither 1 nor 2

136. Which of the following is not an initiative of Atal Innovation Mission?

1. Atal Tinkering Labs
2. Mentor India Campaign
3. ARISE
4. Generation Unlimited

Choose the correct one from the options given below

(a) 1 and 2 only   (b) 2 3 and 4 only
(c) 1, 2 and 3   (d) 4 only

137. Consider the following statements about the National Tiger Conservation Authority

1. It is constituted under enabling provisions of the Wildlife (Protection) Act, 1972
2. It is a statutory body
3. Project Tiger is a Centrally Sponsored Scheme

Which of the statements given above is/are correct?

(a) 1 and 2 only   (b) 2 and 3 only
(c) 1, 2 and 3   (d) 3 only

138. To enlighten about the ancient form of health science- NadiVigyan and its fruitful benefits in curing various spinal disorders, a webinar has been presented by which of the following Ministries?

(a) Ministry of Health and Family Welfare

(b) Ministry of Ayush

(c) Department of Science and Technology

(d) None of the above

139. Consider the following statements about NATGRID

1. It comes under the ambit of External affairs Ministry

2. NATGRID is exempted from the Right to Information Act, 2005

Which of the statements given above is/are correct?

(a) 1 only   (b) 2 only

(c) Both 1 and 2   (d) Neither 1 nor 2

140. Which of the following geographical areas are part of India's tiger landscape

1. Gangetic Plains

2. Central Indian Landscape

3. Western Ghats

4. Brahmaputra Plains

5. The Sundarbans.

Choose the correct one from the options given below

(a) 1 and 5 only   (b) 2, 3, 4 and 5only

(c) 1, 2 and 3   (d) All of the above

141. Consider the following statements about P7 Heavy Drop System

1. It is developed indigenously by DRDO

2. It has been inducted in the Air Force.

Which of the statements given above is/are correct?

(a) 1 only   (b) 2 only

(c) Both 1 and 2   (d) Neither 1 nor 2

142. Consider the following statements about Corosure

1. It has been launched by the Human Resource Development (HRD) Ministry

2. It is RT-PCR based COVID19 diagnostic kit

3. It has been developed by Indian School of Science (ISC)

Which of the statements given above is/are incorrect?

(a) 1 and 2 only   (b) 3 only

(c) 1, 2 and 3   (d) 1and 3 only

143. Consider the following statements about recently launched India Energy Modeling Forum

1. Ministry of Power will initially coordinate the activities of the forum

2. The forum will provide a platform to examine important energy and environmental related issues

Which of the statements given above is/are correct?

(a) 1 only   (b) 2 only

(c) Both 1 and 2   (d) Neither 1 nor 2

144. Consider the following statements about Pneumococcal Polysaccharide Conjugate Vaccine

1. It country's first fully indigenously developed vaccine against pneumonia

2. The vaccine will be used for active immunisation against invasive disease and pneumonia caused by 'Streptococcus pneumonia' among adults.

Which of the statements given above is/are correct?

(a) 1 only   (b) 2 only

(c) Both 1 and 2   (d) Neither 1 nor 2

145. Recently we heard about Kohala project, Karot Hydropower station and Azad Pattan hydel power project in news

These three projects are going to be constructed on which of the following rivers?

(a) Jhelum   (b) Chenab

(c) Sutlej   (d) Brahmaputra

146. Consider the following statements about NISHTHA programme

1. It is a National Initiative for School Heads' and Teachers' Holistic Advancement at the elementary stage

2. It is a flagship programme of MHRD to improve learning outcomes.

3. The first on-line NISHTHA programme has been launched recently in all the States/UTs of India

Which of the statements given above is/are correct?

(a) 1 and 2 only   (b) 3 only

(c) 1, 2 and 3   (d) 1and 3 only

147. Consider the following statements aboutThe Economic and Social Council (ECOSOC)

1. It one of the six main organs of the United Nations.

2. Non-governmental organizations have been granted consultative status to the Council

Which of the statements given above is/are correct?

(a) 1 only　　　　　(b) 2 only

(c) Both 1 and 2　　(d) Neither 1 nor 2

148. Consider the following statements about Animal Husbandry Infrastructure Development Fund

1. There won't be any contribution by the beneficiaries to avail the Fund

2. 100% loan to be made available by scheduled banks.

3. Government of India will provide 3% interest subvention to eligible beneficiaries.

Which of the statements given above is/are incorrect?

(a) 1 and 2 only　　(b) 3 only

(c) 1, 2 and 3　　　(d) 1 only

149. Recently ZyCoV-D has initiated Phase I/ II clinical trials in healthy subjects, making it the first indigenously developed vaccine for COVID-19

With reference to it consider the following statements about ZyCoV-D

1. It is a plasmid DNA vaccine

2. It is developed by Zydus and fully funded by the Department of Biotechnology

Which of the statements given above is/are correct?

(a) 1 only

(b) 2 only

(c) Both 1 and 2

(d) Neither 1 nor 2

150. Consider the following statements about PRASHAD Scheme

1. The objective is integrated development of all the pilgrimage and heritage destinations of India

2. The scheme aimed at infrastructure development

3. It was launched by the Ministry of Culture in the year 2014-15

Which of the statements given above is/are correct?

(a) 1 and 2 only

(b) 3 only

(c) 1, 2 and 3

(d) 2 only

ANSWER KEY

1. (a)	2. (d)	3. (c)	4. (a)	5. (c)	6. (d)	7. (a)	8. (a)	9. (d)	10. (a)
11. (c)	12. (b)	13. (a)	14. (d)	15. (c)	16. (a)	17. (b)	18. (b)	19. (a)	20. (a)
21. (a)	22. (c)	23. (a)	24. (a)	25. (d)	26. (c)	27. (c)	28. (c)	29. (c)	30. (a)
31. (d)	32. (a)	33. (a)	34. (c)	35. (d)	36. (c)	37. (c)	38. (a)	39. (a)	40. (c)
41. (d)	42. (b)	43. (d)	44. (b)	45. (b)	46. (d)	47. (c)	48. (c)	49. (a)	50. (c)
51. (d)	52. (a)	53. (b)	54. (a)	55. (a)	56. (a)	57. (a)	58. (b)	59. (a)	60. (c)
61. (c)	62. (b)	63. (a)	64. (d)	65. (b)	66. (c)	67. (b)	68. (c)	69. (b)	70. (d)
71. (a)	72. (a)	73. (d)	74. (b)	75. (c)	76. (b)	77. (c)	78. (d)	79. (a)	80. (c)
81. (b)	82. (c)	83. (d)	84. (a)	85. (d)	86. (a)	87. (c)	88. (a)	89. (c)	90. (a)
91. (c)	92. (b)	93. (c)	94. (b)	95. (a)	96. (b)	97. (d)	98. (d)	99. (d)	100. (d)
101. (a)	102. (d)	103. (c)	104. (d)	105. (c)	106. (d)	107. (a)	108. (b)	109. (a)	110. (c)
111. (a)	112. (d)	113. (a)	114. (c)	115. (d)	116. (b)	117. (b)	118. (b)	119. (a)	120. (a)
121. (b)	122. (b)	123. (a)	124. (d)	125. (b)	126. (c)	127. (a)	128. (b)	129. (a)	130. (c)
131. (c)	132. (a)	133. (b)	134. (a)	135. (c)	136. (d)	137. (c)	138. (d)	139. (b)	140. (d)
141. (a)	142. (b)	143. (b)	144. (a)	145. (a)	146. (a)	147. (c)	148. (a)	149. (a)	150. (d)

EXPLANATION

1. (a) • India has been a member of ITF, an intergovernmental organisation for transport policy, since 2008.

• The International Transport Forum at the OECD is an intergovernmental organisation with 60 member countries.

• ITF is the only global body that covers all transport modes. The ITF is administratively integrated with the OECD, yet politically autonomous.

• The ITF maintains the International Road Traffic and Accident Database (IRTAD), a comprehensive database of statistics related to road safety. IRTAD also acts as a permanent working group of the ITF.

• The International Transport Forum was created on 18 May 2006 by ministers from 43 countries.

2. (d) • The HRD Ministry has launched an initiative 'YUKTI 2.0 to help systematically assimilate technologies having commercial potential and information related to incubated startups in our higher education institutions.

• It is an initiative of MHRD's Innovation Cell for Higher Education Institutes and AICTE

3. (c) • For the first time in recorded history, the annual Ambubachi rituals at the sacred Kamakhya temple in Guwahati are wearing a deserted look.

• Located atop the Nilachal Hills, Kamakhya temple is one of the 51 Shakti Peeths in the country.

• The Kamakhya temple is one of 51 Shakti Peethas, important shrines in the Hindu tradition of Shaktism (followers of the Shakti cult) that are spread across India, Bangladesh, Nepal, Pakistan, China and Sri Lanka.

4. (a) • Favipiravir is an antiviral medication that was developed in Japan and got approval for treating people with influenza.

• It reportedly showed anti-viral activity against all subtypes of influenza virus strains.

• Favipiravir is among the many drugs currently being trialled to treat COVID-19 (alongside Ebola drug Remdesivir, the HIV drug combination lopinavir/ritonavir, and a combination of lopinavir/ritonavir with Interferon beta, and others).

• Favipiravir can be used in COVID-19 patients with co-morbid conditions such as diabetes and heart disease with mild to moderate COVID-19 symptoms

5. (c) • As for people of Kutch, this day is associated with beginning of rains in Kutch, Gujarat. Kutch is largely a desert area therefore people living valuate rain very much.

• Ashadhi-beej is celebrated mainly at two places in India - Vishvanath temple in Varanasi, UP and Mulesh Mahadev in Umreth, Gujarat.

• Spring season to predict the weather, during the pre-monsoon, there is a small festival called Ashadhi-beej to predict the monsoon.

• During Ashadhi-beej, they check the moisture in the atmosphere to help predict which crop would do best in coming monsoon.

6. (d) • YUKTI 2.0' is a systematic attempt to collate the technologies and innovations developed by students, faculty, startups in HEIs and to ensure that innovators from our education institutes get suitable opportunities and support for commercialization of their innovations.

• YUKTI 2.0 is logical extension of earlier version of 'YUKTI', an initiative of MHRD, to identify ideas relevant in COVID pandemic.

• Earlier, the Minister had launched the YUKTI (Young India combating COVID with Knowledge, Technology and Innovation) web portal on 11 April, 2020.

• Through this portal, the Ministry of Human Resource Development will endeavor to ensure that students, teachers and researchers in higher educational institutions are getting appropriate support to meet the requirements needed to advance their technologies and innovations.

7. (a) • The Tripura government has decided to start a scheme called 'EktuKhelo, EktuPadho' which means 'Play little, Study little', from June 25.

• As per the scheme, the students would be getting audio and video contents on learning activities, projects along with fun and gaming activities via SMS or WhatsApp services.

8. (a) • The current structural temple, built and renovated many times in the period 8th-17th century, gave rise to a hybrid indigenous style that is sometimes called the Nilachal type a temple with a hemispherical dome on a cruciform base.

- The current structure has been built during the Ahom times, with remnants of the earlier Koch temple carefully preserved.

- Nilachal is a style of Hindu temple architecture in Assam, India, that is characterized by a bulbous polygonal dome over a cruciform ratha type bada.

- This hybrid style developed first in the Kamakhya temple on the Nilachal hills under the Koch kingdom and became popular as a style later under the Ahom kingdom.

9. (d)

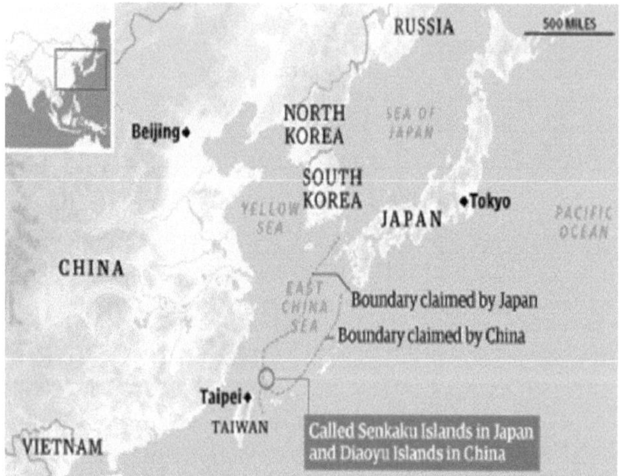

- These are a group of uninhabited islands in the East China Sea. Japan administers and controls the Senkaku islands.

- The islands are known as Diaoyu Islands in China and the Diaoyutai Islands in Taiwan

- Territorial sovereignty over the islands and the maritime boundaries around them are disputed between the People's Republic of China, the Republic of China (Taiwan), and Japan.

10. (a)
- Bharat Skills is a e-learning portal of the Directorate General of Training (DGT), Ministry of Skill Development and Entrepreneurship.

- Bharat Skills is a Central Repository for skills which provides NSQF curriculum, course material, videos, question banks and mock test etc. for ITI/NSTI Students and Teachers.

11. (c)
- Union HRD Minister, launched the Manodarpan initiative of HRD Ministry

- During the COVID pandemic, the HRD Ministry felt the need to focus on continuing education on the academic front and the mental well-being of the students.

12. (b)
- The first Arab space mission to Mars has blasted off aboard a rocket from Japan, with its unmanned probe - called Al-Amal, or Hope

- The Emirati project is one of three racing to Mars, including Tianwen-1 from China and Mars 2020 from the United States, taking advantage of a period when the Earth and Mars are nearest.

- The Hope Probe blasted off from Japan's Tanegashima Space Center for a seven-month journey to the red planet, where it will orbit and send back data about the atmosphere.

13. (a)
- The Bill envisages simplified dispute resolution process, has provision for mediation and e-filing of cases.

- The consumer will be able to file cases in the nearest commission under the jurisdiction of which he resides.

- Consumers can file complaints from anywhere and they do not need to hire lawyer to represent their cases. For mediation, there will be strict timeline fixed in the rules.

- On misleading advertisements there is provision for jail term and fine for manufacturers.

- There is no provision for jail for celebrities but they could be banned for endorsing products if it is found to be misleading.

- A manufacturer or product service provider or product seller will now be responsible to compensate for injury or damage caused by defective product or deficiency in services.

14. (d)
- The Power Ministry also launched "Retrofit of Air-conditioning to improve Indoor Air Quality for Safety and Efficiency" (RAISE) national programme.

- RAISE initiative can potentially alleviate the issue of bad air quality in workspaces across the nation and pioneer ways to make them healthier and greener.

- It is a Joint initiative of EESL and USAID

15. (c)
- Market Integration and Transformation Program for Energy Efficiency (MAITREE) is aimed at accelerating the adoption of cost-effective energy

efficiency measures as a standard practice within buildings, and specifically focuses on cooling.

- MAITREE is a part of the US-India bilateral Partnership between the Ministry of Power and USAID.

16. (a) • DRDO has developed P7 Heavy Drop System which is capable of para dropping military stores up to 7-ton weight class from IL-76 aircraft.

- P-7 Heavy Drop System is used for Para drop of military stores (vehicle/ ammunition/ equipment) of 7 Ton weight class.

- System has been developed successfully with 100% indigenous resources. P-7 HDS has been inducted in the Army.

- The Human Resource Development (HRD) Ministry e-launched the world's most affordable probe free RT-PCR based #COVID19 diagnostic kit, COROSURE developed by Indian Institute of Technology Delhi (IIT)

17. (b) • The Human Resource Development (HRD) Ministry e-launched the world's most affordable probe free RT-PCR based #COVID19 diagnostic kit, COROSURE developed by Indian Institute of Technology Delhi (IIT)

- The test, Corosure, has been billed as the world's most affordable probe free RT-PCR based Covid-19 diagnostic kit.

- The test, Corosure, has been billed as the world's most affordable probe free RT-PCR based Covid-19 diagnostic kit.

- The product is approved by the Indian Council of Medical Research (ICMR) and the Drug Controller General of India (DCGI).

18. (b) • Sustainable Growth Pillar is an important pillar of India-US Strategic Energy Partnership co-chaired by NITI Aayog and USAID.

- The SG pillar entails energy data management, energy modelling and collaboration on low carbon technologies as three key activities.

- In the joint working group meeting of the Sustainable Growth Pillar on July 2, 2020, an India Energy Modeling Forum was launched.

- The forum provides an unbiased platform to discuss the contemporary issues revolving around energy and environment.

19. (a) • The country's first fully indigenously developed vaccine against pneumonia has got approval

from the Drug Controller General of India (DCGI)

- With the help of Special Expert Committee (SEC) for vaccines, the drug regulator reviewed the phase I, II and III clinical trial data submitted by Pune-based firm Serum Institute of India and then granted the market approval for Pneumococcal Polysaccharide Conjugate Vaccine.

- The vaccine will be used for active immunisation against invasive disease and pneumonia caused by 'Streptococcus pneumonia' among infants.

20. (a) Azad Pattan hydel power project

- The 700-MW hydel power project is being built on the Jhelum river in Sudhoti district of Pakistan Occupied Kashmir

- Pakistan and China signed an agreement for the 700 MW Azad Pattan hydel power project on the Jhelum river in Sudhoti district of Pakistan Occupied Kashmir (PoK).

Karot Hydropower station

- The Karot Hydropower station, the third project being executed by China on the Jhelum is on the boundaries of Kotli district in PoK and Rawalpindi district in Pakistan's Punjab province.

- According to the CPEC site, construction is under progress, and the project is expected to be commissioned by the end of 2021.

21. (a) • The first on-line NISHTHA programme for 1200 Key Resources Persons of Andhra Pradesh was launched by Union HRD Minister

- NISHTHA is a National Initiative for School Heads' and Teachers' Holistic Advancement at the elementary stage under Samagra Shiksha -a flagship programme of MHRD to improve learning outcomes.

- NISHTHA in face-to-face mode was launched on 21st August, 2019. Thereafter, 33 states/UTs have launched this programme in their states/ UTs in collaboration under Samagra Shiksha, a Centrally Sponsored Scheme.

- Around 23,000 Key Resource Persons and 17.5 lakh teachers and school heads have been covered under this NISHTHA face to face mode till date.

22. (c) • The Economic and Social Council is at the heart of the United Nations system to advance the three dimensions of sustainable development - economic, social and environmental.

- It is the central platform for fostering debate and innovative thinking, forging consensus on ways forward, and coordinating efforts to achieve internationally agreed goals.
- A number of non-governmental organizations have been granted consultative status to the Council to participate in the work of the United Nations.
- The UN Charter established ECOSOC in 1945 as one of the six main organs of the United Nations

23. (a) • The eligible beneficiaries under the Scheme would be Farmer Producer Organizations (FPOs), MSMEs, Section 8 Companies, Private Companies and individual entrepreneur with minimum 10% margin money contribution by them.
- The balance 90% would be the loan component to be made available by scheduled banks.
- Government of India will provide 3% interest subvention to eligible beneficiaries.
- There will be 2 years moratorium period for principal loan amount and 6 years repayment period thereafter.

24. (a) • ZyCoV-D, the plasmid DNA vaccine designed and developed by Zydus and partially funded by the Department of Biotechnology, has initiated Phase I/ II clinical trials in healthy subjects, making it the first indigenously developed vaccine for COVID-19 to be administered in humans in India.
- The Department of Biotechnology Government of India has partnered with Zydus to address rapid development of an indigenous vaccine for COVID-19 under the National Biopharma Mission.

25. (d) • The project "Development of Pilgrimage Amenities at Somnath, Gujarat" sanctioned under the PRASHAD scheme in March 2017 has been successfully completed with the cost of Rs. 45.36 crores.
- The 'National Mission on Pilgrimage Rejuvenation and Spiritual, Heritage Augmentation Drive' (PRASHAD) launched by the Ministry of Tourism in the year 2014-15 with the objective of integrated development of identified pilgrimage and heritage destinations.
- The scheme aimed at infrastructure development such as entry points (Road, Rail and Water Transport), last mile connectivity, basic tourism

facilities like Information/ Interpretation Centers

26. (c) • The "Decarbonising Transport in India" project will design a tailor-made transport emissions assessment framework for India.
- It will provide the government with a detailed understanding of current and future transport activity and the related CO2 emissions as a basis for their decision-making.
- The India project is carried out in the wider context of the International Transport Forum's "Decarbonising Transport" initiative.
- It is part of the "Decarbonising Transport in Emerging Economies" (DTEE) family of projects, which supports transport decarbonisation across different world regions.
- India, Argentina, Azerbaijan, and Morocco are current participants.

27. (c) • The Organisation for Economic Co-operation and Development (OECD) is an inter governmental economic organisation with 37 member countries, founded in 1961 to stimulate economic progress and world trade. (HQ Paris, France)
- It is a forum of countries describing themselves as committed to democracy and the market economy and to shape policies that foster prosperity, equality, opportunity and well-being for all
- It was founded in 1961 by 18 European nations, and the United States and Canada to stimulate economic progress and world trade.
- India is not a member but key partner and it is invited for annual ministerial conference.
- Generally, OECD members are high-income economies with a very high Human Development Index (HDI) and are regarded as developed countries.

28. (c) • Established in 1927, FICCI is the largest and oldest apex business organisation in India.
- A non-government, not-for-profit organisation, FICCI is the voice of India's business and industry.
- From influencing policy to encouraging debate, engaging with policy makers and civil society, FICCI articulates the views and concerns of industry.

- FICCI draws its membership from the corporate sector, both private and public, including SMEs and MNCs.

- FICCI provides a platform for networking and consensus building within and across sectors and is the first port of call for Indian industry, policy makers and the international business community.

29. (c)
- It is an endangered species of monkey, found only in Assam and parts of Bhutan

- Conservation Status - Endangered

- Golden langurs are endemic to the semi-evergreen and mixed-deciduous forests straddling India and Bhutan

- The golden langurs in Assam are hemmed in by three rivers - Brahmaputra in the south, Manas in east and Sonkosh in west.

30. (a)
- NITI Aayog in collaboration with International Transport Forum (ITF) will launch the "Decarbonising Transport in India" project on 24 June, with the intention to develop a pathway towards a low-carbon transport system for India.

- The "Decarbonising Transport in India" project will design a tailor-made transport emissions assessment framework for India.

- It will provide the government with a detailed understanding of current and future transport activity and the related CO2 emissions as a basis for their decision-making.

31. (d)
- In November 2019, IBM India, in partnership with Directorate General of Training (DGT), Ministry of Skill Development and Entrepreneurship, Government of India, and its implementation partners, made the SkillsBuild online learning platform available to Indian students through Bharatskills (https://bharatskills.gov.in) of DGT.

- Bharat Skills is a e-learning portal of the Directorate General of Training (DGT), Ministry of Skill Development and Entrepreneurship.

32. (a)
- Dairy Processing and Infrastructure Development Fund under NABARD over a period of 3 years (i.e. 2017-18 to 2019-20), was announced in the Union Budget of 2017-18.

- Funding will be in the form of interest bearing loan, which will flow from National Bank for Agriculture and Rural Development (NABARD) to National Dairy Development Board (NDDB) / National Cooperative Development Corporation (NCDC) and in turn to eligible End Borrowers such as Milk Unions, State Dairy Federations, Multi-state Milk Cooperatives, Milk Producer Companies etc

- The scheme will be implemented across the country.

33. (a)
- NITI Aayog, in partnership with Bill and Melinda Gates Foundation (BMGF), Centre for Social and Behavioural Change (CSBC), Ashoka University, and the Ministries of Health and WCD, today launched a behaviour change campaign called 'Navigating the New Normal', and its website.

- Developed under the guidance of Empowered Group 6, constituted by the Government of India and chaired by CEO, NITI Aayog, the campaign has two parts.

34. (c)
- The Society of Indian Defence Manufacturers (SIDM) is a not-for-profit association formed to be the apex body of the Indian defence industry.

- SIDM plays a proactive role as an advocate, catalyst, and facilitator for the growth and capability building of the defence industry in India.

- It works closely with the government towards enabling the growth of the defence industry.

- Collaborate with experts from the armed forces, academia and defence industry to optimize the industry's development capabilities.

35. (d)
- The Health & Family Welfare Ministry has launched the 'eBloodServices' mobile App developed by The Indian Red Cross Society (IRCS)

- This application is developed by the E-Raktkosh team of Centre for Development of Advanced Computing (CDAC) under the Digital India scheme

- This app makes it easy for those in need to request for Blood units at IRCS NHQ.

- Once the request is placed through the app, the requisite units become visible to IRCS, NHQ blood bank in its E-Raktkosh dashboard and this allows assured delivery within the specified time.

36. (c)
- Like in blood banks, where blood is extracted and stored for those who might be in need, the idea is to extract and store plasma from people who have recovered from Covid-19 and give it to someone suffering from the disease.
- Delhi was among the first few states to get ICMR approval to conduct trials with plasma therapy, which is still at trial stage.
- Once a person contracts the virus, the blood produces antibodies and certain cells 'remember' the antigen and produce antibodies when they come in contact with the same virus again.
- The plasma trial is examining if the plasma containing antibodies from recovered patients is beneficial to others as well.

37. (c)
- Tribal Ministry will launch the website - Tribes India e-Mart - on Independence Day on August 15.
- It will be similar to selling your products on e-commerce giants Amazon or Flipkart. The difference is just that it will be only for tribals
- The government had set up Tribal Cooperative Marketing Development Federation of India in 1987 with an aim to provide fair price for products of tribals across the country.
- The agency functions under the Union Tribal Affairs Ministry.
- The tribal artisans will be trained and asked to register themselves as sellers on the website.
- TRIFED will train these tribals and help them get registered.

38. (a)
- The Defence Minister of India has launched a new web portal for issue of No Objection Certificate (NOC) for power projects and Research Survey Exploration Exploitation (RSEE) activities in the Indian Territorial Waters (TW) and Exclusive Economic Zone (EEZ).
- To ensure ease of business and transparency in issuing NOC for such projects, the Ministry has developed the online application portal with the assistance of National e-Governance Division (NeGD), Bhaskaracharya Institute for Space Applications and Geo-informatics (BISAG) and National Informatics Centre (NIC).
- The portal will facilitate the applicants in submitting their proposals online for seeking MoD Security Clearance for undertaking Power Projects/RSEE activities.

39. (a)
- United Nations Convention on the Law of the Sea (UNCLOS) 1982, also known as Law of the Sea divides marine areas into five main zones namely- Internal Waters, Territorial Sea, Contiguous Zone, Exclusive Economic Zone (EEZ) and the High Seas.
- According to rules of UNCLOS, all areas extending up to 12 nautical miles from a country's coastline are its territorial waters (TW). All areas extending up to 200 nautical miles from a country's coastline are its exclusive economic zones (EEZ).

40. (c)
- The World Bank announced the approval of project 'Strengthening Teaching-Learning and Results for States Program (STARS)' for India.
- The project aims to improve the quality and governance of school education in six States.
- The project, Strengthening Teaching-Learning and Results for States Program (STARS), will be implemented through the Samagra Shiksha Abhiyan, the flagship central scheme, in Himachal Pradesh, Kerala, Madhya Pradesh, Maharashtra, Odisha and Rajasthan.

41. (d)
- DGT under the aegis of the Ministry of Skill Development & Entrepreneurship (MSDE), is responsible for implementing long term institutional training to the nation's youth through its network of training institutes and infrastructure.
- It plays a key role in the execution of vocational training schemes and in making 'Digital India' dream become a reality.
- Creating opportunities for Young India with focus on new-age skills like Artificial Intelligence (AI), Big Data, 3D - Technology, Cloud Computing, Cyber Security, etc. which are aligned to Industry 4.0 requirements, has become the prime focus for DGT.

42. (b)
- Japan's Fugaku supercomputer claimed the top spot, carrying out 2.8 times more calculations per second than an IBM machine in the US.
- The US machine, called Summit, came top of the bi-annual Top500 list the previous four times.

43. (d)
- The Cabinet Committee on Economic Affairs, has approved setting up of Animal Husbandry Infrastructure Development Fund (AHIDF) worth Rs. 15000 crore with an interest subsidy scheme to promote investment by private players and MSMEs in dairy, meat processing and

animal feed plants, a move which is expected to create 35 lakh jobs.

- The fund is part of the Rs 20 lakh crore stimulus package announced in May to help people affected by the lockdown to prevent the spread of COVID-19.

- The eligible beneficiaries under the Scheme would be Farmer Producer Organizations (FPOs), MSMEs, Section 8 Companies, Private Companies and individual entrepreneur with minimum 10% margin money contribution by them.

- The balance 90% would be the loan component to be made available by scheduled banks.

44. (b) • Minister of MSME, Nitin Gadkari launched the Credit Guarantee Scheme for Sub-ordinate Debt (CGSSD) which is also called "Distressed Assets Fund-Sub-ordinate Debt for MSMEs".

- This Scheme seeks to extend support to the promoter(s) of the operational MSMEs which are stressed and have become NPA as on 30th April, 2020;

- There will be a moratorium of 7 years on payment of principal whereas maximum tenor for repayment will be 10 years.

45. (b) • Government of India and SIDBI set up the Credit Guarantee Fund Trust for Micro and Small Enterprises (CGTMSE).

- Ministry of Micro, Small & Medium Enterprises (MSME), Government of India launched Credit Guarantee Scheme (CGS) so as to strengthen credit delivery system and facilitate flow of credit to the MSE sector.

- To operationalise the scheme, Government of India and SIDBI set up the Credit Guarantee Fund Trust for Micro and Small Enterprises (CGTMSE) to make collateral-free credit to the micro and small enterprise sector.

- Both the existing and the new enterprises are eligible to be covered under the scheme.

- The Ministry of MSMEs, GoI and Small Industries Development Bank of India (SIDBI) established a trust named Credit Guarantee Fund Trust for Micro and Small Enterprises (CGTMSE) to implement the CGS.

46. (d) • It has been designed and developed indigenously by the Defence Research and Development Organization (DRDO) and it is capable of detecting, locating and neutralizing incoming torpedo.

- The Advanced Torpedo Decoy System Maareech is capable of being fired from all frontline warships.

- Design & Development of this anti-torpedo decoy system has been undertaken indigenously by DRDO labs - Naval Science and Technological Laboratory (NSTL) and Naval Physical & Oceanographic Laboratory (NPOL).

- Bharat Electronics Limited, a Defence PSU, would undertake the production of this decoy system.

47. (c) • Two-day digital conference on the defence & aerospace manufacturing sector 'Defence Conclave 2020, Gujarat' via video conferencing has been inaugurated

- It is jointly organised by Confederation of Indian Industry (CII) Gujarat and Society of Indian Defence Manufacturers (SIDM).

- The Conclave intends to build on the positives of the 'Make in India' vision for boosting the defence manufacturing.

48. (c) • IN-SPACE (Indian National Space Promotion and Authorisation Centre), a new board that provide private players a level playing field

- The body will also perform the role of a regulator and will have on its board members from the private industry

- IN-SPACE will be a separate vertical within the Department of Space (DoS) that will make independent decisions for permitting and regulating activities of the private sector

- It will have its own legal, technological, activity promotion and monitoring directorates and its Board will comprise members from the private industry, academia and government of India

49. (a) • The Khadi and Village Industries Commission (KVIC) is a statutory body formed in April 1957 (as per an RTI) by the Government of India, under the Act of Parliament, 'Khadi and Village Industries Commission Act of 1956'.

- It is an apex organisation under the Ministry of Micro, Small and Medium Enterprises, with regard to khadi and village industries within India

- It seeks to - "plan, promote, facilitate, organise and assist in the establishment and development of khadi and village industries in the rural areas in coordination with other agencies engaged in rural development wherever necessary

50. (c) • NITI Aayog, in partnership with Bill andMelinda Gates Foundation (BMGF), Centre for Social and Behavioural Change (CSBC), Ashoka University, and the Ministries of Health and WCD, today launched a behaviour change campaign called 'Navigating the New Normal', and its website.

• Developed under the guidance of Empowered Group 6, constituted by the Government of India and chaired by CEO, NITI Aayog, the campaign has two parts.

• The first is a web portal, http://www.covidthenewnormal.com/, containing resources informed by behavioural science and the use of nudge and social norms theory, related to Covid-safe behavioural norms during the ongoing Unlock phase, and the second is a media campaign focused on the wearing of masks.

• Developed in consultation with MoHFW and other stakeholders, the website aims to increase public participation and engage CSOs and NGOs.

• It will become a repository of strategies and collaterals to practise Covid-safe behaviours in different sectors.

• It aims to provide open-source access to anyone, including CSOs, NGOs, the public, institutions, anganwadi workers and district administration.

51. (d) • The Indian Navy has inducted an advanced anti-torpedo decoy system called 'Maareech'

• It has been designed and developed indigenously by the Defence Research and Development Organization (DRDO) and it is capable of detecting, locating and neutralizing incoming torpedo.

• The ATDS first detects and then confuse and divert the torpedo attacks on ships from under the water.

• By diverting the torpedoes' original course, it forces it to lose its energy thus preventing it from being effective on target.

• Torpedoes are self propelled weapon with a warhead and can be used under or on the water surface. They are one of the mainstay of sea-warfare attack systems.

52. (a) • NashaMukt Bharat: Annual Action Plan (2020-21) for 272 Most Affected Districts' was e-launched by the Ministry of Social Justice and Empowerment on the occasion of "International Day Against Drug Abuse and Illicit Trafficking"

• The Ministry of Social Justice and Empowerment observes 26th June every year as "International Day Against Drug Abuse and Illicit Trafficking".

• It is the nodal Ministry for drug demand reduction which coordinates and monitors all aspects of drug abuse prevention which include assessment of the extent of the problem, preventive action, treatment and rehabilitation of addicts, dissemination of information and public awareness.

• NashaMukt Bharat Annual Action Plan for 2020-21 would focus on 272 most affected districts and launch a three-pronged attack combining efforts of Narcotics Bureau, Outreach/Awareness by Social Justice and Treatment through the Health Dept.

53. (b) • The AtmaNirbhar Uttar Pradesh Rojgar Abhiyan will cover 31 districts of Uttar Pradesh, which has seen more than 30 lakh migrant labourers return home following the lockdown in the country.

• It will be undertaken as part of the Garib Kalyan Rojgar Abhiyan that the Prime Minister started on June 20 for 116 districts in six states in the country

• Under this, local entrepreneurship will be promoted along with providing employment opportunities to migrant workers.

54. (a) • The Minister of Petroleum and Natural Gas inaugurated Battery Swapping Facility Quick Interchange Service (QIS) at Chandigarh

• India's top oil firm Indian Oil Corporation has launched a battery swapping facility for Electric Vehicles at its petrol pumps, offering to replace discharged batteries with fully charged ones in just couple of minutes.

• QIS will play a pivotal role in providing an alternative energy solution to the 3-wheeler segment and boosting India's economic growth.

• IOC, the country's top fuel retailer is now making a foray into EV charging. It has partnered with Sun Mobility for setting up battery swapping facility, called Quick Interchange Station (QIS).

55. (a) • The Public Sector Enterprise 'New Space India Limited (NSIL)' will endeavour to re-orient space activities from a 'supply driven' model to a 'demand driven' model, thereby ensuring optimum utilisation of space assets.

• NSIL is a Central Public Sector Enterprise of Government of India.

• It is the commercial subsidiary of ISRO

• It was established on 6 March 2019 under the administrative control of Department of Space (DOS), India.

• The main objective of NSIL is to scale up industry participation (mostly private and international customers) in Indian space programmes.

56. (a) • The main highlight was the launch of the TRIBES India products on the Government e-Marketplace (GeM) (with a diverse range on display) and TRIFED's new website (https://trifed.tribal.gov.in)

• The Union Minister of Tribal Affairs inaugurated the TRIBES India store on Government eMarket place which can now help in facilitating purchases by Government and the revamped website (https://trifed.tribal.gov.in/), which has all relevant details about the schemes and initiatives underway to the benefit of tribal communities.

57. (a) • GeM is a short form of one stop Government e-Market Place hosted by Directorate General of Supplies and Disposals (DGS&D) where common user goods and services can be procured.

• GeM is dynamic, self sustaining and user friendly portal for making procurement by Government officers.

• Government e-Marketplace (GeM - gem.gov.in) is a very bold step of the Government with the aim to transform the way in which procurement of goods and services is done by the Government Ministries and Departments, Public Sector Undertakings and other apex autonomous bodies of the Central Government.

• GeM is a completely paperless, cashless and system driven e-market place that enables procurement of common use goods and services with minimal human interface.

58. (b) • Pradhan Mantri Van Dhan Yojana or Van Dhan Scheme launched on 14th April, 2018 by the Prime Minister with Ministry of Tribal Affairs as nodal department at central level and TRIFED as nodal agency at national level

• It is a well thought master plan for the socio-economic development of the tribal population of the country.

Its crucial steps are enumerated below

• Initiative targeting livelihood generation for tribal gatherers and transforming them into entrepreneurs.

• Idea is to set-up tribal community owned Van Dhan Vikas Kendras (VDVKs) in predominantly forested tribal districts.

• A Kendra shall constitute of 15 tribal SHGs, each comprising of up to 20 tribal NTFP gatherers or artisans i.e. about 300 beneficiaries per Van Dhan Kendra.

• 100% Central Government Funded with TRIFED providing Rs. 15 lakhs for each 300 member Van Dhan Kendra.

59. (a) • Co-operative banks are financial entities established on a co-operative basis and belonging to their members.

• In India, co-operative banks are registered under the States Cooperative Societies Act.

• They also come under the regulatory ambit of the Reserve Bank of India (RBI) under two laws, namely, the Banking Regulations Act, 1949, and the Banking Laws (Co-operative Societies) Act, 1955.

• They were brought under the RBI's watch in 1966, a move which brought the problem of dual regulation along with it.

60. (c) • The nearly 100-year-old procurement arm of the Central Government - the Directorate General of Supplies and Disposals (DGS&D) - has been close down on October 31, 2017

• The closure of DGS&D, follows the government's shift to the Commerce Ministry's e-market platform (GeM) set up for public procurement of goods and services.

61. (c) • The 49th Governing Council Meeting of National Productivity Council (NPC), an autonomous body under Department for Promotion of Industry & Internal Trade (DPIIT), Ministry of Commerce & Industry, Government of India was held recently

• It was chaired by the Commerce & Industry Minister and President of NPC Governing Council.

- The GC Meeting has been conducted after a lapse of fifteen years.
- National Productivity Council of India (NPC), established in the year 1958, is an autonomous organization under Department for Promotion of Industry & Internal Trade, Ministry of Commerce and Industry, Government of India.

62. (b)
- The Cairns Group (Cairns Group of Fair Trading Nations) is an interest group of 20 agricultural exporting countries, composed of Argentina, Australia, Bolivia, Brazil, Canada, Chile, Colombia, Costa Rica, Guatemala, Indonesia, Malaysia, New Zealand, Pakistan, Paraguay, Peru, the Philippines, South Africa, Thailand, Uruguay, and Vietnam.
- The Cairns Group seeks to liberalize global trade in agricultural produce.
- In particular, its members aim to abolish export subsidies and trade-distorting ("amber box") domestic support for agricultural products and seek to improve market access for agricultural exports.

63. (a)
- Maharashtra Chief Minister Uddhav Thackeray inaugurated 'Project PLATINA world's largest convalescent plasma therapy trial cum treatment of severe COVID-19 patients.
- Project PLATINA -World's Largest convalescent plasma therapy trial cum treatment of severe COVID-19 patients was launched by Maharashtra Medical Education and Drugs Department

64. (d)
- Canada is leading efforts on WTO reform through the Ottawa Group, which acts as an impartial sounding board for key issues and ideas on how to advance WTO reform.
- In addition to Canada, the Ottawa Group comprises Australia, Brazil, Chile, the European Union, Japan, Kenya, Mexico, New Zealand, Norway, Singapore, Korea, and Switzerland.
- The Ottawa Group supports its members in advancing concrete proposals to improve how the WTO functions over the short, medium, and long terms.

65. (b)
- NPC is a constituent of the Tokyo-based Asian Productivity Organisation (APO), an Inter-Governmental Body of which the Government of India is a founding member.
- The APO is an intergovernmental organization established in 1961 to increase productivity in the Asia-Pacific region through mutual cooperation.
- The APO contributes to the sustainable socioeconomic development of the region through policy advisory services, acting as a think tank, and undertaking smart initiatives in the industry, agriculture, service, and public sectors.

66. (c)
- Samagra Shiksha is an overarching programme for the school education sector extending from pre-school to class 12.
- The scheme has been prepared with the broader goal of improving school effectiveness measured in terms of equal opportunities for schooling and equitable learning outcomes.
- It subsumes the three Schemes of Sarva Shiksha Abhiyan (SSA), Rashtriya Madhyamik Shiksha Abhiyan (RMSA) and Teacher Education (TE).

67. (b)
- MoSPI has instituted a new award 'Prof. P. C. Mahalanobis National Award in Official Statistics' for recognizing outstanding achievement of official statisticians in Central Government, State/UT Governments and institutions.

68. (c)
- An enterprise for this purpose will be known as Udyam and its Registration Process will be known as 'Udyam Registration'.
- An MSME in the country will now be known as 'Udyam' since the term comes closer to the meaning of an enterprise.
- MSME registration process is fully online, paperless and based on self-declaration. No documents or proof are required to be uploaded for registering an MSME
- MSME registration process or Udyam Registration can be filed online based on self-declaration with no requirement for documents of proof, barring Aadhar (Adhaar Number will be required for registration)
- It is a paperless and based on self-declaration. No documents or proof are required to be uploaded for registering an MSME;
- Udyam Registration has also been fully integrated with the IT and GST systems.

69. (b)
- AI enabled MyGov Corona Helpdesk bagged two awards under categories (1) "Best Innovation for Covid-19 - Society" and (2) "People's Choice

Covid-19 Overall Winner", at the recently held CogX 2020, which is a prestigious Global Leadership Summit and Festival of AI & Emerging Technology held annually in London.

- CogX is one of the world's largest events on AI, held annually in London with over 15,000 participants in attendance from the highest levels of business, government, industry, and research.

- The Cogx Awards are given out to the best-of-the-best in AI and emerging technologies across the world.

70. (d) • Union Minister for Fisheries, Animal Husbandry and Dairying, launched the first edition of the Fisheries and Aquaculture Newsletter "MATSYA SAMPADA" published by the Department of Fisheries, Ministry for Fisheries, Animal Husbandry and Dairying, and the Operational Guidelines of the Pradhan Mantri MatsyaSampada Yojana (PMMSY).

- The Government of India in May, 2020 launched a new Flagship Scheme i.e. the Pradhan Mantri MatsyaSampada Yojana (PMMSY) for sustainable and responsible development of fisheries sector at an investment of Rs. 20050 crore.

- PMMSY will be implemented over a period of 5 years from FY 2020-21 to FY 2024-25 in all States/Union Territories.

- The PMMSY will be implemented as an umbrella scheme with two separate Components namely (a) Central Sector Scheme (CS) and (b) Centrally Sponsored Scheme (CSS).

71. (a) • From July, over six crore micro, small and medium enterprises across the country will be classified on the basis of the new criteria approved by the government.

- As per the revised criteria, a unit with Rs 50 crore of investment and Rs 250 crore of turnover will fall under the 'medium' enterprise category.

- Besides, a manufacturing and services unit with Rs 1 crore of investment and Rs 5 crore of turnover will be classified as 'micro' whereas a unit involving Rs 10 crore of investment and Rs 50 crore of turnover will be categorised as a 'small' enterprise.

- Also, a new composite formula of classification for manufacturing and services units has been notified. Now, there will be no difference between the manufacturing and service sectors.

- The new definition and criterion will come into effect from 1 July, 2020

- The existing criterion of definition of MSMEs is based on the MSMED Act, 2006.It was different for manufacturing and services units.

72. (a) • The country is moving towards the institution of 'one nation, one ration card', which will be of immense benefit to the poor who travel to other states in search of work.

- Ration card portability is aimed at providing intra-state as well as inter-state portability of ration cards.

- While the Integrated Management of Public Distribution System (IM-PDS) portal (http://www.impds.nic.in/) provides the technological platform for the inter-state portability of ration cards, enabling a migrant worker to buy foodgrains from any FPS across the country, the other portal (annavitran.nic.in) hosts the data of distribution of foodgrains through E-PoS devices within a state.

- The Annavitran portal enables a migrant worker or his family to avail the benefits of PDS outside their district but within their state. While a person can buy her share of foodgrains as per her entitlement under the NFSA, wherever she is based, the rest of her family members can purchase subsidised foodgrains from their ration dealer back home.

73. (d) • The Union Minister of HRD launched World's first ever online B.Sc. degree in Programming and Data Science

- The programme has been prepared and offered by the Indian Institute of Technology Madras (IIT Madras), which is ranked No.1 in India Rankings 2020 by NIRF.

- This programme is open to anyone who has passed Class XII, with English and Maths at the Class X level, and enrolled in any on-campus UG course.

74. (b) • To provide a single platform for research internships, capacity building programs, and workshops across the country, the Science and Engineering Research Board (SERB) has launched a new scheme called 'Accelerate Vigyan' (AV).

- The primary objective of this inter-ministerial scheme is to give more thrust on encouraging high-end scientific research and preparing scientific manpower, which can lead to research careers and knowledge-based economy.

75. (c) • It is a wing of the National Academy of Medical Sciences and has been conducting Postgraduate Medical Examinations at the national level since 1976.

• The National Board of Examinations came into existence in 1975, as a wing of the National Academy of Medical Sciences and has been conducting Postgraduate Medical Examinations at the national level since 1976.

• The Board was registered as an Autonomous Organization under MoHFW in 1982 with the objective of conducting high standard post-graduate examinations in the field of modern medicine on all India basis, formulating basic training requirements for eligibility, developing curriculum for post graduate training and accreditation of institutions where this training is imparted.

• The students enrolled are called Diplomates of National Board (DNB).

76. (b) • AV will initiate and strengthen mechanisms of identifying research potential, mentoring, training and hands-on workshop on a national scale.

• The vision is to expand the research base, with three broad goals, namely, consolidation / aggregation of all scientific programs, initiating high-end orientation workshops, and creating opportunities for research internships for those who do not have access to such resources / facilities

• Thus, an Inter-Ministerial Overseeing Committee (IMOC) involving all the scientific ministries/departments and a few others has been constituted for the purpose of supporting SERB in implementing the AV scheme in a successful manner.

• Another new component under AV is 'SAMMOHAN' that has been sub-divided into 'SAYONJIKA' and 'SANGOSHTI'.

• SAYONJIKA is an open-ended program to catalogue the capacity building activities in science and technology supported by all government funding agencies in the country. SANGOSHTI is a pre-existing program of SERB.

77. (c) • NITI Aayog and Rocky Mountain Institute (RMI) released Towards a Clean Energy Economy: Post-Covid-19 Opportunities for India's Energy and Mobility Sectors report, which advocates for stimulus and recovery efforts that work towards building a clean, resilient, and least-cost energy future for India.

• These efforts include electric vehicle, energy storage, and renewable energy programs.

78. (d) • Under the 100 % Emergency Credit Line Guarantee Scheme (ECLGS) backed by a Government guarantee , Banks from Public & Private Sectors have sanctioned loans worth over Rs. 1 lakh crore

• This would help more than 30 lakh units of MSMEs & other businesses restart their businesses post the lockdown..

• Government of India through Ministry of Finance, Department of Financial Services has introduced the Emergency Credit Line Guarantee Scheme (ECLGS) for providing 100% guarantee coverage for additional working capital term loans upto 20% of their entire outstanding credit upto Rs. 25 crore i.e. upto Rs. 5 crore

79. (a) • NBE's flagship DNB Programmes are offered in 82 disciplines and subspecialties of modern medicine which includes DNB Programme in 29 Broad and across 703 private and government institutions

• It is a wing of the National Academy of Medical Sciences and has been conducting Postgraduate Medical Examinations at the national level since 1976.

• The National Board of Examinations came into existence in 1975, as a wing of the National Academy of Medical Sciences and has been conducting Postgraduate Medical Examinations at the national level since 1976.

• The Board was registered as an Autonomous Organization under MoHFW in 1982 with the objective of conducting high standard post-graduate examinations in the field of modern medicine

80. (c) • It is an attempt to boost research and development in the country by enabling and grooming potential PG/PhD students by means of developing their research skills in selected areas across different disciplines or fields.

- It has two components: High-End Workshops ('KARYASHALA') and Research Internships ('VRITIKA').
- This is especially important for those researchers who have limited opportunities to access such learning capacities / facilities / infrastructure.
- The current call for applications invites researchers for the winter season (Dec 2020-Jan 2021) 'KARYASHALA' and 'VRITIKA'

81. (b)
- The Union Minister of Health & Family Welfare released the Good Clinical Practice Guidelines Handbook and Prospectus for Fellowship Programme for International Students (FPIS) of National Board of Examinations (NBE)
- The Health & Family Welfare Ministry also electronically released Fellowship Programme for International Students (FPIS) - Prospectus for Current year 2020 - 2021 in 11 specialties spread over 42 premium institutions.
- This is the first time that International Fellowship Programme is being launched for International Students from all countries including SAARC Nations, at Post MD/MS level through common Fellowship Entrance Test

82. (c)
- This Drug Discovery Hackathon is a joint initiative of MHRD's Innovation Cell (MIC), All India Council for Technical Education (AICTE) and Council of Scientific and Industrial Research (CSIR) and supported by Centre for Development of Advanced Computing (CDAC), My Gov as well as private players.
- This Hackathon is first of its kind National initiative for supporting drug discovery process and will see participation from professionals, faculty, researchers and students from varied fields like Computer Science, Chemistry, Pharmacy, Medical Sciences, Basic Sciences and Biotechnology.
- The Hackathon consists of challenges that are posted as problem statements and, are based on specific drug discovery topics which, are open to the participants to solve.
- MyGov portal is being used and any Indian student can participate.
- Professionals and researchers from anywhere in the world can participate.

83. (d)
- Minister for Food Processing Industries launched the PM Formalization of Micro Food Processing Enterprises (PM FME) scheme as a part of "Atmanirbhar Bharat Abhiyan
- The Ministry of Food Processing Industries (MoFPI) has launched an all India "Centrally Sponsored PM Formalisation of Micro food processing Enterprises (PM FME) scheme" to be implemented over a period of five years from 2020-21 to 2024-25 with an outlay of Rs 10,000 crore.
- The objective is to providing financial, technical and business support for upgradation of existing micro food processing enterprises
- The expenditure under the scheme would to be shared in 60:40 ratio between Central and State Governments, in 90:10 ratio with North Eastern and Himalayan States, 60:40 ratio with UTs with legislature and 100% by Centre for other UTs.

84. (a)
- Operation Greens Scheme, being implemented by MoFPI has been extended from tomato, onion and potato (TOP) crops to other notified horticulture crops (to all perishable fruits and vegetables) for providing subsidy for their transportation and storage from surplus production area to major consumption centres.
- Any other fruit/vegetable can be added in future on the basis of recommendation by Ministry of Agriculture or State Government

85. (d)
- The scientists identified the virus through surveillance of influenza viruses in pigs that they carried out from 2011 to 2018 in ten provinces of China.
- In a new research, scientists from China - which has the largest population of pigs in the world - have identified a "recently emerged" strain of influenza virus that is infecting Chinese pigs and that has the potential of triggering a pandemic.
- Named G4, the swine flu strain has genes similar to those in the virus that caused the 2009 flu pandemic.

86. (a)
- NMCG is the implementation wing of National Council for Rejuvenation, Protection and Management of River Ganga (referred as National Ganga Council)
- It was established in the year 2011 as a registered society under Societies Registration Act, 1860
- It has a two tier management structure and comprises of Governing Council and Executive Committee

- In October 2016, National Ganga Council has replaced National Ganga River Basin Authority (NGRBA) which was constituted under the provisions of the Environment (Protection) Act (EPA), 1986.
- With the formation of the NGC, the National Ganga River Basin Authority (NGRBA) was dissolved.
- The functioning of the NGRBA was similar to the NGC, and the prime minister was the chairman of the NGRBA as well.

87. (c) • Union Human Resource Development Minister and Minister of Sports and Youth Affairs and Ministry of Minority Affairs launched Fit Hai to Hit Hai India under the Fit India campaign
- The "Fit Hai To Hit Hai India" program organized under the Fit India campaign.
- 'Fit Hai to Hit Hai India' webinar series for students were also conducted
- The Fit India Talks sessions are being organized in association with the Sports Authority of India and the Ministry of Human Resource Development.

88. (a) • Every year, the Swachh Survekshan is redesigned innovatively, to ensure that the process becomes more robust, with focus on sustaining the behaviour change.
- A new category of awards titled 'Prerak Dauur Samman' as part of Swachh Survekshan 2021 launched
- The PrerakDauurSamman has a total of five additional sub- categories -Divya (Platinum), Anupam (Gold), Ujjwal (Silver), Udit (Bronze), Aarohi (Aspiring) - with top three cities being recognized in each.
- The survey will categorise cities on the basis of six indicator-wise performance criteria -- segregation of waste into wet, dry and hazard categories; processing capacity against wet waste generated; processing and recycling of wet and dry waste; construction & demolition (C&D) waste processing; percentage of waste going to landfills; and sanitation status of cities.

89. (c) • The Dhamma Chakra Day celebrations are being organized by the International Buddhist Confederation (IBC) in partnership with Ministry of Culture, Government of India.
- It aims to keep with the historical legacy of India being the land of Buddha's enlightenment and awakening, his turning of the wheels of Dhamma, and Mahaparinirvana.
- The day marks Buddha's first teaching after attaining Enlightenment to the first five ascetic disciples (pañcavargika) on the full-moon day of Asadha at 'Deer Park', ?i?ipatana in the current day Sarnath, near Varanasi, India.
- Asadha Poornima is the second most sacred day for Buddhists after the Buddha Poornima or Vesak.

90. (a) • The entire state of Jharkhand observed Hul Divas sans the usual festivities because of the prevailing pandemic situation worldwid
- The people observed Hul Divas in a simple manner as people paid tributes to the revolutionaries Sidho-Kanhu, Chand-Bhairav and Phulo-Jhano who blew the bugle of Santal revolution against the British Rulers to free their land of the Raj and take back their 'Jal-Jungle-Zameen' which was rightfully theirs and handed down through generations by their forefathers.
- Hul Divas is observed annually on June 30 in memory of tribals - Sidho and KanhuMurmu - who led the Santhal hul (rebellion) on June 30, 1855, at Bhognadih in Sahebganj district.
- People, mostly Santhals from Jharkhand and neighbouring states, gather there in large number to celebrate what they think was the first people's action against the British

91. (c) • The Prime Minister launched the 'Aatmanirbhar Bharat App Innovation Challenge' to help start-up and tech community achieve the Aatmanirbhar Bharat mission.
- To help our start-up and tech community to achieve the objective, of developing Apps which can satisfy our market as well as compete with the world Ministry of Electronics & Information Technology along with Atal Innovation Mission are coming up with the Aatmanirbhar Bharat Innovation challenge.
- This challenge will run in two tracks: Promotion of Existing Apps and Development of New Apps.
- For the promotion of existing Apps and platforms across the categories of E-learning, Work-from-Home, Gaming, Business, Entertainment, Office Utilities, and Social Networking, Government will provide mentoring, hand-holding and support.

92. (b) • The Central Drugs Standard Control Organisation(CDSCO)under Directorate General of Health Services,Ministry of Health & Family Welfare,Government of India is the National Regulatory Authority (NRA) of India.

• The Drugs & Cosmetics Act,1940 and rules 1945 have entrusted various responsibilities to central & state regulators for regulation of drugs & cosmetics.

• Under the Drugs and Cosmetics Act, CDSCO is responsible for approval of Drugs, Conduct of Clinical Trials, laying down the standards for Drugs, control over the quality of imported Drugs in the country and coordination of the activities of State Drug Control Organizations by providing expert advice with a view of bring about the uniformity in the enforcement of the Drugs and Cosmetics Act.

93. (c) • National Atlas and Thematic Mapping Organization (NATMO) functioning as a subordinate department under the Department of Science & Technology, Ministry of Science & Technology, Government of India published the 4th updated version of COVID-19 Dashboard on its official Portal at http://geoportal.natmo.gov.in/Covid19/

• It is a specialized institution of its kind in the world. This organization was assigned with responsibility in the field of thematic cartography and geographical research at national level.

• A subordinate office under Department of Science & Technology, it is the sole authority for depicting National framework data in the form of thematic maps and atlases to cater the actual picture of the development and planning initiatives of the country among the users.

94. (b) • The Sindhu Darshan festival is celebrated along the banks of the river Sindhu in the UT of Ladakh every year on the full moon day.

• The Sindhu Darshan Festival is a celebration of River Sindhu, also known as the Indus Valley Civilisation.

• The main reason behind the celebration of Sindhu Darshan Festival is to endorse the Indus River (Sindhu River) as an icon of the communal harmony and unity of India.

• Nimu or Nimmu is a small village situated some 45 kms from Leh in the South East part of Ladakh.

• It is a popular tourist attraction as one can see the picturesque confluence of River Indus and Zanskar.

95. (a) • India's Vice President Venkaiah Naidu launched the Elyments app - which claims to be India's first official social media super app.

• The app has been built by over a thousand IT professionals who are also volunteers of the Art of Living, which is helmed by Sri Sri Ravi Shankar.

• In the social media world, the app will be competing with the likes of Facebook, WhatsApp and Instagram.

96. (b) National Atlas and Thematic Mapping Organization

• It is a specialized institution of its kind in the world. This organization was assigned with responsibility in the field of thematic cartography and geographical research at national level.

• A subordinate office under Department of Science & Technology, it is the sole authority for depicting National framework data in the form of thematic maps and atlases to cater the actual picture of the development and planning initiatives of the country among the users.

• The first National Atlas of India in Hindi popularly known as Bharat: Rashtriya Atlas having a 26 multi-colour maps was published in 1957 and was acclaimed the world over as a unique publication.

• Consequent upon the success of Bharat: Rashtriya Atlas, the organization decided to prepare an ambitious project containing 300 plates which covered all the aspects of the land, people and economy of the country.

97. (d) • The Directorate General of Quality Assurance (DGQA) is under Deptt. Of Defence Production, Ministry of Defence.

• This organisation is more than hundred years old and provides Quality Assurance (QA) cover for the entire range of Arms, Ammunitions, Equipments and Stores supplied to Armed Forces.

• Apart from QA activities, the organisation is responsible for import substitution and associates with Defence Research and Development Organisation (DRDO) in the development projects.

• It also ensures Documentation, Codification and

Standardisation Action for minimizing the variety of components / equipments.

98. (d) • The Global Environment Facility (GEF) Trust Fund was established on the eve of the 1992 Rio Earth Summit, to help tackle our planet's most pressing environmental problems.

• GEF funding to support the projects is contributed by donor countries. These financial contributions are replenished every four years (see GEF Replenishment documents) by the 39 GEF donor countries.

• GEF funds are available to developing countries and countries with economies in transition to meet the objectives of the international environmental conventions and agreements.

• The World Bank serves as the GEF Trustee, administering the GEF Trust Fund (contributions by donors).

99. (d) • State-run Indian Oil Corporation Ltd (IOC) launched a special winter-grade diesel that remains unfrozen up to minus 33 degree Celsius.

• The fuel would help provide year-round access to snow-capped border regions, and is part of India's efforts to speed up strategic road connectivity.

• This new fuel will help Indian security forces to stock up on crucial supplies and ammunition that gets cut off due to bad weather in winters.

• Indian Oil has come up with an innovative solution to this problem by introducing a special winter-grade diesel with a low pour-point of -33o Celsius, which does not lose its fluidity function even in extreme winter conditions

100. (d) • Beijing made this claim while objecting to a request to develop the Sakteng wildlife sanctuary in eastern Bhutan's Trashigang district at an online meeting of the Global Environment Facility (GEF).

• Bhutan objected to the Chinese claim and also the GEF council rejected the Chinese claim and approved the project.

• The Sakteng Wildlife Sanctuary is located in the China-Bhutan disputed areas which is on the agenda of China-Bhutan boundary talk, China opposes and does not join the Council decision on this project

101. (a) • The Representation of the People Act, 1951 is an act of Parliament of India to provide for the conduct of election of the Houses of Parliament and to the House or Houses of the Legislature of each State, the qualifications and disqualifications for membership of those Houses, the corrupt practices and other offences at or in connection with such elections and the decision of doubts and disputes arising out of or in connection with such elections.

• It was introduced in Parliament by law minister Dr. B.R. Ambedkar.

• The Act was enacted by the provisional parliament under Article 327 of Indian Constitution, before the first general election.

102. (d) • Antigen from the pathogen and antibodies produced by the human immune cells can be thought of as matching the compatible pair.

• Every pathogen has specific molecular structures called as antigen. They are like the surface with a particular hue and design.

• Once infected by the germ, the human immune system develops antibodies that match the antigen.

• Our immune system has ten thousand types of antibodies. If the pathogen is a known enemy, the immune system can pull the matching antibody (as it has ten thousand types of antibodies).Once the match is made the pathogen is inactivated. No longer it can infect.

103. (c) • An independently operating financial organization, the GEF provides grants for projects related to biodiversity, climate change, international waters, land degradation, the ozone layer, persistent organic pollutants (POPs), mercury, sustainable forest management, food security, sustainable cities.

The GEF also serves as financial mechanism for the following conventions:

• Convention on Biological Diversity (CBD)

• United Nations Framework Convention on Climate Change (UNFCCC)

• United Nations Convention to Combat Desertification (UNCCD)

• Stockholm Convention on Persistent Organic Pollutants (POPs)

• Minamata Convention on Mercury

The GEF, although not linked formally to the Montreal Protocol on Substances that Deplete the Ozone Layer (MP), supports implementation of the Protocol in countries with economies in transition.

104. (d)
- The World Bank's MSME Emergency Response Programme will address the immediate liquidity and credit needs of some 1.5 million viable MSMEs to help them withstand the impact of the current shock and protect millions of jobs. This is the first step among a broader set of reforms that are needed to propel the MSME sector over time.
- This project will support the Government in providing targeted guarantees to incentivize NBFCs and banks to continue lending to viable MSMEs to help sustain them through the crisis
- The World Bank Group, including its private sector arm - the International Finance Corporation (IFC), will support the government's initiatives to protect the MSME sector by "unlocking liquidity, enabling financial innovations" and supporting "key market-oriented channels of credit such as the NBFCs and Small Finance Bank (SFBs)

105. (c)
- Recently Children with Covid-19 infection have shown some symptoms similar to those associated with a rare illness called Kawasaki disease - such as rashes and inflammation - while other symptoms of Kawasaki disease have been absent.
- Such symptoms have also shown in children who tested negative for Covid-19.
- The World Health Organization (WHO) termed this new illness "multisystem inflammatory disorder".
- It affects children. Its symptoms include red eyes, rashes, and a swollen tongue with reddened lips - often termed strawberry tongue - and an inflamed blood vessel system all over the body.

106. (d)
- The Union Cabinet has given its approval to a new pan India Central Sector Scheme-Agriculture Infrastructure Fund.
- The scheme shall provide a medium - long term debt financing facility for investment in viable projects for post-harvest management Infrastructure and community farming assets through interest subvention and financial support.
- All loans under this financing facility will have interest subvention of 3% per annum up to a limit of Rs. 2 crore.
- The National, State and District level Monitoring Committees will be set up to ensure real-time monitoring and effective feed-back.
- The duration of the Scheme shall be from FY2020 to FY2029 (10 years).

107. (a)
- The scheme will be launched under the Pradhan Mantri Awas Yojana (PMAY) by converting government funded housing in the cities into Affordable Rental Housing Complexes under PPP (public-private partnership) mode through concessionaire.
- The Union Cabinet has given its approval for developing of Affordable Rental Housing Complexes (AHRCs) for urban migrants / poor as a sub-scheme under Pradhan Mantri Awas Yojana - Urban (PMAY - U)
- Ministry of Housing & Urban Affairs (MoHUA) has initiated an Affordable Rental Housing Complexes (ARHCs) for urban migrants/poor as a sub-scheme under Pradhan Mantri Awas Yojana (Urban).

108. (b)
- The scheme includes creation of a Motor Vehicle Accident Fund.
- The National Health Authority has been entrusted to implement the scheme.
- The scheme to provide compulsory insurance cover to all road users in the country.
- The fund would be utilized for treatment of road accident victims and for payment of compensation to the injured or to the family of person losing life in hit and run cases. This includes treatment of victims during the crucial Golden hour.

109. (a)
- India's real estate industry has registered one of the largest improvements globally and regionally in Jones Lang LaSalle's (JLL) biennial Global Real Estate Transparency Index (GRETI).
- The country ranks 34th globally on the index with higher levels of transparency observed in India due to regulatory reforms, enhanced market data and sustainability initiatives
- JLL and LaSalle have been tracking real estate transparency and championing higher standards since 1999. This 11th edition of GRETI covers 99 countries and territories, and 163 city regions.

110. (c)
- It is the apex body responsible for implementing India's flagship public health insurance/ assurance scheme called "Ayushman Bharat Pradhan Mantri Jan Arogya Yojana."
- National Health Authority is the successor of the National Health Agency, which was functioning as a registered society since 23rd May, 2018.
- NHA has been set-up to implement PM-JAY, as it is popularly known, at the national level. An

attached office of the Ministry of Health and Family Welfare with full functional autonomy

- NHA is governed by a Governing Board chaired by the Union Minister for Health and Family Welfare.

111. (a) • Assam government has decided to upgrade the DehingPatkai wildlife sanctuary into a national park amid an ongoing row over allowing coal mining within its jurisdiction.

- Assam has five national parks and DehingPatkai, if upgraded, will increase the tally to 6.

112. (d) Wildlife Sanctuaries

- Wildlife sanctuaries refer to an area which provides protection and favourable living conditions to the wild animals.

- Biosphere reserves are the protected areas, which tend to conserve the genetic diversity of the plants, animals birds, etc

- International Union of Conservation of Nature, shortly called as IUCN has grouped wildlife sanctuaries in Category IV of protected areas.

National Parks

- On the other hand, the national park provides protection to the entire set of the ecosystem, i.e. flora, fauna, landscape, etc. of that region.

- National Park implies an area that is exclusively designated by the government for the conservation of wildlife and biodiversity due to its natural, cultural and historical significance.

113. (a) • The bubonic plague, known as the "Black Death" in the Middle Ages, is a highly infectious and often fatal disease that is spread mostly by rodents.

- Plague is an infectious disease caused by Yersinia pestis, a zoonotic bacteria, usually found in small mammals and their fleas

- Bubonic plague is the most common form of plague and is caused by the bite of an infected flea.

- Human to human transmission of bubonic plague is rare.

114. (c) • It is a Statutory Organization and it serves as apex body to review all wildlife-related matters and approve projects in and around national parks and sanctuaries.

- It has been constituted under the Wildlife Protection Act, 1972.

- The NBWL is chaired by the Prime Minister. It has 47 members including the Prime Minister.

- NBWL advises the Central Government on framing policies and measures for conservation of wildlife in the country.

- Its objective is to promote the conservation and development of wildlife and forests.

- It has power to review all wildlife-related matters and approve projects in and around national parks and sanctuaries.

- No alternation of boundaries in national parks and wildlife sanctuaries can be done without approval of the NBWL.

115. (d) Five National Parks of Assam

- Dibru-Saikhowa National Park.

- Kaziranga National Park.

- Manas National Park.

- Nameri National Park.

- Orang National Park.

116. (b) • The National Mission for Manuscripts was launched in February 2003 by the Government of India, under the Ministry of Tourism and Culture, with the mandate of documenting, conserving and disseminating the knowledge preserved in the manuscripts.

- One of the objectives of the mission is to publish rare and unpublished manuscripts so that the knowledge enshrined in them is spread to researchers, scholars and general public at large.

117. (b) • Prime Minister Shri Narendra Modi will dedicate to the nation the 750 MW Solar Project set up at Rewa, Madhya Pradesh on July 10, 2020.

- The Solar Park was developed by the Rewa Ultra Mega Solar Limited (RUMSL), a Joint Venture Company of Madhya Pradesh UrjaVikas Nigam Limited (MPUVN), and Solar Energy Corporation of India (SECI), a Central Public Sector Undertaking.

- Central Financial Assistance of Rs. 138 crore has been provided to RUMSL for development of the Park.

- The Rewa Solar Project was the first solar project in the country to break the grid parity barrier.

118. (b) • Solar Energy Corporation of India ltd" (SECI) is a CPSU under the administrative control of the Ministry of New and Renewable Energy (MNRE), set up on 20th Sept, 2011 to facilitate the implementation of JNNSM and achievement of targets set therein.

- It is the only CPSU dedicated to the solar energy sector. It was originally incorporated as a section-25 (not for profit) company under the Companies Act, 1956.

- However, through a Government of India decision, the company has recently been converted into a Section-3 company under the Companies Act, 2013.

- The mandate of the company has also been broadened to cover the entire renewable energy domain and renamed to Renewable Energy Corporation of India (RECI).

119. (a) • After the recent successful launch of a Colombian satellite by Indian Space Research Organisation (ISRO) along with other countries onboard PSLV-C43, another South American country Brazil is getting ready for launching its satellite in 2020.

- The Indian Space Research and Research Organisation (ISRO) gets ready to launch Brazil's Amazonia-1 satellite next month onboard PSLV.

120. (a) • The Ministry of Culture has taken up the project of reprinting of 108 volumes of Mongolian Kanjur under the National Mission for Manuscripts (NMM).

- The first set of five volumes of Mongolian Kanjur published under the NMM was presented to the President of India Shri Ram Nath Kovind on the occasion of Guru Purnima, also known as Dharma Chakra Day, on 4th July 2020.

121. (b) • The BRO maintains operations in twenty-one states, one UT (Andaman and Nicobar Islands), and neighboring countries such as Afghanistan, Bhutan, Myanmar, and Sri Lanka.

- The BRO operates and maintains over 32,885 kilometers of roads and about 12,200 meters of permanent bridges in the country.

- The BRO consists of Border Roads Wing under the Ministry of Defense and the General Reserve Engineer Force (GREF).

- The BRO operates in 18 Projects namely: Arunank, Beacon, Brahmank, Chetak, Deepak, Dantak, Himank, Hirak, Pushpak, Sampark, Setuk, Sewak, Shivalik, Swastik, Udayak, Vartak, Vijayak and sela tunnel

122. (b) • Prime Minister addressed the inaugural address at India Global Week 2020

- The India Global Week 2020 is a three-day virtual conference, being held from July 9 to July 11, themed 'Be The Revival: India and a Better New World', will have 5,000 global participants from 30 nations being addressed by 250 global speakers across 75 sessions.

- The forum focused on India's trade and foreign investment prospects.

- India Global Week 2020, a virtual conference being organised in the UK

123. (a) • To improve the information flow and bridge the demand-supply gap in the skilled workforce market, the Ministry of Skill Development and Entrepreneurship (MSDE) launched 'Aatamanirbhar Skilled Employee Employer Mapping (ASEEM)' portal to help skilled people find sustainable livelihood opportunities.

- ASEEM will provide employers a platform to assess the availability of skilled workforce and formulate their hiring plans

- Aatamanirbhar Skilled Employee Employer Mapping (ASEEM) refers to all the data, trends and analytics which describe the workforce market and map demand of skilled workforce to supply.

- It will provide real-time granular information by identifying relevant skilling requirements and employment prospects.

- ASEEM helps in recruiting a skilled workforce that spurs business competitiveness and economic growth

124. (d) • The Smart Cities Mission opened the registration for India Cycles4Change Challenge on 10thJuly, 2020.

- The challenge was launched on 25th June, 2020 the Ministry of Housing and Urban Affairs.

- The event was marked by description of the Challenge brief and launch of the online portal for submission of application for participating cities.

- The Challenge aims to help cities connect with their citizens as well as experts to develop a unified vision to promote cycling.

125. (b) • On the occasion of 'National Fish Farmers Day' theNFDB in collaboration with the NBFGR will take up the work to establish "Fish Cryobanks" in different parts of the country, which will facilitate all time availability of 'fish sperms' of desired species to fish farmers.

- This would be the first time in the world when "Fish Cryobank" will be established, which can bring a revolutionary change in the fisheries sector in the country for enhancing fish production and productivity and thereby increasing prosperity among the fish farmers.

- The "Cryomilt" technology developed by the NBFGR in support with NFDB may be helpful in establishment of "Fish Cryobanks", which will provide good quality of fish sperms in hatcheries at any time.

126. (c) • NITI Aayog organized a virtual workshop with 47 Central Ministries/Departments in furtherance of the Government of India's decision to monitor the performance of 29 select Global Indices to drive reforms and growth in the country.

- The participants about various background activities carried out by NITI Aayog, NIC, DPIIT, MoSPI and other Ministries in relation to monitoring of these Global Indices.

- It will measure and monitor India's performance on various important social, economic and other parameters through internationally recognized Indices.

127. (a) • The Atal Innovation Mission of Centre's think-tank, NITI Aayog, has launched a free online app development course for school students across the country.

- Under the Atal Tinkering Lab initiative, AIM, NITI Aayog launched the ATL App Development module for India's young minds

- Named, 'ATL App Development Module', the online course intends to make mobile application-developers of school students under Atal Tinkering Lab initiative of AIM.

- The course has been jointly developed by NITI Aayog's AIM and Indian startup, Plezmo.

128. (b) • Generation Unlimited is a new UNICEF-led global partnership that aims to ensure that every young person age 10-24 is in some form of school, learning, training, self-employment, or age-appropriate employment by 2030.

- It aims to co-create and scale up proven solutions related to secondary age-education, skills for learning, employability and decent work, and empowerment, with a focus on girls.

129. (a) • India has 2,967 tigers - a reported growth of 33% in the fourth cycle of the Tiger Census which has been conducted every four years since 2006.

- In 2006, the census showed that the number of tigers in India was only 1,411. In the next cycle of 2010, the numbers grew to 1,706, and in 2014, the tiger numbers grew to 2,226.

- As per the Tiger Census of 2018, the state of Madhya Pradesh has the highest number of tigers at 526. It is followed by Karnataka with 524 tigers and Uttarakhand at 442 tigers.

- The states of Chhattisgarh and Mizoram saw a decline in tiger numbers while Odisha maintained its population.undertaken using the best available science, technology and analytical tools.

- The M-STrIPES app, CaTRAT software and the Extract Compare programs made this tiger census the most accurate in history.

130. (c) • In ATLs, students of class 6th to 12th acquire a problem-solving attitude, develop innovative solutions leveraging technologies like 3D printers, robotics, miniaturised electronics, IOT and programming and DIY kits, with support from teachers and mentors.

- AIM is the Government of India's flagship initiative to promote a culture of innovation and entrepreneurship in the country.

- AIM's objective is to develop new programmes and policies for fostering innovation in different sectors of the economy, provide platform and collaboration opportunities for different stakeholders, create awareness and create an umbrella structure to oversee innovation ecosystem of the country.

131. (c) • NITI Aayog organized a virtual workshop with 47 Central Ministries/Departments in furtherance of the Government of India's decision to monitor the performance of 29 select Global Indices to drive reforms and growth in the country.

- The participants about various background activities carried out by NITI Aayog, NIC, DPIIT, MoSPI and other Ministries in relation to monitoring of these Global Indices.

- It will measure and monitor India's performance on various important social, economic and other parameters through internationally recognized Indices.

132. (a) • The Atal Innovation Mission of Centre's think-tank, NITI Aayog, has launched a free online app development course for school students across the country.

- Under the Atal Tinkering Lab initiative, AIM, NITI Aayog launched the ATL App Development module for India's young minds

- Named, 'ATL App Development Module', the online course intends to make mobile application-developers of school students under Atal Tinkering Lab initiative of AIM.

- The course has been jointly developed by NITI Aayog's AIM and Indian startup, Plezmo.

133. (b) • Generation Unlimited is a new UNICEF-led global partnership that aims to ensure that every young person age 10-24 is in some form of school, learning, training, self-employment, or age-appropriate employment by 2030.

- It aims to co-create and scale up proven solutions related to secondary age-education, skills for learning, employability and decent work, and empowerment, with a focus on girls.

134. (a) • India has 2,967 tigers - a reported growth of 33% in the fourth cycle of the Tiger Census which has been conducted every four years since 2006.

- In 2006, the census showed that the number of tigers in India was only 1,411. In the next cycle of 2010, the numbers grew to 1,706, and in 2014, the tiger numbers grew to 2,226.

- As per the Tiger Census of 2018, the state of Madhya Pradesh has the highest number of tigers at 526. It is followed by Karnataka with 524 tigers and Uttarakhand at 442 tigers.

- The states of Chhattisgarh and Mizoram saw a decline in tiger numbers while Odisha maintained its population.undertaken using the best available science, technology and analytical tools.

- The M-STrIPES app, CaTRAT software and the Extract Compare programs made this tiger census the most accurate in history.

135. (c) • In ATLs, students of class 6th to 12th acquire a problem-solving attitude, develop innovative solutions leveraging technologies like 3D printers, robotics, miniaturised electronics, IOT and programming and DIY kits, with support from teachers and mentors.

- AIM is the Government of India's flagship initiative to promote a culture of innovation and entrepreneurship in the country.

- AIM's objective is to develop new programmes and policies for fostering innovation in different sectors of the economy, provide platform and collaboration opportunities for different stakeholders, create awareness and create an umbrella structure to oversee innovation ecosystem of the country.

136. (d) Six major initiatives of AIM:

- Atal Tinkering Labs-Creating problem-solving mindset across schools in India.

- Atal Incubation Centers-Fostering world class start-ups and adding a new dimension to the incubator model.

- Atal New India Challenges-Fostering product innovations and aligning them to the needs of various sectors/ministries.

- Mentor India Campaign- A national Mentor network in collaboration with public sector, corporates and institutions, to support all the initiatives of the mission.

- Atal Community Innovation Centre- To stimulate community centric innovation and ideas in the unserved /underserved regions of the country including Tier 2 and Tier 3 cities.

- ARISE-To stimulate innovation and research in the MSME industry.

137. (c) • The National Tiger Conservation Authority is a statutory body under the Ministry of Environment, Forests and Climate Change constituted under enabling provisions of the Wildlife (Protection) Act, 1972,

- 'Project Tiger' is a Centrally Sponsored Scheme of the Environment, Forests and Climate Change, providing funding support to tiger range States, for in-situ conservation of tigers in designated tiger reserves, and has put the endangered tiger on an assured path of recovery by saving it from extinction, as revealed by the recent findings of the All India tiger estimation using the refined methodology.

138. (d) • To enlighten about the ancient form of health science- NadiVigyan and its fruitful benefits in curing various spinal disorders, Ministry of Tourism presented a webinar on 'NadiVigyan: A complete solution for spinal disorders' under Dekho Apna Desh webinar series.

- According to Ayurveda, there are 3 doshas or three internal state of a body namely Vata (air+ether) Pitta(Fire+ water) and Kapha (Earth+ water).

- Any imbalance of these elements in the body leads to several disorders.

- Thus, it is being stated in Ayurveda that the diet plan of an individual should be made in consideration to the body type in sync with these elements.

139. (b) • First conceptualised in 2009, NATGRID (under the Ministry of Home affairs) seeks to become the one-stop destination for security and intelligence agencies to access database related to immigration entry and exit, banking and telephone details of a suspect on a "secured platform". The project aims to go live by December 31.

- The MoU, signed in March, will give NATGRID access to the Crime and Criminal Tracking Network and Systems (CCTNS) database, a platform that links around 14,000 police stations.
- It links intelligence and investigation agencies.
- All State police are mandated to file First Information Reports (FIR) in the CCTNS.

140. (d) • India's five tiger landscapes are: Shivalik Hills and Gangetic Plains, Central Indian Landscape and Eastern Ghats, Western Ghats, North-East Hills and Brahmaputra Plains, and the Sundarbans.

Since tigers occur across varied habitats and a large geographical expanse of India, we divided tiger bearing habitats into five major landscapes

| Shivalik-Gangetic plains | Central India and Eastern Ghats | Western Ghats | North Eastern Hills and Brahmaputra Flood Plains | Sundarbans |

141. (a) • DRDO has developed P7 Heavy Drop System which is capable of para dropping military stores up to 7-ton weight class from IL-76 aircraft.

- P-7 Heavy Drop System is used for Para drop of military stores (vehicle/ ammunition/ equipment) of 7 Ton weight class.
- System has been developed successfully with 100% indigenous resources. P-7 HDS has been inducted in the Army.
- The Human Resource Development (HRD) Ministry e-launched the world's most affordable probe free RT-PCR based #COVID19 diagnostic kit, COROSURE developed by Indian Institute of Technology Delhi (IIT)

142. (b) • The Human Resource Development (HRD) Ministry e-launched the world's most affordable probe free RT-PCR based #COVID19 diagnostic kit, COROSURE developed by Indian Institute of Technology Delhi (IIT)

- The test, Corosure, has been billed as the world's most affordable probe free RT-PCR based Covid-19 diagnostic kit.
- The test, Corosure, has been billed as the world's most affordable probe free RT-PCR based Covid-19 diagnostic kit.
- The product is approved by the Indian Council of Medical Research (ICMR) and the Drug Controller General of India (DCGI).

143. (b) • Sustainable Growth Pillar is an important pillar of India-US Strategic Energy Partnership co-chaired by NITI Aayog and USAID.

- The SG pillar entails energy data management, energy modelling and collaboration on low carbon technologies as three key activities.
- In the joint working group meeting of the Sustainable Growth Pillar on July 2, 2020, an India Energy Modeling Forum was launched.
- The forum provides an unbiased platform to discuss the contemporary issues revolving around energy and environment.

144. (a) • The country's first fully indigenously developed vaccine against pneumonia has got approval from the Drug Controller General of India (DCGI)

- With the help of Special Expert Committee (SEC) for vaccines, the drug regulator reviewed the phase I, II and III clinical trial data submitted by Pune-based firm Serum Institute of India and then granted the market approval for Pneumococcal Polysaccharide Conjugate Vaccine.
- The vaccine will be used for active immunisation against invasive disease and pneumonia caused by 'Streptococcus pneumonia' among infants.

145. (a) Azad Pattan hydel power project

- The 700-MW hydel power project is being built on the Jhelum river in Sudhoti district of Pakistan Occupied Kashmir

- Pakistan and China signed an agreement for the 700 MW Azad Pattan hydel power project on the Jhelum river in Sudhoti district of Pakistan Occupied Kashmir (PoK).

Karot Hydropower station

- The Karot Hydropower station, the third project being executed by China on the Jhelum is on the boundaries of Kotli district in PoK and Rawalpindi district in Pakistan's Punjab province.

- According to the CPEC site, construction is under progress, and the project is expected to be commissioned by the end of 2021.

146. (a) • The first on-line NISHTHA programme for 1200 Key Resources Persons of Andhra Pradesh was launched by Union HRD Minister

- NISHTHA is a National Initiative for School Heads' and Teachers' Holistic Advancement at the elementary stage under Samagra Shiksha -a flagship programme of MHRD to improve learning outcomes.

- NISHTHA in face-to-face mode was launched on 21st August, 2019. Thereafter, 33 states/UTs have launched this programme in their states/ UTs in collaboration under Samagra Shiksha, a Centrally Sponsored Scheme.

- Around 23,000 Key Resource Persons and 17.5 lakh teachers and school heads have been covered under this NISHTHA face to face mode till date.

147. (c) • The Economic and Social Council is at the heart of the United Nations system to advance the three dimensions of sustainable development - economic, social and environmental.

- It is the central platform for fostering debate and innovative thinking, forging consensus on ways forward, and coordinating efforts to achieve internationally agreed goals.

- A number of non-governmental organizations have been granted consultative status to the Council to participate in the work of the United Nations.

- The UN Charter established ECOSOC in 1945 as one of the six main organs of the United Nations

148. (a) • The eligible beneficiaries under the Scheme would be Farmer Producer Organizations (FPOs), MSMEs, Section 8 Companies, Private Companies and individual entrepreneur with minimum 10% margin money contribution by them.

- The balance 90% would be the loan component to be made available by scheduled banks.

- Government of India will provide 3% interest subvention to eligible beneficiaries.

- There will be 2 years moratorium period for principal loan amount and 6 years repayment period thereafter.

149. (a) • ZyCoV-D, the plasmid DNA vaccine designed and developed by Zydus and partially funded by the Department of Biotechnology, has initiated Phase I/ II clinical trials in healthy subjects, making it the first indigenously developed vaccine for COVID-19 to be administered in humans in India.

- The Department of Biotechnology Government of India has partnered with Zydus to address rapid development of an indigenous vaccine for COVID-19 under the National Biopharma Mission.

150. (d) • The project "Development of Pilgrimage Amenities at Somnath, Gujarat" sanctioned under the PRASHAD scheme in March 2017 has been successfully completed with the cost of Rs. 45.36 crores.

- The 'National Mission on Pilgrimage Rejuvenation and Spiritual, Heritage Augmentation Drive' (PRASHAD) launched by the Ministry of Tourism in the year 2014-15 with the objective of integrated development of identified pilgrimage and heritage destinations.

- The scheme aimed at infrastructure development such as entry points (Road, Rail and Water Transport), last mile connectivity, basic tourism facilities like Information/ Interpretation Centers

Practice Questions Set – 2
General Studies Paper I

1. Consider the following statements about Rozgar Yukta Gaon (RYG)
   1. It aims at introducing an subsidy-led business model in place of enterprise-led model
   2. It will be rolled out in all the villages by providing charkhas, looms & warping units to khadi artisans

   Which of the statements given above is/are correct?

   (a) 1 only   (b) 2 only

   (c) Both 1 and 2   (d) Neither 1 nor 2

2. Consider the following statements about Market Promotion and Development Assistance Scheme (MPDA)
   1. It was launched as a unified scheme by merging different schemes implemented by the Khadi sector
   2. Under MPDA grant/subsidy provided for construction of khadi plazas

   Which of the statements given above is/are correct?

   (a) 1 only   (b) 2 only

   (c) Both 1 and 2   (d) Neither 1 nor 2

3. Consider the following statements about the Affordable Rental Housing Complexes (ARHCs) programme
   1. It has been launched to provide rental accommodations to migrant and urban poor.
   2. It has been launched under the Pradhan Mantri AwasYojana Urban (PMAY-U) as part of Atma Nirbhar Bharat Abhiyan

   Which of the statements given above is/are correct?

   (a) 1 only   (b) 2 only

   (c) Both 1 and 2   (d) Neither 1 nor 2

4. Consider the following statements about National Real Estate Development Council (NAREDCO)
   1. It was established as an autonomous self-regulatory body
   2. It is under the aegis of Ministry of Housing and Urban Affairs, Govt. of India.
   3. It is a single platform where government, industry and public would discuss various problems and opportunities of real estate industry in India

   Which of the statements given above is/are correct?

   (a) 1 and 2 only   (b) 2 only

   (c) 1, 2 and 3   (d) 1and 3 only

5. Consider the following statements about recent space missions on Mars by various countries?
   1. China is sending both a rover and an orbiter.
   2. The UAE has launched an orbiter and rover recently.
   3. NASA and the European Space Agency are launching a dune buggy in 2026 to fetch the rock samples

   Which of the statements given above is/are correct?

   (a) 1 only   (b) 2 only

   (c) 2 and 3 only   (d) 1 and 3 only

6. Consider the following statements about Atmospheric Research Testbeds
   1. This is going to be launched in 2021 by the Ministry of Earth Sciences
   2. It will be an open field observatory in tropics
   3. The research testbeds will help in better understanding of the monsoonal clouds

   Which of the statements given above is/are correct?

   (a) 1 only   (b) 1 and 2 only

   (c) 2 and 3only   (d) 1, 2 and 3

7. Consider the following statements about Society for Innovation and Entrepreneurship (SINE)
   1. It is a technology business incubator at IIT Bombay
   2. It is supported by the Ministry of Education

   Which of the statements given above is/are correct?

   (a) 1 only   (b) 2 only

   (c) Both 1 and 2   (d) Neither 1 nor 2

8. Recently an all encompassing digitisation drive has been embarked by which of the following Ministries?

(a) The Ministry of Electronics and Information Technology

(b) TRIFED under Ministry of Tribal Affairs

(c) Ministry of Human Resource and Development

(d) Ministry of Home Affairs

9. Recently the 2nd Empathy e-Conclave was organised on the occasion of World Hepatitis Day by which of the following organisations?

(a) World Health Organisation

(b) The Indian Council of Medical Research

(c) Ministry of Health and Family Welfare

(d) None of the above

10. The Reserve Bank of India (RBI) has signed an agreement for extending a $400-million currency swap facility to Sri Lanka

With reference to it consider the following statements

1. It has signed the agreement under the South Asian Association for Regional Cooperation (SAARC) framework

2. These swap operations carry no exchange rate or other market risk

Which of the statements given above is/are correct?

(a) 1 only   (b) 2 only

(c) Both 1 and 2   (d) Neither 1 nor 2

11. Consider the following statements about the New National Education Policy 2020

1. The draft of the policy was prepared by a panel of experts led by K Kasturirangan.

2. There will be clear cut separation of learning areas in terms of curricular, co-curricular or extra-curricular areas

3. The system of 'affiliated colleges' will be gradually phased out in 15 years.

Which of the statements given above is/are correct?

(a) 1 and 2 only   (b) 2 only

(c) 1, 2 and 3   (d) 1and 3 only

12. Consider the following statements about India's first COVID-19 blockchain platform, BelYo.

1. The Project has been funded jointly by World Health Organisation and Ministry of Health

2. Its objective is to convert COVID-19 related clinical data of developing vaccines currently from the physical form into digital assets

Which of the statements given above is/are correct?

(a) 1 only   (b) 2 only

(c) Both 1 and 2   (d) Neither 1 nor 2

13. Consider the following statements about recently launched iCREST

1. It has been launched by NITI Aayog's Atal Innovation Mission (AIM).

2. Under the initiative, the AIM's incubators are set to be upscaled and provided requisite support to foster the incubation enterprise economy

Which of the statements given above is/are correct?

(a) 1 only   (b) 2 only

(c) Both 1 and 2   (d) Neither 1 nor 2

14. Under a multi-pronged mission, codenamed "Operation Breathing Space" India is working with which of the following nations on four different kinds of rapid tests?

(a) Germany   (b) USA

(c) Japan   (d) Israel

15. Consider the following statements about Blockchain Technology

1. It makes the history of any digital asset unalterable and transparent

2. It creates a decentralized distribution chain that gives everyone access to the document at the same time

3. It is managed by a cluster of computers owned by any single entity

Which of the statements given above is/are correct?

(a) 1 and 2 only   (b) 2 only

(c) 1, 2 and 3   (d) 1 and 3 only

16. The government approved a new education policy that seeks to revamp all aspects of education structure

With reference to it consider the following statements about the New Education Policy

1. It aims to achieve universal access to education to all between age groups of 3-18 years by 2030.

2. The objective is to increase the Gross Enrolment Ratio in primary and secondary education including vocational education from 26.3% to 50% by 2035.

Which of the statements given above is/are correct?

(a) 1 only   (b) 2 only

(c) Both 1 and 2   (d) Neither 1 nor 2

17. Consider the following statements about Subhash Chandra Bose Aapda Prabandhan Puraskar

    1. It has been administered by the Ministry of Home Affairs

    2. Its objective is to recognise the excellent work done only by the individuals in the field of disaster management.

    3. Only Indian nationals and Indian institutions can apply for the award.

    Which of the statements given above is/are correct?

    (a) 1 and 2 only   (b) 2 only

    (c) 1, 2 and 3   (d) 3 only

18. Consider the following statements about UDAN regional connectivity Scheme

    1. The sole objective of this scheme is to enhance the existing regional airports to increase the number of operational airports for scheduled civilian flights

    2. The regional connectivity scheme will be applicable on route length between 200 to 800 km

    Which of the statements given above is/are correct?

    (a) 1 only   (b) 2 only

    (c) Both 1 and 2   (d) Neither 1 nor 2

19. Consider the following statements about Unnat Bharat Abhiyan

    1. It has been launched by the Ministry of Human Resource Development (MHRD)

    2. Its aim is to connect Central government ministries with local communities to address the development challenges through appropriate technologies.

    Which of the statements given above is/are correct?

    (a) 1 only   (b) 2 only

    (c) Both 1 and 2   (d) Neither 1 nor 2

20. Consider the following statements about the recently released New Education Policy

    1. The (BVoc) degrees has been introduced in the New Education Policy

    2. Foreign languages, such as Korean, Japanese etc will be offered at the Higher level.

    3. The undergraduate degree will be of either 3 or 4-year duration, with single exit options

    Which of the statements given above is/are incorrect?

(a) 1 and 2 only   (b) 2 only

(c) 1, 2 and 3   (d) 1and 3 only

21. Consider the following statements about Gramodyog Vikas Yojana

    1. It has been launched by the Minister of Rural Development

    2. This programme will benefit artisans involved in manufacturing of handicrafts

    Which of the statements given above is/are correct?

    (a) 1 only   (b) 2 only

    (c) Both 1 and 2   (d) Neither 1 nor 2

22. Consider the following statements about SKOCH award

    1. It is the highest civilian honour in the country conferred by an independent organisation.

    2. It covers the best of efforts in the area of digital, financial and social inclusion.

    Which of the statements given above is/are incorrect?

    (a) 1 only   (b) 2 only

    (c) Both 1 and 2   (d) Neither 1 nor 2

23. Consider the following Confederation of Real Estate Developers' Associations of India (CREDAI)

    1. It comes under the ambit of Housing and Urban Affairs Ministry

    2. It is the apex body of public and private real estate developers

    Which of the statements given above is/are correct?

    (a) 1 only   (b) 2 only

    (c) Both 1 and 2   (d) Neither 1 nor 2

24. Consider the following statements about the recently launched Mars Rover Perseverance by NASA

    1. The mission objective is to bring the first Martian rock samples back to Earth

    2. The rover also includes equipment for extracting oxygen from Mars' thin carbon-dioxide atmosphere.

    Which of the statements given above is/are correct?

    (a) 1 only   (b) 2 only

    (c) Both 1 and 2   (d) Neither 1 nor 2

25. Consider the following statements about Global Initiative on Sharing All Influenza Data

    1. The World Health Organisation is the official host of the GISAID platform

2. It provides a publicly accessible database designed by scientist for scientist, to improve the sharing of influenza data.

3. The Initiative ensures that open access to data in GISAID is provided free-of-charge to all individuals

Which of the statements given above is/are correct?

(a) 1 and 2 only   (b) 2 only

(c) 2 and 3 only   (d) 1 and 3 only

26. Consider the following statements about Interest Subsidy Eligibility Certificate Scheme (ISEC)

1. It was launched to help food processing institutions in mobilizing the capital funds from banking institutions.

2. ISEC has been implemented by the Ministry of Agriculture and Farmers' Welfare

Which of the statements given above is/are correct?

(a) 1 only   (b) 2 only

(c) Both 1 and 2   (d) Neither 1 nor 2

27. Gramodyog Vikas Yojana has been approved for the benefit of artisans involved in manufacturing of agarbatti

With reference to it consider the following statements

1. Initially four Pilot Projects will be started

2. The Khadi and Village Industries Commission (KVIC), will provide training, and assist artisans working in this area

3. KVIC is a statutory organizations, working under the M/o MSME

Which of the statements given above is/are correct?

(a) 1 and 2 only   (b) 2 only

(c) 2 and 3 only   (d) 1, 2 and 3

28. Consider the following statements about Vidyarthi Vigyan Manthan 2020-21

1. It has been launched by the Ministry of Human Resource and Development

2. It is a national programme for popularizing science among school students of Class 6th to 11th.

Which of the statements given above is/are correct?

(a) 1 only

(b) 2 only

(c) Both 1 and 2

(d) Neither 1 nor 2

29. SpaceX capsule and NASA crew made its first splashdown recently

With reference to it consider the following statements

1. It is the first commercially built and operated spacecraft to carry people to and from orbit.

2. It was the first ever splashdown by US astronauts

3. It was the first time a private company launched people into orbit

Which of the statements given above is/are correct?

(a) 1 and 3 only   (b) 2 only

(c) 2 and 3 only   (d) 1, 2 and 3

30. Consider the following statements about the Electronic Vaccine Intelligence Network (eVIN)

1. It is implemented under National Health Mission (NHM) by Ministry of Health and Family Welfare.

2. eVIN aimed at strengthening immunization supply chain systems across the country.

3. It also provides real-time information on vaccine stocks and flows, and storage temperatures across all cold chain points

Which of the statements given above is/are correct?

(a) 1 and 2 only   (b) 2 only

(c) 2 and 3 only   (d) 1, 2 and 3

31. Consider the following statements about the guidelines issued by the Bureau of Civil Aviation Security (BCAS) for drone operating systems

1. The capacity to retain recording of minimum 30 days shall be in place for all categories of remotely piloted aircraft system (RPAs)

2. An RPA or drone is in nano or mini category if it has weight less than 250 grams.

3. If a drone is between 250 grams and 2 kg, it is in the micro category.

Which of the statements given above is/are correct?

(a) 1 and 2 only   (b) 2 only

(c) 2 and 3 only   (d) 1and 3 only

32. Consider the following statements about the National Cooperative Development Corporation

1. It is an apex-level statutory institution

2. It is under the Ministry of Agriculture and Farmers' Welfare

3. The cooperatives have acquired a huge network of small and marginal farmers and the rural poor

Which of the statements given above is/are correct?

(a) 1 only (b) 2 only

(c) 1, 2 and 3 (d) 1and 3 only

33. The result of national annual innovation Marathon challenge ATL Tinkering Marathon 2019 has been declared recently

With reference to it consider the following statements?

1. It is a flagship event of Atal Innovation Mission (AIM) and NITI Aayog in association with the department of science and technology

2. This year, the challenge was executed by AIM in partnership with MyGOV on MyGov's Innovate Platform.

Which of the statements given above is/are correct?

(a) 1 only (b) 2 only

(c) Both 1 and 2 (d) Neither 1 nor 2

34. Consider the following statements about Habitat Model for Efficiency and Comfort

1. The project has been developed by the Energy and Resources Institute (TERI) in partnership with the Department of Science & Technology

2. They have developed novel external shading solution for windows in both residential and commercial buildings

Which of the statements given above is/are correct?

(a) 1 only (b) 2 only

(c) Both 1 and 2 (d) Neither 1 nor 2

35. Consider the following statements about The Energy and Resources Institute (TERI)

1. It is a not-for-profit organisation

2. It works in the fields of energy, environment, and sustainable development

3. It was formerly known as the Tata Energy Research Institute.

Which of the statements given above is/are correct?

(a) 1 only (b) 2 only

(c) 1, 2 and 3 (d) 1and 3 only

36. Consider the following statements about Sendai Framework

1. It is for Disaster Risk Reduction

2. It is a non-binding agreement, which the signatory nations, including India

3. The Sendai Framework is the successor instrument to the Hyogo Framework for Action (HFA)

Which of the statements given above is/are correct?

(a) 1 and 2 only (b) 1, 2 and 3

(c) 2 and 3 only (d) 1and 3 only

37. Consider the following statements about the National Building Code of India (NBC)

1. It is a national instrument providing guidelines for regulating the building construction activities across the country.

2. It serves as a Model Code for adoption by all agencies involvedin building construction works

Which of the statements given above is/are correct?

(a) 1 only (b) 2 only

(c) Both 1 and 2 (d) Neither 1 nor 2

38. Recently the Indian Railways has commissioned longest bridge in the South Western Zone on Bhima river

Bhima river is the tributary of which of the following rivers?

(a) Krishna River (b) Godavari

(c) Cauvery (d) None of the above

39. Consider the following statements about Innovation and Agri-entrepreneurship Development programme

1. It has been launched under Rashtriya Krishi Vikas Yojana

2. Its objective is to promote innovation and agripreneurship by providing financial support

Which of the statements given above is/are correct?

(a) 1 only (b) 2 only

(c) Both 1 and 2 (d) Neither 1 nor 2

40. Consider the following statements about Abanindranath Tagore

1. He established Bengal school of artto counter the English influence on Indian artists.

2. He was the first major supporter of swadeshi values in Indian art.

3. Indian Society of Oriental Art was established by Abanindranath Tagore

Which of the statements given above is/are correct?

(a) 1 and 2 only (b) 1 only

(c) 2 and 3 only (d) 1, 2 and 3

41. Consider the following statements about the India Water Resources Information System

    1. It contains information related to the level of water in all the dams, reservoirs and canals through dashboards

    2. It is open to the public, and accessible through the web portal

    3. India WRIS receives data from many central and state agencies

    Which of the statements given above is/are correct?

    (a) 1 and 2 only   (b) 1, 2 and 3

    (c) 2 and 3 only   (d) 1 and 3 only

42. Indian Railways is introducing first "Kisan Rail" from Devlali to Danapur

    With reference to it consider the following statements about Kisan Rail

    1. The train will provide seamless supply chain of wheat, rice and other cereals.

    2. It will be the first ever multi commodity trains

    Which of the statements given above is/are correct?

    (a) 1 only   (b) 2 only

    (c) Both 1 and 2   (d) Neither 1 nor 2

43. Consider the following statements about the National Centre for Good Governance (NCGG)

    1. It is an autonomous institute under the aegis of Department of Administrative Reforms and Public Grievances

    2. Its objective is to be a think tank for governance & policy reforms

    Which of the statements given above is/are correct?

    (a) 1 only   (b) 2 only

    (c) Both 1 and 2   (d) Neither 1 nor 2

44. Consider the following statements about the Indian Technical and Economic Cooperation (ITEC)

    1. It is a bilateral programme of assistance of the Government of India.

    2. ITEC Programme was launched in 1964 by the Ministry of External Affairs.

    3. The ITEC Programme, fully funded by the Government of India

    Which of the statements given above is/are correct?

    (a) 1 and 2 only   (b) 2 and 3 only

    (c) 1and 3 only   (d) 1, 2 and 3

45. Consider the following statements about Gustave Trouvé Award

    1. Recently Aditya, India's first solar ferry bagged the prestigious Gustave Trouvé Award

    2. It is the only international award given only to companies, building & innovating in state-of-the-art electric boats.

    Which of the statements given above is/are correct?

    (a) 1 only   (b) 2 only

    (c) Both 1 and 2   (d) Neither 1 nor 2

46. Consider the following statements about recently launched the My Handloom portal

    1. It has been launched only for theindividual weavers

    2. It will act as One-stop shop for information on all handloom schemes

    3. Weavers can apply for various benefits under the various handloom schemes usingMy Handloom portal

    Which of the statements given above is/are correct?

    (a) 1 and 2 only   (b) 1, 2 and 3

    (c) 2 and 3 only   (d) 1 and 3 only

47. Consider the following statements about Clean India Mission

    1. The Clean India Mission (Rural)was financed and monitored through the Ministry of Drinking Water and Sanitation

    2. The Clean India Mission (Urban)was overseen by the Ministry of Housing and Urban Affairs.

    Which of the statements given above is/are correct?

    (a) 1 only   (b) 2 only

    (c) Both 1 and 2   (d) Neither 1 nor 2

48. Consider the following statements about Agriculture Infrastructure Fund

    1. It is a Central Sector Scheme

    2. The Fund will catalyze the creation of pre and post-harvest management infrastructure

    Which of the statements given above is/are correct?

    (a) 1 only   (b) 2 only

    (c) Both 1 and 2   (d) Neither 1 nor 2

49. Consider the following statements about PM - KISAN

    1. It is a Central Sponsored scheme with 100% funding from Government of India.

2. An income support of 6,000/- per year in three equal instalments will be provided to small and marginal farmer families

3. The identification of the farmer families which are eligible to avail the benefits will be administered by the Ministry of Statistics and Programme Implementation

Which of the statements given above is/are correct?

(a) 1 and 2 only   (b) 1, 2 and 3

(c) 2 only   (d) 1 and 3 only

50. Consider the following statements about Indian Textile Sourcing Fair 2020.

1. It has been launched by the Department for Promotion of Industry & Internal Trade.

2. The government is providing online training opportunities to weavers and handloom producers by organising such virtual fairs

Which of the statements given above is/are correct?

(a) 1 only   (b) 2 only

(c) Both 1 and 2   (d) Neither 1 nor 2

51. Consider the following statements about the Handloom Mark Scheme (HLM) app

1. It enables the weaver located at any corner of the country to apply for Handloom Mark registration

2. The app helps ascertain the genuineness of the product through QR code labels affixed on each handloom product.

Which of the statements given above is/are correct?

(a) 1 only   (b) 2 only

(c) Both 1 and 2   (d) Neither 1 nor 2

52. Consider the following statements about the recently inaugurated first ever undersea optical fibre cable project for Andaman and Nicobar Islands

1. The work of laying undersea cable has been executed by a Japanese firm

2. Total eight Islands will be connected with Chennai through the submarine optical fibre cable project

3. The Chennai - Andaman and Nicobar Islands (CANI) connecting submarine optical fibre cable project will be handled by BSNL

Which of the statements given above is/are correct?

(a) 1 and 3 only   (b) 1, 2 and 3

(c) 2 only   (d) 3 only

53. Consider the following statements about Island Development Agency

1. It is chaired by the Union Home Minister

2. Total 10 islands from Andaman & Nicobar, Lakshadweep and Daman & Diu have been identified for holistic development in the first phase.

Which of the statements given above is/are correct?

(a) 1 only   (b) 2 only

(c) Both 1 and 2   (d) Neither 1 nor 2

54. Consider the following statements about IC-IMPACTS (the India-Canada Centre for Innovative Multidisciplinary Partnerships to Accelerate Community Transformation and Sustainability)

1. It has been established through the Indian Networks of Centres of Excellence (NCE) as a new Centre dedicated to the development of research collaborations between Canada and India.

2. The major focus areas of research cooperation under the IC-IMPACT are green buildings and smart cities

3. DST has been working with IC-IMPACTS for research partnerships since 2013.

Which of the statements given above is/are correct?

(a) 1 and 3 only   (b) 1, 2 and 3

(c) 2 and 3 only   (d) 3 only

55. World Elephant Day celebrated on August 1, 2 is an international annual event, dedicated to the preservation and protection of the world's elephants.

With reference to it consider the following statements

1. Asian elephants are listed as "Endangered" on the IUCN Red List of threatened species.

2. The National Portal on human elephant conflict called "Surakhsya" has been launched on this occasion.

3. Indian Elephant has been listed in the Appendix I of the Convention of the Migratory species

Which of the statements given above is/are correct?

(a) 1 and 2 only   (b) 1, 2 and 3

(c) 2 and 3 only   (d) 1 and 3 only

56. Indigenous seed balls named BEEG (Bio -compost Enriched Eco-friendly Globule) which will help people and farmers in plantation with safety in Corona times has been developed by which of the following?

(a) Ministry of Agriculture and Farmers Welfare

(b) Indian Council of Agricultural Research (ICAR)

(c) Department of Biotechnology

(d) None of the above

57. Consider the following statements about KavKaz 2020

   1. India is going to participate in the Russian Kavkaz 2020 strategic command-post exercise.

   2. 150 Army personnel will be heading to Astrakhan in Southern Russia for the exercise

   3. Only those countries which are members of SCO are invited to participate in KavKaz 2020

   Which of the statements given above is/are incorrect?

   (a) 1 only   (b) 2 only

   (c) 1, 2 and 3   (d) 1and 3 only

58. Consider the following statements about the National Technical Advisory Group on Immunisation (NTAGI)

   1. It is India's apex advisory body on immunization

   2. It was established in 2001 by an order of the Parliament

   Which of the statements given above is/are correct?

   (a) 1 only   (b) 2 only

   (c) Both 1 and 2   (d) Neither 1 nor 2

59. Consider the following statements about COVID-19 vaccine Sputnik V

   1. It is based on the DNA of a SARS-CoV-2 type adenovirus

   2. It used inanimate particles created on the basis of adenovirus

   3. Adenovirus is a common cold virus.

   Which of the statements given above is/are correct?

   (a) 1 only   (b) 2 only

   (c) 1, 2 and 3   (d) 1and 3 only

60. Consider the following statements about The Shanghai Cooperation Organisation (SCO)

   1. It is a permanent intergovernmental international organisation

   2. India is one of the founding members of this group

   3. The secretariat of SCO is based in Shanghai, China.

   Which of the statements given above is/are incorrect?

   (a) 3 only   (b) 1 and 3 only

   (c) 2 and 3 only   (d) 1 only

61. Consider the following statements about VijnanaBharati (VIBHA)

   1. It is a non-profit organisation

   2. It is a national movement for the propagation and popularization of science & technology

   3. It is partially funded by the Department of Science and Technology

   Which of the statements given above is/are correct?

   (a) 1 and 2 only   (b) 2 only

   (c) 1, 2 and 3   (d) 1and 3 only

62. Consider the following statements about National Council of Educational Research & Training (NCERT)

   1. It is an organization set up by the Government of India to assist and advise both the central and state governments on academic matters related to school education.

   2. The objective is to undertake, promote and coordinate research in areas related to school and higher education

   Which of the statements given above is/are correct?

   (a) 1 only   (b) 2 only

   (c) Both 1 and 2   (d) Neither 1 nor 2

63. Consider the following statements about the Production Linked Incentive Scheme (PLI)

   1. The scheme is for Small Scale Electronics Manufacturing

   2. This scheme will provide incentive to boost domestic manufacturing

   3. It also attracts large investments in the electronics value chain including mobile phones, electronic components

   Which of the statements given above is/are correct?

   (a) 1 and 2 only   (b) 2 only

   (c) 1, 2 and 3   (d) 1and 3 only

64. 'E-Raksha Bandhan', aimed at creating awareness among the public on cybercrimes across the State and Disha police stations to tackle cases of crimes against women in a speedy manner are launched by which of the following states?

   (a) Andhra Pradesh   (b) Telangana

   (c) Karnataka   (d) Uttar Pradesh

65. Consider the following statements about Vigyan Prasar (VP)

1. It is an autonomous organization under the Department of Science and Technology (DST)

2. Its objective is broadcast science based documentaries to propagate and popularize Science & Technology among students and masses.

Which of the statements given above is/are correct?

(a) 1 only   (b) 2 only

(c) Both 1 and 2   (d) Neither 1 nor 2

66. Consider the following statements about TRIFED

1. It is established under the Multi-State Cooperative Societies Act, 1984 by the Government of India as a national level Cooperative body.

2. TRIFED plays the dual role of both a market developer and a service provider

3. TRIBES India is the private brand under which the sourced handcrafted products from the tribal people are sold.

Which of the statements given above is/are correct?

(a) 1 only   (b) 1 and 2 only

(c) 2 and 3only   (d) 1, 2 and 3

67. The Union Environment Minister, released the detailed report of Tiger Census on the eve of Global Tiger Day

With reference to it consider the following statements?

1. India has 70 percent of world's tiger population.

2. LIDAR based survey technology will be used to get more accuracy in counting number of tigers

3. Guinness World Records recognises India's efforts as the world largest camera trap survey of wildlife.

Which of the statements given above is/are correct?

(a) 1 and 3 only   (b) 2 only

(c) 2 and 3only   (d) 1, 2 and 3

68. Consider the following statements about currency swap agreement

1. Reserve Bank of India has currency swap agreement with Japan, USA and Russia

2. The Reserve Bank of India also offers similar swap lines to central banks in the SAARC and BIMSTEC regions

Which of the statements given above is/are correct?

(a) 1 only   (b) 2 only

(c) Both 1 and 2   (d) Neither 1 nor 2

69. Ministry of Human Resource Development has initiated many projects to assist teachers, scholars and students in their pursuit of learning

Which of the following is/are not an initiative of MHRD?

1. DIKSHA platform

2. SMILE (Social Media Interface for Learning Engagement)

3. Swayam Prabha TV Channel

4. e-PathShala

Choose the correct from the options given below

(a) 1 and 3 only   (b) 2 only

(c) 3only   (d) 1only

70. Consider the following statements about coastal shipping

1. The movement of goods in cargo from one coast to other.

2. Coastal shipping can be national or international.

3. Coastal shipping is within 20 nautical miles of the coastline

Which of the statements given above is/are correct?

(a) 1 only   (b) 2 only

(c) 1 and 2only   (d) 1, 2 and 3

71. Consider the following statements about PASSEX Exercise

1. Recently Indian Army undertook Passage Exercise (PASSEX) with US Army .

2. This is for the first time that any Indian defence force has conducted the Passage Exercise

Which of the statements given above is/are correct?

(a) 1 only   (b) 2 only

(c) Both 1 and 2   (d) Neither 1 nor 2

72. Consider the following statements about Malabar Exercise

1. It is a biennial trilateral naval exercise between the navies of India, Japan, and the USA

2. Japan is a permanent partner of Malabar Exercise since its inception

3. Australia and Singapore also participated as non-permanent participants

Which of the statements given above is/are incorrect?

(a) 1 and 2 only   (b) 2 only

(c) 1, 2 and 3   (d) 1and 3 only

73. Consider the following statements about Delhi serological survey

1. The serological test is performed to diagnose infections and autoimmune illnesses.

2. The survey included the IgG Enzyme-Linked Immunosorbent Assay (ELISA) test

3. The IgG test is also useful for detecting acute infections

Which of the statements given above is/are correct?

(a) 1 and 2 only   (b) 2 only

(c) 1, 2 and 3   (d) 1and 3 only

74. Consider the following statements about India Ideas Summit 2020

1. It is being hosted by NITI Aayog.

2. Indian and European Countries (EU) policymakers, state-level officials and leaders from business and society participated virtually in the summit

Which of the statements given above is/are correct?

(a) 1 only   (b) 2 only

(c) Both 1 and 2   (d) Neither 1 nor 2

75. Consider the following statements about the U.S.-India Business Council

1. It is the premier business advocacy organization, composed of top-tier U.S. and Indian companies

2. The Council is the largest bilateral trade association in the United States

Which of the statements given above is/are correct?

(a) 1 only   (b) 2 only

(c) Both 1 and 2   (d) Neither 1 nor 2

76. Consider the following statements about National Automotive Testing and R&D Infrastructure Project (NATRiP)

1. It is a fully Government of India funded project

2. Ministry of Heavy Industry & Public Enterprises (MoHI&PE) is the focal Ministry for implementation of NATRIP

Which of the statements given above is/are correct?

(a) 1 only   (b) 2 only

(c) Both 1 and 2   (d) Neither 1 nor 2

77. Consider the following statements about ASPIRE portal

1. The portal has been prepared with the help of the UNICEF for the college students

2. Information pertaining to college fee, subjects, admission procedure etc can be obtained from this portal.

Which of the statements given above is/are correct?

(a) 1 only   (b) 2 only

(c) Both 1 and 2   (d) Neither 1 nor 2

78. Consider the following statements about Retrofit of Air Conditioning to Improve Air Quality for Safety and Efficiency" (RAISE)

1. It is initiated Jointly by Energy Efficiency Services Ltd (EESL) and World Energy Forum

2. Its objective is to enhance building and appliance efficiency improve building performance, promote energy conservation, and also to improve indoor air quality.

Which of the statements given above is/are correct?

(a) 1 only   (b) 2 only

(c) Both 1 and 2   (d) Neither 1 nor 2

79. South Asia Women in Energy (SAWIE) platform has been launched by which of the following organisations?

(a) SAARC   (b) USAID

(c) World Bank   (d) NITI Aayog

80. The largest automotive technology event in the country NuGen Mobility Summit is organised by which of the following organisations

(a) The Ministry of Heavy Industries and Public Enterprises

(b) The Ministry of Electronics and Information Technology

(c) The Department for Promotion of Industry and Internal Trade (DPIIT)

(d) None of the above

81. Manodarpan initiatives have been launched recently by which of the following organisations?

(a) Ministry of Culture

(b) Ministry of Health and Family Welfare

(c) HRD Ministry

(d) Ministry of Tourism

82. Consider the following statements about the Hope Probe

1. The Hope Probe blasted off from Japan's Tanegashima Space Center

2. It is the first MARS mission of The Japan Aerospace Exploration Agency (JAXA)

3. It will not land on the planet, but instead orbit it for a whole Martian year

Which of the statements given above is/are incorrect?

(a) 1 and 2 only   (b) 2 only

(c) 1, 2 and 3   (d) 1and 3 only

83. Consider the following statements about the New Consumer Protection Act 2019

1. Consumers can file complaints from anywhere

2. Consumers need to hire lawyer to represent their cases.

3. On misleading advertisements there is fine for manufacturers but no jail term

Which of the statements given above is/are correct?

(a) 1 only   (b) 2 and 3 only

(c) 1, 2 and 3   (d) 1and 3 only

84. Consider the following statement s about Retrofit of Air-conditioning to improve Indoor Air Quality for Safety and Efficiency (RAISE)

1. It has been launched by the Ministry of Environment, Forest and Climate

2. The initiative will alleviate the issue of bad air quality in households across the nation and pioneer ways to make them healthier and greener.

Which of the statements given above is/are correct?

(a) 1 only   (b) 2 only

(c) Both 1 and 2   (d) Neither 1 nor 2

85. Consider the following statements about MAITREE

1. It is a joint naval exercise between India and US

2. Japan and Australia also participated as an observer in the recent MAITREE Exercise

Which of the statements given above is/are incorrect?

(a) 1 only   (b) 2 only

(c) Both 1 and 2   (d) Neither 1 nor 2

86. Consider the following statements about the recently launched Manodarpan Initiative of HRD Ministry

1. The objective is to provide psychosocial support to students and teachers for their mental health & well-being during the COVID outbreak

2. This initiative has been included in the ATMANIRBHAR BHARAT ABHIYAN

Which of the statements given above is/are correct?

(a) 1 only   (b) 2 only

(c) Both 1 and 2   (d) Neither 1 nor 2

87. Recently the largest solar power plant of navy commissioned at Indian Naval Academy, Ezhimala

The Indian Naval Academy, Ezhimala is situated in which of the following states/UTs?

(a) Karnataka   (b) Kerala

(c) Tamil Nadu   (d) Lakshadweep

88. Consider the following statements about Bal Gangadhar Tilak

1. He owned and edited two weekly newspapers i.e Kesari (published in Marathi), and The Mahratta (published in English).

2. He organized two important festivals, Ganesh in 1893 and Shivaji in 1895.

3. In 1916 he concluded the Lucknow Pact with Mohammed Ali Jinnah

Which of the statements given above is/are correct?

(a) 1 and 2 only   (b) 2 only

(c) 1, 2 and 3   (d) 1and 3 only

89. Consider the following statements about Chandra Shekhar Azad.

1. He participated in the Non-Cooperation Movement which was launched by Gandhiji in 1921

2. He formed Hindustan Republican Association (HRA)

Which of the statements given above is/are correct?

(a) 1 only   (b) 2 only

(c) Both 1 and 2   (d) Neither 1 nor 2

90. Consider the following statements about Defence Institute of High Altitude Research (DIHAR)

1. It has been established by DRDO

2. It is located in the Union Territory of Ladakh.

3. It works on cold arid agro-animal technologies.

Which of the statements given above is/are correct?

(a) 1 and 2 only   (b) 2 only

(c) 1, 2 and 3   (d) 1and 3 only

91. Consider the following statements about Vriksharopan Abhiyan

1. It has been organized by the Ministry of Environment, Forest and Climate Change

2. It is an annual event participated by various central and state government organisations along with UNEP

Which of the statements given above is/are correct?

(a) 1 only   (b) 2 only

(c) Both 1 and 2   (d) Neither 1 nor 2

92. Consider the following statements about Jal Jeevan Mission

1. Its objective is to provide safe and adequate quantity drinking water to every household

2. The Jal Jeevan Mission is based on a community approach to water

3. The programme also implement source sustainability measures as mandatory elements like rain water harvesting

Which of the statements given above is/are correct?

(a) 1 and 2 only   (b) 2 only

(c) 2 and 3only   (d) 1, 2 and 3

93. Consider the following statements about Bharat

1. It is an indigenously-developed drone made by DRDO

2. The DRDO has provided the Bharat drones to the Indian Army for accurate surveillance in high altitude areas and mountainous terrain

Which of the statements given above is/are correct?

(a) 1 only   (b) 2 only

(c) Both 1 and 2   (d) Neither 1 nor 2

94. Going Green is an initiative of which of the following Ministries?

(a) Ministry of Coal

(b) Ministry of Environment

(c) Ministry of HRD

(d) Ministry of New and Renewable energy

95. Consider the following statements about Dhruvastra

1. It is India's anti-tank guided missile

2. Dhruvastra is the helicopter version of 'Nag Helina'

3. It has been manufactured in collaboration with Israel

Which of the statements given above is/are correct?

(a) 1 and 2 only   (b) 2 only

(c) 2 and 3only   (d) 1, 2 and 3

96. Consider the following statements about Nag missile (HELINA)

1. HELINA is a first-generation fire and forget class anti-tank guided missile (ATGM) system

2. The HELINA missile can engage targets both in the direct hit mode as well as top attack mode

3. The ATGM is guided by an infrared imaging seeker (IIS)

Which of the statements given above is/are correct?

(a) 1 and 2 only   (b) 2 only

(c) 2 and 3 only   (d) 1, 2 and 3

97. Consider the following statements about National Financial Reporting Authority (NFRA)

1. It was constituted by the Government of India under the provisions of FRBM act

2. It is an independent regulator for the auditing profession

Which of the statements given above is/are correct?

(a) 1 only   (b) 2 only

(c) Both 1 and 2   (d) Neither 1 nor 2

98. Ministry of Defence has issued the formal Government Sanction Letter for grant of Permanent Commission (PC) to Women Officers in the Indian Army

With reference to it consider the following statements?

1. Permanent Commission has been granted to Short Service Commissioned (SSC) Women Officers in all ten streams of the Indian Army

2. At present there is no women appointments in the combat roles

3. Short Service Commission officers are for the maximum period of 14 years

Which of the statements given above is/are correct?

(a) 1 and 2 only   (b) 2 only

(c) 2 and 3only   (d) 1, 2 and 3

99. Consider the following statements about the India-Russia Joint Technology Assessment and Accelerated Commercialization Programme

1. It has been launched by the Ministry of Electronics and Information Technology in partnership with FICCI

2. The programme will connect Indian, and Russian science & technology led SMEs and start-ups only

Which of the statements given above is/are correct?

(a) 1 only   (b) 2 only

(c) Both 1 and 2   (d) Neither 1 nor 2

100. Consider the following statements about HGCO19

1. It is the first-of-its-kind mRNA-based vaccine manufacturing platform in India.

2. It uses a 'self-replicating mRNA platform' that ensures the high injectable dose and sustained antigen release for a shorter duration

3. Lipid inorganic nanoparticle (LION) delivery system used for HGC019 vaccine which reduces the adverse effect

Which of the statements given above is/are correct?

(a) 1 and 2 only   (b) 2 only

(c) 1 and 3only   (d) 1, 2 and 3

101. Consider the following statements about Tianwen-1

1. It is Taiwan's first independent mission to visit Mars

2. It is an unmanned probe to Mars

3. The probe would orbit Mars for about two months without attempting soft landing

Which of the statements given above is/are incorrect?

(a) 1 and 2 only   (b) 2 only

(c) 1, 2 and 3   (d) 1and 3 only

102. Consider the following statements about e-Symposium Series

1. It has been organised by the Ministry of Human Resource and development along with MeiTY

2. It is a platform that brings together policy makers, scholars, institutions, corporates to discuss and deliberate development initiatives only in the North East Region.

Which of the statements given above is/are correct?

(a) 1 only   (b) 2 only

(c) Both 1 and 2   (d) Neither 1 nor 2

103. Consider the following statements about Indian Scholastic Assessment (Ind-SAT) Test

1. Ind-SAT is an exam for grant of scholarships and admissions to SAARC nation students

2. The exam conducted in the proctored internet mode by the National Testing Agency.

Which of the statements given above is/are correct?

(a) 1 only   (b) 2 only

(c) Both 1 and 2   (d) Neither 1 nor 2

104. Consider the following statements about EdCIL (India) Limited

1. It is an not for profit organisation under Ministry of Human Resource Development

2. It offers management and consultancy services in all areas of education and human resource development, both within India and overseas.

Which of the statements given above is/are correct?

(a) 1 only   (b) 2 only

(c) Both 1 and 2   (d) Neither 1 nor 2

105. Consider the following statements about the India-Russia Joint Technology Assessment and Accelerated Commercialization Programme

1. The Department of Science and Technology will fund ten Russian projects over a period of two years

2. Department of Science and technology will directly implement this programme in India

Which of the statements given above is/are correct?

(a) 1 only   (b) 2 only

(c) Both 1 and 2   (d) Neither 1 nor 2

106. Consider the following statements about Study in India as a programme

1. It is a programme jointly implemented by MHRD and Ministry of External affairs

2. The selection of the students is based on their merit in graduation

Which of the statements given above is/are correct?

(a) 1 only   (b) 2 only

(c) Both 1 and 2   (d) Neither 1 nor 2

197. India and which of the following nations have renewed their agreement on scientific and technological cooperation for the next five years (2020-2025)?

(a) India and European Union

(b) India and USA

(c) India and Russia

(d) India and Japan

108. Consider the following statements about high throughput COVID-19 testing facilities

1. These high-throughput testing facilities have been set up strategically across India by ICMR

2. The labs are enabled to test diseases other than COVID as well

Which of the statements given above is/are correct?

(a) 1 only   (b) 2 only

(c) Both 1 and 2   (d) Neither 1 nor 2

109. Consider the following statements about Chambal river

1. It is tributary of the Yamuna River

2. It rises in the Vindhya Range just south of Mhow, western Rajasthan state

3. It forms a portion of the Uttar Pradesh-Madhya Pradesh border

Which of the statements given above is/are correct?

(a) 1 and 2 only   (b) 2 only

(c) 1, 2 and 3   (d) 1and 3 only

110. The National Transit Pass System has been launched recently by which of the following Ministries?

(a) Ministry of Road Transport and Highways

(b) Ministry of Commerce and Industry administers

(c) Ministry of Home affairs

(d) None of the above

111. India-EURATOM Agreement on research and development cooperation in the peaceful uses of nuclear energy signed recently between which of the following countries?

(a) India - Russia   (b) India - Germany

(c) India - Japan   (d) None of the above

112. Consider the following statements about the Bihad area of Gwalior-Chambal region

1. The Centre, in collaboration with the World Bank, has decided to convert large area of ravines in Gwalior-Chambal belt of Madhya Pradesh and Uttar Pradesh into arable land

2. The Chambal is a perennial river originates near the south slope of the Vindhya Range in Madhya Pradesh.

Which of the statements given above is/are correct?

(a) 1 only   (b) 2 only

(c) Both 1 and 2   (d) Neither 1 nor 2

113. Recently the Environment Minister virtually launched the National Transit Pass System

With reference to it consider the following statements about National Transit Pass System

1. It enhances seamless movement of minor forest produce only

2. The National Transit Pass System has been implemented across all the states and UTs

3. National Transit Pass System generates Pan India Transit Passes facilitating seamless movement across India

Which of the statements given above is/are incorrect?

(a) 1 and 2 only   (b) 3 only

(c) 1, 2 and 3   (d) 1and 3 only

114. Consider the following statements about Astrophysics Stratospheric Telescope for High Spectral Resolution Observations at Sub-millimeter-wavelengths (ASTHROS)

1. ASTHROS has been launched recently by NASA from Antarctica

2. The mission will try to find answers about formation of new planets

3. ASTHROS will carry an instrument to measure the motion and speed of gas around newly-formed stars.

Which of the statements given above is/are correct?

(a) 1 and 2 only   (b) 3 only

(c) 1, 2 and 3   (d) 1and 3 only

115. Consider the following statements about recently launched Dare to Dream 2.0 challenge

1. It has been launched by Defence Research and Development Organisation (DRDO)

2. It has been launched for emerging technologies to promote the individuals &startups for innovation in defence and aerospace technologies

Which of the statements given above is/are correct?

(a) 1 only   (b) 2 only

(c) Both 1 and 2   (d) Neither 1 nor 2

116. Consider the following statements about the recently launched mobile app 'BIS-Care'

1. It has been launched by the Ministry of Consumer Affairs, Food & Public Distribution

2. Consumers can check the authenticity of the ISI-marked and hallmarked products and also lodge complaints using this app.

3. The Bureau of Indian Standards (BIS) comes under the aegis of Ministry of Heavy Industries and Public Enterprises

Which of the statements given above is/are correct?

(a) 1 and 2 only
(b) 2 only
(c) 2 and 3only
(d) 1, 2 and 3

117. Consider the following statements about Global Tiger Day.

1. It was established in 2010 at Saint Petersburg Tiger Summit in Russia.

2. The governments of tiger-populated countries voted to double tiger population by 2020.

3. None of the countries have achieved the target of doubling tiger population yet

Which of the statements given above is/are correct?

(a) 1 only
(b) 1 and 2 only
(c) 3 only
(d) 1, 2 and 3

118. Consider the following statements about the new coastal vessel "SAGAR ANVESHIKA

1. It is a coastal patrolling vessel

2. It is being built for the coast guard

Which of the statements given above is/are correct?

(a) 1 only
(b) 2 only
(c) Both 1 and 2
(d) Neither 1 nor 2

119. Integrated Flood Warning System for Mumbai (IFLOWS-Mumbai) has been developed by which of the following organisations?

(a) Ministry of Earth Sciences (MoES)

(b) National Disaster Management Authority.

(c) NITI Aayog

(d) None of the above

120. Consider the following statements about the Tiger Census 2018

1. The state of Madhya Pradesh has the highest number of tigers

2. Mizoram is the only state that saw a decline in tiger numbers

3. The M-STrIPES app, CaTRAT software and the Extract Compare programs were used for the first time in tiger census 2018

Which of the statements given above is/are incorrect?

(a) 1 only
(b) 1 and 2 only
(c) 2 and 3 only
(d) 1, 2 and 3

121. Consider the following statements about Tigers

1. The Bengal tiger is found primarily in India

2. Project Tiger' is a Centrally Sponsored Scheme

3. India has the presence of all the different species of tigers across five tiger landscapes

Which of the statements given above is/are correct?

(a) 1 only
(b) 1 and 2 only
(c) 2 and 3only
(d) 1, 2 and 3

122. Consider the following statements about recently launched Knowledge Resource Centre Network (KRCNet)

1. It is an initiative of Ministry of Human Resource and Development or Ministry of Education

2. Under this initiative the traditional libraries of the MHRD system will be upgraded into a top-notch Knowledge Resource Centres (KRC).

Which of the statements given above is/are correct?

(a) 1 only
(b) 2 only
(c) Both 1 and 2
(d) Neither 1 nor 2

123. Consider the following statements about mobile App Mausam

1. Ministry of Earth Sciences has launched it for India Meteorological Department.

2. This Mobile App is dedicated to the general public

3. It is designed to communicate both the weather information and forecasts in a lucid manner

Which of the statements given above is/are correct?

(a) 1 only
(b) 1 and 2 only
(c) 2 and 3only
(d) 1, 2 and 3

124. Consider the following statements about Centre for Augmenting WAR with COVID-19 Health Crisis (CAWACH)

1. It is a joint initiative by the Department of Science and Technology and Health Ministry

2. It supports market-ready innovations for the control of COVID-19

Which of the statements given above is/are correct?

(a) 1 only
(b) 2 only
(c) Both 1 and 2
(d) Neither 1 nor 2

125. Consider the following statements about Lyfas COVID score.

   1. It is a digital functional biomarker smartphone tool for screening, early detection and home monitoring of chronic diseases

   2. It has been developed by a start-up Acculi Labs with support from the DST

   Which of the statements given above is/are correct?

   (a) 1 only   (b) 2 only

   (c) Both 1 and 2   (d) Neither 1 nor 2

126. Consider the following statements about National Biopharma Mission.

   1. It is an Industry-Academia Collaborative Mission

   2. It is co-funded by the World Bank

   3. It is implemented the Department of Pharmaceuticals

   Which of the statements given above is/are incorrect?

   (a) 1 and 2 only   (b) 3 only

   (c) 1 and 3   (d) 1 only

127. Consider the following statements about Biotechnology Industry Research Assistance Council (BIRAC)

   1. It is a not-for-profit Public Sector Enterprise

   2. It objective is to strengthen and empower the emerging Biotech enterprise

   3. It set up by Department of Biotechnology (DBT)

   Which of the statements given above is/are correct?

   (a) 1 and 2 only   (b) 3 only

   (c) 1, 2 and 3   (d) 1 and 3 only

128. Consider the following statements about PM SVANidhi Mobile App

   1. It has been launched by the Ministry of Labour & Employment

   2. The objective is to provide affordable Working Capital loan to all the unskilled migrant labourers to resume their livelihoods

Which of the statements given above is/are incorrect?

(a) 1 only

(b) 2 only

(c) Both 1 and 2

(d) Neither 1 nor 2

129. Consider the following statements about International Centre of Automotive Technology (ICAT)

   1. It is a division of NATRIP (National Automotive Testing and R&D Infrastructure Project) Implementation Society (NATIS)

   2. It is under Department of Heavy Industries, Government of India.

   Which of the statements given above is/are correct?

   (a) 1 only

   (b) 2 only

   (c) Both 1 and 2

   (d) Neither 1 nor 2

130. Consider the following statements about Animal Husbandry Infrastructure Development fund (AHIDF)

   1. Government of India would set up Credit Guarantee Fund of Rs. 750 crore to be managed by SIDBI .

   2. The fund will be provided for existing dairy and meat processing and value addition infrastructure

   3. The beneficiaries can apply for loan in the scheduled bank through "UdyamiMitra" portal of SIDBI.

   Which of the statements given above is/are correct?

   (a) 1 and 2 only

   (b) 3 only

   (c) 1, 2 and 3

   (d) 1 and 3 only

ANSWER KEY

1. (d)	2. (c)	3. (c)	4. (c)	5. (d)	6. (d)	7. (a)	8. (b)	9. (d)	10. (c)
11. (d)	12. (d)	13. (c)	14. (d)	15. (a)	16. (a)	17. (d)	18. (b)	19. (a)	20. (c)
21. (d)	22. (d)	23. (d)	24. (c)	25. (c)	26. (d)	27. (d)	28. (b)	29. (a)	30. (d)
31. (c)	32. (c)	33. (b)	34. (c)	35. (c)	36. (b)	37. (c)	38. (a)	39. (c)	40. (d)
41. (c)	42. (b)	43. (c)	44. (d)	45. (a)	46. (c)	47. (c)	48. (a)	49. (c)	50. (d)
51. (c)	52. (c)	53. (a)	54. (c)	55. (b)	56. (d)	57. (c)	58. (a)	59. (c)	60. (c)
61. (a)	62. (a)	63. (c)	64. (a)	65. (a)	66. (b)	67. (a)	68. (d)	69. (b)	70. (d)
71. (d)	72. (a)	73. (a)	74. (d)	75. (c)	76. (c)	77. (b)	78. (b)	79. (b)	80. (d)
81. (c)	82. (b)	83. (a)	84. (d)	85. (c)	86. (c)	87. (b)	88. (b)	89. (b)	90. (d)
91. (d)	92. (c)	93. (c)	94. (a)	95. (a)	96. (c)	97. (b)	98. (d)	99. (b)	100. (c)
101. (d)	102. (b)	103. (b)	104. (b)	105. (d)	106. (d)	107. (a)	108. (b)	109. (c)	110. (d)
111. (d)	112. (b)	113. (a)	114. (b)	115. (c)	116. (a)	117. (a)	118. (d)	119. (a)	120. (c)
121. (b)	122. (d)	123. (d)	124. (b)	125. (c)	126. (b)	127. (c)	128. (c)	129. (c)	130. (b)

EXPLANATION

1. (d) • To bring in a new component of 'RozgarYukt Gaon' to introduce enterprise-based operation in the Khadi sector and to create employment opportunities for thousands of new artisans

   • It aims at introducing an 'Enterprise-led Business Model' in place of 'Subsidy-led model' through partnership among 3 stakeholders- KRDP-assisted Khadi Institution, Artisans and Business Partner.

   • It will be rolled out in 50 villages by providing 10,000 charkhas, 2000 looms & 100 warping units to khadi artisans, and would create direct employment for 250 artisans per village.

2. (c) • MPDA was launched as a unified scheme by merging different schemes implemented by the khadi sector including publicity, marketing, market promotion, and marketing development assistance.

   • Grant/subsidy was also provided for construction of khadi plazas. The overall objective of the scheme is to ensure increased earnings for artisans.

3. (c) • The Ministry also released the knowledge pack of the government's 'Affordable Rental Housing Complexes' (ARHCs) programme, which has been recently launched to provide rental accommodations to migrant and urban poor.

   • The ARHCs scheme, which has been launched under the Pradhan Mantri Awas Yojana Urban (PMAY-U) as part of AtmaNirbhar Bharat Abhiyan, will help in providing dignified and affordable living spaces for urban migrants/ poor in need

   • The ARHCs scheme would also help real estate developers in retaining labour force on their sites

4. (c) • National Real Estate Development Council (NAREDCO) was established as an autonomous self-regulatory body in 1998 under the aegis of Ministry of Housing and Urban Affairs, Govt. of India.

   • NAREDCO, is the apex national body for the real estate industry and it is visualized as a single platform where Government, industry and public would discuss various problems and opportunities face to face which would result in speedy resolution of issues

- NAREDCO works to create and sustain an environment conducive to the growth of real estate industry in India, partnering industry and government alike through advisory and consultative processes.

5. (d) • NASA and the European Space Agency are launching a dune buggy in 2026 to fetch the rock samples, along with a rocket ship that will put the specimens into orbit around Mars. Then another spacecraft will capture the orbiting samples and bring them home.

- Two other NASA landers are also operating on Mars - 2018's InSight and 201, 2's Curiosity rover.

- Six other spacecraft are exploring the planet from orbit: three from the U.S., two from Europe and one from India.

- China is sending both a rover an orbiter.

- The UAE, a newcomer to outer space, has an orbiter en route.(only orbiter)

6. (d) • On the setting up of Atmospheric Research Testbeds, a unique facility in Tropics will be launched in 2021 with the first phase of instrumentation.

- This open field observatory is planned to be spread over 100 acres of land (50 km away from Bhopal) and is proposed for a better understanding of the monsoon clouds and land surface processes.

- This centre will have state-of-the-art observational systems such as radars, wind profilers, UAVs etc.

7. (a) • The Society for Innovation and Entrepreneurship (SINE), a technology business incubator at IIT Bombay supported by DST has been identified as the Implementing Agency of CAWACH to source and support startups having solutions to fight pandemic COVID-19 by way of funding.

- SINE is supported by Indian STEPs and Business Incubator Association (ISBA) in implementation of the program.

8. (b) • TRIFED under Ministry of Tribal Affairs has embarked on an 'all-encompassing digitisation drive' to only promote tribal commerce

- The drive also maps and links its village-based tribal producers and artisans to national and international markets by setting up state of art e-

platforms benchmarked to international standards.

- The strategy is aimed to effectively promote tribal commerce.

- TRIFED is in the process of digitising all the information related to the forest dwellers associated with the Van Dhan Yojana, village haats and their warehouses.

9. (d) • On the occasion of "World Hepatitis Day", 2nd Empathy e-Conclave was organised

- The event was organised by Institute of Liver and Biliary Sciences (ILBS) in collaboration with Airport Authority of India (AAI) for creating awareness among the parliamentarians.

- India is committed to the WHO goals of elimination of Hepatitis C and of reducing the burden of Hepatitis B by 2030.

- The theme of this year's conclave is "Keep your Liver Safe in COVID times"

10. (c) • Sri Lanka entered into an agreement with the RBI for a currency swap worth \$400 million under the South Asian Association for Regional Cooperation (SAARC) framework in April

- Reserve Bank of India signs document for \$400 million currency swap facility to Sri Lanka till Nov 2022

- These swap operations carry no exchange rate or other market risks, as transaction terms are set in advance.

- In the swap arrangement, a country provides dollars to a foreign central bank, which, at the same time, provides the equivalent funds in its currency to the former, based on the market exchange rate at the time of the transaction.

11. (d) • The draft of the policy was prepared by a panel of experts led by former Indian Space Research Organisation Chairman K Kasturirangan.

- According to the draft policy, there will be no hard separation of learning areas in terms of curricular, co-curricular or extra-curricular areas and all subjects, including arts, music, crafts, sports, yoga, community service, etc. will be curricular

- Single-stream higher education institutions will be phased out over time, and all will move towards becoming multidisciplinary.

- The system of 'affiliated colleges' will be gradually phased out in 15 years.

12. (d) • Gobal blockchain start-up BelfricsBT, along with YoSync, a startup incubated at IIITB-IMACX Studios, has signed research collaboration in agreement with IIIT Bangalore to jointly develop India's first COVID-19 blockchain platform, BelYo.

• The project has been funded by the Mphasis F1 Foundation as a part of their larger outreach programme to tackle the pandemic in India.

• BelYo uses the BelfricsBTBelrium blockchain platform to convert COVID-19 related clinical and vaccination data of citizens currently from the physical form into digital assets that can be retrieved by any contact tracing apps like AarogyaSetu via APIs.

13. (c) • To encourage and enable holistic progress in the incubator ecosystem across the country, NITI Aayog's Atal Innovation Mission (AIM), has launched AIM iCREST - an Incubator Capabilities enhancement program for a Robust Ecosystem focused on creating high performing Startups.

• This is a first of its kind initiative for advancing innovation at scale in India.

• AIM has joined hands with Bill & Melinda Gates Foundation and Wadhwani Foundation - organizations that can lend credible support and expertise in the entrepreneurship and innovation space.

• AIM iCREST, has been designed to enable the incubation ecosystem and act as a growth hack for AIM's Atal and Established incubators across the country.

14. (d) • Under a multi-pronged mission, codenamed "Operation Breathing Space" the authorities of India and Israel are working on four different kinds of rapid tests, which will be jointly developed after trials on Indian COVID-19 patients

• The tests that the Israeli teams will be conducting trials for include an audio test, a breath test, thermal testing, and a polyamino test which seeks to isolate proteins related to COVID-19.

15. (a) • It is also referred as Distributed Ledger Technology (DLT),as it makes the history of any digital asset unalterable and transparent through the use of decentralization and cryptographic hashing.

• It creates a decentralized distribution chain that gives everyone access to the document at the same time.

• It is managed by a cluster of computers and not owned by any single entity; therefore, it is decentralized.

16. (a) • The government approved a new education policy that seeks to revamp all aspects of education structure and aims to achieve universal access to education to all between age groups of 3-18 years by 2030.

• The Union Cabinet, approved the New Education Policy that also proposed to change the name of the Ministry of Human Resource Development to the Ministry of Education.

• The aim will be to increase the Gross Enrolment Ratio in higher education including vocational education from 26.3% to 50% by 2035.

17. (d) • The Government of India has instituted Subhash Chandra Bose Aapda Prabandhan Puraskaar to recognise the excellent work done by the individuals and institutions in the field of disaster management.

• In addition to a certificate, these awards carry a cash award of Rs 51 lakhs for an Institution and Rs 5 lakhs for an Individual.

• An individual can apply for the award as well as nominate other person or institution.

• It is administered by National Disaster Management Authority Award:

• Only Indian nationals and Indian institutions can apply for the award.

• The nominated individual or institution should have worked in any area of disaster management like Prevention, Mitigation, Preparedness, Rescue, Response, Relief, Rehabilitation, Research, Innovation or early warning in India.

18. (b) • The scheme has two components. The first component is to develop new airports and enhance the existing regional airports to increase the number of operational airports for scheduled civilian flights

• The regional connectivity scheme will be applicable on route length between 200 to 800 km with no lower limit set for hilly, remote, island and security sensitive regions.

• The Central government will provide concessions to the tune of 2 per cent excise on Value Added Tax (VAT).

• A Regional Connectivity Fund (RCF) will be created to fund the scheme via a levy on certain flights. States are expected to contribute 20 per cent to the fund.

19. (a) • The Ministry of Human Resource Development (MHRD) has launched a programme called Unnat Bharat Abhiyan in the year 2014 with an aim to connect institutions of higher education, including Indian Institutes of Technology (IITs), National Institutes of Technology (NITs) and Indian Institutes of Science Education & Research (IISERs) etc. with local communities to address the development challenges through appropriate technologies.

20. (c) • The B.Voc. degrees introduced in 2013 will continue to exist, but vocational courses will also be available to students enrolled in all other Bachelor's degree programmes, including the 4-year multidisciplinary Bachelor's programmes.

• Foreign languages, such as Korean, Japanese, Thai, French, German, Spanish, Portuguese, and Russian, will also be offered at the secondary level.

• The undergraduate degree will be of either 3 or 4-year duration, with multiple exit options.

21. (d) • Ministry of Micro Small and Medium Enterprises (MSME), Government of India, approved a programme for the benefit of artisans involved in manufacturing of Agarbatti and to develop village industry under 'Gramodyog Vikas Yojana'

• As per the programme, initially four Pilot Projects will be started, including one in North Eastern part of the country.

22. (d) • SKOCH Award, instituted in 2003, is the highest civilian honour in the country conferred by an independent organisation.

• It recognises people, projects and institutions that go the extra mile to make India a better nation.

• SKOCH Award covers the best of efforts in the area of digital, financial and social inclusion.

• SKOCH Group is India's leading Think Tank, dealing with socio-economic issues, with a focus on inclusive growth since 1997.

• SKOCH Group has instituted India's highest independent civilian honours in the field of finance, technology, economics and social sector.

23. (d) • CREDAI is a not-for-profit company registered under Section 25 of Companies Act, 1956, seeks to create a favourable policy climate to ensure housing for all.

• Confederation of Real Estate Developers' Associations of India (CREDAI) established in 1999 is the apex body of private real estate developers

• CREDAI strives to make the Real Estate industry more organized and progressive by working closely with all stakeholders: government representatives, policy makers, investors, finance companies, consumers, and real estate professionals.

• CREDAI a recognized partner for the government and is represented on several committees working at policy formulations and various committees of the Government

24. (c) • The biggest, most sophisticated Mars rover (Perseverance) ever built blasted off for the red planet to bring the first Martian rock samplesback to Earth to be analysed for evidence of ancient life.

• Perseverance will aim for treacherous unexplored territory

• It also will release a mini helicopter that will attempt the first powered flight on another planet

• It includes equipment for extracting oxygen from Mars' thin carbon-dioxide atmosphere.

25. (c) • The GISAID platform was launched on the occasion of the Sixty-first World Health Assembly in May 2008.

• GISAID provides a publicly accessible database designed by scientist for scientist, to improve the sharing of influenza data.

• In 2010 the Federal Republic of Germany became the official host of the GISAID platform and EpiFlu™ database providing sustainability of the platform and stability through its public-private-partnership with the GISAID Initiative to this day.

• The GISAID Initiative promotes the rapid sharing of data from all influenza viruses and the coronavirus causing COVID-19.

• The Initiative ensures that open access to data in GISAID is provided free-of-charge to all individuals that agreed to identify themselves and agreed to uphold the GISAID sharing mechanism governed through its Database Access

26. (d) • It was launched in May 1977 to help Khadi and Poly vastra producing institutions in mobilizing the capital funds from banking institutions.

- Under the Scheme, implementing agencies can avail of bank loan as per the ISEC issued by the KVIC on payment of only 4 percent of interest and difference between the actual interest charged by the bank and 4 percent is borne by KVIC as interest subsidy.

27. (d) • Ministry of Micro Small and Medium Enterprises (MSME), Government of India, approved a programme for the benefit of artisans involved in manufacturing of Agarbatti and to develop village industry under 'Gramodyog Vikas Yojana'

- As per the programme, initially four Pilot Projects will be started, including one in North Eastern part of the country.
- The Khadi and Village Industries Commission (KVIC), a statutory organisation under the Ministry of Micro Small and Medium Enterprises (MSME), will provide training, and assist artisans working in this area, with Agarbatti manufacturing machines.
- Under this Mission, Khadi and Village Industries Commission (KVIC), one of the statutory organizations, working under the M/o MSME, will provide training, and assist artisans working in this area

28. (b) • Health and Family Welfare Minister launched 'Vidyarthi Vigyan Manthan, 2020-21.

- This initiative is a national programme for popularizing science among school students of Class 6th to 11th.
- It is an initiative of Vijnana Bharati (VIBHA), in collaboration with Vigyan Prasar and National Council of Educational Research and Training (NCERT).
- It was designed to identify the bright minds with a scientific aptitude among the student community.
- This is a platform to identify the talent in the field of science and to promote the scientific acumen among the students.

29. (a) • Two NASA astronauts returned to Earth, their capsule parachuting into the Gulf of Mexico to close out an unprecedented test flight by Elon Musk's SpaceX company.

- It was the first splashdown by US astronauts in 45 years, with the first commercially built and operated spacecraft to carry people to and from orbit.
- The return clears the way for another SpaceX crew launch as early as next month and possible tourist flights next year.

- It was the first time a private company launched people into orbit and also the first launch of NASA astronauts from home turf in nearly a decade.

30. (d) • The Electronic Vaccine Intelligence Network (eVIN) is an innovative technological solution aimed at strengthening immunization supply chain systems across the country.

- This is being implemented under National Health Mission (NHM) by Ministry of Health and Family Welfare.
- eVIN aims to provide real-time information on vaccine stocks and flows, and storage temperatures across all cold chain points in the country.
- This robust system has been used with the requisite customization during the COVID pandemic for ensuring continuation of the essential immunization services and protecting our children and pregnant mothers against vaccine preventable diseases.

31. (c) • The BCAS has listed out rules that should be followed for cyber security, storage facility, training and background check of staff for drone operating systems or remotely piloted aircraft systems.

- A remotely piloted aircraft (RPA), its associated remote pilot station, its required command and control links and any other components constitute a remotely piloted aircraft system (RPAS).
- The capacity to retain recording of minimum 30 days shall be in place for all categories of RPAs except for mini and micro
- An RPA or drone is in nano or mini category if it has weight less than 250 grams.
- If its weight is between 250 grams and 2 kg, it is in the micro category.
- Each RPA and RPAS operator must establish, implement and maintain a security programme, based on the aforementioned guidelines, and it must be submitted to BCAS before its operation
- The operator of RPAS must obtain relevant permissions from the local administration and the Directorate General of Civil Aviation (DGCA) before operating the RPAS,

32. (c) • NCDC as an apex-level statutory institution under the Ministry of Agriculture and Farmers' Welfare has achieved tremendous success with a cumulative financial assistance to cooperatives to the tune of Rs 1,54,000 crore.

- Cooperatives in India have come a long way and have proven their success in improving the condition of farmers and economic development.

- Largely as associations of small and marginal farmers and the rural poor, the cooperatives have acquired a huge network of over 8.50 lakh organisations and 290 million members.

- Cooperatives lend support to farmers in minimising risks in the agriculture and allied sector and act as a shield against exploitation

33. (b) • Atal Innovation Mission (AIM), NITI Aayog declared the results of its flagship national annual innovation Mthe results of its flagship national annual innovation Marathon challenge ATL Tinkering Marathon 2019 arathon challenge ATL Tinkering Marathon 2019 held over 5000+ Atal Tinkering Labs across the country and announced 150 winners of the Marathon.

- This year, the challenge was executed by AIM in partnership with MyGOV on MyGov's Innovate Platform.

- With the central theme as "Research, Ideate, Innovate, Implement - Mindful Innovation for the greater good", this year's marathon was uniquely designed by the students themselves.

34. (c) • The Energy and Resources Institute (TERI) in partnership with the Department of Science & Technology, Government of India has developed novel external shading solution for windows in residential and commercial buildings under the project Habitat Model for Efficiency and Comfort.

35. (c) • It is a not-for-profit, policy research organization - working in the fields of energy, environment, and sustainable development

- Established in 1974, it was formerly known as the Tata Energy Research Institute.

- As the scope of its activities widened, it was renamed The Energy and Resources Institute in 2003.

- TERI's mission is to usher transitions to a cleaner and sustainable future through the conservation and efficient use of energy and other resources, and innovative ways of minimizing and reusing waste.

36. (b) • The Sendai Framework for Disaster Risk Reduction 2015-2030 (Sendai Framework) was the first major agreement of the post-2015 development agenda and provides Member States with concrete actions to protect development gains from the risk of disaster. It is a non-binding agreement, which the signatory nations, including India

- The Framework aims to achieve the substantial reduction of disaster risk and losses in lives, livelihoods and health and in the economic, physical, social, cultural and environmental assets of persons, businesses, communities and countries over the next 15 years.

- The Sendai Framework is the successor instrument to the Hyogo Framework for Action (HFA) 2005-2015: Building the Resilience of Nations and Communities to Disasters.

37. (c) • The National Building Code of India (NBC), a comprehensive building Code, is a national instrument providing guidelines for regulating the building construction activities across the country.

- It serves as a Model Code for adoption by all agencies involved in building construction works be they Public Works Departments, other government construction departments, local bodies or private construction agencies.

- The Code mainly contains administrative regulations, development control rules and general building requirements; fire safety requirements; stipulations regarding materials, structural design and construction (including safety); building and plumbing services; approach to sustainability; and asset and facility management.

- The Code was first published in 1970 at the instance of Planning Commission and then first revised in 1983.

38. (a) • The Bhima River is a major river in Western India and South India. It flows southeast for 861 kilometres through Maharashtra, Karnataka, and Telangana states, before entering the Krishna River.

- It is a major tributary of the Krishna River

- In the Bhimashankar heights of the Western Ghats, it rises and flows southeastward for 450 miles or 725 km in Maharashtra to join the Krishna in Karnataka.

- The major tributaries are the Sina and Nira rivers.
- The drainage area of the Bhima is defined by the Western Ghats (west), the Balaghat Range (north), and the Mahadeo Hills (south).

39. (c) • A component, Innovation and Agri-entrepreneurship Development programme has been launched under Rashtriya Krishi Vikas Yojana in order to promote innovation and agripreneurship by providing financial support and nurturing the incubation ecosystem.

- These start-ups are in various categories such as agro-processing, artificial intelligence, digital agriculture, farm mechanisation, waste to wealth, dairy, fisheries etc.

40. (d) • Abanindranath Tagore,, the nephew of Rabindranath Tagore, was one of the most prominent artists of India.

- He was the first major supporter of swadeshi values in Indian art.
- Abanindranath first created the 'Indian Society of Oriental Art' and later went on to establish Bengal school of art.
- His sole aim for establishing the school was to counter the English influence on Indian artists.
- Abanindranath is also regarded as a proficient and accomplished writer.
- Some of his books like 'BudoAngla', 'KhirerPutul' and 'Rajkahini' are best examples of Bengali children's literature.

41. (c) • The Ministry of Jal Shakti has launched a new version of the India Water Resources Information System (India-WRIS) with new functionalities and features.

- Open to the public, and accessible through the web portal www.indiawris.gov.in, this portal contains information related to Water Resources through dashboards for rainfall, water levels & discharge of rivers, water bodies, ground water levels, reservoir storages, evapotranspiration and soil moisture, as well as modules on water resources projects, water bodies, hydro-met data availability and tools for GIS layer editing.
- The Ministry of Jal Shakti (MoJS), under the National Hydrology Project, launched the first version of India Water Resources Information System (India-WRIS) in July, 2019.

- India WRIS is, at present, receiving data from many central and state agencies like CWC, CGWB, IMD, NRSC, Andhra Pradesh, Uttar Pradesh and Gujarat etc. on regular basis.

42. (b) • In the Union Budget 2020-21, Minister of Finance had made an announcement 'to build a seamless national cold supply chain for perishables, inclusive of milk, meat, and fish'.

- It was also stated that the Indian Railways will set up a KISAN RAIL.
- Indian Railways is introducing first "Kisan Rail" from Devlali to Danapur
- The train will provide seamless supply chain of Perishable produce.
- This train will help in bringing perishable agricultural products like vegetables, fruits to the market in a short period of time.
- The train with frozen containers is expected to build a seamless national cold supply chain for perishables, inclusive of fish, meat and milk.
- Indian Railways have earlier run single commodity special trains like Banana Specials etc. But this will be the first ever multi commodity trains and will carry fruits

43. (c) • The National Centre for Good Governance (NCGG) is an autonomous institute under the aegis of Department of Administrative Reforms and Public Grievances, Government of India. Its head office is at New Delhi and registered office at Mussoorie.

Its main objectives are :

- To be a think tank for governance & policy reforms, working across administrative, social, financial and political arenas
- To initiate and participate in research and training on various aspects of regulatory and developmental administration, public policy, governance and public management.

44. (d) • The Indian Technical and Economic Cooperation (ITEC) Programme was instituted by a decision of the Indian Cabinet as a bilateral programme of assistance of the Government of India.

- ITEC Programme was launched in 1964 by the Ministry of External Affairs.
- The ITEC Programme, fully funded by the Government of India, has evolved and grown over the years.

45. (a) • Aditya, India's first solar ferry that bagged the prestigious Gustave Trouvé Award for Excellence in Electric Boats and Boating

• Recently, on July 27th, Aditya bagged the prestigious Gustave Trouvé Award for Excellence in Electric Boats and Boating.

• It is the only international award given to individuals & companies building & innovating in state-of-the-art electric boats.

46. (c) • The Union Minister of Textiles also launched the "My Handloom" portal for individual weavers as well as other organizations for applying for various benefits under the various handloom schemes like Block Level Clusters, Handloom Marketing Assistance and Awards.

• The "India Handloom" brand was launched in 2015 on the occasion of the 1st National Handloom Day.

• The portal with a single "sign-in" is to act as One-stop shop for information on all handloom schemes which will retain information, and will ensure transparency and provide real-time status update on applications under National handloom Development programme

47. (c) • In rural areas "SBM - Gramin" was financed and monitored through the Ministry of Drinking Water and Sanitation; whereas "SBM - urban" was overseen by the Ministry of Housing and Urban Affairs.

• As part of the campaign, volunteers, known as Swachhagrahis, or "Ambassadors of cleanliness", promoted indoor plumbing and community approaches to sanitation (CAS) at the village level.

48. (a) • The Union Cabinet has approved the Central Sector Scheme of financing facility under "Agriculture Infrastructure Fund" of Rs. 1 Lakh Crore.

• The Fund will catalyze the creation of post-harvest management infrastructure and community farming assets such as cold storage, collection centres, processing units, etc.

• These assets will enable farmers to get greater value for their produce, as they will be able to store and sell at higher prices, reduce wastage, and increase processing and value addition.

49. (c) • PM Kisan is a Central Sector scheme with 100% funding from Government of India.

• It has become operational from 1.1, 2.2018.

• Under the scheme an income support of 6,000/- per year in three equal installments will be provided to small and marginal farmer families having combined land holding/ownership of upto 2 hectares.

• Definition of family for the scheme is husband, wife and minor children.

• State Government and UT administration will identify the farmer families which are eligible for support as per scheme guidelines.

• The fund will be directly transferred to the bank accounts of the beneficiaries.

50. (d) • The Union Minister of Textiles also inaugurated the virtual Indian Textile Sourcing Fair 2020.

• The Government is providing online marketing opportunities to weavers and handloom producers.

• The fair will connect more than 150 participants from different regions of the country showcasing their products with unique designs and skills.

51. (c) • On this occasion the textile Ministry launched the Mobile App & Backend Website for Handloom Mark Scheme (HLM).

• The Handloom Mark is being promoted to provide collective identity to the authentic handloom products.

• Textiles Committee Mumbai has developed the Mobile App with a backend web portal to completely digitise the process of registration.

• The App will enable the weavers located at any corner of the country to apply for Handloom Mark registration through the comfort of their homes by click of a button on their mobiles.

• This app helps ascertain the genuineness and originality of the product through unique and dynamic QR code labels affixed on each handloom product.

52. (c) • Prime Minister inaugurated the first ever undersea optical fibre cable project for Andaman and Nicobar Islands

" It will provide high speed broadband connections in the union territory at par with services in the mainland.

100 GIGABIT PER SEC SPEED

Representative Image

➤ The CANI cable system will have speed of 100 gigabit per second	telecom facility to these islands
➤ The eight islands to be connected with Chennai include Port Blair, Little Andaman (Hut bay), Car Nicobar, Kamorta, Great Nicobar (Campbell bay), Havelock, Long and Rangat Islands	➤ The total route length of the project is estimated to be 2,200 km
➤ It will provide secure, reliable, robust, affordable	➤ NEC Corporation, a Japanese company, will handle the project

- Work of laying undersea cable has been executed by BSNL in a record time of less than 24 months.

- This project will give a boost to 4G mobile services and digital services like tele-education, tele-health, e-governance services, and tourism on the islands.

53. (a) • The Island Development Agency was formed 3 years ago (2017) for the holistic development of islands. It is chaired by the Union Home Minister

- The Island Development Agency analysed the developments taken place in favour of the programme "Holistic development of islands".

- 10 islands namely Smith, Ross, Aves, Long and Little Andaman in Andaman & Nicobar and Minicoy, Bangaram, Suheli, Cherium and Tinnakara in Lakshadweep have been identified for holistic development in the first phase.

54. (c) • IC-IMPACTS (the India-Canada Centre for Innovative Multidisciplinary Partnerships to Accelerate Community Transformation and Sustainability) is the first, and only, Canada-India Research Centre of Excellence established through the Canadian Networks of Centres of Excellence (NCE) as a new Centre dedicated to the development of research collaborations between Canada and India.

- The Conference was organised virtually by the India-Canada Centre for Innovative Multidisciplinary Partnership to Accelerate Community Transformation and Sustainability (IC-IMPACTS) on 6 August 2020.

- DST has been working with IC-IMPACTS for research partnerships since 2013. This partnership is aimed towards working hand-in-hand with communities in the two countries to develop community-based solutions for the most urgent needs.

- The major focus areas of research cooperation under the IC-IMPACT are green buildings and smart cities; occupants survivability in buildings during fires; integrated water management & safe and sustainable infrastructure; and health problems arising from water-borne and infectious diseases.

55. (b) • Ministry also launched beta version of a portal on Human-Elephants Conflict.

- The National Portal on human elephant conflict called "Surakhsya" for collection of real time information & also for managing the conflicts on a real time basis will help to set the data collection protocols, data transmission pipelines and data visualization tools to enable policy-makers to leverage HEC data for policy formulation and for preparation of Action Plans for mitigation of conflicts.

- Asian elephants are listed as "Endangered" on the IUCN Red List of threatened species.

- The current population estimates indicate that there are about 50,000 -60000 Asian elephants in the world. More than 60 % of the population is held in India.

- Indian Elephant has also been listed in the Appendix I of the Convention of the Migratory species in the recently concluded Conference of Parties of CMS 13 at Gandhi Nagar, Gujarat in February 2020.

56. (d) • IIT Kanpur has developed indigenous seed balls named BEEG (Bio -compost Enriched Eco-friendly Globule) which will help people and farmers in plantation with safety in Corona times and will also provide employment to people.

- The BEEG is developed in collaboration with Agnys Waste Management Private Limited (start-up at IIT Kanpur).

- The Seed Balls are comprised of indigenous variety of seeds, compost, and clay.

- There is no need for digging pits for planting saplings .

57. (c) • India turned down Russia's invitation to participate in next month's multilateral defence exercise, which is scheduled to be held in southern Russia between September 15 and 27.

- India had earlier planned to send a company-level strength of approximately 180 troops from an infantry battalion, 40 personnel of the Air Force, and two Navy officers as observers

- China and Pakistan are also invited to participate in KavKaz 2020 as both countries are members of the Shanghai Cooperation Organisation (SCO).

- The exercise is scheduled for September 15-26 and there will be participation from atleast 18 countries in KavKaz 2020 including countries from Central Asian Republics who are part of SCO as well as China, Iran, Pakistan and Turkey.

58. (a) • The National Technical Advisory Group on Immunisation (NTAGI) was established by an order of the Ministry of Health and Family Welfare (MoHFW) in 2001.

- As India's apex advisory body on immunization, the NTAGI provides guidance and advice to the MoHFW on provision of vaccination and immunization services for the effective control of vaccine preventable diseases in the country.

59. (c) • Russia became the first country in the world to register a COVID-19 vaccine after less than two months of human testing

- The vaccine is expected to provide immunity from the coronavirus for up to two years

- Vaccine used inanimate particles created on the basis of adenovirus

- It is based on the DNA of a SARS-CoV-2 type adenovirus, a common cold virus.

- To make it effective, the vaccine uses the weakened virus to deliver small parts of a pathogen and stimulate an immune response.

60. (c) • SCO is a eight-member economic and security bloc and India and Pakistan were admitted as full members back in 2017.

- It is a permanent intergovernmental international organisation founded in 2001 with its secretariat based in Beijing, China.

- The founding members of this grouping include China, Russia, Kazakhstan, Kyrgyzstan, Tajikistan and Uzbekistan.

61. (a) • Vijnana Bharati or VIBHA, previously known as "Swadeshi Science Movement" is a Non-profit organisation, working for science popularization & implementation of modern technology & ancient sciences in India.

- It was founded by the eminent scientists of Indian Institute of Science, Bengaluru led by Prof. K.I. Vasu.

- It is a dynamic Science Movement with Swadeshi Spirit interlinking traditional and modern

sciences on one hand, and natural and spiritual sciences on the other hand, adapted to national needs.

- It is a national movement for the propagation and popularization of Science & Technology among students and masses.

62. (a) • National Council of Educational Research & Training (NCERT) is an organization set up by the Government of India in the year 1961 to assist and advise the central and state governments on academic matters related to school education.

- The major objectives of NCERT and its constituent units are to: undertake, promote and coordinate research in areas related to school education; prepare and publish model textbooks, supplementary material, newsletters, and journals and develop educational kits, multimedia digital materials, etc.

63. (c) • PLI scheme has been huge success in terms of the applications received from Global as well as Domestic Mobile Phone manufacturing companies and electronic components manufacturers.

- Production Linked Incentive Scheme (PLI)for Large Scale Electronics Manufacturing was notified on 1st April, 2020.

- The Production Linked Incentive Scheme (PLI) for Large Scale Electronics Manufacturing proposes a financial incentive to boost domestic manufacturing and attract large investments in the electronics value chain including mobile phones, electronic components and ATMP units.

- Production Linked Incentives of up to INR 40,951 crores will be awarded over a period of 5 years.

64. (a) • Chief Minister Y.S. Jagan Mohan Reddy launched 'E-Raksha Bandhan', aimed at creating awareness among the public on Cybercrimes across the State

- The Andhra Pradesh Police, Crime Investigation Department (CID), FM Radio, Cyber Crime Prevention Against Women and Children (CCPWC), Cyber Peace Foundation and other organisations are organising the month-long online awareness drive.

- The Andhra Pradesh government has opened up Disha police stations across 18 police district headquarters to tackle cases of crimes against women in a speedy manner.

65. (a) • It is an autonomous organization under the Department of Science and Technology (DST), Government of India.

• The principal objective of VP is to serve India's science popularization agenda.

• This is achieved through several strategically important two - way stakeholder specific approaches to communicate about principles and practice of science and technology and implications for development and quality of life.

66. (b) • TRIFED was established in August 1987 under the Multi-State Cooperative Societies Act, 1984 by the Government of India as a National level Cooperative body.

• Under the administrative control of the then Ministry of Welfare of India, TRIFED is mandated to ringing about socio-economic development of tribals of the country by institutionalising the trade of Minor Forest Produce (MFP) & Surplus Agricultural Produce (SAP) collected/ cultivated by them.

• TRIFED plays the dual role of both a market developer and a service provider

• TRIBES India is the brand under which the sourced handcrafted products from the tribal people are sold.

67. (a) • India has 70 percent of world's tiger population.

• India is tirelessly working with all 13 tiger range countries towards nurturing the tiger.

• To deal with the challenge of human-animal conflict which is causing deaths of animals, LIDAR based survey technology will be used for the first time.

• Lidar is a method for measuring distances by illuminating the target with laser light and measuring the reflection with a sensor.

• With the presence of nearly 30 percent of India's tigers outside tiger reserves, India had embarked upon assessing management interventions through the globally developed Conservation Assured | Tiger Standards (CA|TS) framework, which will now be extended to all fifty tiger reserves across the country.

• A feather in India's cap was added with the Guinness World Records recognizing the country's efforts as the world largest camera trap survey of wildlife.

68. (d) • This facility provides the country, which is getting the dollars, with the flexibility to use these reserves at any time in order to maintain an appropriate level of balance of payments or short-term liquidity.

• The RBI also offers similar swap lines to central banks in the SAARC region within a total corpus of $2 billion.

• India already has a $75 billion bilateral currency swap l ine with Japan, which has the second highest dollar reserves after China.

• India is working with the United States to secure a dollar swap line that would help in better management of its external account and provide extra cushion in the event of an abrupt outflow of funds, according to banking industry and government sources.

• In 2019, India signed a $75 billion bilateral currency swap line agreement with Japan, which has the second largest dollar reserves after China. This facility provides India with the flexibility to use these reserves at any time in order to maintain an appropriate level of balance of payments or short-term liquidity.

• The Reserve Bank of India also offers similar swap lines to central banks in the SAARC region within a total corpus of $2 billion.

69. (b) Ministry of Human Resource Development has initiated many projects to assist teachers, scholars and students in their pursuit of learning like

• DIKSHA platform

• Swayam Prabha TV Channel

• Online MOOC courses

• On Air - Shiksha Vani

• DAISY by NIOS for differently-abled

• e-PathShala

• National Repository of Open Educational Resources (NROER) to develop e-content

Some of the major digital initiatives by State Governments are

• SMILE (Social Media Interface for Learning Engagement) in Rajasthan

• Project Home Classes in Jammu

• PadhaiTunharduvaar (Education at your doorstep) in Chhattisgarh

- Unnayan Initiatives in Bihar through portal and mobile application
- Mission Buniyaad in NCT of Delhi

70. (d) • Coastal Shipping means movement of goods in cargo from one coast to other. Coastal shipping can be national or international.

- Coastal shipping is within 20 nautical miles of the coastline. The requirements for movement of vessels in this part of the sea are different from standard requirements of deep sea shipping.
- Coastal ship movements require smaller vessels and lesser draft, and therefore, involve lower costs
- Coastal shipping cannot operate on its own; it needs support from road and rail to move the cargo from factories and warehouses to the ports and then deliver it to customers from the destination ports.

71. (d) • Four frontline warships of the Indian Navy participated in the "PASSEX" exercise when the US carrier strike group was transiting through the Indian Ocean Region on its way from the South China Sea

- Indian Navy units undertook Passage Exercise (PASSEX) with US Navy.
- Indian Navy had conducted similar PASSEXs with Japan Maritime Self-Defense Force and French Navy in recent past.

72. (a) • It is an annual trilateral naval exercise between the navies of India, Japan, and the USA which is held alternately in the Indian and Pacific Oceans.

- Originally begun in 1992 as a bilateral exercise between India and the United States, Japan became a permanent partner in 2015.
- Past non-permanent participants are Australia and Singapore.
- The Malabar exercise is expected to take place later this year.

73. (a) • A serological survey is an exercise to check the prevalence of the disease in a population by detecting the presence of specific antibodies against the virus.

- The serological test is performed to diagnose infections and autoimmune illnesses. It can also be conducted to check if a person has developed immunity to certain diseases.
- The survey included the IgG Enzyme-Linked Immunosorbent Assay (ELISA) test which

estimates the proportion of the population exposed to SARS-CoV-2 infection.

- The IgG test is not useful for detecting acute infections but it indicates episodes of infections that have happened in the past. The test has been approved by ICMR for its high sensitivity and specificity.

74. (d) • The Summit is being hosted by the US-India Business Council.

- This year marks the 45th anniversary of the formation of the Council.
- The theme for this year's India Ideas Summit is 'Building a Better Future'
- The virtual summit will see high-level presence from Indian and US government policymakers, state-level officials and thought leaders from business and society.
- The Summit convenes business and government leaders for discussions on the future of the U.S.-India Partnership and the trends shaping globalization, trade and investment, and the future of work in the COVID-era and beyond.

75. (c) • Formed in 1975 at the request of the U.S. and Indian governments, the U.S.-India Business Council is the premier business advocacy organization, composed of more than 350 top-tier U.S. and Indian companies advancing U.S.-India commercial ties.

- The Council is the largest bilateral trade association in the United States, with liaison presence in New York, Silicon Valley, and New Delhi.
- The Council aims to create an inclusive bilateral trade environment between India and the United States by serving as the voice of industry, linking governments to businesses, and supporting long-term commercial partnerships that will nurture the spirit of entrepreneurship, create jobs, and successfully contribute to the global economy.

76. (c) • NATRiP is a fully Government of India funded project with a total project cost of Rs. 3727.30 crore.

- This is the largest and one of the most significant initiatives in Automotive sector so far.
- Ministry of Heavy Industry & Public Enterprises (MoHI&PE) is the nodal Ministry of the Government for automotive industry in India

and is in charge of framing and administering Auto Policy of the Government of India.

- MoHI&PE is the focal Ministry for implementation of NATRIP. Secretary, MoHI&PE chairs the NATRIP Implementation Society (NATIS) Governing Council.

77. (b) • The Minister for School Education launch portal 'Aspire' at Mantralya

- The Portal has been prepared with the help of the UNICEF for the students of class 9th to 1, 2th of the government schools.

- The 'Aspire' is in fact a future opportunity portal. Information pertaining to college fee, subjects, admission procedure etc. of all the colleges of national and state level can be obtained from this portal.

- Students by self login on this portal can gather information as regard to subjects of their own interest

78. (b) • The United States and India have been working to enhance building and appliance efficiency through enhanced building codes, design and operation of smart buildings of the future, smart meters and demand side response, as well as retrofit of buildings to improve building performance, promote energy conservation, and improve indoor air quality.

- USAID and Energy Efficiency Services Ltd (EESL) jointly initiated a new activity, "Retrofit of Air Conditioning to Improve Air Quality for Safety and Efficiency" (RAISE) for healthy and energy efficient buildings. The initiative will be scaled in public sector buildings

79. (b) • USAID launched the South Asia Women in Energy (SAWIE) platform focused on the power sector and the sides are working to incorporate gender-focused activities across the technical pillars.

- The U.S. Agency for International Development (USAID) and the U.S.-India Strategic Partnership Forum (USISPF) have officially launched the "South Asia Women in Energy (SAWIE) platform to promote women's empowerment and gender sensitization in the energy sector in South Asia region.

80. (d) • The International Centre for Automotive Technology (ICAT) is organizing a NuGen Mobility Summit, 2019

- The objective of the Summit is to share new ideas, learnings, global experiences, innovations and future technology trends for faster adoption, assimilation and development of advanced automotive technologies for a smarter and greener future.

- This event will help in building a platform for bringing together all stakeholders in the automotive industry to understand global advancements in technologies.

81. (c) • Union HRD Minister, launched the Manodarpan initiative of HRD Ministry

- During the COVID pandemic, the HRD Ministry felt the need to focus on continuing education on the academic front and the mental well-being of the students.

82. (b) • The first Arab space mission to Mars has blasted off aboard a rocket from Japan, with its unmanned probe - called Al-Amal, or Hope

- The Emirati project is one of three racing to Mars, including Tianwen-1 from China and Mars 2020 from the United States, taking advantage of a period when the Earth and Mars are nearest.

- The Hope Probe blasted off from Japan's Tanegashima Space Center for a seven-month journey to the red planet, where it will orbit and send back data about the atmosphere.

83. (a) • The Bill envisages simplified dispute resolution process, has provision for Mediation and e-filing of cases.

- The Consumer will be able to file cases in the nearest commission under the jurisdiction of which he resides.

- Consumers can file complaints from anywhere and they do not need to hire lawyer to represent their cases. For mediation, there will be strict timeline fixed in the rules.

- On misleading advertisements there is provision for jail term and fine for manufacturers.

- There is no provision for jail for celebrities but they could be banned for endorsing products if it is found to be misleading.

- A manufacturer or product service provider or product seller will now be responsible to compensate for injury or damage caused by defective product or deficiency in services.

84. (d) • The Power Ministry also launched "Retrofit of Air-conditioning to improve Indoor Air Quality for Safety and Efficiency" (RAISE) national programme.

• RAISE initiative can potentially alleviate the issue of bad air quality in workspaces across the nation and pioneer ways to make them healthier and greener.

• It is a Joint initiative of EESL and USAID

85. (c) • Market Integration and Transformation Program for Energy Efficiency (MAITREE) is aimed at accelerating the adoption of cost-effective energy efficiency measures as a standard practice within buildings, and specifically focuses on cooling.

• MAITREE is a part of the US-India bilateral Partnership between the Ministry of Power and USAID.

86. (c) • NATRiP is a fully Government of India funded project with a total project cost of Rs. 3727.30 crore.

• This is the largest and one of the most significant initiatives in Automotive sector so far.

• Ministry of Heavy Industry & Public Enterprises (MoHI&PE) is the nodal Ministry of the Government for automotive industry in India and is in charge of framing and administering Auto Policy of the Government of India.

• MoHI&PE is the focal Ministry for implementation of NATRIP. Secretary, MoHI&PE chairs the NATRIP Implementation Society (NATIS) Governing Council.

87. (b) • The Minister for School Education launch portal 'Aspire' at Mantralya

• The Portal has been prepared with the help of the UNICEF for the students of class 9th to 1, 2th of the government schools.

• The 'Aspire' is in fact a future opportunity portal. Information pertaining to college fee, subjects, admission procedure etc. of all the colleges of national and state level can be obtained from this portal.

• Students by self login on this portal can gather information as regard to subjects of their own interest

88. (b) • The United States and India have been working to enhance building and appliance efficiency through enhanced building codes, design and operation of smart buildings of the future, smart meters and demand side response, as well as retrofit of buildings to improve building performance, promote energy conservation, and improve indoor air quality.

• USAID and Energy Efficiency Services Ltd (EESL) jointly initiated a new activity, "Retrofit of Air Conditioning to Improve Air Quality for Safety and Efficiency" (RAISE) for healthy and energy efficient buildings. The initiative will be scaled in public sector buildings

89. (b) • USAID launched the South Asia Women in Energy (SAWIE) platform focused on the power sector and the sides are working to incorporate gender-focused activities across the technical pillars.

• The U.S. Agency for International Development (USAID) and the U.S.-India Strategic Partnership Forum (USISPF) have officially launched the "South Asia Women in Energy (SAWIE) platform to promote women's empowerment and gender sensitization in the energy sector in South Asia region.

90. (d) • The International Centre for Automotive Technology (ICAT) is organizing a NuGen Mobility Summit, 2019

• The objective of the Summit is to share new ideas, learnings, global experiences, innovations and future technology trends for faster adoption, assimilation and development of advanced automotive technologies for a smarter and greener future.

• This event will help in building a platform for bringing together all stakeholders in the automotive industry to understand global advancements in technologies.

91. (d) • Union Home Minister will launch Vriksharopan Abhiyan in the presence of Union Minister of Coal, Mines and Parliamentary affairs

• It will be organized by Ministry of Coal involving all Coal/Lignite PSUs which large scale plantation would be carried out in mines, colonies, offices and other suitable areas of Coal/Lignite PSUs and seedlings will be distributed in the nearby areas for promoting plantation by the society.

92. (c) • Government of India initiated the Jal Jeevan Mission to provide safe and adequate quantity drinking water to every rural household of the country by 2024 with the motto "Har Ghar Jal".

• The programme also implement source sustainability measures as mandatory elements, such as recharge and reuse through grey water management, water conservation, rain water harvesting.

• The Jal Jeevan Mission is based on a community approach to water and has extensive Information, Education and Communication as a key components of the mission.

93. (c) • DRDO has provided its indigenously-developed drone named Bharat to the Indian Army for carrying out accurate surveillance in high altitude areas and mountainous terrain along the Line of Actual Control in Eastern Ladakh.

• The Indian Army requires drones for accurate surveillance in the ongoing dispute in the Eastern Ladakh area. For this requirement, the DRDO has provided the Bharat drones to it.

94. (a) • Going green is the key thrust area of coal sector involving maximization of green cover through ecological reclamation of mined out areas and overburden dumps, plantation in and around mines and avenue plantation at suitable places.

• Ministry's Going Green initiative will kick start through active participation of coal/lignite PSUs as well as private miners.

95. (a) • The flight trial of India`s anti-tank guided missile `Dhruvastra` were successfully conducted at the Interim Test Range (ITR) in Odisha recently.

• The trials of the helicopter-launched Nag Missile (HELINA), which has now been named as Dhruvastra anti-tank guided missile, were conducted in direct and top attack mode.

• Dhruvastra is the helicopter version of 'Nag Helina' with several new features and meant to be fired from air to destroy enemy bunkers, armoured vehicles and main battle tanks.

• The helicopter-launched anti-tank guided missile (ATGM) is one of the most advanced anti-tank weapons in the world.

96. (c) • HELINA is a third-generation fire and forget class anti-tank guided missile (ATGM) system mounted on the Advanced Light Helicopter (ALH).

• The system has all-weather day and night capability and can defeat battle tanks with conventional armour as well as explosive reactive armour.

• The ATGM is guided by an infrared imaging seeker (IIS) operating in the lock-on before-launch mode and helps in further strengthening the defence capabilities of the country.

• The HELINA missile can engage targets both in the direct hit mode as well as top attack mode.

97. (b) • The National Financial Reporting Authority (NFRA) was constituted on 01st October,2018 by the Government of India under Sub Section (1) of section 132 of the Companies Act, 2013

• The establishment of NFRA as an independent regulator for the auditing profession will improve the transparency and reliability of financial statements and information presented by listed companies and large unlisted companies in India.

98. (d) • The order specifies grant of PC to Short Service Commissioned (SSC) Women Officers in all ten streams of the Indian Armyi.e Army Air Defence (AAD), Signals, Engineers, Army Aviation, Electronics and Mechanical Engineers (EME), Army Service Corps (ASC), Army Ordnance Corps (AOC), and Intelligence Corps in addition to the existing streams of Judge and Advocate General (JAG) and Army Educational Corps (AEC).

• After that Short Service Commission (SSC) came with an appointment for 10 years (expandable upto 14 years) and the first batch under this entered in 2008.

• Short Service Commission officers are for the maximum period of 14 years

• Till now Women officers are not eligible for command or criteria appointments

• This Supreme Court ruling does not grant women the right to serve in combat units. At Present there is No Women appointments in the Combat Roles

99. (b) • The Department of Science and Technology has launched the India-Russia Joint Technology Assessment and Accelerated Commercialization Programme in partnership with the Federation of Indian Chambers of Commerce and Industry (FICCI) and Foundation for Assistance to Small Innovative Enterprises (FASIE) of the Russian Federation.

- The programme will connect Indian, and Russian Science & Technology (S&T) led SMEs and Start-ups for joint R&D for technology development and for cross-country technology adaptation.

100. (c)
- DBT-BIRAC has facilitated the establishment of 'first-of-its-kind' mRNA-based vaccine manufacturing platform in India.
- DBT has provided seed funding for the development of Gennova's novel self-amplifying mRNA-based vaccine candidate for COVID19.
- In collaboration with HDT Biotech Corporation, Seattle, USA, Gennova has developed an mRNA vaccine candidate (HGCO19), with demonstrated safety, immunogenicity, neutralization antibody activity in the rodent and non-human primate models.
- HGCO19 uses a 'self-replicating mRNA platform' that ensures the low injectable dose(dose-sparing effect) and sustained antigen release for a longer duration.
- The novel mRNA vaccine candidate, HGCO19, has all the necessary arsenal to guide the host cells to make the antigen -spike protein of the virus, reported to interact with host cells receptor, and supported by 'lipid inorganic nanoparticle (LION)' as a delivery vehicle.
- 'LION delivery system' used for HGCO19 has adjuvant property, enhanced storage stability, reduced adverse effects, improved permeability and bioavailability.

101. (d)
- China launched an unmanned probe to Mars in its first independent mission to visit another planet
- The probe is expected to reach Mars in February where it will attempt to deploy a rover to explore the planet for 90 days.
- If successful, the Tianwen-1, or "Questions to Heaven", which is the name of a poem written two millennia ago, will make China the first country to orbit, land and deploy a rover in its inaugural mission.
- The probe would orbit Mars for about two and a half months and look for an opportunity to enter its atmosphere and make a soft landing.

102. (b)
- The Union Minister for Tribal Affairs inaugurated an e-Symposium on Handicrafts titled "Emergent North-East India: Strategic and Developmental Imperatives in Handicrafts" organized by Dr. APJ Abdul Kalam Centre for Policy Research and Analysis, Indian Institute of Management (IIM), Shillong
- The e-Symposium Series is conceived as a platform that brings together policy makers, scholars, institutions, corporates and civil society to discuss and deliberate development initiatives in the North East Region.

103. (b)
- The Ministry of HRD conducted the first ever Indian Scholastic Assessment (Ind-SAT) Test 2020 under its 'Study in India'
- Nearly five thousand candidates from Nepal, Ethiopia, Bangladesh, Bhutan, Uganda, Tanzania, Rwanda, Sri-Lanka, Kenya, Zambia, Indonesia and Mauritius appeared for the exam conducted in the proctored internet mode by the National Testing Agency.
- Ind-SAT is an exam for grant of scholarships and admissions to foreign students for studying in select Indian universities under the Study in India programme.
- The exam is designed to gauge the scholastic capability of students applying to study in India.
- The exam was held in 1, 2 countries on a pilot basis this year. There are plans to extend this to other countries in the future.

104. (b)
- It is a Mini Ratna Category-1 CPSE continously profit making and fast growing CPSE under Ministry of Human Resource Development offering management and consultancy services in all areas of education and human resource development, both within India and overseas. The company has in the recent past registered rapid growth with the turnover has grown more than 04 times in the last 05 years to INR 321 crore in FY 18-19.
- EdCIL (India) Limited, a PSU under MHRD and the implementing agency of SII handled the registrations and other aspects of the examination.

105. (d)
- The Department of Science and Technology has launched the India-Russia Joint Technology Assessment and Accelerated Commercialization Programme in partnership with the Federation of Indian Chambers of Commerce and Industry (FICCI) and Foundation for Assistance to Small Innovative Enterprises (FASIE) of the Russian Federation.
- On behalf of DST, FICCI will implement the program in India.

- Over a period of two years, the Department of Science and Technology will fund up to INR 15 Crores to ten Indian SMEs/Start-ups and FASIE will provide similar funding to the Russian projects.

106. (d) • The Study in India is a programme of MHRD under which foreign students come to study in 116 select higher education institutions in India for under graduate and post graduate programmes.

- The selection of the students is based on their merit in the class 1, 2 / school leaving exam.

- About top 2000 students are given scholarships, while some others are given fee discounts by the institutions. Around 780 students had taken admission under the programme during its first year - 2018-19. In the second year this number rose to about 3200.

107. (a) • India and European Union have renewed its Agreement on Scientific and Technological Cooperation for the next five years (2020-2025).

- The Agreement was initially signed in on 23 November 2001 and renewed two times in past in 2007 and 2015.

- The cooperation has been focused on water, green transport, e-mobility, clean energy, circular economy, bio-economy, health, and ICT.

108. (b) • The Prime Minister launched high throughput COVID-19 testing facilities on 27th July via video conferencing.

- These facilities will ramp up testing capacity in the country and help in strengthening early detection and treatment, thus assisting in controlling the spread of the pandemic.

- These three high-throughput testing facilities have been set up strategically at ICMR-National Institute of Cancer Prevention and Research, Noida; ICMR-National Institute for Research in Reproductive Health, Mumbai; and ICMR-National Institute of Cholera and Enteric Diseases, Kolkata, and will be able to test over 10,000 samples in a day.

- The labs are enabled to test diseases other than COVID as well, and post the pandemic, will be able to test for Hepatitis B and C, HIV, Mycobacterium tuberculosis, Cytomegalovirus, Chlamydia, Neisseria, Dengue, etc.

109. (c) • The Chambal is the chief tributary of the Yamuna River and rises in the Vindhya Range just south of Mhow, western Madhya Pradesh state.

- From its source it flows north into southeastern Rajasthan state. Turning northeast, it flows past Kota and along the Rajasthan-Madhya Pradesh border; shifting east-southeast, it forms a portion of the Uttar Pradesh-Madhya Pradesh border and flows through Uttar Pradesh to empty into the Yamuna after a 550-mile (900-km) course.

110. (d) • Environment Minister Prakash Javadekar virtually launched piloting of the National Transit Pass System

- The National Transit Pass System enhances seamless movement of forest produce.

- Now, people can apply for Passes from their mobile phones as well as receive e passes in their mobile phones.

111. (d) Joint Statement of the 15th India-EU Summit (July 15, 2020)

- The leaders adopted the "India-EU Strategic Partnership: A Roadmap to 2025" to guide cooperation between India and the EU over the next five years.

- They welcomed the signing of the India-EURATOM Agreement on research and development cooperation in the peaceful uses of nuclear energy.

- They also adopted a Joint Declaration on Resource Efficiency and Circular Economy and welcomed the upcoming renewal of the India-EU Science and Technology Agreement for another five years.

112. (b) • The Centre, in collaboration with the World Bank, has decided to convert large area of ravines in Gwalior-Chambal belt of Madhya Pradesh into arable land

- The Union Minister of Agriculture & Farmers held a meeting with the representatives of World Bank

- During this meeting it was decided that the substantive project would be prepared in collaboration and support from World Bank to accomplish the integrated development of the Bihad area in Gwalior - Chambal region.

113. (a) • The National Transit Pass System enhances seamless movement of forest produce.

- Now, people can apply for Passes from their mobile phones as well as receive e passes in their mobile phones.

- It will make the process of getting permits faster and without physically going to" forest department offices.

- The pilot project will be functional in Madhya Pradesh and Telangana for now.

- NTPS will replace manual paper-based transit system by online transit system and will bring in one permit for whole India for transit of timber, bamboo and other minor forest produce for ease of doing business

- Transit of timber, bamboo and other forest produce is governed by various state specific acts and rules.

- National Transit Pass System generates Pan India Transit Passes facilitating seamless movement of forest produce across India

- NTPS will ensure seamless movement of forest produce across all states thereby resulting in enhancing the income of rural people and also facilitating the ease of doing business in the country

114. (b) • NASA has started work on a new mission to send a telescope, on a football stadium-sized balloon, high into the stratosphere to observe wavelengths of light invisible from the Earth.

- The mission will try to find answers about formation of giant stars in the galaxy.

- The telescope mission called Astrophysics Stratospheric Telescope for High Spectral Resolution Observations at Submillimeter-wavelengths (ASTHROS) is likely to be launched in December 2023 from Antarctica.

- The balloon included a telescope, science instruments, and subsystems such as the cooling and electronic systems.

- ASTHROS will carry an instrument to measure the motion and speed of gas around newly-formed stars.

- During the flight, the mission will study four main targets, including two star-forming regions in the Milky Way galaxy.

- It will also for the first time detect and map the presence of two specific types of nitrogen ions which can reveal places where winds from massive stars and supernova explosions have reshaped the gas clouds.

115. (c) • Defence Research and Development Organisation (DRDO) has launched its

innovation contest 'Dare to Dream 2.0' on the 5th death anniversary of former President and noted scientist Dr APJ Abdul Kalam

- The scheme is being launched for emerging technologies to promote the individuals &startups for innovation in defence and aerospace technologies in the country after the call of 'Atmanirbhar Bharat' given by Prime Minister

- The 'Dare to Dream 2.0' is an open challenge to promote the innovators and startups of the country.

116. (a) • Union Minister for Consumer Affairs, Food & Public Distribution launched the Bureau of Indian Standard's Mobile App 'BIS-Care' and three portals - the Standardization, Conformity Assessment and Training Portals of e-BIS on www.manakonline.in for consumers.

- Consumers can check the authenticity of the ISI-marked and hallmarked products and lodge complaints using this app.

- The Bureau of Indian Standards (BIS) is the national Standards Body of India working under the aegis of Ministry of Consumer Affairs, Food & Public Distribution, Government of India.

- It is established by the Bureau of Indian Standards Act, 1986 which came into effect on 23 December 1986.

117. (a) • The Heads of the Governments of Tiger Range countries at St. Petersburg, Russia, had resolved to double tiger numbers across their global range by 2022 by signing the St. Petersburg declaration on tiger conservation.

- During the said meeting it was also decided to celebrate July 29 as Global Tiger Day across the world, which is since, being celebrated to spread and generate awareness on tiger conservation.

- It was during this day last year, when the Prime Minister declared to the world India's fulfilment of its resolve to double tiger numbers, four years in advance to the target year of 2022 as decided during the St. Petersburg declaration on tiger conservation in Russia in 2010. India now has nearly 70% of the global tiger population.

118. (d) • A new Coastal Research Vessel "SAGAR ANVESHIKA" was commissioned in February 2020.

- It is Coastal Research Vessels which was built for National Institute of Ocean Technology, Ministry of Earth Sciences, Govt. of India,

- This is by far one of the most remarkable developments in the history of India's coastal research with India's private sector partnering the Government and boosting the vision of 'Make in India'.
- SAGAR ANVESHIKA, the second vessel will enable scientists to conduct various oceanographic research missions aboard her.
- 'SAGAR ANVESHIKA' will house state of the art laboratories equipped with modern scientific instruments.

119. (a) • MoES has developed and commissioned an Integrated Flood Warning System for Mumbai (IFLOWS-Mumbai) in close coordination with Municipal Corporation of Greater Mumbai, Govt of Maharashtra. to aid in the mitigation activities of the flood prone city of Mumbai.

120. (c) • As per the Tiger Census of 2018, the state of Madhya Pradesh has the highest number of tigers at 526. It is followed by Karnataka with 524 tigers and Uttarakhand at 442 tigers.

- The states of Chhattisgarh and Mizoram saw a decline in tiger numbers while Odisha maintained its population using the best available science, technology and analytical tools.
- The M-STrIPES app (used in last census also), CaTRAT software and the Extract Compare programs made this tiger census the most accurate in history.

121. (b) • Tigers are scattered among Bangladesh, Bhutan, Cambodia, China, Indonesia, Laos PDR, Malaysia, Myanmar, Nepal, Russian Federation, Thailand and Vietnam.

- India's five tiger landscapes are: Shivalik Hills and Gangetic Plains, Central Indian Landscape and Eastern Ghats, Western Ghats, North-East Hills and Brahmaputra Plains, and the Sundarbans.
- There are different species of tigers - Siberian tigers, Bengal tigers, Indochinese tigers, Malayan tigers and South China tigers.
- The Bengal tiger is found primarily in India, with smaller a population of them in Bangladesh, Nepal, Bhutan, China and Myanmar as well.
- 'Project Tiger' is a Centrally Sponsored Scheme of the Environment, Forests and Climate Change, providing funding support to tiger range States

122. (d) • On the occasion of its foundation day MoES-Knowledge Resource Centre Network (KRCNet)

- The traditional libraries of the MoES system will be upgraded into a top-notch Knowledge Resource Centres (KRC).
- KRCs will be connected with each other and integrated into the KRCNet portal. It will be a single point entry to the intellectual world of Ministry of Earth Sciences (MoES).
- The resources and services of MoES system will be accessible 24X7 through a one point dynamic, updated and integrated KRCNet portal.

123. (d) • India Meteorological Department, Ministry of Earth Sciences has taken various initiatives in recent years for improvement in dissemination of weather forecast and warning services based on latest tools and technologies.

- To further enhance this initiative, Ministry of Earth Sciences launched the mobile App "Mausam" for India Meteorological Department.
- This Mobile App is dedicated to the general public and designed to communicate the weather information and forecasts in a lucid manner without technical jargons.
- Users can access observed weather, forecasts, radar images and be proactively warned of impending weather events.
- The Mausam mobile app will be an important tool for dissemination of weather information and warnings in an attractive and user friendly manner which will meet the requirements of public.
- The mobile app has been designed and developed jointly by ICRISAT's Digital Agriculture & Youth (DAY) team, Indian Institute of Tropical Meteorology (IITM), Pune and India Meteorological Department

The MAUSAM mobile App has the following 5 services:

- Current Weather -
- Nowcast
- City Forecast
- Warnings
- Radar products

124. (b) • CAWACH is an initiative by National Science & Technology Entrepreneurship Development Board (NSTEDB), Department of Science and Technology (DST), Government of India.

- It aims to support market-ready innovations for the control of COVID-19 and startup ideas to address associated challenges.

125. (c)
- Acculi Labs is armed with 'Lyfas' a clinical-grade, non-invasive, digital functional biomarker smartphone tool for screening, early detection, root cause analysis, acute event risk assessment, prognosis, and home monitoring of chronic diseases

- The new technology developed with support from the DST, will detect the possible infection in an asymptomatic individual to prioritise the conventional testing queue as well as carry out a risk assessment of an asymptomatic individual to become symptomatic and risk assessment of an asymptomatic individual for recovery.

126. (b)
- The Industry-Academia Collaborative Mission of Department of Biotechnology (DBT), Govt of India for accelerating discovery research to early development for Biopharmaceuticals approved by the Cabinet for a total cost US$ 250 million and 50% co-funded by the World Bank is being implemented at Biotechnology Research Assistance Council (BIRAC).

- This program is dedicated to deliver affordable products to the nation with an aim to improve the health standards of India's population.

- Vaccines, medical devices and diagnostics and biotherapeutics are few of its most important domains, besides, strengthening the clinical trial capacity and building technology transfer capabilities in the country.

127. (c)
- Biotechnology Industry Research Assistance Council (BIRAC) is a not-for-profit Section 8, Schedule B, Public Sector Enterprise, set up by Department of Biotechnology (DBT), Government of India as an Interface Agency to strengthen and empower the emerging Biotech enterprise to undertake strategic research and innovation, addressing nationally relevant product development needs.

128. (c)
- The Ministry of Housing and Urban Affairs launched the Mobile Application of PM Street Vendor's AtmaNirbhar Nidhi (PM SVANidhi)

- Ministry of Housing and Urban Affairs, on June 01, 2020, for providing affordable Working Capital loan to street vendors to resume their livelihoods that have been adversely affected due to Covid-19 lockdown.

- The launch of Mobile App will give impetus to the implementation strategy of the Scheme besides promoting paper-less digital accessing of micro-credit facilities by the Street Vendors.

129. (c)
- Department of Heavy Industry (DHI), Govt of India, has embarked on a mission to promote innovation, R&D and product development in India for various sectors.

- The International Centre for Automotive Technology (ICAT) was established in 2006 at Manesar, Haryana, India.

- It is a division of NATRIP (National Automotive Testing and R&D Infrastructure Project) Implementation Society (NATIS) under Department of Heavy Industries, Government of India.

- ICAT is providing quality services to the industry in all the domains of automotive and non automotive development, such as Powertrain, Noise Vibration and Harshness, Component, Fatigue, Photometry, Tyre & Wheel, Passive Safety, EMC and CAD & CAE.

130. (b)
- Government has been implementing several schemes for incentivizing the investment made by dairy cooperative sector for development of dairy infrastructure.

- AHIDF would facilitate much needed incentivisation of investments in establishment of such infrastructure for dairy and meat processing and value addition infrastructure and establishment of animal feed plant in the private sector.

- Government of India would also set up Credit Guarantee Fund of Rs. 750 crore to be managed by NABARD.

- Credit guarantee would be provided to those sanctioned projects which are covered under MSME defined ceilings. Guarantee Coverage would be upto 25% of Credit facility of borrower.

- The beneficiaries intending to invest for establishing dairy and meat processing and value addition infrastructure or strengthening of the existing infrastructure can apply for loan in the scheduled bank through "Udyami Mitra" portal of SIDBI.

Practice Questions Set – 3
General Studies Paper I

1. Consider the following statements about the One Nation One Ration Card Plan

   1. The objective is to ensure the delivery of food security entitlements to all beneficiaries covered under the National Nutrition Mission or POSHAN Abhiyaan

   2. The nation-wide portability of ration cards to be implemented under the ongoing central sponsored scheme on 'Integrated Management of Public Distribution System (IM-PDS)

   Which of the statements given above is/are correct?

   (a) 1 only   (b) 2 only

   (c) Both 1 and 2   (d) Neither 1 nor 2

2. Consider the following statements about National Programme for Civil Services Capacity Building (NPCSCB)

   1. The Programme will be delivered by setting up an Integrated Government offline Training- iGOT Karmayogi Platform.

   2. It aims to prepare the Indian civil servant empowered with specific role-competencies

   Which of the statements given above is/are correct?

   (a) 1 only   (b) 2 only

   (c) Both 1 and 2   (d) Neither 1 nor 2

3. Consider the following statements about the US- India Strategic Partnership Forum (USISPF)

   1. It is a non-profit organization, with the primary objective of strengthening the U.S.-India bilateral and strategic partnership.

   2. It plays a significant role in fostering a robust and dynamic relationship between the two countries through policy advocacy

   Which of the statements given above is/are incorrect?

   (a) 1 only   (b) 2 only

   (c) Both 1 and 2   (d) Neither 1 nor 2

4. Consider the following statements about Public Human Resources Council

   1. It includes only the Union Ministers, Chief Ministers and Public Service functionaries under the Chairmanship of Prime Minister

   2. It will act as the apex body for providing strategic direction to the task of Human Resource development

   Which of the statements given above is/are correct?

   (a) 1 only   (b) 2 only

   (c) Both 1 and 2   (d) Neither 1 nor 2

5. Consider the following statements about the National Food Security Act, (NFSA) 2013

   1. The existing Antyodaya Anna Yojana (AAY) has been merged under the National Food Security Act

   2. The Act has a special focus on the nutritional support to women and children.

   3. The eligible persons will be entitled to receive 5 kgs of foodgrains per person per month at subsidised prices

   Which of the statements given above is/are correct?

   (a) 1 only   (b) 2 only

   (c) 2 and 3 only   (d) 1and 3 only

6. Consider the following statements about All India Management Association (AIMA)

   1. It is the apex body for management in India

   2. It is a non-lobbying, not for profit organisation, working closely with industry, government, academia and students

   Which of the statements given above is/are correct?

   (a) 1 only   (b) 2 only

   (c) Both 1 and 2   (d) Neither 1 nor 2

7. Consider the following statements about the Agency for Non-Conventional Energy and Rural Technology (ANERT)

   1. ANERT is an autonomous organisation established functioning under power department

   2. ANERT is the State Nodal Agency (SNA) for the Ministry of New and Renewable Energy (MNRE), to carry out the Centrally Assisted Programmes in Kerala

   Which of the statements given above is/are correct?

(a) 1 only   (b) 2 only

(c) Both 1 and 2   (d) Neither 1 nor 2

8. Which of the following nations are discussing building a "supply chain resilience initiative"?

   (a) Japan, India and Australia

   (b) Taiwan, Hong-Kong, Philippines

   (c) France, USA and India

   (d) India, USA and Japan

9. Swasthya Portal has been launched by which of the following Ministries?

   (a) The Ministry of Tribal Affairs

   (b) The Ministry of Health and Family Welfare

   (c) The Ministry of Women and Child Development

   (d) The Ministry of Social Justice and Empowerment

10. Consider the following statements about Energy Efficiency Services Limited (EESL)

    1. EESL is world's largest public Energy Service Company (ESCO) under the administrative control of Ministry of Power

    2. It is a joint venture of state-owned NTPC Limited, Power Finance Corporation, REC Limited and Power Grid Corporation of India Ltd.

    Which of the statements given above is/are correct?

    (a) 1 only   (b) 2 only

    (c) Both 1 and 2   (d) Neither 1 nor 2

11. Consider the following statements about the Business Reform Action Plan (BRAP)

    1. The recent Business Reform Action Plan (BRAP) ranking of states was declared by the World Bank

    2. It includes 180 reform points covering 12 business regulatory areas

    3. State Rankings have been released earlier also for the years 2015, 2016 and 2017-18.

    Which of the statements given above is/are correct?

    (a) 1 and 3 only   (b) 3 only

    (c) 2 and 3 only   (d) 2 only

12. Consider the following statements

    1. In a recent finding the Chandrayaan-II Moon data indicates that the Moon's poles are home to water

    2. The mission objective of Chandrayaan-2 (Indian lunar mission) was to explore the unchartered south pole of the celestial body by landing a rover.

Which of the statements given above is/are correct?

(a) 1 only   (b) 2 only

(c) Both 1 and 2   (d) Neither 1 nor 2

13. The Chief Minister of which of the following states has released a book titled "Tangams:An Ethnolinguistic Study Of The Critically Endangered Group?

    (a) Chhattisgarh   (b) Telangana

    (c) Arunachal Pradesh   (d) None of the above

14. 'RCF SAFEROLA' has been introduced by a 'mini ratna' company Rashtriya Chemicals and Fertilizers Limited (RCF).

    RCF SAFEROLA is related to which of the following?

    (a) Hand Cleansing IPA Gel

    (b) New Variety of Urea

    (c) Fortified edible oil

    (d) Generic Vitamin C capsules

15. Consider the following statements about the Mental Health Rehabilitation Helpline "KIRAN"

    1. It has been launched jointly by the Ministry of Health and Family Welfare and the Department of Empowerment of Persons with Disabilities (DEPwD)

    2. It offers mental health rehabilitation services with the objective of early screening, first-aid, psychological support and mental well-being

    Which of the statements given above is/are correct?

    (a) 1 only   (b) 2 only

    (c) Both 1 and 2   (d) Neither 1 nor 2

16. A Mental Health Rehabilitation Helpline "KIRAN" has been launched by which of the following Ministries/State/Organisations?

    (a) Ministry of Health and Family Welfare

    (b) State government of Andhra Pradesh

    (c) Minister of Social Justice and Empowerment

    (d) NITI Aayog

17. Consider the following statements about recently launched Project Dolphin

    • Share on Facebook

    • Share on Twitter

    1. The project is aimed at saving both river and marine dolphins.

    2. Project Dolphin is to be implemented by National Mission for Clean Ganga (NMCG)

3. Project Dolphin will be on the lines of Project Tiger

Which of the statements given above is/are correct?

(a) 1 and 3 only　　　(b) 2 only

(c) 1 2 and 3　　　(d) 1and 3 only

18. The Kalasa-Banduri Project undertaken by which of the following state governments?

(a) Karnataka government

(b) Goa government

(c) Maharashtra government

(d) Andhra government

19. Consider the following statements about Start-Up Village Entrepreneurship Programme (SVEP)

1. It is implemented by Deendayal Antyodaya Yojana -National Rural Livelihoods Mission (DAY-NRLM), Ministry of Rural Development

2. SVEP focusses on providing self-employment opportunities by providing training in business management without any financial assistance

Which of the statements given above is/are correct?

(a) 1 only　　　(b) 2 only

(c) Both 1 and 2　　　(d) Neither 1 nor 2

20. Consider the following statements about Gangetic dolphin

1. The Gangetic dolphin listed as critically endangered by the International Union for the Conservation of Nature.

2. It is included in the First Schedule of the Indian Wildlife (Protection), Act 1972.

Which of the statements given above is/are correct?

(a) 1 only　　　(b) 2 only

(c) Both 1 and 2　　　(d) Neither 1 nor 2

21. Consider the following statements about the International Day of Clean Air For Blue skies

1. World Health Organisation has adopted a resolution to observe the International Day of Clean Air for Blue Skies on 07th September every year starting from 2020.

2. It was introduced to acknowledge the threats posed by air pollution and to encourage every country in the world to take preventive measures.

Which of the statements given above is/are correct?

(a) 1 only　　　(b) 2 only

(c) Both 1 and 2　　　(d) Neither 1 nor 2

22. Consider the following statements

1. Rocket engine carries its own supply of oxygen for combustion

2. Jet engine utilizes oxygen from the atmosphere for combustion.

Which of the statements given above is/are correct?

(a) 1 only　　　(b) 2 only

(c) Both 1 and 2　　　(d) Neither 1 nor 2

23. Consider the following statements about recently tested Hypersonic Test Demonstrator Vehicle (HSTDV)

1. It has been developed by the Defence Research and Development Organisation (DRDO)

2. HSTDV is an unmanned ramjet demonstration aircraft for hypersonic speed flight.

Which of the statements given above is/are correct?

(a) 1 only　　　(b) 2 only

(c) Both 1 and 2　　　(d) Neither 1 nor 2

24. Consider the following statements about Mandovi / Mahadayi river

1. The Mandovi originates from Karnataka's Belgaum district.

2. The Mandovi river basin falls into the states of Goa, Karnataka and Maharashtra.

3. Kalasa and Banduri are two tributaries of the Mahadayi river

Which of the statements given above is/are correct?

(a) 1 and 3 only　　　(b) 2 only

(c) 1, 2 and 3　　　(d) 1 and 3 only

25. Consider the following statements about the National Clean Air Programme (NCAP)

1. The target is to achieve 20 to 30 percent reduction in PM 10 and PM 2.5 concentrations by 2024 keeping 2017 as base year.

2. NCAP has been implemented across all the States and Union Territories

Which of the statements given above is/are incorrect?

(a) 1 only　　　(b) 2 only

(c) Both 1 and 2　　　(d) Neither 1 nor 2

26. The government launched the Air Quality Index (AQI) monitoring and tracking the levels of Pollution on eight parameters.

Which of the following parameters is/are part of those eight parameters?

1. NO_2
2. SO_2
3. CO_2
4. O_3
5. Pb

Choose the correct one from the options given below

(a) 1 and 5 only
(b) 1, 3 and 5 only
(c) 1, 2, 4 and 5 only
(d) 1, 2, 3 and 4 only

27. Consider the following statements about Global Innovation Index

   1. GII 2020 has been released solely by the World Intellectual Property Organization (WIPO)

   2. India has joined the group of top 50 countries in the Global Innovation Index for the first time

   Which of the statements given above is/are correct?

   (a) 1 only
   (b) 2 only
   (c) Both 1 and 2
   (d) Neither 1 nor 2

28. Consider the following statements about Special Frontier Force (SFF)

   1. It is under the administrative control of Defence Ministry

   2. The special frontier force trained in mountain warfare

   3. SFF's commandos are drawn from various battalions of Indian Army

   Which of the statements given above is/are incorrect?

   (a) 1 and 3 only
   (b) 2 only
   (c) 1, 2 and 3
   (d) 1and 3 only

29. The nationwide investigation, has disrupted the operation of illegal software called "Real Mango" used for cornering confirmed Railway reservation.

   This investigation was carried out by which of the following organisations?

   (a) Delhi Police Cyber Cell
   (b) The Ministry of Electronics and Information Technology
   (c) Ministry of Home affairs
   (d) None of the above

30. The India Innovation Index has been released last year by which of the following Organisation

   (a) NITI Aayog
   (b) The Department for Promotion of Industry and Internal Trade (DPIIT)
   (c) Ministry of Housing and Urban Affairs
   (d) World Intellectual Property Organization

31. Consider the following statements

   1. AYURAKSHA is a joint venture of All India Institute of Ayurveda (AIIA) and Health Ministry

   2. Its objective is to provide the Ayurveda Preventive and Promotive health services to all the frontline workers

   Which of the statements given above is/are correct?

   (a) 1 only
   (b) 2 only
   (c) Both 1 and 2
   (d) Neither 1 nor 2

32. Cabinet approves Constitution of 22nd Law Commission of India

   With reference to it consider the following statements about Law Commission of India

   1. The 22nd Law Commission has been constituted for a term of three years

   2. It is a non-statutory body

   3. Its recommendations are advisory in nature

   Which of the statements given above is/are correct?

   (a) 1 and 3 only
   (b) 2 only
   (c) 1 2 and 3
   (d) 1and 2 only

33. Consider the following statements about National Recruitment Agency (NRA)

   1. NRA will conduct a Common Eligibility Test (CET) to shortlist candidates for both the technical and non-technical posts of Group B and C

   2. NRA will have representatives of Ministry of Railways, Ministry of Finance, Education Ministry, the SSC, RRB & IBPS.

   Which of the statements given above is/are incorrect?

   (a) 1 only
   (b) 2 only
   (c) Both 1 and 2
   (d) Neither 1 nor 2

34. Consider the following statements about Students' Learning Enhancement Guidelines

   1. These guidelines have been prepared and released by NITI Aayog

   2. These guidelines are model of suggestions for those children, who do not have digital resources to get learning opportunities at home

   Which of the statements given above is/are correct?

   (a) 1 only
   (b) 2 only
   (c) Both 1 and 2
   (d) Neither 1 nor 2

35. A mobile unit called Dhanwantari Rath equipped with health care services and team of doctors to outreach OPD services has been launched

It is an initiative of which of the following organisations?

(a) All India Institute of Ayurveda (AIIA)

(b) Ministry of Health and Family Welfare

(c) State government of Delhi

(d) None of the above

36. The government has taken several initiatives to boost private players in space sector

With reference to it consider the following statements

1. New Space India Ltd (NSIL) will allow space activities and usage of department of Space owned facilities by non-government private entities (NGPEs)

2. IN-SPACE is a commercial arm of ISRO established to scale up the industry participation in Indian space programmes.

Which of the statements given above is/are correct?

(a) 1 only   (b) 2 only

(c) Both 1 and 2   (d) Neither 1 nor 2

37. India has signed a contract for development of five eco-tourism zones in Addu atoll of the island nation.

Addu atoll is situated in which of the following countries?

(a) Maldives   (b) Mauritius

(c) Seychelles   (d) Sri Lanka

38. Consider the following statements about Atoll

1. It is a ring-shaped coral reef

2. It surrounds a body of water called a lagoon

3. Atolls develop with underwater volcanoes, called seamounts.

Which of the statements given above is/are correct?

(a) 1 only   (b) 2 only

(c) 1 2 and 3   (d) 1 and 3 only

39. Consider the following statements about Nasha Mukt Bharat: Annual Action Plan (2020-21)

1. The annual action plan has been launched only for the 272 Most Affected Districts

2. It has been launched by the Narcotics Bureau

Which of the statements given above is/are correct?

(a) 1 only   (b) 2 only

(c) Both 1 and 2   (d) Neither 1 nor 2

40. Consider the following statements about Parsi New Year Navroz

1. It is celebrated to mark the beginning of the Iranian calendar.

2. In India and across the world it is celebrated in accordance with the Shahenshahi calendar.

3. It is observed by Iranians and the Parsi community around the world.

Which of the statements given above is/are correct?

(a) 1 and 3 only   (b) 2 only

(c) 1 2 and 3   (d) 1and 2 only

41. Consider the following statements about India-Sweden Healthcare Innovation Centre

1. It is collaboration between the Ministry of Health and Family Welfare and Business Sweden.

2. The India Sweden Healthcare Innovation Centre has agreed to support the goals of Atal Innovative Mission

Which of the statements given above is/are correct?

(a) 1 only   (b) 2 only

(c) Both 1 and 2   (d) Neither 1 nor 2

42. Consider the following statements about Millennium Alliance

1. The objective is to identify test and scale Indian innovations that address global development solutions.

2. It is a consortium of public-private partnership including the Department of Science and Technology, Govt. of India

Which of the statements given above is/are correct?

(a) 1 only   (b) 2 only

(c) Both 1 and 2   (d) Neither 1 nor 2

43. Consider the following statements about the fifth edition of the annual cleanliness urban survey Swachh Survekshan 2020 conducted by the Ministry of Housing and Urban Affairs (MoHUA)

1. It saw the introduction of a new performance category, the Prerak DAUUR Samman which has a total of five additional sub- categories

2. 25% weightage integrated into the final Swachh Survekshan results by considering the performance of cities, in Swachh Survekshan League, a quarterly cleanliness assessment

Which of the statements given above is/are correct?

(a) 1 only   (b) 2 only

(c) Both 1 and 2   (d) Neither 1 nor 2

44. Which of the following nations are discussing building a "supply chain resilience initiative to counter China's dominance as trade and geopolitical tensions escalate across the region

(a) Japan, India and Australia

(b) Japan, India and USA

(c) Russia, India and Australia

(d) None of the above

45. Consider the following statements about the Digital Quality of Life Index 2020

  1. India ranks among the lowest in the world in terms of Internet quality

  2. India makes it into the top 10 in terms of Internet affordability.

  3. The Index has been released by TRAI

Which of the statements given above is/are correct?

(a) 1 and 3 only   (b) 2 only

(c) 1, 2 and 3   (d) 1 and 2 only

46. Consider the following statements about the Cantonment Boards

  1. It is a defence administration body in India under control of the Ministry of Defence

  2. Cantonments are areas which comprise of both military and civil population.

Which of the statements given above is/are correct?

(a) 1 only   (b) 2 only

(c) Both 1 and 2   (d) Neither 1 nor 2

47. Consider the following statements about the Agricultural Finance Corporation Ltd or AFC India Ltd.

  1. It is wholly owned by Commercial Banks, NABARD and EXIM Bank

  2. It provides consulting, policy advisory and implementation support for agriculture and rural development

Which of the statements given above is/are correct?

(a) 1 only   (b) 2 only

(c) Both 1 and 2   (d) Neither 1 nor 2

48. Consider the following statements about Agricultural and Processed Food Products Export Development Authority (APEDA)

  1. It is an apex body under the Ministry of Food Processing Industries

  2. It responsible for the export promotion of agricultural products.

Which of the statements given above is/are correct?

(a) 1 only   (b) 2 only

(c) Both 1 and 2   (d) Neither 1 nor 2

49. Consider the following statements

  1. Central sector schemes, is 100% funded by the Union government and implemented by the State Government machinery.

  2. Centrally Sponsored Schemes are formulated in subjects from the State List

Which of the statements given above is/are correct?

(a) 1 only   (b) 2 only

(c) Both 1 and 2   (d) Neither 1 nor 2

50. Consider the following statements about Chhavni COVID: Yodha Sanrakshan Yojana

  1. It has been launched by the Ministry of Defence

  2. It is a group life insurance scheme which will cover the defence personnel

Which of the statements given above is/are correct?

(a) 1 only   (b) 2 only

(c) Both 1 and 2   (d) Neither 1 nor 2

51. National Survey on Extent and Pattern of Substance Use in India has been commissioned and funded by which of the following Ministries/Organisations?

(a) Ministry of Social Justice and Empowerment

(b) Ministry of Health and Family Welfare

(c) Department of Chemicals and Petrochemicals, Ministry of Chemicals and Fertilizers

(d) None of the above

52. Consider the following statements about BRICS

  1. It is an informal group of states

  2. The New Development Bank (NDB) and the Contingent Reserve Arrangement (CRA) are the important institutions of BRICS

Which of the statements given above is/are correct?

(a) 1 only   (b) 2 only

(c) Both 1 and 2   (d) Neither 1 nor 2

53. The Uttar Pradesh government had sent a request for renaming the railway station in Varanasi district.

With reference to it consider the following statements

  1. The Ministry of Railways considers proposals for name change according to the existing guidelines

  2. The Ministry of Railways gives its approval after taking no-objections from the Department of Posts and Survey of India

Which of the statements given above is/are correct?

(a) 1 only   (b) 2 only

(c) Both 1 and 2   (d) Neither 1 nor 2

54. Consider the following statements about Atal Ranking of Institutions on Innovation Achievements (ARIIA) 2020.

    1. A special category for higher educational institutions for women has been introduced for the first time

    2. ARIIA is an initiative to systematically rank all major higher educational institutions and universities in India

Which of the statements given above is/are correct?

(a) 1 only   (b) 2 only

(c) Both 1 and 2   (d) Neither 1 nor 2

55. Consider the following statements about Swadeshi Microprocessor Challenge

    1. It has been launched by NITI Aayog

    2. It invites innovators, start-ups and students to develop microprocessors

Which of the statements given above is/are correct?

(a) 1 only   (b) 2 only

(c) Both 1 and 2   (d) Neither 1 nor 2

56. The Union Cabinet has given its approval for creation of National Recruitment Agency (NRA)

With reference to it consider the following statements about NRA

    1. NRA will conduct the first-level /Tier I Examination only

    2. The CET score of the candidate shall be valid for a period of three years

Which of the statements given above is/are correct?

(a) 1 only   (b) 2 only

(c) Both 1 and 2   (d) Neither 1 nor 2

57. Recently the 'eSanjeevani' telemedicine service records 2 lakh tele-consultations

With reference to it consider the following statements

    1. E-Sanjeevani platform enables only Patient-to-Doctor Tele-consultations service

    2. It has been implemented across all the states

Which of the statements given above is/are correct?

(a) 1 only   (b) 2 only

(c) Both 1 and 2   (d) Neither 1 nor 2

58. Consider the following statements about the Food Safety and Standards Authority of India (FSSAI)

    1. It is an autonomous body established under the Ministry of Health & Family Welfare

    2. The FSSAI has been established under the Food Safety and Standards Act, 2006

Which of the statements given above is/are correct?

(a) 1 only   (b) 2 only

(c) Both 1 and 2   (d) Neither 1 nor 2

59. Recently a Mobile App for Urban Local Bodies (ULB) functionaries. This App aims to provide user friendly digital interface for the functionaries of ULBs to source loan applications of street vendors.

The above app has been launched for which of the following Schemes?

(a) PM SVANidhi   (b) PM KISAN

(c) PM Ujjwala   (d) None of the above

60. Consider the following statements about National Recruitment Agency (NRA)

    1. The final selection for recruitment shall be made through separate specialised Tiers (II, III etc) of examination which shall be conducted by NRA itself

    2. There shall be no restriction on the number of attempts to be taken by a candidate to appear in the CET

Which of the statements given above is/are correct?

(a) 1 only   (b) 2 only

(c) Both 1 and 2   (d) Neither 1 nor 2

61. India's only overseas air base is located in Farkhor. Farkhor is situated in which of the following countries?

(a) Kyrgyzstan   (b) Kazakhstan

(c) Uzbekistan   (d) Tajikistan

62. Consider the following statements about the recent amendments done in Prime Minister Employment Generation Program (PMEGP)

    1. KVIC is the nodal agency for implementing the scheme.

    2. The role of District Level Task Force Committee (DLTFC) in approving the PMEGP projects has been diluted

    3. KVIC has been entrusted the task of clearing the applications from prospective entrepreneurs and forward it to the Banks

Which of the statements given above is/are correct?

(a) 1 only   (b) 2 only

(c) 1, 2 and 3   (d) 1 and 3 only

63. Consider the following statements about the Trifood Project

   1. It has been implemented by the Ministry of Food Processing Industry (MoFPI)

   2. It aims to enhance the income of farmers through better utilization of and value addition to the Minor Forest Products collected by the farmers

Which of the statements given above is/are incorrect?

(a) 1 only   (b) 2 only

(c) Both 1 and 2   (d) Neither 1 nor 2

64. Consider the following statements about Connect Central Asia Policy of India

   1. It is a broad-based approach, which includes political, security, and economic as well as cultural connections.

   2. It focuses on five nations namely Kyrgyzstan, Kazakhstan, Uzbekistan, Tajikistan, Turkmenistan

Which of the statements given above is/are correct?

(a) 1 only   (b) 2 only

(c) Both 1 and 2   (d) Neither 1 nor 2

65. The Golden Crescent region comprises of which of the following countries?

(a) Afghanistan, Iraq, and Pakistan

(b) Afghanistan, Iran, and Pakistan

(c) Kyrgyzstan, Iran and Afghanistan

(d) Kazakhstan, Kyrgyzstan Tajikistan

66. Consider the following statements about Kawasaki disease

   1. Kawasaki typically affects children under five years of age

   2. WHO termed this new illness multisystem inflammatory disorder.

Which of the statements given above is/are correct?

(a) 1 only   (b) 2 only

(c) Both 1 and 2   (d) Neither 1 nor 2

67. Consider the following statements about Biotechnology Industry Research Assistance Council (BIRAC)

   1. It is a not-for-profit Public Sector Enterprise

   2. It objective is to strengthen and empower the emerging Biotech enterprise

   3. It set up by Department of Biotechnology (DBT)

Which of the statements given above is/are correct?

(a) 1 and 2 only   (b) 3 only

(c) 1 2 and 3   (d) 1and 3 only

68. World Press Freedom Index is released by

(a) World Economic Forum

(b) International Federation of Journalists

(c) United Nations Development Programme (UNDP)

(d) None of the above

69. Deeksharambh - a guide to Student Induction Programme was recently released by which of the following ministries?

(a) Ministry of Human Resource Development

(b) Ministry of Women and Child Development

(c) Ministry of Social Justice and Empowerment

(d) NITI Aayog under AIM

70. India has signed a deal with which of the following nations for acquiring Strum Ataka anti-tank missile for its fleet of Mi-35 attack choppers of Indian Air Force (IAF).

(a) Russia   (b) USA

(c) Israel   (d) None of the above

71. Nuakhai is an agricultural festival of which of the following states?

(a) Odisha   (b) Jharkhand

(c) Madhya Pradesh   (d) Karnataka

72. Which of the following countries is/are part of ASEAN Plus Six initiative

   1. India   2. Australia

   3. New Zealand   4. China

Choose the correct from the options given below

(a) 1 and 4 only   (b) 1 and 3 only

(c) 1 2 and 3 only   (d) All of the above

73. Consider the following statements about the Technical group on population projections

   1. It is constituted by the National Commission on Population (NCP) under the Ministry of Home Affairs

   2. Its mandate is to provide population projections for the period 2011 to 2036.

   3. The report states that India will overtake China as the world's most populous country around 2022

Which of the statements given above is/are correct?

(a) 1 and 2 only   (b) 3 only

(c) 1, 2 and 3   (d) 2 only

74. Consider the following statements about the National Payments Corp. of India (NPCI)

1. NPCI was incorporated as a not-for-profit company under the provisions of the Companies Act

2. It has been promoted by the RBI and 10 core banks including SBI and ICICI

Which of the statements given above is/are correct?

(a) 1 only   (b) 2 only

(c) Both 1 and 2   (d) Neither 1 nor 2

75. Consider the following statements about the National Population Commission

1. Its objective is to review, monitor and give directions for the implementation of Census, every 10 years

2. It is chaired by the prime minister

Which of the statements given above is/are correct?

(a) 1 only   (b) 2 only

(c) Both 1 and 2   (d) Neither 1 nor 2

76. Consider the following statements about East Asia Summit

1. EAS is an initiative of ASEAN and is based on the premise of the centrality of ASEAN.

2. It is a forum of 18 countries of the Asia-Pacific region formed

3. China, India, Russian Federation and the USA are members of EAS

Which of the statements given above is/are correct?

(a) 1 and 2 only   (b) 3 only

(c) 1, 2 and 3   (d) 1and 3 only

77. Recently the Reserve Bank of India (RBI) unveiled the framework to set up a pan-India umbrella entity

With reference to it consider the following statements

1. It must have a minimum paid-up capital of Rs 500 crore

2. Applicants must also have at least three years of experience in the payments ecosystem.

3. No single promoter or promoter group should have more than 40% investment in the capital of this entity.

Which of the statements given above is/are incorrect?

(a) 1 and 2 only   (b) 2 and 3 only

(c) 1, 2 and 3   (d) None of the above

78. Uttar Pradesh government signed a cooperation agreement with which of the following countries for resolving water crisis in Bundelkhand region?

(a) Russia   (b) Israel

(c) France   (d) Germany

79. AarogyaSetu team has worked on a new innovative feature which is called 'Open API Service'.

With reference to it consider the following statements about the Open API Service

1. It can be availed by organizations and business entities, who are registered in India with more than 50 employees

2. Once enrolled the Open API will provide the Aarogya Setu status and name of the Aarogya Setu User without taking any consent from the user

Which of the statements given above is/are correct?

(a) 1 only   (b) 2 only

(c) Both 1 and 2   (d) Neither 1 nor 2

80. Consider the following statements about recently launched "Chunauti"- Next Generation Start-up Challenge Contest

1. It has been launched by the Ministry of Electronics and Information Technology

2. The objective is to boost start-ups and software products with special focus on Tier-II towns of India.

Which of the statements given above is/are correct?

(a) 1 only   (b) 2 only

(c) Both 1 and 2   (d) Neither 1 nor 2

81. Consider the following statements about Aryabhatta Research Institute of Observational Sciences (ARIES)

1. It is an autonomous research institute under the Department of Science and Technology (DST)

2. ARISE focus in Atmospheric Sciences division is mainly in the lower part of the atmosphere and covers the studies on aerosols and trace gases.

Which of the statements given above is/are correct?

(a) 1 only   (b) 2 only

(c) Both 1 and 2   (d) Neither 1 nor 2

82. The Aegean dispute is a set of interrelated controversies between which of the following nations?

    (a) China - Japan   (b) China - Vietnam
    (c) China - Philippines(d) None of the above

83. Consider the following statements about the National Council for Transgender Persons

    1. The council will have joint secretary-level members from the ministries of health, home, minority affairs, education, rural development, labour and law.

    2. There will be a member from the department of pensions, Niti Aayog, National Human Rights Commission and National Commission for Women.

    3. Representatives from all states or Union Territories will be the members of the commission.

    Which of the statements given above is/are correct?

    (a) 1 and 2 only   (b) 2 and 3 only
    (c) 1 2 and 3   (d) None of the above

84. Consider the following statements about the Atal BimitVyakti Kalyan Yojana

    1. It is a welfare measure being implemented by the Ministry of Social Justice and Empowerment

    2. It offers cash compensation to insured persons when they are rendered unemployed

    3. The relief become due for payment 90 days after unemployment

    Which of the statements given above is/are correct?

    (a) 1 and 2 only   (b) 2 only
    (c) 1 2 and 3   (d) 1 and 3 only

85. Consider the following statements about Employees' State Insurance

    1. It is a self-financing social security and health insurance scheme for Indian workers.

    2. The fund is managed by the Employees' State Insurance Corporation (ESIC)

    3. ESIC is a Statutory Body

    Which of the statements given above is/are correct?

    (a) 1 and 2 only   (b) 2 only
    (c) 1 and 3 only   (d) 1 2 and 3

86. The Odisha government has announced to give a facelift to the 11th century Lingaraja Temple.

    With reference to it consider the following statements

    1. The Lingaraja Temple is dedicated to Shiva

    2. It is built by the kings from the Somavamsi dynasty

    Which of the statements given above is/are correct?

    (a) 1 only   (b) 2 only
    (c) Both 1 and 2   (d) Neither 1 nor 2

87. The eVIN has reached 32 States and Union Territories (UTs) and will soon be rolled out in the remaining States and UTs

    With reference to it consider the following statements about eVIN

    1. It is aimed at strengthening pharmaceutical supply chain systems across the country.

    2. It is implemented under the National Health Mission (NHM)

    Which of the statements given above is/are correct?

    (a) 1 only   (b) 2 only
    (c) Both 1 and 2   (d) Neither 1 nor 2

88. The JNU got approval for a fund from the Higher Education Funding

    With reference to it consider the following statements about Higher Education Funding Agency (HEFA)

    1. The HEFA is a joint venture company of Canara Bank and the Ministry of Human Resource Development.

    2. All the centrally funded higher educational institutions will be eligible to join as members of the HEFA.

    Which of the statements given above is/are correct?

    (a) 1 only   (b) 2 only
    (c) Both 1 and 2   (d) Neither 1 nor 2

89. The Manodarpan initiative has been launched by which of the following Ministries?

    (a) Ministry of Human Resource and Development
    (b) Ministry of Health and Family Welfare
    (c) NITI Aayog
    (d) Ministry of Home Affairs

90. Consider the following statements about the Kumhar Sashaktikaran Yojana

    1. It is an initiative of the Khadi and Village Industries Commission(KVIC)

    2. It objective is to empower the potters' community in the remotest of locations in the country.

Which of the statements given above is/are incorrect?

(a) 1 only   (b) 2 only

(c) Both 1 and 2   (d) Neither 1 nor 2

91. Recently the Siddi community gets its first lawmaker in Karnataka.

With reference to it consider the following statements about Siddi community

1. They are included as the Scheduled Tribes in Karnataka.

2. They are an ethnic group inhabiting India and Pakistan.

3. They are primarily Hindus

Which of the statements given above is/are correct?

(a) 1 and 3 only   (b) 2 only

(c) 1, 2 and 3   (d) 1and 2 only

92. Natesa, a rare sandstone idol from the 9th century (Pratihara Style) has been retrieved recently after 22 years

With reference to it consider the following statements about Pratihara Style

1. It is a famous temple architecture belonging to the Gurjara- Pratihara dynasty of Rajasthan.

2. The greatest development of their style of building is at Khajuraho, Madhya Pradesh

Which of the statements given above is/are correct?

(a) 1 only   (b) 2 only

(c) Both 1 and 2   (d) Neither 1 nor 2

93. Consider the following statements about Bru Tribes

1. They are recognized as a Particularly Vulnerable Tribal Group (PVTG) in Tripura

2. They are spread across the north eastern states of Tripura, Assam, Manipur, and Mizoram

Which of the statements given above is/are correct?

(a) 1 only   (b) 2 only

(c) Both 1 and 2   (d) Neither 1 nor 2

94. Consider the following statements about the Naval Innovation and Indigenisation Organisation (NIIO)

1. It has been launched by the Ministry of Electronics and Information Technology

2. The objective of NIIO is to boost self-reliance in the service and manufacturing sector.

Which of the statements given above is/are correct?

95. Two villages of which of the following states were designated as 'Tsunami Ready' for their preparedness by UNESCO?

(a) Andhra Pradesh   (b) Odisha

(c) Karnataka   (d) West Bengal

96. Consider the following statements about the Directorate General of Defence Estates (DGDE)

1. It is an Inter Services Organisation of the Ministry of Defence

2. It directly controls the Cantonment Administration.

3. It can't levy any tax.

Which of the statements given above is/are correct?

(a) 1 and 3 only   (b) 2 only

(c) 1, 2 and 3   (d) 1and 2 only

97. Consider the following statements about Dedicated Freight Corridor Corporation India Limited (DFCCIL)

1. It is a Public Sector Undertaking (PSU) corporation run by government of India's Ministry of Railways

2. It was registered as a company under the Companies Act

3. It has been set up as a special purpose vehicle

Which of the statements given above is/are correct?

(a) 1 and 2 only   (b) 3 only

(c) 1, 2 and 3   (d) 1and 3 only

98. Which of the following infrastructure Projects is/ are financed by AIIB

1. Bangalore Metro Rail Project

2. Gujarat Rural Roads (MMGSY)

3. Jaipur Metro Rail Project

4. Mumbai Urban Transport Project

Choose the correct answer from the options given below

(a) 1 and 2 only   (b) 1 2 and 4 only

(c) 1, 2, 3 and 4   (d) 1and 3 only

99. Consider the following statements about National Investment and Infrastructure Fund (NIIF).

1. It is an Indian-government backed entity

2. It has been established to provide long-term capital to the infrastructure sector.

Which of the statements given above is/are correct?

(a) 1 only   (b) 2 only

(c) Both 1 and 2   (d) Neither 1 nor 2

100. Consider the following statements about the Dedicated Freight Corridor Corporation India Limited (DFCCIL).

1. The Eastern & western dedicated freight corridor projects are partly funded by the World Bank and Japan International Cooperation Agency (JICA) respectively.

2. Private containers will also be allowed to use the freight corridor without any extra charges

3. The Eastern Corridor will connect Dadri in Uttar Pradesh to Jawaharlal Nehru Port (JNPT) in Mumbai

Which of the statements given above is/are incorrect?

(a) 1 and 2 only   (b) 3 only

(c) 2 and 3only   (d) 1 only

101. Consider the following statements about the Asian Infrastructure Investment Bank (AIIB)

1. India is a founding member of AIIB

2. It is open to all members of the World Bank or the Asian Development Bank

3. It doesn't allow for non-sovereign entities to apply for AIIB membership

Which of the statements given above is/are incorrect?

(a) 3 only   (b) 2 only

(c) 2 and 3only   (d) 1 and 3 only

102. Consider the following statements about the recently launched "Chunauti"- Next Generation Start-up Challenge Contest

1. It has been launched by NITI Aayog

2. It objective is to boost start-ups and software products with special focus on Tier-II towns of India.

3. The start-ups selected through Chunauti will be provided support from the government only in the form of funds

Which of the statements given above is/are correct?

(a) 1 and 3 only

(b) 2 only

(c) 2 and 3only

(d) 1and 3 only

103. Consider the following statements about the Association of Renewable Energy Agencies of States (AREAS)

1. Union Minister for New & Renewable Energy is the ex-officio President of the Association.

2. It is an autonomous body under the Minister for New & Renewable Energy

Which of the statements given above is/are correct?

(a) 1 only   (b) 2 only

(c) Both 1 and 2   (d) Neither 1 nor 2

104. Consider the following statements about Eklavya Model Residential Schools (EMRS)

1. It has been established under Ministry of Social Justice and Empowerment

2. Every block with more than 50% SC/ST and Minority population will have an Eklavya Model Residential School by the year 2022.

3. These schools will have special facilities for preserving local art and culture

Which of the statements given above is/are correct?

(a) 1 and 3 only   (b) 2 only

(c) 2 and 3only   (d) 1 and 3 only

105. Consider the following statements about recently launched the national GIS-enabled land bank system

1. It will be used to get real-time information about the availability of industrial land and resources.

2. It is being developed by integrating the Industrial Information System (IIS) with Central GIS (Geographic Information System).

Which of the statements given above is/are correct?

(a) 1 only   (b) 2 only

(c) Both 1 and 2   (d) Neither 1 nor 2

106. Consider the following statements about the Pradhan Mantri Jan-Dhan Yojana (PMJDY)

1. PMJDY account is treated as inoperative if there are no customer induced transactions in the account for over a period of six months

2. The free accidental insurance cover on RuPay cards increased from Rs. 1 lakh to Rs. 2 lakh for all the account holders of PMJDY

Which of the statements given above is/are correct?

(a) 1 only   (b) 2 only

(c) Both 1 and 2   (d) Neither 1 nor 2

107. Consider the following statements about Exercise Kavkaz 2020

1. India has participated in Kavkaz 2020 with 180 troops from an infantry battalion, 40 personnel of the Air Force, and two Navy officers as observers.

2. The aim of the exercise is to "provide real-time training to counter international terrorism in the Northern and Caucasus region

Which of the statements given above is/are correct?

(a) 1 only
(b) 2 only
(c) Both 1 and 2
(d) Neither 1 nor 2

108. Consider the following statements about SCO

1. India and China were admitted as full members back in 2017.

2. It is a permanent inter- ministerial international organisation

3. The group has developed Regional Anti-Terrorist Structure (RATS).

Which of the statements given above is/are correct?

(a) 1 and 3 only
(b) 3 only
(c) 1, 2 and 3
(d) 2 only

109. Consider the following statements about India and ASEAN relations

1. Both sides have agreed to review the ASEAN - India Trade in Goods Agreement (AITIGA) signed in 2009

2. The ASEAN-India Trade in Goods Agreement was signed but yet to enter into force

Which of the statements given above is/are correct?

(a) 1 only
(b) 2 only
(c) Both 1 and 2
(d) Neither 1 nor 2

110. Recently the Pradhan Mantri Jan-Dhan Yojana (PMJDY) completed 6 years. With reference to it consider the following statements about the Pradhan Mantri Jan-Dhan Yojana (PMJDY)

1. It was launched in 2015 with an objective to focus on every Unbanked Adult

2. In the extension of PMJDY the Over Draft limit has been doubled from Rs 5,000/- to Rs 10,000/ without conditions

Which of the statements given above is/are incorrect?

(a) 1 only
(b) 2 only
(c) Both 1 and 2
(d) Neither 1 nor 2

111. Vallam Kali and Pulikali are dance and art forms specific to which of the following states?

(a) Kerala
(b) Karnataka
(c) Tamil Nadu
(d) Telangana

112. Consider the following statements about Phalcon airborne warning and control systems (AWACS)

1. India doesn't yet have a single Phalcon AWACS

2. It is capable of tracking the movement of troops across the border without crossing territorial limits.

Which of the statements given above is/are correct?

(a) 1 only
(b) 2 only
(c) Both 1 and 2
(d) Neither 1 nor 2

113. Consider the following statements about Airborne Warning And Control System (AWACS)

1. It is a mobile, long-range radar surveillance and control centre for air and land defence.

2. It is mounted in a specially modified aircraft and can also be mounted on any submarine

Which of the statements given above is/are incorrect?

(a) 1 only
(b) 2 only
(c) Both 1 and 2
(d) Neither 1 nor 2

114. Consider the following statements about India - SCO relations

1. India, Pakistan and all Shanghai Cooperation Organisation (SCO) member-nations had participated in a strategic command and staff exercise as part of Exercise Tsentr.

2. India has never participated in SCO peace mission exercise

Which of the statements given above is/are correct?

(a) 1 only
(b) 2 only
(c) Both 1 and 2
(d) Neither 1 nor 2

115. India's first toy manufacturing cluster is going to be established at Koppal(a) Koppala is situated in which of the following states?

(a) Uttarakhand
(b) Karnataka
(c) Gujarat
(d) Uttar Pradesh

116. Consider the following statements

1. NETRA also known as Airborne Early Warning and Control System is a project of India's Defence Research and Development Organisation

2. India had signed a USD 5 billion deal with the USA to buy five units of the S-400 air defence missile systems

Which of the statements given above is/are correct?

(a) 1 only   (b) 2 only

(c) Both 1 and 2   (d) Neither 1 nor 2

117. The World's largest solar tree has been developed and installed by which of the following organisations?

(a) Ministry of New and Renewable Energy

(b) ISRO

(c) DRDO

(d) None of the above

118. Consider the following statements about Pinaka Multiple Launch Rocket System (MLRS)

1. It has been indigenously designed and developed by DRDO

2. It was designed to replace the BM-21 Grad multiple rocket launcher systems of the Indian Army.

3. The launch system of Pinaka is comprised up of two pods, which are mounted on a Tatra launcher vehicle.

Which of the statements given above is/are correct?

(a) 1 only   (b) 2 only

(c) 1, 2 and 3   (d) 1and 3 only

119. Consider the following statements about Agriota-E Marketplace platform.

1. It has been launched by the Ministry of Agriculture and Farmers' Welfare

2. It is a new technology-driven agri-commodity trading and sourcing e-market platform

Which of the statements given above is/are correct?

(a) 1 only

(b) 2 only

(c) Both 1 and 2

(d) Neither 1 nor 2

120. Consider the following statements about the Global Food Security Index

1. It is managed and updated annually by the Food and Agriculture Organization

2. It measures food security across most of the developing countries of the world.

Which of the statements given above is/are incorrect?

(a) 1 only   (b) 2 only

(c) Both 1 and 2   (d) Neither 1 nor 2

121. An extreme-UV light has been detected from one of the farthest galaxy called AUDFs01 located 9.3 billion light-years away from earth by which of the following observatories

(a) Compton Gamma Ray Observatory

(b) Spitzer Space Telescope.

(c) AstroSat

(d) Hubble Space Telescope

122. Consider the following statements about Green Term Ahead Market (GTAM)

1. GTAM platform would lessen the burden on agriculture-rich states

2. GTAM platform will lead to increase in number of participants involved in agriculture and allied sector.

Which of the statements given above is/are correct?

(a) 1 only   (b) 2 only

(c) Both 1 and 2   (d) Neither 1 nor 2

123. Consider the following statements about Pradhan Mantri Kisan SAMPADA Yojana

1. It is a Central Sector Scheme

2. It is implemented by Ministry of Agriculture and Farmer's welfare

3. The objective is to create modern infrastructure with efficient supply chain management

Which of the statements given above is/are correct?

(a) 1 only   (b) 2 only

(c) 1 2 and 3   (d) 1and 3 only

124. Consider the following statements about the Mega Food Park Scheme

1. Mega Food Park typically consists of supply chain infrastructure excluding food processing units.

2. It is implemented by a Special Purpose Vehicle (SPV) which is a body Corporate registered under the Companies Act.

Which of the statements given above is/are correct?

(a) 1 only

(b) 2 only

(c) Both 1 and 2

(d) Neither 1 nor 2

125. Consider the following statements about India's first Space Observatory AstroSat

1. It was launched by the Indian Space Research Organization (ISRO)

2. It is aimed at studying celestial sources in X-ray, optical and UV spectral bands one at a time.

Which of the statements given above is/are correct?

(a) 1 only

(b) 2 only

(c) Both 1 and 2

(d) Neither 1 nor 2

126. Consider the following statements about the Regional Anti-Terrorist Structure (RATS).

1. It is a permanent organ of the SCO

2. Its headquarters is based in Tashkent.

3. RATS plays a very critical role in fight against terrorism, extremism and separatism

Which of the statements given above is/are correct?

(a) 1 only   (b) 2 only

(c) 1, 2 and 3   (d) 1and 3 only

127. The National Technical Advisory Group on Immunisation (NTAGI) includes a Standing Technical Sub-Committee (STSC).

With reference to it consider the following statements about STSC

1. It is tasked with undertaking technical review of scientific evidence on matters related to immunization policy and programmes.

2. Final recommendations are drafted by the STSC by taking the consent of NATGI

Which of the statements given above is/are correct?

(a) 1 only   (b) 2 only

(c) Both 1 and 2   (d) Neither 1 nor 2

128. Consider the following statements about the Online Performance Dashboard Empowering Tribals, Transforming India

1. The Online Performance Dashboard has been launched recently by NITI Aayog

2. It has been developed by the Ministry of Tribal Affairs (MoTA)

3. The Dashboard showcases updated & real-time details of schemes / initiatives of the Ministry for achieving these SDGs.

Which of the statements given above is/are correct?

(a) 1 only   (b) 2 only

(c) 1, 2 and 3   (d) 1and 3 only

129. Consider the following statements about the AI Step Up Module

1. This Step up module is specifically devised considering students as young as 12 years of age

2. The step-up module needs no previous knowledge and introduces the concepts to students from the basics

Which of the statements given above is/are correct?

(a) 1 only   (b) 2 only

(c) Both 1 and 2   (d) Neither 1 nor 2

130. Consider the following statements about Transiting Exoplanet Survey Satellite (TESS)

1. It is designed to discover thousands of large size planets orbiting around the brightest dwarf stars in the sky.

2. It is a joint initiative of European Space Agency and Japan Aerospace Exploration Agency

Which of the statements given above is/are correct?

(a) 1 only   (b) 2 only

(c) Both 1 and 2   (d) Neither 1 nor 2

ANSWER KEY

1. (d)	**2.** (b)	**3.** (d)	**4.** (d)	**5.** (c)	**6.** (c)	**7.** (c)	**8.** (a)	**9.** (a)	**10.** (c)
11. (c)	**12.** (b)	**13.** (c)	**14.** (a)	**15.** (b)	**16.** (c)	**17.** (d)	**18.** (a)	**19.** (a)	**20.** (b)
21. (b)	**22.** (c)	**23.** (a)	**24.** (c)	**25.** (b)	**26.** (c)	**27.** (b)	**28.** (d)	**29.** (d)	**30.** (a)
31. (d)	**32.** (c)	**33.** (c)	**34.** (b)	**35.** (a)	**36.** (d)	**37.** (a)	**38.** (c)	**39.** (a)	**40.** (a)
41. (b)	**42.** (c)	**43.** (b)	**44.** (a)	**45.** (d)	**46.** (b)	**47.** (c)	**48.** (b)	**49.** (b)	**50.** (a)
51. (a)	**52.** (c)	**53.** (d)	**54.** (c)	**55.** (d)	**56.** (c)	**57.** (d)	**58.** (c)	**59.** (a)	**60.** (b)
61. (d)	**62.** (c)	**63.** (c)	**64.** (c)	**65.** (b)	**66.** (c)	**67.** (c)	**68.** (d)	**69.** (a)	**70.** (a)
71. (a)	**72.** (d)	**73.** (d)	**74.** (a)	**75.** (b)	**76.** (c)	**77.** (d)	**78.** (b)	**79.** (a)	**80.** (c)
81. (c)	**82.** (d)	**83.** (a)	**84.** (b)	**85.** (d)	**86.** (c)	**87.** (b)	**88.** (c)	**89.** (a)	**90.** (d)
91. (d)	**92.** (c)	**93.** (c)	**94.** (d)	**95.** (b)	**96.** (c)	**97.** (c)	**98.** (b)	**99.** (c)	**100.** (c)
101. (a)	**102.** (b)	**103.** (d)	**104.** (a)	**105.** (a)	**106.** (d)	**107.** (b)	**108.** (b)	**109.** (a)	**110.** (c)
111. (a)	**112.** (b)	**113.** (c)	**114.** (a)	**115.** (b)	**116.** (a)	**117.** (d)	**118.** (c)	**119.** (b)	**120.** (c)
121. (c)	**122.** (d)	**123.** (d)	**124.** (b)	**125.** (a)	**126.** (c)	**127.** (a)	**128.** (c)	**129.** (b)	**130.** (d)

EXPLANATION

1. (d) • The 'One Nation One Ration Card' plan is an ambitious endeavour of the government to ensure the delivery of food security entitlements to all beneficiaries covered under the National Food Security Act, 2013 (NFSA), irrespective of their physical location anywhere in the country, by implementing nation-wide portability of ration cards under the ongoing central sector scheme on 'Integrated Management of Public Distribution System (IM-PDS)' in association with all States/UTs.

• Through this system, the migratory NFSA beneficiaries are now enabled with an option to lift their entitled quota of foodgrains from any Fair Price Shop (FPS) of their choice anywhere in the country by using their same/existing ration card

2. (b) • The Union Cabinet has approved launching of a National Programme for Civil Services Capacity Building (NPCSCB)

• Mission Karmayogi aims to prepare the Indian Civil Servant for the future by making him more creative, constructive, imaginative, innovative, proactive, professional, progressive, energetic, enabling, transparent and technology-enabled.

• Empowered with specific role-competencies, the civil servant will be able to ensure efficient service delivery of the highest quality standards.

3. (d) • The US-India Strategic Partnership Forum (USISPF) is a non-profit organization, with the primary objective of strengthening the U.S.-India bilateral and strategic partnership.

• Dedicated to strengthening economic and commercial ties, USISPF plays a significant role in fostering a robust and dynamic relationship between the two countries through policy advocacy that will lead to driving economic growth, entrepreneurship, employment-creation, and innovation to create a more inclusive society.

4. (d) • A Public Human Resources Council comprising of select Union Ministers, Chief Ministers, eminent public HR practitioners, thinkers, global thought leaders and Public Service functionaries under the chairmanship of Prime Minister

• It will serve as the apex body for providing strategic direction to the task of Civil Services Reform and capacity building.

5. (c) • The enactment of the National Food Security Act, (NFSA) 2013 on July 5, 2013 marks a paradigm shift in the approach to food security from welfare to rights based approach.

• The National Food Security Act, (NFSA) 2013 is being implemented in all the States/UTs, on an all India basis.

• The eligible persons will be entitled to receive 5 kgs of foodgrains per person per month at subsidised prices of Rs. 3/2/1 per Kg for rice/wheat/coarse grains.

• The existing Antyodaya Anna Yojana (AAY) households, which constitute the poorest of the poor, will continue to receive 35 kgs of foodgrains per household per month.

• The Act also has a special focus on the nutritional support to women and children. Besides meal to pregnant women and lactating mothers during pregnancy and six months after the child birth, such women will also be entitled to receive maternity benefit of not less than Rs. 6,000.

6. (c) • The All India Management Association (AIMA) is the apex body for management in India with over 38000 members and close to 6000 corporate /institutional members through 66 Local Management Associations affiliated to it.

• AIMA was formed over 60 years ago and is a non-lobbying, not for profit organisation, working closely with industry, government, academia and students, to further the cause of the management profession in India.

• The association is represented on a number of policy making bodies of the Government of India and national associations including All India Council for Technical Education (AICTE), which is the apex regulatory body for professional education in the country under the Ministry of Human Resource Development; National Board of Accreditation (NBA)

7. (c) • ANERT is an autonomous organisation established during 1986 under Societies Act by the Government of Kerala, now functioning under power dept; with its headquarters at Thiruvananthapuram.

• ANERT is guided by an Executive Committee chaired by the Chairman, Secretary power dept; and a Governing Body chaired by the Minister of Electricity, Govt. of Kerala to provide guidelines for ANERT's activities in various energy related areas.

• ANERT is the State Nodal Agency (SNA) for the Ministry of New and Renewable Energy (MNRE), Govt. of India, to carry out the Centrally Assisted Programmes in Kerala.

8. (a) • Japan, India and Australia are seeking to build stronger supply chains to counter China's dominance as trade and geopolitical tensions escalate across the region

• The three nations are discussing building a supply chain resilience initiative

• The Supply Chain Resilience Initiative first proposed by Japan.

• The objective is to reduce the dependency in China.

9. (a) • Union Tribal Affairs Minister launched Swasthya, a first of its kind Tribal Health & Nutrition Portal: One-stop solution for the health & nutrition status of the tribal population of India

• The Ministry of Tribal Affairs in collaboration with Piramal Swasthya, the Centre of Excellence has developed this Tribal Health and Nutrition Portal 'Swasthya', a one-stop solution presenting all information pertaining to tribal health and nutrition related to Scheduled Tribe people.

10. (c) • Energy Efficiency Services Limited (EESL), a Super Energy Service Company (ESCO) under the administrative control of Ministry of Power, Government of India

• It is an energy service company (ESCO) of the Government of India and is the world's largest public ESCO.

• It is 100% government-owned, a joint venture of state-owned NTPC Limited, Power Finance Corporation, REC Limited and POWERGRID.

• EESL was formed under India's Ministry of Power to facilitate energy efficiency projects.

11. (c) • Union Minister of Finance and Corporate Affairs announced the 4thedition of Business Reform Action Plan (BRAP) ranking of states.

• Andhra Pradesh retained its top position in ease of doing business ranking 2019, followed by Uttar Pradesh and Telangana.

• Till date, State Rankings have been released for the years 2015, 2016 and 2017-18.

• The Business Reform Action Plan 2018-19 includes 180 reform points covering 12 business regulatory areas such as Access to Information,

Single Window System, Labour, Environment, etc.

12. (b) • The sign of this finding is that even though the surface of the Moon is known to have iron - rich rocks, it is not known for the presence of water and oxygen, which are the two elements needed to interact with iron to create rust

- This could be because the Earth's own atmosphere could be protecting the Moon as well.

- Chandrayaan-1 Moon data indicates that the Moon's poles are home to water; this is what the scientists are trying to decipher.

Chandrayaan -2

- Chandrayaan-2 is an Indian lunar mission to explore the unchartered south pole of the celestial body by landing a rover.

- On September 7 2019, India attempted to make a soft landing on to the lunar surface.

- However, lander Vikram missed the primary landing site and went for the second. The visuals went missing henceforth.

- If India does succeed, it will be the fourth country to land on the moon, after the erstwhile USSR, US and China, to cement its place among the world's space-faring nations.

13. (c) • A book titled 'The Tangams: An Ethnolinguistic Study Of The Critically Endangered Group of Arunachal Pradesh' by the Centre for Endangered Languages (CFEL) under Arunachal Institute of Tribal Studies (AITS) of Rajiv Gandhi University here, was released by Chief Minister

- The book has valuable data on endangered oral narratives like ritual songs, lamentation songs, lullabies and festival songs in Tangam language spoken by the Tangam community, which has reportedly 253 speakers left now.

- Tangam People is a little-known community within the larger Adi tribe of Arunachal Pradesh.

- Tangam is an oral language that belongs to the Tani group, under the greater Tibeto- Burman language family.

- It has been marked 'critically endangered' by the UNESCO World Atlas of Endangered Languages (2009).

14. (a) • State-owned RCF has introduced a hand sanitiser in the market as part of its effort to control spread of coronavirus disease.

- To assist government in its effort to combat COVID-19, Rashtriya Chemicals and Fertilizers Ltd (RCF) has introduced a Hand Cleansing IPA Gel RCF SAFEROLA

15. (b) • Union Minister for Social Justice and Empowerment will launch the 24x7 Toll-Free Mental Health Rehabilitation Helpline KIRAN (1800-500-0019).

- This Helpline has been developed by the Department of Empowerment of Persons with Disabilities (DEPwD), Ministry of Social Justice & Empowerment to provide relief and support to persons with Mental Illness.

- This helpline will offer mental health rehabilitation services with the objective of early screening, first-aid, psychological support, distress management, mental well-being, promoting positive behaviors, psychological crisis management etc.

16. (c) • Union Minister for Social Justice and Empowerment will launch the 24x7 Toll-Free Mental Health Rehabilitation Helpline KIRAN (1800-500-0019).

- This Helpline has been developed by the Department of Empowerment of Persons with Disabilities (DEPwD), Ministry of Social Justice & Empowerment to provide relief and support to persons with Mental Illness.

- This helpline will offer mental health rehabilitation services with the objective of early screening, first-aid, psychological support, distress management, mental well-being, promoting positive behaviors, psychological crisis management etc.

17. (d) • Prime Minister has announced the launching of the Project Dolphin for the conservation and protection of the Dolphins in the rivers and in oceans of the country.

- The proposed project is aimed at saving both river and marine dolphins.

- Project Dolphin will be on the lines of Project Tiger, which has helped increase the tiger population

- It got in-principle approval in December last year, at the first meeting of the National Ganga Council (NGC), headed by the Prime Minister.

- So far, the National Mission for Clean Ganga (NMCG), which implements the government's flagship scheme NamamiGange, has been taking some initiatives for saving dolphins.

- Now, Project Dolphin is expected to be implemented by the Ministry of Environment, Forest and Climate Change.

18. (a) • The conflict on the Mandovi / Mahadayi river - flowing through Goa, Karnataka and Maharashtra

- The Kalasa-Banduri Project undertaken by the Karnataka government proposes to divert Mandovi river water from Kalasa and Banduri canals into the Malaprabha river in the state to facilitate drinking water to 13 towns of Karnataka

19. (a) • Start-Up Village Entrepreneurship Programme (SVEP) is implemented by Deendayal Antyodaya Yojana -National Rural Livelihoods Mission (DAY-NRLM), Ministry of Rural Development, as a sub-scheme since 2016.

- Its objective is to support the rural poor come out of poverty, supporting them setup enterprises and provide support till the enterprises stabilize

- SVEP focuses on providing self-employment opportunities with financial assistance and training in business management and soft skills while creating local community cadres for promotion of enterprises.

- SVEP addresses three major pillars of rural start-ups namely - finances, incubation and skill ecosystems.

20. (b) • The Gangetic dolphin remains listed as endangered by the International Union for the Conservation of Nature.

- After the launch of Ganga Action Plan in 1985, the government on November 24, 1986 included Gangetic dolphins in the First Schedule of the Indian Wildlife (Protection), Act 1972.

- The Conservation Action Plan for the Ganges River Dolphin 2010-2020, which identified threats to Gangetic Dolphins and impact of river traffic, irrigation canals and depletion of prey-base on Dolphins populations.

21. (b) • The General Assembly of United Nations on 19 December 2019 adopted a resolution to observe the International Day of Clean Air for Blue Skies on 07th September every year starting from 2020.

- The very first International Day of Clean Air for blue skies held on September 7th, 2020.

- The United Nations General Assembly invited the United Nations Environment Programme (UNEP) to facilitate the observance of the International Day, in collaboration with other relevant organizations.

- The International Day of Clean Air for Blue Skies was introduced to acknowledge the threats posed by air pollution and to encourage every country in the world to take preventive measures.

22. (c) • A scramjet is a supersonic combusting ramjet.

- This is a variant of a ramjet jet engine in which combustion takes place in supersonic airflow.

- Rocket engine - It carries its own supply of oxygen for combustion (less energy efficient)

- Jet engine - It utilizes oxygen from the atmosphere for combustion. (high energy efficient)

23. (a) • DRDO has successfully flight tested the Hypersonic Technology Demonstrator Vehicle using the indigenously developed scramjet propulsion system

- The HSTDV is an unmanned scramjet demonstration aircraft for hypersonic speed flight.

- Besides its utility for long-range cruise missiles of the future, the technology has multiple civilian applications also.

- The HSTDV cruise vehicle is mounted on a solid rocket motor, which will take it to a required altitude, and once it attains certain mach numbers for speed, the cruise vehicle will be ejected out of the launch vehicle. Subsequently, the scramjet engine will be ignited automatically.

24. (c) • The Mandovi originates from Karnataka's Belagaum district. The Mandovi river basin falls into the states of Goa, Karnataka and Maharashtra.

- The river is 81 kilometres (km) in length; 35 km of which flows in Karnataka, 1 km in Maharashtra and 45 km in Goa.

- The Kalasa-Banduri canal - part of the 11-dam project on the river Mandovi.- aims to improve drinking water supply to the districts of Belagavi, Bagalkot, Dharwad and Gadag.

25. (b) • In January last year, the Environment Ministry had launched National Clean Air Programme (NCAP) to tackle the problem of air pollution in

a comprehensive manner with a target to achieve 20 to 30 percent reduction in PM 10 and PM 2.5 concentrations by 2024 keeping 2017 as base year.

- The plan identified earlier 102 non-attainment cities, across 23 States and Union Territories.

- 20 more non-attainment cities have been included under NCAP based on latest data trend on air quality.

- It involves building across Kalasa and Banduri, two tributaries of the Mahadayi river, to initially divert 7.56 thousand million cubic feet (TMC) of water to the Malaprabha river, which supplies drinking water needs of the said four districts.

26. (c) • The AQI is an index for reporting daily air quality.

- It tells you how clean or polluted your air is, and what associated health effects might be a concern for you.

- The objective of an AQI is to quickly disseminate air quality information (almost in real-time) that entails the system to account for pollutants which have short-term impacts.

- Eight parameters (PM10, PM2.5, NO_2, SO_2, CO, O_3, NH_3, and Pb) having short-term standards have been considered for near real-time dissemination of AQI.

27. (b) • India has joined the group of top 50 countries in the Global Innovation Index for the first time in history.

- India moves up four places to the 48th rank.

- The Global Innovation Index (GII) 2020, released jointly by the World Intellectual Property Organization (WIPO), Cornell University and INSEAD Business School, ranks 131 economies.

- India ranks in the top 15 in indicators such as ICT (Information and Communication Technology) services exports, government online services, graduates in science and engineering, and R&D-intensive global companies.

28. (d) • A secret force also known as the Special Frontier Force (SFF) under the administrative control of the Cabinet secretariat and the PMO.

- Raised towards the end of the 1962 war, SFF's commandos are drawn from Tibetan refugees settled in India.

- The SFF has played an important role in multiple military operations - from the 1971 India-Pakistan war to the 1999 Kargil battle - but has largely functioned under the shadows. SFF units, also known as Vikas battalions, come under the direct purview of the Cabinet Secretariat, and is operationally involved with the Army.

29. (d) • A drive against touts was intensified by Railway Protection Force (RPF) of Indian Railways.

- In a nationwide investigation, RPF has disrupted the operation of illegal software called "Real Mango" used for cornering confirmed Railway reservation.

- A drive against touts was intensified by Railway Protection Force (RPF) of Indian Railways.

- Operation of an illegal software called "Rare Mango" (later changed its name to "Real Mango)" was intensified by Railway Protection Force (RPF) of Indian Railways.

30. (a) • The India Innovation Index, which was released last year by NITI Aayog, has been widely accepted as a major step in the direction of decentralisation of innovation across all states of the country

31. (d) • A MoU was signed between All India Institute of Ayurveda (AIIA) and Delhi Police for extending the Ayurveda Preventive and Promotive health services in the residential colonies of Delhi Police.

- These services are to be provided through a mobile unit named 'DhanwantariRath' and Police Wellness Centres and are to be catered by AIIA, supported by Ministry of AYUSH.

- AYURAKSHA a joint venture of AIIA, an autonomous Institute under Ministry of AYUSH and Delhi Police aims for maintaining the health of frontline COVID warriors like Delhi police personal through Ayurveda immunity boosting measures.

32. (c) • The Union Cabinet has approved Twenty-second Law Commission of India for a period of three years

- The Law Commission of India is a non-statutory body constituted by the Government of India from time to time.

- The Commission was originally constituted in 1955 and is re-constituted every three years. The tenure of twenty-first Law Commission of India was upto 31st August, 2018.

- The various Law Commissions have been able to make important contribution towards the progressive development and codification of Law of the country. The Law Commission has so far submitted 277 reports.

33. (c) • The Union Cabinet has given its approval for creation of National Recruitment Agency (NRA), paving the way for a transformational reform in the recruitment process for central government jobs.

- A multi-agency body called the National Recruitment Agency (NRA) will conduct a Common Eligibility Test (CET) to screen/ shortlist candidates for the Group B and C (non-technical) posts.

- NRA will have representatives of Ministry of Railways, Ministry of Finance/Department of Financial Services, the SSC, RRB & IBPS.

34. (b) • Union Education Minister virtually releases Students' Learning Enhancement Guidelines

- In view of this, NCERT has prepared Students' Learning Enhancement Guidelines on the direction of the Ministry of Education for the present situation and also for post pandemic situation.

- These guidelines emphasize upon the community working closely with the school to get learning materials such as workbooks, worksheets, etc. delivered at the doorsteps of children by teachers and volunteers.

- It also suggests teaching local students by volunteers or teachers setting up television at the community centre and maintaining social distance norms.

- These guidelines will help children, who do not have digital resources to get learning opportunities at home with their teachers or volunteers.

35. (a) • DhanwantariRath and Police wellness centres would be outreach OPD services of AIIA and aimed to benefit the Families of Delhi Police through Ayurveda Preventive health care services.

- DhanwantariRath - Mobile unit of Ayurveda health care services would consist a team of Doctors who would be visiting Delhi Police colonies regularly.

36. (d) • The union cabinet recently approved private player participation in space in June 2020 to transform the sector.

Indian National Space Promotion and Authorization Center (IN-SPACe)

- IN-SPACe is an independent nodal agency under Department of Space for allowing space activities and usage of department of Space owned facilities by non-government private entities (NGPEs) as well as to prioritise the launch manifest.

New Space India Ltd (NSIL

- It is a Central Public Sector Enterprise under Department of Space and Commercial Arm of ISRO established to scale up the industry participation in Indian space programmes.

37. (a) • India and Maldives signed a contract for development of five eco-tourism zones in Addu atoll of the island nation.

- These eco tourism zones are part of grant projects being implemented under the High-Impact Community Development project (HICDP) scheme which involves a total grant assistance of 5.5 million US dollars to the Maldives.

- Currently, there are 9 such high-impact projects being implemented in the Maldives.

38. (c) • An atoll is a ring-shaped coral reef, island, or series of islets.

- An atoll surrounds a body of water called a lagoon.

- Sometimes, atolls and lagoons protect a central island.

- Channels between islets connect a lagoon to the open ocean or sea.

- Atolls develop with underwater volcanoes, called seamounts.

39. (a) • NashaMukt Bharat: Annual Action Plan (2020-21) for 272 Most Affected Districts' was launched by the Ministry of Social Justice and Empowerment on the occasion of International Day Against Drug Abuse and Illicit Trafficking. The Ministry of Social Justice and Empowerment observes 26th June every year as International Day Against Drug Abuse and Illicit Trafficking.

- It is the nodal Ministry for drug demand reduction which coordinates and monitors all aspects of drug abuse prevention

40. (a) • Parsi New Year, also known as Navroz or Nowroz, is celebrated to mark the beginning of the Iranian calendar.

- In Persian, 'Nav' stands for new, and 'Roz' stands for the day, which literally translates to 'new day'.
- The tradition is believed to have been celebrated for the past 3,000 years, and is observed by Iranians and the Parsi community around the world.
- Navroz is celebrated in March globally, however, in India, the Shahenshahi calendar is followed that doesn't account for leap years, hence Navroz arrives 200 days later, in August.

41. (b) • India-Sweden Healthcare Innovation Centre is collaboration between AIIMS Delhi, AIIMS Jodhpur and Business Sweden.
- The Innovation Centre aims to create an ecosystem of open innovation and is built under strategic guidance from Government of India's Ministry of Health and Family Welfare, Indian Council of Medical Research (ICMR), Government of Sweden's Ministry of Health and Social Affairs and Embassy of Sweden in India.
- Through this collaboration with Atal Innovation Mission, the India-Sweden Healthcare Innovation centre ecosystem will be further strengthened to provide all the required support to the innovators for faster scale-up of their solutions.
- The India Sweden Healthcare Innovation Centre has agreed to support the goals of AIM by enabling synergies towards creating a sustainable ecosystem of innovation and entrepreneurship between the two countries.

42. (c) • The Millennium Alliance is an innovation-driven and impact-focused initiative leveraging collaborative resources to identify test and scale Indian innovations that address global development solutions.
- It is a consortium of partners (Public-Private Partnership) including the Department of Science and Technology, Govt. of India, United States Agency for International Development (USAID), Federation of Indian Chambers of Commerce and Industry (FICCI), UK Government's Department for International Development (DFID), Facebook and Marico Innovation Foundation.

43. (b) • The fifth edition of the annual cleanliness urban survey conducted by the Ministry of Housing and Urban Affairs (MoHUA), Government of India
- Going a step forward, to ensure sustainability of on-ground performance of cities, the Ministry

had also introduced Swachh Survekshan League last year, a quarterly cleanliness assessment of cities and towns done in three quarters with 25% weightage integrated into the final Swachh Survekshan results for this year.
- MoHUA launched the sixth edition of the survey, Swachh Survekshan 2021.
- Swachh Survekshan 2021 saw the introduction of a new performance category, the Prerak DAUUR Samman which has a total of five additional sub- categories
- Divya (Platinum), Anupam (Gold), Ujjwal (Silver), Udit (Bronze), Aarohi (Aspiring).

44. (a) • Japan, India and Australia are seeking to build stronger supply chains to counter China's dominance as trade and geopolitical tensions escalate across the region
- The three nations are discussing building a supply chain resilience initiative
- The talks are at a working level currently, but Japan would like to bring them to a higher level at some point
- India's government is considering the plan and will make a decision soon about whether to participate
- The Supply Chain Resilience Initiative first proposed by Japan.
- The objective is to reduce the dependency in China.

45. (d) • India ranks among the lowest in the world in terms of Internet quality, according to a global research released by online privacy solutions provider SurfShark.

Digital Quality of Life Index 2020 highlights
- It researches on the quality of a digital wellbeing in 85 countries
- India stands at the overall rank of 57 out of the 85 countries.
- In terms of e-infrastructure, India occupies 79th place
- India makes it into the top 10 in terms of Internet affordability. (Rank-9)
- In terms of Internet Quality India is at the bottom of the pillar (Rank 78
- In terms of Electronic Security, it stands at 57th Rank
- Its Rank is 15 in terms of e-government

46. (b) • It is a civic administration body in India under control of the Ministry of Defence

• There are 62 Cantonments in the country which have been notified under the Cantonments Act, 1924 (succeeded by the Cantonments Act, 2006).

• The overall municipal administration of the notified Cantonments is the function of the Cantonment Boards which are democratic bodies.

• Cantonments are different from the Military Stations in that the Military Stations are purely meant for the use and accommodation of the armed forces and these are established under an executive order whereas the Cantonments are areas which comprise of both military and civil population.

47. (c) • AFC India Ltd., is a deemed to be Govt. organization, wholly owned by Commercial Banks, NABARD and EXIM Bank, established in 1968.

• It is a multi-disciplinary cross-functional development organization providing consulting, policy advisory and implementation support for agriculture, rural development and other strategic socio-economic sectors in India.

48. (b) • Agricultural and Processed Food Products Export Development Authority (APEDA) is an apex body under the Ministry of Commerce and Industry, Government of India, responsible for the export promotion of agricultural products.

• The Agricultural and Processed Food Products Export Development Authority (APEDA) was established by the Government of India under the Agricultural and Processed Food Products Export Development Authority Act passed by the Parliament in December, 1985.

• The Authority replaced the Processed Food Export Promotion Council (PFEPC).

49. (b)

Central sector schemes

• Under Central sector schemes, it is 100% funded by the Union government and implemented by the Central Government machinery.

• Central sector schemes are mainly formulated on subjects from the Union List.

Centrally Sponsored Scheme (CSS)

• Under Centrally Sponsored Scheme (CSS) a certain percentage of the funding is borne by the States in the ratio of 50:50, 70:30, 75:25 or 90:10 and the implementation is by the State Governments.

• Centrally Sponsored Schemes are formulated in subjects from the State List to encourage States to prioritise in areas that require more attention.

50. (a) • Raksha Mantri launched the 'Chhavni COVID: Yodha Samrakshan Yojana', a group life insurance scheme through Life Insurance Corporation (LIC), which will cover more than 10,000 employees in all 62 Cantonment Boards in event of any unfortunate fatal calamity with an insurance cover of Rs five lakhs each.

• The Scheme will benefit permanent and contractual employees including doctors, paramedics and sanitation staff.

51. (a) • This report is an output from the project National Survey on Extent and Pattern of Substance Use in India which was commissioned and funded by Ministry of Social Justice and Empowerment, Government of India.

• Based on the finding of the National Survey on Extent and Pattern of Substance Use in India and list of districts which are vulnerable from the supply point of view provided by Narcotics Control Bureau, the Ministry of Social Justice and Empowerment would undertake intervention programmes in vulnerable districts across the country

52. (c) • BRICS is an informal group of states comprising the Federative Republic of Brazil, the Russian Federation, the Republic of India, the People's Republic of China and the Republic of South Africa.

• At the Fortaleza Summit (2014), in Brazil, important institutions were created: the New Development Bank (NDB) and the Contingent Reserve Arrangement (CRA).

53. (d) • The Uttar Pradesh government had sent a request for renaming the railway station in Varanasi district.

• A 'no objection certificate' has been issued for changing the name of the Manduadih railway station to 'Banaras'

• The home ministry considers proposals for name change according to the existing guidelines in consultations with agencies concerned.

• It gives its approval to any proposal for change of name of any place after taking no-objections from the Ministry of Railways, Department of Posts and Survey of India

54. (c) • The Vice-President of India Shri M. Venkaiah Naidu virtually announced Atal Ranking of Institutions on Innovation Achievements (ARIIA) 2020.

 • This year, a special category for higher educational institutions for women has been introduced to encourage women and bringing gender parity in the areas of innovation and entrepreneurship, top place for which was secured by Avinashilingam Institute for Home Science and Higher Education for Women under this category.

 • Atal Ranking of Institutions on Innovation Achievements (ARIIA) is an initiative of Ministry of Human Resource Development (MHRD), Govt. of India to systematically rank all major higher educational institutions and universities in India on indicators related to "Innovation and Entrepreneurship Development" amongst students and faculties.

55. (d) • Union Minister of Communications and Electronics & Information Technology, launched "Swadeshi Microprocessor Challenge- Innovate Solutionsfor #Aatmanirbhar Bharat" to provide further impetus to the strong ecosystem of Start-up, innovation and research in the country.

 • IIT Madras and Center for Development of Advance Computing (CDAC) have developed two microprocessors named SHAKTI (32 bit) and VEGA (64 bit) respectively using Open Source Architecture under the aegis of Microprocessor Development Programme of Ministry of Electronics and IT.

 • "Swadeshi Microprocessor Challenge- Innovate Solutions for #Aatmanirbhar Bharat" seeks to invite innovators, startups and students to use these microprocessors to develop various technology products.

 • The "Swadeshi Microprocessor Challenge" is part of the series of proactive, preemptive and graded measures taken by Ministry of Electronics and IT to spur the technology led innovation ecosystem in the country

56. (c) • It is envisioned that the NRA would be a specialist body bringing the state-of-the-art technology and best practices to the field of Central Government recruitment.

 • Under the NRA, the candidates by appearing in one examination will get an opportunity to compete for many posts.

 • NRA will conduct the first-level /Tier I Examination which is the stepping stone for many other selections.

 • The CET score of the candidate shall be valid for a period of three years from the date of declaration of the result.

57. (d) • eSanjeevani platform has enabled two types of telemedicine services viz. Doctor-to-Doctor (eSanjeevani) and Patient-to-Doctor (eSanjeevani OPD) Tele-consultations.

 • eSanjeevani has been implemented so far by 23 States and other States are in the process of rolling it out.

 • The top five States which have been utilizing the e-health services being offered through this platform are Tamil Nadu (56,346 consultations), Uttar Pradesh (33,325), Andhra Pradesh (29,400), Himachal Pradesh (26,535) and Kerala (21,433).

58. (c) • The Food Safety and Standards Authority of India (FSSAI) has been established under Food Safety and Standards , 2006 which consolidates various acts & orders that have hitherto handled food related issues in various Ministries and Departments.

 • Ministry of Health & Family Welfare, Government of India is the Administrative Ministry for the implementation of FSSAI.

59. (a) • Prime Minister Street Vendors AtmaNirbhar Nidhi (PM SVANidhi) Scheme which has been launched to provide credit for working capital to street vendors to resume their business.

 • Minister launched a Mobile App for ULB functionaries. This App aims to provide user friendly digital interface for the functionaries of ULBs to source loan applications of street vendors.

 • With the purpose of taking the microcredit facility to the door step of the vendors a Mobile App for Lending Institutions has already been launched by the Ministry

60. (b) • There shall be no restriction on the number of attempts to be taken by a candidate to appear in the CET subject to the upper age limit.

 • NRA shall conduct a separate CET each for the three levels of graduate, higher secondary (12th pass) and the matriculate (10th pass) candidates for those non-technical posts to which recruitment is presently carried out by the Staff Selection Commission (SSC), the Railway

Recruitment Boards (RRBs) and by the Institute of Banking Personnel Selection (IBPS).

- Based on the screening done at the CET score level, final selection for recruitment shall be made through separate specialised Tiers (II, III etc) of examination which shall be conducted by the respective recruitment agencies.

61. (d) • Farkhor Air Base is a military air base located near the town of Farkhor in Tajikistan, 130 kilometres (81 mi) southeast of the capital Dushanbe.

- It is operated by the Indian Air Force in collaboration with the Tajik Air Force. Farkhor is India's first military base outside its territory.

62. (c) • The flagship Prime Minister Employment Generation Program (PMEGP) implemented by Khadi and Village Industries Commission (KVIC) progressed at a much rapid pace.

- PMEGP is the flagship employment generation program of the Central government and KVIC is the nodal agency for implementing the scheme.

- The Ministry on April 28, this year amended the guidelines to do away with the role of the District Level Task Force Committee (DLTFC) in approving the PMEGP projects.

- The role of DLTFC, headed by the District Collectors, was time consuming.

- As per the amended guidelines, KVIC, the nodal agency for implementing PMEGP scheme, was entrusted the task of clearing the applications from prospective entrepreneurs and forward it to the Banks for taking credit decisions.

63. (c) • TRIFOOD Scheme is a joint initiative of Ministry of Food Processing Industry, Ministry of Tribal Affairs and TRIFED. Under this scheme a tertiary value addition center will be set up in Jagdalpur in Chhattisgarh and Raigad in Maharashtra at a cost of approximately Rs.11 crores.

- TRIFOOD Scheme, implemented in the backdrop of VanDhan Yojana will promote value addition to Minor Forest Produce (MFP).

- TRIFOOD aims to enhance the income of tribals through better utilization of and value addition to the MFPs collected by the tribal forest gatherers.

- To achieve this, as a start, two Minor Forest Produce (MFP) processing units will be set up.

- This scheme draws its strength from The Forest Rights Act of 2005,aims to provide remunerative and fair prices to tribal gatherers of forest produces.

64. (c) • India's 'Connect Central Asia' Policy is a broad-based approach, including political, security, economic and cultural connections.

- On 12 June 2012 India's Minister Of State for External Affairs gave a Keynote address at First India-Central Asia Dialogue.

- Central Asia consists of five nations: Kazakhstan, Kyrgyzstan, Tajikistan, Turkmenistan, and Uzbekistan.

- All five nations became independent after the collapse of the USSR in 1991.

65. (b)

The Golden Crescent is the slice of the opium-producing area that cuts across Iran, Pakistan and Afghanistan. It has now become one of the most important opium-producing centres of the world

66. (c) • The World Health Organization (WHO) termed this new illness multisystem inflammatory disorder.

- It is an immunological reaction to an infection or a virus. A child's immunity system responds to a particular infection and develops these symptoms.

- Kawasaki typically affects children aged under five.

67. (c) • Biotechnology Industry Research Assistance Council (BIRAC) is a not-for-profit Public Sector Enterprise, set up by Department of Biotechnology (DBT)

- It is as an Interface Agency to strengthen and empower the emerging Biotech enterprise to undertake strategic research and innovation, addressing nationally relevant product development needs.

68. (d) • 201 9 World Press Freedom Index compiled by Reporters Without Borders (RSF), covering 180 countries and territories.

- India dropped down by 2 places 140 out of 180

69. (a) • The Union Minister of HRD, released a guide to Student Induction Programme, Deeksharambh, to help new students adjust and feel comfortable in the new environment, help them inculcate the ethos and culture of the institution, help them build bonds with other students and faculty members, and expose them to a sense of larger purpose and self-exploration.

70. (a) • India has signed a deal with Russia for acquiring Strum Ataka anti-tank missile for its fleet of Mi-35 attack choppers of Indian Air Force (IAF).

71. (a) • Nuakhai is a regional public holiday in the Indian state of Odisha on the day after the Ganesh Chaturthi festival.

• This is the panchamitithi (fifth day) of the lunar fortnight of the month of Bhadrapada or Bhadraba.

• This is an agricultural festival of the people of Odisha.

• The festival is observed across the state, but it is particularly important in the life and culture of Western Odisha.

72. (d) • ASEAN Plus Three was the first of attempts for further integration to improve existing ties of Southeast Asia with East Asian countries of China, Japan and South Korea.

• This was followed by the even larger East Asia Summit (EAS), which included ASEAN Plus Three as well as India, Australia, and New Zealand.

• EAS is an initiative of ASEAN and is based on the premise of the centrality of ASEAN.

• The final report of the East Asian Study Group in 2002, established by the ASEAN+3 countries (i.e. China, Japan and ROK), recommended EAS as an ASEAN led development limited to the ASEAN +3 countries.

• The ASEAN Ministerial Meeting (AMM) held in Vientiane on July 26, 2005 welcomed the participation of ASEAN, China, Japan, Republic of Korea, Australia, India and New Zealand, in the first EAS.

73. (d) • The group was constituted by the National Commission on Population (NCP) under the Ministry of Health and Family Welfare with the mandate to provide population projections for the period 2011 to 2036.

• India's population growth rate is expected to decline to its lowest since the Independence in the 2011-2021 decade, with a decadal growth rate of 12.5%.

• It will decline further to 8.4% in the 2021-2031 decade

• India will overtake China as the world's most populous country around 2031 - almost a decade later than the United Nations projection of 2022.

74. (a) • NPCI was incorporated as a not-for-profit company under the provisions of the Companies Act to provide infrastructure to the entire banking system in India.

• The 10 core promoter banks are SBI, Punjab National Bank, Canara Bank, Bank of Baroda, Union Bank of India, Bank of India, ICICI Bank, HDFC Bank, Citibank and HSBC.

75. (b) • The National Commission on Population (NCP) was constituted in May 2000, to fulfil the objectives of the National Population Policy 2000.

• The objectives of this commission are to review, monitor and give directions for the implementation of the National Population Policy (NPP) 2000.

• It is chaired by the prime minister with the Deputy Chairman Planning Commission (now NITI Aayog) as vice chairman.

• Presently this Commission is functioning under Ministry of Health.

76. (c) • The East Asia Summit is a unique Leaders-led forum of 18 countries of the Asia-Pacific region formed to further the objectives of regional peace, security and prosperity.

• Established in 2005, EAS allows the principal players in the Asia-Pacific region to discuss issues of common interest and concern, in an open and transparent manner, at the highest level.

• The membership of EAS consists of ten ASEAN Member States (i.e. Brunei Darussalam, Cambodia, Indonesia, Lao PDR, Malaysia, Myanmar, Singapore, Thailand, the Philippines and Vietnam), Australia, China, India, Japan, New Zealand, Republic of Korea, Russian Federation and the USA.

77. (d) • Any new umbrella organization for retail payments on the lines of the National Payments Corp. of India (NPCI) must have a minimum paid-up capital of ?500 crore and strive for inter-operability with NPCI systems

• No single promoter or promoter group should have more than 40% investment in the capital of this entity.

• The promoter can bring down shareholding in the entity to a minimum of 25% after five years

• Applicants must also have at least three years of experience in the payments ecosystem.

• A minimum net-worth of Rs 300 crore should be maintained at all times,

- The proposed entity may be a 'for-profit' or a Section 8 company as may be decided by it

78. (b) **AIR**

- India and Israel signed a cultural agreement that outlines a three-year programme of cooperation to further strengthen their strategic bilateral relations.
- Israel also signed a cooperation agreement with the Uttar Pradesh government on August 20 for resolving water crisis in Bundelkhand region.

79. (a)
- In order to help businesses and economy to start functioning while being safe, the Open API Service enables organizations to check the status of AarogyaSetu and integrate it into its various Work from Home features.
- The Open API Service of AarogyaSetu, can be availed by organizations and business entities, who are registered in India with more than 50 employees, and they can use the Open API Service to query the AarogyaSetu Application in real-time and get the health status of their employees or any other AarogyaSetu User, who have provided their consent for sharing their health status with the organization.
- The Open API shall only provide the AarogyaSetu status and name of the AarogyaSetu User (with User's consent). No other personal data shall be provided through the API.

80. (c)
- Union Minister for Electronics and Information Technology launched "Chunauti"- Next Generation Startup Challenge Contest to boost startups and software products with special focus on Tier-II towns of India.
- It aims to identify around 300 startups working in identified areas and provide them seed fund of upto Rs. 25 lakh and other facilities
- The government has earmarked a budget of Rs. 95.03 Crore over a period of three years for this programme.

81. (c)
- Aryabhatta Research Institute of Observational Sciences (ARIES), Nainital an autonomous research institute under the Department of Science and Technology (DST), Govt. of India ARIES, Nainital, started research activities in the field of atmospheric science and climate change about two decades ago.
- It is one of the leading research Institutes which specializes in observational Astronomy & Astrophysics and Atmospheric Sciences.
- The main research interests of Astronomy & Astrophysics division are in solar, planetary, stellar, galactic and extra-galactic astronomy including stellar variabilities, X-ray binaries, star clusters, nearby galaxies
- Research focus in Atmospheric Sciences division is mainly in the lower part of the atmosphere and covers the studies on aerosols and trace gases.

82. (d)
- The Aegean dispute is a set of interrelated controversies between Greece and Turkey over sovereignty and related rights in the region of the Aegean Sea.
- This set of conflicts has strongly affected Greek-Turkish relations since the 1970s

83. (a)
- The council will have joint secretary-level members from the ministries of health, home, minority affairs, education, rural development, labour and law.
- In addition, there will be a member from the department of pensions, Niti Aayog, National Human Rights Commission and National Commission for Women.
- Representatives from five states or Union Territories, on a rotational basis, will be members of the commission.
- The first such clutch comprises Jammu and Kashmir, Andhra Pradesh, Odisha, Tripura and Gujarat.
- Five members of the community and five experts, from non-governmental organisations, have also been named to the commission.
- The tenure of the community members and expert shall be three years.

84. (b)
- The ESIC also decided to extend the relaxation in eligibility criteria and enhancement of unemployment benefit under the 'Atal BimitVyakti Kalyan Yojana' with retrospective effect from March 24 to December 31, 2020.
- Under the relaxed eligibility norm and enhancement, payment would now be made at 50 per cent of average wages payable for a maximum 90 days unemployment instead of 25 per cent earlier.
- Instead of the relief becoming payable 90 days after unemployment, it shall now become due for payment after 30 days.
- The ESIC is implementing the 'Atal Bimit Vyakti Kalyna Yojna' under which unemployment

benefit is paid to the workers covered under the ESI Scheme.

- It is a welfare measure being implemented by the Employee's State Insurance (ESI) Corporation.
- It offers cash compensation to insured persons when they are rendered unemployed.

85. (d) • Employees' State Insurance (abbreviated as ESI) is a self-financing social security and health insurance scheme for Indian workers.

- The fund is managed by the Employees' State Insurance Corporation (ESIC) according to rules and regulations stipulated in the ESI Act 1948.
- ESIC is a Statutory Body and Administrative Ministry is Ministry of Labour and Employment, Government of India.

86. (c) • The Lingaraja Temple is dedicated to Shiva and is one of the oldest temples in Bhubaneswar.

- It represents the quintessence of the Kalinga Architecture and culminating the medieval stages of the architectural tradition at Bhubaneswar.
- The temple is believed to be built by the kings from the Somavamsi dynasty, with later additions from the Ganga rulers.
- It is built in the Deula style that has four components namely, vimana (structure containing the sanctum), jagamohana (assembly hall), natamandira (festival hall) and bhoga-mandapa (hall of offerings), each increasing in the height to its predecessor.

87. (b) • The eVIN is an innovative technological solution aimed at strengthening immunization supply chain systems across the country.

- This is being implemented under the National Health Mission (NHM) by the Ministry of Health and Family Welfare.
- It aims to provide real-time information on vaccine stocks and flows, and storage temperatures across all cold chain points in the country.
- This system has been used during the COVID pandemic for ensuring the continuation of the essential immunization services and protecting our children and pregnant mothers against vaccine-preventable diseases.

88. (c) • Higher Education Funding Agency (HEFA) for the construction of new infrastructure.

- The HEFA is a joint venture company of Canara Bank and the Ministry of Human Resource Development.
- It provides financial assistance for the creation of educational infrastructure and R&D in India's premier educational institutions.
- All the Centrally Funded Higher Educational Institutions will be eligible to join as members of the HEFA.

89. (a) • The Union HRD Ministry launched the Manodarpan initiative

- The 'Manodarpan' covers a wide range of activities to provide psychosocial support to students, teachers and families for Mental Health and Emotional Well-being during the COVID outbreak and beyond.

90. (d) • KumbharSashaktikaran Program is an initiative of the Khadi and Village Industries Commission (KVIC) for empowerment of potters community in the remotest of locations in the country.

- The program reaches out to the potters in : U.P., M.P., Maharashtra, J&K, Haryana, Rajasthan, West Bengal, Assam, Gujarat, Tamil Nadu, Odisha, Telangana and Bihar.

91. (d) • The Siddi also known as Sidi, Siddhi, Sheedi or Habshi, are an ethnic group inhabiting India and Pakistan.

- They are sometimes referred to as Afro-Indians. They are descendants of Bantu people of the East African region.
- They are primarily Muslims, although some are Hindus and others belong to the Catholic Church.

92. (c) • It is a famous temple architecture belonging to the Gurjara- Pratihara dynasty of Rajasthan.

- The architecture is known for their sculptures, carved panels and open pavilion style temples belonging to Nagara Style of temple architecture.
- They used most common sandstones for idols that have various shades of red, caused by iron oxide (rust).
- The greatest development of their style of building is at Khajuraho, Madhya Pradesh, now a UNESCO World Heritage Site.

93. (c) • They are also known as Reang.

- They are spread across the north eastern states of Tripura, Assam, Manipur, and Mizoram.
- They are one of the 21 scheduled tribes of Tripura.

- In Tripura, they are recognized as a Particularly Vulnerable Tribal Group (PVTG).
- They speak the Reang dialect of Bru language which is of Tibeto- Burmese origin and is locally referred to as Kau Bru.
- A 1997 intercommunity ethnic violence forced thousands of people from the Bru tribe to leave their homes in Mizoram.
- The murder of a Mizo forest guard allegedly by Bru militants led to a violent backlash against the community, forcing several thousand people to flee to neighbouring Tripura.

94. (d)
- The Union Minister of Defence, launched the Naval Innovation and Indigenisation Organisation (NIIO) to boost self-reliance in the defence manufacturing sector.
- It will provide dedicated structures for the end-users to interact with academia and industry towards fostering innovation and indigenisation for self-reliance in defence.

95. (b)
- Odisha has become the first State in the country and India, the first country, to implement the programme in the Indian Ocean region.
- The National Board, after verification of the implementation of the indicators at these villages as per guidelines, decided to recognize them nationally and recommended to UNESCO-IOC.
- Based on the recommendations, UNESCO-IOC approved recommendation of the two villages.
- Tsunami ready is a community performance-based programme initiated by UNESCO-Intergovernmental Oceanographic Commission (IOC).
- It aims to promote preparedness through active collaboration of public, community leaders, national and local emergency management agencies.

96. (c)
- Directorate General, Defence Estates (DGDE) is an Inter Services Organisation of the Ministry of Defence which directly controls the Cantonment Administration.
- The Directorate General Defence Estates (DGDE), monitors all 62 cantonments in the country
- The cantonment board takes care of mandatory duties such as provision of public health, water supply, sanitation, primary education, and street lighting etc.

- As the resources are owned by government of India, it can't levy any tax. Government of India provides the financial assistance.

97. (c)
- Dedicated Freight Corridors (DFC) is one of the largest rail infrastructure projects undertaken by the Government of India. The overall cost is pegged at Rs 81,459 crores.
- DFCCIL has been set up as a special purpose vehicle to undertake planning, development, mobilization of financial resources, construction, maintenance and operation of Dedicated Freight Corridors.
- It is a Public Sector Undertaking (PSU) corporation run by government of India's Ministry of Railways to undertake planning, development, and mobilisation of financial resources and construction, maintenance and operation of the Dedicated Freight Corridors (DFC).
- The DFCCIL was registered as a company under the Companies Act 1956 in 2006.

98. (b)
- India is the largest beneficiary of AIIB financing for infrastructure projects
- The total loan sanctioned by AIIB to five Indian projects is USD 1.074 billion.

Approved projects
- Bangalore Metro Rail Project
- Gujarat Rural Roads (MMGSY)
- India Infrastructure Fund.
- Andhra Pradesh 24×7 - Power For All Project.
- Covid-19 support for India.
- Mumbai Urban Transport Project-III

99. (c)
- NIIF is an Indian-government backed entity established to provide long-term capital to the country's infrastructure sector.
- Its portfolio includes investments in ports and logistics, real estate and renewables.

100. (c)
- It is expected that Western Corridor connecting Dadri in Utttar Pradesh to Jawaharlal Nehru Port (JNPT) in Mumbai and Eastern Corridor starting from Sahnewal near Ludhiana (Punjab) to terminate at Dankuni in West Bengal shall be completed by December, 2021.
- The Eastern & western dedicated freight corridors entail an investment of $12 billion, with the World Bank and Japan International Cooperation Agency (JICA) partly funding the project with around $1.86 bn and $5.2 bn respectively.

- Private containers will also be allowed to use the freight corridor but they have to pay track usage charges.

101. (a)
- AIIB invests in sustainable infrastructure and other productive sectors in Asia and beyond,
- Membership in the AIIB is divided into regional (Asia) and non-regional(other continent) members.
- India is a founding member of AIIB
- It is open to all members of the World Bank or the Asian Development Bank
- AIIB allows for non-sovereign entities to apply for AIIB membership, assuming their home country is a member. (eg- sovereign wealth funds of a member country)

102. (b)
- Union Minister for Electronics and Information Technology launched "Chunauti"- Next Generation Startup Challenge Contest to boost startups and software products with special focus on Tier-II towns of India.
- It aims to identify around 300 startups working in identified areas and provide them seed fund of upto Rs. 25 Lakh and other facilities
- The startups selected through Chunauti will be provided various support from the Government through Software Technology Parks of India centers across India.

103. (d)
- Association of Renewable Energy Agencies of the States (AREAS) has been formed on MNRE initiative to interact and learn from each other's experiences and also share their best practices and knowledge regarding technologies and schemes/programmes.
- The AREAS got registered under Society Registration Act 1860 on 27 August 2014.
- Union Minister for New & Renewable Energy is the Patron of the Association and Secretary, MNRE is the ex-officio President of the Association.

104. (a)
- Eklavya Model Residential Schools (EMRS) established under Ministry of Tribal Affairs witnessed its first NAT Awardee
- EMRS started in the year 1997-98 to impart quality education to ST children in remote areas in order to enable them to avail of opportunities in high and professional educational courses and get employment in various sectors.
- As per revised 2018 EMRS Scheme, every block with more than 50% ST population and at least 20,000 tribal persons, will have an Eklavya Model Residential School by the year 2022.
- These schools will be on par with Navodaya Vidyalayas and will have special facilities for preserving local art and culture besides providing training in sports and skill development.

105. (a)
- Commerce and Industry Minister launched the national GIS-enabled land bank system, which will help investors to get real-time information about the availability of industrial land and resources.
- The system is being developed by integrating the Industrial Information System (IIS) with state GIS (Geographic Information System). The project has been launched for six states.
- The IIS portal is a GIS-enabled database of industrial areas/clusters across the states.

106. (d)
- Focus shift from 'Every Household' to Every Unbanked Adult'
- RuPay Card Insurance - Free accidental insurance cover on RuPay cards increased from Rs. 1 lakh to Rs. 2 lakh for PMJDY accounts opened after 28.8.2018.
- PMJDY account is treated as inoperative if there are no customer induced transactions in the account for over a period of two years

107. (b)
- India turned down Russia's invitation to participate in next month's multilateral defence exercise, which is scheduled to be held in southern Russia between September 15 and 27.
- India had earlier planned to send a company-level strength of approximately 180 troops from an infantry battalion, 40 personnel of the Air Force, and two Navy officers as observers.
- The aim of the exercise is to provide real-time training to counter international terrorism in the Northern and Caucasus region, and the setting will involve both offensive and defensive operations against international terror

108. (b)
- SCO is a eight-member economic and security bloc and India and Pakistan were admitted as full members back in 2017.
- It is a permanent intergovernmental international organisation founded in 2001 with its secretariat based in Beijing, China.
- The founding members of this grouping include China, Russia, Kazakhstan, Kyrgyzstan, Tajikistan and Uzbekistan.

- The grouping has been having multilateral drills and has developed Regional Anti-Terrorist Structure (RATS).

109. (a) • Commerce and Industry Ministry of India and Industry and Trade Ministry of Vietnam co-chaired the 17th ASEAN-India Economic Ministers Consultations

- The Ministers' discussion centred on the review of the ASEAN India Trade in Goods Agreement (AITIGA).

- In 2003, India and ASEAN signed a Framework Agreement on Comprehensive Economic Cooperation to establish an ASEAN -India Regional Trade and Investment Area, which would provide a basis for subsequent FTAs covering goods, services and investment.

- The ASEAN -India Trade in Goods Agreement (AITIGA) was signed in 2009 and it is this that both sides have agreed to review.

- The ASEAN-India Trade in Goods Agreement was signed and entered into force on 1 January 2010.

110. (c) **Extension of PMJDY**

- Focus shift from 'Every Household' to Every Unbanked Adult'

- RuPay Card Insurance - Free accidental insurance cover on RuPay cards increased from Rs. 1 lakh to Rs. 2 lakh for PMJDY accounts opened after 28.8.2018.

- Enhancement in overdraft facilities -

- OD limit doubled from Rs 5,000/- to Rs 10,000/-; OD upto Rs 2,000/- (without conditions).

- Increase in upper age limit for OD from 60 to 65 years

111. (a) **Onam**

- The festival is celebrated in the month of Chingam according to the Malayalam calendar

- The festival is spread over 10 days and culminates with Thiruvonam, the most important day.

- Women participate in Pookolam (rangoli made of flowers) and perform Kaikottikali, a dance form.

- Boat race (Vallam Kali), Pulikali (folk dance in the disguise of a tiger) and other dance and art forms specific to Kerala.

112. (b) • The government is all set to clear acquisition of two PHALCON airborne warning and control systems (AWACS)

- India has three PHALCON AWACS with a 360 degree rotodome mounted on top of the aircraft and two DRDO-built AWACS with 240 degree rotodome. (China has 28 AWACS and Pakistan has seven)

- The Indian Air Force already has three Phalcon AWACS and addition of two more is expected to significantly boost the country's air defencemechanism.

- The Phalcon AWACS is capable of tracking enemy aircraft, hostile missiles, movement of troops across the border without crossing territorial limits.

113. (c) • It is a mobile, long-range radar surveillance and control centre for air defense.

- It is mounted in a specially modified aircraft.

- The radar system can detect, track, and identify low-flying aircraft and high-level targets at much greater distances.

- It also can track maritime traffic, and it operates in any weather over any terrain.

- An airborne computer can assess enemy action and keep track of the location and availability of any aircraft within range.

114. (a) • In 2018, Exercise Vostok saw the participation of China and Mongolia.

- Exercise Tsentr last year had the participation of India, Pakistan and all Shanghai Cooperation Organisation (SCO) member-nations.

- India had participated in SCO peace mission exercise in 2018, and in 2019, for the first time, was involved in a strategic command and staff exercise as part of Exercise Tsentr.

115. (b) • India's First Toy Manufacturing Cluster. To Come Up At Koppal, Karnataka

- In Line With The Vision Of Vocalforlocal And Boosting Toy Manufacturing, Koppala Will Have India's First Toy Manufacturing Cluster.

- The Karnataka Government Is Inviting Global Toy Makers To The First Of Its Kind· Toy Manufacturing Cluster In India At Koppala And Had Recently Held A Webinar Cum Panel Discussion With A Panel Of Leading Toys Manufacturers.

116. (a) • The DRDO Airborne Early Warning and Control System (AEW&CS) is a project of India's Defence Research and Development Organisation to develop an airborne early warning and control system for the Indian Air Force.

• It is also referred to as 'NETRA' Airborne Early Warning and Control System (AEW&CS).

• In October 2018, India had signed a USD 5 billion deal with Russia to buy five units of the S-400 air defence missile system

• India is also integrating the Brahmos supersonic cruise missiles into over 40 Sukhoi fighter jets under a closely-guarded project.

117. (d) • CSIR-CMERI has developed the World's Largest Solar Tree, which is installed at CSIR-CMERI Residential Colony, Durgapur.

• The installed capacity of the Solar Tree is above 11.5 kWp. It has the annual capacity to generate 12,000-14,000 units of Clean and Green Power.

• The Central Mechanical Engineering Research Institute is a public engineering research and development institution in Durgapur, West Bengal, India.

• It is a constituent laboratory of the Indian Council of Scientific and Industrial Research (CSIR).

• This institute is the only national level research institute in the field of mechanical engineering in India.

118. (c) • Its weapon system has a state-of-the-art guidance kit bolstered by an advanced navigation and control system.

• Pinaka was designed to replace the BM-21 Grad multiple rocket launcher systems of the Indian Army.

• The complete MBRL system of Pinaka is comprised of six launcher vehicles, each having 12 rockets with six loader-replenishment vehicles, two command post vehicles with fire control computer and a DIGICORA MET radar.

• The launch system of Pinaka is comprised up of two pods, which are mounted side-by-side to each other on a Tatra launcher vehicle.

• Each launcher has the ability to fire all the rockets in one go or only a few - in a different direction than others with the help of its control computer.

119. (b) • UAE has launched Agriota, a new technology-driven agri-commodity trading and sourcing e-market platform that will bridge the gap between millions of rural farmers in India and the Gulf nation's food industry.

• Under the initiative, launched by the Dubai Multi Commodities Centre (DMCC) millions of Indian farmers will get an opportunity to connect directly with the entire food industry in the UAE, including food processing companies, traders and wholesalers through the Agriota-E Marketplace platform.

• The marketplace allows the farmers to bypass intermediaries, optimising the supply chain and ensuring traceability to create value for all stakeholders

120. (c) • The Global Food Security Index consists of a set of indices from 113 countries.

• It measures food security across most of the countries of the world.

• It was first published in 2012, and is managed and updated annually by The Economist's intelligence unit.

• The Global Food Security Index considers the core issues of affordability, availability, and quality across a set of 113 countries.

• The index is a dynamic quantitative and qualitative benchmarking model, constructed from 34 unique indicators, that measures these drivers of food security across both developing and developed countries.

• India Rank (2019) - 72/113

121. (c) • India's first Multi-Wavelength Space Observatory. AstroSat has detected extreme-UV light from a galaxy located 9.3 billion light-years away from Earth.

• The galaxy called AUDFs01 was discovered by a team of Astronomers from the Inter-University Centre for Astronomy and Astrophysics(IUCAA) Pune.

• India's AstroSat/UVIT (Ultra-Violet Imaging Telescope) was able to achieve this unique feat because the background noise in the UVIT detector is much less than one on the Hubble Space Telescope of US based NASA.

122. (d) • As a first step towards Greening the Indian short term power Market, launched pan-India Green Term Ahead Market (GTAM) in electricity

• The introduction of GTAM platform would lessen the burden on RE-rich States and incentivize them to develop RE capacity beyond their own RPO.

- GTAM platform will lead to increase in number of participants in renewable energy sector.
- It will benefit buyers of RE through competitive prices and transparent and flexible procurement.
- It will also benefit RE sellers by providing access to pan- India market

123. (d) • Government of India (GOI) has approved a new Central Sector Scheme - Pradhan Mantri Kisan SAMPADA Yojana (Scheme for Agro-Marine Processing and Development of Agro-Processing Clusters) with an allocation of Rs. 6,000 crore for the period 2016-20
- The scheme will be implemented by Ministry of Food Processing Industries (MoFPI).
- It is a comprehensive package which will result in creation of modern infrastructure with efficient supply chain management from farm gate to retail outlet.

124. (b) • It aims at providing a mechanism to link agricultural production to the market by bringing together farmers, processors and retailers so as to ensure maximizing value addition, minimizing wastage, increasing farmers income and creating employment opportunities particularly in rural sector.
- The Mega Food Park Scheme is based on Cluster approach and envisages creation of state of art support infrastructure in a well-defined agri / horticultural zone for setting up of modern food processing units in the industrial plots provided in the park with well-established supply chain.
- Mega food park typically consist of supply chain infrastructure including collection centers, primary processing centers, central processing centers, cold chain and around 25-30 fully developed plots for entrepreneurs to set up food processing units.
- The Mega Food Park project is implemented by a Special Purpose Vehicle (SPV) which is a Body Corporate registered under the Companies Act.

125. (a) • It was launched by the Indian Space Research Organization (ISRO) on September 28, 2015
- AstroSat is the first dedicated Indian astronomy mission aimed at studying celestial sources in X-ray, optical and UV spectral bands simultaneously.
- One of the unique features of AstroSat mission is that it enables the simultaneous multi-wavelength observations of various astronomical objects with a single satellite.

126. (c) • It is a permanent organ of the SCO and regarded as very important in the counterterrorism operations by the member countries and has its headquarters based in Tashkent.
- Security officials of all the eight countries sit at the RATS Headquarters in Tashkent.
- In fight against terrorism, extremism and separatism, RATS plays a very critical role, as it gives a chance to all to test their intelligence gathering and exchange; technology complement mechanisms between the members states of SCO.

127. (a) • The National Technical Advisory Group on Immunisation (NTAGI) was established by an order of the Ministry of Health and Family Welfare (MoHFW) in 2001.
- Since its establishment, the NTAGI has been reconstituted twice, in 2010 and 2013.
- The STSC is tasked with undertaking technical review of scientific evidence on matters related to immunization policy and programmes.
- Final recommendations are drafted by the NTAGI taking into account the scientific review by the STSC and any other relevant evidence.

128. (c) • CEO, NITI Aayog inaugurated the Online Performance Dashboard Empowering Tribals, Transforming India developed by the Ministry of Tribal Affairs (MoTA)
- The launch was made during the meeting taken by NITI Aayog to review the progress of Centrally Sponsored Scheme / Central sector schemes of MoTA in the light of national development agenda, Sustainable Development Goals (SDGs), strategy for New India and other policy initiatives.
- Performance Dashboard is an interactive and dynamic online platform that showcases updated & real-time details of 11 schemes / initiatives of the Ministry for achieving these SDGs.

129. (b) • This module is the next step in bringing AI to Indian classrooms and is a successor to the AI Base module launched in February this year.
- The step-up module needs no previous knowledge and introduces the concepts to students from the basics using interactive tools and activities so as to keep their attention undivided.

- The Base module was specifically devised considering students as young as 12 years of age, with absolutely no prior background of AI to ignite curiosity on AI in their young minds and to contribute to the ecosystem of innovation.

- Step up module has been exquisitely designed and presented to involve young students across the country to induce inclusive learning and to empower youngsters of our country to create AI integrated innovations

130. (d) • NASA's Transiting Exoplanet Survey Satellite (TESS), finished its primary mission imaging about 75 per cent of the starry sky as part of a two-year-long survey.

- The Transiting Exoplanet Survey Satellite (TESS) is designed to discover thousands of exoplanets in orbit around the brightest dwarf stars in the sky.

- In its prime mission, a two-year survey of the solar neighborhood, TESS monitored the brightness of stars for periodic drops caused by planet transits.

Practice Questions Set – 4
General Studies Paper I

1. Shanti Swarup Bhatnagar Prize recognizes outstanding Indian work in which of the following fields?

   (a) Science and technology

   (b) Human Resources

   (c) Health Sector

   (d) Social Welfare

2. Consider the following statements regarding Atal Bhujal Yojana:

   1. It is a central sector scheme.

   2. The scheme is to be implemented for a three-year period from 2020-21 to 2022-23.

   3. One of the components is incentivizing the States for achievements in improved groundwater management practices.

   Which of the statements given above is/are correct?

   (a) 1 and 3 only   (b) 2 and 3 only

   (c) 1, 2 and 3   (d) 3 only

3. Consider the following statements with respect to Global Initiative on Sharing All Influenza Data (GISAID) :

   (a) It is a public platform started by the United Nation General Assembly (UNGA) in 2008.

   (b) It only includes data associated with human viruses and does not include avian and other animal viruses.

   Which of the statements given above is/are correct?

   (a) 1 only   (b) 2 only

   (c) Both 1 and 2   (d) Neither 1 nor 2

4. Global Nutrition Report 2020 is released by:

   (a) WHO   (b) UNICEF

   (c) UNGA   (d) None of the above

5. World Risk Index which is a part of the World Risk Report has been released by which of the following organisations?

   (a) World Bank

   (b) World Economic Forum

   (c) IMF

   (d) None of the above

6. Consider the following statements about the Consulting Engineers Association of India (CEAI)

   1. It is an autonomous body which works as an attached office of National Highway Authority of India (NHAI)

   2. CEAI is the apex body of Consulting Engineers in India.

   Which of the statements given above is/are correct?

   (a) 1 only   (b) 2 only

   (c) Both 1 and 2   (d) Neither 1 nor 2

7. ICAR-National Bureau of Plant Genetic Resources (NBPGR) comes under the ministry of?

   (a) Ministry of Agriculture

   (b) Ministry of AYUSH

   (c) Ministry of Science & Technology

   (d) Ministry of Environment and Forests

8. The government of Bangladesh is financing a film on the life of Pritilata Waddedar.

   Pritilata Waddedar was a

   (a) Bengali poet   (b) Social activist

   (c) Freedom fighter   (d) None of the above

9. Knowledge Resource Centre Network (KRCNet), recently seen in news, is an initiative of which of the following union ministry?

   (a) Ministry of Agriculture and Farmers Welfare

   (b) Ministry of Earth Sciences

   (c) Ministry of Human Resource Development

   (d) Ministry of Environment, Forest and Climate Change

10. Consider the following statements about the Partnership for Maternal, Newborn & Child Health (PMNCH)

    1. It is a multi-constituency partnership hosted by the World Health Organisation

    2. It is the world's largest alliance for women's, children's and adolescents' health (WCAH), bringing together over 1,000 partner organizations across 192 countries.

    Which of the statements given above is/are correct?

(a) 1 only   (b) 2 only

(c) Both 1 and 2   (d) Neither 1 nor 2

11. Recently the proposal to introduce ISO Tank Containers for domestic movement was initiated by which of the following organisations/ministries?

(a) DRDO

(b) ISRO

(c) Ministry of road and transportation

(d) None of the above

12. Consider the following statements about NATGRID

1. It is established under the National Security Act.

2. It is an integrated intelligence grid which will connect databases of security agencies and economic institutions.

3. It works under the effective control of the Ministry of Home Affairs.

Which of the statements given above is/are correct?

(a) 1 only   (b) 1 and 3 only

(c) 2 and 3 only   (d) 1, 2 and 3

13. With reference to the Earth Day, consider the following statements:

1. Earth Day is observed every year on April 22.

2. Every year UNESCO leads Earth Day worldwide.

Which of the statements given above is/are correct?

(a) 1 only   (b) 2 only

(c) Both 1 and 2   (d) Neither 1 nor 2

14. A Special Report on Sustainable Recovery has been released recently by which of the following organisations?

(a) Ministry of Environment in association with NITI Aayog

(b) United Nations Environment Programme

(c) World Bank

(d) None of the above

15. Consider the following statements about the International Energy Agency

1. It is autonomous intergovernmental organisation

2. It is established in the framework of the Organisation for Economic Co-operation and Development (OECD)

3. It also works with non-member countries, especially China, India, and Russia.

Which of the statements given above is/are correct?

(a) 1 only   (b) 1 and 3 only

(c) 2 and 3 only   (d) 1, 2 and 3

16. Consider the following statements about the Epidemic Diseases (Amendment) Bill, 2020

1. The act is applicable to healthcare service personnel from public and clinical healthcare service providers

2. Healthcare service providers includes doctors, nurses, paramedical workers and community health workers

Which of the statements given above is/are correct?

(a) 1 only   (b) 2 only

(c) Both 1 and 2   (d) Neither 1 nor 2

17. Consider the following statements about NashaMukt Bharat Abhiyaan

1. It has been launched in 272 most affected districts

2. It is formulated and implemented by the Ministry of Social Justice and Empowerment

Which of the statements given above is/are correct?

(a) 1 only   (b) 2 only

(c) Both 1 and 2   (d) Neither 1 nor 2

18. Human Capital Index 2020 has been released by which of the following Organisations?

(a) World Bank

(b) World Economic Forum

(c) IMF

(d) None of the above

19. Consider the following statements about E-Gram Swaraj Portal

1. It unifies the planning, accounting and monitoring functions of Gram Panchayats

2. It has been launched by the Ministry of Panchayati Raj and implemented by The Ministry of Electronics and Information Technology

Which of the statements given above is/are correct?

(a) 1 only   (b) 2 only

(c) Both 1 and 2   (d) Neither 1 nor 2

20. Consider the following statements about the National Nutrition Mission

1. The Ministry of Women and Child Development (WCD) is the nodal ministry

2. The Ministry of Drinking Water and Sanitation and Ministry of Health and Family Welfare is in-charge of immunisation.

3. It is a scheme for holistic nourishment

Which of the statements given above is/are correct?

(a) 1 only　　　　(b) 1 and 3 only

(c) 2 and 3 only　　(d) 1, 2 and 3

21. Consider the following statements about Mid-day Meal Scheme

    1. It is a Centrally-Sponsored Scheme

    2. It comes under the HRD Ministry's Department of School Education and Literacy.

    3. The scheme covers all government and government aided schools and also Madarsa and Maqtabs

    Which of the statements given above is/are correct?

    (a) 1 only　　　　(b) 2 only

    (c) 1, 2 and 3　　(d) 1 and 3 only

22. Recently the Union Ministry of Jal Shakti has excavated an ancient river or a paleochannel in India with reference to it consider the following statements about paleochannel

    1. It is a remnant of an active river or stream channel only

    2. Paleochannel has been filled or buried by younger sediment.

    Which of the statements given above is/are correct?

    (a) 1 only　　　　(b) 2 only

    (c) Both 1 and 2　　(d) Neither 1 nor 2

23. Consider the following statements about immunity passports

    1. It has been backed by the World Health Organization

    2. It is a nasal spray that helps in developing antibodies against COVID 19

    Which of the statements given above is/are correct?

    (a) 1 only　　　　(b) 2 only

    (c) Both 1 and 2　　(d) Neither 1 nor 2

24. National Initiative for Developing and Harnessing Innovations (NIDHI) is going to be implemented by which of the following ministries?

    (a) Ministry of Skill Development and Entrepreneurship

    (b) Department of Science and Technology (DST)

    (c) NITI Aayog

    (d) None of the above

25. Consider the following statements with reference to Pradhan Mantri Jan Arogya Yojana

    1. PM-JAY offers a sum insured of Rs.5 lakh per family for primary and secondary care only

    2. The entire insurance cost is borne by the central government.

    Which of the statements given above is/are incorrect?

    (a) 1 only　　　　(b) 2 only

    (c) Both 1 and 2　　(d) Neither 1 nor 2

26. Consider the following statements about Atal Tunnel

    1. The tunnel is built with ultra-modern specifications in the Pir Panjal range of Himalayas

    2. It connects Manali to Lahaul-Spiti valley throughout the year.

    3. It is the longest highway tunnel in the world.

    Which of the statements given above is/are correct?

    (a) 1 only　　　　(b) 2 only

    (c) 1, 2 and 3　　(d) 1 and 3 only

27. Consider the following statements about Mahila Police Volunteers (MPVS):

    1. It is a joint initiative of the Union Ministry of Home Affairs and Union Ministry of Women & Child Development.

    2. Kerala is the first state to adopt the initiative.

    Which of the statements given above is/are correct?

    (a) 1 only　　　　(b) 2 only

    (c) Both 1 and 2　　(d) Neither 1 nor 2

28. Consider the following statements about the Fair and Remunerative Price for the sugarcane farmers.

    1. FRP is a legal price guaranteed to the farmers by the state governments

    2. Centre can also give higher price than the FRP

    Which of the statements given above is/are correct?

    (a) 1 only　　　　(b) 2 only

    (c) Both 1 and 2　　(d) Neither 1 nor 2

29. The National Board for Wildlife's (NBWL) has recently recommended coal mining in a part of land from the Saleki proposed reserve forest, Assam.

    Saleki is a part of the DehingPatkai Elephant Reserve that includes the DehingPatkai Wildlife Sanctuary

Dehing Patkai Wildlife Sanctuary is situated in which of the following states?

(a) Karnataka   (b) Kerala

(c) Assam   (d) Uttarakhand

30. Consider the following statements about anti-tank guided missile (ATGM)

   1. It is indigenously developed Anti Tank Guided Missile (ATGM)

   2. It uses laser designation to lock and track the targets for better accuracy.

   Which of the statements given above is/are correct?

   (a) 1 only   (b) 2 only

   (c) Both 1 and 2   (d) Neither 1 nor 2

31. Consider the following statements about ARISE-ANIC programme

   1. It will be driven by NITI Aayog's Atal Innovation Mission (AIM), in collaboration with DRDO

   2. The programme will support deserving applied research-based innovations by providing funding support of up to Rs 50 lakh

   Which of the statements given above is/are correct?

   (a) 1 only   (b) 2 only

   (c) Both 1 and 2   (d) Neither 1 nor 2

32. The Prime Minister held 'SvanidhiSamvaad' with street vendors

   With reference to it consider the following statements about PM Svanidhi scheme

   1. It was launched by the Ministry of Housing and Urban Affairs

   2. It provides a grant of Rs.10000 as working capital to street vendors to resume their livelihoods

   3. Small Industries Development Bank of India (SIDBI) is the implementation agency for PM Svanidhi scheme

   Which of the statements given above is/are correct?

   (a) 1 only   (b) 2 only

   (c) 1, 2 and 3   (d) 1 and 3 only

33. Consider the following statements about Interactive Research School for Health Affairs (IRSHA)

   1. It is an autonomous institute under the Ministry of Health and Family Welfare

   2. The institute is mandated to conduct research in priority areas of human health in co-ordination with other constituents of the university

   Which of the statements given above is/are correct?

(a) 1 only   (b) 2 only

(c) Both 1 and 2   (d) Neither 1 nor 2

34. Consider the following statements about the recently inaugurated National Immunogenicity & Biologics Evaluation Center

   1. This facility has been supported by the Department of Biotechnology (DBT)

   2. The facility is established through the National Biopharma Mission with 100 percent funding from it.

   Which of the statements given above is/are correct?

   (a) 1 only   (b) 2 only

   (c) Both 1 and 2   (d) Neither 1 nor 2

35. Consider the following statements about Pradhan Mantri MatsyaSampada Yojana

   1. It is a flagship scheme for focused and sustainable development of fisheries and animal husbandry sectors

   2. It primarily focuses on adopting cluster or area based approaches

   Which of the statements given above is/are correct?

   (a) 1 only   (b) 2 only

   (c) Both 1 and 2   (d) Neither 1 nor 2

36. Consider the following statements about Biotechnology Industry Research Assistance Council (BIRAC)

   1. It is a not-for-profit public sector enterprise

   2. It is an autonomous body under the Department for Promotion of Industry and Internal Trade (DPIIT)

   Which of the statements given above is/are correct?

   (a) 1 only   (b) 2 only

   (c) Both 1 and 2   (d) Neither 1 nor 2

37. Consider the following statements about recently launched e-Gopala App

   1. It will provide a direct platform to the farmers for buying and selling livestock

   2. It will also guide farmers for animal nutrition and treatment

   Which of the statements given above is/are correct?

   (a) 1 only

   (b) 2 only

   (c) Both 1 and 2

   (d) Neither 1 nor 2

38. Consider the following statements about SAROD-Ports' (Society for Affordable Redressal of Disputes - Ports)

    1. It will advise and assist in settlement of disputes through arbitrations in the maritime sector

    2. It consists members from Indian Ports Association (IPA) and Indian Private Ports and Terminals Association (IPTTA) .

    Which of the statements given above is/are correct?

    (a) 1 only   (b) 2 only

    (c) Both 1 and 2   (d) Neither 1 nor 2

39. The Five Star Villages Scheme has been launched by which of the following Ministries/Aayog/Organisations?

    (a) NITI Aayog

    (b) Swatch Bharat Abhiyaan - Grameen

    (c) Ministry of Health and Family Welfare

    (d) None of the above

40. Consider the following statements about the National Biopharma Mission

    1. It is co-funded by the World Bank

    2. One of its objectives is to deliver affordable biopharmaceuticals products

    3. Strengthening the clinical trial capacity is also one of its important domain

    Which of the statements given above is/are correct?

    (a) 1 only   (b) 2 only

    (c) 1, 2 and 3   (d) 1 and 3 only

41. Consider the following statements about the second edition of the States' Start-up Ranking Exercise

    1. It has been conducted by the Department for Promotion of Industry and Internal Trade (DPIIT)

    2. All of the States and Union Territories participated in the exercise.

    Which of the statements given above is/are correct?

    (a) 1 only   (b) 2 only

    (c) Both 1 and 2   (d) Neither 1 nor 2

42. Consider the following statements about the Million Minds Augmenting National Aspirations and Knowledge (MANAK) programme

    1. This programme invite students from both government and private schools to send original and innovative ideas having potential to solve common problems.

    2. It was launched by the Ministry of Education in partnership with the National Innovation Foundation (NIF)

    Which of the statements given above is/are correct?

    (a) 1 only   (b) 2 only

    (c) Both 1 and 2   (d) Neither 1 nor 2

43. Consider the following statements about National Science and Technology Entrepreneurship Development Board (NSTEDB)

    1. It was established in 1982 by the Government of India under the aegis of All India Council of Technical Education (AICTE)

    2. The Board have representation only from the Ministry of Education

    3. It is an institutional mechanism to help promote knowledge driven and technology intensive enterprises.

    Which of the statements given above is/are correct?

    (a) 1 and 2 only   (b) 3 only

    (c) 1, 2 and 3   (d) 1 only

44. Consider the following statements about the Integrated Road Accident Database Project (iRAD)

    1. The development and implementation of iRAD has been entrusted to the Ministry of Road Transport & Highways

    2. This project is proposed on IT based system for capturing the spot accident and vehicle data using mobile app configured for this purpose.

    Which of the statements given above is/are correct?

    (a) 1 only   (b) 2 only

    (c) Both 1 and 2   (d) Neither 1 nor 2

45. Consider the following statements about NIDHI (National Initiative for Development and Harnessing Innovations)

    1. It is conceived and developed by the Department for Promotion of Industry and Internal Trade (DPIIT), Government of India

    2. Financial institutions, angel investors, venture capitalists and private sectors are some of the key stakeholders of NIDHI

    Which of the statements given above is/are correct?

    (a) 1 only

    (b) 2 only

    (c) Both 1 and 2

    (d) Neither 1 nor 2

46. Consider the following statements about the United Nations Day for South-South Cooperation

1. South-South Cooperation describes the exchange of resources, technology and knowledge between developed and developing countries

2. It also refers to the exchange of expertise, technical cooperation or collaboration between all the countries of the global south.

Which of the statements given above is/are correct?

(a) 1 only   (b) 2 only

(c) Both 1 and 2   (d) Neither 1 nor 2

47. India recently signed the "Agreement on Reciprocal Provision of Supplies and Services" with which of the following countries?

(a) Australia   (b) Japan

(c) USA   (d) None of the above

48. A motion for breach of privilege was moved in the Maharashtra Assembly against Republic TV's Managing Director

With reference to it consider the following statements about Parliamentary Privileges

1. The powers, privileges and immunities of either House of the Indian Parliament do not mentioned in the Constitution

2. It refers to the right and immunity enjoyed by legislatures, only against civil liability for actions done in the course of their legislative duties.

Which of the statements given above is/are incorrect?

(a) 1 only   (b) 2 only

(c) Both 1 and 2   (d) Neither 1 nor 2

49. Consider the following statements about NISHTHA

1. Its objective is to improve learning outcomes at the Elementary level through an Integrated Teacher Training Programme called NISHTHA

2. The aim of this integrated teacher training programme was to build the capacities of around 42 lakh teachers and heads of schools

Which of the statements given above is/are correct?

(a) 1 only   (b) 2 only

(c) Both 1 and 2   (d) Neither 1 nor 2

50. Consider the following statements about the United Nations Economic and Social Council (ECOSOC)

1. It is one of the six principal organs of the United Nations

2. Apart from UN members the non-governmental organizations also have consultative status with the Council

Which of the statements given above is/are correct?

(a) 1 only   (b) 2 only

(c) Both 1 and 2   (d) Neither 1 nor 2

51. Consider the following statements about Biotech-Krishi Innovation Science Application Network (Biotech-KISAN)

1. It has been implemented in all 15 agro-climatic zones of India

2. It aims to link farmers, scientists and science institutions across the country in a network that identifies and helps solve their problems in a cooperative manner.

Which of the statements given above is/are correct?

(a) 1 only   (b) 2 only

(c) Both 1 and 2   (d) Neither 1 nor 2

52. Consider the following statements about Living Planet Report

1. It is based on data produced by the Zoological Society of London (ZSL) .

2. The report shows that freshwater biodiversity is declining far faster than that in oceans or forests

Which of the statements given above is/are correct?

(a) 1 only   (b) 2 only

(c) Both 1 and 2   (d) Neither 1 nor 2

53. Consider the following statements about Association of World Election Bodies (A-WEB)

1. It is the largest association of Election Management Bodies (EMBs)

2. ECI took over as Chair of A-WEB for 2019-2021 term.

Which of the statements given above is/are correct?

(a) 1 only   (b) 2 only

(c) Both 1 and 2   (d) Neither 1 nor 2

54. Consider the following statements about the Farmers' Produce Trade and Commerce (Promotion and Facilitation) Act, 2020

1. The act will promote barrier-free inter-state and intra-state trade

2. The farmers will not be charged any cess or levy for sale of their produce

3. The farmers can also do trading at farmgate, cold storage, warehouse, processing units etc.

Which of the statements given above is/are correct?

(a) 1, 2 and 3   (b) 1 and 2 only

(c) 2 only   (d) 1 and 3 only

55. Logistics Performance Index is released by which of the following Organisations?

(a) World Economic Forum

(b) World Bank

(c) The International Transport Forum

(d) World Trade Union

56. Consider the following statements about the successful flight test of ABHYAS

1. It is designed & developed by Aeronautical Development Establishment (ADE), DRDO.

2. It is a High-speed Expendable Aerial Target missile

Which of the statements given above is/are correct?

(a) 1 only   (b) 2 only

(c) Both 1 and 2   (d) Neither 1 nor 2

57. With reference to the National Initiative for Developing and Harnessing Innovations (NIDHI), consider the following statements:

1. It is an end to end plan for start-ups to double the number of incubators and start-ups in the duration of five years.

2. It is being implemented by the Ministry of Skill Development and Entrepreneurship.

Which of the statements given above is/are not correct?

(a) 1 only   (b) 2 only

(c) Both 1 and 2   (d) Neither 1 nor 2

58. Consider the following statements with reference to UJALA scheme:

1. Under the scheme LED bulbs are distributed.

2. Its objective is to promote energy efficiency.

Which of the statements given above is/are correct?

(a) 1 only   (b) 2 only

(c) Both 1 and 2   (d) Neither 1 nor 2

59. Consider the following statements with reference to Pradhan Mantri Jan Arogya Yojana:

1. It is a medical insurance scheme under which Rs.5 lakh per family is provided for secondary care and tertiary care.

2. It is a central sector scheme.

Which of the statements given above is/are correct?

(a) 1 only   (b) 2 only

(c) Both 1 and 2   (d) Neither 1 nor 2

60. Consider the following statements about the Indian Tsunami Early Warning Centre (ITEWC)

1. It has been established by the Ministry of Earth Science in collaboration with the World Meteorological Organization

2. It provides tsunami services to 25 Indian Ocean Countries

Which of the statements given above is/are correct?

(a) 1 only   (b) 2 only

(c) Both 1 and 2   (d) Neither 1 nor 2

61. Consider the following statements

1. Recently both Kisan Rail and Kisan Udaan services have been inaugurated

2. The first and only Kisan Rail was flagged off between Devlali in Maharashtra and Danapur in Bihar

Which of the statements given above is/are correct?

(a) 1 only   (b) 2 only

(c) Both 1 and 2   (d) Neither 1 nor 2

62. Consider the following statements about the Radar MFSTAR (for Multi-Function Surveillance Track and missile guidance Radar)

1. It has long-distance target detection and tracking ability for both, air and surface targets.

2. It is capable to undertake Target Designation of hostile targets for timely weapon engagement

Which of the statements given above is/are correct?

(a) 1 only   (b) 2 only

(c) Both 1 and 2   (d) Neither 1 nor 2

63. The keel laying ceremony of the third ship (Yard-12653) of the prestigious P17A class stealth frigates conducted virtually

With reference to it consider the following statements about Project 17A

1. It is a follow-up of the Project 17 Shivalik-class frigate for the Indian Coast Guard.

2. The Project has adopted the modern technology called Integrated Construction (IC)

3. The P17A class frigates are being built in joint collaboration with the French government

Which of the statements given above is/are correct?

(a) 1 only   (b) 2 only

(c) 1, 2 and 3   (d) 1 and 3 only

64. Consider the following statements about the SCO Culture Ministers' Meeting

1. It marks India's Chairpersonship of Council of Heads of Government this year.

2. The first SCO Exhibition on Shared Buddhist Heritage is going to be organised by the National Museum of India

Which of the statements given above is/are correct?

(a) 1 only   (b) 2 only

(c) Both 1 and 2   (d) Neither 1 nor 2

65. Consider the following statements about Five Star Villages Scheme

1. The scheme has been implemented nation-wide.

2. The scheme will be implemented by a team of five Gramin Dak Sevaks assigned by the Gram Panchayat

Which of the statements given above is/are correct?

(a) 1 only   (b) 2 only

(c) Both 1 and 2   (d) Neither 1 nor 2

66. Consider the following statements about EASE Banking Reforms Index

1. The Index measures the performance of each Schedule Commercial Bank on various objective metrics across six themes.

2. The latest edition of Ease 3.0 reform agenda aims at providing smart, tech-enabled public sector banking for aspiring India.

Which of the statements given above is/are correct?

(a) 1 only   (b) 2 only

(c) Both 1 and 2   (d) Neither 1 nor 2

67. Consider the following statements about Aero India 2021

1. It offers a unique platform to international aviation sector to bolster business.

2. It is one of the major exhibition only for defence industries with a public air show

3. It s organized every alternate year.

Which of the statements given above is/are correct?

(a) 1 and 3 only   (b) 3 only

(c) 1, 2 and 3   (d) 1 only

68. Institute of Pesticide Formulation Technology-IPFT is an autonomous Institution under which of the following Ministries/Departments?

(a) Ministry of Education

(b) All India Council of Technical Education

(c) Ministry of Agriculture and Farmer's welfare

(d) None of the above

69. Climate Smart Cities Assessment Framework (CSCAF) 2.0 and 'Streets for People Challenge' have been launched by which of the following Ministries/Organisations?

(a) Ministry of Housing and Urban Affairs

(b) Ministry of Environment

(c) NITI Aayog

(d) UNESCO

70. Consider the following statements

1. Gross NPAs has been reduced from the period starting from March-2018 to March-2020

2. The net NPA has increased from the period starting from March 2018 to March 2020

3. Asset quality has improved significantly

Which of the statements given above is/are correct?

(a) 1 and 3 only   (b) 3 only

(c) 1, 2 and 3   (d) 1 only

71. Recently India has been elected as the member of the Commission on Status of Women (CSW)

With reference to it consider the following statements about CSW

1. It is an intergovernmental body dedicated to the promotion of gender equality and the empowerment of women.

2. It a body of the Economic and Social Council (ECOSOC)

3. India will be a member for four years from 2021 to 2025.

Which of the statements given above is/are correct?

(a) 1 only

(b) 2 only

(c) 1, 2 and 3

(d) 1 and 3 only

72. SPICES (Scheme for Promoting Interests, Creativity and Ethics among Students) has been launched by which of the following Ministries?

(a) Ministry of Electronics and Information Technology

(b) Ministry of Education

(c) NITI Aayog

(d) None of the above

73. The term Key Resource Persons sometimes found in news, it refers to the Scheme of which of the following Ministries/Organisations?

(a) Central Board of Secondary Education

(b) Department of Science and Technology

(c) Ministry of Education

(d) None of the above

74. K.N. Dikshit Committee has been constituted

(a) To study the origin and evolution of Indian culture

(b) To study the ancient port cities

(c) To study the evolution of Vedic civilization

(d) None of these

75. Consider the following statements about Pradhan Mantri Van Dhan Yojana

1. TRIFED is the nodal agency both at national and State level

2. The objective is to set-up tribal community owned Van Dhan Vikas Kendras (VDVKs) in predominantly forested tribal districts.

3. It is 100% Central Government funded

Which of the statements given above is/are correct?

(a) 1 only   (b) 2 only

(c) 2 and 3 only   (d) 1 and 3 only

76. Consider the following statements about the Institute of Teaching and Research in Ayurveda (ITRA) Bill 2020

1. ITRA will be the first institution with INI status in the AYUSH Sector

2. The ITRA is sought to be established by conglomerating the presently existing Ayurveda institutes

Which of the statements given above is/are correct?

(a) 1 only   (b) 2 only

(c) Both 1 and 2   (d) Neither 1 nor 2

77. Consider the following statements about India's First Anti Satellite Missile (A-SAT)

1. The (A-SAT) missile test Mission Shakti was successfully conducted by ISRO

2. The missile successfully engaged an Indian orbiting target satellite in Low Earth Orbit (LEO) in a 'Hit to Kill' mode.

Which of the statements given above is/are correct?

(a) 1 only   (b) 2 only

(c) Both 1 and 2   (d) Neither 1 nor 2

78. Consider the following statements about Union for the Protection of Plant Varieties

1. This is the inter-governmental organization based in Geneva and primary intension is to protect the commercial interests of the plant breeders.

2. India is a member of UPOV.

Which of the above is/are correct?

(a) 1 only   (b) 2 only

(c) Both 1 and 2   (d) Neither 1 nor 2

79. Consider the following statements about the 'Pradhan Mantri Garib Kalyan Package Insurance Scheme for Health Workers Fighting COVID-19'

1. There is no age limit for this scheme

2. Individual enrolment is not required.

3. The entire amount of premium for this scheme is being borne by the Ministry of Health and Family Welfare, Government of India.

Which of the statements given above is/are correct?

(a) 2 only   (b) 2 and 3 only

(c) 1 and 2 and 3   (d) 3 only

80. Consider the following statements about the Institute of National Importance (INI)

1. It is a status that may be conferred on a premier public higher education institution only

2. The status can be conferred by passing an ordinance or executive order

Which of the statements given above is/are correct?

(a) 1 only   (b) 2 only

(c) Both 1 and 2   (d) Neither 1 nor 2

81. The Global Initiative to Reduce Land Degradation and Coral Reef program has been launched recently in which of the following global meet?

(a) G20 Environment Ministers meeting

(b) UNFCC ministerial meeting

(c) UNEP

(d) None of the following

82. Consider the following statements about the Biotech-KISAN programme

1. It is an initiative the department of Biotechnology, to empower farmers, especially women farmers.

2. It aims to understand the problems of water, soil, seed and market faced by the farmers and provide simple solutions to them.

Which of the statements given above is/are correct?

(a) 1 only   (b) 2 only

(c) Both 1 and 2   (d) Neither 1 nor 2

83. Living Planet Report 2020 has been released by which of the following organisations?

(a) World Economic Forum

(b) World Wide Fund

(c) United Nations Environment Programme

(d) None of the above

84. Consider the following statements

1. The Bengal tiger is found only in India

2. 'Project Tiger' is a centrally sponsored scheme of the Environment, Forests and Climate Change

Which of the statements given above is/are correct?

(a) 1 only   (b) 2 only

(c) Both 1 and 2   (d) Neither 1 nor 2

85. Consider the following statements about Pradhan Mantri Surakshit Matritva Abhiyan

1. The programme is rolled out in government hospitals only.

2. It gives minimum package of antenatal care services to the women in 1st and 2nd trimesters of pregnancy at the designated health facilities.

Which of the statements given above is/are correct?

(a) 1 only   (b) 2 only

(c) Both 1 and 2   (d) Neither 1 nor 2

86. Consider the following statements about the BrahMos Land-Attack Cruise Missile (LACM)

1. It is surface-to-surface sub-sonic cruise missile

2. Booster, Airframe Section, propulsion system and power supply are some of the major components of BrahMoS produced indigenously

Which of the statements given above is/are correct?

(a) 1 only   (b) 2 only

(c) Both 1 and 2   (d) Neither 1 nor 2

87. Consider the following statements about Ambedkar Social Innovation Incubation Mission (ASIIM)

1. This Mission has been launched by the Department for Promotion of Industry and Internal Trade (DPIIT)

2. The objective is to identify 1000 rural youth in the next 4 years with start-up ideas

Which of the statements given above is/are correct?

(a) 1 only   (b) 2 only

(c) Both 1 and 2   (d) Neither 1 nor 2

88. Consider the following statements about the Unnat Bharat Abhiyan

1. It is a flagship programme of Ministry of Education conceptualised and launched in IIT Delhi

2. It aims to link all the educational institutions with a set of villages across India

Which of the statements given above is/are correct?

(a) 1 only   (b) 2 only

(c) Both 1 and 2   (d) Neither 1 nor 2

89. Recently India has signed a Statement of Intent (SoI) to support the decarbonization and energy transition agenda for accommodating cleaner and more energy with which the following nations

(a) Germany   (b) Singapore

(c) Netherlands   (d) Finland

90. The Minister of Science & Technology, launched CSIR Technologies for rural development under a joint initiative of which of the following organisations?

1. Unnat Bharat Abhiyan (UBA)

2. Indian Institute of Technology Delhi (IITD)

3. Vijnana Bharti (VIBHA)

4. All India Council of Technical Education

Choose the correct one from the options given below

(a) 1, 2 and 3 only   (b) 1, 3 and 4 only

(c) 1, and 2 only   (d) 1, 2 and 3 only

91. Government has proposed to set up Neutrino Observatory in the country and site identified is in Bodi West Hills

Bodi West Hills is situated in which of the following states?

(a) Tamil Nadu   (b) Karnataka

(c) Kerala   (d) Himachal Pradesh

92. Consider the following statements about Sohrai Khovar painting

1. It is a traditional and ritualistic mural art of Hazaribagh district, Jharkhand.

2. It is practised by local tribal women in the area of Hazaribagh district, Jharkhand.

3. It is traditionally painted on the walls of mud houses

Which of the statements given above is/are correct?

(a) 1 and 2 only   (b) 1 and 3 only

(c) 2 and 3 only   (d) All of the above

93. "Ruhdaar" often seen in the news recently is a/an?

(a) Supersonic missile

(b) Mechanical ventilator

(c) Customised train coaches for COVID patients

(d) Cyber surveillance

94. Covid-19 Active Response and Expenditure Support (CARES) Program" is an initiative of which of the following?

(a) The World Bank

(b) New Development Bank

(c) Asian Development Bank

(d) African Development Bank

95. Consider the following statements about the Optical Fibre Village Connectivity project

1. It will be implemented by BSNL

2. The project aims to provide broadband connectivity in every village through Aerial Optical Fibre.

Which of the statements given above is/are correct?

(a) 1 only   (b) 2 only

(c) Both 1 and 2   (d) Neither 1 nor 2

96. Consider the following statements about Shanti Swarup Bhatnagar Prize

1. It is given annually by the Council of Scientific and Industrial Research (CSIR)

2. It is given for notable and outstanding research, applied or fundamental, in the field of biotechnology only

Which of the statements given above is/are correct?

(a) 1 only   (b) 2 only

(c) Both 1 and 2   (d) Neither 1 nor 2

97. Global Climate Risk Index is published by:

(a) United Nations Environment Programme

(b) UN Habitat

(c) Germanwatch

(d) World Economic Forum

98. Vande Bharat Mission' was sometimes seen in news. It is related to:

(a) Semi-high speed train also called as Train 18.

(b) Evacuation exercise to bring back Indian citizens

(c) Rehabilitation measures taken for the flood affected people in Assam.

(d) Achieving renewable energy target before 2024

99. Recently there has been a growing awareness in our country regarding 'Nisargruna plant'. It is used for which of the following purposes?

(a) Its extracts are used in cosmetic industry.

(b) It is a rich source of biodiesel.

(c) It helps in degrading the plastic waste.

(d) It offers eco-friendly process of methane generation.

100. Consider the following statements about National Child Labour Project (NCLP) Scheme.

1. The Ministry of Education is implementing the NCLP Scheme since 1988 for rehabilitation of child labourers.

2. The children in the age group of 9-14 years are rescued/ withdrawn from work and linked directly to the formal education system through a close coordination with the Samagra Shiksha Abhiyan.

Which of the statements given above is/are correct?

(a) 1 only   (b) 2 only

(c) Both 1 and 2   (d) Neither 1 nor 2

ANSWER KEY

1. (a)	**2.** (a)	**3.** (d)	**4.** (d)	**5.** (d)	**6.** (b)	**7.** (a)	**8.** (c)	**9.** (b)	**10.** (c)
11. (d)	**12.** (c)	**13.** (a)	**14.** (d)	**15.** (d)	**16.** (c)	**17.** (a)	**18.** (a)	**19.** (a)	**20.** (d)
21. (c)	**22.** (b)	**23.** (d)	**24.** (b)	**25.** (c)	**26.** (c)	**27.** (a)	**28.** (d)	**29.** (c)	**30.** (c)
31. (b)	**32.** (d)	**33.** (b)	**34.** (a)	**35.** (b)	**36.** (a)	**37.** (b)	**38.** (c)	**39.** (d)	**40.** (c)
41. (a)	**42.** (a)	**43.** (b)	**44.** (d)	**45.** (b)	**46.** (d)	**47.** (b)	**48.** (c)	**49.** (c)	**50.** (c)
51. (b)	**52.** (c)	**53.** (c)	**54.** (a)	**55.** (b)	**56.** (c)	**57.** (b)	**58.** (c)	**59.** (a)	**60.** (b)
61. (d)	**62.** (c)	**63.** (b)	**64.** (c)	**65.** (d)	**66.** (b)	**67.** (a)	**68.** (d)	**69.** (a)	**70.** (a)
71. (c)	**72.** (b)	**73.** (a)	**74.** (a)	**75.** (c)	**76.** (c)	**77.** (b)	**78.** (a)	**79.** (c)	**80.** (a)
81. (a)	**82.** (c)	**83.** (b)	**84.** (b)	**85.** (a)	**86.** (b)	**87.** (d)	**88.** (a)	**89.** (c)	**90.** (d)
91. (a)	**92.** (d)	**93.** (b)	**94.** (c)	**95.** (b)	**96.** (a)	**97.** (c)	**98.** (b)	**99.** (d)	**100.** (d)

EXPLANATION

1. (a) • The Shanti Swarup Bhatnagar Prize for Science and Technology (SSB) is a science award in India given annually by the Council of Scientific and Industrial Research (CSIR) for notable and outstanding research, applied or fundamental, in biology, chemistry, environmental science, engineering, mathematics, medicine and Physics.

• The prize recognizes outstanding Indian work (according to the view of CSIR awarding committee) in science and technology.

2. (a) Atal Bhujal Yojana

• To address the criticality of ground water resources

• To improve ground water management in priority areas through community participation

• Identified districts: 78 districts - Gujarat, Haryana, Karnataka, M. P., Maharashtra, Rajasthan & Uttar Pradesh

• To promote panchayat-led ground water management and behavioural change with primary focus on demand side management.

• To be implemented for a 5-year period - 2020-21 to 2024-25

• A Central Sector Scheme - Total outlay - Rs. 6000 Crores - 50% support from World Bank through loans.

Two Components :

• Institutional Strengthening and Capacity Building Component

• Incentive Component for incentivizing the States for achievements in improved groundwater management practices

3. (d) • GISAID is a public platform started by the World Health Organization (WHO) in 2008 for countries to share genome sequences.

• The GISAID Initiative promotes the international sharing of all influenza virus sequences, related clinical and epidemiological data associated with human viruses, and geographical as well as species-specific data associated with avian and other animal viruses.

• This helps researchers understand how the viruses evolve, spread and potentially become pandemics.

• It actively promotes the development of novel research tools for the analysis of influenza data by helping developers to facilitate the integration or connection of their tools to analyze GISAID data.

4. (d) • This report has been produced by the Independent Expert Group of the Global Nutrition Report, supported by the Global Nutrition Report Stakeholder Group.

   • The Global Nutrition Report was conceived following the first Nutrition for Growth Initiative Summit (N4G) in 2013. The first report was published in 2014.

   • The Global Nutrition Report acts as a report card on the world's nutrition-globally, regionally, and country by country-and on efforts to improve it.

   • It assesses progress in meeting Global Nutrition Targets established by the World Health Assembly.

   • The World Health Organization (WHO) is a Global Nutrition Report Partner.

5. (d) • WRI is part of the World Risk Report 2020 released by the United Nations University Institute for Environment and Human Security (UNU-EHS) and BundnisEntwicklungHilft, in cooperation with the University of Stuttgart in Germany.

   • The WRI is calculated on a country-by-country basis, through the multiplication of exposure and vulnerability.

6. (b) • In order to further improve the ease of doing business, NHAI has agreed to most of the suggestions made by industry body, the Consulting Engineers Association of India (CEAI).

   • Consulting Engineers Association of India (CEAI) is the apex body of Consulting Engineers in India.

   • CEAI represents the Indian Engineering Consultancy professional at the International Federation of Consulting Engineers (FIDIC).

   • Two erstwhile professional bodies of consulting engineers, Association of Consulting Engineers (ACE) and National Association of Consulting Engineers (NACE) amalgamated in to CEAI in the year 1996

   • CEAI Membership comprises of practicing consultants, private and public sector firms engaged in the entire range of engineering consultancy services.

7. (a) • National Medicinal Plants Board (NMPB) and ICAR-National Bureau of Plant Genetic Resources (NBPGR) have entered into a MoU to conserve the Medicinal and Aromatic Plants Genetic Resources (MAPGRs).

   • The conservation will be done at designated space of ICAR-NBPGR in long-term storage module in the National Gene bank and/or at Regional Station for medium term storage module.

   • National Medicinal Plants Board (NMPB) is under Ministry of AYUSH. ICAR-National Bureau of Plant Genetic Resources (NBPGR) is under Department of Agricultural Research and Education.

8. (c) • The government of Bangladesh is financing a film on the life of revolutionary freedom fighter Pritilata Waddedar.

   • The film 'Bhalobasha Pritilata' will be based on the first woman Bengali revolutionary nationalist of the Indian subcontinent against the British regime

9. (b) • Ministry of Earth Sciences (MoES) aims to develop a World-Class Knowledge Resource Centre Network (KRCNet).

   • Under it, the traditional libraries of the MoES system will be upgraded into a top-notch Knowledge Resource Centres (KRC). KRCs will be connected with each other and integrated into the KRCNet portal.

10. (c) • PMNCH seeks to achieve universal access to comprehensive, high-quality reproductive, maternal, newborn and child health care.

    • PMNCH describes itself as a platform for knowledge, advocacy and accountability to improve women and children's health.

    • It is the world's largest alliance for women's, children's and adolescents' health (WCAH), bringing together over 1,000 partner organizations across 192 countries.

11. (d) • Department for Promotion of Industry and Internal Trade (DPIIT), M/o Commerce and Industry, has given permission to the Petroleum and Explosives Safety Organisation (PESO) to introduce ISO Tank Containers for movement of Liquid Oxygen for domestic transport.

    • The proposal to introduce ISO Tank Containers for domestic movement was initiated by DPIIT after a consultation meeting with cryogenic oxygen manufacturers.

12. (c)
- National Intelligence Grid or NATGRID which works under the aegis of the Ministry of Home affairs was established in 2009, in the wake of Mumbai terrorist attacks 2008, through governmental notifications rather than legislation passed in Parliament.
- NATGRID was formed with an aim to collect comprehensive patterns of intelligence that can be readily accessed by intelligence agencies, and will link 10 user agencies with certain databases that would be procured from 21 organisations.
- The project aims to allow investigation and law enforcement agencies to access real-time information from data stored with agencies such as the Income Tax Department, banks, insurance companies, Indian Railways, credit card transactions, and more.

13. (a)
- Earth Day Network (EDN) is the not for profit organisation that leads Earth Day worldwide.
- April 22, 2020 marks 50 years of Earth Day. The theme for Earth Day 2020 is climate action.
- Earth Day is observed every year on April 22. It was first celebrated in 1970. On April 22, 1970, millions of people took to the streets to protest the negative impacts of 150 years of industrial development.
- Objective is to increase the awareness among common public, especially among youngsters, to get full effect of the campaign of environmental safety.

14. (d)
- International Energy Agency (IEA), in collaboration with NITI Aayog, presented a 'Special Report on Sustainable Recovery'
- Part of IEA's flagship World Energy Outlook series, the report proposes a number of actions that could be taken over the next three years to revitalize economies and boost employment while making energy systems cleaner and more resilient.
- The IEA's report, prepared in cooperation with IMF, details energy-focused policies and investments that could help boost economic growth, create jobs and put emissions into structural decline while making energy systems lower-cost, secure and resilient.

15. (d)
- IEA is a Paris-based autonomous intergovernmental organisation established in the framework of the Organisation for Economic Co-operation and Development (OECD) in 1974 in the wake of the 1973 oil crisis.
- The IEA acts as a policy adviser to its member states, but also works with non-member countries, especially China, India, and Russia.
- The Agency's mandate has broadened to focus on the "3Es" of effectual energy policy: energy security, economic development, and environmental protection.

16. (c)
- The act is applicable to healthcare service personnel from public and clinical healthcare service providers such as doctors, nurses, paramedical workers and community health workers; any other persons empowered under the act to take measures to prevent the outbreak of the disease or spread.
- Once a crime is legally registered, the offence will be investigated by an officer of the rank of inspector within a period of 30 days and the trial has to be completed within a year, unless extended by the court.
- Anyone found guilty of such acts of violence against healthcare personnel will be punishable with an imprisonment for a term of three months to five years, and with a fine of Rs 50,000 to Rs 2,00,000.

17. (a)
- The Ministry of Social Justice and Empowerment has formulated and is implementing a National Action Plan for Drug Demand Reduction (NAPDDR) for 2018-2025.
- The Plan aims at reduction of adverse consequences of drug abuse through a multi-pronged strategy.
- The Ministry has launched NashaMukt Bharat Abhiyaan in 272 most affected districts with focus on institutional support, community outreach and awareness generation.

18. (a)
- India has been ranked at the 116th position in the latest edition of the World Bank's annual Human Capital Index that benchmarks key components of human capital across countries.
- India's score increased to 0.49 from 0.44 in 2018, as per the Human Capital Index report
- Last year India was ranked 115 out of 157 countries. This year India finds itself at 116th from among 174 countries.

19. (a)
- With a vision to strengthen digitalization in Panchayats for the purpose of empowering rural India, a unified tool e-Gram SWARAJ portal

(https://egramswaraj.gov.in/) has been developed by the Ministry for effective monitoring and evaluation of works taken up in the Gram Panchayats.

- e-Gram SWARAJ unifies the planning, accounting and monitoring functions of Gram Panchayats.

- It's combination with the Area Profiler application, Local Government Directory (LGD) and the Public Financial Management System (PFMS) renders easier reporting and tracking of Gram Panchayat's activities.

- It provides a single window for capturing Panchayat information with the complete Profile of the Panchayat, details of Panchayat finances, asset details, activities taken up through Gram Panchayat Development Plan (GPDP)

20. (d) • NNM will be an apex body to monitor, supervise, fixing the targets and guiding the nutrition related interventions across the Ministries.

- It would be executed with the Ministry of Women and Child Development (WCD) as the nodal ministry along with Ministry of Drinking Water and Sanitation and Ministry of Health and Family Welfare which is in-charge of immunisation.

- POSHAN Abhiyaan is a scheme for holistic Nourishment

- Objective - to reduce the level of stunting, under-nutrition, anaemia and low birth weight in children.

- The focus is on adolescent girls, pregnant women, children and lactating mothers.

- To ensure a holistic approach, all 36 states and UTs will be covered in a phased manner.

- The Abhiyaan empowers frontline functionaries; i.e Anganwadi and lady supervisors by providing them with smartphones

21. (c) • Union Government has recently announced around 11 per cent increase in annual central allocation of cooking cost under Mid-day meal scheme to eight thousand 100 crore rupees in view of situation arising out of COVID-19.

- Mid-day Meal Scheme

- It is a Centrally-Sponsored Scheme, aimed at increasing enrolment, retention and attendance of students in schools.

- The Midday Meal Scheme comes under the HRD Ministry's Department of School Education and Literacy.

- The scheme covers all government and government aided schools and also Madarsa and Maqtabs supported under the Sarva Shiksha Abhiyan (SSA).

22. (b) • A palaeo channel, or paleochannel, is a remnant of an inactive river or stream channel that has been filled or buried by younger sediment. The sediments that the ancient channel is cut into or buried by can be unconsolidated, semi-consolidated, consolidated or lithified.

- The Union Water Ministry has excavated an old, dried-up river in Prayagraj (formerly Allahabad) that linked the Ganga and Yamuna rivers. The aim is to develop it as a potential groundwater recharge source

23. (d) • A few countries have started considering issuing •immunity passports or some kind of certificates indicating a person has immunity to COVID-19.

- However, the World Health Organization has warned against idea of 'immunity passport'.

- The idea for the immunity passport or a back to work pass is this: If you've been infected with SARS-CoV-2, the virus that causes COVID-19, and recover, then you have immunity that will protect you from getting the disease again for some amount of time.

- WHO says that there is currently no evidence that people who have recovered from COVID-19 and have antibodies are protected against a second infection.

24. (b) • National Initiative for Developing and Harnessing Innovations (NIDHI) is an end to end plan for startups to double the number of incubators and startups in the duration of five years.

- It is being implemented by the Department of Science and Technology (DST) under the Ministry of Science and Technology.

25. (c) • PM-JAY offers a sum insured of Rs.5 lakh per family for secondary care (which doesn't involve a super specialist) as well as tertiary care (which involves a super specialist).

- It is a central sponsored scheme. The insurance cost is shared by the centre and the state mostly in the ratio of 60:40. Under the central sector scheme the entire cost is borne by the central government.

26. (c) • Atal Tunnel is the longest highway tunnel in the World.

• The 9.02 Km long tunnel connects Manali to Lahaul-Spiti valley throughout the year.

• Earlier the valley was cut off for about 6 months each year owing to heavy snowfall.

• The Tunnel is built with ultra-modern specifications in the PirPanjal range of Himalayas at an altitude of 3000 Mtrs (10,000 Feet) from the Mean Sea Level (MSL)

• The tunnel reduces the road distance by 46 Kms between Manali and Leh and the time by about 4 to 5 hours.

27. (a) • Ministry of Women and Child Development in collaboration with the Ministry of Home Affairs has envisaged engagement of Mahila Police Volunteers (MPVs) in the States/UTs who will act as a link between police and community and help women in distress.

• Haryana was the first state to adopt the initiative at Karnal and Mahindergarh District on a pilot basis under Nirbhaya Fund

28. (d) • FRP is a legal price guaranteed to the farmers by the Centre government and it paid by the sugar mills to the farmers

• States can give higher price than FRP, as several State Advised prices are higher than FRP

29. (c) • The NBWL's Standing Committee discussed a proposal for use of 98.59 hectares of land from the Saleki proposed reserve forest land for a coal mining project by North-Easter Coal Field (NECF), a unit of Coal India Limited.

• Saleki is a part of the DehingPatkai Elephant Reserve that includes the DehingPatkai Wildlife Sanctuary covering 111.19 sq km of rainforest and several reserve forests in Sivasagar, Dibrugarh and Tinsukia districts of Assam

30. (c) • The indigenously developed Laser Guided Anti Tank Guided Missile (ATGM) was successfully test fired today on 1st Oct 2020 defeating a target located at longer range.

• The test was conducted from MBT Arjun at KK ranges (ACC&S) Ahmednagar in continuation of successful trial done on 22nd Sep 2020.

• The ATGM employs a tandem HEAT warhead to defeat Explosive Reactive Armour (ERA)

protected armoured vehicles in ranges from 1.5 to 5 km.

• These missiles use laser designation to lock and track the targets for better accuracy.

31. (b) • Atal Innovation Mission (AIM), NITI Aayog, launched the Aatmanirbhar Bharat ARISE-Atal New India Challenges, to spur applied research and innovation in Indian MSMEs and startups.

• The Indian government has launched 15 challenges for Indian MSMEs and Indian startups to solve for a grant of ?50 lakh each

The programme will be driven by Indian Space Research Organization (ISRO), four ministries-

• Ministry of Defence;

• Ministry of Food Processing Industries;

• Ministry of Health and Family Welfare; and

• Ministry of Housing and Urban Affairs-and associated industries to facilitate innovative solutions to sectoral problems.

• The Aatmanirbhar Bharat ARISE-ANIC programme will support deserving applied research-based innovations by providing funding support of up to Rs 50 lakh for speedy development of the proposed technology solution and/or product.

32. (d) • The Government of India had launched PM Svanidhi scheme on 1st June, 2020 to help poor street vendors, impacted by COVID-19, resume livelihood activities.

• The PM Street Vendor's AtmaNirbhar Nidhi (PM SVANidhi) was launched by the Ministry of Housing and Urban Affairs on June 01, 2020 for providing affordable Working Capital loan to street vendors to resume their livelihoodsthat have been adversely affected due to Covid-19 lockdown

• The duration of the scheme is until March 2022.

• Vendors can avail a working capital loan of up to Rs. 10,000, which is repayable in monthly instalments in the tenure of one year.

Implementation agency

• Small Industries Development Bank of India (SIDBI)

33. (b) • Interactive Research School for Health Affairs (IRSHA) is a unique constituent unit of Bharati Vidyapeeth (Deemed to be University), totally dedicated to research.

- The institute was established in 2001. The institute is mandated to conduct research in priority areas of human health in co-ordination with other constituents of the university like Medical, Ayurveda, Homeopathy, Dental colleges, Rajiv Gandhi Institute of IT & BT, Environmental sciences etc.

34. (a)
- National Immunogenicity & Biologics Evaluation Center, a facility supported by the Department of Biotechnology (DBT) was inaugurated in Pune.
- For assessing the clinical immunogenicity of viral vaccines, a facility, the National Immunogenicity & Biologics Evaluation Center (NIBEC) has begun operations after it was inaugurated through an e-inauguration.
- The facility is established jointly by BIRAC-DBT, the Government of India through the National Biopharma Mission, and Bharati Vidyapeeth University through the Interactive Research School for Health Affairs (IRSHA), its constituent unit.

35. (b)
- The Pradhan Mantri MatsyaSampada Yojana (PMMSY) is a flagship scheme for focused and sustainable development of fisheries sector in the country with an estimated investment of Rs. 20,050 crores for its implementation during a period of 5 years from FY 2020-21 to FY 2024-25 in all States/Union Territories, as a part of AatmaNirbhar Bharat Package.
- PMMSY aims at enhancing fish production by an additional 70 lakh tonne by 2024-25, increasing fisheries export earnings to Rs.1,00,000 crore by 2024-25, doubling of incomes of fishers and fish farmers
- PMMSY scheme primarily focuses on adopting 'Cluster or Area based approaches' and creation of Fisheries clusters through backward and forward linkages.

36. (a)
- Biotechnology Industry Research Assistance Council (BIRAC) is a not-for-profit Section 8, Schedule B, Public Sector Enterprise, set up by Department of Biotechnology (DBT), Government of India as an Interface Agency to strengthen and empower the emerging Biotech enterprise to undertake strategic research and innovation, addressing nationally relevant product development needs

37. (b)
- e-Gopala App is a comprehensive breed improvement marketplace and information portal for direct use of farmers.

- At present no digital platform is available in the country for farmers managing livestock including buying and selling of disease free germplasm in all forms (semen, embryos, etc); availability of quality breeding services (Artificial Insemination, veterinary first aid, vaccination, treatment etc) and guiding farmers for animal nutrition, treatment of animals using appropriate ayurvedic medicine/ethno veterinary medicine.
- There is no mechanism to send alerts (on due date for vaccination, pregnancy diagnosis, calving etc) and inform farmers about various government schemes and campaigns in the area.
- The e-Gopala App will provide solutions to farmers on all these aspects.

38. (c)
- Union Minister of State for Shipping launched 'SAROD-Ports' (Society for Affordable Redressal of Disputes - Ports)
- SAROD-Ports consists members from Indian Ports Association (IPA) and Indian Private Ports and Terminals Association (IPTTA).
- SAROD-Ports will advise and assist in settlement of disputes through arbitrations in the maritime sector, including ports and shipping sector in Major Port Trusts, Non-major Ports, including private ports, jetties, terminals and harbours.

39. (d)
- The Department of Posts has launched a scheme called Five Star Villages, to ensure universal coverage of flagship postal schemes in rural areas of the country.
- The scheme seeks to bridge the gaps in public awareness and reach of postal products and services, especially in interior villages.
- All postal products and services will be made available and marketed and publicized at village level, under the Five Star Villages scheme.
- Branch offices will function as one-stop shop to cater all post office - related needs of villagers.

40. (c)
- The Industry-Academia Collaborative Mission of Department of Biotechnology (DBT), Govt of India for accelerating discovery research to early development for Biopharmaceuticals approved by the Cabinet for a total cost US$ 250 million and 50% co-funded by the World Bank is being implemented at Biotechnology Research Assistance Council (BIRAC).

- This program is dedicated to deliver affordable products to the nation with an aim to improve the health standards of India's population.
- National Biopharma Mission identifies the needs and gaps of Biotherapeutics, Vaccine and Devices Industry and address those capacity bottlenecks.
- Vaccines, medical devices and diagnostics and biotherapeutics are few of its most important domains, besides, strengthening the clinical trial capacity and building technology transfer capabilities in the country

41. (a)
- The Department for Promotion of Industry and Internal Trade (DPIIT) conducted the second edition of the States' Startup Ranking Exercise, with the key objective to foster competitiveness and propel States and Union Territories to work proactively towards uplifting the startup ecosystem.
- The States' Startup Ranking Framework 2019 has 7 broad reform area, consisting of 30 action points ranging from Institutional Support, Easing Compliances, Relaxation in Public Procurement norms, Incubation support, Seed Funding Support, Venture Funding Support, and Awareness & Outreach.
- A total of 22 States and 3 Union Territories participated in the exercise.

42. (a)
- The Million Minds Augmenting National Aspirations and Knowledge (MANAK) programme was launched by the Department of Science and Technology (DST) in partnership with the National Innovation Foundation (NIF) in 2017.
- It emphasises on the power of ideas in young minds to create a pipeline of innovative students who can recognise problems and find solutions to them.
- Aiming to harness the power of bright minds spread across 6 lakhs school in the country, DST invites students from government and private schools to send original and innovative ideas having potential to solve common problems.

43. (b)
- It was established in 1982 by the Government of India under the aegis of Department of Science & Technology
- It is an institutional mechanism to help promote knowledge driven and technology intensive enterprises.

- The Board, having representations from socio-economic and scientific Ministries/Departments, aims to convert job-seekers into job-generators through Science & Technology (S&T) interventions.
- To promote and develop high-end entrepreneurship for S&T manpower as well as self-employment by utilising S&T infrastructure and by using S&T methods.

44. (d)
- The Ministry of Road Transport & Highways is in the process of implementing 'Integrated Road Accident Database Project (iRAD)' which will be applicable across the country.
- The development and implementation of iRAD has been entrusted to IIT Madras and National Informatics Centre Services Inc.
- The App when developed and functional, will enable the stakeholders such as the Police, Transport, Health, etc to use their mobile phones to collect accident data on the spot.
- This project is proposed on IT based system for capturing the spot accident data using mobile app configured for this purpose.

45. (b)
- It is an umbrella programme conceived and developed by the Innovation & Entrepreneurship division, Department of Science & Technology, Government of India, for nurturing ideas and innovations (knowledge-based and technology-driven) into successful startups.
- NIDHI aims to nurture start-ups through scouting, supporting and scaling of innovations.
- The key stakeholders of NIDHI includes various departments and ministries of the central government, state governments, academic and R & D institutions, mentors, financial institutions, angel investors, venture capitalists and private sectors.

46. (d)
- South-South Cooperation is a general term often used to describe the exchange of resources, technology and knowledge between developing countries (who are sometimes referred to as the global south).
- It also refers to the exchange of expertise between actors (governments, organizations and individuals) in developing countries.
- So South-South Cooperation is a general term to describe political, economic, social, cultural,

environmental or technical cooperation or collaboration between countries of the global south.

47. (b) • The signing of the Agreement on Reciprocal Provision of Supplies and Services between the Indian Armed Forces and the Self-Defense Forces of Japan.

• After years of negotiations, India and Japan have inked a landmark agreement that will allow their militaries to access each other's bases for logistics support, a key development that comes in the backdrop of growing concerns over China's military muscle flexing in the region

48. (c) • The powers, privileges and immunities of either House of the Indian Parliament and of its Members and committees are laid down in Article 105 of the Constitution.

• Article 194 deals with the powers, privileges and immunities of the State Legislatures, their Members and their committees.

• Parliamentary privilege refers to the right and immunity enjoyed by legislatures, in which legislators are granted protection against civil or criminal liability for actions done or statements made in the course of their legislative duties.

49. (c) • The Department of School Education and Literacy launched a National Mission to improve learning outcomes at the Elementary level through an Integrated Teacher Training Programme called NISHTHA - National Initiative for School Heads' and Teachers' Holistic Advancement on 21st August, 2019.

• The aim of this integrated teacher training programme was to build the capacities of around 42 lakh teachers and Heads of Schools, faculty members of SCERTs and DIETs and Block Resource Coordinators and Cluster Resource Coordinators.

50. (c) • It is one of the six principal organs of the United Nations, responsible for coordinating the economic and social fields of the organization

• ECOSOC serves as the central forum for discussing international economic and social issues and formulating policy recommendations addressed to member states and the United Nations system.

• In addition to a rotating membership of 54 UN member states, over 1,600 nongovernmental organizations have consultative status with the Council to participate in the work of the United Nations

51. (b) • Biotech-Krishi Innovation Science Application Network (Biotech-KISAN) is being implemented in 15 agro-climatic zones of India in phased manner

• This programme aims to work with small and marginal farmers especially the woman farmer for better agriculture productivity through scientific intervention and evolving best farming practices in the Indian context

• Biotech-KISAN aims to link farmers, scientists and science institutions across the country in a network that identifies and helps solve their problems in a cooperative manner.

52. (c) • The Living Planet Report is based on data from the Living Planet Index produced by the Zoological Society of London (ZSL).

• The index is statistically created from journal studies, online databases and government reports for 20,000 populations of 4,200 species of mammal, bird, reptile, amphibian and fish, or approximately 6 percent of the world's vertebrate species.

• About 75 percent of the earth's ice-free land surface has already been significantly altered, most of the oceans are polluted, and more than 85 percent of the area of wetlands has been lost

• The rate of decline is not uniform. The Freshwater Living Planet Index shows that freshwater biodiversity is declining far faster than that in oceans or forests

53. (c) • The Association of World Election Bodies (A-WEB) is largest association of Election Management Bodies (EMBs) worldwide.

• At present A-WEB has 115 EMBs as Members & 16 Regional Associations/Organisations as Associate Members.

• ECI has been very closely associated with the process of formation of A-WEB since 2011

• ECI hosted the 4th General Assembly of A-WEB on 03 Sep 2019 at Bengaluru and took over as Chair of A-WEB for 2019-2021 term.

54. (a) • The new legislation will create an ecosystem where the farmers and traders will enjoy freedom of choice of sale and purchase of agri-produce.

• It will also promote barrier-free inter-state and intra-state trade and commerce outside the physical premises of markets notified under State Agricultural Produce Marketing legislations.

- The farmers will not be charged any cess or levy for sale of their produce and will not have to bear transport costs.

- The Bill also proposes an electronic trading in transaction platform for ensuring a seamless trade electronically.

- In addition to mandis, freedom to do trading at farmgate, cold storage, warehouse, processing units etc.

- Farmers will be able to engage in direct marketing thereby eliminating intermediaries resulting in full realization of price.

55. (b) • The Logistics Performance Index is released once in 2 years by the World Bank. India ranks 44

56. (c) • Successful flight test of ABHYAS - High-speed Expendable Aerial Target (HEAT) was today conducted by Defence Research and Development Organisation (DRDO) from the Interim Test Range, Balasore in Odisha.

- During the trials, two demonstrator vehicles were successfully test flown. The vehicle can be used as target for evaluation of various missile systems.

- Abhyas is designed & developed by Aeronautical Development Establishment (ADE), DRDO. The air vehicle is launched using twin underslung booster.

- It is powered by a small gas turbine engine and has MEMS based Inertial Navigation System (INS) for navigation along with the Flight Control Computer (FCC) for guidance and control.

57. (b) • National Initiative for Developing and Harnessing Innovations (NIDHI) is an end to end plan for start-ups to double the number of incubators and startups in the duration of five years.

- It is being implemented by the Department of Science and Technology (DST) under the Ministry of Science and Technology.

58. (c) Unnat Jyoti by Affordable LEDs for All (UJALA)

- It was launched in 2015 with a target of replacing 77 crore incandescent lamps with LED bulbs and to nullify the high-cost of LEDs that acted as a barrier previously in the adoption of energy-efficient systems.

- The scheme was implemented to set up a phase-wise LED distribution.

- The objective is to promote efficient lighting, enhance awareness on using efficient equipment that will reduce electricity bills and preserve the environment.

- It is the world's largest domestic lighting project.

59. (a) • PM-JAY offers a sum insured of Rs.5 lakh per family for secondary care (which doesn't involve a super specialist) as well as tertiary care (which involves a super specialist).

- It is a central sponsored scheme. The insurance cost is shared by the centre and the state mostly in the ratio of 60:40. Under the central sector scheme the entire cost is borne by the central government.

60. (b) • It was established at Indian National Centre for Ocean Information Services (INCOIS), Hyderabad, an autonomous body under Ministry of Earth Sciences which continues to provide timely tsunami advisories to stake holders and has functioned flawlessly since its establishment in October 2007.

- The ITEWC is also providing tsunami services to 25 Indian Ocean Countries as part of the Intergovernmental Oceanographic Commission (IOC) of UNESCO framework.

61. (d) • Kisan Rail and Kisan Udaan had been announced in this year's budget so that farm produce is able to be transported all over the country in less time.

- On 7th August, the first Kisan Rail was flagged off between Devlali in Maharashtra and Danapur in Bihar as a weekly service, which was later made bi-weekly due to increasing demand.

- Kisan Udaan service will also be started soon.

- India's second and South India's first Kisan Train commenced its inaugural run from Anantapur in Andhra Pradesh to Adarsh Nagar in New Delhi

62. (c) • The Radar MFSTAR (for Multi-Function Surveillance Track and missile guidance Radar) Frigate version shall bring in long-distance target detection and tracking ability for both, Air and Surface targets.

- The MFSTAR is also capable to undertake Target Designation of hostile targets for timely weapon engagement and achieve optimal utilization of Fleet resources.

- This unique MFSTAR feature makes an anti-missile countermeasure (as part of self-defense tactics) highly effective, especially against the sea-skimming missile threat to the Ship

63. (b)
- The keel laying ceremony was conducted through an e-platform
- In all, seven ships of P-17 A with advanced stealth capability has been ordered by the Indian Navy, with the ship, construction to take place at MDL (for four) and GRSE, Kolkata (for three).
- The Nilgiri-class frigate or Project 17A is a follow-on of the Project 17 Shivalik-class frigate for the Indian Navy.
- The P17A class frigates are being built using indigenously developed steel and fitted with weapons and sensors along with Integrated Platform Management System. These ships are having stealth features.
- Construction of P17A ships differ in the very concept of warship building by way of adoption of the modern technology 'Integrated Construction (IC)' where the blocks are pre-outfitted before joining to reduce the build period of warships.

64. (c)
- One of the important aspects that unites and connects Shanghai Cooperation Organization countries to each other is shared heritage of Buddhist philosophy and art.
- To promote the mutual bonding, the National Museum of India is in process of organizing the first SCO Exhibition on Shared Buddhist Heritage this year.
- The Exhibition marks India's Chairpersonship of Council of Heads of Government this year.
- The year 2021 is the 20th Anniversary year of the founding of this Organization and India supports the proposal of declaring 2021 the Year of Culture of the SCO to celebrate the occasion.

65. (d)
- The scheme seeks to bridge the gaps in public awareness and reach of postal products and services, especially in interior villages.
- All postal products and services will be made available and marketed and publicized at village level, under the Five Star Villages scheme.
- Branch offices will function as one-stop shop to cater all post office - related needs of villagers.

- The schemes covered under the Five Star scheme include:
- If a village attains universal coverage for four schemes from the above list, then that village gets four-star status; if a village completes three schemes, then that village get three-star status and so on.
- The scheme is being launched on pilot basis in Maharashtra; based on the experience here, it will be implemented nation-wide.
- The scheme will be implemented by a team of five GraminDakSevaks who will be assigned a village for marketing of all products, savings and insurance schemes of the Department of Posts.
- The team of GraminDakSevaks will conduct door-to-door awareness campaign on all schemes, covering all eligible villagers.
- Required training and infrastructure, covering all schemes, would be provided to all branch offices in identified villages.

66. (b) EASE Banking Reforms Index
- A common reform agenda for PSBs, EASE Agenda is aimed at institutionalizing clean and smart banking.
- It was launched in January 2018
- EASE 2.0 built on the foundation laid in EASE 1.0 and furthered the progress on reforms.
- Reform Action Points in EASE 2.0 aimed at making the reforms journey irreversible,
- The Index measures the performance of each PSB on 120+objective metrics across six themes.
- It provides all PSBs a comparative evaluation showing where banks stand vis-à-vis benchmarks and peers on the Reforms Agenda.
- The Index follows a fully transparent scoring methodology, which enables banks to identify precisely their strengths as well as areas for improvement.

67. (a)
- The 13th edition of Aero India-21 will be held at Air Force Station, Yelahanka, Bengaluru, Karnataka from 3rd to 07th February 2021.
- Aero India exhibition is organized every alternate year.
- It is one of the major exhibition for aerospace and defence industries with a public air show.
- Aero India offers a unique platform to international aviation sector to bolster business

- Aero India 2021 is the 13th edition of Aero India being organised at Bengaluru, Karnataka from 03-07 February 2021.

68. (d)
- Institute of Pesticide Formulation Technology-IPFT an autonomous Institution under the Department of Chemicals & Petrochemicals, Ministry of Chemicals & Fertilizers has successfully developed two new technologies namely Disinfectant spray for surface application and Disinfectant spray for Vegetables & fruits.

69. (a)
- The Minister of State for Housing and Urban Affairs has launched the Climate Smart Cities Assessment Framework (CSCAF) 2.0, along with the 'Streets for People Challenge' in a virtual event organized by the Smart Cities Mission

70. (a)

Major Reform achievements
- Gross NPAs reduced from Rs 8.96 lakh crore in March-2018 to Rs 6.78 lakh crore in March-2020
- Record recovery of Rs 2.27 lakh crore in FY19-FY20 driven by newly setup dedicated stressed account management verticals in PSBs;
- Asset quality has improved significantly, with the net NPA ratio reducing from 7.97% in March 2018 to 3.75% in March 2020
- Number of PSBs under PCA down to three;
- PSBs have adopted digital platforms such as online OTS, e-B????, e-DRT for expedited recovery. 88% of one-time settlement (OTS) cases are now tracked through dedicated IT systems.

71. (c)
- India has been elected as the member of the Commission on Status of Women (CSW), a body of the Economic and Social Council (ECOSOC).
- India will be a member of the prestigious body for four years from 2021 to 2025.
- The CSW is the principal global intergovernmental body exclusively dedicated to the promotion of gender equality and the empowerment of women.
- 45 member states of the United Nations serve as members of the Commission at any one time.

72. (b)
- SPICES (Scheme for Promoting Interests, Creativity and Ethics among Students) has been launched by Union Education Minister to promote healthy co-curricular activity amongst the students for their all-round development.

73. (a)
- Central Board of Secondary Education also keeps organizing Prospective Resource Persons training programmes for the key resource persons.
- These Key Resource Persons, in turn, train other teachers of the schools affiliated to CBSE in various subjects through online as well as in-person training programmes organized by CBSE.

74. (a)
- The government has formed an expert committee for conducting a study on the origin and evolution of Indian culture dating back to around 12,000 years ago
- The 16-member committee will include K.N. Dikshit, chairman, Indian Archaeological Society, New Delhi and former Joint Director General, Archaeological Survey of India, among others.

75. (c)
- The Ministry of Tribal Affairs is the nodal department at central level and TRIFED is the nodal agency at national level
- Initiative targeting livelihood generation for tribal gatherers and transforming them into entrepreneurs
- Idea is to set-up tribal community owned Van Dhan Vikas Kendras (VDVKs) in predominantly forested tribal districts.
- A Kendra shall constitute of 15 tribal SHGs, each comprising of up to 20 tribal NTFP gatherers or artisans i.e. about 300 beneficiaries per Van Dhan Kendra.
- 100% Central Government Funded with TRIFED providing Rs. 15 lakhs for each 300 member Van Dhan Kendra.

76. (c)
- The Institute of Teaching and Research in Ayurveda Bill 2020 has been passed by Rajya Sabha The Bill was earlier passed in Lok Sabha
- This paves the way to establish a state-of-the-art Ayurvedic institution called the Institute of Teaching and Research in Ayurveda (ITRA) at Jamnagar, Gujarat, and to confer the status of Institution of National Importance (INI) to it.
- The ITRA is sought to be established by conglomerating the presently existing Ayurveda institutes at Gujarat Ayurved University campus Jamnagar. This is a cluster of highly reputed institutions
- ITRA will be the first institution with INI status in the AYUSH Sector, and this will enable the

institution to be independent and innovative in the matter deciding course content and pedagogy.

77. (b) • A Customized My Stamp on India's First Anti Satellite Missile (A-SAT) launch was released by Department of Posts on the occasion of Engineers Day

• Defence Research and Development Organisation (DRDO) successfully conducted an Anti-Satellite (A-SAT) missile test 'Mission Shakti' from Dr APJ Abdul Kalam Island in Odisha on 27th March 2019.

• A DRDO developed A-SAT Missile successfully engaged an Indian orbiting target satellite in Low Earth Orbit (LEO) in a 'Hit to Kill' mode.

78. (a) • The Union for the Protection of Plant Varieties is an international agreement, primarily looking at the rights of plant breeders.

• Though it offers limited rights to the farmers, the basic idea of subscribing to UPOV is to uphold commercial interests of the seed developers.

• India not joined UPOV. There is constant pressure on India from advanced countries to subscribe to UPOV, but India resisted due to the reason the farmers' interests far outweigh the breeders interests in India.

79. (c) • The 'Pradhan Mantri Garib Kalyan Package Insurance Scheme for Health Workers Fighting COVID-19' was announced on 30 March 2020 for a period of 90 days.

• This was extended for a further period of 90 days i.e. up to 25th Sept, 2020.

• The scheme has now been extended for another 180 days i.e. 6 months.

• There is no age limit for this scheme and individual enrolment is not required.

• The entire amount of premium for this scheme is being borne by the Ministry of Health and Family Welfare, Government of India.

80. (a) • Institute of National Importance (INI) is a status that may be conferred on a premier public higher education institution in India by an act of Parliament of India, an institution which "serves as a pivotal player in developing highly skilled personnel within the specified region of the country/state".

• Institutes of National Importance receive special recognition and funding from the government of India.

81. (a) • Union Minister applauded the launch of Global Initiative to Reduce Land Degradation and Coral Reef program at the G20 Environment Ministers meeting.

• The Global Initiative on Reducing Land Degradation aims to strengthen the implementation of existing frameworks to prevent, halt, and reverse land degradation within G20 member states and globally, taking into account possible implications on the achievement of other SDGs and adhering to the principle of doing no harm.

• The Global Coral Reef R&D Accelerator Platform is an innovative action-oriented initiative aimed at creating a global research and development (R&D) program to advance research, innovation and capacity building in all facets of coral reef conservation, restoration, and adaptation.

82. (c) • The Biotech-Krishi Innovation Science Application Network (Biotech-KISAN) programme focuses on taking innovative technologies to the farmers.

• Biotech-Krishi Innovation Science Application Network (Biotech-KISAN) is a Department of Biotechnology, Ministry of Science and Technology initiative that empowers farmers, especially women farmers.

• It aims to understand the problems of water; soil, seed and market faced by the farmers and provide simple solutions to them.

83. (b) • The Living Planet Report 2020, published by WWF after two years (WWF report published once every two years) has revealed a global species loss of 68 percent in less than 50 years (from 1970 to 2016) a catastrophic decline never seen before.

• The Living Planet Report is based on data from the Living Planet Index produced by the Zoological Society of London (ZSL).

• The index is statistically created from journal studies, online databases and government reports for 20,000 populations of 4,200 species of mammal, bird, reptile, amphibian and fish, or approximately 6 percent of the world's vertebrate species.

84. (b) • The Bengal tiger is found primarily in India, with smaller a population of them in Bangladesh, Nepal, Bhutan, China and Myanmar as well.

- 'Project Tiger' is a Centrally Sponsored Scheme of the Environment, Forests and Climate Change, providing funding support to tiger range States
- There are different species of tigers - Siberian tigers, Bengal tigers, Indochinese tigers, Malayan tigers and South China tigers.

85. (a)
- The programme is rolled out in specific Government hospitals, both in urban and rural areas.
- It gives assured, comprehensive and quality antenatal care, free of cost universally to all pregnant women on the 9th of every month. However
- It provides minimum package of services for the women in 2nd and 3rd trimesters of pregnancy and the 1st trimester is not included.

86. (b)
- India successfully test fired a new version of the surface-to-surface supersonic cruise missile BrahMos having a range of around 400 km from an integrated test range at Balasore in Odisha
- BrahMos surface-to-surface supersonic cruise missile featuring indigenous Booster, Airframe Section, propulsion system, power supply and many other major components.

87. (d)
- Union Minister for Social Justice and Empowerment-launched the Ambedkar Social Innovation and Incubation Mission (ASIIM) under Venture Capital Fund for SCs with a view to promoting innovation and enterprise among SC students studying in higher educational institutions.
- The Ministry has decided to launch ASIIM through the Venture Capital Fund for Scheduled Castes (VCFSC).
- Under named "Ambedkar Social Innovation Incubation Mission (ASIIM)" initiative, 1,000 SC youth would be identified in the next 4 years with start-up ideas through the Technology Business Incubators (TBIs) in various higher educational institutions.

88. (a)
- It is a flagship programme of Ministry of Education conceptualised and launched in IIT Delhi, with a vision of transformational change in rural development processes by leveraging knowledge institutions to help build the architecture of an Inclusive India.
- The Mission of Unnat Bharat Abhiyan is to enable higher educational institutions to work with the people of rural India in identifying development challenges and evolving appropriate solutions for accelerating sustainable growth
- Till date, a total of 13,760 villages have been adopted under Unnat Bharat Abhiyan

89. (c)
- NITI Aayog and Embassy of the Netherlands, signed a Statement of Intent (SoI) to support the decarbonization and energy transition agenda for accommodating cleaner and more energy.
- Through this collaboration, NITI Aayog and the Dutch embassy seek a strategic partnership to create a platform that enables a comprehensive collaboration among stakeholders
- The focus of the partnership is on co-creating innovative technological solutions by leveraging the expertise of the two entities.

90. (d)
- The Minister of Science & Technology launched CSIR Technologies for rural development under a joint initiative of Council of Scientific & Industrial Research (CSIR), Unnat Bharat Abhiyan (UBA), Indian Institute of Technology Delhi (IITD) and Vijnana Bharti (VIBHA).
- The event was organized through online platform on the occasion of CSIR-NISTADS 40th Foundation Day
- These technologies will now be disseminated to society through the Higher Education Institutional network of UBA and local chapters of VIBHA.
- CSIR- National Institute of Science, Technology and Development Studies (CSIR-NISTADS) is acting as a nodal CSIR Lab to establish linkages between CSIR laboratories, UBA, VIBHA, and stakeholders.

91. (a)
- India based Neutrino Observatory (INO) will observe neutrinos produced in the atmosphere of the Earth.
- This observation will tell us more about the properties of neutrino particles, whose main source is the Sun and the Earth's atmosphere.
- The neutrino detector will be a magnetized iron calorimeter, which will be the heaviest one made by any country.
- The site identified is in Bodi West Hills, in Theni district, Tamil Nadu.

92. (d)
- It is a traditional and ritualistic mural art being practised by local tribal women in the area of Hazaribagh district of Jharkhand.

- It is primarily being practised only in the district of Hazaribagh. However, in recent years, for promotional purposes, it has been seen in other parts of Jharkhand.
- It is prepared during local harvest and marriage seasons using local, naturally available soils of different colours in the area.
- It is traditionally painted on the walls of mud houses, they are now seen on other surfaces, too.
- Its style features a profusion of lines, dots, animal figures and plants, often representing religious iconography.

93. (b)
- A team of engineering students from IIT Bombay, NIT Srinagar and Islamic University of Science &Technology (IUST) have come up with a low-cost ventilator using locally available materials.
- The team has named the low-cost ventilator as •Ruhdaar•.

94. (c)
- The Asian Development Bank (ADB) has recently announced $1.5 billion loan (over Rs. 11,400 crore) to India for its fight against Covid-19 pandemic.
- The funding is part of the Covid-19 Active Response and Expenditure Support (CARES) Program.
- CARES programme will contribute directly to the improvement of access to health facilities and care, as well as social protection for more than 80 crore people, including families below the poverty line, farmers, healthcare workers, women, senior citizens, people with disabilities, low wage earners, and construction workers.
- The CARES Program is funded through the Covid-19 Pandemic Response Option (CPRO) under the ADB's Countercyclical Support Facility.

95. (b)
- On 15th August, 2020, the P.M announced that connectivity is to be taken up to the all more than 6 lakh villages (from the existing Gram Panchayat level) within 1000 days.
- This project will be implemented in a short span of 180 days and will be completed by 31.03.2021 at an approximate cost of Rs. 1,000 crore through CSC SPV
- This project will be executed by combined efforts of Department of Telecom which has already connected 1.5 lakh Gram Panchayats across India with optical fibre internet service, along with Ministry of Electronics & Information Technology and Common Service Centres.
- The Optical Fibre Village Connectivity project has been launched by Department of Telecommunications in order to achieve the dreams of Digital Gram
- It will be implemented by CSC e-Governance Services Ltd., an SPV of Ministry of Electronics & IT.

96. (a)
- The names of 12 scientists who received the country's highest science award Shanti Swarup Bhatnagar Prize for 2020 were announced during the foundation day of the Council for Scientific and Industrial Research (CSIR)
- The Shanti Swarup Bhatnagar Prize for Science and Technology (SSB) is a science award in India given annually by the Council of Scientific and Industrial Research (CSIR) for notable and outstanding research, applied or fundamental, in biology, chemistry, environmental science, engineering, mathematics, medicine and Physics.

97. (c)

Global Climate Risk Index :
- Published by Germanwatch.
- Analysis on the impacts of extreme weather events and associated socio-economic data.
- Published once in a year.
- Purpose: to contextualize ongoing climate policy debates - especially the international climate negotiations - looking at real-world impacts over the last year and the last 20 years.

98. (b)
- Vande Bharat Mission is the biggest evacuation exercise to bring back Indian citizens stranded abroad amidst the coronavirus-induced travel restrictions.
- It is also considered as the largest exercise to bring back Indian citizens since the evacuation of 177,000 from the Gulf region in the early 1990s at the start of hostilities between Iraq and Kuwait during the first Gulf War.
- Vande Bharat Express or Train 18 which is the India's semi-high speed intercity electric multiple unit train is different from Vande Bharat Mission.

99. (d)
- Nisargruna plant is a bio- methanization plant for digesting kitchen food waste and green vegetable wastes from agriculture markets to methane gas which can be used for cooking/ generating electricity or even for running biogas vehicles. This plant can digest animal waste from slaughter house also.
- It offers Zero garbage and Zero effluent and provides high quality manure and methane gas. Weed-free manure obtained from such waste has high nitrogen contents and acts as an excellent soil conditioner.
- The Department of Atomic Energy (DAE), Government of India, recently organized a two-day exhibition on DAE spin-off technologies for non-power applications at New Delhi.

100. (d)
- The Ministry of Labour and Employment is implementing the NCLP Scheme since 1988 for rehabilitation of child labourers.
- Under the NCLP, the children in the age group of 9-14 years are rescued/ withdrawn from work and enrolled in the NCLP Special Training Centres, where they are provided with bridge education, vocational training, mid-day meal, stipend, health care, etc. before being mainstreamed into formal education system.
- The children in the age group of 5-8 years are directly linked to the formal education system through a close coordination with the Samagra Shiksha Abhiyan.

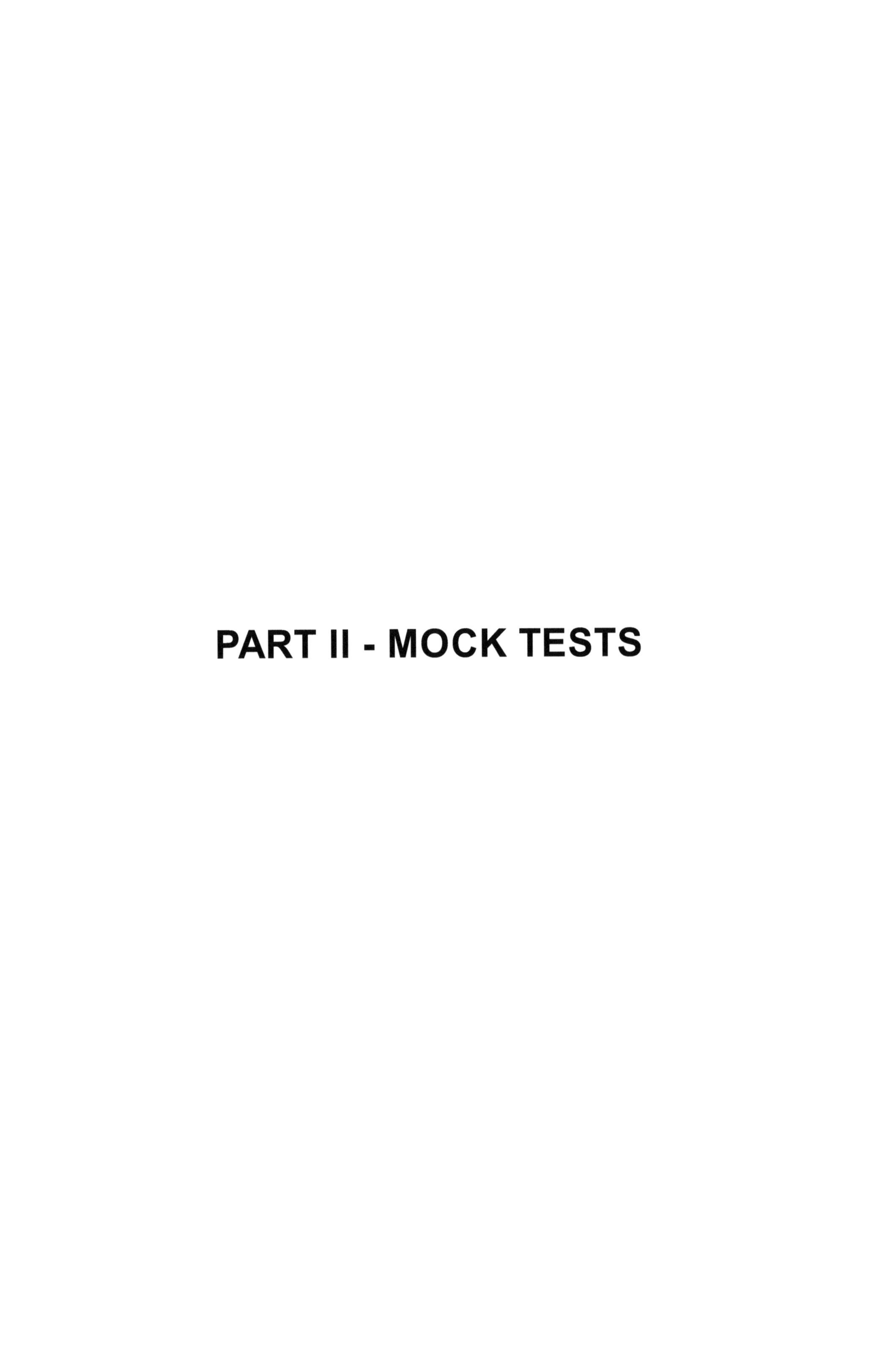

PART II - MOCK TESTS

1. Consider the following statements regarding Social Service League:

1. It was founded by Gopal Hari Deshmukh.

2. It was opened in Bombay with an aim to secure better conditions of life and work for masses.

3. It organized schools, libraries and cooperative societies.

Which of the statements given above is/are correct?

(a) 1 only   (b) 2 and 3 only

(c) 1 and 3 only   (d) 1, 2 and 3

2. Which of the following personality was not associated with Rahnumai Mazadayasnam Sabha?

(a) Dadabhai Naoroji   (b) K R Cama

(c) Bhikaji Cam   (d) S S Bengaleee

3. Consider the following statements regarding Bengal Partition, 1905:

1. Congress session of 1905 was held under the Presidentship of Dadabhai Naoroji.

2. Congress condemn the partition of Bengal and reactionary policies of British government.

3. Congress supported anti-partition and Swadeshi Movement of Bengal.

Which of the statements given above is/are correct?

(a) 1 and 2 only   (b) 2 and 3 only

(c) 3 only   (d) 1, 2 and 3

4. Which of the following statements is/are correct regarding Morley-Minto reforms?

1. Indians were allowed to participate in election of various legislative councils.

2. Separate electorates for Muslim for election to the central and provincial councils was established.

3. Expansion of Imperial Legislative Council and Provincial Legislative council.

Select the correct answer using the code given below:

(a) 2 only   (b) 1 and 3 only

(c) 2 and 3 only   (d) 1, 2 and 3

5. Consider the following statements regarding revolutionary movement in India:

1. Savarkar and his brother organised Mitra Mela in 1899 which merged with Abhinav Bharat in 1904.

2. Lala Lajpat Rai brought journal Punjabee having motto of self-help at any cost.

3. Ajit Singh organized Anjuman-i-Mohisban-i-Watan in Lahore with its journal, Bharat Mata.

Which of the statements given above is/are correct?

(a) 1 only   (b) 2 and 3 only

(c) 1 and 2 only   (d) 1, 2 and 3

6. Consider the following statements:

1. Backward castes are the communities other than SCs and STs who have suffered economical backwardness.

2. Implementation of Mandal Commission recommendation further aggravated the politics of backward classes.

Which of the statements given above is/are correct regarding backward caste politics?

(a) 1 only   (b) 2 only

(c) Both 1 and 2   (d) Neither 1 nor 2

7. Consider the following pairs:

(Jurisdiction)		(Description)
1. Original	:	Settles disputes between union and states and amongst the states
2. Appellate	:	Tries appeal from lower courts in criminal and constitutional cases
3. Advisory	:	Advises the President on matters of public importance and law

Which of the pairs given above is/are correctly matched?

(a) 2 only   (b) 1 and 3 only

(c) 2 and 3 only   (d) 1, 2 and 3

8. The Constitution establishes the Supreme Court as the protector of fundamental rights of the citizen on the one hand and interpreter of Constitution on the other through which of the following way?

1. Restoring fundamental rights by issuing writs.
2. Declaring the concerned law as unconstitutional and non-operational.

Select the correct answer using the code given below:

(a) 1 only   (b) 2 only

(c) Both 1 and 2   (d) Neither 1 nor 2

9. Through which of the following ways local self-government established during British government?

1. Establishment of local boards by Lord Ripon
2. Government of India Act 1909
3. Government of India Act 1919

Select the correct answer using the code given below:

(a) 1 and 2 only   (b) 2 and 3 only

(c) 3 only   (d) 1, 2 and 3

10. Consider the following statements:

1. State Election Commissioner is an independent officer and is not linked to the control of the Election Commission of India.
2. State Finance Commission (SFC) examines the financial position of the local governments in the State.
3. SFC would also review the distribution of revenues between the State and local governments on the one hand and between rural and urban local governments on the other.

Which of the statements given above is/are correct?

(a) 1 and 2 only   (b) 3 only

(c) 2 and 3 only   (d) 1, 2 and 3

11. Which of the following is **NOT** a part of the M1?

(a) Currency with public

(b) Demand deposit in all banks

(c) Other deposits with RBI

(d) Interbank deposits

12. Consider the following statements with respect to Payments Banks:

1. Payments Banks have witnessed remarkable success since its inception.

2. The main driver of the success is the increase in yield of the G-Secs in recent times.

Select the correct answer using the code below:

(a) 1 only   (b) 2 only

(c) Both 1 and 2   (d) Neither 1 nor 2

13. A reduction in per capita income of India can happen due to:

1. Heavy dependence on imports with sluggish imports.
2. Negative net income from abroad
3. Sliding GDP

Select the correct answer using the code below:

(a) 1 and 2 only   (b) 2 and 3 only

(c) 1 and 3 only   (d) 1, 2 and 3

14. Consider the following statements about Non-Banking Financial Companies (NBFCs):

1. RBI is the sole regulator of all the NBFCs.
2. Not all the NBFCs can collect public deposits.
3. NBFCs can also collect savings deposits.

Which of the statements given above is/are correct?

(a) 1 and 2 only   (b) 2 and 3 only

(c) 2 only   (d) 1, 2 and 3

15. With respect to Zero-Budget Natural Farming , consider the following statements:

1. It suits all crops in all agro-climatic zones.
2. It is a method of chemical-free agriculture drawing from traditional Indian practices.

Which of the statements given above is/are correct?

(a) 1 only   (b) 2 only

(c) Both 1 and 2   (d) Neither 1 nor 2

16. Which of the following is/are **not** the consequence of Ozone layer depletion:

1. Increased UV
2. eye cataracts
3. Bioaccumulation
4. Planktons are greatly affected
5. skin cancers
6. Harmful Algal Bloom

Select the correct answer using the code given below:

(a) 1, 2, 3 and 6 only   (b) 2, 4, 5 and 6 only

(c) 3 and 6 only   (d) 2, 4 and 6 only

17. With reference to Bharat Stage Emission Standards, consider the following statements:

    1. It introduced in the year 2010.
    2. They are based on European (EURO) emission standards.
    3. All vehicles will have to follow new standards (BS-VI) from 1st April, 2020.

    Which of the statements given above is/are correct?

    (a) 1 only
    (b) 1 and 2 only
    (c) 2 and 3 only
    (d) 1, 2 and 3

18. With reference to Salinity of Ocean, consider the following statements:

    1. More saline water freezes slower than lesser saline water.
    2. Variation in salinity causes ocean currents.
    3. Salinity decreases the density of sea water.

    Which of the following statements given above is/are **incorrect**?

    (a) 1 and 2 only
    (b) 3 only
    (c) 1 and 3 only
    (d) 1, 2 and 3

19. With reference to ocean current, consider the following statements:

    1. Temperature difference and salinity difference are the secondary forces.
    2. Deep water currents make up the other 90 per cent of the ocean water.

    Which of the statements given above is/are correct?

    (a) 1 only
    (b) 2 only
    (c) Both 1 and 2
    (d) Neither 1 nor 2

20. With reference to mountain building processes, consider the following statements:

    1. Mt.Fujiyama in Japan are examples of Fold mountains.
    2. Block mountains are created when large areas are broken and displaced vertically.
    3. Fold mountains have rugged relief and high conical peaks.

    Which of the statements given above is/are correct?

    (a) 1 and 3 only
    (b) 2 only
    (c) 1, 2 and 3
    (d) 2 and 3 only

21. All the Schemes of the Ministry of Women and Child Development, have been classified under which of the following umbrella schemes?

    1. Mission Poshan 2.0
    2. Mission Vatsalya
    3. Mission Shakti
    4. Mission Nirbhaya

    Select the correct answer using the code below:

    (a) 1 and 2 only
    (b) 2 and 3 only
    (c) 1, 2 and 3 only
    (d) 1, 2, 3 and 4

22. Consider the following statements about Pradhan Mantri YUVA (PM YUVA) Yojana:

    1. It is implemented by the Ministry of Skill Development and Entrepreneurship (MSDE).
    2. It is a pilot scheme, for creating an enabling ecosystem through entrepreneurship education and training.

    Which of the statements given above is/are correct?

    (a) 1 only
    (b) 2 only
    (c) Both 1 and 2
    (d) Neither 1 nor 2

23. Deendayal Antyodaya Yojana - National Rural Livelihoods Mission (DAY-NRLM) has been implemented by which of the following ministries?

    (a) Ministry of Rural Development
    (b) Ministry of Health and Family Welfare
    (c) Ministry of agriculture
    (d) Ministry of Social Justice and Empowerment

24. Consider the following statements:

    1. Ministry of Micro, Small and Medium Enterprises (MSME) is implementing the Prime Minister's Employment Generation Programme (PMEGP), which has the target to generate self-employment opportunities through establishment of micro enterprises for farm and non-farm sector.
    2. Ministry of Rural Development is implementing Skill development program through Small Industries Development Bank of India is a development financial institution (SIDBI) enabling a trainee to take Bank credit and start his/her own Micro-enterprise.

    Which of the statements given above is/are correct?

    (a) 1 only
    (b) 2 only
    (c) Both 1 and 2
    (d) Neither 1 nor 2

25. Consider the following statements about the Economic Empowerment of Women Entrepreneurs and Startups by Women:

1. It is implemented by the Ministry of Skill Development and Entrepreneurship (MSDE) in collaboration with the Ministry of Women and child development.

2. It is a central sectored scheme that has been implemented across India.

Which of the statements given above is/are correct?

(a) 1 only

(b) 2 only

(c) Both 1 and 2

(d) Neither 1 nor 2

26. Consider the following statements regarding The Quantum Key Distribution technology:

1. It uses the Quantum Communication technology which ensures the unconditional data security using the principles of the quantum mechanics on the basis of Laws of Physics.

2. This technology can be used with the conventional encryption systems.

3. The conventional cryptosystems are used for the data-encryption rely on complexity of the mathematical algorithms.

Which of the statements given above is/are correct?

(a) 1 and 3 only

(b) 3 only

(c) 2 and 3 only

(d) 1, 2 and 3

27. Consider the following statements regarding Indian Regional Navigation Satellite System (IRNSS):

1. NAVIC is an autonomous regional satellite navigation system which provides the accurate real-time positioning and timing services.

2. The satellite covers India and the region extending up to 1,500 km across it.

3. This system currently comprises of the constellation of seven satellites with two additional stand-by satellites on ground.

Which of the statements given above are correct?

(a) 1 and 3 only   (b) 1 and 2 only

(c) 2 and 3 only   (d) 1, 2 and 3

28. Consider the following statements regarding ARGOS:

1. ARGOS is a satellite-based system which is involved in the collecting, processing and disseminating the environmental data from a fixed and a mobile platform worldwide.

2. This makes the Argos more useful in geographically locating the data source from any location on the Earth using the Doppler Effect.

Which of the statements given above is/are correct?

(a) 1 only   (b) 2 only

(c) Both 1 and 2   (d) Neither 1 nor 2

29. Consider the following statements regarding OCEANSAT-3:

1. The mission seeks to provide the continuity of ocean colour data along with the improvements to enhance the operational services such as potential fishery zone and the primary productivity.

2. It is a global mission which has been configured to cover the global oceans and to provide a continuity of ocean colour data.

Which of the statements given above is/are **incorrect**?

(a) 1 only   (b) 2 only

(c) Both 1 and 2   (d) Neither 1 nor 2

30. Which of the statements given below is/are correct regarding 'Energy Swaraj Yatra'?

1. The "Energy Swaraj Yatra" bus runs on the wind energy.

2. The bus allows the occupant to perform all the daily activities such as bathing, cooking, sleeping, working, meeting and training.

Select the correct answer using the code given below:

(a) 1 only   (b) 2 only

(c) Both 1 and 2   (d) Neither 1 nor 2

31. Which of the following leaders accompanied Gandhi during Champaran Satyagrah?

1. Anugraha Narayan Sinha

2. Mahadeo Desai

3. Brijkishore Prasad

4. J B Kriplani

Select the correct answer using the code given below:

(a) 1, 2 and 3 only   (b) 3 and 4 only

(c) 2, 3 and 4 only   (d) 1, 2, 3 and 4

32. Hunter Committee was appointed for which of the following reason?

(a) Jallianwala bagh massacre

(b) Education reform

(c) To examine diarchy system of government

(d) Against Rowlatt act

33. Which of the following leaders wanted to expose the basic weakness of legislative council by entering into it?

1. Ajmal Khan

2. Vallabhbhai Patel

3. C R Das

4. M A Ansari

Select the correct answer using the code given below:

(a) 1, 2 and 3 only   (b) 3 and 4 only

(c) 1 and 3 only   (d) 1, 2, 3 and 4

34. In the context of Indian National Movement, Atmasakti, Sarathi and Bijoli were –

(a) Journals publishing articles extolling the self-sacrifice of revolutionaries.

(b) Revolutionary groups working outside the country.

(c) Journals published by moderates to educate the masses regarding the demands of Congress.

(d) Newspapers whose licences were cancelled during Bengal Partition.

35. Which of the following statements is/are correct regarding Lahore session?

1. Round Table conference was decided to be boycotted.

2. Aim of congress was declared to get Complete Independence.

Select the correct answer using the code given below:

(a) 1 only

(b) 2 only

(c) Both 1 and 2

(d) Neither 1 nor 2

36. Consider the following statements regarding tawarikh:

1. They were craftsmen living in the towns.

2. They worked for sultans in hope of rich rewards.

3. They advised ruler to preserve an ideal social order.

Which of the statements given above is/are correct?

(a) 1 only

(b) 2 and 3 only

(c) 1 and 3 only

(d) 1, 2 and 3

37. Consider the following statements:

1. The Lok Sabha and the State Legislative Assemblies are directly elected by the people.

2. The entire country is divided into territorial constituencies of roughly equal population.

Which of the statements given above is/are **incorrect?**

(a) 1 only   (b) 2 only

(c) Both 1 and 2   (d) Neither 1 nor 2

38. Which of the following is/are the powers of Rajya Sabha?

1. Approves constitutional amendments and suggest changes in money bills.

2. Exercise control over executive through asking questions, introducing motions and resolutions.

3. Establishes commissions and committees.

Select the correct answer using the code given below:

(a) 3 only   (b) 2 and 3 only

(c) 1 and 2 only   (d) 1, 2 and 3

39. Which of the following are the instruments of parliamentary control?

1. Deliberation and discussion

2. Approval and refusal of laws

3. Financial control

4. No confidence motion

Select the correct answer using the code given below:

(a) 1, 2 and 3 only

(b) 2, 3 and 4 only

(c) 3 and 4 only

(d) 1, 2, 3 and 4

40. Consider the following statements regarding parliamentary form of government:

    1. Guaranteeing universal adult franchise for all citizens.
    2. People directly play role in election of representatives.
    3. Candidates contest election irrespective of their social background except restriction imposed in Constitution.
    4. Representatives are accountable to the legislature.

    Which of the statements given above are correct?

    (a) 1 and 2 only   (b) 3 and 4 only
    (c) 2, 3 and 4 only   (d) 1, 2, 3 and 4

41. Consider the following statements regarding fundamental rights:

    1. Every citizen must be in a position to claim these rights.
    2. These rights must be binding to every authority that got power to make laws.
    3. It works as a guide to the independent Indian state to institute laws and policies.

    Which of the statements given above is/are correct?

    (a) 2 and 3 only   (b) 1 and 2 only
    (c) 3 only   (d) 1, 2 and 3

42. Consider the following statements with respect to Expense:

    1. This is the charge levied by the Asset Management Companies on the investors who invest through Mutual Funds / Exchange Traded Funds and similar instruments.
    2. For the recently launched Bharat Bond ETF, the expense ratio is slightly lower than that for Mutual Funds.

    Select the correct answer using the code below:

    (a) 1 only
    (b) 2 only
    (c) Both 1 and 2
    (d) Neither 1 nor 2

43. Philip Curve gives relation between which of the following two quantities?

    (a) Inflation and unemployment
    (b) Inflation and Bank Rate
    (c) Bond yield and unemployment
    (d) Repo rate and inflation

44. Consider the following statements about Repo Rate:

    1. It is the rate at which banks as well as NBFCs borrow from the RBI to meet their day-to-day asset-liability mismatches.
    2. Collateral security is required for such borrowings.
    3. The amount of such borrowings by the banks hovers around 5-10% of their annual total loans.

    Select the correct answer using the code below:

    (a) 1 and 2 only   (b) 2 and 3 only
    (c) 2 only   (d) 1, 2 and 3

45. Consider the following statements with respect to Payment Banks and Small Finance Banks:

    1. Both can accept deposits without restrictions.
    2. Both have to comply with the Priority Sector Lending criteria.
    3. Both need to have 25% branches in unbanked rural areas.

    Select the correct answer using the code below:

    (a) 1 and 2 only   (b) 1, 2 and 3
    (c) 1 and 3 only   (d) None of the above

46. Union Minister for MSME inaugurated 50 artisan-based SFURTI clusters, spread over 18 States.

    With reference to it consider the following statements about SFURTI:

    1. It is implemented by the Ministry of MSME.
    2. The focus is to organize traditional industries and artisans into clusters.

    Which of the statements given above is/are correct?

    (a) 1 only   (b) 2 only
    (c) Both 1 and 2   (d) Neither 1 nor 2

47. Companies have been selected for the prestigious National Technology Awards to be given by the Technology Development Board (TDB). With reference to it consider the following statements about Technology Development Board (TDB):

    1. It is a statutory body of Government of India functioning under Department of Science of Technology.
    2. It provides financial assistance only to the companies working for commercialization of indigenous technologies.

    Which of the statements given above is/are correct?

    (a) 1 only   (b) 2 only
    (c) Both 1 and 2   (d) Neither 1 nor 2

48. Recently a 100-day campaign called 'Catch the Rain' launched to promote water conservation in the country by which of the following organisations?

(a) Ministry of Environment

(b) Atal Bhujal Yojana

(c) National Water Mission

(d) NITI Aayog

49. Consider the following statements about Satellite Launch Vehicle PSLV-C51:

1. It launched Amazonia-1 of Brazil and 18 other foreign satellites.

2. Launch Vehicle PSLV-C51 is the first flight of PSLV in DL configuration having 4 strap on motors.

Which of the statements given above is/are correct?

(a) 1 only   (b) 2 only

(c) Both 1 and 2   (d) Neither 1 nor 2

50. Which of the following intervention are included under the Scheme of Fund for Regeneration of Traditional Industries (SFURTI)?

1. Procurement of new machineries

2. Creating raw material banks

3. Improvement of marketing Infrastructure

4. Improved skills and capacity development through training

Select the correct answer using the code below:

(a) 1, 2 and 3 only   (b) 1 and 3 only

(c) 1 and 2 only   (d) 1, 2, 3 and 4

51. With reference to World Environment Day, consider the following statements:

1. The theme of World Environment Day 2020 is 'Celebrating Biodiversity'—a concern that is both urgent and existential.

2. It is observed on the 10 May every year.

Which of the following statement above is/are correct?

(a) 1 only   (b) 2 only

(c) Both 1 and 2   (d) Neither 1 nor 2

52. Consider the following statements:

1. National Tiger Conservation Authority is a Constitutional body under the Ministry of Environment, Forests and Climate Change.

2. It was constituted under enabling provisions of the Environment Protection Act,1986.

Which of the statements given above is/are correct?

(a) 1 only   (b) 2 only

(c) Both 1 and 2   (d) Neither 1 nor 2

53. With reference to Plastic Pollution, consider the following statements:

1. India generates close to 26,000 tonnes of plastic a day and over 10,000 tonnes a day of plastic waste remains uncollected.

2. India's per capita plastic consumption of less than 11kg, is nearly a tenth of the United States of America (109 kg).

3. The plastic processing industry is estimated to grow to 22 million tonnes (MT) a year by 2020

Which of the following statements is/are correct?

(a) 1 only   (b) 1 and 2 only

(c) 2 and 3 only   (d) 1, 2 and 3

54. With reference to Homeostasis in Ecosystem, consider the following statements :

1. It is the maintenance of stable equilibrium, especially through physiological.

2. Cooling of your body through sweating processes is an example of Homeostasis.

Which of the statements given above is/are correct?

(a) 1 only   (b) 2 only

(c) Both 1 and 2   (d) Neither 1 nor 2

55. Which of the following results will be visible in Divergent plate Boundary?

1. Formation of Island arcs

2. Volcanic activity of fissure flow of basaltic magma.

3. Creation of new oceanic crust

Select the correct answer using the code given below:

(a) 2 and 3 only   (b) 1 and 3 only

(c) 3 only   (d) 1, 2 and 3

56. With respect to Internal structure of the earth, consider the following statements:

1. Core forms about 83 per cent of the earth's volume and holds 67% of the earth's mass.

2. Lithosphere includes the crust and the upper part of the mantle.

Which of the statements given above is/are correct?

(a) 1 only   (b) 2 only

(c) Both 1 and 2   (d) Neither 1 nor 2

57. Consider the following statements:

1. Professor Alfred Wegner of Germany was primarily a meteorologist.
2. Arthur Holmes in 1930s discussed the possibility of convection currents in the mantle.

Which of the statements given above is/are correct?

(a) 1 only
(b) 2 only
(c) Both 1 and 2
(d) Neither 1 nor 2

58. Consider the following statements:

1. The actual amount of the water vapour present in the atmosphere is known as the absolute humidity.
2. The specific humidity of saturated air increases rapidly with increasing temperature.

Which of the statements given above is/are correct?

(a) 1 only
(b) 2 only
(c) Both 1 and 2
(d) Neither 1 nor 2

59. Suez Canal connects which of the following two water bodies?

(a) Mediterranean Sea to Red Sea
(b) Mediterranean Sea to Black Sea
(c) Red Sea to Black Sea
(d) Red Sea to Caspian Sea

60. Zabarwan Mountain is situated between-

(a) The Pir Panjal and the Middle Himalayan Range
(b) The Pir Panjal and the Great Himalayan Range
(c) The Zanskar Range and the Great Himalayan Range
(d) The Pir Panjal and the Zanskar Range

61. Consider the following statements:

1. The artificial photosynthesis method was developed in order to capture excess carbon dioxide from the atmosphere.
2. This method harnesses the solar energy and converts the captured carbon dioxide into oxygen and water.

Which of the statements given above is/are correct?

(a) 1 only
(b) 2 only
(c) Both 1 and 2
(d) Neither 1 nor 2

62. Which of the following statements are correct regarding Autism?

1. It is a developmental disorder which is characterized by difficulties of social interaction and communication.
2. The condition is also characterised by a restricted and repetitive behaviour.
3. This disorder is associated with the combination of genetic and environmental factors.

Select the correct answer using the code given below:

(a) 1 and 3 only
(b) 1 and 2 only
(c) 2 and 3 only
(d) 1, 2 and 3

63. Consider the following statements regarding RH-560:

1. The rocket was launched in order to study "attitudinal variations" in the neutral winds and plasma dynamics.
2. ISRO had started launching the indigenously made sounding rockets from the year 1965.

Which of the statements given above is/are correct?

(a) 1 only
(b) 2 only
(c) Both 1 and 2
(d) Neither 1 nor 2

64. Consider the following statements:

1. Early atmosphere composed of Hydrogen and Helium and these were destroyed due to the impact of solar winds.
2. The process of Degassing is responsible for the formation of present atmosphere.

Which of the statements given above is/are **incorrect**?

(a) 1 only
(b) 2 only
(c) Both 1 and 2
(d) Neither 1 nor 2

65. Consider the following statements regarding Nuclear DNA (Deoxyribonucleic Acid) and Mitochondrial DNA (Deoxyribonucleic Acid):

1. Both Nuclear DNA and mitochondrial DNA are inherited from mother and father.
2. Both Nuclear DNA and Mitochondrial DNA contain 46 chromosomes each.
3. Nuclear DNA is responsible for genetic make-up, whereas Mitochondrial DNA is responsible for metabolic activities.

Which of the statements given above is/are **incorrect**?

(a) 3 only
(b) 1 and 2 only
(c) 2 and 3 only
(d) 1, 2 and 3

66. Consider the following statements regarding Lead Poisoning:

1. Lead is a heavy metal with high toxicity.
2. Lead in its organic form could be absorbed through the skin upon application of cosmetics.
3. Lead exposure can make the body susceptible to anaemia as it prevents the formation of haemoglobin.

Which of the statements given above is/are correct?

(a) 1 and 2 only   (b) 1, 2 and 3

(c) 3 only   (d) 2 and 3 only

67. Which of the following statements is/are the feature of Indian secularism?

1. Indian state is not ruled by any particular religious group but can support to any religion.
2. Government offices like courts, police stations, government schools and offices do not promote any one religion.

Select the correct answer using the code given below:

(a) 1 only   (b) 2 only

(c) Both 1 and 2   (d) Neither 1 nor 2

68. Constitution of India has recognized right to water as –

1. Fundamental rights
2. Civil rights
3. Legal rights

Select the correct answer using the code given below:

(a) 1 only   (b) 1 and 3 only

(c) 2 and 3 only   (d) 3 only

69. Horn of Africa comprises which of the following countries?

1. Djibouti
2. Eritrea
3. Ethiopia
4. Somalia

Select the correct answer using the code given below:

(a) 2 and 4 only

(b) 1, 3 and 4 only

(c) 2 and 3 only

(d) 1, 2, 3 and 4

70. Which of the following pair is/are correctly matched?

	(River)		(Source)
1.	Chenab	:	spring at Verinag
2.	Satluj	:	Mansarovar lake
3.	Beas	:	Kullu hills

Select the correct answer using the code given below:

(a) 1 and 2 only

(b) 2 and 3 only

(c) 1 and 3 only

(d) 2 only

71. Consider the following statements about Global Bio-India-2021:

1. It showcase the strength and opportunities of the India's biotechnology sector at both national level and to the global community.
2. It is co-organised by the Department of Biotechnology, Ministry of Science & Technology, Government of India along with NITI Aayog.

Which of the statements given above is/are correct?

(a) 1 only   (b) 2 only

(c) Both 1 and 2   (d) Neither 1 nor 2

72. Consider the following statements about Land Ports Authority of India (LPAI):

1. LPAI for the crucial role taken in facilitating safe and seamless cross-border movement of trade and passengers through land ports.
2. The Land Ports Authority of India or LPAI is a statutory body.
3. It works under the Ministry of Home Affairs, Government of India.

Which of the statements given above is/are correct?

(a) 1 and 2 only   (b) 1 only

(c) 1 and 3 only   (d) 1, 2 and 3

73. Consider the following statements about Association of Biotechnology Led Enterprises (ABLE):

1. It is an autonomous body set up by Department of Biotechnology (DBT).
2. It is an exclusive forum to represent the Indian Biotechnology Sector only.

Which of the statements given above is/are correct?

(a) 1 only   (b) 2 only

(c) Both 1 and 2   (d) Neither 1 nor 2

74. A professional training programmes inaugurated on the occasion of the anniversary of the Central Sector Scheme titled 'Formation and Promotion of 10,000 Farmer Produce Organizations (FPOs)'. With reference to it consider the following statements:

1. In each district there should be an FPO which acts as catalyst for institutional infrastructure.

2. FPOs are already being registered in the all the UTs and States of India.

Which of the statements given above is/are correct?

(a) 1 only   (b) 2 only

(c) Both 1 and 2   (d) Neither 1 nor 2

75. Consider the following statements about Biotechnology Industry Research Assistance Council (BIRAC) :

1. It is a not-for-profit Public Sector Enterprise, set up by Department of Biotechnology (DBT).

2. It is an industry-academia interface and implements its mandate through a wide range of impact initiatives.

Which of the statements given above is/are correct?

(a) 1 only   (b) 2 only

(c) Both 1 and 2   (d) Neither 1 nor 2

76. Consider the following pairs:

(Architecture)		(Description)
1. Masji-i-jami	:	Prayer place
2. Khutba	:	Prayers
3. Qibla	:	Reading namaz facing west

Which of the pairs given above is/are correct?

(a) 1 and 3 only   (b) 2 only

(c) 2 and 3 only   (d) 1, 2 and 3

77. Which of the following features of Buddhist sculptures are associated with Mathura school of art?

1. Large images are carved with boldness.

2. Faces are round and smiling.

3. Sculptural volume is reduced by relaxing flesh.

4. Garments are clearly visible and covers left shoulder.

Select the correct answer using the code given below:

(a) 1 and 2 only   (b) 2 and 3 only

(c) 3 and 4 only   (d) 1, 2, 3 and 4

78. Consider the following types of shikhara in Nagara style temple architecture:

1. Rekha Prasad type is square at base whose walls slope inward till the top point.

2. Phamsana slope upwards on a straight incline.

3. Valabhi is square at base and roof rises into a vaulted chamber.

Which of the statements given above is/are correct?

(a) 1 and 2 only   (b) 2 and 3 only

(c) 3 only   (d) 1, 2 and 3

79. Consider the following pairs:

(Title)		(Office)
1. Sandhi-vigrahika	:	Chief judicial officer
2. Kumar Amatya	:	Minister
3. Nagar-Shreshthi	:	Merchant or chief banker
4. Sarthavaha	:	Chief craftsman

Which of the following pairs is/are correct?

(a) 1 only   (b) 2 and 3 only

(c) 1, 2 and 3 only   (d) 2, 3 and 4 only

80. Consider the following statements:

1. The first plant to colonize an area is called the pioneer community.

2. The final stage of succession is called the climax community.

Which of the statements given above is/are correct?

(a) 1 only   (b) 2 only

(c) Neither 1 nor 2   (d) Both 1 and 2

81. With reference to Ecological pyramid, consider the following statements:

1. Pyramid of Biomass represents the total number of individuals of different species (population) at each trophic level.

2. A pyramid of numbers for the aquatic ecosystem is inverted form.

Which of the statements given above is/are correct?

(a) 1 only   (b) 2 only

(c) Both 1 and 2   (d) Neither 1 nor 2

82. The Nagzira Wildlife Sanctuary (NWS) is located in which state?

(a) Maharashtra   (b) Himachal Pradesh

(c) Jammu & Kashmir   (d) Nagaland

83. Which of the following sources emits Nitrogen Oxides into the atmosphere?

1. Thermal power plants
2. Industries
3. Vehicular emissions

Select the correct answer using the code below:

(a) 1 and 2 only   (b) 2 and 3 only

(c) 3 only   (d) 1, 2 and 3

84. Which of the following are part of UNESCO's World Network of Biosphere Reserves?

1. Nilgiri Biosphere Reserve
2. Manas Biosphere Reserve
3. Nokrek Biosphere Reserve
4. Kachchh Biosphere Reserve
5. Great Nicobar Biosphere Reserve

Select the correct answer using the code below:

(a) 1, 2 and 5 only   (b) 1, 3 and 5 only

(c) 1, 2, 3 and 4 only   (d) 1, 3, 4 and 5 only

85. With reference to cloud seeding, consider the following statements:

1. It is a kind of a weather modification technology to create artificial rainfall.
2. The Pune-based Indian Institute of Tropical Meteorology has been carrying out cloud seeding experiments for several years now.

Which of the statements given above is/are correct?

(a) 1 only   (b) 2 only

(c) Neither 1 nor 2   (d) Both 1 and 2

86. With reference to Seismic wave, consider the following statements:

1. Love wave is the fastest surface wave and moves the ground from side-to-side.
2. Primary wave is least destructive among the earthquake waves.
3. Most of the shaking felt from an earthquake is due to the Rayleigh wave.

Which of the statements given above is/are correct?

(a) 1 and 3 only   (b) 2 and 3 only

(c) 1, 2 and 3   (d) 2 only

87. Consider the following statements:

1. The most popular argument regarding the origin of the universe is the Nebular Hypothesis theory.
2. The formation of moon, as a satellite of the earth, is an outcome of 'giant impact'

Which of the statement given above is/are correct?

(a) 1 only   (b) 2 only

(c) Both 1 and 2   (d) Neither 1 nor 2

88. Find the correct statements about NBFCs in India:

1. There is no separate ombudsman for NBFCs
2. An NBFC that does not fall under any other regulator is regulated by RBI.
3. Prompt Corrective Action is also applicable for the NBFCs
4. Deposits with the NBFCs are not insured.

Select the correct answer using the code below:

(a) 1, 2 and 3 only   (b) 2, 3 and 4 only

(c) 1, 2 and 4 only   (d) 2 and 4 only

89. Which of the following indices is/are released as part of the Human Development Index?

1. Multidimensional Poverty Index (
2. Gender Development Index (
3. Inequality-Adjusted Human Development Index (
4. Gender Inequality Index

Select the correct answer using the code below:

(a) 1, 2 and 3 only   (b) 2, 3 and 4 only

(c) 1, 2, 3 and 4   (d) 1 and 3 only

90. The Enhanced Access and Service Excellence (EASE) was released by which of the following ?

(a) Department of Financial Services.

(b) Bimal Jalan Committee

(c) Reserve Bank of India

(d) National Payment Corporation of India (

91. Consider the following statements with respect to the All India Financial Institutions:

1. RBI is the regulator over all the All India Financial Institutions.
2. BASEL Norms are not applicable for All India Financial Institutions.

Select the correct answer using the code below:

(a) 1 only   (b) 2 only

(c) Both 1 and 2   (d) Neither 1 nor 2

92. Electric bulbs are filled with Nitrogen and Argon gases in order to-
1. Increase the illumination of the bulb.
2. Prolong the life of filament.
3. Increase the heat radiation of the filament.
4. Reduce the power consumption of the bulb.

Select the correct answer using the code given below:

(a) 1 and 4 only   (b) 2 and 4 only
(c) 1, 2 and 3 only   (d) 2 only

93. E-waste is used in various industries as a cheap source of rich metals. Which of the following metals can be obtained through the recycling of e-waste?
1. Platinum
2. Lithium
3. Gold
4. Thorium
5. Cobalt

Select the correct answer using the code given below:

(a) 1, 3, 4 and 5 only   (b) 1, 2, 3, 4 and 5
(c) 1, 2 and 4 only   (d) 2, 3 and 5 only

94. Which of the following statements is/are the examples of Colloids around us?
1. The blue colour of the sky
2. Fog, mist and rain
3. Formation of River deltas

Select the correct answer using the code given below:

(a) 1 only   (b) 1 and 2 only
(c) 2 and 3 only   (d) 1, 2 and 3

95. Consider the following statements regarding enriched uranium:
1. The natural uranium obtained constitutes predominantly U-238.
2. Centrifuges enrich the content of U-235.
3. The primary purpose of enrichment of uranium i.e., increasing U-235 is to manufacture nuclear weapons.

Which of the statements given above is/are correct?

(a) 1 and 2 only   (b) 2 only
(c) 2 and 3 only   (d) 1, 2 and 3

96. Consider the following statements about Deep-tech startup:
1. It is a high level technology and innovation that has the potential to transform the world, and has a deep impact on society.
2. It is disruptive technologies based on scientific discoveries, engineering, mathematics, physics and medicine.

Which of the statements given above is/are correct?

(a) 1 only   (b) 2 only
(c) Both 1 and 2   (d) Neither 1 nor 2

97. Consider the following statements about DakPay Payment app:
1. It has been launched by the department of Posts (DoP) and India Post Payments Bank (IPPB).
2. It provides interoperable banking services to the customers with any bank in the country.

Which of the statements given above is/are correct?

(a) 1 only   (b) 2 only
(c) Both 1 and 2   (d) Neither 1 nor 2

98. Which of the following is/are the major initiatives of AIM?
1. Atal Tinkering Labs
2. Atal Incubation Centers
3. Atal New India Challenges
4. Mentor India Campaign
5. ARISE

Select the correct answer using the code below:

(a) 1 and 3 only   (b) 1, 2, 3 and 4 only
(c) 2, 3 and 5 only   (d) 1, 2, 3, 4 and 5

99. The term Quality, Uniqueness, Innovation, Eco-friendliness and Thrill (QUIET) has been associated with which of the following sector:

(a) Indian Toys
(b) Handicraft Industry
(c) The Khadi and Village Industries Commission
(d) None of the above

100. Atal Innovation Mission (AIM), NITI Aayog partners with MathWorks- to strengthen the Deep-tech startup ecosystem of India. With reference to it consider the following statements:
1. The startups supported by AIM, will get access to steps of the art MathWorks tools.
2. MathWorks is the leading developer of mathematical computing software.

Which of the statements given above is/are correct?

(a) 1 only
(b) 2 only
(c) Both 1 and 2
(d) Neither 1 nor 2

ANSWER KEY

1. (b)	**2.** (c)	**3.** (c)	**4.** (b)	**5.** (d)	**6.** (b)	**7.** (b)	**8.** (c)	**9.** (a)	**10.** (d)
11. (d)	**12.** (d)	**13.** (d)	**14.** (c)	**15.** (c)	**16.** (c)	**17.** (c)	**18.** (b)	**19.** (c)	**20.** (d)
21. (c)	**22.** (c)	**23.** (a)	**24.** (d)	**25.** (d)	**26.** (a)	**27.** (d)	**28.** (c)	**29.** (d)	**30.** (b)
31. (d)	**32.** (a)	**33.** (c)	**34.** (a)	**35.** (c)	**36.** (b)	**37.** (d)	**38.** (c)	**39.** (d)	**40.** (a)
41. (b)	**42.** (a)	**43.** (a)	**44.** (c)	**45.** (d)	**46.** (c)	**47.** (a)	**48.** (c)	**49.** (a)	**50.** (d)
51. (a)	**52.** (d)	**53.** (d)	**54.** (c)	**55.** (a)	**56.** (b)	**57.** (c)	**58.** (c)	**59.** (a)	**60.** (b)
61. (a)	**62.** (d)	**63.** (c)	**64.** (d)	**65.** (b)	**66.** (b)	**67.** (b)	**68.** (a)	**69.** (d)	**70.** (d)
71. (a)	**72.** (d)	**73.** (b)	**74.** (d)	**75.** (c)	**76.** (a)	**77.** (d)	**78.** (a)	**79.** (b)	**80.** (d)
81. (d)	**82.** (a)	**83.** (d)	**84.** (b)	**85.** (d)	**86.** (c)	**87.** (b)	**88.** (d)	**89.** (c)	**90.** (a)
91. (a)	**92.** (d)	**93.** (b)	**94.** (d)	**95.** (a)	**96.** (c)	**97.** (c)	**98.** (d)	**99.** (a)	**100.** (c)

EXPLANATION

1. b **Social Service League:** A follower of Gokhale, Narayan Malhar Joshi founded the Social Service League in Bombay with an aim to secure for the masses better and reasonable conditions of life and work. They organised many schools, libraries, reading rooms, day nurseries and cooperative societies. Their activities also included police court agents' work, legal aid and advice to the poor and illiterate, excursions for slum dwellers, facilities for gymnasia and theatrical performances, sanitary work, medical relief and boys' clubs and scout corps. Joshi also founded the All India Trade Union Congress (1920).

2. c The Rahnumai Mazdayasnan Sabha (Religious Reform Association) was founded in 1851 by a group of Englisheducated Parsis for the "regeneration of the social conditions of the Parsis and the restoration of the Zoroastrian religion to its pristine purity". The movement had Naoroji Furdonji, Dadabhai Naoroji, K.R. Cama and S.S. Bengalee as its leaders.

3. c The Indian National Congress, meeting in 1905 under the presidentship of Gokhale, resolved to (i) condemn the partition of Bengal and the reactionary policies of Curzon, and (ii) support the anti-partition and Swadeshi Movement of Bengal.

4. b
- The elective principle was recognised for the nonofficial membership of the councils in India. Indians were allowed to participate in the election of various legislative councils, though on the basis of class and community.
- For the first time, separate electorates for Muslims for election to the central council was established—a most detrimental step for India.
- The number of elected members in the Imperial Legislative Council and the Provincial Legislative Councils was increased. In the provincial councils, non-official majority was introduced, but since some of these non-officials were nominated and not elected, the overall non-elected majority remained.

5. d
- Savarkar and his brother organised Mitra Mela, a secret society, in 1899 which merged with Abhinav Bharat (after Mazzinni's 'Young Italy') in 1904.
- The Punjab extremism was fuelled by issues such as frequent famines coupled with rise in land revenue and irrigation tax, practice of 'begar' by zamindars and by the events in Bengal.
- Among those active here were Lala Lajpat Rai who brought out Punjabee (with its motto of self-help at any cost) and Ajit Singh (Bhagat

Singh's uncle) who organised the extremist Anjuman-i-Mohisban-i-Watan in Lahore with its journal, Bharat Mata.

6. b One long-term development of this period was the rise of Other Backward Classes as a political force. This refers to the administrative category 'Other Backward Classes'. These are communities other than SC and ST who suffer from educational and social backwardness. These are also referred to as 'backward castes'. The decision of the National Front government to implement the recommendations of the Mandal Commission further helped in shaping the politics of 'Other Backward Classes'.

7. b • **Original jurisdiction:** Settles disputes between Union and States and amongst States.

  • **Appellate:** Tries appeals from lower courts in Civil, Criminal and Constitutional cases

  • **Advisory:** Advises the President on matters of public importance and law

  • **Writ:** Can issue writs of Habeas Corpus, Mandamus, Prohibition, Certiorari and Quo warranto to protect the Fundamental Rights of the individual.

8. c The Constitution provides two ways in which the Supreme Court can remedy the violation of rights.

  • First it can restore fundamental rights by issuing writs of Habeas Corpus; mandamus etc. (article 32). The High Courts also have the power to issue such writs (article 226).

  • Secondly, the Supreme Court can declare the concerned law as unconstitutional and therefore non-operational (article 13).

Together these two provisions of the Constitution establish the Supreme Court as the protector of fundamental rights of the citizen on the one hand and interpreter of Constitution on the other. The second of the two ways mentioned above involves judicial review.

9. a In modern times, elected local government bodies were created after 1882. Lord Rippon, who was the Viceroy of India at that time, took the initiative in creating these bodies. They were called the local boards. However, due to slow progress in this regard, the Indian National Congress urged the government to take necessary steps to make all local bodies more effective. Following the Government of India Act 1919, village panchayats were established in a number of provinces. This trend continued after the Government of India Act of 1935.

10. d The State government is required to appoint a State Election Commissioner who would be responsible for conducting elections to the Panchayati Raj institutions. However, the State Election Commissioner is an independent officer and is not linked to nor is this officer under the control of the Election Commission of India.

The State government is also required to appoint a State Finance Commission once in five years. This Commission would examine the financial position of the local governments in the State. It would also review the distribution of revenues between the State and local governments on the one hand and between rural and urban local governments on the other.

11. d M1 excludes India's deposits with IMF, World bank, Foreign Government etc and Interbank deposits

12. d • Payments Banks are considered as a failure till now, because of their flawed business model.

  • There is sharp fall in the yields of G-secs in recent times, and hence, the margins of the Payments Banks were squeezed. They have to deposit 75% of their deposits in Government Securities.

13. d Per capita income = NNP at factor cost/Divided by population

NNP = GDP – Depreciation + Net income from abroad. As the variables involved in the formula vary, the per capita income change accordingly.

Heavy dependence on imports with sluggish imports results in depreciation of Rupee and further decreases the NNP.

14. c • All NBFCs are not regulated by Reserve Bank of India. To explain further, Non-Banking Financial Companies are into several domains like asset management, insurance sector, microfinance etc. RBI regulates only some of them, for example NBFC-MFIs. Some of them are regulated by SEBI. So, Non-Banking Financial Companies are regulated by various financial sector regulators.

  • Only specific NBFCs are mandated to collect public deposits. Collecting the public deposits involves risk and hence all are not allowed.

  • Under no circumstances, NBFCs can collect savings deposits. Only the banks can collect savings deposits.

15. c • Zero budget natural farming is a method of chemical-free agriculture drawing from traditional Indian practices.

- It was originally promoted by agriculturist Subhash Palekar, who developed it in the mid-1990s as an alternative to the Green Revolution's methods that are driven by chemical fertilizers and pesticides and intensive irrigation.

- It is a unique model that relies on Agro-ecology.

- It aims to bring down the cost of production to nearly zero and return to a pre-green revolution style of farming.

- It claims that there is no need for expensive inputs such as fertilisers, pesticides and intensive irrigation.

Benefits of ZBNF

- The ZBNF method promotes soil aeration, minimal watering, intercropping, bunds and topsoil mulching and discourages intensive irrigation and deep ploughing.

- It suits all crops in all agro-climatic zones.

- Citing the benefits of ZBNF, in June 2018, Andhra Pradesh rolled out an ambitious plan to become India's first State to practise 100% natural farming by 2024.

16. c Ozone layer depletion causes increased UV radiation levels at the Earth's surface, which is damaging to human health.

Negative effects include increases in certain types of skin cancers, eye cataracts and immune deficiency disorders. UV radiation also affects terrestrial and aquatic ecosystems, altering growth, food chains and biochemical cycles. Aquatic life just below the water's surface, the basis of the food chain, is particularly adversely affected by high UV levels. UV rays also affect plant growth, reducing agricultural productivity.

17. c **Introduced in the year 2000:**

- They are set by the Central Pollution Control Board under the Ministry of Environment and Climate Change.

- **Objective:** To keep air pollutants emitted by the internal combustion engine of vehicles under control.

- They are based on European (EURO) emission standards.

- Bharat Stage (BS) emission norms were first brought into effect in 2000 under the head "India 2000". This was followed by BS2 in 2001 and BS3 in 2005.

- However, the emission norms were made more stringent only with the enforcement of Bharat Stage IV (BS4). Thereafter, the Government of India skipped the implementation of BS5 in 2016 and decided to introduce Bharat Stage VI (BS6) in 2020 instead.

18. b The oceanic salinity affects the life of marine plants, marine animals and also the physical properties of oceans like temperature, pressure, density, waves, currents, etc.

More saline water freezes slower than lesser saline water.

i. The boiling point of saline water is higher than fresh water.

ii. Salinity increases the density of sea water.

iii. Evaporation is lower over more saline water.

iv. Variation in salinity causes ocean currents.

19. c **Secondary Forces Responsible For Ocean Currents :**

- Temperature difference and salinity difference are the secondary forces.

- Differences in water density affect vertical mobility of ocean currents (vertical currents).

- Water with high salinity is denser than water with low salinity and in the same way cold water is denser than warm water.

Based on depth

The ocean currents may be classified based on their depth as surface currents and deep water currents:

- Surface currents constitute about 10 per cent of all the water in the ocean, these waters are the upper 400 m of the ocean;

- Deep water currents make up the other 90 per cent of the ocean water. These waters move around the ocean basins due to variations in the density and gravity.

- Deep waters sink into the deep ocean basins at high latitudes, where the temperatures are cold enough to cause the density to increase.

20. d - Volcanic Mountains are formed due to volcanic activity. Mt.Kilimanjaro in Africa and Mt.Fujiyama in Japan are examples of such mountains.

- The Himalayan Mountains and the Alps are young fold mountains with rugged relief and high conical peaks. The Aravali range in India is one of the oldest fold mountain systems in the world.

- The range has considerably worn down due to the processes of erosion. The Appalachians in North America and the Ural mountains in Russia have rounded features and low elevation. They are very old fold mountains.

- Block Mountains are created when large areas are broken and displaced vertically. The uplifted blocks are termed as horsts and the lowered blocks are called graben. The Rhine valley and the Vosges Mountain in Europe are examples of such mountain systems.

21. c • For effective implementation of various schemes and programmes of the Ministry of Women and Child Development, all major schemes of the Ministry have been classified under 3 umbrella schemes viz.

All the Schemes of the Ministry of Women and Child Development, have been classified under which of the above umbrella schemes

- **Mission Poshan 2.0**
- **Mission Vatsalya**
- **Mission Shakti**

All Major Schemes of WCD Ministry classified under 3 Umbrella Schemes

- The prime objective of the Ministry is to address gaps in State action for women and children and to promote inter-ministerial and inter-sectoral convergence to create gender equitable and child centred legislation, policies and programmes.

- Women are key agents for achieving transformational economic, environmental and social changes required for sustainable development. To achieve this objective, continuation of existing schemes with suitable modifications is inevitable and necessary which can be achieved through **Mission Shakti.**

- Children are the future of our country. Well-being of children is essential for the country's development as they contribute to the future human resource of the country.

- To strengthen nutritional content, delivery, outreach, and outcomes, Government is merging the Supplementary Nutrition Programme and Poshan Abhiyan to launch **Mission POSHAN 2.0.**

- The Ministry of Women and Child Development has taken many initiatives to ensure safety and well-being of children. **Mission VATSALYA** will ensure the same going ahead.

22. c • The Ministry of Skill Development and Entrepreneurship (MSDE) is implementing Pradhan Mantri YUVA (PM YUVA) Yojana, a pilot scheme, for creating an enabling ecosystem through entrepreneurship education, training, advocacy and easy access to entrepreneurship network.

- The scheme covers 10 States and 2 Union Territories (viz. i.e. Uttar Pradesh, Uttarakhand, Bihar, West Bengal, Assam, Meghalaya, Maharashtra, Tamil Nadu, Telangana, Kerala, Delhi and Puducherry).

23. a • Ministry of Rural Development is also implementing Deendayal Antyodaya Yojana - National Rural Livelihoods Mission (DAY-NRLM) which aims at eliminating rural poverty through promotion of multiple livelihoods for each rural poor household.

- Out of the SHG beneficiaries of 60,18,886 covered under NRLM Pan-India, 5,54,200 are from West Bengal (Darjeeling GT Area including Kalimpong – 5315 and Uttar Darjeeling – 7,898).

- Under the Sub-scheme i.e. Start-up Village Entrepreneurship Programme (SVEP) covered under DAY-NRLM, a total of 194,144 enterprises have been set-up

24. d • Ministry of Micro, Small and Medium Enterprises (MSME) is implementing the Prime Minister's Employment Generation Programme (PMEGP), which has the target to generate self-employment opportunities through establishment of micro enterprises for non-farm sector.

- Furthermore, Ministry of Rural Development is implementing Skill development program through Rural Self Employment Training Institutes (RSETIs) enabling a trainee to take Bank credit and start his/her own Micro-enterprise.

- RSETIs is a Bank led initiative of Ministry of Rural Development, set up with dedicated infrastructure in each district of the country sponsored, managed and run by Banks with active co-operation from the Government of India and State Government.

- Presently 585 RSETIs are functional in 27 states (except Goa) and 6 UTs (except Delhi, Chandigarh and Daman & Diu).

- The scheme is applicable to all the categories including women. Any unemployed youth in the age group of 18-45 years, irrespective of caste, creed, religion, gender and economic status, having aptitude to take up self-employment or wage employment and having some basic knowledge in the related field can undergo training under RSETI.

25. d
- To encourage women entrepreneurship within the Country, Ministry of Skill Development and Entrepreneurship (MSDE) is implementing the pilot project, 'Economic Empowerment of Women Entrepreneurs and Startups by Women' in collaboration with Deutsche Gesellschaftfür Internationale Zusammenarbeit (GIZ) Germany.
- The project pilots incubation and acceleration programmes for women micro entrepreneurs to start new businesses and scale up existing enterprises in Assam, Rajasthan and Telangana.
- The project has the target to pilot the incubation programme with 250 women and the acceleration programme with 100 women.
- The first cohort of the support programme ended in April-May, 2020 and the second cohort has commenced in July, 2020.

26. a The Quantum Key Distribution technology uses the Quantum Communication technology which ensures the unconditional data security using the principles of the quantum mechanics on the basis of Laws of Physics. This technology cannot be used with the conventional encryption systems. The conventional cryptosystems are used for the data-encryption rely on complexity of the mathematical algorithms. Quantum Cryptography is the future-proof because no future advancements in computational power can break the quantum-cryptosystem.

Recently ISRO's demonstration of the Free Space Quantum Communication includes the live video conferencing using the quantum-key-encrypted signals. It is a major milestone to achieve the unconditionally secured satellite data communication using the quantum technologies.

27. d Indian Regional Navigation Satellite System (IRNSS) or NAVIC - NAVIC is an autonomous regional satellite navigation system which provides the accurate real-time positioning and timing services. The satellite covers India and the region extending up to 1,500 km across it. The extended service area of the satellite lies in between primary service area and the rectangle area which is enclosed by 30th parallel south to 50th parallel north and 30th meridian east to 130th meridian east. This system currently comprises of the constellation of seven satellites with two additional stand-by satellites on ground.

28. c ARGOS is a satellite-based system which is involved in the collecting, processing and disseminating the environmental data from a fixed and a mobile platform worldwide. It also helps in the data collection by the satellite. This makes the Argos more useful in geographically locating the data source from any location on the Earth using the Doppler Effect. It was established in the year 1978. The ARGOS has provided the data for the environmental research and protection of communities.

29. d The ISRO spacecraft Oceansat-3 is being developed in order to provide the service continuity for the operational users of Ocean Colour Monitor data from Oceansat 2. It also seeks to enhance the application potential in other areas. It is a global mission which has been configured to cover the global oceans and to provide a continuity of ocean colour data. The mission seeks to provide the continuity of ocean colour data along with the improvements to enhance the operational services such as potential fishery zone and the primary productivity.

30. b The "Energy Swaraj Yatra" bus runs on the solar energy. It comprises of a complete work-cum-residential unit. The professor has been travelling on the bus to raise awareness regarding the use of solar power since the year 2020. This yatra will continue till 2030. The bus allows the occupant to perform all the daily activities such as bathing, cooking, sleeping, working, meeting and training. This bus has been fitted with the 3.2 kW solar panels. It is having the capacity of 6 kWh of battery storage. The concept of "Energy Swaraj Yatra" is based on "Gandhian ideologies" to mitigate the climate change and to ensure the energy sustainability. Climate change has become an emergency which requires public efforts in order to mitigate it. The Energy Swaraj Movement was started to bring about the public awareness and their involvement to solve climate change problem.

31. d When Gandhi, joined now by Rajendra Prasad, Mazharul-Haq, Mahadeo Desai, Narhari Parekh, and J.B. Kripalani, reached Champaran to probe into

the matter, the authorities ordered him to leave the area at once. Other popular leaders associated with Champaran Satyagraha were Brajkishore Prasad, Anugrah Narayan Sinha, Ramnavmi Prasad and Shambhusharan Varma.

32. a The massacre at Jallianwalla Bagh shocked Indians and many British as well. The Secretary of State for India, Edwin Montagu, ordered that a committee of inquiry be formed to investigate the matter. On October 14, 1919, the Government of India announced the formation of the Disorders Inquiry Committee, which came to be more widely and variously known as the Hunter Committee/ Commission after the name of chairman, Lord William Hunter, former Solicitor-General for Scotland and Senator of the College of Justice in Scotland. The purpose of the commission was to "investigate the recent disturbances in Bombay, Delhi and Punjab, about their causes, and the measures taken to cope with them.

33. c One section led by C.R. Das, Motilal Nehru and Ajmal Khan wanted an end to the boycott of legislative councils so that the nationalists could enter them to expose the basic weaknesses of these assemblies and use these councils as an arena of political struggle to arouse popular enthusiasm.

The other school of thought led by C. Rajagopalachari, Vallabhbhai Patel, Rajendra Prasad and M.A. Ansari came to be known as the 'No changers'.

34. a Journals publishing memoirs and articles extolling the self-sacrifice of revolutionaries, such as Atmasakti, Sarathi and Bijoli.

35. c The following major decisions were taken at the Lahore session.

- The Round Table Conference was to be boycotted.
- Complete independence was declared as the aim of the Congress.
- Congress Working Committee was authorised to launch a programme of civil disobedience including non-payment of taxes and all members of legislatures were asked to resign their seats.
- January 26, 1930 was fixed as the first Independence (Swarajya) Day, to be celebrated everywhere.

36. b Although inscriptions, coins and architecture provide a lot of information, especially valuable are "histories", tarikh (singular)/tawarikh (plural), written in Persian.

1. The authors of tawarikh lived in cities (mainly Delhi) and hardly ever in villages.

2. They often wrote their histories for Sultans in the hope of rich rewards.

3. These authors advised rulers on the need to preserve an "ideal" social order based on birthright and gender distinctions. Their ideas were not shared by everybody.

37. d The Lok Sabha and the State Legislative Assemblies are directly elected by the people. For the purpose of election, the entire country (State, in case of State Legislative Assembly) is divided into territorial constituencies of roughly equal population. One representative is elected from each constituency through universal adult suffrage where the value of vote of every individual would be equal to another. At present there are 543 constituencies. This number has not changed since 1971 census.

38. c Powers of Rajya Sabha

- Considers and approves non money bills and suggests amendments to money bills.
- Approves constitutional amendments.
- Exercises control over executive by asking questions, introducing motions and resolutions.
- Participates in the election and removal of the President, Vice President, Judges of Supreme Court and High Court.
- It can alone initiate the procedure for removal of Vice President.
- Can give the Union parliament power to make laws on matters included in the State list.

39. d The legislature in parliamentary system ensures executive accountability at various stages: policy making, implementation of law or policy and during and post-implementation stage. The legislature does this through the use of a variety of devices:

- Deliberation and discussion
- Approval or Refusal of laws
- Financial control
- No confidence motion

40. a Constitution of India guarantees universal adult suffrage for all citizens. When they were making the Constitution, the members of the Constituent Assembly felt that the freedom struggle had prepared the masses for universal adult suffrage and that this

would help encourage a democratic mindset and break the clutches of traditional caste, class and gender hierarchies. This means that the people of India have a direct role in electing their representatives. Also, every citizen of the country, irrespective of his/her social background, can also contest in elections. These representatives are accountable to the people.

41. b The Constitution, therefore, also guarantees the rights of minorities against the majority. As Dr Ambedkar has said about these Fundamental Rights, their object is two-fold. The first objective is that every citizen must be in a position to claim those rights. And secondly, these rights must be binding upon every authority that has got the power to make laws.

In addition to Fundamental Rights, the Constitution also has a section called Directive Principles of State Policy. This section was designed by the members of the Constituent Assembly to ensure greater social and economic reforms, and to serve as a guide to the independent Indian State to institute laws and policies that help reduce the poverty of the masses.

42. a • The expense ratio is the percentage of asset funds charged by the Asset Management Companies for operating mutual funds and similar instruments. For example, if you are investing Rs. 10,000 and the expense ratio is 1%, the AMC will charge Rs. 100 to cover their expenses and other incidental costs including their profit.

• The expense ratio for the Bharat Bond ETF is not slightly lower, but abysmally low compared with any other mutual fund product. It is just 0.0005 per cent. As the expense ratio is less, the net returns for the investors will be high.

43. a As per the Philips Curve, inflation is indirectly proportional to unemployment

44. c Only banks, not NBFCs, can borrow from RBI to meet their day-to-day asset-liability mismatches through the repo platform.

Loans are granted through repo by RBI against Government securities as collateral, in which the banks have already invested. Such borrowing accounts for only 0.3 to 0.35% of bank's total loan portfolio.

45. d • While the Small Financial Banks can accept deposits without restrictions, the Payment Banks can accept maximum 1 Lakh of deposits per person per year. Priority Sector Lending criteria is not applicable for Payment Banks.

• Small Finance Banks have 25% branches in unbanked rural areas but for Payment Banks, 25% access points must be in rural areas like Business correspondence (BC), Kirana Stores.

46. c • In the 50 clusters inaugurated, over 42,000 artisans have been supported in the traditional segments of muslin, khadi, coir, handicraft, handlooms, wood craft, leather, pottery, carpet weaving, bamboo, agro processing, tea, etc.

• The Ministry of MSME, Govt. of India has funded an amount of around Rs.85 crore for development of these 50 clusters.

• The Ministry of MSME is implementing a Scheme of Fund for Regeneration of Traditional Industries (SFURTI) with a view to organize traditional industries and artisans into clusters to make them competitive and increase their income.

• As on date, there are 371 numbers of Clusters which have are being funded by the Ministry, supporting 2.18 lakh artisans with a total Government assistance of Rs. 888 cr. More than Rs.708 crore has been the budgetary allocation under the scheme, of which more than Rs.567 crore has been released for the implementation of the scheme so far.

• SFURTI clusters are of two types i.e., Regular Cluster (500 artisans) with Government assistance of up to Rs.2.5 crore and Major Cluster (more than 500 artisans) with Government assistance up to Rs.5 crore.

47. a • A total of 12 companies have been selected for the National Technology Awards 2020 for commercialization of successful commercialization of innovative indigenous technologies.

• Every year, for furtherance of its mandate, TDB seeks applications for prestigious National awards for commercialization of technologies under these three categories.

• These awards conferred to various industries provides a platform of recognition to Indian industries and their technology provider, who have worked as a team, to bring innovation to the market and contributed to the vision of "Aatma Nirbhar Bharat".

• The awards were given by the Technology Development Board (TDB), a statutory body of Government of India functioning under Department of Science of Technology for the year 2019-20.

- The Technology Development Board is a statutory body of Government of India functioning under Department of Science of Technology which provides financial assistance to companies working for commercialization of indigenous technologies and adaptation of imported technologies for domestic applications.
- TDB was established in 1996 with a novel aim of providing financial assistance to Indian companies for commercialization of innovative indigenous technologies.
- Since its inception, TDB has funded more than 300 companies for commercialization of technologies.

48. c
- The Centre's Jal Shakti Ministry is about to launch a 100-day campaign called 'Catch the Rain' to promote water conservation in the country.
- The Prime Minister made the statement while addressing this year's second 'Mann Ki Baat' radio programme.
- National Water Mission's (NWM) campaign "Catch The Rain" with the tagline "Catch the rain, where it falls, when it falls" is to nudge the states and stake-holders to create appropriate Rain Water Harvesting Structures (RWHS) suitable to the climatic conditions and sub-soil strata before monsoon.
- It was launched by. the National Water Mission, Ministry of Jal Shakti in collaboration with Nehru Yuva Kendra Sangathan (NYKS), Ministry of Youth Affairs & Sports

49. a
- Satellite Launch Vehicle PSLV-C51 carrying Amazonia-1 of Brazil and 18 other satellites lifted off from the first launch pad of the Satish Dhawan Space Centre (SHAR), over 100 km from Chenna
- The four-stage 44.4 metre tall PSLV, a workhorse launch vehicle of ISRO in its 53rd mission, soared into clear sky and every stage performed as programmed
- PSLV-C51 is the 53rd flight of PSLV and 3rd flight of PSLV in 'DL' configuration (with 2 strap-on motors).
- PSLV-C51 is the 53rd flight of PSLV and 3rd flight of PSLV in 'DL' configuration (with 2 strap-on motors).
- This was the 78th launch vehicle mission from SDSC SHAR, Sriharikota and the first dedicated commercial launch of PSLV-C51/Amazonia-1 Mission

50. d
- The Ministry of MSME is implementing a Scheme of Fund for Regeneration of Traditional Industries (SFURTI) with a view to organize traditional industries and artisans into clusters to make them competitive and increase their income.
- Under the Scheme, the Ministry supports various interventions including setting up of infrastructure through Common Facility Centers (CFCs), procurement of new machineries, creating raw material banks, design intervention, improved packaging, improvement of marketing Infrastructure, improved skills and capacity development through training and exposure visits, etc.
- Besides, the scheme focuses on strengthening the cluster governance systems with the active participation of the stakeholders, so that they are able to gauge the emerging challenges and opportunities and respond to them through building innovative and traditional skills, improved technologies, advanced processes, market intelligence and new models of public-private partnerships, so as to gradually replicate similar models of cluster- based traditional Industries.

51. a The **World Environment Day** is observed on the **5th** of June every year for encouraging worldwide awareness and action to protect our environment.
- The day has been celebrated since 1974 by **engaging governments, businesses, celebrities and citizens** to focus their efforts on a pressing environmental issue.
- India will be focusing on the Nagar Van (Urban Forests) in addition to the official theme of the World Environment Day.
- Further, the **Indian Navy** has also marked the day through various initiatives which are intended to reduce its environmental footprint.
- The **theme** of World Environment Day 2020 is 'Celebrating Biodiversity'—a concern that is both urgent and existential.
- Almost one million species are facing extinction worldwide and thus there has never been a more important time to focus on biodiversity.

- The day will **be hosted** in Colombia in partnership with Germany.

52. d
- National Tiger Conservation Authority (NTCA) is a statutory body under the Ministry of Environment, Forests and Climate Change.
- It was established in 2005 following the recommendations of the Tiger Task Force.
- It was constituted under enabling provisions of the Wildlife (Protection) Act, 1972, as amended in 2006, for strengthening tiger conservation, as per powers and functions assigned to it.

53. d
- Plastic pollution is caused by the accumulation of plastic waste in the environment. It can be categorized in primary plastics, such as cigarette butts and bottle caps, or secondary plastics, resulting from the degradation of the primary ones.
- According to the Central Pollution Control Board (CPCB), India generates close to 26,000 tonnes of plastic a day and over 10,000 tonnes a day of plastic waste remains uncollected.
- According to a Federation of Indian Chambers of Commerce and Industry (FICCI) study the plastic processing industry is estimated to grow to 22 million tonnes (MT) a year by 2020 from 13.4 MT in 2015 and nearly half of this is single-use plastic.
- India's per capita plastic consumption of less than 11 kg, is nearly a tenth of the United States of America (109 kg).

54. c
- Homeostasis is the maintenance of stable equilibrium, especially through physiological (through bodily part functions. E.g. Cooling your body through sweating processes.
- Organisms try to maintain the constancy of its internal environment despite varying external environmental conditions that tend to upset their homeostasis.

55. a Divergent movement of plates result in:
1. Volcanic activity of fissure flow of basaltic magma.
2. Creation of new oceanic crust
3. Formation of submarine mountain ridges
4. Occurrence of shallow focus earthqaukes
5. Drifting of oceanic plates
6. Creation of transform faults.

56. b
- Mantle It forms about 83 per cent of the earth's volume and holds 67% of the earth's mass.
- It extends from Moho's discontinuity to a depth of 2,900 km.
- The density of the upper mantle varies between 2.9 g/cm^3 and 3.3 g/cm^3.
- The lower mantle extends beyond the asthenosphere. It is in a solid state.
- The lithosphere is the rigid outer part of the earth with thickness varying between 10-200 km.
- It is includes the crust and the upper part of the mantle.
- The lithosphere is broken into tectonic plates (lithospheric plates), and the movement of these tectonic plates cause large-scale changes in the earth's geological structure (folding, faulting).

57. c
- Continental Drift theory was given by Alfred Wegener in 1912.
- Professor Alfred Wegner of Germany was primarily a meteorologist.
- The CDT of wegner ' grew out of the need of explaining the major variations of climate in the past.
- Convection Current Theory is the soul of Seafloor Spreading Theory.
- Arthur Holmes in 1930s discussed the possibility of convection currents in the <u>mantle</u>.
- These currents are generated due to radioactive elements causing thermal differences in the <u>mantle</u>.

58. c
- The actual amount of the water vapour present in the atmosphere is known as the absolute humidity.
- It is the weight of water vapour per unit volume of air and is expressed in terms of grams per cubic metre. (g/m^3).
- The absolute humidity differs from place to place on the surface of the earth.
- Specific humidity is mass of water vapour in a unit mass of moist air, usually expressed as grams of vapour per kilogram of air. It is the actual amount of water vapour present per kg of mass of air.
- For instance- if 1 kg air holds 10 grams of water vapour, the specific humidity will be 10 grams per kg of air i.e. 10 g/kg.

- The specific humidity of saturated air increases rapidly with increasing temperature.

59. a Suez Canal, sea-level waterway running north-south across the Isthmus of Suez in Egypt to connect the Mediterranean and the Red seas. The canal separates the African continent from Asia, and it provides the shortest maritime route between Europe and the lands lying around the Indian and western Pacific oceans. It is one of the world's most heavily used shipping lanes. The canal extends 120 miles (193 km) between Port Said in the north and Suez in the south, with dredged approach channels north of Port Said, into the Mediterranean, and south of Suez.

Its significance-

- The Suez Canal provides a crucial link for oil, natural gas and cargo being shipping from East to West.

- It provides a major shortcut for ships moving between Europe and Asia, who before its construction had to sail around Africa to complete the same journey.

- Around 10 % of the world's trade flows through the waterway and it remains one of Egypt's top foreign currency earners.

- As per a report, the canal is a major source of income for Egypt's economy, with the African country earning $5.61 billion in revenues from it last year.

[* File contains invalid data | In-line.JPG *]

60. b The Zabarwan Range is a short (32 km) long sub-mountain range between Pir Panjal and Great Himalayan Range in the central part of the Kashmir Valley in the Union Territory of Jammu and Kashmir in India.

- The Zabarwan Range borders the central part of the Kashmir Valley in the east.

- Literally it is the mountain range between Sind Valley and Lidder Valley on the north and south, and between the Zanskar Range and Jehlum Valley on the east and west, respectively.

- Specifically the range is known to be what overlooks the Dal Lake and holds the Mughal gardens of Srinagar. The north end of the range lies in Ganderbal, while the south end lies in Pampore.

- The highest peak of this range is Mahadev Peak at 13,013 feet (3,966 m), which forms the distant background of the eastern mountain wall.

61. a A team of Scientists from Jawaharlal Nehru Centre for Advanced Scientific Research have found a method that mimic the Photosynthesis which is the natural process of reducing the carbon dioxide in the atmosphere.

- The artificial photosynthesis method was developed in order to capture excess carbon dioxide from the atmosphere.

- This method harnesses the solar energy and converts the captured carbon dioxide into carbon monoxide (CO). The Carbon monoxide in turn can be used as a fuel for the internal combustion engines.

- In the process, the teams of scientists are conducting the same process as in the natural photosynthesis but using the simple nanostructures.

- The team of Scientists has designed and fabricated the integrated catalytic system which is based on the metal-organic framework (MOF-808). The system comprises of a photosensitizer. The photosensitizer can harness the solar power and the catalytic centre. This in turn reduces the CO2.

62. d It is a developmental disorder which is characterized by difficulties of social interaction and communication. The condition is also characterised by a restricted and repetitive behaviour. The signs of the autism are usually identified during first three years of the child. The signs of the autism are developed gradually. This disorder is associated with the combination of genetic and environmental factors. Autism is estimated to affect about 24.8 million people across the world as of 2015. As of 2017, in the developed countries, 1.5% of children are diagnosed with this disorder. This disorder occurs more often in males than in females.

63. c Recently, the Indian Space Research Organisation (ISRO) has launched the sounding rocket called RH-560. The rocket was launched in order to study "attitudinal variations" in the neutral winds and plasma dynamics.

- The RH-560 rocket was launched from Satish Dhawan Space Centre (SDSC) Sriharikota Range (SHAR). ISRO highlighted that the sounding rockets are one or two-stage solid propellant rockets.

- These rockets are used to probe the upper atmospheric regions and conduct the space research.

- The rockets would also serve as easily affordable platforms which can test or prove the prototypes of new components or subsystems for use in the launch vehicles and satellites.
- ISRO had started launching the indigenously made sounding rockets from the year 1965.

64. d
- The early atmosphere, with hydrogen and helium, is supposed to have been stripped off as a result of the solar winds. This happened not only in case of the earth, but also in all the terrestrial planets, which were supposed to have lost their primordial atmosphere through the impact of solar winds.
- During the cooling of the earth, gases and water vapour were released from the interior solid earth. This started the evolution of the present atmosphere. The early atmosphere largely contained water vapour, nitrogen, carbon dioxide, methane, ammonia and very little of free oxygen. The process through which the gases were outpoured from the interior is called degassing.

65. b
- Nuclear DNA is inherited from both the parents, whereas Mitochondrial DNA is inherited only from the mother. DNA in a cell exists both in nucleus and mitochondria. Nuclear DNA is longer as compared to the Mitochondrial DNA. Other important aspect is Nuclear DNA contain around 20,000 to 25,000 genes, while mitochondrial DNA contains only 37 genes.
- Nuclear DNA consists of 46 chromosomes, whereas Mitochondrial DNA consists of only 1 chromosome.
- The chromosomes in Nuclear DNA are responsible for genetic make-up of a human being, while the chromosome of the Mitochondrial DNA is responsible for the metabolic activities.

66. b
- **All the statement is correct:** Lead is a heavy metal with high toxicity.
- It can be easily moulded and shaped and can easily form alloys with other metals. Hence, it is widely used in industries.
- This wide use of lead has increased incidences of lead-poisoning.
- Lead poisoning is a type of metal poisoning caused by lead in the body. Exposure to lead can occur by contaminated air, water, dust, food, or consumer products.
- Children are at greater risk as they are more likely to put objects in their mouth such as those that contain lead paint and absorb a greater proportion of the lead that they eat.
- Widespread use of lead-acid batteries is a major cause poisoning especially for the workers and people living around the industries.
- Lead in its organic form could be absorbed through the skin upon application of cosmetics.
- Lead exposure also makes the body susceptible to anaemia as it prevents the formation of haemoglobin.
- Lead replaces minerals, notably iron and calcium, in the body and prevents haemoglobin formation, resulting in anaemia.

67. b The Indian State works in various ways to prevent the above domination. First, it uses a strategy of distancing itself from religion. The Indian State is not ruled by a religious group and nor does it support any one religion. In India, government spaces like law courts, police stations, government schools and offices are not supposed to display or promote any one religion.

68. a The Constitution of India recognises the right to water as being a part of the Right to Life under Article 21. It means that it is the right of every person, whether rich or poor, to have sufficient amount of water to fulfil his/her daily needs at a price that he/she can afford. In other words, there should be universal access to water.

69. d The Horn of Africa is a peninsula and its adjacent regions in East Africa, and it is the easternmost projection of the African continent, excluding African islands. It lies along the southern boundary of the Red Sea and extends hundreds of kilometers into the Gulf of Aden, Somali Sea and Guardafui Channel. The Horn of Africa consists of the internationally-recognized countries of Djibouti, Eritrea, Ethiopia and Somalia, as well as Somaliland, an unrecognized sovereign state that is internationally considered to be part of Somalia. It covers approximately two million square kilometers (770,000 square miles) and is inhabited by roughly 115 million people.

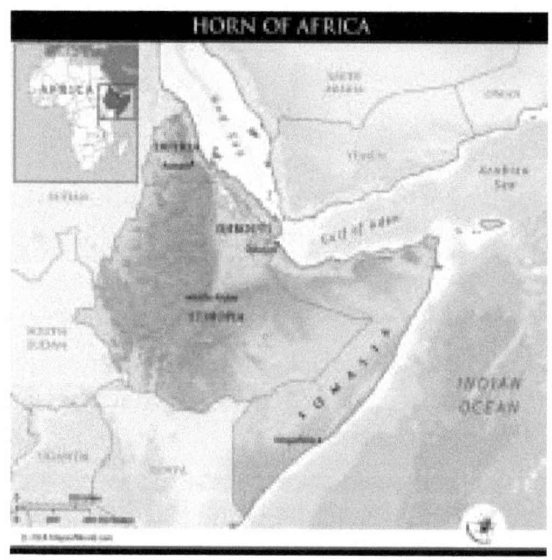

70. d • The Chenab originates from near the Bara Lacha Pass in the Lahul-Spiti part of the Zaskar Range. The Jhelum has its source in a spring at Verinag in the south-eastern part of the Kashmir Valley.

• Two small streams on opposite sides of the pass, namely Chandra and Bhaga, form its headwaters at an altitude of 4,900 m.

• The Satluj rises from the Manasarovar-Rakas Lakes in western Tibet at a height of 4,570 m within 80 km of the source of the Indus.

• Like the Indus, it takes a north-westerly course upto the Shipki La on the Tibet-Himachal Pradesh boundary.

• The Beas originates near the Rohtang Pass, at a height of 4,062 m above sea level, on the southern end of the PirPanjal Range, close to the source of the Ravi.

71. a • The Union Minister for Science & Technology inaugurated the second edition of Global Bio-India-2021 in New Delhi through virtual mode.

• The 3-day event will showcase the strength and opportunities of the India's biotechnology sector at national level and to the global community.

• Being one of the largest biotechnology stakeholder conglomerates, this event is being co-organised by the Department of Biotechnology, Ministry of Science & Technology, Government of India along with its Public Sector Undertaking, and Biotechnology Industry Research Assistance Council (BIRAC) in partnership with industry association Confederation of Indian Industry (CII), Association of Biotechnology Led Enterprises (ABLE) and Invest India.

72. d • The Land Ports Authority of India (LPAI) celebrated its 9th Foundation Day at its Headquarter in New Delhi.

• LPAI work done by the organisation in building infrastructure for facilitation of India's land borders.

• LPAI for the crucial role taken in facilitating safe and seamless cross-border movement of trade and passengers through land ports during the recent COVID-19 pandemic.

• The Land Ports Authority of India or LPAI is a statutory body (created through the Land Ports Authority of India Act, 2010) working under the Ministry of Home Affairs, Government of India is responsible for creating, upgrading, maintaining and managing border infrastructure in India.

• It manages several Integrated Check Posts (ICPs) all across Borders of India.

73. b • Association of Biotechnology Led Enterprises - ABLE is a not-for-profit pan-India forum that represents the Indian Biotechnology Sector.

• It was launched in April 2003, after industry leaders felt a need to form an exclusive forum to represent the Indian Biotechnology Sector.

74. d • Union Ministers of State for Agriculture and Farmers Welfare inaugurated professional training programmes designed and developed for CEOs, Board of Directors, Accountants of FPOs on the occasion of the anniversary of the Central Sector Scheme titled 'Formation and Promotion of 10,000 Farmer Produce Organizations (FPOs)'.

• In each block there should be an FPO which acts as catalyst for institutional infrastructure.

• More than 2200 FPOs produce clusters have been allocated for the formation of FPOs in the current year, of which 100 FPOs for specialized Organic produce, 100 FPOs from Oilseeds & 50 commodity-specific FPOs with value chain development will be formed.

• FPOs are already being registered in the UT of Kashmir, Rajasthan, Maharashtra, Madhya Pradesh, Odisha, Bihar, West Bengal, Uttar Pradesh, Tamil Nadu and also in North Eastern State of Arunachal Pradesh. In other states, it is in progress.

75. c
- It is a not-for-profit Section 8, Schedule B, Public Sector Enterprise, set up by Department of Biotechnology (DBT), Government of India as an Interface Agency to strengthen and empower the emerging Biotech enterprise to undertake strategic research and innovation, addressing nationally relevant product development needs.
- BIRAC is a industry-academia interface and implements its mandate through a wide range **of impact initiatives,** be it providing access to risk capital through targeted funding, technology transfer, IP management and handholding schemes that help bring **innovation excellence** to the biotech firms and make them globally competitive.

76. a A mosque is called a masjid in Arabic, literally a place where a Muslim prostrates in reverence to Allah. In a "congregational mosque" (masjid-i-jami or jama masjid) Muslims read their prayers (namaz) together. Members of the congregation choose the most respected, learned male as their leader (imam) for the rituals of prayer. He also delivers the sermon (khutba) during the Friday prayer. During prayer, Muslims stand facing Mecca. In India this is to the west. This is called the qibla.

77. d Images of Vaishnava (mainly Vishnu and his various forms) and Shaiva (mainly the lingas and mukhalingas) faiths are also found at Mathura but Buddhist images are found in large numbers. It may be noted that the images of Vishnu and Shiva are represented by their ayudhas (weapons). There is boldness in carving the large images, the volume of the images is projected out of the picture plane, the faces are round and smiling, heaviness in the sculptural volume is reduced to relaxed flesh. The garments of the body are clearly visible and they cover the left shoulder. Images of the Buddha, Yakshas, Yakshinis, Shaivite and Vaishnavite deities and portrait statues are profusely sculpted. In the second century CE, images in Mathura get sensual, rotundity increases, they become fleshier.

78. a There are many subdivisions of nagara temples depending on the shape of the shikhara. There are different names for the various parts of the temple in different parts of India; however, the most common name for the simple shikhara which is square at the base and whose walls curve or slope inward to a point on top is called the 'latina' or the rekha-prasada type of shikara.

The second major type of architectural form in the nagara order is the phamsana. Phamsana buildings tend to be broader and shorter than latina ones. Phamsana roofs do not curve inward, instead they slope upwards on a straight incline.

The third main sub-type of the nagara building is what is generally called the valabhi type. These are rectangular buildings with a roof that rises into a vaulted chamber.

79. b Some important administrative posts were hereditary during Pallavas and, Chalukyas
1. maha-danda-nayaka was chief judicial officer
2. kumar-amatya, meaning an important minister
3. sandhi-vigrahika, meaning a minister of war and peace
4. nagarashreshthi was chief banker or merchant of the city
5. the sarthavaha was leader of the merchant caravans
6. prathama-kulika was the chief craftsman

80. d
- The first plant to colonize an area is called the pioneer community.
- The final stage of succession is called the climax community.
- A climax community is stable, mature, more complex and long-lasting.
- The stage leading to the climax community is called successional stages or seres.
- Each transitional community that is formed and replaced during succession is called a stage in succession or a seral community.
- **Succession is characterized by the following:** increased productivity, the shift of nutrients from the reservoirs, increased diversity of organisms, and a gradual increase in the complexity of food webs.
- Succession would occur faster in area existing in the middle of the large continent. This is because here seeds of plants belonging to the different seres would reach much faster.

81. d
- Pyramid of numbers represents the total number of individuals of different species (population) at each trophic level.
- Depending upon the size, the pyramid of numbers may not always be upright, and may even be completely inverted.
- In aquatic ecosystems, the pyramid of biomass may assume an inverted form. (In contrast, a pyramid of numbers for the aquatic ecosystem is upright)

82. a   The Nagzira Wildlife Sanctuary (NWS) is located between the Bhandara district and Gondia district of Maharashtra.

83. d   Nitrogen oxides are a group of seven gases and compounds which is composed of nitrogen and oxygen and collectively known as NOx gases. Some of the sources of Nitrogen oxides emission are Thermal power plants, industries, and vehicles.

84. b   11 of the eighteen biosphere reserves are a part of the World Network of Biosphere Reserves, based on the UNESCO Man and the Biosphere (MAB) Programme list.

Name	States	Year
Nilgiri Biosphere Reserve	Tamil Nadu, Kerala, Karnataka	2000
Gulf of Mannar Biosphere Reserve	Tamil Nadu	2001
Sundarbans Biosphere Reserve	West Bengal	2001
Nanda Devi Biosphere Reserve	Uttarakhand	2004
Nokrek Biosphere Reserve	Meghalaya	2009
Pachmarhi Biosphere Reserve	Madhya Pradesh	2009
Simlipal Biosphere Reserve	Odisha	2009
Great Nicobar Biosphere Reserve	Great Nicobar	2013
Achanakmar-Amarkantak Biosphere Reserve	Chhattisgarh, Madhya Pradesh	2012
Agasthyamalai Biosphere Reserve	Kerala and Tamil Nadu	2016
Khangchendzonga National Park	Sikkim	2018

85. d
- Cloud seeding is a kind of a weather modification technology to create artificial rainfall. It works only when there is enough pre-existing clouds in the atmosphere. Rain happens when moisture in the air reaches levels at which it can no longer be held, and cloud seeding aims to facilitate and accelerate that process by making available chemical 'nuclei' around which condensation can take place.
- These 'seeds' of rain can be the iodides of silver or potassium, dry ice (solid carbon dioxide), or liquid propane. The seeds can be delivered by plane or simply by spraying from the ground.
- The Pune-based Indian Institute of Tropical Meteorology has been carrying out cloud seeding experiments for several years now. These experiments have been done in areas around Nagpur, Solapur, Hyderabad, Ahmedabad, Jodhpur, and recently Varanasi. The success rate of these experiments in inducing rains is about 60 to 70 per cent, depending on local atmospheric conditions, the amount of moisture in the air and cloud characteristics.

86. c
- The first kind of surface wave is called a Love wave, named after A.E.H. Love, a British mathematician who worked out the mathematical model for this kind of wave in 1911.
- It's the fastest surface wave and moves the ground from side-to-side. Confined to the surface of the crust, Love waves produce entirely horizontal motion.
- Primary waves are called so because they are the fastest among the seismic waves and hence are recorded first on the seismograph.
- These waves are of relatively high frequency and are the least destructive among the earthquake waves.
- A Rayleigh wave rolls along the ground just like a wave rolls across a lake or an ocean. Because it rolls, it moves the ground up and down, and side-to-side in the same direction that the wave is moving.
- Most of the shaking felt from an earthquake is due to the Rayleigh wave, which can be much larger than the other waves.

87. b
- The most popular argument regarding the origin of the universe is the Big Bang Theory. It is also called expanding universe hypothesis. Edwin Hubble, in 1920, provided evidence that the universe is expanding. As time passes, galaxies move further and further apart.

- It is now generally believed that the formation of moon, as a satellite of the earth, is an outcome of 'giant impact' or what is described as "the big splat". A body of the size of one to three times that of mars collided into the earth sometime shortly after the earth was formed. It blasted a large part of the earth into space. This portion of blasted material then continued to orbit the earth and eventually formed into the present moon about 4.44 billion years ago.

88. d
   - RBI's separate Ombudsman for NBFCs started since 2018.
   - Any NBFC that is not regulated by any other regulator, falls under RBI's purview.
   - Prompt Corrective Action is NOT applicable for the NBFCs.
   - Deposits with the NBFCs are not insured.

89. c   The Human Development Report releases five composite indices each year: Human Development Index (HDI), Inequality-Adjusted Human Development Index (IHDI), Gender Development Index (GDI), Gender Inequality Index (GII), and the Multidimensional Poverty Index (MPI). (

90. a   In January 2018,Dept of Financial Services released EASE framework with 6 pillars to make PSBs Responsive and Responsible viz. Customer Responsiveness; Responsible Banking: Reduce NPA, prevent frauds; Credit Off Take; Help MSME entrepreneurs via SIDBI's Udyamimitra.com portal; Deepening Financial Inclusion & Digitalization; Employees' Human Resource Management (HRM).

91. a
   - AIFIs are not 'banks' because they can't accept direct deposits from people at large. RBI is the regulator over AIFI.
   - BASEL norms applicable but RBI can prescribe different / slabs norms / deadlines.

92. d   Filling of inert gases like nitrogen and argon prevents oxidation of the filament and increase its life. Inert gases do not play any other role like increasing power efficiency, illumination, changing heat profile of the filament etc. They may even reduce the heat emitted by the bulb to some extent as the bulb's inside is properly insulated.

93. b
   - Electronic waste or e-waste describes discarded electrical or electronic devices.
   - Some computer components can be reused in assembling new computer products, while others are reduced to metals that can be reused in applications as varied as construction, flatware, and jewellery.

> Substances found in large quantities include epoxyresins, fiberglass, PCBs, PVC (polyvinyl chlorides), thermosetting plastics, lead, tin, copper, silicon, beryllium, carbon, iron, and aluminium.

> Elements found in small amounts include cadmium, mercury, and thallium.

> Elements found in trace amounts include americium, antimony, arsenic, barium, bismuth, boron, cobalt, europium, gallium, germanium, gold, indium, lithium, manganese, nickel, niobium, palladium, platinum, rhodium, ruthenium, selenium, silver, tantalum, terbium, thorium, titanium, vanadium, and yttrium.

Smartphones, tablets and other popular electronic products contain precious materials, including gold, copper, palladium, silver, platinum, cobalt, and more.

94 .d   A colloid is a heterogeneous system in which one substance is dispersed (dispersed phase) as very fine particles in another substance called dispersion medium.

   - **The blue colour of the sky:** Dust particles along with water suspended in the air scatter blue light which reaches our eyes and the sky looks blue to us.

   - **Fog, mist and rain:** When a large mass of air containing dust particles, is cooled below its dew point, the moisture from the air condenses on the surfaces of these particles forming fine droplets. These droplets being colloidal in nature continue to float in the air in the form of mist or fog.

   - **Formation of delta:** River water is a colloidal solution of clay. Seawater contains a number of electrolytes. When river water meets the sea water, the electrolytes present in seawater coagulate the colloidal solution of clay resulting in its deposition with the formation of a delta.

95. a
   - Natural uranium constitutes around 99.3% of U-238 and around 0.7% of U-235. To make a nuclear reactor, the uranium needs to be enriched (increasing U 235) so that up to 20% of it is Uranium 235. For nuclear bombs, U-235 needs to be increased to 80 or 90%. Hence enrichment of uranium is undertaken for different purposes. If we enrich up to particular level, we can produce nuclear power and if we enrich up to much higher levels of U-235, we can make nuclear bombs.

- Centrifuges are used for enrichment of Uranium.
- The primary purpose is not producing nuclear weapons. Enrichment has several other purposes; one such purpose is producing nuclear power.

96. c
- Deeptech, at a high level, refers to technology and innovation that has the potential to disrupt and transform the world, and has a deep impact on society.
- In the context of software/hardware, entrepreneurs are building new business models using recent technological advances in areas such as artificial intelligence (AI), machine learning (ML), big data, augmented reality (AR) / virtual reality (VR), blockchain, industry 4.0, robotics, cyber security, internet of things (IoT) and others.
- When utilized optimally, these technologies and the associated IPs can create significant entry barriers for any startup, giving them an edge over competition.
- Deep tech is that set of cutting-edge and disruptive technologies based on scientific discoveries, engineering, mathematics, physics and medicine.

97. c
- Department of Posts (DoP) and India Post Payments Bank (IPPB) has unveiled a new digital payment app 'DakPay' at a virtual event held recently.
- The App is launched as part of its ongoing efforts to provide Digital Financial inclusion at the last mile across India.
- DakPay is not just a digital payment app but a suite of digital financial and assisted banking services provided by India Post & IPPB through the trusted Postal ('Dak') network across the nation to cater to the financial needs ('Pay') of various sections of the society.
- The app will also provide interoperable banking services to the customers with any bank in the country.

98. d Six major initiatives of AIM:
- Atal Tinkering Labs-Creating problem-solving mindset across schools in India.
- Atal Incubation Centers-Fostering world class start-ups and adding a new dimension to the incubator model.
- Atal New India Challenges-Fostering product innovations and aligning them to the needs of various sectors/ministries.

- Mentor India Campaign- A national Mentor network in collaboration with public sector, corporates and institutions, to support all the initiatives of the mission.
- Atal Community Innovation Centre- To stimulate community centric innovation and ideas in the unserved /underserved regions of the country including Tier 2 and Tier 3 cities.
- ARISE-To stimulate innovation and research in the MSME industry.

99. a
- Toys can become a symbol to demonstrate India's Quality, Uniqueness, Innovation, Eco-friendliness and Thrill (QUIET) of Indian Toys.
- India Toy Fair (TITF)2021 has created a window of opportunity for our artisans, MSMEs, Startups, young designers & thinkers.
- There were 225 entries in the Toy Design challenge in two categories: 1. Professional 2. Amateur.
- In each category, there were cash prizes of Rs. 1.0 lakh, Rs. 50,000 & Rs.25,000 to the first, second and third prize winners and 'Certificate' of recognition

100. c
- Under this partnership, startups supported by AIM, will get access to steps of the art MathWorks tools (including MATLAB and Simulink), engineering support, online trainings, access to MATLAB community, and opportunities for developing awareness of the startup products through their domestic and global reach.
- MathWorks product portfolioincludes the MATLAB technical computing platform and Simulink, a block diagram environment for simulation and Model-Based Design, in addition to 100+ toolboxes and specialized products.
- AIM and MathWorks plan to organize series of knowledge sharing sessions for incubators and startups to train and support them on various relevant topics.
- MathWorks is the leading developer of mathematical computing software. Engineers and scientists worldwide rely on these product families to accelerate the pace of discovery, innovation, and development in automotive, aerospace, electronics, renewable energy, financial services, biotech, and other industries.
- MathWorks supports over 3,000 startups and 300 Accelerators worldwide.

Mock Test 2
General Studies Paper I

1. Consider the following statements regarding PM Swasth Bharat Yojana:
   1. It will provide primary, secondary and tertiary healthcare facilities.
   2. It aims to create new institutions and facilities to cater to detection and cure of new and emerging diseases.
   3. This will be in addition of Ayushman Bharat yojana.

   Which of the statements given above is/are correct?
   (a) 1 and 2 only   (b) 3 only
   (c) 2 and 3 only   (d) 1, 2 and 3

2. Which of the following statements is/are correct regarding vehicle scrapping policy?
   1. It is a voluntary programme to phase out old and unfit vehicles.
   2. This will help in encouraging fuel-efficient, environment friendly vehicles, by reducing vehicular pollution and oil import bill.
   3. Personal and commercial vehicles would go under fitness test after 20 years.

   Select the correct answer using the code given below:
   (a) 3 only   (b) 2 and 3 only
   (c) 1 and 2 only   (d) 1, 2 and 3

3. Which of the following are objectives of MITRA Scheme?
   1. To enable textile industry to become globally competitive.
   2. Attract large investments
   3. Boost employment generation

   Select the correct answer using the code given below:
   (a) 1 and 2 only   (b) 2 and 3 only
   (c) 1 and 3 only   (d) 1, 2 and 3

4. Two new technologies namely, MetroLite and MetroNeo are announced to be deployed for which of the following?
   (a) To provide metro rail system at lesser cost in Tier 2 and tier 3 cities.
   (b) Cost effective with similar convenience metro rail system in tier 2 and periphery of tier 1 cities.
   (c) To boost smart city initiative in tier 2 and tier 3 cities.
   (d) Solid waste management in tier 2 and tier 3 cities.

5. Consider the following statements:
   1. Ujjwala Scheme which has benefited 8 crores households will be extended to cover 1 crores more beneficiaries.
   2. 100 more districts have to be added to the City Gas Distribution network in next 3 years.
   3. A gas pipeline project will be taken up in Union Territory of Jammu & Kashmir and North East.

   Which of the statements given above is/are correct?
   (a) 3 only   (b) 2 and 3 only
   (c) 1 and 2 only   (d) 1, 2 and 3

6. Towards the development of modern fishing harbours and fish landing centres, GOI has identified 5 fishing harbours. Which of the following centres are identified?
   1. Kochi
   2. Petuaghat
   3. Bharoch
   4. Chennai
   5. Vishakhapatnam

   Select the correct answer using the code given below:
   (a) 1, 2, 4 and 5 only   (b) 2, 3, 4 and 5 only
   (c) 1, 2, 3 and 4 only   (d) 1, 2, 3, 4 and 5

7. Consider the following statements:
   1. Budget 2021 abolished Dividend Distribution Tax.
   2. It was abolished with the objective to incentivized investments.
   3. Dividend was made taxable in the hands of shareholders.

   Which of the statements given above is/are correct regarding Divided Distribution Tax?
   (a) 2 and 3 only   (b) 1 only
   (c) 1 and 3 only   (d) 1, 2 and 3

8. Which of the following sectors are considered as strategic sectors?
   1. Atomic energy, space and defence
   2. Transport and telecommunication
   3. Investments in manufacturing sector
   4. Banking, insurance and financial sectors

   Select the correct answer using the code given below:
   (a) 3 and 4 only   (b) 1, 2 and 4 only
   (c) 1, 2 and 3 only   (d) 1, 2, 3 and 4

9. Consider the following statements regarding Pradhan Mantri Gareeb kalyan Yojana:
   1. It ensured food security through public distribution system.
   2. It provided direct benefit transfers to widows, pensioners and women.
   3. Cash support was provided to farmers.
   4. Additional funds were given to MGNREGA projects.

   Which of the statements given above is/are correct?
   (a) 3 only   (b) 2, 3 and 4 only
   (c) 1, 2, 3 and 4   (d) 1, 2 and 4 only

10. Which of the following statements is/are correct regarding structural reforms in mining sector?
    1. To increase participation of the private sector in mineral exploration.
    2. To redefine the norms of exploration for auction of mineral blocks to ensure a seamless exploration-cum-mining-cum-production regime.
    3. It aims to reduce dependence on imported coal, to create a strong, self-reliant domestic energy sector.

    Select the correct answer using the code given below:
    (a) 1 and 2 only   (b) 3 only
    (c) 2 and 3 only   (d) 1, 2 and 3

11. Consider the following statements regarding fiscal policy during COVID-19 in India:
    1. The counter-cyclical fiscal policy stabilizes the business cycle by being expansionary in good times and contractionary in bad times.
    2. A pro-cyclical fiscal policy is the one wherein fiscal policy reinforces the business cycle by being contractionary during good times and expansionary during recessions.

    Which of the statements given above is/are **incorrect**?
    (a) 1 only   (b) 2 only
    (c) Both 1 and 2   (d) Neither 1 nor 2

12. Consider the following statements:
    1. India's public debt-to-GDP has been significantly low compared to high global debt levels.
    2. India's overall debt levels as a per cent of GDP are the lowest amongst the group of G-20 OECD countries and BRICS nations.
    3. The public debt and overall debt level for India has declined since 2003 and continued the same since 2011.

    Which of the statements given above is/are correct?
    (a) 1 and 2 only   (b) 3 only
    (c) 2 and 3 only   (d) 1, 2 and 3

13. In the context of 'Bare Necessity Index', which of the following statements is/are correct?
    1. Access to bare necessities has improved across all the states from 2012 to 2018.
    2. Odisha, Jharkhand, West Bengal and Tripura have improved their access.
    3. Access to water, housing and macro-environment are dimensions on which improvement has been measured.

    Select the correct answer using the code given below:
    (a) 1 only   (b) 2 and 3 only
    (c) 1 and 3 only   (d) 1, 2 and 3

14. Consider the following statements regarding Global Innovation Index:
    1. India has improved its rank from 81 in 2015 to 48 in 2020.
    2. India ranked first in Central and South Asia and second among lower middle-income group countries.
    3. India has entered in top 50 innovating countries for the first time in 2020.

    Which of the statements given above is/are correct?
    (a) 1 and 2 only   (b) 2 only
    (c) 1 and 3 only   (d) 1, 2 and 3

15. In the context of Non-Performing Assets (NPAs), consider the following statements:
    1. RBI constituted J P Nayak committee who suggested for ever-greening of loans to get rid of NPAs.

2. Asset Quality Review tool started using by RBI to get to know the exact amount of NPA in banking system.

3. Bank crisis due to NPA problem has been aggravated by forbearance policy.

Which of the statements given above is/are correct?

(a) 1 and 2 only   (b) 2 and 3 only

(c) 3 only   (d) 1, 2 and 3

16. Zombie firms were used to identify which of the following firm types?

(a) Shell companies

(b) Firms existing on papers with such other features to divert the loan amount.

(c) Unproductive firms who used to lend money from banks.

(d) None of the above

17. Consider the following statements:

1. The hospitalisation rates in India are among the lowest in the world.

2. India has one of the highest levels of (Out-of-the-pocket expenditure) OOPE in the world.

Which of the statements given above is/are correct regarding healthcare in India?

(a) 1 only   (b) 2 only

(c) Both 1 and 2   (d) Neither 1 nor 2

18. Which of the following are parameters for sovereign ratings?

1. Rule of law

2. Ease of doing business

3. General government debt to GDP ratio

4. Political stability and control of corruption

5. GDP growth rate

Select the correct answer using the code given below:

(a) 1, 2, 3 and 4 only

(b) 2, 3 and 4 only

(c) 3, 4 and 5 only

(d) 1, 2, 3, 4 and 5

19. Which of the following initiatives are taken for education during COVID-19 pandemic?

1. PM eVIDYA for higher education under Atma Nirbhar Bharat programme.

2. PRAGYATA guidelines

3. DAISY

Select the correct answer using the code given below:

(a) 1 and 2 only   (b) 2 and 3 only

(c) 1 and 3 only   (d) 1, 2 and 3

20. Which of the following are considered as workers in usual status (PS+SS)?

1. The persons who worked for a relatively long part of the 365 days preceding the date of survey.

2. The persons from among the remaining population who had worked at least for 30 days during the reference period of 365 days preceding the date of survey.

Select the correct answer using the code given below:

(a) 1 only   (b) 2 only

(c) Both 1 and 2   (d) Neither 1 nor 2

21. Consider the following statements regarding unemployment in India:

1. The highest decline in unemployment rates is seen among those who have received formal vocational/ technical training.

2. The level of unemployment rate is higher among the urban youth and lowest among the illiterates.

3. Bihar, Himachal Pradesh and Maharashtra having equal rural and urban youth unemployment.

Which of the statements given above is/are correct?

(a) 3 only   (b) 2 and 3 only

(c) 1 and 2 only   (d) 1, 2 and 3

22. Which of the following committees were constituted for labor reforms?

1. Mitra Committee

2. National Commission on Rural Labor

3. IX and X Five Year Plans

Select the correct answer using the code given below:

(a) 1 and 2 only   (b) 2 and 3 only

(c) 1 and 3 only   (d) 1, 2 and 3

23. Which of the following activities is/are called unpaid activities?

1. Taking care of children and elderly households

2. Production of goods and services for own consumption

3. Self-employment

Select the correct answer using the code given below:

(a) 1 and 2 only   (b) 3 only

(c) 2 and 3 only   (d) 1, 2 and 3

24. COVID-19 demonstrated the importance of investing and strengthening public health system. In this context, which of the following statements is/are correct regarding India's health outcome?

1. Total Fertility Rate (TFR) has reduced sharply from 3.6 in 1991 to 2.2 in 2018.

2. Decline in Maternal Mortality Ratio (MMR).

3. Polio, Guinea worm disease, Yaws and maternal & neonatal Tetanus and Swine flu is eliminated.

Select the correct answer using the code given below:

(a) 3 only   (b) 2 and 3 only

(c) 1 and 2 only   (d) 1, 2 and 3

25. Consider the following statements regarding FDI in India:

1. The gross FDI equity inflows into the services sector jumped 34 per cent (Year-on-Year) YoY during April-September 2020.

2. High growth in FDI inflows received in Computer software and hardware, retail trading, agricultural services, education and healthcare equipment.

Which of the statements given above is/are correct?

(a) 1 only   (b) 2 only

(c) Both 1 and 2   (d) Neither 1 nor 2

26. World Investment Report 2020 was published by which of the following organization?

(a) International Monetary Fund

(b) World Economic Forum

(c) World Bank

(d) United Nations Conference on Trade and Development

27. Which of the following statements is/are correct regarding Travel Bubble?

1. It is a temporary arrangements between two countries aimed at restarting commercial passenger services during pandemic.

2. Airlines from source and destination countries can enjoy the biased and limited benefits.

3. They are reciprocal in nature.

Select the correct answer using the code given below:

(a) 2 only   (b) 1 and 3 only

(c) 2 and 3 only   (d) 1, 2 and 3

28. Which of the following is considered as vision of Sagarmala Programme?

1. Reduce logistics cost of export-import and domestic trade with minimal infrastructure investment.

2. Lower down logistics cost of bulk commodities by location future industrial capacity near the coast.

3. Improving export competitiveness by developing port proximities.

Select the correct answer using the code given below:

(a) 1, 2 and 3   (b) 2 and 3 only

(c) 1 and 2 only   (d) 1 and 3 only

29. CHAMPIONS online platform was launched by GoI for which of the following purpose?

(a) To promote online education in rural and urban areas.

(b) To conduct online examination of universities.

(c) To provide online coaching to northeastern students for the preparation of UPSC/SPCS examination.

(d) To help and handhold the MSMEs.

30. Consider the following pairs:

(Scheme)	(Objective)
1. Samarth	: World class infrastructure facilities to India textiles industries
2. Scheme for Integrated textiles park (SITP)	: Capacity building in the textile sector
3. Amended Technology Upgradation Fund Scheme	: Modernization and upgradation of the technology of the Indian textile industry

Which of the pairs given above is/are **incorrectly** matched regarding textile industries in India?

(a) 3 only   (b) 2 and 3 only

(c) 1, 2 and 3   (d) 1 and 2 only

31. Consider the following statements regarding New India New railway initiative:

1. Private entities will operate railways through PPP model.

2. Operation, financing, procurement and maintenance of trains will go in the hands of private entities.

3. Government kept the decision regarding fare charges in their own control.

Which of the statements given above is/are correct?

(a) 2 and 3 only   (b) 1 and 2 only

(c) 3 only   (d) 1, 2 and 3

32. Kisan Rail services will provide which of the following services?

1. Market opportunity by transporting perishable items

2. Transportation of agri-products

3. Transportation of marine and dairy products to markets

Select the correct answer using the code given below:

(a) 3 only   (b) 2 and 3 only

(c) 1 and 2 only   (d) 1, 2 and 3

33. Consider the following statements:

1. AMRUT would have thrust on municipal bonds and municipal finance reform.

2. It has decreased an overall outlay of municipality.

3. Municipal bodies have to publish audited annual accounts and present notification of floor rates for property tax.

Which of the statements given above is/are correct in the context of 15th Finance Commission?

(a) 2 only   (b) 2 and 3 only

(c) 1, 2 and 3   (d) 1 and 3 only

34. Which of the following are parameters of fiscal conservatism?

1. Tax concession

2. Reduction in corporate taxes

3. Misconceived Goods and Services Tax

4. Reduction in fiscal deficit

Select the correct answer using the code given below:

(a) 1, 2 and 3 only   (b) 2, 3 and 4 only

(c) 1, 3 and 4 only   (d) 1, 2, 3 and 4

35. Which of the following are considered as economic inequality?

1. Fall in employment

2. Decline in real wages

3. Rise in the number of people in poverty

4. An expected rise in the proportion of undernourished children.

Select the correct answer using the code given below:

(a) 1 and 2 only   (b) 2, 3 and 4 only

(c) 1, 3 and 4 only   (d) 1, 2, 3 and 4

36. Consider the following statements:

1. Anganwadi and Mid-day Meal programme are called direct nutrition programme.

2. Ministry of health and Family Welfare is the implementing agency of anganwadi services.

3. Anganwadi services are clubbed together with other services under 'Saksham Anganwadi and Poshan 2.0'.

Which of the statements given above are correct?

(a) 1 and 3 only

(b) 2 and 3 only

(c) 1 and 2 only

(d) 1, 2 and 3

37. Consider the following statements:

1. Both IMF and World Bank have urged a departure from fiscal orthodoxy in the wake of the pandemic.

2. They are urging the advanced economies to cut its spending when the debt to GDP ratio is poised to rise to 125% by the end of 2021.

Which of the statements given above is/are correct?

(a) 1 only   (b) 2 only

(c) Both 1 and 2   (d) Neither 1 nor 2

38. Consider the following statements:

1. Agriculture is remained the top of the sector for which allocation of fund was announced.

2. Urea is put under the nutrient-based subsidy regime.

3. The goal of $5 trillion economy is depends on the manufacturing sector boost.

Which of the statements given above is/are **incorrect**?

(a) 1 only   (b) 2 and 3 only

(c) 1 and 3 only   (d) 1, 2 and 3

39. Consider the following statements:
    1. Tax holiday has extended to the affordable housing projects.
    2. Infrastructure activities will get a boost with the widening of financing avenues.
    3. The proposal to set up a Development Finance Institution is a huge positive which will reinvigorate investment.

    Which of the statements given above is/are correct regarding economic recovery?

    (a) 1 and 2 only
    (b) 3 only
    (c) 2 and 3 only
    (d) 1, 2 and 3

40. Which of the following statements is/are correct?
    1. Global Risk Report of WEF states that environmental risks continue to threaten the global economy.
    2. A study by Swiss Re Institute have founded that 20% of countries including India is have fragile ecosystems.
    3. The Dasgupta Review stresses the need to find new measures for growth and development to avoid a catastrophic breakdown.

    Select the correct answer using the code given below:

    (a) 1 and 2 only
    (b) 3 only
    (c) 2 and 3 only
    (d) 1, 2 and 3

41. Consider the following statements:
    1. Drug prices in India are regulated to ensure continued availability and affordability of essential lifesaving drugs with improved access to consumers.
    2. National Pharmaceutical Pricing Authority (NPPA) is an independent regulator who fix pricing of drugs and improve its accessibility and affordability.

    Which of the statements given above is/are correct regarding regulation of drug prices in India?

    (a) 1 only
    (b) 2 only
    (c) Both 1 and 2
    (d) Neither 1 nor 2

42. Consider the following statements regarding inflation calculation in India:
    1. Momentum of inflation captures the price changes year to year.
    2. Base effect of inflation captures the price changes a year ago.

Which of the statements given above is/are correct?

(a) 1 only
(b) 2 only
(c) Both 1 and 2
(d) Neither 1 nor 2

43. CPI-C (Combined) inflation is not considered as appropriate due to which of following reasons?
    1. Food inflation due to supply side shock.
    2. Several components of food inflation are transitory with wide variations within the food and beverages group.
    3. Food inflation due to higher weight of food items in the index.

    Select the correct answer using the code given below:

    (a) 1 only
    (b) 2 and 3 only
    (c) 1 and 2 only
    (d) 1, 2 and 3

44. Consider the following statements regarding Insolvency and Bankruptcy code:
    1. Nearly 23 per cent of the cases admitted were settled or withdrawn after the commencement of Corporate Insolvency Resolution Process (CIRP).
    2. Manufacturing Sector, Real Estate, IT sector and Construction are among the top sectors initiating CIRP.

    Which of the statements given above is/are correct?

    (a) 1 only
    (b) 2 only
    (c) Both1 and 2
    (d) Neither 1 nor 2

45. Consider the following statements regarding insurance sector:
    1. Insurance penetration is calculated as ratio of insurance premium to population.
    2. Insurance density is calculated as percentage of insurance premium to GDP.

    Which of the statements given above is/are **incorrect**?

    (a) 1 only
    (b) 2 only
    (c) Both 1 and 2
    (d) Neither 1 nor 2

46. Consider the following statements regarding Non-Banking Financial Companies (NBFCs):
    1. It witnessed slowdown in their growth in 2019-20 largely due to isolated credit events in few large NBFCs and challenges in accessing funds.
    2. It benefitted from the liquidity infusing measures announced by the Reserve Bank during the pandemic by included Targeted Long-Term Repo (TLTRO) Operations.

3. Cost of funds for all types of borrowings by NBFCs marginally increased in June 2020.

Which of the statements given above is/are correct?

(a) 3 only   (b) 1 and 2 only

(c) 2 and 3 only   (d) 1, 2 and 3

47. Which of the following are technological initiatives by GoI for trade related logistics?

1. SWIFT
2. FOIS
3. VAHAN
4. ICEGATE

Select the correct answer using the code given below:

(a) 1, 2, 3 and 4   (b) 2, 3 and 4 only

(c) 3 and 4 only   (d) 1, 2 and 3 only

48. Consider the following statements:

1. RBI's policy on the exchange rate of the rupee has been to allow it to be determined by market forces.
2. India experienced unprecedented FPI outflows of US$ 15.92 billion in March 2020.
3. India is the fifth largest foreign exchange reserves holder among all countries of the world after China, Japan, Switzerland and Russia.

Which of the statements given above is/are correct?

(a) 1 and 3 only   (b) 3 only

(c) 1 and 2 only   (d) 1, 2 and 3

49. Consider the following statements:

1. Indian pharmaceutical industry is third largest in the world in terms of volume
2. It is ahead of China and Italy and 14th largest in terms of value.
3. India was at 11th position in terms of share in world pharma exports in 2019 with Germany, Switzerland and USA occupying the top three positions.

Which of the statements given above is/are correct regarding India pharmaceutical industry?

(a) 1 and 3 only   (b) 2 only

(c) 2 and 3 only   (d) 1, 2 and 3

50. Goods trade barometer index is published by which of the following organization?

(a) World Trade Organization

(b) United Nations Conference on Trade and Development

(c) International Monetary Fund

(d) World Economic Forum

51. Which of the following situations can be categorized as the 'Black Swan Event'?

1. Nuclear apocalypse.
2. Climate changes reaching beyond its tipping point
3. An expected spread of pandemic

Select the correct answer using the codes given below:

(a) 1 and 2 only   (b) 2 only

(c) 1 and 3 only   (d) 1, 2 and 3

52. The Economic Survey 2021 predicts that India Would follow V-shaped recovery in the post pandemic phase. This projection is based on which of the following parameters?

1. E-way Bills
2. Rail freights
3. GST collections
4. Power consumptions

Select the correct answer using the codes given below:

(a) 1 and 2 only   (b) 2, 3 and 4 only

(c) 1, 2 and 3 only   (d) 1, 2, 3 and 4

53. Which of the following measures is/are correct with reference to the fiscal policy measures taken by the Government to assist the revival of economy from COVID 19?

1. Emergency health fund
2. Special Credit Facility to Street Vendors
3. Deferring compliance requirements for FPIs under Voluntary Retention Route
4. Liquidity Injection for DISCOMs

Select the correct answer using the codes given below:

(a) 1, 2 and 4 only   (b) 2 and 4 only

(c) 1, 2, 3 and 4   (d) 3 and 4 only

54. Consider the following statements with reference to the new definition of Micro, Small and Medium Enterprises (MSMEs):

1. The new definition of MSME covers more than 80% of all the such firms.
2. The new definition distinguished between the manufacturing and service MSMEs.

Which of the statements given above is/are correct?

(a) 1 only
(b) 2 only
(c) Both 1 and 2
(d) Neither 1 nor 2

55. Which of the following statements is/are correct with reference to the steps taken by the Government with reference to the steps taken by the Government for corporate sector?

1. Minor technical defaults of the Companies Act have been decriminalised.
2. Removal of penalties for defaults for Small Companies, One-person Companies.
3. Creation of specialised branched of National Companies Law Appellate Tribunal.

Select the correct answer using the codes given below:

(a) 1 and 2 only
(b) 2 only
(c) 1 and 3 only
(d) 1, 2 and 3

56. Which of the following benefits is/are associated with the Counter Cyclic Policy?

1. Liquidity constraints on households is eased.
2. Makes credit expensive and repels investment.
3. Positive consumer sentiment for future productivity.

Select the correct answer using the codes given below:

(a) 1 and 2 only
(b) 2 only
(c) 1 and 3 only
(d) 1, 2 and 3

57. Consider the following statements with reference to the Fiscal Multipliers:

1. It captures the aggregate return derived by the economy from an additional Rupee of fiscal spending.
2. It is greater during economic crises.

Which of the statements given above is/are correct?

(a) 1 only
(b) 2 only
(c) Both 1 and 2
(d) Neither 1 nor 2

58. Consider the following statements:

1. In a Pro-cyclic contractionary fiscal policy, there is increase in Government expenditure and decrease in taxes.
2. In a counter-cyclic expansionary fiscal policy, there is decrease in Government expenditure and increase in taxes.

Which of the statements given above is/are correct?

(a) 1 only
(b) 2 only
(c) Both 1 and 2
(d) Neither 1 nor 2

59. Consider the following statements with reference to the Interest Rate Growth Differential (IGRD):

1. It is the difference between nominal rate of interest in an economy and the nominal rate of growth.
2. A positive IRGD reflects an economic situation where the Government can ensure debt sustainability.
3. Over the last two decades India's IRGD has been negative.

Which of the statements given above is/are correct?

(a) 1 and 2 only
(b) 1 and 3 only
(c) 1 only
(d) 1, 2 and 3

60. Which of the following statements is/are correct with reference to the trend in the GDP Growth rates in India?

1. GDP growth rates have been greater than interest rates over the last two decades.
2. The interest rates have generally been more variable than the GDP growth rates.

Select the correct answer using the codes given below:

(a) 1 only
(b) 2 only
(c) Both 1 and 2
(d) Neither 1 nor 2

61. Consider the following statements:

1. Wealth effect refers to the phenomenon when people tend to spend more as the value of their assets decrease.
2. When a bond is turned again to a new bond, it may lead to Rollover Risk.

Which of the statements given above is/are correct?

(a) 1 only
(b) 2 only
(c) Both 1 and 2
(d) Neither 1 nor 2

62. Which of the following statements is/are correct with reference to the Global Burden of diseases?

1. More than two-thirds of the global deaths and more than half of deaths in India are caused by Non Communicable Diseases.
2. The Economic Survey suggests a specific focus on communicable diseases to deal with possible future pandemics.

Select the correct answer using the codes given below:

(a) 1 only   (b) 2 only

(c) Both 1 and 2   (d) Neither 1 nor 2

63. The World Rule of Law Index is released by which of the following institutions?

(a) World Justice Project

(b) World Economic Forum

(c) United Nations Conference on Trade and Development

(d) World Trade Organization

64. According to the Economic Survey 2021, the prolonged period of forbearance has led to which of the following consequences?

1. Undercapitalization
2. Enhanced lending to zombie firms
3. Weakening of corporate governance.

Select the correct answer using the codes given below:

(a) 1 and 2 only   (b) 2 only

(c) 1 and 3 only   (d) 1, 2 and 3

65. According to the 'Solow Growth Model', the output per unit worker depends on which of the following parameters?

1. Savings
2. Population growth
3. Biodiversity

Select the correct answer using the codes given below:

(a) 1 and 2 only   (b) 2 only

(c) 1 and 3 only   (d) 1, 2 and 3

66. Consider the following statements:

1. More than 50% of India's sovereign external foreign currency denominated debt in 2020 was owed to multilaterals and IMF.
2. India has a history of zero sovereign default.

Which of the statements given above is/are **incorrect**?

(a) 1 only   (b) 2 only

(c) Both 1 and 2   (d) Neither 1 nor 2

67. The Economic Survey 2021 refers to the 'Home Bias', which is associated to which of the following sectors?

(a) Foreign Exchange

(b) Currency Manipulation

(c) Credit rating Agencies

(d) Trade war

68. Consider the following statements with reference to India's public debt:

1. The public debt in India has declined since 2003.
2. The Government's external debt is less than 2% of the GDP.

Which of the statements given above is/are correct?

(a) 1 only   (b) 2 only

(c) Both 1 and 2   (d) Neither 1 nor 2

69. Consider the following statements:

1. V-shaped recovery in industrial production was observed over the year.
2. E-way bills, electronic toll collection, rail freight and port cargo traffic recovered.
3. Indian services sector sustained its recovery from the pandemic driven declines.

Which of the statements given above is/are correct?

(a) 1 only   (b) 2 and 3 only

(c) 1 and 2 only   (d) 1, 2 and 3

70. The Budget 2021-22 proposes to launch the MITRA scheme in which of the following sectors?

(a) Electronics   (b) Solar panels

(c) Textiles   (d) Food Processing

71. Which of the following statements is **NOT** correct with respect to the key takeaways of Budget 2021-22?

1. It provides the highest ever increase in the overall capital expenditure.
2. In the road sector, the capital expenditure provided is the highest ever so far.
3. Railways sector has received the highest ever allocation till date.

Select the correct answer using the code given below:

(a) 1 and 2 only   (b) 1, 2 and 3

(c) 1 and 3 only   (d) None of the above

72. Consider the following statements with respects to the specific target set up the Budget 2021-22 in Railway sector:

1. 100% electrification of Broad-Gauge routes will be completed by 2025.
2. The Western Dedicated Freight Corridor (DFC) and Eastern DFC will be commissioned by the end of 2021.

Which of the statements given above is/are correct?

(a) 1 only
(b) 2 only
(c) Both 1 and 2
(d) Neither 1 nor 2

73. Which of the following existing schemes underwent an expansion in scope in the Budget 2021-22?

1. Ujjwala yojana
2. Operation Green
3. SWAMITVA scheme
4. Ayushman Bharat

Select the correct answer using the code given below:

(a) 1, 2, 3 and 4
(b) 3 and 4 only
(c) 4 only
(d) 1, 2 and 3 only

74. Consider the following statements with respect to the 'Scraping Policy' of vehicles proposed in the Budget 2021-22:

1. It proposes the mandatory requirement of scrapping both commercial and private vehicles.
2. Fitness Tests are mandated for commercial vehicles after 15 years.

Which of the statements given above is/are correct?

(a) 1 only
(b) 2 only
(c) Both 1 and 2
(d) Neither 1 nor 2

75. Consider the following statements about deficits :

1. The difference between revenue expenditure and revenue receipt is known as revenue deficit.
2. The primary deficit is the fiscal deficit minus interest payments

Which of the statements given above is/are correct?

(a) 1 only
(b) 2 only
(c) Both 1 and 2
(d) Neither 1 nor 2

76. Consider the following statements regarding PM AtmaNirbhar Swasth Bharat Yojana:

1. It is a central-sector scheme.
2. It will be launched with an outlay of about 64,180 crores over 6 years.
3. This will develop capacities of primary, secondary, and tertiary care Health Systems, strengthen existing national institutions, and create new institutions, to cater to detection and cure of new and emerging diseases.
4. This will be in addition to the National Health Mission.

Which of the statements given above are correct?

(a) 2, 3 and 4 only
(b) 1 and 4 only
(c) 2 and 3 only
(d) 1, 2 and 3 only

77. Which of the statements given below is/are **incorrect** about The Jal Jeevan Mission (Urban)?

1. It aims at universal water supply in all 4,378 Urban Local Bodies with 2.86 crores household tap connections, as well as liquid waste management in 500 AMRUT cities.
2. It will be implemented over 2 years, with an outlay of 2,87,000 crores.

Select the correct answer using the code given below:

(a) 1 only
(b) 2 only
(c) Both 1 and 2
(d) Neither 1 nor 2

78. Consider the following statements:

1. The New Space India Limited (NSIL), a PSU under the Department of Space will execute the PSLV-CS51 launch, carrying the Amazonia Satellite from Brazil, along with a few smaller Indian satellites.
2. As part of the Gaganyaan mission activities, four Indian astronauts are being trained on Generic Space Flight aspects, in Russia.
3. The first unmanned launch is slated for December 2022.

Which of the statements given above is/are correct?

(a) 1 and 2 only
(b) 3 only
(c) 2 and 3 only
(d) 1, 2 and 3

79. Which of the statements given below is/are correct?

1. A Deep Ocean Mission with a budget outlay of more than 4,000 crores, over five years.
2. This Mission will cover deep ocean survey exploration and projects for the conservation of deep sea bio-diversity.

Select the correct answer using the code given below:

(a) 1 only
(b) 2 only
(c) Both 1 and 2
(d) Neither 1 nor 2

80. Consider the following statements regarding Pradhan Mantri Jan Arogya Yojana (PM-JAY):

1. This ambitious program was launched by Government of India in 2018 to provide healthcare access to the most vulnerable sections.
2. PM-JAY is being used significantly for high frequency, low cost care such as dialysis.

Which of the statements given above is/are **incorrect?**

(a) 1 only   (b) 2 only

(c) Both 1 and 2   (d) Neither 1 nor 2

81. Consider the following statements regarding progress of Pradhan Mantri Jan Arogya Yojana (PM-JAY):

1. The scheme is implementing by 32 states and UTs.

2. Under the scheme 13.48 crore E-cards have been issued.

3. 1.5 crore users have registered on the scheme's website.

Which of the statements given above is/are correct?

(a) 1 and 2 only   (b) 3 only

(c) 2 and 3 only   (d) 1, 2 and 3

82. Consider the following statements regarding Bare Necessities Index (BNI):

1. The BNI summarises 26 indicators on five dimensions viz., water, sanitation, housing, micro-environment, and other facilities.

2. The BNI has been created for all states for 2012 and 2018 using data from two NSO rounds viz., 69th and 76th on Drinking Water, Sanitation, Hygiene and Housing Condition in India.

Which of the statements given above is/are correct?

(a) 1 only   (b) 2 only

(c) Both 1 and 2   (d) Neither 1 nor 2

83. Consider the following statements:

1. The 2030 agenda for Sustainable Development with 17 Sustainable Development Goals (SDGs) and 169 associated targets.

2. It encompasses a comprehensive developmental agenda integrating social, economic and environmental dimensions.

Which of the statements given above is/are **incorrect?**

(a) 1 only   (b) 2 only

(c) Both 1 and 2   (d) Neither 1 nor 2

84. According to Nationally Determined Contribution (NDC) submitted India has sought to-

1. Reduce the emissions intensity of its GDP by 33 to 35 per cent below 2005 levels by the year 2030.

2. Achieve 40 per cent of cumulative electric power installed capacity from non-fossil fuel sources by 2030.

3. Enhance forest and tree cover to create additional carbon sink equivalent to 2.5 to 3 billion tons of carbon dioxide by 2030.

Which of the statements given above is/ are correct?

(a) 1 and 2 only   (b) 2 only

(c) 3 only   (d) 1, 2 and 3

85. Which of the following statements is/are correct?

1. India has taken several proactive steps at both the national and the sub national level to mainstream the SDGs into the policies, schemes and programmes of the Government.

2. In 2020, the highlight of India's SDG initiatives has been the Voluntary National Review (VNR) presented to the United Nations High-Level Political Forum (HLPF) on Sustainable Development which is the highest international platform for review and follow-up of the SDGs under the auspices of the United Nations Economic and Social Council.

Select the correct answer using the code given below:

(a) 1 only   (b) 2 only

(c) Both 1 and 2   (d) Neither 1 nor 2

86. Consider the following statements regarding localization of the SDGs:

1. Localisation of SDGs is crucial to any strategy aimed at achieving the goals under the 2020 Agenda.

2. Essentially, localising SDGs involves the process of adapting, planning, implementing and monitoring the SDGs from national to local levels by relevant institutions and stakeholders.

Which of the statements given above is/are correct?

(a) 1 only   (b) 2 only

(c) Both 1 and 2   (d) Neither 1 nor 2

87. Consider the following statements regarding National Solar Mission (NSM):

1. Its objective is to achieve 100 GW of solar power in seven years starting from 2014-15.

2. The cumulative capacity of 36.9 GW was commissioned till November 2020.

3. Around 36 GW solar energy capacities are under installation, and an additional 19 GW capacity has been tendered.

Which of the statements given above are correct?

(a) 1 and 2 only   (b) 2 and 3 only

(c) 1 and 3 only   (d) 1, 2 and 3

88. Consider the following statements regarding National Mission for Enhanced Energy Efficiency (NMEEE):
   1. Its aim is to achieve growth with ecological sustainability.
   2. The Perform Achieve and Trade (PAT) Scheme is one of the initiatives under the NMEEE, and was initiated in 2019.

   Which of the statements given above is/are correct?
   (a) 1 only   (b) 2 only
   (c) Both 1 and 2   (d) Neither 1 nor 2

89. Consider the following statements regarding National Mission for a Green India (GIM):
   1. It aimed for improved ecosystem services by Increasing forest/tree cover by 5 m ha and improving quality of forest cover on another 5 m ha (a total of 10 m ha).
   2. A sum of 343.08 crore rupees has been released to 13 states during the period 2015-16 to 2019-20 for undertaking afforestation activities over an area of 1.42 lakh ha.

   Which of the statements given above is/are correct?
   (a) 1 only   (b) 2 only
   (c) Both 1 and 2   (d) Neither 1 nor 2

90. Which of the following statements is/are correct regarding National Mission on Sustainable Habitat (NMSH)?
   1. The mission is being implemented through three programmes: Atal Mission on Rejuvenation and Urban Transformation, Swachh Bharat Mission, and Smart Cities Mission.
   2. Under the Smart Cities Mission, 1987 projects have already been completed so far, while 4375 projects are under completion. Smart Cities Mission requires cities to have at least 50 percent energy coming from solar and at least 50 per cent buildings to be energy efficient and green.

   Select the correct answer using the code given below:
   (a) 1 only   (b) 2 only
   (c) Both 1 and 2   (d) Neither 1 nor 2

91. Which of the following statements is/are correct regarding National Water Mission (NWM)?
   1. The National Institute of Hydrology is the nodal agency to get the State Specific Action Plan (SSAP) for the water sector for all states/UTs.
   2. It focuses on monitoring of ground water, aquifer mapping, capacity building, water quality monitoring and other baseline studies.

   Select the correct answer using the code given below:
   (a) 1 only   (b) 2 only
   (c) Both 1 and 2   (d) Neither 1 nor 2

92. Which of the following statements is/are correct regarding National Mission for Sustainable Agriculture?
   1. It aims at enhancing food security by making agriculture more productive, sustainable, remunerative, and climate resilient.
   2. Under the mission 7960 farm machinery banks established in 2018-19 to reduce crop residue burning.

   Select the correct answer using the code given below:
   (a) 1 only   (b) 2 only
   (c) Both 1 and 2   (d) Neither 1 nor 2

93. Consider the following statements regarding National Mission for Sustaining Himalayan Ecosystems:
   1. Its objective is to continuously assess the health status of the Himalayan Ecosystem. Enable policy bodies in their policy formulation functions.
   2. The key achievements include setting up of the Centre of Glaciology at Wadia Institute of Himalayan Geology.

   Which of the statements given above is/are **incorrect**?
   (a) 1 only   (b) 2 only
   (c) Both 1 and 2   (d) Neither 1 nor 2

94. Consider the following statements regarding National Mission on Strategic Knowledge for Climate Change (NMSKCC):
   1. Its aim is to gain a better understanding of climate science, formation of knowledge networks among the existing knowledge institutions engaged in research and development.
   2. Key achievements include setting up of 12 Centres of Excellence and 10 State Climate Change Centres.

   Which of the statements given above is/are correct?
   (a) 1 only   (b) 2 only
   (c) Both 1 and 2   (d) Neither 1 nor 2

95. Which of the following are aims of the Jawaharlal Nehru National Solar Mission (JNNSM)?

1. Deploy 20,000 MW of grid connected solar power by 2022 to be achieved in 3 phases.
2. 2,000 MW of off-grid solar applications including 20 million solar lights by 2022.
3. 20 million sq. m. solar thermal collector area.

Select the correct answer using the code given below:

(a) 1 and 2 only   (b) 1 and 3 only
(c) 2 and 3 only   (d) 1, 2 and 3

96. Consider the following statements regarding Agriculture Infrastructure Fund:

1. This scheme is operational from the year 2020-21 to 2029-30.
2. Under the scheme, 1 lakh crores rupees will be provided by banks and financial institutions as loans to primary agricultural credit societies (PACS), marketing cooperative societies, farmer producers organizations (FPOs), self-help group (SHG), farmers, joint liability groups (JLG), multipurpose cooperative societies, agri-entrepreneurs, startups and central/ state agency or local body sponsored public private partnership project, etc.

Which of the statements given above is/are correct?

(a) 1 only   (b) 2 only
(c) Both 1 and 2   (d) Neither 1 nor 2

97. Consider the following statements regarding India's International Trade in Agricultural Commodities:

1. In 2019-20, India's agricultural and allied exports amounted to approximately 252 thousand crores rupees.
2. The major export destinations were USA, Saudi Arabia, Iran, Nepal and Bangladesh.
3. The top agriculture and related products exported from India were marine products, basmati rice, buffalo meat, spices, non-basmati rice, cotton raw, oil meals, sugar, castor oil and tea.

Which of the statements given above is/are correct?

(a) 1 only   (b) 2 and 3 only
(c) 2 only   (d) 1, 2 and 3

98. Consider the following statements regarding Prime Minister-Formalisation of Micro Food Processing Enterprises (PM-FME):

1. Under the Atma Nirbhar Bharat Abhiyan, Ministry of Food Processing Industries (MoFPI) has launched a new Centrally Sponsored Scheme, Prime Minister-Formalisation of Micro Food Processing Enterprises (PM-FME) with a total outlay of 10,000 crores rupees over the period 2020-2025.
2. The scheme is expected to benefit 2 lakh micro food processing units through credit linked subsidy.

Which of the statements given above is/are correct?

(a) 1 only   (b) 2 only
(c) Both 1 and 2   (d) Neither 1 nor 2

99. Consider the following statements regarding Production-Linked Incentive (PLI) Scheme:

1. It is introduced in 10 key sectors, including food processing sector, for enhancing India's manufacturing capabilities and improving exports.
2. The scheme will not support the branding and marketing abroad.

Which of the statements given above is/are correct?

(a) 1 only   (b) 2 only
(c) Both 1 and 2   (d) Neither 1 nor 2

100. Which of the following statements is/are correct regarding Pradhan Mantri Garib Kalyan Anna Yojana (PM-GKAY)?

1. It was launched for additional allocation of foodgrains from the Central Pool at the rate of 5 kg per person per month free of cost for all the beneficiaries covered under Targeted Public Distribution System (TPDS).
2. The PMGKAY scheme was extended for a further period of 5 months i.e. July – November, 2020.

Select the correct answer using the code given below:

(a) 1 only   (b) 2 only
(c) Both 1 and 2   (d) Neither 1 nor 2

ANSWER KEY

1. (a)	2. (c)	3. (d)	4. (b)	5. (c)	6. (a)	7. (a)	8. (b)	9. (d)	10. (d)
11. (c)	12. (a)	13. (a)	14. (c)	15. (d)	16. (c)	17. (c)	18. (d)	19. (d)	20. (c)
21. (d)	22. (d)	23. (a)	24. (c)	25. (a)	26. (d)	27. (b)	28. (a)	29. (d)	30. (d)
31. (b)	32. (d)	33. (d)	34. (d)	35. (d)	36. (a)	37. (a)	38. (d)	39. (d)	40. (d)
41. (c)	42. (b)	43. (d)	44. (c)	45. (c)	46. (b)	47. (a)	48. (d)	49. (a)	50. (a)
51. (d)	52. (d)	53. (c)	54. (a)	55. (c)	56. (c)	57. (c)	58. (d)	59. (b)	60. (a)
61. (b)	62. (a)	63. (a)	64. (d)	65. (a)	66. (d)	67. (c)	68. (a)	69. (d)	70. (c)
71. (d)	72. (d)	73. (d)	74. (b)	75. (c)	76. (a)	77. (b)	78. (a)	79. (c)	80. (d)
81. (d)	82. (c)	83. (d)	84. (d)	85. (c)	86. (b)	87. (d)	88. (a)	89. (c)	90. (a)
91. (b)	92. (c)	93. (d)	94. (c)	95. (d)	96. (c)	97. (d)	98. (c)	99. (a)	100. (c)

EXPLANATION

1. a   A new centrally sponsored scheme, PM AtmaNirbhar Swasth Bharat Yojana, will be launched with an outlay of about Rs. 64,180 crores over 6 years. This will develop capacities of primary, secondary, and tertiary care Health Systems, strengthen existing national institutions, and create new institutions, to cater to detection and cure of new and emerging diseases. This will be in addition to the National Health Mission.

2. c   A voluntary vehicle scrapping policy, to phase out old and unfit vehicles was announced. This will help in encouraging fuel-efficient, environment friendly vehicles, thereby reducing vehicular pollution and oil import bill. Vehicles would undergo fitness tests in automated fitness centres after 20 years in case of personal vehicles, and after 15 years in case of commercial vehicles.

3. d   To enable the textile industry to become globally competitive, attract large investments and boost employment generation, a scheme of Mega Investment Textiles Parks (MITRA) will be launched in addition to the PLI scheme. This will create world class infrastructure with plug and play facilities to enable create global champions in exports. 7 Textile Parks will be established over 3 years.

4. b   A total of 702 km of conventional metro is operational and another 1,016 km of metro and RRTS is under construction in 27 cities. Two new technologies i.e., 'MetroLite' and 'MetroNeo' will be deployed to provide metro rail systems at much lesser cost with same experience, convenience and safety in Tier-2 cities and peripheral areas of Tier-1 cities.

5. c   Government has kept fuel supplies running across the country without interruption during the COVID-19 lockdown period. Taking note of the crucial nature of this sector in people's lives, the following key initiatives are being announced:

   a. Ujjwala Scheme which has benefited 8 crores households will be extended to cover 1 crores more beneficiaries.

   a. We will add 100 more districts in next 3 years to the City Gas Distribution network.

   b. A gas pipeline project will be taken up in Union Territory of Jammu & Kashmir.

   c. An independent Gas Transport System Operator will be set up for facilitation and coordination of booking of common carrier capacity in all-natural gas pipelines on a non-discriminatory open access basis.

6. a   Substantial investments in the development of modern fishing harbours and fish landing centres had proposed. To start with, 5 major fishing harbours – Kochi, Chennai, Visakhapatnam, Paradip, and Petuaghat – will be developed as hubs of economic activity. Government will also develop inland fishing harbours and fish-landing centres along the banks of rivers and waterways.

7. a Government introduced a series of reforms in the Direct tax system for the benefit of taxpayers and the economy. Few months prior to the pandemic, in order to attract investments they slashed Corporate tax rate to make it among the lowest in the world. The Dividend Distribution Tax too was abolished. The burden of taxation on small taxpayers was eased by increasing rebates. In 2020, the return filers saw a dramatic increase to 6.48 crore from 3.31 crore in 2014. In the previous Budget, the government abolished the Dividend Distribution Tax (DDT) in order to incentivise investment. Dividend was made taxable in the hands of shareholders.

8. b In Budget 2021, various sectors are classified as strategic and non-strategic sectors. The strategic sectors classified are:

   i)   Atomic energy, Space and Defence

   ii) Transport and Telecommunications

   iii) Power, Petroleum, Coal and other minerals

   iv) Banking, Insurance and financial services

9. d The Pradhan Mantri Garib Kalyan Yojana (PMGKY) for ensuring food security through public distribution system, direct benefit transfers to widows, pensioners and women, additional funds for MGNREGS, and debt moratoria and liquidity support for businesses.

10. d The proposed structural reforms in the mining sector aim to increase participation of the private sector in mineral exploration, redefine the norms of exploration for auction of mineral blocks to ensure a seamless exploration-cum-mining-cum-production regime. They will also redefine the standard of exploration required for auctioning of blocks for prospecting license-cum mining lease and open acreage licensing policy for allocation of mining rights which will give a major boost to the production of minerals in the country. These reforms aim to reduce dependence on imported coal, to create a strong, self-reliant domestic energy sector, attract private investments, generate jobs and stimulate the economic growth in the medium-term.

11. c Indian Kings used to build palaces during famines and droughts to provide employment and improve the economic fortunes of the private sector. Economic theory, in effect, makes the same recommendation: in a recessionary year, Government must spend more than during expansionary times. Such counter-cyclical fiscal policy stabilizes the business cycle by being contractionary (reduce spending/increase taxes) in good times and expansionary (increase spending/reduce taxes) in bad times. On the other hand, a pro-cyclical fiscal policy is the one wherein fiscal policy reinforces the business cycle by being expansionary during good times and contractionary during recessions.

12. a After analyzing the key parameters of debt dynamics and their implications, it is imperative to understand the structure and characteristics of India's public debt. India's public debt-toGDP has been significantly low compared to high global debt levels. A cross-country comparison of debt levels points out that for India, the government debt level as a proportion of GDP is equal to the median in the group of G-20 OECD countries and in the group of BRICS nations. India's overall debt levels as a per cent of GDP are the lowest amongst the group of G-20 OECD countries and also among the group of BRICS nations. Moreover, public debt and overall debt level for India has declined since 2003 and has been stable since 2011.

13. a Compared to 2012, access to "the bare necessities" has improved across all States in the country in 2018. Access to bare necessities is the highest in the States such as Kerala, Punjab, Haryana and Gujarat while it is the lowest in Odisha, Jharkhand, West Bengal and Tripura. The improvements are widespread as they span each of the five dimensions viz., access to water, housing, sanitation, micro-environment and other facilities. InterState disparities in the access to "the bare necessities" have declined in 2018 when compared to 2012 across rural and urban areas. This is because the States where the level of access to "the bare necessities" was low in 2012 have gained relatively more between 2012 and 2018.

14. c India entered the top 50 innovating countries for the first time in 2020 since the inception of the Global Innovation Index (GII) in 2007, by improving its rank from 81 in 2015 to 48 in 2020. To herald this significant achievement while setting out the path for further progress, the Survey examines India's innovation performance on various dimensions. India ranks first in Central and South Asia, and third amongst lower middle-income group economies

15. d The P. J. Nayak Committee (2014), constituted by RBI, highlighted in its report submitted in May 2014 the twin concerns stemming from the forbearance regime: ever-greening of loans by classifying NPAs as restructured assets and the resultant undercapitalization of banks. Once the forbearance policy was discontinued in 2015, RBI conducted an Asset Quality Review to know the exact amount

of bad loans present in the banking system. As a result, banks' disclosed NPAs increased significantly from 2014-15 to 2015-16. In the absence of forbearance, banks preferred disclosing NPAs to the restructuring of loans. Thus, the roots of the present banking crisis go back to the prolonged forbearance policies followed between 2008 and 2015.

16. c Precisely, the forbearance period witnessed an increase in lending to unproductive firms, popularly referred to as "zombies". Zombies are typically identified using the interest coverage ratio, the ratio of a firm's profit after tax to its total interest expense. Firms with an interest coverage ratio lower than one are unable to meet their interest obligations from their income and are categorized as zombies. This increased lending to zombies could merely be a reflection of the poor financial performance of firms during the forbearance regime. To assess whether it is indeed the case of risky lending, a revised definition of zombie firms is considered. Under this alternative definition, zombie firms are those whose interest coverage ratio lies in the bottom quartile. This definition ensures that the proportion of zombies remains the same across all years.

17. c At 3-4 per cent, the hospitalisation rates in India are among the lowest in the world; the average for middle income countries is 8-9 per cent and 13-17 per cent for OECD countries (OECD Statistics). Given the increasing burden of NCD, lower life expectancy, higher MMR and IMR, the low hospitalisation rates are unlikely to reflect a more healthy population as compared to middle income or OECD countries. Thus, the low hospitalisation rates reflect lower access and utilisation of healthcare in India. India has one of the highest levels of OOPE in the world.

18. d Never in the history of sovereign credit ratings has the fifth largest economy in the world been rated as the lowest rung of the investment grade (BBB-/Baa3). China and India are the only exceptions to this rule – China was rated A-/A2 in 2005 and now India is rated BBB-/Baa3.

Within its sovereign credit ratings cohort – countries rated between A+/A1 and BBB-/ Baa3 for S&P/ Moody's – India is a clear outlier on several parameters, i.e. a sovereign whose rating is significantly lower than mandated by the effect on the sovereign rating of the parameter. These include GDP growth rate, inflation, general government debt (as per cent of GDP), cyclically adjusted primary balance (as per cent of potential GDP), current account balance (as per cent of GDP), political stability, rule of law, control of corruption, investor protection, ease of doing business, short-term external debt (as per cent of reserves), reserve adequacy ratio and sovereign default history. The outlier status remains true not only now but also during the last two decades.

19. d • **PM eVIDYA:** This initiative was announced for school and higher education under the Atma Nirbhar Bharat programme in May, 2020. It is a comprehensive initiative to unify all efforts related to digital/online/on-air education to enable multi-mode and equitable access to education for students and teachers.

• **One nation, one digital education infrastructure:** Under this component all States/UTs have free access to a single digital infrastructure i.e, DIKSHA. It is artificial intelligence based, highly scalable, and can be accessed through a web-portal and mobile application. It provides access to a large number of curricula linked e-content through several use cases and solutions such as QR coded Energized Textbooks (ETBs), courses for teachers, quizzes and others. DIKSHA has experienced more than 800 crore hits since lockdown. In April, 2020, VidyaDaan portal was launched on Diksha as a national content contribution program that leverages the DIKSHA platform and tools to seek and allow contribution/donation of e-learning resources for school education by educational bodies, private bodies, and individual experts.

• **For the differently-abled:** One DTH channel is being operated specifically for hearing impaired students in sign language. For visually and hearing-impaired students, study material has been developed in Digitally Accessible Information System (DAISY) and in sign language; both are available on NIOS website/ YouTube. 25 NCERT textbooks have also been converted into DAISY format.

• PRAGYATA guidelines on digital education was developed with a focus on online/blended/ digital education for students who are presently at home due to the closure of schools.

• **MANODARPAN:** The 'Manodarpan' initiative for psychosocial support has been included in the Atmanirbhar Bharat Abhiyan, as part of strengthening and empowering the human capital to increase productivity and efficiency through reforms and initiatives in the education sector.

20. c The workers in the usual status (ps+ss) are obtained by considering the usual principal status (ps) and the subsidiary status (ss) together. The workers in the usual status (ps+ss) include (a) the persons who worked for a relatively long part of the 365 days preceding the date of survey and (b) the persons from among the remaining population who had worked at least for 30 days during the reference period of 365 days preceding the date of survey.

21. d The decline in unemployment rate is widespread across all the categories. The highest decline in unemployment rates is seen among those who have received formal vocational/ technical training. The level of unemployment is recorded the highest, 20.2 per cent, among urban youth (age 15-29 years) and the lowest for the subgroup 'not literates' at 1.1 per cent among the persons of age 15 years and above with different educational attainments. The youth unemployment rates varies widely across States in India. The States like Arunachal Pradesh, Kerala, Manipur, and Bihar are on the high extreme while the States such as Gujarat, Karnataka, West Bengal and Sikkim are on the lower extreme. States/UTs on the red line or close to it, such as Bihar, Himachal Pradesh and Maharashtra, indicates that their youth unemployment rate in urban areas is almost equal to the unemployment rate in rural areas, and the States/UTs above the line indicate higher youth unemployment in urban than rural. It is quite visible that unemployment rates in urban are much higher than the rural sector in most of the States/UTs.

22. d National Commission on Rural Labour by Prof. C. H. Hanumantha Rao: Made recommendations for specific categories of workers, definition of migrant workers to cover all migrants, recommended a minnimum wage of Rs. 20 per day at 1990 prices.

Mitra Committee by Shri Mitra: Major recommendations in IR Act, definition of workman should have no nexus with wages drawn by workman, and should be made uniform in all labour legislations.

Ninth Five Year Plan Vol-2, Human & Social Development: Existing labour laws cover a small segment of workforce. Ninth Plan aims at reducing the number of laws, with the objective that a smaller number of laws reach the entire workforce.

Tenth Five Year Plan, Vol-I & II, Labour Welfare & Social Security: Rigid labour laws applied to the organised sector make it difficult for the entrepreneur to rationalise labour than to dispose of capital assets when the need arises. Effective cost of labour to the entrepreneur can be many times the nominal wage bill. Reform labour laws

23. a Unpaid activities include taking care of children, elderly in the household, production of goods and services for own consumption, while paid activities include self-employment, regular wage/salary jobs and casual work. SNA production activity include employment, Unpaid direct volunteering for other households for production of goods or for production of goods/services for market/non-market units, Unpaid community and organization-based volunteering for production of goods or for production of goods/services for market/non-market units,etc and Non-SNA Production includes Unpaid domestic services for household members, Unpaid caregiving services for household members, Unpaid direct volunteering for other households for production of services for the households and Unpaid community- and organization-based volunteering for production of services for the households.

24. c COVID-19 demonstrated the importance of investing and strengthening public health system. India has made significant progress in improving its health outcomes over the last two decades by eliminating Polio, Guinea worm disease, Yaws and maternal & neonatal Tetanus. Health indicators shows, Total Fertility Rate (TFR) has reduced sharply from 3.6 in 1991 to 2.2 in 2018. Maternal Mortality Ratio (MMR) was 113 per 1,00,000 live births for the period 2016- 2018 and Under Five Mortality Rate (U5MR) was 36 per 1000 live births in 2018. But in 2020, it was the COVID-19 pandemic that put to test the health infrastructure of India. The pandemic brought forth the inherent strengths of the medical fraternity in effectively managing the spread of the disease. There are more than 1 crore Covid-19 cases reported in India, with recovery of more than 95 per cent. However, the country lost around 1.52 lakh lives due to the Covid-19 pandemic.

25. a The gross FDI equity inflows (excluding re-invested earnings) into the services sector jumped 34 per cent YoY during April-September 2020 to reach US$ 23.61 billion, accounting for almost four-fifth of the total gross FDI equity inflows into India during this period (Table 4). The jump in FDI equity inflows was driven by strong inflows into the 'Computer Software & Hardware' sub-sector, wherein FDI inflows increased to US$ 17.55 billion which is over 336 per cent higher over the corresponding period last year. High growth in FDI inflows was also present in subsectors such as 'Retail Trading', 'Agriculture Services', and 'Education'.

26. d India improved its position from 12th in 2018 to 9th in 2019 in the list of the world's largest FDI recipients according to the latest World Investment Report 2020 by United Nations Conference on Trade and Development (UNCTAD). FDI into India recorded almost 17 per cent jump during April-September 2020 over the corresponding period last year, despite the global slowdown, the COVID-19 pandemic, lockdown measures and supply chain disruptions.

27. b Transport Bubbles" or "Air Travel Arrangements" are temporary arrangements between two countries aimed at restarting commercial passenger services when regular international flights are suspended as a result of the COVID-19 pandemic. They are reciprocal in nature, meaning airlines from both countries enjoy similar benefits.

28. a To harness the coastline, 14,500 km of potentially navigable waterways and strategic location on key international maritime trade routes, the Government has embarked on the ambitious Sagarmala Programme to promote port-led development in the country. The vision of the Programme is to reduce logistics cost of Exports-Imports and domestic trade with minimal infrastructure investment. This includes reducing the cost of transporting domestic cargo; lowering logistical cost of bulk commodities by locating future industrial capacities near the coast; improving export competitiveness by developing port proximate discrete manufacturing clusters, etc.

29. d In a major initiative, on 9th May, 2020, the GoI launched CHAMPIONS online platform to help and handhold the MSMEs. 'CHAMPIONS' stands for Creation and Harmonious Application of Modern Processes for Increasing the Output and National Strength. It is an ICT based technology system aimed at making the smaller units big by solving their grievances, encouraging, supporting, helping and handholding them throughout the business lifecycle. The platform facilitates a single window solution for all the needs of the MSMEs

30. d The GoI is implementing several schemes cutting across sectors such as the Amended Technology Upgradation Fund Scheme (ATUFS), Scheme for Integrated textiles park (SITP) and a scheme called Samarth. ATUFS, is a revised version of TUFS and has the objective to modernize and upgrade the technology of the Indian textile industry. SITP is for providing world class infrastructure facilities. Of the 56 textile parks which were sanctioned under SITP, 23 have been completed so far. Samarth focusses on capacity building in the textile sector. In addition, other schemes specific to silk, jute, wool, handloom and handicraft sectors are also being implemented.

31. b The GoI has allowed the private players to operate in the Railways sector through the PPP mode under the "New India New Railway" initiative. The initiative is expected to garner an investment of about Rs. 30,000 crores from the private sector. Ministry of Railways has identified over 150 pairs of train services for the introduction of 151 modern train sets or rakes through private participation. The private entity shall be responsible for financing, procuring, operating, and maintenance of the trains and shall have the freedom to decide on the fare to be charged from its passengers. The private entities that would undertake the project is being selected through a two-stage competitive bidding process. The bidding process is expected to be completed by May 2021 and the private trains are likely to be introduced in 2023-24.

32. d The Union Budget 2020-21 made an announcement to run the Kisan Rail services to provide better market opportunity by transporting perishables and agri-product, including milk, meat, and fish. Railways had actively pursued with various stakeholders – including the Ministry of Agriculture, state governments, and local bodies – to rollout the Kisan Rail services. The Railways has so far operated Kisan Rail services on thirteen routes. Till 8th January 2021, a total of 120 trips of Kisan Rail have been operated, transporting more than 34,000 tonnes of consignments.

33. d
- Building on the track record of previous finance commissions, the XV FC Commission has significantly raised the bar on financial governance of India's municipalities in the interim report in at least four specific ways.
- If the final report furthers or even maintains these four specific agendas, it could be a watershed moment in the otherwise stolid journey of financial governance reforms of India's municipalities.
- First, the XV FC in its interim report has tried to significantly increase the overall outlay for municipalities.
- Second, two very important entry conditions have been set for any municipality (there are approximately 4,500 of them) in India to receive FC grants: Publication of audited annual accounts and notification of floor rates for property tax.
- There is also a thrust on municipal bonds and municipal finance reform conditions under AMRUT.

- Third, the XV FC has adopted a nuanced approach of distinguishing between million-plus urban agglomerations, and other cities.

34. d Persisting fiscal conservatism

- Fiscal conservatism is the economic philosophy of prudence in government spending and debt.
- Tax concessions, such as the sharp reduction in corporate tax rates in September 2019, and the misconceived Goods and Services Tax regime, underlie the erosion of the revenue base.
- Though presented before the COVID-19 pandemic was officially acknowledged, the Budget for 2020-21 had projected only a modest increase in the revenue receipts of the Centre, from Rs. 16.8 lakh crore in 2019-20 to Rs. 20.2 lakh crore.
- The revised estimates suggest that revenue receipts actually fell to Rs.15.6 lakh crore.
- Moreover, the government's ambitious disinvestment agenda that was expected to pull in Rs. 2.1 lakh crore of non-debt capital receipts seems to have been completely derailed. The sum garnered was just Rs. 32,000 crore.
- In the event, if spending had to be hiked significantly, deficit concerns had to be dropped.
- The government was clearly not willing to go in that direction, keeping expenditure growth low relative to requirement. That conservatism seems to persist.
- Total expenditure is projected to rise by just 0.95% in 2021-22 relative to revised estimates for 2020-21, even if 14.5% relative to the Budget estimate for 2020-21.

35. d

- The novel coronavirus pandemic and the resultant lockdown led to massive job and livelihood losses.
- Unlike most advanced countries and emerging market economies, India's response to address the distress of the masses has been meagre.
- The government's additional public spending to cope with the unprecedented crisis has been a little over 1% of GDP.
- As is widely known, the output (GDP) contraction in 2020-21 has come on top of a slowdown in GDP growth over much of the previous decade (the 2010s), fall in employment, the decline in real wages, rise in the number of people in poverty, and, hence, an expected rise in the proportion of undernourished children.

- Much of the decline in the growth rate is on account of an unprecedented fall in fixed investment rate as a ratio of GDP, especially in infrastructure sectors.

36. a

- The partial National Family Health Survey-5 results released recently showed that child malnutrition levels in 2019 were higher than in 2016 in most States.
- The fall in incomes witnessed by most poor and working-class households in the last one year would have made this situation even worse.
- Recent field surveys conducted by Hunger Watch and the Azim Premji University between October 2020 and December 2020 found that for two-thirds of the respondents, food intake was still not back to pre-lockdown levels.
- Malnutrition has multiple determinants with access to food, health and care being the immediate.
- In this context, direct nutrition programmes such as the anganwadi programme and school mid-day meals make a crucial contribution to the diets of children and pregnant and lactating women.
- There are large gaps in delivery of supplementary nutrition. It is not clear whether the revised estimates reflect a true picture, because data of the Controller General of Accounts show that the expenditure of the entire Ministry of Women and Child Development (which implements anganwadi services among other things) up to December 2020 was only Rs. 14,607.1 crore (49% of Budget estimates).
- In the current Budget, different schemes have been clubbed together and anganwadi services are now part of something called 'Saksham Anganwadi and Poshan 2.0' which has an allocated budget of Rs. 20,105 crore.

37. a

- The International Monetary Fund (IMF) and the World Bank, both flag-bearers of the Washington Consensus, have been urging a departure from fiscal orthodoxy in the wake of the pandemic.
- Both these institutions used to be wary of any increase in the public debt to GDP ratio beyond 100%.
- Today, they are urging the advanced economies to spend more by running up deficits even when the debt to GDP ratio is poised to rise to 125% by the end of 2021.
- The Survey argues that in India, the growth rate is higher than the interest rate most of the time.

- So the conventional restraints on fiscal policy need to be questioned, especially when there is a serious contraction of the sort the Indian economy faced in 2020-21.

- It says that, in the current situation, expansionary fiscal policy will boost growth and cause debt to GDP ratios to be lower, not higher.

- Given India's growth potential, we do not have to worry about debt sustainability until 2030.

- These points are by no means novel; the conditions for debt sustainability are well known.

- However, the Survey's line was not accepted in the past. Indian fiscal policy has adhered to orthodoxy even during a downturn, such as the one we faced in the years preceding the pandemic.

38. d
- Sector-specific targeted proposals, barring production-linked incentives for industry are few as agriculture and the micro and small industries segment — which shores up demand with their consumption multipliers — seem to have been accorded lower priority.

- There are no radical reform proposals for the agriculture sector, with no announcements with regard to bringing urea under the nutrient-based subsidy regime or rationalising the Public Distribution System issue prices of foodgrains.

- In fact, the recent growth performance of the sector has led the Finance Minister not to have any increase in cash transfers under the Pradhan Mantri Kisan Samman Nidhi Scheme (PM-KISAN) from the existing Rs. 6,000 per Year.

- Manufacturing growth, which is expected to be a catalyst in pushing the economy toward the $5- trillion economy goal (by 2025), would depend entirely on how private investments pick up.

- While the textile sector is the focal point to push employment and industrialisation, a lack of concrete policies towards export promotion at a time when the exchange rate is appreciating and a pedalling with tariffs to increase protection is frequent, might undermine the competitiveness of manufacturing exports.

39. d
- Tax holidays extended to affordable housing projects, together with the extended deduction on loans for affordable housing will give relief to the real estate sector, one of the hardest hit by the pandemic.

- Infrastructure activities will get a boost with the widening of financing avenues. The ambitious targets laid down under the National Infrastructure Pipeline necessitate promoting new mechanisms for raising capital.

- The proposal to set up a Development Finance Institution is a huge positive which will reinvigorate investment.

- FICCI has been advocating the need for such an institution for a while, and we hope that the government will consider expanding the proposed DFI's scope to long-gestation projects besides infrastructure.

- Foreign portfolio investments being allowed in the debt financing of InVITs (infrastructure investment trust) and REITs (real estate investment trusts) will further boost the infrastructure and real estate sectors.

40. d
- The WEF's Global Risks report for 2021 states that environmental risks continue to threaten the global economy.

- The top five risks are extreme weather, climate action failure, human environmental damage, infectious diseases and biodiversity loss.

- A study by Swiss Re Institute published in 2020 introduces a new biodiversity and ecosystem services index.

- It found that globally, 20% of countries, including India, have fragile ecosystems.

- It also states that 55% of the global GDP depends on high-functioning biodiversity and ecosystem services.

- The Economics of Biodiversity: The Dasgupta Review, commissioned by HM Treasury and released on February 2, 2021, highlights the grave risks faced by the world because of the failure of economics to take into account the rapid degradation of nature.

- The review stresses the need to find new measures for growth and development to avoid a catastrophic breakdown.

- The world's governments need to come up with a form of national accounting that is different from the GDP model, and the new system has to account for the depletion of nature and natural resources.

41. c Drug prices in India are regulated to ensure continued availability and affordability of essential lifesaving drugs with improved access to consumers. National Pharmaceutical Pricing Authority (NPPA), which is an independent regulator for pricing of drugs and to ensure availability and accessibility of medicines at affordable prices, has played an active role in addressing the exigencies arising out of COVID-19 pandemic and undertook necessary measures to ensure continued availability of life saving essential medicines throughout the country. It invoked extraordinary powers in public interest to ensure that policy enhances access to life saving drugs like Heparin and Medical Oxygen.

42. b When changes in the CPI in the base month have a considerable effect on changes in YoY inflation, this is referred to as base effect. Base effects are therefore the contribution to changes in the annual rate of measured inflation from abnormal changes in the CPI in the base period. Hence, we need to distinguish whether changes in inflation are caused by price changes in the current month, or by extreme price changes in the base period.

   1. Momentum: It captures the recent price changes.

   2. Base effect: It captures the price changes a year ago.

43. d The Survey finds that sole focus on CPI-C inflation may not be appropriate for four reasons. First, food inflation, which contributes significantly to CPI-C is driven primarily by supply-side factors. Second, given its role as the headline target for monetary policy, changes in CPI-C anchor inflation expectations. This occurs despite inflation in CPI-C being driven by supplyside factors that drive food inflation. Third, several components of food inflation are transitory with wide variations within the food and beverages group. Finally, food inflation has been driving overall CPI-C inflation due to the relatively higher weight of food items in the index.

44. c Since the inception of the Code in December 2016, 4,117 applications have been admitted as on December 31, 2020 (Figure 19). Nearly 23 per cent of the cases admitted were settled or withdrawn after the commencement of Corporate Insolvency Resolution Process (CIRP). Out of the 1420 cases for which the CIRP process has been completed, liquidation as an outcome has happened nearly 3.6 times the resolution. Manufacturing Sector, Real Estate and Construction are among the top three sectors initiating CIRP.

45. c The performance and potential of insurance sector is assessed using two indicatorsInsurance penetration and Insurance Density. Insurance penetration is calculated as percentage of insurance premium to GDP and insurance density is calculated as ratio of insurance premium to population. 4.51 In India, Insurance penetration which was 2.71 per cent in 2001 has steadily increased to 3.76 per cent in 2019. In contrast, insurance penetration in Asia, i.e., Malaysia, Thailand and China was 4.72, 4.99 and 4.30 per cent respectively in 2019. The insurance density in India which was US$ 11.5 in 2001 reached to approximately US$ 78 in 2019. The comparative figuresfor Malaysia, Thailand and China in 2019 were much higher at US$ 536, US$ 389 and US$ 430 respectively.

46. b
- NBFCs witnessed slowdown in their growth in 2019-20 largely due to isolated credit events in few large NBFCs and challenges in accessing funds.
- Total assets of NBFCs had increased from Rs. 23.41 lakh crore in March 2018 to 29.23 lakh crore in March 2019, and further to Rs. 33.91 lakh crore in March 2020, resulting in an annual growth of 16.01 per cent during 2019-20 as compared with 24.86 per cent in 2018-19.
- Banks continued to support NBFCs with their lending expanding 9.2 per cent (YoY) till October 2020, well above the overall bank credit growth.
- The sector also benefitted from the liquidity infusing measures announced by the Reserve Bank during the pandemic that also included Targeted Long-Term Repo (TLTRO) Operations covering the NBFC sector.
- Cost of funds for all types of borrowings by NBFCs marginally declined in June 2020, compared to March 2020 or June 2019, except for Non-Convertible Debentures (NCDs). Cost of NCDs, which contribute to major source of funds for NBFCs, increased marginally from 8.1 per cent in March 2020 to 8.2 per cent in June 2020.

47. a India Logistics Platform (iLOG) - Several IT-based solutions have been deployed by government over the years such as Indian Customs EDI Gateway (ICEGATE) and Single Window Interface for Trade (SWIFT) developed for trade facilitation; Port Community System (PCS) for cargo handling at seaports; Freight Operations Information System (FOIS) by Indian Railways and VAHAN (National Vehicle Registration System) by Ministry of Road Transport and Highways. However, each system owner has adopted a different approach, leaving critical gaps that require manual or offline processing at various stages. Therefore, a comprehensive platform iLOG is being developed for integrating all logistics related digital portals.

48. d RBI's policy on the exchange rate of the rupee has been to allow it to be determined by market forces, with interventions only to maintain orderly market conditions by containing excessive volatility in the exchange rate, without reference to any pre-determined target level or band. India experienced unprecedented FPI outflows of US$ 15.92 billion in March 2020, after recording cumulative inflows of US$ 1.42 billion in January 2020 and February 2020, with high volatility in the INR. RBI deployed several conventional and unconventional tools in order to ensure financial stability and orderly conditions in financial markets and has been largely successful in controlling the volatility in the rupee. India is the fifth largest foreign exchange reserves holder among all countries of the world after China, Japan, Switzerland and Russia.

49. a Indian pharmaceutical industry is third largest in the world, in terms of volume, behind China and Italy and 14th largest in terms of value. India almost doubled its share in world pharma exports in a span of ten years from 1.4 per cent in 2010 to 2.6 per cent in 2019. India was at 11th position in terms of share in world pharma exports in 2019 with Germany, Switzerland and USA occupying the top three positions. India enjoys a consistent and long run Revealed Comparative Advantage (RCA) in its pharmaceutical exports since 2009. However, in a cross-country perspective, India's revealed comparative advantage (RCA) stands at 12th spot.

50. a WTO's goods trade barometer index is a leading indicator that signals changes in world trade growth two to three months ahead of merchandise trade volume statistics. Its baseline value is 100, a value greater than 100 suggests above-trend growth while a value below 100 indicates below-trend growth.

51. d
- A black swan is an unpredictable situation that is much beyond what is normally expected of a situation and has potentially severe consequences.
- Black swan events are characterized by their extreme rarity, severe impact, and the widespread insistence they were obvious in hindsight.
- All the situations listed above can lead to Black swan event. In the Economic Survey 2021, the COVID 19 pandemic is referred to as the Black swan event.

52. d
- **All the statements are correct.**
- The economy witnessed a sharp contraction of 23.9 per cent in the first quarter FY 2020-21 and 7.5 per cent in 2nd Quarter of FY 2020-21 due to the stringent lockdown imposed during March-April 2020.

- Since then, several high frequency indicators (such as E-way Bills) have demonstrated a V-shaped recovery. Indicators like E-way bills, rail freight, GST collections and power consumption not only reached pre-pandemic levels but also surpassed previous year levels.

53. c
- To assist the revival of economy from COVID 19, several fiscal policy measures were announced by the Government that included
  - o Emergency health fund
  - o Special Credit Facility to Street Vendors
  - o Liquidity Injection for DISCOMs
  - o Pradhan Mantri Garib Kalyan Yojana
  - o Increment in daily wage under MGNREGS
  - o Tax & contribution policy changes
  - o Support to States, linking borrowings to Reforms; etc.
- "Deferring compliance requirements for FPIs under Voluntary Retention Route" is part of the monetary policy (not fiscal policy) announced by the Central Bank.

54. a
- New MSME definition covering almost 99 per cent of all firms enabling MSMEs to grow in size and create jobs. **Hence, the 1st statement is correct.**
- Removal of artificial separation between manufacturing and service MSMEs. **Hence, the 2nd statement is incorrect.**

55. c
- Many structural reforms have been taken by the Government for the corporate sector:
- Minor technical and procedural defaults of the Companies Act have been decriminalised. **Hence, the 1st statement is correct.**
- Power for the creation of additional/ specialized benches for NCLAT. **Hence, the 3rd statement is correct.**
- Lower penalties for all defaults for Small Companies, One-person Companies, Producer Companies & Start Ups. **Hence, the 2nd statement is incorrect.**
- Simplified Proforma for Incorporating Company Electronically Plus (SPICe +) introduced.
- Including the provisions of Part IXA (Producer Companies) of Companies Act, 1956 in Companies Act, 2013.

56. c
- The Survey points out that counter-cyclical fiscal policy is necessary to smooth out economic cycles, more so in the case of a crisis like the pandemic.

- A binding liquidity constraint on households is imposed in case of economic crisis due to less disposable income. Thus a fiscal stimulus by the government eases the liquidity situation of the households and leads to consequent increase in consumption levels. **Hence, the 1st statement is correct.**

- Investment sentiment turns negative and growth is impacted during a crisis. Fiscal expansion increases market liquidity, thus making credit cheaper and stimulating investment and growth. **Hence, the 2nd statement is incorrect.**

- An increase in government investment spending provides sends the positive signal for future productivity. **Hence, the 3rd statement is correct.**

57. c   **Both the statements are correct.**

- Fiscal multipliers capture the aggregate return derived by the economy from an additional Rupee of fiscal spending. These are undoubtedly greater during economic crises, when compared to economic expansion, due to following reasons:
  - o The liquidity situation of the households is eased with increased government expenditure and this leads to consequent increase in consumption levels.
  - o Credit becomes cheaper, stimulating investment and growth, as the fiscal expansion increases market liquidity.
  - o Fiscal multipliers are likely to be higher in recessionary periods because private savings increase through the precautionary motive to save.

58. d   **Both the statements are incorrect.**

- In a Pro-cyclic contractionary fiscal policy, there is decrease in Government expenditure and increase in taxes.

- In a counter-cyclic expansionary fiscal policy, there is increase in Government expenditure and decrease in taxes.

59. b   • It refers to the difference between nominal rate of interest in an economy and the nominal rate of growth. **Hence, the 1st statement is correct.**

- More negative the IRGD, the easier (and quicker) it is for the Government to ensure debt sustainability. **Hence, the 2nd statement is incorrect.**

- Cross country evidence also suggests that, within countries, growth rates vary far more across time than interest rates.

- Since 2003, India's IRGD has been negative and the lowest for the major OECD economies. **Hence, the 3rd statement is correct.**

60. a   • For more than two decades, GDP growth rates have been greater than interest rates. **Hence, the 1st statement is correct.**

- The variability(in the GDP growth rates in India is higher than variability in interest rates. Thus the changes in Interest Rate Growth Differential are mostly attributable to changes in growth rates rather than the changes in interest rates. Thus, it is a higher growth that provides the key to the sustainability of debt for India. **Hence, the 2bd statement is incorrect.**

61. b   • The wealth effect is a economic theory that refers to the behaviour of people to spend more as the value of their assets rise. The rationale behind this behaviour is that consumers feel more financially secure and confident about their wealth when their homes or investment portfolios increase in value. **Hence, the 1st statement is incorrect.**

- Rollover risk is a risk associated with the refinancing of debt. When a loan or other debt obligation (like a bond) is about to mature and needs to be converted, or rolled over, into new debt, it may lead to Rollover risk. **Hence, the 2nd statement is correct.**

62. a   • 71% of global deaths and about 65% of deaths in India are caused by NCDs. The the contribution of NCDs increased 37% to 61% of all deaths between 1990 and 2016. **Hence, the 1st statement is correct.**

- As the next health crisis could possibly be drastically different from COVID-19, the Economic Survey suggests that the focus must be on building the healthcare system generally rather than a specific focus on communicable diseases. **Hence, the 2nd statement is incorrect.**

63. a   • As per the World Justice Project's 'World Rule of Law Index', for the category of 'following due process in administrative proceedings', India's ranking has improved significantly (from 75 in 2015 to 45 in 2020).

- But it is low (>90) in the categories of Effective enforcement of regulations and Timeliness of Administrative proceedings.

64. d   • **All the statements are correct.**

- According to the Economic Survey 2021, the prolonged period of forbearance has led to the following consequences:

o Undercapitalization,

o enhanced lending to zombie firms,

o ever-greening of loans.

o Borrower firms benefitting from forbearance witnessed weakening of corporate governance,

o deterioration in the quality of Boards,

o inefficient allocation of capital,

o mis- appropriation of resources,

o deterioration in economic performance and increased defaults.

65. a • Solow Growth Model refers to the model of economic growth that analyses changes in the level of output in an economy over time as a result of changes in the population.

• The model highlighted that that output per worker mainly depends on **savings, population growth and technological progress.**

66. d • **Both the statements are correct.**

• India's its zero sovereign default history unquestionably demonstrates it willingness to pay.

• India's sovereign external debt as per cent of GDP stood at a 4% (September 2020). Moreover, 54% of India's sovereign external foreign currency denominated debt was owed to multilaterals and IMF, which is not expected to impact credit rating assessments.

67. c • The Economic Survey 2021 refers to the 'Home Bias', which is associated to the sovereign credit ratings given by Credit Rating Agencies.

• The respective home country of CRAs, countries with linguistic and cultural similarity, and countries with higher home-bank exposures received higher ratings than justified by their political and economic fundamentals.

68. a • For India, the Public debt and overall debt level has declined since 2003 and has been stable since 2011. **Hence, the 1st statement is correct.**

• The Government's external debt is only 2.7 per cent of GDP. Thus debt portfolio is having very low foreign exchange risk. **Hence, the 2nd statement is incorrect.**

• Also, small share of floating rate debt (floating rate debt of Central Government is less than 5 per cent of public debt) tends to limit rollover risks and insulates the debt portfolio from interest rate volatility.

69. d A palpable V-shaped recovery in industrial production was observed over the year. Manufacturing rebounded and industrial value started to normalize. Headwinds, however, lingered on. Revitalized inter and intra-state movement along with a sustained spurt in industrial and commercial activity heralded the economy's returning to normalcy. E-way bills, electronic toll collection, rail freight and port cargo traffic not just recovered but surpassed previous year levels in Q3: 2020-21, Indian services sector sustained its recovery from the pandemic driven declines.

70. c • The Budget 2021-22 proposes a new scheme of Mega Investment Textiles Parks (MITRA) with the objective making the textile industry globally competitive and attract large investments and boost employment generation.

• This will create world-class infrastructure with plug and play facilities to enable create global champions in exports. 7 Textile Parks will be established over 3 years.

Hence the correct option is (c).

71. d • **All the statements are correct.** For 2021-22, the Budget proposes a sharp increase in capital expenditure, allocating Rs. 5.54 lakh crores which are 34.5% more than the BE of 2020-21.

• A record sum of Rs. 1,10,055 crores is provided for Railways of which Rs. 1,07,100 crores is for capital expenditure.

• An enhanced outlay of Rs. 1,18,101 lakh crores is provided for Ministry of Road Transport and Highways, of which Rs. 1,08,230 crores is for capital, the highest ever.

Hence the correct option is (d).

72. d • **Both statements are incorrect.** Bringing down the logistic costs for the industry lies at the core of the 'Make in India' initiative. IN this context, the budget expects that the Western Dedicated Freight Corridor (DFC) and Eastern DFC will be commissioned by June 2022. **Thus, the second statement is incorrect.**

• Broad Gauge Route Kilometres (RKM) electrified is expected to reach 46,000 RKM i.e., 72% by end of 2021. 100% electrification of Broad-Gauge routes will be completed by December 2023. **Thus, the first statement is incorrect. Hence the correct option is (d).**

73. d • Ujjwala Scheme which has benefited 8 crores households will be extended to cover 1 crore more beneficiaries.

SWAMITVA Scheme was launched to provide an integrated property validation solution for rural India. It is proposed to expand the scheme to all states/UTs during FY21-22

- The 'Operation Green Scheme', which presently covers the processing of tomato, potato and onions; will be expanded to include 22 perishable products.

- There is no such enhancement of Ayushman Bharat Scheme. **Hence the correct option is (d).**

74. b
- With an objective to improve the air quality, a separate voluntary vehicle scrapping policy will be announced that will incentivize the use of fuel-efficient vehicle and reduce the vehicular pollution and import bill. **Thus, the first statement is incorrect.**

- Besides this, personal vehicles would be made to undergo fitness tests in automated fitness centres after 20 years. The commercial vehicle would undergo this test after 15 years. **Thus, the second statement is correct. Hence, the correct option is (b).**

75. c **Fiscal Deficit**
- When the government's non-borrowed receipts fall short of its entire expenditure, it has to borrow money from the public to meet the shortfall.

- The excess of total expenditure over total non-borrowed receipts is called the fiscal deficit.

Revenue Deficit
- The difference between revenue expenditure and revenue receipt is known as revenue deficit. It shows the shortfall of government's current receipts over current expenditure.

Primary Deficit
- The primary deficit is the fiscal deficit minus interest payments. It tells how much of the Government's borrowings are going towards meeting expenses other than interest payments. **Hence, both statements are correct.**

76. a A new centrally sponsored scheme, PM AtmaNirbhar Swasth Bharat Yojana, will be launched with an outlay of about 64,180 crores over 6 years. This will develop capacities of primary, secondary, and tertiary care Health Systems, strengthen existing national institutions, and create new institutions, to cater to detection and cure of new and emerging diseases. This will be in addition to the National Health Mission. The main interventions under the scheme are:

- Support for 17,788 rural and 11,024 urban Health and Wellness Centers

- Setting up integrated public health labs in all districts and 3382 block public health units in 11 states;

- Establishing critical care hospital blocks in 602 districts and 12 central institutions;

- Strengthening of the National Centre for Disease Control (NCDC), its 5 regional branches and 20 metropolitan health surveillance units;

- Expansion of the Integrated Health Information Portal to all States/UTs to connect all public health labs;

- Operationalisation of 17 new Public Health Units and strengthening of 33 existing Public Health Units at Points of Entry, that is at 32 Airports, 11 Seaports and 7 land crossings;

- Setting up of 15 Health Emergency Operation Centers and 2 mobile hospitals; and

- Setting up of a national institution for One Health, a Regional Research Platform for WHO South East Asia Region, 9 Bio-Safety Level III laboratories and 4 regional National Institutes for Virology.

77. b The Jal Jeevan Mission (Urban) will be launched. It aims at universal water supply in all 4,378 Urban Local Bodies with 2.86 crores household tap connections, as well as liquid waste management in 500 AMRUT cities. It will be implemented over 5 years, with an outlay of 2,87,000 crores.

78. a
- The New Space India Limited (NSIL), a PSU under the Department of Space will execute the PSLV-CS51 launch, carrying the Amazonia Satellite from Brazil, along with a few smaller Indian satellites.

- As part of the Gaganyaan mission activities, four Indian astronauts are being trained on Generic Space Flight aspects, in Russia. The first unmanned launch is slated for December 2021.

79. c Our oceans are a storehouse of living and non-living resources. To better understand this realm, we will launch a Deep Ocean Mission with a budget outlay of more than 4,000 crores, over five years. This Mission will cover deep ocean survey exploration and projects for the conservation of deep sea bio-diversity.

80. d The Pradhan Mantri Jan Arogya Yojana (PM-JAY) – the ambitious program launched by Government of India in 2018 to provide healthcare access to the most vulnerable sections. PM-JAY is being used significantly for high frequency, low cost care such as dialysis and continued to be utilised without disruption even during the Covid pandemic and

the lockdown. PM-JAY enhanced health insurance coverage. Across all the states, the proportion of households with health insurance increased by 54 per cent for the states that implemented PM-JAY while falling by 10 per cent in states that did not.

81. d As per the latest annual report of PM-JAY released by the National Health Authority (NHA, 2019), the status of implementation is as follows:

- 32 states and UTs implement the scheme
- 13.48 crore E-cards have been issued
- Treatments worth INR 7,490 crore have been provided (1.55 crores hospital admission)
- 24,215 hospitals empaneled
- 1.5 crore users have registered on the scheme's website (mera.pmjay.gov.in).

82. c Access to "the bare necessities" such as housing, water, sanitation, electricity and clean cooking fuel are a sine qua non to live a decent life. The BNI summarises 26 indicators on five dimensions viz., water, sanitation, housing, micro-environment, and other facilities. The BNI has been created for all states for 2012 and 2018 using data from two NSO rounds viz., 69th and 76th on Drinking Water, Sanitation, Hygiene and Housing Condition in India. Compared to 2012, access to "the bare necessities" has improved across all States in the country in 2018. Access to bare necessities is the highest in the States such as Kerala, Punjab, Haryana and Gujarat while it is the lowest in Odisha, Jharkhand, West Bengal and Tripura. The improvements are widespread as they span each of the five dimensions viz., access to water, housing, sanitation, micro-environment and other facilities.

83. d The 2030 agenda for Sustainable Development with 17 Sustainable Development Goals (SDGs) and 169 associated targets encompasses a comprehensive developmental agenda integrating social, economic and environmental dimensions. Several initiatives have been taken at both the national and the sub national level to mainstream the SDGs into the policies, schemes and programmes of the Government. India has been taking several proactive climate actions to fulfill its obligations as per the principles of common but differentiated responsibilities and respective capabilities and equity.

84. d In its NDC, India has sought to reduce the emissions intensity of its GDP by 33 to 35 per cent below 2005 levels by the year 2030; achieve 40 per cent of cumulative electric power installed capacity from non-fossil fuel sources by 2030; and enhance forest and tree cover to create additional carbon sink equivalent to 2.5 to 3 billion tons of carbon dioxide by 2030.

85. c India has taken several proactive steps at both the national and the sub national level to mainstream the SDGs into the policies, schemes and programmes of the Government. In 2020, the highlight of India's SDG initiatives has been the Voluntary National Review (VNR) presented to the United Nations High-Level Political Forum (HLPF) on Sustainable Development which is the highest international platform for review and follow-up of the SDGs under the auspices of the United Nations Economic and Social Council. The reviews are voluntary and country-led and are aimed at facilitating the sharing of experiences, including successes, challenges and lessons learned.

86. b Localisation of SDGs is crucial to any strategy aimed at achieving the goals under the 2030 Agenda. Essentially, localising SDGs involves the process of adapting, planning, implementing and monitoring the SDGs from national to local levels by relevant institutions and stakeholders. In terms of engagement and collaboration of institutions, it is consequential how the Centre, State and Local Governments work together to achieve the SDGs at the national level; and how SDGs provide a framework for subnational and local policy, planning and action for realisation of the SDG targets at local levels. To accelerate SDG achievements, the country has adopted the approach of cooperative and competitive federalism which is based on Centre-State collaboration in nation building and healthy competition among the States in various development outcomes. The SDG India Index and Dashboard, designed and developed by NITI Aayog, is the principal tool to measure and monitor SDG performance at the national and sub-national levels. The states are institutionally empowered and positioned to achieve the SDGs with the support of the Central Government and allied institutions. Hence, the States are the key actors in the process of localisation of SDGs with the Central Government playing an enabling role.

87. d National Solar Mission (NSM) - Achieve 100 GW of solar power in seven years starting from 2014-15. The cumulative capacity of 36.9 GW was commissioned till November 2020. Around 36 GW solar energy capacities are under installation, and an additional 19 GW capacity has been tendered.

88. a National Mission for Enhanced Energy Efficiency (NMEEE) –

- To achieve growth with ecological sustainability.
- Mandating reduction in energy consumption in large energyconsuming industries,

- Financing for PPP to reduce energy consumption through demand-side management programs in the municipal, buildings, and agricultural sectors,
- Energy incentives, including reduced taxes on energy-efficient appliances.
- The Perform Achieve and Trade (PAT) Scheme is one of the initiatives under the NMEEE, and was initiated in March 2012.
- PAT Cycle I (2012-2015) has overachieved the target, saving around 31 million tonnes of CO2 (Mt CO2).
- PAT Cycle II (2016-17 to 2018-19) - emission reduction of 61.34 MtCO2 was achieved.
- PAT Cycle III (2017-18 to 2019- 20) concluded on 31 March 2020, results of this cycle are awaited.
- Currently PAT Cycle IV is under implementation.

89. c   National Mission for a Green India (GIM) - Improved ecosystem services by Increasing forest/tree cover by 5 m ha and improving quality of forest cover on another 5 m ha (a total of 10 m ha). A sum of 343.08 crore rupees has been released to 13 states during the period 2015-16 to 2019-20 for undertaking afforestation activities over an area of 1.42 lakh ha.

90. a
- National Mission on Sustainable Habitat (NMSH) – its objectives are as follow:
  - Development of sustainable habitat standards.
  - Promoting energy efficiency as a core component of urban planning by extending the existing Energy Conservation Building Code (ECBC).
  - Strengthening the enforcement of automotive fuel economy standards, and
  - Using pricing measures to encourage the purchase of efficient vehicles and incentives for the use of public transportation.
- The mission is being implemented through three programmes: Atal Mission on Rejuvenation and Urban Transformation, Swachh Bharat Mission, and Smart Cities Mission.
- Under the ECBC, 335 demonstration buildings have been supported with technical assistance for compliance in the states/UTs. Cumulative builtup area of 0.16 billion m^2 ensures an approximate energy saving of 0.17 BU.

- Under the Smart Cities Mission, 1987 projects have already been completed so far, while 4375 projects are under completion. Smart Cities Mission requires cities to have at least 10 percent energy coming from solar and at least 80 per cent buildings to be energy efficient and green.
- Urban Transport Modal Shift: As on June, 2020, 700 km of metro rail was operational in 18 major cities and a Bus Rapid Transit (BRT) network of about 450 km was operational in 11 cities across the country carrying 10 million passengers daily.
- Smart Cities Mission: As on June 2020, the value of tendered smart city projects was over 1,66,000 crores rupees, including 1,25,000 crores rupees of work orders issued and 27,000 crores rupees of completed projects.
- Smart roads, smart solar, smart water, PPPs and vibrant public spaces projects are being implemented under the Mission.
- Swachh Bharat Mission: 6.2 million household toilets, against the mission target of 5.8 million, and 0.59 million community & public toilets, against the mission target of 0.50 million, have been constructed as in December 2020. Under the mission, 100 per cent door-to-door waste collection has been achieved in more than 83 thousand wards.
- 4340 (99 per cent) of the total 4372 cities have been declared Open Defecation Free (ODF) in the country.

91. b
- National Water Mission (NWM) – its aims are as follow:
  - Focuses on monitoring of ground water, aquifer mapping, capacity building, water quality monitoring and other baseline studies.
  - Promoting citizen and state action for water conservation, augmentation, and preservation.
  - Focusing attention on overexploited areas.
  - Promoting basin-level integrated water resources management.
- The National Institute of Hydrology is the nodal agency to get the State Specific Action Plan (SSAP) for the water sector for 16 selected states. Five States have completed the first phase of SSAP.
- 6,376 new ground water monitoring wells created.

92. c National Mission for Sustainable Agriculture aims at enhancing food security by making agriculture more productive, sustainable, remunerative, and climate resilient.

- 7960 farm machinery banks established in 2018-19 to reduce crop residue burning.
- Under Rainfed Area Development Programme, an area of about 74,175.41 ha and 55,902.92 ha was brought under different Integrated Farming System approach in 2018-19 and 2019-20 respectively.
- During 2018-19 & 2019-20, an area of 4.14 lakh ha was covered under organic farming. At present, 25.34 lakh ha, is under organic farming.

93. d • National Mission for Sustaining Himalayan Ecosystems- its objectives are as follow:

> ➢ To continuously assess the health status of the Himalayan Ecosystem. Enable policy bodies in their policy formulation functions.
> ➢ Start of new centres relevant to climate change in the existing institutions in the Himalayan States.
> ➢ Regional cooperation with neighbouring countries in Glaciology.

- The key achievements include setting up of the Centre of Glaciology at Wadia Institute of Himalayan Geology.
- A national network programme on Himalayan Cryosphere has been launched.
- A mega programme named Human and Institutional Capacity Building (HICAB) programme for the Indian Himalayan Region was launched during the 2018-19 and six state level knowledge networks have been supported in the states of Jammu & Kashmir, Himachal Pradesh, Assam, Meghalaya, Manipur and Arunachal Pradesh in the Himalayan Region. Under this programme, 18 projects and 7 Major R&D programmes are getting implemented.
- In addition, three Centres of Excellence, one each at Kashmir University, Sikkim University and Tezpur University have been supported under the mission.

94. c National Mission on Strategic Knowledge for Climate Change (NMSKCC) –

- To gain a better understanding of climate science, formation of knowledge networks among the existing knowledge institutions engaged in research and development.

- Development of national capacity for modeling the regional impact of climate change on different ecological zones within the country.
- Key achievements include setting up of 12 Centres of Excellence and 10 State Climate Change Centres.
- 8 Global Technology Watch Groups (GTWGs) in the areas of Renewable Energy Technology, Advance Coal Technology, Enhanced Energy Efficiency, Green Forest, Sustainable Habitat, Water, Sustainable Agriculture and Manufacturing have been set up.

95. d The Government launched the Jawaharlal Nehru National Solar Mission (JNNSM) in 2010 with the aim to (i) deploy 20,000 MW of grid connected solar power by 2022 to be achieved in 3 phases, (ii) 2,000 MW of off-grid solar applications including 20 million solar lights by 2022 and (iii) 20 million sq. m. solar thermal collector area.

96. c This scheme is operational from the year 2020-21 to 2029-30. The scheme provides for medium to long term debt financing facility for investment in viable projects for post-harvest management infrastructure and community farming assets Under the scheme, 1 lakh crores rupees will be provided by banks and financial institutions as loans to primary agricultural credit societies (PACS), marketing cooperative societies, farmer producers organizations (FPOs), self-help group (SHG), farmers, joint liability groups (JLG), multipurpose cooperative societies, agri-entrepreneurs, startups and central/ state agency or local body sponsored public private partnership project, etc. All loans under this financing facility will have interest subvention of 3 per cent per annum up to a limit of 2 crores rupees. This subvention will be available for a maximum period of 7 years. Further, credit guarantee coverage will be available for eligible borrowers from this financing facility under Credit Guarantee Fund Trust for Micro and Small Enterprises (CGTMSE) scheme for a loan up to 2 crores rupees.

97. d In 2019-20, India's agricultural and allied exports amounted to approximately 252 thousand crores rupees. The major export destinations were USA, Saudi Arabia, Iran, Nepal and Bangladesh. The top agriculture and related products exported from India were marine products, basmati rice, buffalo meat, spices, non-basmati rice, cotton raw, oil meals, sugar, castor oil and tea. While India occupies a leading position in global trade of aforementioned agri- products, its total agri-export basket accounts for a little over 2.5 per cent of world agri-trade.

98. c   Under the Atma Nirbhar Bharat Abhiyan, Ministry of Food Processing Industries (MoFPI) has launched a new Centrally Sponsored Scheme, Prime Minister-Formalisation of Micro Food Processing Enterprises (PM-FME) with a total outlay of 10,000 crores rupees over the period 2020- 2025. The scheme is expected to benefit 2 lakh micro food processing units through credit linked subsidy. The Scheme adopts One District One Product (ODOP) approach to reap benefit of scale in terms of procurement of inputs, availing common services and marketing of products. The States need to identify one food product per district keeping in view the existing clusters and availability of raw material. Support for common infrastructure and branding & marketing would be for that product. The Scheme also places focus on waste to wealth products, minor forest products and Aspirational Districts.

99. a   Government gave its approval in November 2020 to introduce the Production-Linked Incentive (PLI) Scheme in 10 key sectors, including food processing sector, for enhancing India's manufacturing capabilities and improving exports. The approved financial outlay for the PLI scheme in food processing is 10,900 crores rupees. The food segments identified includes ready to eat/ready to cook, marine products, processed fruits & vegetables, mozzarella cheese, and innovative/organic products of SMEs. The scheme would also support the branding and marketing abroad.

100. c   In pursuance of the pro-poor announcement made under Pradhan Mantri Garib Kalyan Package, Government of India launched the Pradhan Mantri Garib Kalyan Anna Yojana (PMGKAY) scheme for additional allocation of foodgrains from the Central Pool at the rate of 5 kg per person per month free of cost for all the beneficiaries covered under Targeted Public Distribution System (TPDS) (AAY & PHH) including those covered under Direct Benefit Transfer (DBT) for a period of 3 months i.e. April-June, 2020. Accordingly, about 121 LMT of foodgrains was allotted to approximately 80.96 crores beneficiaries entailing subsidy outgo of nearly 46061 crores rupees. The PMGKAY scheme was extended for a further period of 5 months i.e. July – November, 2020. Accordingly, about 201 LMT of foodgrains have been allocated for free of cost distribution to beneficiaries entailing subsidy outgo of nearly 76062.11 Crores rupees.

Mock Test 3
General Studies Paper I

1. Recently India proposed the creation of a special working group on innovation and start-ups and an expert working group on traditional medicine in which of the following summits?
   (a) G20 Summit
   (b) SCO (Heads of State Council)summit
   (c) BRICS Summit
   (d) None of the above

2. Consider the following statements about paleochannel:
   1. It is a remnant of an inactive fossil fuel sediments that has been filled or buried by younger sediment.
   2. Paleochannels constitute the most important preferred pathways away from the active channel.
   Which of the statements given above is/are correct?
   (a) 1 only
   (b) 2 only
   (c) Both 1 and 2
   (d) Neither 1 nor 2

3. Consider the following statements about the Hornbill Festival:
   1. It is an annual cultural and tourism extravaganza that showcases the rich and diverse ethnicity of all the North Eastern States.
   2. All the tribes of North Eastern States take part in this festival.
   Which of the statements given above is/are correct?
   (a) 1 only
   (b) 2 only
   (c) Both 1 and 2
   (d) Neither 1 nor 2

4. Consider the following statements about Merchant Discount Rate (MDR):
   1. MDR is the percentage of the digital transaction that a merchant pays to the banks.
   2. It is always borne by the merchant.
   Which of the statements given above is/are correct?
   (a) 1 only
   (b) 2 only
   (c) Both 1 and 2
   (d) Neither 1 nor 2

5. Consider the following statements about the Shanghai Cooperation Organisation (SCO):
   1. The council of heads of government is SCO's highest decision making body.
   2. The SCO's official languages are Russian and Chinese.
   Which of the statements given above is/are correct?
   (a) 1 only
   (b) 2 only
   (c) Both 1 and 2
   (d) Neither 1 nor 2

6. Consider the following statements regarding the National Capital Region Transport Corporation (NCRTC):
   1. It is a joint venture of the Government of India and State Governments of Haryana, NCT Delhi, Uttar Pradesh (12.5%) and Rajasthan (12.5%).
   2. It is mandated for implementing the Regional Rapid Transit System (RRTS) project across the National Capital Region (NCR) only.
   Which of the statements given above is/are correct?
   (a) 1 only
   (b) 2 only
   (c) Both 1 and 2
   (d) Neither 1 nor 2

7. Department of Biotechnology (DBT) has facilitated Transfer of Technology of novel Brucella vaccine. With reference to it, consider the following statements about Brucella abortus S19 delta per vaccine:
   1. It can play an important role in National Tuberculosis Control Programme.
   2. Brucella disease can also get transmitted to human beings.
   Which of the statements given above is/are correct?
   (a) 1 only
   (b) 2 only
   (c) Both 1 and 2
   (d) Neither 1 nor 2

8. Six women led startups have won COVID-19 Shri Shakti Challenge. Shri Shakti Challenge has been organised by which of the following organisation/Ministry?
   (a) Ministry of Women and Child Development
   (b) NITI Aayog
   (c) Ministry of Health and Family Welfare
   (d) None of the above

9. Consider the following statements about Brucellosis:

1. It is a zoonotic disease which causes production losses in livestock.
2. There is no vaccine available to protect humans against Brucella.

Which of the statements given above is/are correct?

(a) 1 only
(b) 2 only
(c) Both 1 and 2
(d) Neither 1 nor 2

10. Consider the following statements about Bhasan Char:

1. This newly created island is located near the mouth of the river Ganga where it flows into the Bay of Bengal.
2. Bhasan Char surfaced only in 2006 from the sediment deposited through volcanic eruption and cyclone.

Which of the statements given above is/are correct?

(a) 1 only
(b) 2 only
(c) Both 1 and 2
(d) Neither 1 nor 2

11. Consider the following statements about Partners in Population and Development (PPD):

1. It is an intergovernmental initiative launched in 1994 to help implement the Cairo Program of Action (POA).
2. PPD has been created for expanding and improving all the developing countries collaboration in the fields of reproductive health, population, and development.

Which of the statements given above is/are correct?

(a) 1 only
(b) 2 only
(c) Both 1 and 2
(d) Neither 1 nor 2

12. Consider the following statements about recently announced CoWIN app:

1. It is an app through which one would be able to self-register for any vaccines including COVID 19.
2. It is an upgraded version of the Electronic Vaccine Intelligence Network (eVIN).

Which of the statements given above is/are correct?

(a) 1 only
(b) 2 only
(c) Both 1 and 2
(d) Neither 1 nor 2

13. With reference to the New Development Bank (NDB), consider the following statements:

1. NDB has an observer status in the United Nations General Assembly.
2. NDB was jointly founded by the BRICS countries at the 6th BRICS Summit in Fortaleza, Brazil in 2014.

Which of the statements given above is/are correct?

(a) 1 only
(b) 2 only
(c) Both 1 and 2
(d) Neither 1 nor 2

14. Education for Justice (E4J) initiative, recently seen in the news, is launched by:

(a) UNESCO
(b) Pratham International
(c) Ministry of Human Resource Development
(d) United Nations Office on Drugs and Crimes

15. Consider the following statements about South-South cooperation:

1. It refers to the technical cooperation among all the countries in the Global South.
2. The countries share knowledge, skills, expertise and resources to meet their development goals through concerted efforts.

Which of the statements given above is/are correct?

(a) 1 only
(b) 2 only
(c) Both 1 and 2
(d) Neither 1 nor 2

16. Consider the following statements regarding Pradhan Mantri Rojgar Protsahan Yojana (PMRPY):

1. The scheme incentivise employers for generation of new employment.
2. It is targeted for employees earning wages less than or equal to Rs 15,000/- per month.

Which of the statements given above is/are correct?

(a) 1 only
(b) 2 only
(c) Both 1 and 2
(d) Neither 1 nor 2

17. Consider the following statements about Integrated Road Accident Database (IRAD):

1. IRAD has been developed and implemented by the National Informatics Centre (NIC).
2. This project is supported by the world Bank.
3. It has been implemented across all the states and working as a central accident database management system.

Which of the statement given above is/are **incorrect**?

(a) 2 only   (b) 1 and 3 only

(c) 2 and 3 only   (d) None of the above

18. The concept of Significant Economic Presence (SEP) has been introduced to capture which of the following areas?

    (a) Tax evasion cases

    (b) Online tax complains

    (c) Digital taxation

    (d) None of the above

19. Consider the following statements about the recently launched AYUSH Sanjivani App:

    1. It is developed by the Ministry of AYUSH and the Ministry of Electronics and Information Technology (MEITY).

    2. It intends to generate data on usage of AYUSH advocacies and its impact in prevention of Covid-19.

    Which of the statements given above is/are correct?

    (a) 1 only   (b) 2 only

    (c) Both 1 and 2   (d) Neither 1 nor 2

20. Consider the following statements about Pulse Oximeter:

    1. It is used to measure the oxygen of the blood.

    2. It measures the saturation of oxygen in red blood cells (RBCs).

    Which of the statements given above is/are correct?

    (a) 1 only   (b) 2 only

    (c) Both 1 and 2   (d) Neither 1 nor 2

21. Consider the following statements about the Quick Reaction Surface to Air Missile (QRSAM) System:

    1. It can also operates on the move.

    2. The recently launched QRSAM system consists of all indigenously developed subsystems.

    Which of the statements given above is/are correct?

    (a) 1 only   (b) 2 only

    (c) Both 1 and 2   (d) Neither 1 nor 2

22. Consider the following statements about the deep sea mission:

    1. It will explore Exclusive Economic Zone only.

    2. This mission is going to be launched by the Ministry of Earth Science in coordination with the Indian Coast Guard.

Which of the statements given above is/are **incorrect**?

(a) 1 only   (b) 2 only

(c) Both 1 and 2   (d) Neither 1 nor 2

23. Abhayam app designed for safe and secure travel for women commuting by autos and taxis has been launched by which of the following organisation/ministry?

    (a) Ministry of Women and Child development

    (b) Ministry of Home Affairs

    (c) Delhi Police

    (d) None of the above

24. Consider the following statements about International Financial Services Centres (IFSCs):

    1. It can provide Indian corporates with easier access to global financial markets.

    2. It aids in promotion of financial markets in India.

    3. The first IFSC in India has been set up in Gandhinagar.

    Which of the statements given above are correct?

    (a) 1 and 2 only   (b) 1 and 3 only

    (c) 2 and 3 only   (d) 1, 2 and 3

25. Consider the following statements about Open Skies treaty:

    1. The treaty provides for inspection flights over member countries' territories to monitor nuclear activities.

    2. Recently both Russia and USA exited from the Open Skies treaty.

    Which of the statements given above is/are correct?

    (a) 1 only   (b) 2 only

    (c) Both 1 and 2   (d) Neither 1 nor 2

26. Government of India & AIIB signed an agreement for $304 million to improve reliability, capacity and security of the power transmission network in which of the following states?

    (a) Nagaland   (b) Assam

    (c) Manipur   (d) Tripura

27. Which of the following surveys are entrusted by Labor Bureau?

    1. All India Survey of Migrant workers,

    2. All India survey of Domestic Workers,

    3. All India survey of employment generated by Professionals

4. All India survey of employment generated in Transport Sector

Select the correct answer using the code given below:

(a) 1 and 2 only
(b) 1, 3 and 4 only
(c) 2, 3 and 4 only
(d) 1, 2, 3 and 4

28. Saras Aajeevika Mela 2021 inaugurated recently by which of the following Ministry?

(a) Ministry of Rural Development

(b) TRIFED

(c) The Khadi and Village Industries Commission

(d) Ministry of Minority Affairs

29. The Waste to Wealth Mission is an initiative of which of the following organisation?

(a) Ministry of Environment

(b) Ministry of Housing and Urban Affairs

(c) NITI Aayog

(d) None of the above

30. Consider the following statements about Solar Rooftop Financing Program:

1. The World Bank is working with the Ministry of New and Renewable Energy to bring in a credit guarantee mechanism to help MSMEs investing in rooftop solar to reduce their energy expenses.

2. In 2016, The World Bank launched the 'Solar Rooftop Financing Program' being implemented by the State Bank of India (SBI).

Which of the statements given above is/are correct?

(a) 1 only
(b) 2 only
(c) Both 1 and 2
(d) Neither 1 nor 2

31. India has recently signed an agreements for the defence line of credit and developing the harbour at Uthuru Thila Falhu naval base with which of the following countries?

(a) Maldives
(b) Mauritius
(c) Sri Lanka
(d) Seychelles

32. Consider the following statements about EDISON Alliance:

1. It is as an international organization for public-private partnership.

2. World Bank will serve as the secretariat and platform for the EDISON.

Which of the statements given above is/are correct?

(a) 1 only
(b) 2 only
(c) Both 1 and 2
(d) Neither 1 nor 2

33. Consider the following statements about Corruption Perception Index (CPI):

1. It uses a scale of 0 to 100, where 0 is highly corrupt and 100 is very clean.

2. It is released annually by Oxfam International.

Which of the statements given above is/are correct?

(a) 1 only
(b) 2 only
(c) Both 1 and 2
(d) Neither 1 nor 2

34. Urs festival celebrated recently in which of the following states?

(a) Chhattisgarh
(b) Gujrat
(c) Rajasthan
(d) Andhra Pradesh

35. Consider the following statements about Mega Investment Textiles Parks (MITRA):

1. The objective is to develop seven Mega Integrated Textile Region and Apparel (MITRA) parks as part of a plan to double the industry size to $300 billion by 2025-26.

2. MITRA will lead to increased investments and enhanced employment opportunities with the support from the Production Linked Incentive (PLI) scheme.

Which of the statements given above is/are correct?

(a) 1 only
(b) 2 only
(c) Both 1 and 2
(d) Neither 1 nor 2

36. After over two year the National Mineral Development Corporation (NMDC) has resumed production of iron ore from Donimalai Mines. It is situated in which of the following state?

(a) Kerala
(b) Karnataka
(c) Chhattisgarh
(d) Odisha

37. Consider the following statements about the Development Finance Institutions (DFIs):

1. DFIs cannot access soft loans from international market.

2. Rupee bonds sold by the DFIs do not qualify as Statutory Lending Ration.

3. At present, DFIs cannot participate in the Long Term Operation of the RBI.

Which of the statements given above is/are correct?

(a) 1 and 2 only
(b) 2 and 3 only
(c) 3 only
(d) 1, 2 and 3

38. The Adaptation Action Agenda was launched by which of the following organization/summit?

(a) UNFCC

(b) World Economic Forum

(c) UNEP

(d) None of the above

39. Consider the following statements about Rohini Commission:

1. The Rohini Commission was appointed in accordance with the Article 340 to suggest the sub-categorization of SC/ST.

2. The Centre has extended the tenure of the Rohini Commission until 31st July, 2021 to submit its report.

Which of the statements given above is/are correct?

(a) 1 only   (b) 2 only

(c) Both 1 and 2   (d) Neither 1 nor 2

40. Recently India and Mauritius sign Comprehensive Economic Cooperation and Partnership Agreement. With reference to it consider the following statements:

1. It is the first trade agreement signed by India with a country in Africa.

2. The CECPA between India and Mauritius covers both trades in goods and services.

Which of the statements given above is/are correct?

(a) 1 only   (b) 2 only

(c) Both 1 and 2   (d) Neither 1 nor 2

41. Consider the following statements about Intergovernmental Negotiations framework (IGN):

1. It is a group of nation-states working within the United Nations to further reform on the Non- Proliferation of Nuclear Weapon treaty.

2. India, along with Brazil, Japan and Germany are the prominent participants of IGN.

Which of the statements given above is/are correct?

(a) 1 only   (b) 2 only

(c) Both 1 and 2   (d) Neither 1 nor 2

42. Consider the following statements about Bharat Parv:

1. It is celebrated every year from 26th to 31st January across India.

2. It is organised Jointly by the Ministry of Tourism and the Ministry of Culture.

Which of the statements given above is/are correct?

(a) 1 only   (b) 2 only

(c) Both 1 and 2   (d) Neither 1 nor 2

43. Consider the following statements about the UN Capital Development Fund(UNCDF):

1. It provides micro-finance access to Least Developed Countries (LDCs) only.

2. UNCDF programmes also help to empower women.

Which of the statements given above is/are correct?

(a) 1 only   (b) 2 only

(c) Both 1 and 2   (d) Neither 1 nor 2

44. Consider the following statements:

1. It is common in low-income populations in developing regions of Africa, Asia, and the Americas.

2. Dengue, Rabies, Leprosy, Buruli ulcer, Endemic treponematoses (yaws) are few examples of it.

Above mentioned statements belongs to which of the following disease?

(a) COVID – 19

(b) Tuberculosis

(c) Neglected tropical disease

(d) None of the above

45. Consider the following statements:

1. Spices board of India is an autonomous body responsible for the export promotion of the 52 scheduled spices and development of Cardamom.

2. India is the world's largest exporter of chili and turmeric.

Which of the statements given above is/are correct?

(a) 1 only   (b) 2 only

(c) Both 1 and 2   (d) Neither 1 nor 2

46. Recently, the Union Minister of Health & Family Welfare addressed the fourth edition of Future Investment Initiative Forum. With reference to it consider the following statements about Future Investment Initiative Forum:

1. It is an international platform for expert-led debate between global leaders, investors and innovators with the power to shape the future of global investment.

2. It is hosted by the Public Investment Fund of Saudi Arabia (PIF).

Which of the statements given above is/are correct?

(a) 1 only   (b) 2 only

(c) Both 1 and 2   (d) Neither 1 nor 2

47. Consider the following statements about Leatherback Turtles:

1. They are the largest sea turtle species.
2. It is one of the most migratory, crossing both the Atlantic and Pacific Oceans.
3. Globally the IUCN status of leatherback is listed as Vulnerable.

Which of the statements given above is/are correct?

(a) 1 and 2 only   (b) 2 and 3 only

(c) 3 only   (d) 1, 2 and 3

48. Union Home Minister has recently participated in an event commemorating one year of the signing of the Boda Accord, 2020. With reference to it consider the following statements:

1. It was the first ever peace deal with Bodo rebel groups that was signed in January 2020 by the Centre.
2. This accord has triggered the process of ending insurgency in the North-East.

Which of the statements given above is/are correct?

(a) 1 only   (b) 2 only

(c) Both 1 and 2   (d) Neither 1 nor 2

49. The Framework for Strategic Partnership between the International Energy Agency (IEA) members and the Government of India was signed recently. With reference to it consider the following statements:

1. It will lead to an extensive exchange of knowledge and will enhance global energy security, stability and sustainability.
2. India is a full time member of IEA.

Which of the statements given above is/are correct?

(a) 1 only   (b) 2 only

(c) Both 1 and 2   (d) Neither 1 nor 2

50. Consider the following statements about Bodoland Territorial Council (BTC):

1. It is an autonomous body under the Sixth Schedule of the Constitution.
2. Bodo Tribes are the single largest community among the notified Scheduled Tribes in Assam.

51. Consider the following statements regarding Development Finance Institution (DFI):

1. DFI will be a specialized institution to provide funds for the manufacturing units.
2. The DFI will help in funding the projects under the National Infrastructure Pipeline (NIP).
3. It is also the principal financial institution and development bank to build and sustain a supportive ecosystem during the life cycle of the infrastructure projects.

Which of the statements given above is/are correct?

(a) 2 and 3 only   (b) 1 only

(c) 1 and 2 only   (d) 3 only

52. Consider the following statements regarding Prabuddha Bharata:

1. It is a monthly magazine of the Ramakrishna Order.
2. This magazine was founded in the year 1896 by P. Aiyasami, B. R. Rajam Iyer, G. G. Narasimhacharya, and B. V. Kamesvara Iyer under the guidance of Swami Vivekananda.

Which of the statements given above is/are correct?

(a) 1 only   (b) 2 only

(c) Both 1 and 2   (d) Neither 1 nor 2

53. Consider the following statements regarding FAC T-81:

1. The Indian Naval Fast Attack Craft, IN FAC T-81, of the Super Dvora MK II class was commissioned in January, 2020 in Mumbai.
2. It has the capability of day or night surveillance and reconnaissance.

Which of the statements given above is/are correct?

(a) 1 only   (b) 2 only

(c) Both 1 and 2   (d) Neither 1 nor 2

54. Consider the following statements regarding Asia-Pacific Personalised Health Index:

1. The index measures the readiness in adopting the personalised healthcare of 11 health systems in the Asia-Pacific region.
2. The health systems that were evaluated includes: India, China, Singapore, Australia, Malaysia, Taiwan, Japan, Thailand, Indonesia, South Korea, and New Zealand.

Which of the statements given above is/are **incorrect**?

(a) 1 only   (b) 2 only

(c) Both 1 and 2   (d) Neither 1 nor 2

55. Consider the following statements:

1. The Larsen & Toubro (L&T) has bagged a contract worth Rs 1390 crore for the Mumbai-Ahmedabad bullet train project.

2. The bullet rain project or the Mumbai-Ahmedabad high-speed rail corridor is being executed by the Indian railway.

Which of the statements given above is/are correct?

(a) 1 only   (b) 2 only

(c) Both 1 and 2   (d) Neither 1 nor 2

56. Consider the following statements regarding Start-up India Seed Fund Scheme (SISFS):

1. The scheme was launched with the aim of providing the financial assistance to start-ups for the product trials, market-entry, and proof of concept, prototype development and commercialization.

2. The scheme will be in mission mode for the year 2021-22.

3. The overall execution and monitoring of the SISFS will be done by the DPIIT.

4. The funds under the Start-up India Seed Fund Scheme will be disbursed through the selected incubators across the country.

Which of the statements given above are correct?

(a) 1, 3 and 4 only   (b) 1 and 4 only

(c) 1 and 2 only   (d) 1, 2, 3 and 4

57. Which of the following statements is/are correct regarding STARS Project?

1. STARS project is a central sector scheme that seeks to strengthen the school education system.

2. The 6 Indian states include- Kerala, Maharashtra, Himachal Pradesh, Rajasthan, Madhya Pradesh, Rajasthan, and Odisha.

3. The STARS Project carries forward the vision of the National Education Policy 2020 that envisages the equitable education for all.

Select the correct answer using the code given below:

(a) 2 only   (b) 2 and 3 only

(c) 1 and 2 only   (d) 3 only

58. Which of the following statements is/are correct regarding Neglected Tropical Diseases (NTD)?

1. The NTDs are a diverse group of communicable diseases that prevail in tropical and subtropical conditions.

2. These diseases affect more than one billion people every year.

Select the correct answer using the code given below:

(a) 1 only   (b) 2 only

(c) Both 1 and 2   (d) Neither 1 nor 2

59. Consider the following statements:

1. The United Nations Development Programme (UNDP) has released its "Global Climate Litigation Report 2021".

2. As per the report, climate cases have nearly doubled over the last three years.

Which of the statements given above is/are correct?

(a) 1 only   (b) 2 only

(c) Both 1 and 2   (d) Neither 1 nor 2

60. Which of the following statements is/are correct regarding the Davos Dialogue of World Economic Forum?

1. This is the 51st annual meeting of the World Economic Forum.

2. The theme of the annual meeting was announced as 'The Great Reset'.

Select the correct answer using the code given below:

(a) 1 only   (b) 2 only

(c) Both 1 and 2   (d) Neither 1 nor 2

61. Consider the following statements:

1. The National Non-Communicable Disease Monitoring Survey (NNMS) was recently released in India by the Ministry of health.

2. The survey was conducted for the period of 2019-20.

3. It covers the age groups of 15-69 years, males and females from the urban and rural areas.

Which of the statements given above is/are correct?

(a) 1 and 3 only

(b) 2 only

(c) 1 and 2 only

(d) 1, 2 and 3

62. Which of the following statements is/are correct regarding off-budget borrowings?

1. The loans that are taken by any public institution and not by the Centre directly are called as the "Off-Budget Borrowings".

2. These borrowings are used to fulfil the expenditure needs of the government.

Select the correct answer using the code given below:

(a) 1 only   (b) 2 only

(c) Both 1 and 2   (d) Neither 1 nor 2

63. Which of the following statements is/are **incorrect** regarding National Mission for Edible Oil (NMEO)?

1. The Ministry of Agriculture has proposed for the National Mission for Edible Oil in order to increase the domestic availability and reduce the import dependency.

2. The mission has been proposed for next five years in the span of 2020-21 to 2024-25.

Select the correct answer using the code given below:

(a) 1 only   (b) 2 only

(c) Both 1 and 2   (d) Neither 1 nor 2

64. Consider the following statements regarding "Green Tax":

1. The Ministry of Environment, forest and Climate Change has decided to impose the additional taxes on old vehicles that are no more fit on road. This additional tax is being called as the "Green Tax".

2. The decision was taken to curb pollution.

Which of the statements given above is/are correct?

(a) 1 only   (b) 2 only

(c) Both 1 and 2   (d) Neither 1 nor 2

65. Consider the following statements regarding Akash-NG:

1. Akash-NG is a medium-range mobile surface-to-air missile defense system.

2. It has been developed by the Defence Research and Development Organisation (DRDO).

3. The missile has the capability of targeting the aircraft up to 50-60 km away at altitudes of 18,000 m.

4. Missile is in operation with the Indian Army and the Indian Air Force.

Which of the statements given above are correct?

(a) 1, 3 and 4 only   (b) 1 and 4 only

(c) 1 and 2 only   (d) 1, 2, 3 and 4

66. Consider the following statements regarding AMPHEX–21:

1. The Indian Armed forces conducted a large-scale tri-service joint amphibious exercise AMPHEX–21 in Andaman and Nicobar group of islands in January, 2021.

2. The exercise was conducted with the aim of validating India's capabilities to safeguard the territorial integrity of the island territories.

Which of the statements given above is/are correct?

(a) 1 only   (b) 2 only

(c) Both 1 and 2   (d) Neither 1 nor 2

67. Consider the following statements regarding RoDTEP Scheme:

1. Under the scheme, a mechanism will be created for reimbursement of levies, taxes or duties at central, state and local levels.

2. The RoDTEP Scheme was launched in 2020 to boost exports of India in International markets.

Which of the statements given above is/are correct?

(a) 1 only   (b) 2 only

(c) Both 1 and 2   (d) Neither 1 nor 2

68. Which of the following statements is/are correct Sagarmala Seaplane Services Project?

1. The project aims to provide air connectivity to numerous tourists, religious, remote and unexplored locations near water bodies.

2. Ministry of Transport is the implementing agency.

Select the correct answer using the code given below:

(a) 1 only   (b) 2 only

(c) Both 1 and 2   (d) Neither 1 nor 2

69. Which of the following statements is/are correct Sea Vigil-21?

1. The Sea Vigil exercise will be undertaken along the 7,516 kilo metres coastline.

2. It involves all the thirteen coastal states, Union Territories and the Exclusive Economic Zone.

3. The exercise is conducted by the Indian Navy.

Which of the statements given above is/are correct?

(a) 1 and 3 only   (b) 2 only

(c) 1 and 2 only   (d) 1, 2 and 3

70. Consider the following statements regarding Pradhan Mantri Kausal Vikas Yojana 3.0:

1. The third Phase is to be implemented by the Ministry of Skill Development and Entrepreneurship.

2. Pradhan Mantri Kaushal Vikas Yojana 3.0 is to train more than 1 lakh candidates for a period of one year with an investment of 950 crores of Rupees.

Which of the statements given above is/are correct?

(a) 1 only   (b) 2 only

(c) Both 1 and 2   (d) Neither 1 nor 2

71. Which of the following statements is/are correct regarding Jarosite?

1. It is a rare maritime mineral found in the Antarctica ice.

2. Jarosite is a mineral from mars which is scarcely seen on earth.

Select the correct answer using the code given below:

(a) 1 only

(b) 2 only

(c) Both 1 and 2

(d) Neither 1 nor 2

72. Consider the following statements regarding CollabCAD software:

1. The National Informatics centre and the Central Board of Secondary Education (CBSE) jointly launched the CollabCAD software.

2. It aims to provide a platform to students across the country to create and modify digital designs.

Which of the statements given above is/are incorrect?

(a) 1 only   (b) 2 only

(c) Both 1 and 2   (d) Neither 1 nor 2

73. Consider the following statements regarding Abell 370:

1. It is a galaxy cluster located four billion light years away from the earth. The galaxy cluster is located in the constellation called Cetus.

2. The Abell 370 galaxy cluster was first discovered in 2002 using the lensing effect.

74. Which of the following statements is/are correct regarding "Lost Galaxy"?

1. It is also known as NGC 4535.

2. The galaxy is located about 50 million light-years from Earth.

3. The Galaxy was discovered in 1785 by William Herschel who found the planet Uranus.

Select the correct answer using the code given below:

(a) 3 only   (b) 1 and 2 only

(c) 1 only   (d) 1, 2 and 3

75. Consider the following statements regarding Kraken Mare:

1. Kraken Mare is huge liquid body located in the north pole of Titan.

2. Kraken Mare was discovered by the space probe Cassini.

Which of the statements given above is/are correct?

(a) 1 only

(b) 2 only

(c) Both 1 and 2

(d) Neither 1 nor 2

76. WHR 20 Happiness Report published by which of the following organization?

(a) World Economic Forum

(b) International Monetary Fund

(c) World Bank

(d) United Nations

77. Consider the following statements:

1. Training of women on animal husbandry are been conducted by National Dairy Development Board (NDDB).

2. Women-led cooperatives provide fertile ground for grooming women from rural areas for leadership positions.

Which of the statements given above is/are correct?

(a) 1 only   (b) 2 only

(c) Both 1 and 2   (d) Neither 1 nor 2

78. Consider the following statements regarding electoral bonds:

1. It removes all pre-existent limits on political donations.
2. Trace of donor can be find out through banks where they purchase these bonds.
3. This scheme helps to curb the issue of black money.

Which of the statements given above is/are correct?

(a) 3 only   (b) 1 and 2 only
(c) 2 and 3 only   (d) 1, 2 and 3

79. Consider the following statements:

1. Maitri setu connects Sabroom in India with Ramgarh in Bangladesh.
2. Bangladesh allows the shipment of goods from its Mongla and Chattogram (Chittagong).
3. Bangladesh accounts for more than 35% of India's international medical patients and contributes more than 50% of India's revenue from medical tourism.

Which of the statements given above is/are correct?

(a) 1 and 2 only   (b) 3 only
(c) 2 and 3 only   (d) 1, 2 and 3

80. Consider the following statements:

1. Employee PF contributions beyond Rs 1.5 lakh are not tax-deductible under Section 80C of the I-T Act.
2. The income on GPF contributions up to Rs 5 lakh would be tax-free.

Which of the statements given above is/are correct?

(a) 1 only   (b) 2 only
(c) Both 1 and 2   (d) Neither 1 nor 2

81. Which of the following viruses are water-transmitted pathogens?

1. Astrovirus
2. Hepatitis A
3. Nonovirus
4. Nepah virus

Select the correct answer using the code given below:

(a) 1, 2 and 3 only
(b) 4 only
(c) 2, 3 and 4 only
(d) 1, 2, 3 and 4

82. Consider the following statements:

1. 40% of the world CO_2 emitted by coal.
2. Zero-carbon target can be achieved through production, storage and distribution of renewable energy.
3. India is the primary buyer of coal produced in Australia and becomes a largest contributor of CO_2 emission in 2019.

Which of the statements given above is/are correct?

(a) 3 only   (b) 1 and 2 only
(c) 2 and 3 only   (d) 1, 2 and 3

83. Consider the following statements:

1. India ambitions to anchor a global super-grid called One Sun One World One Grid.
2. It will connect to West Asia and Southeast Asia and then spread to Africa and South America.
3. Multi-country grids allow for the unpredictable outputs from renewable energy plants to be balanced across countries.

Which of the statements given above is/are correct?

(a) 2 only
(b) 1 and 3 only
(c) 2 and 3 only
(d) 1, 2 and 3

84. Which of the following are the fields where India-Taiwan cooperate each other?

1. Modern democratic values
2. Healthcare
3. Telemedicine
4. Tourism

Select the correct answer using the code given below:

(a) 1 and 2 only
(b) 2, 3 and 4 only
(c) 1, 2 and 3 only
(d) 1, 2, 3 and 4

85. Consider the following statements:

1. The pregnancies terminable subject to the opinion of one medical practitioner is raised from 12 weeks to 20 weeks.
2. The pregnancies terminable subject to the opinion of two medical practitioners is raised to include those exceeding 20 but not exceeding 24 weeks.

Which of the statements given above is/are correct regarding MTP Bill, 2021?

(a) 1 only   (b) 2 only

(c) Both 1 and 2   (d) Neither 1 nor 2

86. Consider the following statements regarding Balakrishna Committee:

1. It was constituted to examine the status of Delhi.

2. On the basis of recommendation of this committee, Delhi was given the status of UT having legislative Assembly.

Which of the statements given above is/are correct?

(a) 1 only   (b) 2 only

(c) Both 1 and 2   (d) Neither 1 nor 2

87. Consider the following statements regarding Ken-Betwa linking project:

1. Both are tributaries of River Yamuna.

2. After linking, water from Betwa River will be transferred to Ken River.

3. This project will affect the core region of Pench Tiger Reserve.

Which of the statements given above is/are correct?

(a) 3 only   (b) 1 and 2 only

(c) 2 and 3 only   (d) 1, 2 and 3

88. Consider the following statements regarding scrappage policy:

1. It envisages whether the commercial and private vehicles are roadworthy after 15 and 20 years.

2. It seen as a route to rejuvenate COVID-19 affected economies by privileging green technologies.

Which of the statements given above is/are correct?

(a) 1 only   (b) 2 only

(c) Both 1 and 2   (d) Neither 1 nor 2

89. What are the possible reasons for being India a favorable destination for the growth of multinational companies?

1. Growing purchasing power of people

2. Change in geopolitics

3. Cheap mobile data

Select the correct answer using the code given below:

(a) 1 and 2 only   (b) 2 and 3 only

(c) 1 and 2 only   (d) 1, 2 and 3

90. Consider the following statements:

1. The overriding powers given to the Governor-General in the Government of India Act, 1935.

2. In NCT bill, the constitutional objectivity is distribution and separation of powers with denial of absolute power to any one functionary being the ultimate goal.

Which of the statements given above is/are correct?

(a) 1 only   (b) 2 only

(c) Both 1 and 2   (d) Neither 1 nor 2

91. Diamond of democracies is often seen in news, which defines –

(a) Shanghai Cooperation Organization

(b) BRICS

(c) BIMSTEC

(d) QUAD

92. Consider the following statements regarding democracy index:

1. It was published by Freedom House based out in USA and the Varieties of Democracy project of Sweden.

2. Their methodologies and indicators are transparently public, and the data sets they provide are widely analysed by researchers worldwide.

Which of the statements given above is/are correct?

(a) 1 only   (b) 2 only

(c) Both 1 and 2   (d) Neither 1 nor 2

93. Consider the following statements regarding BrahMos:

1. It has attaining a speed of Mach 2.8.

2. It is an air-to-air missile system.

3. It has indigenously manufactured in India.

Which of the statements given above is/are correct?

(a) 1 and 2 only

(b) 3 only

(c) 2 and 3 only

(d) 1, 2 and 3

94. Artificial intelligence is useful in which of the following areas?

1. Crop yields

2. Cancer treatment

3. Access to credit

4. Increase in business productivity

Select the correct answer using the code given below:

(a) 1 and 2 only   (b) 2, 3 and 4 only

(c) 1, 3 and 4 only   (d) 1, 2, 3 and 4

95. Consider the following statements:

1. Quad cooperation was a result of tsunami in Indian Ocean.

2. India will produce one billion COVID -19 vaccines by 2022.

3. All the members emphasized on security challenge and rules-based maritime order in the East and South China Seas.

Which of the statements is/are correct regarding Quad summit 2021?

(a) 1 only   (b) 2 and 3 only

(c) 1 and 3 only   (d) 1, 2 and 3

96. Consider the following statements regarding POCSO act:

1. The consent of under 18 is irrelevant.

2. It believed that a uniform age of 18 would ensure that trials of child rape would focus on the conduct of the accused and the circumstances of the offence.

Which of the statements given above is/are correct?

(a) 1 only   (b) 2 only

(c) Both 1 and 2   (d) Neither 1 nor 2

97. Which of the following are necessary for population stabilization?

1. Incentivize late marriages and child birth

2. Easy access to contraception

3. Promote labor force participation of women

Select the correct answer using the code given below:

(a) 1 and 2 only   (b) 2 and 3 only

(c) 1 and 3 only   (d) 1, 2 and 3

98. What is ShadowPad which was seen in the news recently?

(a) COVID-19 Vaccine

(b) A life threatening virus

(c) A backdoor 'Trojan' malware

(d) Super computer

99. Consider the following statements regarding Enabling Business of Agriculture report:

1. It is based on eight indicators which were published by World Bank and IMF jointly.

2. India ranked 49 among 101 countries.

3. France, Croatia, and the Czech Republic are the three top-ranking countries.

Which of the statements given above is/are correct?

(a) 1 only

(b) 2 and 3 only

(c) 1 and 2 only

(d) 1, 2 and 3

100. Consider the following statements regarding scorpene-submarine:

1. The Scorpene class of submarines were designed by French naval shipbuilding firm DCNS in partnership with Spanish shipbuilding firm Navantia.

2. INS Karanj is the first truly indigenous submarine which encapsulates the spirit of 'Make in India' and digital India.

Which of the statements given above is/are correct?

(a) 1 only

(b) 2 only

(c) Both 1 and 2

(d) Neither 1 nor 2

ANSWER KEY

1. (d)	**2.** (b)	**3.** (d)	**4.** (a)	**5.** (b)	**6.** (c)	**7.** (b)	**8.** (d)	**9.** (c)	**10.** (d)
11. (a)	**12.** (b)	**13.** (c)	**14.** (d)	**15.** (b)	**16.** (c)	**17.** (b)	**18.** (c)	**19.** (c)	**20.** (c)
21. (c)	**22.** (c)	**23.** (d)	**24.** (d)	**25.** (d)	**26.** (b)	**27.** (d)	**28.** (a)	**29.** (d)	**30.** (b)
31. (a)	**32.** (a)	**33.** (a)	**34.** (c)	**35.** (c)	**36.** (b)	**37.** (c)	**38.** (d)	**39.** (b)	**40.** (c)
41. (b)	**42.** (d)	**43.** (c)	**44.** (c)	**45.** (c)	**46.** (c)	**47.** (d)	**48.** (b)	**49.** (a)	**50.** (c)
51. (a)	**52.** (c)	**53.** (b)	**54.** (d)	**55.** (a)	**56.** (a)	**57.** (b)	**58.** (c)	**59.** (b)	**60.** (c)
61. (a)	**62.** (c)	**63.** (d)	**64.** (b)	**65.** (d)	**66.** (c)	**67.** (c)	**68.** (a)	**69.** (d)	**70.** (c)
71. (c)	**72.** (d)	**73.** (c)	**74.** (d)	**75.** (c)	**76.** (d)	**77.** (c)	**78.** (b)	**79.** (d)	**80.** (c)
81. (a)	**82.** (b)	**83.** (b)	**84.** (d)	**85.** (c)	**86.** (c)	**87.** (b)	**88.** (c)	**89.** (d)	**90.** (c)
91. (d)	**92.** (c)	**93.** (a)	**94.** (d)	**95.** (d)	**96.** (c)	**97.** (d)	**98.** (c)	**99.** (b)	**100.** (a)

EXPLANATION

1. d
- Prime Minister Narendra Modi didn't participate in the Shanghai Cooperation Organisation's (SCO) council of heads of government summit.
- The virtual summit was chaired by Vice president M Venkaiah Naidu.
- This was the first time India hosted a meeting of the body since it was admitted into the eight-member grouping in 2017.
- India proposed the creation of a special working group on innovation and start-ups and an expert working group on traditional medicine.

2. b
- A palaeo channel, or paleochannel, is a remnant of an inactive river or stream channel that has been filled or buried by younger sediment. The sediments that the ancient channel is cut into or buried by can be unconsolidated, semi-consolidated, consolidated or lithified.
- The Union Water Ministry has excavated an old, dried-up river in Prayagraj (formerly Allahabad) that linked the Ganga and Yamuna rivers. The aim is to develop it as a potential groundwater recharge source, according to officials at the National Mission for Clean Ganga (NMCG), a body under the Union Jal Shakti Ministry that coordinates the cleaning of the Ganga.

3. d
- Nagaland will be taking its 21st edition of the Hornbill Festival to a virtual platform from December 1 to 5, on three national and regional audio visual news channels.
- It is a 10-day annual cultural and tourism extravaganza that elaborately showcases the rich and diverse Naga ethnicity through folk dances, traditional music, local cuisine, handicrafts, art, craft workshops highlighting indigenous textiles and designs, among various other Naga experiences.
- Hornbill Festival is held at Naga Heritage Village, Kisama which is about 12 km from Kohima. All the tribes of Nagaland take part in this festival.
- The Festival is named after the Indian Hornbill, the large and colourful forest bird which is displayed in folklore in most of the state's tribes.

4. a
- MDR is the percentage of the digital transaction that a merchant pays to the banks.
- Sometimes it may be passed on to the customer, sometimes it may be borne by the merchant himself.
- The Merchant Discount Rate is shared among three players i.e., the bank which facilitated the mechanism with shopkeeper, the bank of the

customer who paid the amount through the debit card or otherwise and third is the payment platform i.e., Visa / RuPay etc.

5. b
- It is a permanent intergovernmental international organisation, the creation of which was announced on 15 June 2001 in Shanghai (China) by the Republic of Kazakhstan, the People's Republic of China, the Kyrgyz Republic, the Russian Federation, the Republic of Tajikistan, and the Republic of Uzbekistan. It was preceded by the Shanghai Five mechanism.
- On the meeting the status of a full member of the Organization was granted to the Republic of India and the Islamic Republic of Pakistan.
- The **Heads of State Council (HSC)** is the supreme decision-making body in the SCO.
- The **council of heads of government is SCO's second highest body** and is responsible for handling the trade and economic agenda.
- The SCO Heads of Government Council (HGC) meets once a year to discuss the organisation's multilateral cooperation strategy and priority areas, to resolve current important economic and other cooperation issues, and also to approve the organisation's annual budget.
- The SCO's official languages are Russian and Chinese.

6. c
- The National Capital Region Transport Corporation (NCRTC) is mandated for implementing the **Regional Rapid Transit System (RRTS)** project across the National Capital Region (NCR), ensuring a balanced and sustainable urban development through better connectivity and access.
- NCRTC is a joint venture of the Government of India (50%) and State Governments of Haryana (12.5%), NCT Delhi (12.5%), Uttar Pradesh (12.5%) and Rajasthan (12.5%).
- It is mandated to **design, construct, finance, operate and maintain RRTS in NCR** and works under the administrative control of **Ministry of Housing & Urban Affairs, GOI.**

NCRTC is mandated to implement India's first RRTS in NCR.

7. b
- Department of Biotechnology (DBT), facilitated Transfer of Technology of novel Brucella vaccine viz. **Brucella abortus S19 delta per vaccine**
- This vaccine was developed by **ICAR-Indian Veterinary Research Institute (ICAR-IVRI),** Izatnagar, Uttar Pradesh through a Network project on Brucellosis supported by DBT in which a gene was knocked out from Brucella abortus S19 strain.
- *Brucella abortus* S19 delta per vaccine can play an important role in **National Brucellosis Control Programme** initiated by Department of Animal Husbandry & Dairying, Ministry of Fisheries, Animal Husbandry & Dairying, Government of India.
- Brucella is a disease of economic importance worldwide. Not only does it impact cattle, sheep, goat and swine, but it also gets transmitted to human beings.
- Immunization with Brucella vaccine also helps cattle to remain healthy, thereby improving their milk production.

8. d
- Six women led startups have won COVID-19 Shri Shakti Challenge organized by MyGov in collaboration with UN Women.
- With an objective to encourage and involve women led startups to come up with innovative solutions that can help in the fight against COVID19 or solve problems that impact a large number of women, MyGov in collaboration with UN Women, launched the COVID-19 Shri Shakti Challenge in April 2020.
- This was a unique challenge hosted on the Innovate platform of MyGov that called for applications from women led startups as well as startups who have solutions that address issues faced by a larger number of women.
- The Challenge was implemented in two stages: Ideation stage and Proof of Concept (PoC) Stage.

9. c
- Brucellosis is a zoonotic disease which causes production losses in livestock. The disease induces abortion at the last stage of pregnancy, infertility and other reproductive problem which causes losses in production of milk and meat.
- Globally the disease is reported in approximately half a million human population every year.

- In India huge population involved in dairy farming is directly affected with the Brucellosis.

- Incidentally there is no vaccine available to protect humans against Brucella.

10. d
- Located near the mouth of the river Meghna where it flows into the Bay of Bengal, Bhasan Char surfaced only in 2006 from the sediment deposited by the river.

- Bhasan Char is less an island and more mud flat, and is vulnerable to going under water from tides and flooding.

- Much of it is submerged during the monsoon. Located near the mouth of the river Meghna where it flows into the Bay of Bengal, Bhasan Char surfaced only in 2006 from the sediment deposited by the river.

- Located close to the much larger Sandwip, Bhasan Char spans 40 sq km. The government has built shelters, hospitals and masjids.

11. a **Partners in Population and Development (PPD)**

- It is an intergovernmental initiative created specifically for the purpose of expanding and improving South-to-South collaboration in the fields of reproductive health, population, and development.

- PPD was launched at the 1994 International Conference on Population and Development (ICPD), when ten developing countries from Asia, Africa and Latin America formed an intergovernmental alliance to help implement the Cairo Program of Action (POA).

- This POA, endorsed by 179 nations, stresses the need to establish mechanisms to promote development through the sharing of experiences in reproductive health (RH) and family planning (FP) within and among countries and to promote effective partnerships among the governments, Non- Governmental- Organizations (NGOs), research institutions and the private sector.

- The PPD is the "only organization in the world fully dedicated to South-South partnerships."

12. b
- Health secretary revealed the details of CoWIN app through which one would be able to self register for vaccine

- With three vaccine-makers, including Pfizer, having applied for emergency use authorisation of their vaccine candidates in India, the vaccination drive is likely to begin shortly.

- Co-WIN, the new app which will be available for free download, is an upgraded version of the Electronic Vaccine Intelligence Network (eVIN).

- The app will also send real-time data of the temperature of the cold-storage units to the main server

13. c
- It is a multilateral development bank jointly founded by the BRICS countries (Brazil, Russia, India, China and South Africa) at the 6th BRICS Summit in Fortaleza, Brazil in 2014.

- It was formed to support infrastructure and sustainable development efforts in BRICS and other underserved, emerging economies for faster development through innovation and cutting-edge technology.

- It is headquartered at Shanghai, China.

- In 2018, the NDB received observer status in the United Nations General Assembly, establishing a firm basis for active and fruitful cooperation with the UN.

14. d
- The Education for Justice (E4J) initiative was launched by the United Nations Office on Drugs and Crimes to teach next generation about crime prevention and address problems under law.

- The initiative seeks to prevent crime and promote a culture of lawfulness through education activities designed for primary, secondary and tertiary levels.

- The E4J initiative is under the Global Programme for the Implementation of the Doha Declaration.

15. b
- South-South cooperation refers to the technical cooperation among developing countries in the Global South.

- It is a broad framework of collaboration among countries of the South in the political, economic, social, cultural, environmental and technical domains.

- Involving two or more developing countries, it can take place on a bilateral, regional, intraregional or interregional basis.

- Developing countries share knowledge, skills, expertise and resources to meet their development goals through concerted efforts.

16. c PMRPY

- Aim - To incentivise employers for generation of new employment.

- Government of India will pay the full employer's contribution towards Employee Pension Scheme (EPS) and Employees' Provident Fund (EPF): for the first three years of their employment.

- Implemented by the Ministry of Labour & Employment.

- The employer is incentivised for increasing the employment base of workers in the establishment.

- A large number of workers will find jobs and they will have access to social security benefits of the organized sector.

17. b Integrated Road Accident Database (IRAD):

- A central accident database management system to analyse causes of road crashes and helps in devising safety interventions to reduce such accidents in the country

- Developed by Indian Institute of Technology, Madras Will be implemented by National Informatics Centre (NIC) Supported by the world Bank

- Aims to develop and implement 'data-led' road safety interventions in order to reduce the road accidents

- This system shall be first launched in the Six States: Karnataka, Madhya Pradesh, Maharashtra, Rajasthan, Tamil Nadu and Uttar Pradesh.

18. c

- Digital taxation refers to a taxation regime which is aimed at taxation of companies which derive large revenues from countries through their digital presence instead of physical presence.

- India imposed a 6% equalization levy on online advertising in 2016. Under this, the levy is withheld by the recipient of services from the payment it's making for services.

- The concept of Significant Economic Presence (SEP) has been introduced in India under the income-tax law to capture business models that operate digitally/remotely in India, subject to certain thresholds in terms of users and revenue.

19. c

- It is developed by the Ministry of AYUSH and the Ministry of Electronics and Information Technology (MEITY).

- It targets to reach out to 50 lakh people in the country.

- The app intends to generate data on usage of AYUSH (Ayurveda, Yoga & Naturopathy, Unani, Siddha, Sowa-rigpa and Homoeopathy) advocacies and measures among the population and its impact in prevention of Covid-19.

- The data collected through this app will be analyzed to find out usage of AYUSH interventions and its efficacy in maintaining health by enhancing immunity.

20. c

- It is a test used to measure the oxygen level (oxygen saturation) of the blood.

- It measures the saturation of oxygen in red blood cells (RBCs) and can be attached to a person's fingers, toes, nose, feet, ears or forehead.

- It is easy and painless and the device can be reused or disposed of after use.

- It is generally used to check the health of patients with known conditions that affect blood oxygen levels like heart and lung conditions.

21. c

- In yet another flight test, the Quick Reaction Surface to Air Missile (QRSAM) System tracked the target accurately and successfully neutralised the airborne target.

- The flight test was conducted in the deployment configuration of the weapon system comprising of Launcher, fully Automated Command and Control System, Surveillance System and Multi -Function Radars.

- The QRSAM weapon system, which can operate on the move, consists of all indigenously developed subsystems. All objectives of the test were fully met. The launch was carried out in the presence of the users from Indian Army.

- A number of range instruments like Radar, Telemetry and Electro Optical Sensors were deployed which captured the complete flight data and verified the performance of the missile.

- The first in the series test of QRSAM took place on 13th Nov 2020 achieving the milestone of a direct hit. Second test proved the performance parameters of warhead.

22. c
- The Ministry of Earth Sciences will soon launch an ambitious 'Deep Ocean Mission' that envisages exploration of minerals, energy and marine diversity of the underwater world
- The mission, which is expected to cost over Rs 4,000 crore, will give a boost to efforts to explore India's vast Exclusive Economic Zone and Continental Shelf
- The mission will also involve developing technologies for different deep ocean initiatives.

23. d
- Andhra Pradesh Chief Minister launched the 'Abhayam' app designed for safe and secure travel for women commuting by autos and taxis
- The app aims at providing emergency help to those in distress and instills confidence among women, especially those traveling alone.
- The app is brought not because of lack of trust in auto, taxi drivers, but to build confidence among women passengers of safe travel in those vehicles.
- Like Ola, Uber, even our local autos and taxis offer a much safer transport, and women need not fear to board these vehicles

The first Internet of Things (IoT)-based women safety project aims to bring one lakh autos under the Abhayam initiative.

24. d
- An IFSC enables bringing back the financial services and transactions that are currently carried out in offshore financial centres by Indian corporate entities and overseas branches/subsidiaries of Financial Institutions (such as banks, insurance companies, etc.) to India.
- IFSCs are intended to provide Indian corporates with easier access to global financial markets, and to complement and promote further development of financial markets in India.
- The first IFSC in India has been set up at the Gujarat International Finance Tec-City (GIFT City) in Gandhinagar.

25. d
- The US has exited the Open Skies treaty, which allows countries to observe one another's militaries.
- Six months after US President Donald Trump announced his administration's decision to withdraw from the Open Skies accord
- The treaty provides for inspection flights over member countries' territories to monitor military activities.
- US officials claim that Russia violated the Open Skies treaty by blocking surveillance flights around certain areas, including the Russian enclave of Kaliningrad and the border with Georgia.
- Russia has denied the allegations and warned that the withdrawal will affect the interests of all of 35 participating countries.
- However, Russia intended to fully follow all the rights and obligations under the treaty as long as the treaty is in force.

26. b
- The Government of India and the Asian Infrastructure Investment Bank (AIIB signed a loan agreement for a $304 million Assam Intra-State Transmission System Enhancement Project to improve reliability, capacity and security of the power transmission network in the State of Assam.

The project aims to strengthen Assam's electricity transmission system by

(a) constructing 10 transmission substations and laying transmission lines with the associated infrastructure;

(b) upgrading 15 existing substations, transmission lines and existing ground wire to optical power ground wire; and

(c) providing technical assistance to support project implementation.

27. d
- All-India Quarterly Establishment based Employment Survey
- The Ministry of Labour launched the trainers' training programme for the All India Surveys being conducted by Labour Bureau, an attached office of Ministry of Labour & Employment by releasing the Instruction Manuals & Questionnaires for the surveys and the software application developed.

The Labour Bureau is entrusted with five All India surveys

(a) All India Survey of Migrant workers,

(b) All India survey of Domestic Workers,

(c) All India survey of employment generated by Professionals,

   (d) All India survey of employment generated in Transport Sector and

   (e) All-India Quarterly Establishment based Employment Survey

28. a
- The Ministry of Rural Development inaugurated Saras Aajeevika Mela 2021 at Noida Haat
- The Saras Aajeevika Mela 2021 is being organized from 26th February to 14th March 2021 by the Ministry of Rural Development.
- More than 300 rural self-help groups and craftsman from 27 states are participating in the Mela.

29. d
- The Waste to Wealth Mission of the Office of the Principal Scientific Adviser to the Government of India, and the Municipal Corporation of Faridabad (MCF), launched a pilot technology today to clean the Gaunchi Drain at Sanjay Colony, Faridabad.
- The Gaunchi Drain is a key arterial drainage system in Faridabad.
- Gaunchi is amongst the 11 most polluted drains of Haryana that together release 1002 million litres of polluted water in the Yamuna every day
- The project has deployed a RISE (Research Initiative For Scientific Enhancement) machine from DESMI EnviRo-CLEAN A/S, a Danish company that specialises in cleaning water bodies.

30. b
- The World Bank – SBI's $625 million has supported India's significant Rooftop Solar roll out.
- The MSME sector, through SBI's current rooftop solar (RTS) lending portfolio can leverage concessional debt and fulfil India's ambitious target for large scale implementation of rooftop solar.
- The World Bank is working with the Ministry of Micro, Small & Medium Enterprises, to bring in a credit guarantee mechanism catering to lending to MSMEs who would like to reduce their energy expenses in the long term by investing in rooftop solar.
- In 2016, The World Bank launched the 'Solar Rooftop Financing Program' being implemented by the State Bank of India (SBI).
- With a view to addressing the issues on the debt side and to give a fillip to the sector, SBI has availed a $625 million line of credit from World Bank specifically, for financing RTS projects across the country through its identified branches.

31. a
- India extended a $50-million line of credit to the Maldives for defence projects and the two countries signed an agreement to develop and maintain a key naval facility for the armed forces of the Indian Ocean archipelago.

Uthuru Thila Falhu naval base
- The agreements for the defence line of credit and developing the harbour at Uthuru Thila Falhu naval base were signed on the second and final day of external affairs minister S Jaishankar's visit to the Maldives.
- Five other agreements, including one for a $25-million line of credit for the development of roads, were signed
- The agreement between India's EXIM Bank and the Maldivian government for the defence line of credit will facilitate capability building in the maritime domain, Jaishankar said without giving details.

32. a
- The World Economic Forum (WEF) has announced the launch of an Essential Digital Infrastructure and Services Network
- It is as an international organization for public-private partnership, WEP will serve as the secretariat and platform for the EDISON Alliance.
- Its prime goal is to ensure an unprecedented level of cross-sectoral collaboration between the technology industry and other critical sectors of the economy, according to the WEF.

33. a
- Recently, the Transparency International has released the Corruption Perception Index (CPI) 2020.
- The CPI scores 180 countries and territories by their perceived levels of public sector corruption, according to experts and businesspeople.
- It uses a scale of 0 to 100, where 0 is highly corrupt and 100 is very clean.
- The CPI aggregates data from a number of different sources that provide perceptions among business-people and country experts of the level of corruption in the public sector

34. c • Afghanistan President has sent the first ever sacred chadar to Ajmer Sharif Dargah during the Urs festival.

• It is an annual festival held in Ajmer, Rajasthan.

• It is held over 6 days and involves night long dhikr and qawwali singing.

35. c • Recently, the Union Finance Minister in her Budget Speech 2021-22 has announced the Mega Investment Textiles Parks (MITRA) scheme.

• The textiles ministry has proposed to develop seven Mega Integrated Textile Region and Apparel (MITRA) parks as part of a plan to double the industry size to $300 billion by 2025-26

• The parks to be setup over 1,000 acres of land with world class infrastructure, and plug-and-play facilities.

• It will enable the textile industry to become globally competitive, attract large investments, boost employment generation and exports.

• It will create world class infrastructure with plug and play facilities to enable create global champions in exports.

• MITRA will lead to increased investments and enhanced employment opportunities with the support from the Production Linked Incentive (PLI) scheme. MITRA will give the domestic manufacturers a level-playing field in the international textiles market through emphasis on state- of-the-art infrastructure.

36. b • After over two years, state- owned NMDC Ltd. resumed production of iron ore from Donimalai Mines in Karnataka

In December 2018, suspended mining in Donimalai due to a legal battle with the Karnataka government over the issue of imposition of premium on the sale price of the iron ore extracted from the mines.

37. c • DFIs were meant to fund industrial initiatives that had long gestations as well as high project risks, which often meant that they could not get funding from the commercial banks of the time.

• DFIs benefitted from financial repression, as the rupee bonds they sold qualified as statutory liquidity ratio (SLR) holdings for banks.

• DFIs benefitted from financial repression, as the rupee bonds they sold qualified as statutory liquidity ratio (SLR) holdings for banks.

38. d • The Climate Adaptation Summit (CAS 2021) 2021, is an online global conference to accelerate, innovate and scale up the world's efforts in adapting our societies and economies to the inevitable effects of climate change over the coming decade.

• It will have a focus on securing new investments to ensure that millions of smallholder farmers can adapt to the stresses of climate on food production.

• During the event, the Adaptation Action Agenda (AAA) was launched.

• CAS 2021 is a multi-stakeholder event, with participation by governments from all continents as well as business leaders, mayors, international organisations, academia, civil society, and youth representatives.

• The Adaptation Action Agenda (AAA) is an instrument to accelerate action on climate adaptation by promoting, guiding, monitoring and sharing experience on climate resilience, and building together. It offers an integral framework in which individual actions and coalitions are brought together to reach the ambition of a climate-resilient future by 2030 (as stated in the SDGs).

• The Adaptation Action Agenda will present a comprehensive and accessible overview of key actions taken to enhance resilience, and their envisioned outcomes.

39. b • The Rohini Commission was appointed in accordance with the Article 340 of the constitution in October 2017. The Centre has extended the tenure of the Rohini Commission until 31st July, 2021 to submit its report.

• In 2015, the National Commission for Backward Classes (NCBC) had recommended that OBCs should be categorised into extremely backward classes, more backward classes and backward classes

• It was decided in Census 2021, data of OBCs will also be collected, but no consensus has been reached regarding enumeration of OBCs in the Census.

40. c • Government of India, and Government of Mauritius signed the India-Mauritius Comprehensive Economic Cooperation and Partnership Agreement (CECPA) in Port Louis

- CECPA is the first trade Agreement signed by India with a country in Africa.
- The Agreement is a limited agreement, which will cover Trade in Goods, Rules of Origin, Trade in Services, Technical Barriers to Trade (TBT), Sanitary and Phytosanitary (SPS) measures, Dispute Settlement, Movement of Natural Persons, Telecom, Financial services, Customs Procedures and Cooperation in other Areas
- As regards trade in services, Indian service providers will have access to around 115 sub-sectors from the 11 broad service sectors, such as professional services, computer related services, research & development, other business services, telecommunication, construction, distribution, education, environmental, financial, tourism & travel related, recreational, yoga, audio-visual services, and transport services.

41. b
- It is a group of nation-states working within the United Nations to further reform of the United Nations Security Council (UNSC).
- It has been nearly 13 years after the start of the Intergovernmental Negotiations (IGN) but it has made no progress.
- India, along with Brazil, Japan and Germany are pressing for urgent reform of the U.N. Security Council and for a permanent seat in the reformed 15-member top organ of the world body.

42. d
- It will be celebrated every year from 26th to 31st January, 2020 in New Delhi by the Ministry of Tourism
- It aims to encourage Indians to visit different tourist places of India and to inculcate the spirit of 'DekhoApnaDesh'.
- It includes highlights of the Republic Day Parade Tableaux, performances by the Armed Forces Bands, theme pavilions of different States and Central Ministries and cultural performances from different regions of the country.

43. c
- The UN Capital Development Fund has appointed Indian-origin investment and development banker Preeti Sinha as its Executive Secretary, whose focus will be on providing micro-finance assistance to women, youth, small and medium-sized enterprises in under-served communities.
- Established in 1966, the New York-headquarted organisation **provides micro-finance access to Least Developed Countries (LDCs),** with the mandate to unlock the full potential of public and private finance.
- The United Nations Capital Development Fund (UNCDF) is the capital investment agency of the United Nations for the LDCs
- It provides access to microfinance and investment capital.
- **UNCDF programmes help to empower women,** and are designed to catalyze larger capital flows from the private sector, national Governments and development partners, for maximum impact towards the internationally agreed developments goals.

44. c
- Neglected tropical diseases (NTDs) are a diverse group of tropical infections which are common in low-income populations in developing regions of Africa, Asia, and the Americas.
- Dengue, Rabies, Leprosy (Hansen disease), Blinding trachoma, Buruli ulcer, Endemic treponematoses (yaws) are few examples of NTD.
- 1 in 5 people around the world are affected by NTDs.
- India is home to the world's largest absolute burden of at least 11 of major neglected tropical diseases.

45. c
- India is the world's largest exporter of chili and turmeric, the exports of which have recorded a steady progress, over the years.

Spices Board India
- It is the flagship organization for the development and worldwide promotion of Indian spices.
- It is one of the five Commodity Boards functioning under the Ministry of Commerce & Industry.
- It is an autonomous body responsible for the export promotion of the 52 scheduled spices and development of Cardamom (Small & Large).
- The Board is an international link between the Indian exporters and the importers abroad.

46. c
- It is an international platform for expert-led debate between global leaders, investors and innovators with the power to shape the future of global investment.
- It is focused on utilizing investment to drive growth opportunities, enable innovation and disruptive technologies, and address global challenges.
- It is hosted by the Public Investment Fund of Saudi Arabia (PIF).
- The fourth edition is held under the theme of "The Neo-Renaissance" that will link leaders, investors and policymakers as they reimagine the global economy amid the Covid-19 pandemic.

47. d
- They are named for their shell, which is leather-like rather than hard, like other turtles.
- They are extremely vulnerable to temperature extremes.
- It is the only species without scales and a hard shell.
- They are the largest sea turtle species and also one of the most migratory, crossing both the Atlantic and Pacific Oceans.
- Although their distribution is wide, numbers of leatherback turtles have seriously declined during the last century as a result of intense egg collection and fisheries bycatch.
- Globally, leatherback status according to IUCN is listed as Vulnerable, but many subpopulations (such as in the Pacific and Southwest Atlantic) are Critically Endangered.

48. b
- It is the third peace deal with Bodo rebel groups that was signed in New Delhi on January 2020 by the Centre.
- It was signed with all four factions of National Democratic Front of Bodoland (NDFB), the All Bodo Students Union (ABSU) and United Bodo Peoples' Organisation (UBPO).
- The Bodoland Territorial Region (BTR) Accord has triggered the process of ending insurgency in the North-East and was able to bring peace to the troubled region in Assam.

49. a
- The development comes at a time when international energy markets have been volatile and amid rising tensions between China and India, the world's second- and third-largest crude oil importers.

Strategic Partnership Framework
- It will strengthen mutual trust and cooperation & enhance global energy security, stability and sustainability.
- This partnership will lead to an extensive exchange of knowledge and would be a stepping stone towards India becoming a full member of the IEA.
- The contents of the Strategic partnership will be jointly decided by IEA members and India.

50. c
- It is an autonomous body under the Sixth Schedule of the Constitution.
- There have been two Bodo Accords earlier, and the second one led to the formation of BTC.
- The area under the jurisdiction of BTC, formed under the 2003 Accord, was called the Bodo Territorial Autonomous District (BTAD).
- Later, BTAD was renamed as Bodoland Territorial Region (BTR).
- BTAD comprises Kokrajhar, Chirang, Baksa and Udalguri districts, accounting for 11% of Assam's area and 10% of its population.

Bodo Tribes
- They are the single largest community among the notified Scheduled Tribes in Assam.

Part of the larger umbrella of Bodo-Kachari, the Bodos constitute about 5-6% of Assam's population.

51. a The government is considering introducing a new bill "National Bank for Financing Infrastructure and Development Bill, 2021" in the ongoing budget session of the parliament. This bill will be passed with the objective of setting up a new development finance institution (DFI) so as to finance the infrastructure projects. Development Finance Institution (DFI)-
- The finance ministry had started working on the structure of a new DFI in the year 2020.
- DFI will be a specialized institution to provide funds for the infrastructure projects. The DFI will be backed by government.
- The DFI will help in funding the projects under the National Infrastructure Pipeline (NIP).
- The new DFI will act as a provider, enabler and catalyst for infrastructure financing.
- It is also the principal financial institution and development bank to build and sustain a

supportive ecosystem during the life cycle of the infrastructure projects.

NIP is a group of social and economic infrastructure projects. The project has been launched for a period of five years. The project has an initial sanctioned amount of Rs. 102 lakh crore. The pipeline project was first announced by the Prime Minister of India during the 2019 Independence Day speech.

52. c The publication of the Prabuddha Bharata magazine was started from Madras (Present day Chennai). The journal was published in Chennai for 2 years. After that, the magazine started publishing from Almora. From April 1899, the magazine started publishing from Advaita Ashrama. Since then, Advaita Ashram continuously edit the magazine and it is published and printed in Kolkata. In the history, many great personalities have contributed to the magazine namely, Bal Gangadhar Tilak, Former President Sarvepalli Radhakrishnan, Netaji Subhas Chandra Bose, Sister Nivedita and Sri Aurobindo. Presently, it is edited by Swami Vireshananda.

- It is a monthly magazine of the Ramakrishna Order.

- This magazine was founded in the year 1896 by P. Aiyasami, B. R. Rajam Iyer, G. G. Narasimhacharya, and B. V. Kamesvara Iyer under the guidance of Swami Vivekananda.

- Prabuddha Bharata magazine was of great significance in spreading the message of the ancient spiritual wisdom of the country.

- The magazine comprises of the articles and translations by monks, scholars and other writers on humanities and social sciences.

53. b The Indian Naval Fast Attack Craft, IN FAC T-81, of the Super Dvora MK II class was decommissioned in January in Mumbai. The IN FAC T-81 was decommissioned after providing service for more than 20 years.

IN FAC T-81:

- It is a 25 meters long vessel having 60 tonnes of displacement.

- The craft was built at Goa Shipyard Ltd. in collaborations with M/s Ramta of Israel.

- It was commissioned into the service of Indian Navy on June 5, 1999.

- The commissioning of the craft was done by

the then Governor of Goa, Lt Gen JFR Jacob (Retd).

- It was specially designed for shallow waters.

- It has the capability of day or night surveillance and reconnaissance.

- The craft was also involved in the beach insertion, extraction of Marine Commandoes, high-speed interception of intruder craft and Search & Rescue.

- The craft could achieve the speeds up to 45 knots.

- It was the 2nd ship of the Extra Fast Attack Craft (XFAC) Super Dvora MK II Class.

54. d Asia-Pacific Personalised Health Index was recently released by the Economist Intelligence Unit (EIU). The index measures the readiness in adopting the personalised healthcare of 11 health systems in the Asia-Pacific region. This is a newly launched index. The health systems that were evaluated includes: India, China, Singapore, Australia, Malaysia, Taiwan, Japan, Thailand, Indonesia, South Korea, and New Zealand. It measured the performance across 27 indicators of the personalised health across 4 categories that are called as the 'Vital Signs'. The four vital signs include Policy Context, Health Information, Personalised Technologies and Health Services. India was ranked at 10th position overall.

55. a The Larsen & Toubro (L&T) has bagged a contract worth

Rs. 1390 crore for the Mumbai-Ahmedabad bullet train project. This project is India's first such project. L&T has bagged the contract for the project from the National High-Speed Rail Corporation Limited (NHSRCL). The contract for the Mumbai-Ahmedabad bullet corridor has been given to Larsen & Toubro (L&T) – IHI Infrastructure Systems Consortium. L&T has been given the contract for the procurement and fabrication of 28 steel bridges for Crossing Over Rivers, roads, railway lines, highways and other structures for the Mumbai Ahmedabad high-speed rail corridor.

56. a **Start-up India Seed Fund Scheme (SISFS)-**

- The scheme will be launched with a corpus of Rs 945 crore.

- The scheme was launched with the aim of providing the financial assistance to start-ups for the product trials, market-entry, proof of concept, prototype development and commercialization.

- The funds under the Start-up India Seed Fund Scheme will be disbursed through the selected incubators across the country.
- The scheme will be in mission mode for the year 2021-25.
- The official notification on the launch of SISFS was released by the Department for Promotion of Industry and Internal Trade (DPIIT).
- The overall execution and monitoring of the SISFS will be done by the DPIIT. The DPIIT will form an Experts Advisory Committee (EAC) to look after the same.
- The Expert Advisory Committee (EAC) will evaluate and select the incubators in order to allot the Seed Funds, take all required measures for efficient utilization of funds and to monitor the progress.
- The seed support will be provided only once to any start-up.

57. b The Department of School Education and Literacy under the Ministry of Education, and the World Bank have signed the Strengthening Teaching-Learning and Results for States Program (STARS) project in January, 2021. The project is a financial support agreement.

- STARS project is a centrally sponsored scheme that seeks to strengthen the school education system.
- The agreement has been signed with an aim of improving the quality and governance of school education in six states of India.
- The 6 Indian states include- Kerala, Maharashtra, Himachal Pradesh, Rajasthan, Madhya Pradesh, Rajasthan, and Odisha.
- The STARS project will be benefitting approximately 250 million students in the age group of 6 to 17 years coming from the 1.5 million schools.
- Apart from the students, the project will also benefit 10 million teachers across the six states.
- The project was launched with the aim of strengthening the public-school education.
- It also supports India's aim of "Education for All".

- The STARS Project carries forward the vision of the National Education Policy 2020 that envisages the equitable education for all.

58. c The NTDs are a diverse group of communicable diseases that prevail in tropical and subtropical conditions. These diseases affect more than one billion people every year. In combating the disease, the countries invest billions of dollars every year. The Populations who are living in poverty, where there is no adequate sanitation, those who are in close contact with infectious vectors, domestic animals & livestock are highly affected by such diseases. As per the WHO major NTDs are: Buruli Ulcers, Chagas Disease, Dengue, Chikungunya, Sleeping Sickness (Human African Trypanosomiasis), Hansens' disease (Leprosy), Trachoma Mycetoma, chromo-blastomycosis, deep mycoses etc. As per the data, one in five people across the world are affected by NTD. India is home to the world's largest absolute burden of 11 of the major neglected tropical diseases.

59. b The United Nations Environment Programme (UNEP) has released its "Global Climate Litigation Report 2021". The report was published by the UNEP in cooperation with the Sabin Center for Climate Change Law at Columbia University. The report highlights that the Climate litigation cases have increased in recent years. The litigations have made the courtroom increasingly relevant to efforts to address the climate change across the world.

- As per the report, climate cases have nearly doubled over the last three years.
- Increasing climates cases are increasingly compelling the governments and corporate actors to implement their climate commitments.
- The cases are also compelling the government to pursue more ambitious climate change mitigation and adaptation goals.
- As per the data provided by the report, in 2017 884 cases were brought in 24 countries. While as of 2020, cases have increased to 1,550 filed in 38 countries and the European Union courts.
- Report finds that the climate litigation continues to be concentrated in high-income countries and the trend might further grow in the global south.

- The report has also identified the trends in climate litigation like Violations of "climate rights". That means the cases are increasingly relying on fundamental human rights such as right to life, food, health and water.

60. c	The virtual session will be attended by more than 400 top industry leaders from across the world. This is the 51st annual meeting of the World Economic Forum. The World Economic Forum annual meeting in Davos will bring together the top leaders of the world. These leaders will help in shaping the regional, global and industry agendas for 2021. The Davos Dialogue 2021 will also significant in the light of the launch of the "Great Reset Initiative" by the World Economic Forum in the post-COVID-19 world. The theme of the annual meeting was announced as 'The Great Reset'.

61. a	The National Non-Communicable Disease Monitoring Survey (NNMS) was recently released in India by the Ministry of health. The survey was conducted for the period of 2017-18. This is the first of its kind of a comprehensive survey on NCDs. It covers the age groups of 15-69 years, males and females from the urban and rural areas.

- The report highlights that, two in five adults have three or more risk factors for non-communicable diseases (NCD) in India.

- Further, the status of health system to respond to the disease burden is underscored.

- It also states that more than one in every four adults and 6.2% adolescents were overweight or obese.

- Three out of ten adults had raised blood pressure.

- 3% had raised blood glucose.

- It also shows that more than two in five adults and one in four adolescents were doing insufficient physical activity. The average daily intake of salt was 8 grams for these children.

- One in every three adults and more than one-fourth proportion of men were involved in tobacco consumption and consumed alcohol in past 12 months.

62. c	The loans that are taken by any public institution and not by the Centre directly are called as the "Off-Budget Borrowings". The public institution borrows on the directions of the central government. These borrowings are used to fulfil the expenditure needs of the government. Under such borrowing norms, Centre use to finance its expenditures while keeping the debt off the books. Thus, the debt is not counted while calculating the fiscal deficit. The liability of the loan is not formally on the Centre and is not included in the national fiscal deficit. Thus, it helps in keeping the fiscal deficit of the country within acceptable limits.

63. d	The Ministry of Agriculture has proposed for the National Mission for Edible Oil in order to increase the domestic availability and reduce the import dependency. The mission has been proposed for next five years in the span of 2020-21 to 2024-25. The NMEO comprises of the three Sub-Missions into it with the objective of increasing the production of oilseeds and edible oils from the three sources:

1.	Primary Sources- it includes the Annual Crops, Plantation Crops and Edible TBOs

2.	Secondary Sources- it includes the Rice bran oil and Cotton seed oil.

3.	Consumer Awareness to maintain the edible oil consumption constant at 19.00 kg per person per annum.

64. b	The Ministry of road transport has decided to impose the additional taxes on old vehicles that are no more fit on road. This additional tax is being called as the "Green Tax". The decision was taken to curb pollution. It will also motivate people to switch to environment-friendly alternatives to the vehicles. The Green tax will reduce the pollution level. It will also make the polluter to pay for creating pollution. Revenue collected from the green tax will be kept in a separate account. The amount will be used for tackling the problem of pollution. The states have been asked to set up state-of-art facilities to monitor the emission.

65. d	**Akash-NG:-**

- Akash-NG is a medium-range mobile surface-to-air missile defense system.

- It has been developed by the Defence Research and Development Organisation (DRDO).

- The missile has been produced jointly by the Bharat Dynamics Limited (BDL) that developed the Missile Systems and the Bharat Electronics (BEL), Tata Power Strategic Engineering Division & Larsen & Toubro that developed the radars, control centers, launcher systems.

- The missile has the capability of targeting the aircraft up to 50-60 km away at altitudes of 18,000 m.

- The missile can neutralize the aerial targets such as the fighter jets, cruise missiles and air-to-surface missiles.

- Missile is in operation with the Indian Army and the Indian Air Force.

- It utilizes an integrated ramjet-rocket propulsion system. This propulsion system provides sustained thrust for the missile after initial rocket motor burnout until its interception.

66. c The Indian Armed forces conducted a large-scale tri-service joint amphibious exercise AMPHEX – 21 in Andaman and Nicobar group of islands in January, 2021.

- In this exercise, the naval ships, amphibious troops of the Army and different types of aircraft from the Air force participated.

- The exercise was conducted with the aim of validating India's capabilities to safeguard the territorial integrity of the island territories.

- The exercise was also aimed at enhancing the operational synergy and joint warfighting capabilities between the three Services.

- In the exercise there were a series of engagements ranging from the multi-faceted maritime operations by synergised employment of amphibious assault ships, execution of maritime airstrikes, surveillance platforms and complex manoeuvres at sea.

- The exercise also involved the airborne insertion of Marine Commandos of Navy and Special Forces of the Army, naval gunfire support, the amphibious landing of forces and follow-on operations.

- Exercise KAVACH for the defence of Andaman & Nicobar Islands was also the part of AMPHEX – 21.

67. c The Government of India announced that the benefit of RoDTEP (Remission of Duties and Taxes on Exported Products) scheme is to be extended to all goods. The RoDTEP Scheme was launched in 2020 to boost exports of India in International markets. Under the scheme, a mechanism will be created for reimbursement of levies, taxes or duties at central, state and local levels. Prior to the scheme, the reimbursements were not done under any mechanism.

68. a The Government of India is to initiate the project of Sagarmala Seaplane Services on selected routes. Ministry of ports, shipping and waterways is the implementing agency. The project aims to provide air connectivity to numerous tourists, religious, remote and unexplored locations near water bodies. This is to make the journey easier and simulate tourism on these new locations. Ultimately the project will contribute to boost the GDP of the country in the long run. Seaplane service will work under Udan scheme.

69. d The second edition of coastal Defence Exercise Sea Vigil-21 is had been conducted in January, 2021. The Sea Vigil exercise will be undertaken along the 7,516 kilo metres coastline. It involves all the thirteen coastal states, Union Territories and the Exclusive Economic Zone. Also, the exercise involves the fishing and coastal communities. The exercise is conducted by the Indian Navy. The Sea Vigil is a build-up towards the major theatre level exercise TROPEX that the Indian Navy conducts every two years. Both Sea Vigil and TROPEX will together cover the entire spectrum of maritime security challenges. This includes transition from peace to conflict.

70. c The Government of India had launched the third phase of Pradhan Mantri Kaushal Vikas Yojana. The third Phase is to be implemented by the Ministry of Skill Development and Entrepreneurship. Under the third phase of Pradhan Mantri Kaushal Vikas Yojana, 729 Pradhan Mantri Kaushal Kendra are to be established and more than 200 ITIs are to be rolled out under Skill India mission. This will build a robust pool of skilled professionals. Pradhan Mantri Kaushal Vikas Yojana 3.0 is to train more than 1 lakh candidates for a period of one year with an investment of 950 crores of Rupees.

71. c A rare maritime mineral, Jarosite, has been found in the Antarctica ice. It was discovered after drilling deep into Antarctic ice. The recently discovered mineral was examined and it was found that it was formed in pockets within the ice. This supports the theory of presence of jarosite on MARS in as similar manner. It signifies that, the minerals are able to form in thick deposits on mars because the planet is a lot dustier than Antarctica.

- Jarosite is a mineral from mars which is scarcely seen on earth.
- It is a sulphate of potassium and iron.
- The mineral can be formed by both water and acidic conditions.
- It was first discovered on Mars in 2004 by a rover named "opportunity".
- Other Jarosite minerals include silver, sodium, lead and ammonium.
- It can be found are in the mining and ore processing wastes where they act as sinks for other toxic elements such as lead and arsenic.

72. d The National Informatics centre and the Central Board of Secondary Education (CBSE) jointly launched the CollabCAD software. The CollabCAD software provides engineering solution for students and Faculty of Engineering Graphics curriculum. It aims to provide a platform to students across the country to create and modify digital designs.

The aim is to provide a good platform to the students of Atal tinkering labs across the country. With the software the students of Atal tinkering labs will be able to create and modify 3D designs with free flow of creativity. It will enable students to create data across the network and access the same design data for storage and visualisation.

73. c NASA recently shared the picture of a huge cluster of galaxies called Abell 370.

Abell 370

- It is a galaxy cluster located four billion light years away from the earth. The galaxy cluster is located in the constellation called Cetus.
- The core of Abell 370 is made of more than hundred galaxies.
- The Galaxy was catalogued by George Abell and hence the name.
- Abell 370 has several arcs of light. These arcs are the mirages caused by gravitational lensing of dark and massive objects located between the observer and the distant galaxies.
- The Abell 370 galaxy cluster was first discovered in 2002 using the lensing effect.

74. d Recently, the Hubble Space Telescope of NASA captured the images of the NGC 4535 which is also known as the "Lost Galaxy". The image highlights that the young and hot stars that hang out are the bright blue spots. On the other hand, older and cooler stars are highlighted by the bright shades nearer to the center.

Lost Galaxy

- It is also known as NGC 4535.
- The galaxy is one of the largest of some 2,000 galaxies in the Virgo Cluster.
- The galaxy is located about 50 million light-years from Earth.
- It is a barred spiral galaxy that means a vast swirl of stars having a distinct bar structure at its center.
- The galaxy gives the yellowish glow at its central bulge. The yellowish glow suggests the way to the oldest and coldest retinue of stars in the Lost Galaxy.
- The Galaxy was discovered in 1785 by William Herschel who found the planet Uranus.
- The galaxy was termed as the Lost Galaxy by Copeland because then he had a glimpse of NGC 4535 using his small yard lenses.

75. c The researchers have recently found that the largest sea in Titan (moon of Saturn) is thousand feet deep in its centre. Also, it is the size of five great lakes combined together.

Kraken Mare

- Kraken Mare is huge liquid body located in the north pole of Titan.
- It is made of ethane and methane.
- The sea covers 154,000 square miles.
- Kraken Mare was discovered by the space probe Cassini.

76. d
- The WHR20 Happiness Report released in March 2021 by the UN Sustainable Development Solutions Network compares citizens' own perceptions of their well-being in 153 countries.
- According to the report, Indian citizens are amongst the least happy in the world: India ranks a very low 144th.

77. c
- Importantly, women-led cooperatives also provide fertile ground for grooming women from rural areas for leadership positions.
- In many instances, this becomes the first step for women in breaking free from traditional practices.

- This was amply demonstrated through the testimonials of women dairy farmers highlighted by the Department of Animal Husbandry and Dairying on the International Women's Day earlier this month.
- Recent years have seen the rise of women-led dairy unions and companies.
- To this end, the NDDB has played a proactive role in setting up women-led producer enterprises like Shreeja Mahila Milk Producer Company, which was started with 24 women and now has more than 90,000 members, with an annual turnover of approximately Rs. 450 crore.

78. b
- The electoral bonds scheme, however, removes all pre-existing limits on political donations, and effectively allows well-resourced corporations to buy politicians by paying immense sums of money.
- However, not only do electoral bonds violate basic democratic principles by allowing limitless and anonymous donations to political parties, they do so asymmetrically.
- Since the donations are routed through the State Bank of India, it is possible for the government to find out who is donating to which party, but not for the political opposition to know.
- This, in turn, means that every donor is aware that the central government can trace their donations back to them.
- The government has attempted to justify the electoral bonds scheme by arguing that its purpose is to prevent the flow of black money into elections.
- That apart, this justification falls apart under the most basic scrutiny: it is entirely unclear what preventing black money has to do with donor anonymity, making donations limitless, and leaving citizens in the dark.

79. d
- Recently, a 1.9 kilometre long bridge, the Maitri Setu, was inaugurated by Prime Minister Narendra Modi, connecting Sabroom in India with Ramgarh in Bangladesh.
- Bangladesh allows the shipment of goods from its Mongla and Chattogram (Chittagong) seaports carried by road, rail, and water ways to Agartala (Tripura) via Akhura; Dawki (Meghalaya) via Tamabil; Sutarkandi (Assam) via Sheola, and Srimantpur (Tripura) via Bibirbazar.
- This allows landlocked Assam, Meghalaya and Tripura to access open water routes through the Chattogram and Mongla ports.

80. c
- The employee PF contributions beyond Rs. 1.5 lakh are not tax-deductible under Section 80C of the I-T Act, but income on such contributions beyond Rs. 2.5 lakh will be taxable and employer contributions into the EPF, NPS or any superannuation pension fund are capped at Rs. 7.5 lakh.
- And the income on GPF contributions up to Rs. 5 lakh would be tax-free
- To top this off, the new Wages Code will compel employers to pay higher EPF contributions by linking them to at least half of their total pay on a cost to company basis, rather than 24% of basic pay presently.

81. a
- This is an alarming prospect for us as river water or lake water, which carries human waste, sewage, and toxic waste, can be a very generous host for viruses of different kinds and we do not know where and how they can mutate and strike.
- Some water-transmitted viral pathogens are astrovirus, hepatitis A and norovirus.
- Unlike in the developed world, a huge section of the population in India uses polluted water from sources like rivers, lakes, or groundwater for drinking.

82. b
- Coal mining provides incomes for Australia's local economy, but the health and environmental harm from mining and combustion represents a big net loss for the world.
- CO_2 emissions, the chief cause of climate change, totalled 36 billion metric tonnes globally in 2019, of which nearly 40% came from coal.
- The Carmichael mine is set to become Australia's largest coal mine, producing up to 60 million tonnes of coal annually and 2.3 billion tonnes over its 60- year lifespan.
- As India is the primary buyer of the Carmichael coal, the project will significantly add to its emissions.

- Australia's coal mining and coal exports generate incomes and jobs, but when the destruction from pollution, soil erosion, and biodiversity loss is included, the net contribution for India is negative.

83. b
- India's ambition of anchoring a global super-grid called One Sun One World One Grid, or OSOWOG needs an institutional vision.

- It aims to begin with connections to West Asia and Southeast Asia and then spread to Africa and beyond.

- The South Asian lesson, contained in these latest rules, is that political realities will constantly collide with, and damage, expansive visions of borderless trade.

- Impartial institutions for planning, investments and conflict resolution are crucial to multi-country power pools.

- Multi-country grids allow for the unpredictable outputs from renewable energy plants to be balanced across countries, thus avoiding expensive country-specific balancing technologies such as hydropower and gas plants.

84. d The mutual efforts between Delhi and Taipei have enabled a range of bilateral agreements covering agriculture, investment, customs cooperation, civil aviation, industrial cooperation and other areas, the time has come to recalibrate India-Taiwan relations.

85. c The Medical Termination of Pregnancy (Amendment) Bill is being hailed as a much-needed departure from the existing legal regime under the Medical Termination of Pregnancy Act, 1971 for two reasons — first, the bill replaces "any married woman or her husband" with "any woman or her partner" while contemplating termination of pregnancies resulting from contraception failures, thus ostensibly destigmatising pregnancies outside marriage; and second, the time limit within which pregnancies are legally terminable is increased.

While the limit for the first category (pregnancies terminable subject to the opinion of one medical practitioner) is raised from 12 weeks to 20 weeks, the limit for the second category (pregnancies terminable subject to the opinion of two medical practitioners) is raised to include those exceeding 20 but not exceeding 24 weeks, instead of the present category of cases exceeding 12 but not exceeding 20 weeks.

86. c
- In 1987, the Balakrishnan Committee was set up to submit its recommendations with regard to the status to be conferred on Delhi.

- In 1989, the Committee recommended that Delhi should continue to be a Union Territory but that there must be a Legislative Assembly and Council of Ministers responsible to the said Assembly with appropriate powers; and to ensure stability, appropriate constitutional measures should be taken to confer the National Capital a special status.

- Based on this report, the Constitution (69th) Amendment Act and the Government of National Capital Territory of Delhi (GNCT) Act, 1991 were passed.

- They roughly restored the kind of governance system that was offered to Delhi in 1952: a Union Territory with a Legislative Assembly, a Council of Ministers and an elected Chief Minister.

- This limited reincarnation has continued to hold the field to date, despite several efforts to progress to full or near-statehood.

87. b
- The Ken-Betwa Link Project lies in Bundelkhand, a drought-prone region, which spreads across 13 districts of Uttar Pradesh and Madhya Pradesh.

- According to the Jal Shakti Ministry, the project will be of immense benefit to the water-starved region of Bundelkhand, especially in the districts of Panna, Tikamgarh, Chhatarpur, Sagar, Damoh, Datia, Vidisha, Shivpuri and Raisen of Madhya Pradesh and Banda, Mahoba, Jhansi and Lalitpur of Uttar Pradesh.

- It will pave the way for more interlinking of river projects to ensure that scarcity of water does not become an inhibitor for development in the country.

- According to a written reply given by Minister of State for Jal Shakti Rattan Lal Kataria, out of the 6,017 ha of forest area coming under submergence of Daudhan dam of Ken Betwa Link Project, 4,206 ha of area lies within the core tiger habitat of Panna Tiger Reserve.

88. c
- It will take until April 1, 2022 for vehicles belonging to the government and the public sector to be scrapped, another year thereafter to identify junk heavy commercial vehicles

through mandatory fitness checks, and finally other vehicles by 2024, it is a constructive road map.

- It will be no easy task, however, to put in place a credible system of automated fitness checking centres with help from States to assess whether commercial and private vehicles are roadworthy after 15 and 20 years, respectively, as the policy envisages.

- Equally important, enforcement will be key to get them scrapped once they are found unfit for use and to stop them from moving to smaller towns.

- States must also come on board to provide road tax and registration concessions, while the automobile industry is expected to sweeten the deal with genuine discounts on new vehicles.

89. d
- Four core dynamics drive this calculus and explain why multinational companies are making India an essential part of their growth story.

- **First, sheer demographics.** What India offers through its nearly 1.4 billion people and their growing purchasing power is uniquely valuable for multinationals with global ambitions.

- No other country outside of China has a market that houses nearly one in six people on the planet and a rising middle class of 600 million.

- **Second, shifting geopolitics.** Rising U.S.-China competition is redefining the global landscape for investment and manufacturing, forcing multinationals to rethink their footprints and production hubs.

- Major multinational companies such as Samsung have invested billions in the Indian market, and manufacturers such as Cisco, Nokia, Ericsson, and Flex are reportedly weighing new investments that take advantage of fresh incentive programs.

- **Third, rising digital connectivity.** Cheap mobile data have powered a revolution across India's digital economy and connected an estimated 700 million Indians to the Internet.

- More than 500 million Indians still remain offline, and the rise of these 'next gen netizens' is a key reason why leading global tech companies are investing in India and weathering acute policy pressure.

- **Fourth, national resilience.** Despite facing the scourge of the novel coronavirus head on, India has managed the pandemic better than many of its western peers and restored economic activity even before implementing a mass vaccination programme.

90. c
- There are several disagreements with both the reports, yet who can deny that we are not doing enough to preserve our democratic capital and unnecessarily enacting laws or coming up with policies that have possibilities of tilting our democracy towards authoritarianism.

- The overriding powers given to the Governor-General in the Government of India Act, 1935 was opposed by the leaders of our freedom movement, and this opposition prevented the legislation from being enforced at the Centre. The Delhi Bill takes us back to British era.

- Such Bills could strengthen the international perception of India becoming an electoral autocracy.

- The then CJI also talked of "constitutional objectivity" as the key to checks and balances between the legislature and executive — one that ensures that the two operate within their allotted spheres since "legitimate constitutional trust" is based on distribution and separation of powers with denial of absolute power to any one functionary being the ultimate goal.

91. d
- The Quad's ideology of a "diamond of democracies" can only succeed if it does not insist on exclusivity in India's strategic calculations.

- Those who speak of Robert Kaplan's book, Monsoon, which proposed a greater role for the U.S. in the Indian Ocean as the inspiration for America's current Quad strategy, would do well to also read Mr. Kaplan's sequel, The Revenge of Geography, in which he makes the case that the world "continues to evolve according to the dictates of physical terrain, frustrating the proponents of human agency".

- The truth is, despite last week's Quad Summit, India's choices for its Quad strategy will continue to be guided as much by its location on land as it is by its close friendships with fellow democracies, the U.S., Japan and Australia, across the seas.

92. c
- Freedom House (based in Washington DC) and the Varieties of Democracy project (VDEM, based in Gothenburg, Sweden) are two of the more well-regarded efforts to conceptualise and measure the state of democracy globally each year.
- Their methodologies and indicators are transparently public, and the data sets they provide are widely analysed by researchers worldwide.

93. a
- Research and development of the BrahMos cruise missile systems began in the late 1990s.
- Manufactured by BrahMos Aerospace Limited, a joint venture between the Defence Research and Development Organisation and the joint stock company Military Industrial Consortium NPO Mashinostroyenia (earlier known as the Federal State Unitary Enterprise NPOM of Russia), this is the first supersonic cruise missile to enter service.
- Capable of attaining a speed of Mach 2.8 (almost three times the speed of sound), it has a range of at least 290 km (a new version can reach up to 400 km).
- Travelling with such velocity means that it would be difficult for air defence systems utilising surface-to-air missiles to intercept the BrahMos while making it easier for it to target and neutralise advanced fighter jets such as the Chinese J-20 fighter aircraft moving at less than Mach 2.
- Even so, efforts to increase the speed and range of the missile in its next iterations are under way, with a goal of achieving hypersonic speeds (at or above Mach 5) and a maximum range of 1,500 km.
- Early naval and land variants of the BrahMos were inducted into service by the Indian Navy in 2005 and the Indian Army in 2007.

94. d
- AI has helped increase crop yields, raised business productivity, improved access to credit and made cancer detection faster and more precise.
- It could contribute more than $15 trillion to the world economy by 2030, adding 14% to global GDP.
- Google has identified over 2,600 use cases of "AI for good" worldwide. A study published in Nature reviewing the impact of AI on the Sustainable Development Goals (SDGs) finds that AI may act as an enabler on 134 — or 79% — of all SDG targets.

95. d
- The Indian Ocean tsunami of 2004 triggered cooperation among the navies and governments of the Quad powers.
- They sought to forge diplomatic cooperation on regional issues in 2006-08, but gave up mainly because China objected to it and the hostility to China was not yet a potent enough glue.
- It is both a laudable and doable objective, given the firm commitment of financial support by the U.S. and Japan, logistics and some funding from Australia, and the manufacturing and anagerial capabilities of India.
- This new synergy is a real highlight that should result in the production of one billion vaccine doses in India by 2022.
- Now is the time to back political commitment with a strong mix of resolve, energy, stamina and the fresh ideas of stakeholders and experts outside of government to fulfill the promise of the Quad.

96. c
- The Parliamentary Committee (Rajya Sabha) which considered the POCSO Bill, 2011 had, in fact, criticised the clause providing for the possibility of consent in cases of sexual intercourse with minors between the ages of 16 and 18.
- It believed that a uniform age of 18 would ensure that trials of child rape would focus on the conduct of the accused and the circumstances of the offence, instead of putting victims on trial as is often the case when the consent of the victim is in question.
- This would indicate that adolescent sexuality was not meant to be an exception to POCSO's bright-line approach.
- The five State studies on the functioning of Special Courts under the POCSO Act, conducted by the Centre for Child and the Law, National Law School of India University, Bengaluru, have demonstrated that these de facto consensual cases are complicated.
- While adolescents can and do choose to have sex, it is a fact that they are still children, and their nascent sexual autonomy is susceptible to abuse.
- This contradiction created by the very nature of adolescence has led to inconsistent and unprincipled adjudication.

- The absolute age line of POCSO has not prevented the insensitive assessment of minors' consent.

97. d
- The National Family Health Survey-4 has shown how TFR has reduced even among illiterate women from all religions in the southern states — even in Kerala and Telangana which have a high proportion of Muslims.
- The question that arises is how could the Southern states achieve population stabilisation so early and several others could follow suit, while Uttar Pradesh and Bihar continue to drift?
- Three things are needed: Incentivise later marriages and child births; make contraception easy for women and promote women's labour force participation.
- The population momentum, if managed properly in the Hindi belt, will remain India's biggest asset until 2055. By 2040, India will be the undisputed king of human capital.
- But alongside some other disturbing nationwide trends must also be counteracted without delay because stabilisation isn't only about controlling population growth.
- A balanced sex ratio is essential to secure social cohesion. Son preference, falling sex ratios, and an abhorrence towards begetting a second or third female child are negative developments that have penetrated even into rural areas.

98. c
- ShadowPad is a network intrusion malware affiliated to both the Chinese Ministry of State Security and the People's Liberation Army.
- ShadowPad is depicted as a "backdoor 'Trojan' malware which creates a secret path from a targeted system to a command and control server to extract information".
- If indeed the future is digital, and if China has indeed embarked on an all-out offensive of this nature, India needs to adopt comprehensive measures to forestall a potential 'Cyber Pearl Harbour', as far as India is concerned.

99. b
- A recent publication by the World Bank titled Enabling the Business of Agriculture (EBA) 2019 provides some interesting insights on this question.
- Based on eight indicators, the EBA measures the extent to which government regulatory systems in 101 countries worldwide make it easier for their farmers to operate agricultural activities.
- The indicators are supplying seed, registering fertilizer, securing water, registering machinery, sustaining livestock, protecting plant health, trading food, and accessing finance.
- These indicators measure the strength of a country's agricultural regulatory environment pertaining to market integration and entrepreneurship in agriculture.
- The EBA is akin to the Doing Business project of the World Bank, which ranks the ease of doing business in countries.

100. a
- The Scorpene class submarines are one of the most advanced conventional submarines in the world.
- The submarine has superior stealth features, such as advanced acoustic silencing techniques, low radiated noise levels and ability to attack with precision-guided weapons on board.
- The Indian Navy intends to use the submarines for missions such as area surveillance, intelligence gathering, anti-submarine warfare, anti-surface warfare and minelaying operations.
- The submarines are armed with six torpedo-launching tubes, 18 heavy weapons, tube-launched MBDA SM-39 Exocet anti-ship missiles and precision-guided weapons. It can launch crippling attacks on surface and underwater enemy targets.
- Moreover, the attack submarines can travel at a maximum submerged speed of approximately 20 knots and have the ability to remain submerged for 21 days. It has a diving depth of more than 350m.
- The Scorpene class of submarines were designed by French naval shipbuilding firm DCNS in partnership with Spanish shipbuilding firm Navantia.
- INS Karanj has been equipped with the best sensors in the world and is fitted with an integrated platform management system to provide centralised propulsion and machinery control.

Mock Test 4
General Studies Paper I

1. Consider the following statements regarding Cooperative Federalism:
   1. The concept is taken from the Constitution of Britain.
   2. The concept of cooperative federalism regards division of power as well as means to promote the prosperity and well-being of the people.

   Which of the statements given above is/are correct?
   - (a) 1 only
   - (b) 2 only
   - (c) Both 1 and 2
   - (d) Neither 1 nor 2

2. Consider the following statements regarding Zonal Councils:
   1. The zonal councils are constitutional bodies empowered by Article 263 of our Constitution.
   2. We have five zonal councils dividing the states into five groups.
   3. Geographical proximity and connectivity along with infrastructure were considered for dividing the zones.

   Which of the statements given above are correct?
   - (a) 1 and 2 only
   - (b) 1 and 3 only
   - (c) 2 and 3 only
   - (d) 1, 2 and 3

3. Consider the following statements regarding the step towards decentralization that was taken in 1992:
   1. It became constitutionally mandatory to hold regular elections to local government bodies.
   2. At least one-third of all the positions were reserved for women.
   3. State Election Commission was created in each state to conduct panchayat and municipal elections.

   Which of the statements given above is/are correct?
   - (a) 1 only
   - (b) 1 and 2 only
   - (c) 2 and 3 only
   - (d) 1, 2 and 3

4. Which of the following features of Fundamental Rights is/are correct?
   1. All the rights are available to citizens, foreigners and legal persons.
   2. They are absolute in nature.
   3. Most of them are available against arbitrary action of state.
   4. These are justiciable in nature.

   Select the correct answer using the code given below:
   - (a) 1 and 2 only
   - (b) 3 and 4 only
   - (c) 4 only
   - (d) 1, 2, 3 and 4

5. Consider the following statements regarding Chilika Lake:
   1. It is considered as home to the highest single lagoon dolphin population.
   2. It is the largest winter ground for migratory birds on Indian sub-continent.
   3. Nalabana Bird Sanctuary is situated inside the periphery of Chilika Lake.
   4. Kalijai Temple is located on an island in Chilika Lake.

   Which of the statements given above is/are correct?
   - (a) 2 only
   - (b) 1 and 2 only
   - (c) 1 and 3 only
   - (d) 1, 2, 3 and 4

6. Consider the following statements regarding International Tropical Timber Organisation (ITTO):
   1. The International Tropical Timber Organization (ITTO) is an intergovernmental organization.
   2. It promotes sustainable tropical timber supply chains and also helps to develop capacity in tropical forestry.
   3. India is a member of this organisation.

   Which of the statements given above is/are correct?
   - (a) 2 only
   - (b) 1 and 3 only
   - (c) 2 and 3 only
   - (d) 1, 2 and 3

7. Consider the following statements regarding the Polycrack Technology:
   1. The technology is the world's very first patented heterogeneous catalytic process which converts multiple feedstocks into hydrocarbon liquid fuels, gas, carbon as well as water.

2. This technology can even use unsegregated municipal solid waste with moisture content and all types of plastic as well as E-waste as feedstock material.

Which of the statements given above is/are **incorrect?**

(a) 1 only
(b) 2 only
(c) Both 1 and 2
(d) Neither 1 nor 2

8. Consider the following statements:

1. Prokaryotic cells lack nuclear membrane.
2. Eukaryotic cells possess nuclear membrane.
3. All prokaryotic organisms are single celled organisms.

Which of the statements given above is/are correct?

(a) 1 only
(b) 1 and 2 only
(c) 2 and 3 only
(d) 1, 2 and 3

9. Consider the following statements regarding Saline soil:

1. Saline soils are rich in sodium, potassium and magnesium but lack in nitrogen and calcium.
2. Excessive irrigation in areas of green revolution converts the fertile alluvial soils into saline.
3. Farmers are advised to add gypsum to the saline soil to solve the problem of salinity in the soil.

Which of the statements given above is/are correct?

(a) 1 and 2 only
(b) 3 only
(c) 2 and 3 only
(d) 1, 2 and 3

10. Consider the following statements:

1. Chambal, a tributary of Ganga emerges from glaciers present in Uttarakhand.
2. River Gandak rises in Nepal Himalayas.
3. Narmada is one among those long rivers that flow westwards.
4. Son River of central India is the second largest of the Ganges' southern tributaries.

Which of the statements given above are correct?

(a) 1 and 4 only
(b) 2 and 3 only
(c) 1 and 3 only
(d) 2, 3 and 4 only

11. Consider the following statements regarding distribution of minerals in India:

1. About 95% of total reserves of Iron are located in north-eastern region of India.
2. Manganese deposits are found in almost all geological formations except Dharwar system.

3. Over 97 per cent of coal reserves occur in the valleys of Damodar, Sone, Mahanadi and Godavari.

Which of the statements given above is/are **incorrect?**

(a) 1 and 3 only
(b) 2 and 3 only
(c) 1 and 2 only
(d) 3 only

12. The leeward side of mountain gets less rainfall by the process of Orographic rain. Consider the following statements:

1. When the air mass comes across a leeward side of mountain, the temperature falls and the capacity to take in moisture decreases.
2. The descending of air masses on the leeward side makes moisture taking capacity higher.

Which of the statements given above is/are correct?

(a) 1 only
(b) 2 only
(c) Both 1 and 2
(d) Neither 1 nor 2

13. Consider the following statements:

1. During the previous decade, the Consumer Price Index-based inflation came down to less than half of what it was a decade ago.
2. During the past five years, the annual average Wholesale Price Index is always lesser than Consumer Price Index.

Which of the statements given above is/are **incorrect?**

(a) 1 only
(b) 2 only
(c) Both 1 and 2
(d) Neither 1 nor 2

14. Consider the following statements regarding Special Drawing Rights (SDR):

1. It is an artificial currency instrument used by the International Monetary Fund.
2. Renminbi is having lowest weightage in Special Drawing Rights basket of currencies.
3. It is held with the central bank of the member countries.

Which of the statements given above is/are correct?

(a) 1 only
(b) 2 and 3 only
(c) 1 and 3 only
(d) 1, 2 and 3

15. Consider the following statements regarding Operation Twist:

1. It can be considered as an example of open market operations.
2. It is expected to facilitate monetary transmission.

3. Operation Twist first appeared in 1961 as a way to strengthen the U.S. dollar and stimulate cash flow into the economy.

Which of the statements given above are correct?

(a) 1 and 2 only

(b) 2 and 3 only

(c) 1 and 3 only

(d) 1, 2 and 3

16. When the fiscal deficit target slips by 0.5% in comparison to the original budget estimates, which of the following is/are most likely to occur?

1. Less domestic savings will be available for the investments of the private sector.

2. The Capital Expenditure of the centre will increase commensurately by 0.5%.

Select the correct answer using the code given below:

(a) 1 only   (b) 2 only

(c) Both 1 and 2   (d) Neither 1 nor 2

17. Consider the following statements regarding the Stone Age in India:

1. The domestication of animals was observed for the first time in the Neolithic age.

2. No traces of Neolithic people were found in Kashmir valley.

3. First human colonization of the Ganga plains was started in Mesolithic Period.

Which of the statements given above is/are correct?

(a) 1 and 2 only   (b) 3 only

(c) 1 and 3 only   (d) 1, 2 and 3

18. Which of the places where associated with the life of Buddha?

1. Kapilavastu

2. Sravanabelagola

3. Vaisali

4. Gaya

Select the correct answer using the code given below:

(a) 1, 2 and 3 only   (b) 2 and 4 only

(c) 3 and 4 only   (d) 1, 3 and 4 only

19. Consider the following statements regarding the architecture of Hampi:

1. It is located in the Krishna-Tungabhadra basin which formed the nucleus of the Vijaynagara Empire.

2. It was a well-fortified city, mortar or cementing agent was used in the construction of these walls.

3. Splendid arches and domes were part of the Hampi architecture.

4. One of the unique features of temples at Hampi is the wide chariot streets flanked by the row of pillared mandapas.

Which of the statements given above are correct?

(a) 1 and 2 only   (b) 2 and 3 only

(c) 1, 3 and 4 only   (d) 1, 2, 3 and 4

20. Consider the following statements regarding Upanishads:

1. These are the examples of Guru-Shishya tradition of India.

2. They are also known as the end of the Vedas.

3. The oldest Upanishads are Brihadaranyaka and Chandogya Upanishads.

Which of the statements given above are correct?

(a) 1 and 3 only   (b) 2 and 3 only

(c) 1 and 2 only   (d) 1, 2 and 3

21. Alma-Ata Declaration of WHO is related to –

(a) Role of State Legislature in the development of health infrastructure during COVID -19.

(b) Role of local government to focus on water, sanitation and shelter.

(c) Redressal mechanism against vaccine nationalism

(d) None of the above

22. Through which of the following ways federalism is promoted in India?

1. Creation of NITI Aayog

2. Acceptance of Fifteenth Finance Commission's recommendations for greater devolution.

3. Establishment of GST Council

4. Restructuring of centre-state level schemes

Select the correct answer using the code given below:

(a) 1, 2 and 3 only   (b) 2, 3 and 4 only

(c) 3 and 4 only   (d) 1, 2, 3 and 4

23. Shahtoot dam recently seen in the news due to which of the following reason?

(a) India has constructed this dam in Iran

(b) A hydroelectric power project in Afghanistan

(c) India has signed an agreement to construct this is Kabul, Afghanistan

(d) A disputed territory between India and Pakistan

24. Consider the following statements:

1. The return on the most popular PPF scheme was pegged at 6.4% which remains lower in the last 50 years.

2. PPF interest rate was reduced in Q1 from 7.9 to 7.1 percent.

Which of the statements given above is/are correct?

(a) 1 only   (b) 2 only

(c) Both 1 and 2   (d) Neither 1 nor 2

25. Consider the following statements:

1. The Preamble in the Constitution gives prominent importance to liberty of belief, faith and worship to all citizens.

2. The concepts of faith, belief and worship are the foundations of Articles 25 and 26 of the Constitution of India.

3. Prohibiting citizens from approaching appropriate courts proceedings to handover the land of any temple is against the fundamental right under Article 14.

Which of the statements given above is/are correct?

(a) 3 only   (b) 2 and 3 only

(c) 1 and 2 only   (d) 1, 2 and 3

26. Consider the following statements:

1. Early atmosphere composed of Hydrogen and Helium and these were destroyed due to the impact of solar winds.

2. The process of degassing is responsible for the formation of present atmosphere.

Which of the statements given above is/are **incorrect?**

(a) 1 only   (b) 2 only

(c) Both 1 and 2   (d) Neither 1 nor 2

27. Which of the following public sector companies is/are stakeholders in Energy Efficiency Services Limited (EESL)?

1. National Thermal Power Corporation Limited

2. Power Finance Corporation Limited

3. Rural Electrification Corporation Limited

4. Nuclear Power Corporation of India.

Select the correct answer using the code given below:

(a) 2, 3 and 4 only   (b) 2 and 3 only

(c) 1, 3 and 4 only   (d) 1, 2 and 3 only

28. Consider the following statements regarding optical communication (OC):

1. In optical communication, signal in the form of light waves is transmitted through optical fibres to the remote end.

2. Optical communication signal can be transmitted through medium of electrical channel.

Which of the statements given above is/are **incorrect?**

(a) 1 only   (b) 2 only

(c) Both 1 and 2   (d) Neither 1 nor 2

29. Consider the following statements regarding SARS-CoV-2:

1. Like other coronaviruses, SARS-CoV-2 particles are spherical and have proteins called spikes protruding from their surface.

2. SARS-CoV-2 spikes bind to receptors on the human cell surface called angiotensin-converting enzyme 2 (ACE2).

3. The researchers found that the SARS-CoV-2 spike was 10 to 20 times more likely to bind ACE2 on human cells than the spike from the SARS virus from 2002.

Which of the statements given above are correct?

(a) 1 and 2 only   (b) 2 and 3 only

(c) 1 and 3 only   (d) 1, 2 and 3

30. The members of the State Legislative Assembly participate in which of the following elections?

1. The President

2. The Vice-President

3. Members of the Legislative Council

Select the correct answer using the code given below:

(a) 1, 2 and 3   (b) 1 and 3 only

(c) 1 only   (d) 1 and 2 only

31. Consider the following statements regarding the Salary and the Allowances of Leader of Opposition in Parliament Act, 1977:

1. One-tenth of the total number of members of Lok Sabha is mandatory to get the recognition of the Leader of the Opposition.

2. Under the Act, discretionary powers are given to the Speaker of Lok Sabha.

Which of the statements given above is/are correct?

(a) 1 only   (b) 2 only

(c) Both 1 and 2   (d) Neither 1 nor 2

32. Which of the following comes under the ambit of Doctrine of Double Jeopardy, as enshrined under Article 20(2)?

1. A Civil servant prosecuted and convicted by a court of law can be punished under departmental proceedings for the same offence.
2. A person punished departmentally may be prosecuted in a court of law.

Select the correct answer using the code given below:

(a) 1 only   (b) 2 only

(c) Both 1 and 2   (d) Neither 1 nor 2

33. Consider the following statements regarding organisation of Panchayats:

1. A Gram Sabha consists of all the adults i.e. voters living in the area of a Gram Panchayat.
2. Gram Sabha is an executive committee but not a legal body.
3. Gram Panchayat is the Village assembly of Gram Sabha.

Which of the statements given above is/are correct?

(a) 1 only   (b) 1 and 2 only

(c) 2 and 3 only   (d) 1, 2 and 3

34. Consider the following statements:

1. Wastelands are barren and uncultivated land lying unproductive or which is not being utilized to its potential.
2. Wetlands include areas of marine water at the depth of which low tide does not exceed six metres.

Which of the statements given above is/are correct?

(a) 1 only   (b) 2 only

(c) Both 1 and 2   (d) Neither 1 nor 2

35. Which of the following species naturally found in India?

1. Nicobar Megapode
2. Sarus Crane
3. Asiatic Wild Ass
4. One-horned rhinoceros

Select the correct answer using the code given below:

(a) 1 and 4 only   (b) 2 and 4 only

(c) 1 and 3 only   (d) 1, 2 and 3 only

36. Consider the following statements regarding International Convention for the Regulation of Whaling (ICRW):

1. Its purpose is to provide for the proper conservation of whale stocks and orderly development of the whaling industry.
2. The convention provides for two types of whaling activities only i.e. commercial whaling and aboriginal/indigenous whaling.
3. India is a party to the convention.

Which of the statements given above are correct?

(a) 1 and 2 only   (b) 1 and 3 only

(c) 2 and 3 only   (d) 1, 2 and 3

37. Consider the following statements regarding Maputo Bay Seagrass Restoration Project:

1. Maputo Bay is situated in Western Indian Ocean.
2. The bay is the northern termination of the series of lagoons which line the coast from Saint Lucia Bay.
3. The carbon storage potential of both seagrass and tropical rainforests is almost the same.
4. Overfishing may lead to destruction of seagrass.

Which of the statements given above are correct?

(a) 2 and 4 only   (b) 1, 2 and 4 only

(c) 1 and 2 only   (d) 1, 2 and 3 only

38. Consider the following statements regarding 'Indian Monsoon':

1. The arrival of Indian Monsoon is gradual but its withdrawal is sudden.
2. The Islands of Arabian Sea receives very first monsoon showers.
3. Indian monsoon shows complete reversal of wind.

Which of the statements given above is/are **incorrect?**

(a) 1 and 3 only   (b) 1 only

(c) 2 and 3 only   (d) 1, 2 and 3

39. Consider the following statements regarding Urban Heat Island:

1. It refers to a metropolitan area which is lot warmer than its surrounding rural areas.
2. The factors responsible for Urban Heat Islands are building materials, waste heat and dense population.
3. Night time temperatures above ground level in Urban Heat Islands remain high.

Which of the statements given above are correct?

(a) 1 and 2 only

(b) 2 and 3 only

(c) 1 and 3 only

(d) 1, 2 and 3

40. Which of the following are the features of Shola grasslands?
    1. Tropical montane forests
    2. Sky islands
    3. High water retention capacity
    4. Domination of pioneer species of vegetation
    Select the correct answer using the code given below:
    (a) 1 and 2 only   (b) 2 and 4 only
    (c) 1, 2 and 3 only   (d) 1, 2, 3 and 4

41. Consider the following statements regarding estuaries:
    1. It is an area of fine deposits where the rivers divide and joins the sea.
    2. It constitutes a variety of fauna including worms, oysters, crabs and waterfowl.
    3. It is a region which has low tides.
    4. Estuaries form a transition zone between river environments and maritime environments.
    Which of the statements given above are correct?
    (a) 2 and 4 only   (b) 1 and 2 only
    (c) 3 and 4 only   (d) 2 and 3 only

42. Consider the following statements regarding Purchasing Managers Index:
    1. This index is released for both the manufacturing sector and service sector.
    2. It broadly reflects the health of the private sector companies.
    3. Index above 100 indicates expansion.
    4. The PMI is usually released at the beginning of every month.
    Which of the statements given above are correct?
    (a) 1 and 3 only   (b) 1, 2 and 4 only
    (c) 1 and 2 only   (d) 1, 2, 3 and 4

43. Consider the following statements about Gig Economy:
    1. Majority of the jobs created under this is of temporary and flexible in nature.
    2. Gig economy jobs are cheaper for the companies in comparison to the Conventional Economy.
    3. The existing regulatory framework in various countries is generally considered insufficient to regulate gig economy jobs.
    4. An estimated 56% of new employment in India is being generated by the gig economy companies.

Which of the statements given above is/are correct?
(a) 1 only   (b) 1 and 2 only
(c) 2 and 3 only   (d) 1, 2, 3 and 4

44. Which of the following statements is/are correct regarding Reserve Bank of India's Utkarsh 2022?
    1. It is a roadmap to improve regulation and supervision functions of the central bank.
    2. It will strengthen the trust of citizens and other Institutions in the RBI.
    3. It will ensure environment friendly digital as well as physical infrastructure.
    Select the correct answer using the code given below:
    (a) 2 and 3 only   (b) 1 and 3 only
    (c) 2 only   (d) 1, 2 and 3

45. Consider the following statements regarding Board for Financial Supervision (BFS):
    1. Reserve Bank of India performs the supervisory function under the guidance of the Board for Financial Supervision.
    2. The primary objective of Board for Financial Supervision is a consolidated supervision of the financial sector.
    3. The board is chaired by one of the Deputy Governors of Reserve Bank of India.
    Which of the statements given above are correct?
    (a) 1 and 2 only   (b) 1 and 3 only
    (c) 2 and 3 only   (d) 1, 2 and 3

46. Consider the following statements:
    1. India has had a trade surplus with Pakistan.
    2. Pakistan was a Most Favored Nation for India which was revoked after Kargil war.
    3. Pakistan is lifting ban from Indian trade due to shortage of cotton for raw material which can be fulfilled by India on reasonable price.
    Which of the statements given above is/are correct?
    (a) 1 and 3 only   (b) 2 only
    (c) 1 and 2 only   (d) 1, 2 and 3

47. Consider the following statements:
    1. RBI has announced inflation targeting for quinquennial ending on 31st March 2026.
    2. The upper tolerance level is kept at 6 percent and lower at 2 percent from the baseline of 4 percent.
    Which of the statements given above is/are correct?
    (a) 1 only   (b) 2 only
    (c) Both 1 and 2   (d) Neither 1 nor 2

48. Consider the following statements regarding climate justice:

1. Distributive justice pertains to how resources should be distributed in terms of principles of equality, equity and merit.
2. Corrective justice pertains to the righting of wrongs.
3. Commutative justice refers to agreements or commitments, and other kinds of social contracts.

Which of the statements given above is/are correct?

(a) 1 only   (b) 2 and 3 only
(c) 1 and 2 only   (d) 1, 2 and 3

49. Consider the following statements:

1. Right to education was initially kept in DPSP to achieve within a decade.
2. RTE was given fundamental rights status under 86th Amendment Act, 2002.
3. After its implementation, it directly discriminate between students studying in minority and non-minority institutions.

Which of the statements given above is/are correct?

(a) 1 and 2 only   (b) 3 only
(c) 2 and 3 only   (d) 1, 2 and 3

50. What are the actions taken by UNESCO against racism?

1. Education
2. Science
3. Culture
4. Communication

Select the correct answer using the code given below:

(a) 3 and 4 only   (b) 1, 2, 3 and 4
(c) 2, 3 and 4 only   (d) 1, 2 and 4

51. Consider the following statements regarding Mahajanapadas:

1. Location of all Mahajanapadas was in Ganga-Yamuna river valley.
2. The archaeological linkage of the era of Mahajanapadas relates with the Northern Black Polished Ware (NBPW) era.
3. All the Mahajanapadas were monarchical.

Which of the statements given above is/are **incorrect**?

(a) 1 and 2 only   (b) 1 and 3 only
(c) 2 only   (d) 3 only

52. Consider the following statements regarding Swaraj party:

1. The Swaraj party was formed after differences occurred in congress over issue of council entry.
2. The council entry was opposed by no-changers on the ground that parliamentary work would neglect constructive work and loss of revolutionary zeal.
3. After the defeat of Swarajists proposal at Gaya session of congress, both Motilal Nehru and C.R. Das announced the formation of Swarajist party.
4. No-changers in congress was led by M.K Gandhi.

Which of the statements given above are correct?

(a) 1 and 2 only   (b) 2 and 4 only
(c) 1, 2 and 3 only   (d) 1, 2, 3 and 4

53. Consider the following statements regarding Kuchipudi dance:

1. It emerged out of a long rich tradition of dance-drama.
2. It is based on the themes of Bhagavata Purana.
3. "Tarangam" is a unique feature of this dance form.

Which of the statements given above is/are correct?

(a) 1 and 2 only   (b) 2 and 3 only
(c) 3 only   (d) 1, 2 and 3

54. Which of the following statements are correct regarding agriculture and domestication of animals in Indus Valley civilization?

1. The Harappans probably used the wooden ploughshare to plough the fields.
2. Cereals were probably received as taxes from peasants.
3. The Harappan culture was horse-centred.

Select the correct answer using the code given below:

(a) 1 and 2 only   (b) 1 and 3 only
(c) 2 and 3 only   (d) 1, 2 and 3

55. Consider the following statements regarding the Draft National Policy for Rare Diseases:

1. National Registry for Rare Diseases will be created by Indian Medical Association which will help to arrive at a definition of rare diseases.
2. The policy proposes two categories of rare diseases including diseases require long term treatment at low cost and lifelong treatment at high cost.

3. Rare diseases are also called as orphan diseases and the drugs to treat them are called orphan drugs.

4. The policy takes to the concept of crowd funding to treat rare diseases.

Which of the statements given above are correct?

(a) 1, 2 and 3 only   (b) 2, 3 and 4 only

(c) 3 and 4 only   (d) 1 and 4 only

56. Ruthenium (Ru) is in the news in which of the following context?

(a) It is the fourth element to have magnetic properties at room temperature.

(b) It is the element which is identified as a probable material in the future manufacturing of solar panels.

(c) It is the element used in preparing nanomotors.

(d) It is the material identified with the highest tensile strength.

57. Consider the following statements regarding Small Satellite Launch Vehicle (SSLV):

1. Small Satellite Launch Vehicle can carry payloads up to 1,000 kg.

2. The primary idea is to ensure mass production of SSLVs through the private sector.

3. It has three stage solid propulsion systems.

Which of the statements given above are correct?

(a) 1 and 2 only

(b) 2 and 3 only

(c) 1 and 3 only

(d) 1, 2 and 3

58. Consider the following statements:

1. Nitrogen fixation is the process of converting nitrogen from air into ammonia and then into nitrates in which nitrogen is converted into a usable form by the plants.

2. Formation of biofilms on the surface of soil particles to trap water in the soil.

3. Formation of networks of hyphae in the root system to facilitate the uptake of nutrients from the soil.

In which of the above complex relations between plants and microbes, the bacteria play a primary and key role?

(a) 1 only   (b) 1 and 2 only

(c) 1 and 3 only   (d) 1, 2 and 3

59. Which of the following statement is **incorrect** regarding the Attorney General for India?

(a) He represents government of India in any reference made by the President under Article 143.

(b) His consent is necessary for Initiating proceedings for contempt in certain cases.

(c) His consent is necessary for finalization of appointments of Judges of State High Courts.

(d) He appears in courts of law on behalf of the House of Parliament or the Speaker.

60. Consider the following statements regarding the President of India:

1. The Presidential address is a parliamentary convention and is not mentioned in the constitution.

2. The President of India is not elected by an open ballot system.

3. The President of India is not the part of Union Executive.

Which of the statements given above are correct?

(a) 1 and 2 only

(b) 2 and 3 only

(c) 1 and 3 only

(d) 1, 2 and 3

61. Consider the following statements regarding Tribal Advisory Council:

1. Article 244 of the Constitution provides for the establishment of Tribal Advisory Council in tribal areas.

2. This Council should consist of not more than twenty members.

3. Not less than two-third members of council shall be the representatives of the Scheduled Tribes in the Legislative Assembly of the State.

Which of the statements given above are correct?

(a) 1 and 2 only   (b) 1 and 3 only

(c) 2 and 3 only   (d) 1, 2 and 3

62. Consider the following statements:

1. The term Federation has not used anywhere in the constitution of India.

2. Legislative competence of Parliament can be extended without amending the constitution.

Which of the statements given above is/are correct?

(a) 1 only   (b) 2 only

(c) Both 1 and 2   (d) Neither 1 nor 2

63. Consider the following statements regarding the adaptation techniques in Organisms:

1. Animals living in deserts dilute their urine to save water.

2. Animals living in cold regions accumulate glycerol or antifreeze proteins that lower the freezing point of their body.

3. Animals living in colder regions have shorter limbs than those living in warmer regions.

Which of the statements given above is/are correct?

(a) 2 and 3 only   (b) 1 and 3 only

(c) 2 only   (d) 1, 2 and 3

64. Consider the following statements regarding Sarus crane:

1. It is naturally found in India only.

2. It has been protected under schedule I of Wildlife Protection Act.

3. The Sarus Crane is the tallest flying bird in the world.

Which of the statements given above is/are correct?

(a) 1 and 2 only   (b) 2 and 3 only

(c) 3 only   (d) 1, 2 and 3

65. Consider the following statements regarding the plastic waste recycling in India:

1. Out of all the major plastic components, Polyethylene Terephthalate (PET) is getting recycled up to the maximum extent.

2. This is due to the strict implementation of Extended Producer Responsibility.

Which of the statements given above is/are correct?

(a) 1 only   (b) 2 only

(c) Both 1 and 2   (d) Neither 1 nor 2

66. Consider the following statements regarding the United Nations Environment Assembly (UNEA):

1. The UNEA is the world's highest-level decision-making body on the environment.

2. The UNEA was created during the United Nations Conference on Sustainable Development, also referred to as RIO+20.

3. The Assembly is the governing body of the UN Environment Programme.

4. It addresses the critical environmental challenges facing the world today.

Which of the statements given above is/are correct?

(a) 1 only   (b) 1 and 3 only

(c) 2 and 3 only   (d) 1, 2, 3 and 4

67. Consider the following statements regarding Plate Tectonics Theory:

1. The rigid plates move horizontally over the asthenosphere as rigid units.

2. The arctic plates move faster than the pacific plates.

3. The mobile rock beneath the rigid plates is believed to be moving in a circular manner.

Which of the statements given above is/are **incorrect**?

(a) 1 and 3 only   (b) 2 only

(c) 2 and 3 only   (d) 1, 2 and 3

68. Consider the following statement regarding Zero Budget Natural Farming:

1. It is a method of farming done without using any credit and without spending any money on purchased inputs.

2. It aims to eliminate the use of chemical pesticides.

3. It is yet to be practiced in India

Which of the statements given above is/are correct?

(a) 1 and 2 only   (b) 3 only

(c) 2 and 3 only   (d) 1, 2 and 3

69. Which of the following lakes are found in Ladakh region?

1. Pangong Tso Lake

2. Chandra Taal Lake

3. Tso-Kar Lake

4. Tso Moriri Lake

Select the correct answer using the code given below:

(a) 1 and 3 only   (b) 1, 2 and 4 only

(c) 1, 2, 3 and 4   (d) 1, 3 and 4 only

70. Consider the following Indirect Taxes:

1. Union Excise Duty

2. Customs Duty

3. Goods and Services Tax

4. Dividend Distribution Tax

5. Corporate Tax

6. Fringe Benefit Tax

7. Octroi

Which of the above mentioned taxes are Indirect Taxes?

(a) 1, 2, 3 and 7 only   (b) 2, 4, 5 and 6 only

(c) 1, 3, 4, 5 and 6 only   (d) 1, 2, 3, 4, 5, 6 and 7

71. Which of the following are considered as challenges in the employment in India?

1. Creating productive jobs
2. Correction of mismatch in demand and supply of labors
3. Relying on manufacturing by doing some structural change

Select the correct answer using the code given below:

(a) 1 and 2 only   (b) 2 and 3 only
(c) 1 and 3 only   (d) 1, 2 and 3

72. Consider the following statements regarding IBC code:

1. Pre-pack is the resolution of the debt of a distressed company.
2. It is an agreement between secured creditors and investors instead of a public bidding process.

Which of the statements given above is/are correct?

(a) 1 only   (b) 2 only
(c) Both 1 and 2   (d) Neither 1 nor 2

73. Consider the following statements:

1. Saudi-Arabia is the largest source of crude oil import for India.
2. Reduction in crude oil imports from Saudi Arabia would likely lead to increased imports from other gulf countries.
3. OPEC+ is a group of 23 countries who have cut down the crude oil prices during pandemic.

Which of the statements given above is/are correct?

(a) 1 and 3 only   (b) 2 only
(c) 2 and 3 only   (d) 1, 2 and 3

74. Consider the following statements:

1. India's per-capita emissions are a third of the global average.
2. Annual emissions make India the fourth largest emitter.
3. India contributes 30% carbon in the atmosphere which is much higher than USA and China.

Which of the statements given above is/are correct?

(a) 3 only   (b) 2 and 3 only
(c) 1 and 2 only   (d) 1, 2 and 3

75. Consider the following statement s:

1. The Act fails to recognise the absolute right of a woman over her body in taking decisions regarding abortions and reproductive health.
2. The time limit of abortion has been pushed back from 20 to 24 weeks.
3. The right to seek termination is restricted to such category of women as may be prescribed by rules.

Which of the statements given above is/are correct regarding MTP act, 2021?

(a) 1 only   (b) 2 and 3 only
(c) 1 and 2 only   (d) 1, 2 and 3

76. Consider the following statements regarding Exchange Traded Funds (ETFs):

1. ETFs are mutual funds traded on stock exchanges.
2. The Bharat 22 ETF allows government to park its holdings in selected private commercial banks.
3. Transaction can be done on a real time basis through ETF.
4. ETF reflects the composition of an Index in BSE Sensex.

Which of the statements given above are correct?

(a) 1 and 2 only   (b) 2 and 4 only
(c) 1, 3 and 4 only   (d) 1, 2 and 3

77. Consider the following statements:

1. National Stock Exchange is Asia's oldest stock exchange.
2. NSE was established on the recommendation of Pherwani committee.
3. Sensex measures the price movement of 30 companies.
4. It was the second exchange in India to provide fully computerized electronic trading.

Which of the statements given above are correct?

(a) 1 and 3 only   (b) 2 and 3 only
(c) 3 and 4 only   (d) 1, 2, 3 and 4

78. Consider the following statements regarding Nationalization of banks in India:

1. Nationalisation aimed to provide stability to the banking system by preventing bank failures.
2. Nationalisation led to balanced flow of credit to all realms of economy.
3. It led to increase in nexus between banks and the business tycoons.

Which of the statements given above is/are correct?

(a) 1 and 2 only   (b) 2 only
(c) 1 and 3 only   (d) 1, 2 and 3

79. Consider the following statements regarding the Zamindars during the Mughal period:
    1. Milkiyat was a personal land held by the Zamindars.
    2. They could collect revenue on behalf of the state.
    3. They were forbidden from having any units of cavalry, artillery and infantry in order to consolidate the central power.

    Which of the statements given above is/are correct?

    (a) 1 and 2 only   (b) 2 and 3 only
    (c) 2 only   (d) 1, 2 and 3

80. Consider the following statements regarding Swami Vivekananda:
    1. He was one of the most prominent figures of India who Introduced Indian philosophies of Vedanta and Yoga to the 'Western world'.
    2. He is also considered as the major force in the revival of Hinduism in India and contributed to the concept of nationalism in colonial India.

    Which of the statements given above is/are correct?

    (a) 1 only   (b) 2 only
    (c) Both 1 and 2   (d) Neither 1 nor 2

81. Consider the following statements in the context of medieval Indian history:
    1. Kingdom was divided into eight tarafs which was governed by tarafdars.
    2. Nobles were paid in form of salary or jagir.
    3. A tract of khalisa was used to keep a part for the expenses of sultan.

    Which of the statements above given is/are correct regarding Bahmani Kingdom?

    (a) 1 only
    (b) 1 and 2 only
    (c) 2 and 3 only
    (d) 1, 2 and 3

82. Consider the following statements regarding temple entry movement in Kerala:
    1. Gandhiji took a tour in Kerala in support of this movement.
    2. Many higher caste Hindus organization supported temple entry movement in Kerala.

    Which of the statements given above is/are correct?

    (a) 1 only
    (b) 2 only
    (c) Both 1 and 2
    (d) Neither 1 nor 2

83. Consider the following statements regarding Sodium hypochlorite:
    1. It is corrosive and is not recommended to be used on human beings, certainly not as a spray or shower.
    2. Sodium hypochlorite is commonly used as a bleaching agent and also to sanitise swimming pools.
    3. The diluted form of sodium hypochlorite is commonly used as an antacid to treat heartburn, indigestion and upset stomach.

    Which of the statements given above are correct?

    (a) 1 and 2 only   (b) 2 and 3 only
    (c) 1 and 3 only   (d) 1, 2 and 3

84. Consider the following statements regarding Nuclear DNA and Mitochondrial DNA:
    1. Both Nuclear DNA and mitochondrial DNA are inherited from mother and father.
    2. Both Nuclear DNA and Mitochondrial DNA contain 46 chromosomes each.
    3. Nuclear DNA is responsible for genetic make-up, whereas Mitochondrial DNA is responsible for metabolic activities.

    Which of the statements given above is/are **incorrect**?

    (a) 3 only   (b) 1 and 2 only
    (c) 2 and 3 only   (d) 1, 2 and 3

85. The prices of Rhodium and Palladium increased sharply in recent times and the primary reason is?

    (a) Huge demand from electric battery manufacturers, as these are used in electric batteries.
    (b) Recent invention of their use in the solar panels manufacturing.
    (c) Increased demand from jewelers due to their use with Platinum.
    (d) Their increased usage in catalytic converters in internal combustion engines due to the stringent pollution norms.

86. Consider the following statements:
    1. Event Horizon Telescope project captured the first-ever image of a black hole.
    2. The light which escapes from a black hole is measured directly for the first time.

    Which of the statements given above is/are correct?

    (a) 1 only   (b) 2 only
    (c) Both 1 and 2   (d) Neither 1 nor 2

87. Which of the following is/are the devices used by the Parliament to exercise its control over the ministers?

1. Question hour
2. Discussions
3. No-confidence motion

Select the correct answer using the code given below:

(a) 1 only   (b) 2 and 3 only

(c) 1 and 3 only   (d) 1, 2 and 3

88. Consider the following statements regarding the amendment of the Constitution:

1. A private member can introduce a bill for the amendment of the constitution only after the prior permission of the President.
2. A bill which seeks to amend the federal provisions of the Constitution is presented to the President after it is duly passed by both the houses of the Parliament and the state legislatures.

Which of the statements given above is/are **incorrect?**

(a) 1 only   (b) 2 only

(c) Both 1 and 2   (d) Neither 1 nor 2

89. Consider the following statements regarding the constitutional provisions for the creation of All India Judicial Service for appointments to the lower judiciary:

1. At present, the powers of recruitment and the appointments to the lower judiciary lies with the State Public Service Commission only.
2. To create All-India Judicial Service, a constitutional amendment under Article 368 with ratification by the state legislatures becomes mandatory.

Which of the statements given above is/are correct?

(a) 1 only   (b) 2 only

(c) Both 1 and 2   (d) Neither 1 nor 2

90. Consider the following statements:

1. Supreme Court has power to entertain appeal from any court or tribunal within India.
2. Supreme Court has power to deliver advisory opinion of any question of fact or law referred to it by the President.
3. Salaries of the judges of Supreme Court are subject to vote by the Parliament.

4. It's judgement is binding on all other courts within India.

Which of the statements given above are correct?

(a) 1 and 3 only   (b) 2, 3 and 4 only

(c) 2 and 4 only   (d) 1, 2 and 4 only

91. Consider the following statements regarding UNESCO's Man and the Biosphere (MAB) Programme:

1. MAB is an Intergovernmental Scientific Programme that aims to establish a scientific basis for the improvement of relationships between people and their environment.
2. It study and compare the dynamic inter-relationships between natural or near-natural ecosystems and socio-economic processes.
3. Department of Environment is the nodal agency for Biosphere Reserve programmes in India.

Which of the statements given above is/are correct?

(a) 1 and 3 only   (b) 2 and 3 only

(c) 1, 2 and 3   (d) 3 only

92. Consider the following statements regarding the Multidisciplinary drifting Observatory for the Study of Arctic Climate (MOSAiC) mission:

1. The prime objective of the MOSAiC mission is to study the impact of climate change on the Antarctic region.
2. India is spearheading the MOSAiC Scientific expedition.

Which of the statements given above is/are **incorrect?**

(a) 1 only   (b) 2 only

(c) Both 1 and 2   (d) Neither 1 nor 2

93. Consider the following statements regarding Corporate Social Responsibility (CSR):

1. India is the first country in the world to make CSR mandatory.
2. The amount spent by a company towards CSR cannot be claimed as business expenditure.
3. No specific tax exemption has been extended to the expenditure incurred on CSR.
4. Injeti Srinivas panel had been set up to study CSR expenditure.

Which of the statements given above is/are correct?

(a) 1 only   (b) 2 and 4 only

(c) 1 and 3 only   (d) 1, 2, 3 and 4

94. Consider the following statements regarding the Champaran Satyagraha:

1. Rajkumar Shukla requested Gandhiji to look into the problem of Indigo planters of Champaran in Bihar.
2. British government made a committee to look into the matter of Champaran indigo planters without inclusion of Gandhiji.
3. Committee came up with an agreement that granted farmers more control over what they wanted to grow on their own lands along with other benefits.

Which of the statements given above is/are correct?

(a) 1 only   (b) 1 and 3 only

(c) 1 and 2 only   (d) 1, 2 and 3

95. Consider the following statements:

1. He restored all the territories up to the river Krishna into Vijayanagar by compelling the ruler of Orissa.
2. Itallian traveller Domingo Paes spent some years in his court.
3. He built a new town near Vijayanagar and dug a tank for irrigation purpose.
4. He prevailed justice and equity in his empire.

Above mentioned statements are related to which of the following ruler of Vijayanagar?

(a) Dev Raya II   (b) Krishna Dev Raya

(c) Harihar I   (d) Rama Raja

96. Consider the following statements regarding the Balkan Plan:

1. It was the first such plan that proposed the idea of separation of different provinces.
2. Both the Balkan Plan and the Cabinet Mission were in favor of creation of Pakistan.

Which of the statements give above is/are correct?

(a) 1 only   (b) 2 only

(c) Both 1 and 2   (d) Neither 1 nor 2

97. Consider the following statements regarding Centre for Augmenting WAR with COVID-19 Health Crisis (CAWACH):

1. This initiative is launched by Ministry of AYUSH.
2. It is mandated to extend timely support to potential start-ups by way of the requisite financial assistance targeting innovations that are deployable in the market within the next 6 months.

3. Society for Innovation and Entrepreneurship (SINE) is the Implementing Agency of the CAWACH.

Which of the statements given above is/are correct?

(a) 2 only   (b) 2 and 3 only

(c) 1, 2 and 3   (d) 2 and 3 only

98. When does the Parliament legislate on a subject in the State List?

1. When Lok Sabha passes a resolution by 2/3rd majority that it is in national interest to do so.
2. When Legislatures of two or more states requests Parliament to legislate on a subject in the State List.
3. During the proclamation of national emergency.

Select the correct answer using the code given below:

(a) 1 and 3 only   (b) 2 and 3 only

(c) 1, 2 and 3   (d) 1 and 2 only

99. Consider the following pairs:

(Cloud type)	(Description)
1. Cumulonimbus Cloud:	It is the thunder cloud with tremendous vertical height and varying shapes
2. Nimbostratus Cloud :	It is low cloud that brings heavy rain
3. Cirrostratus Cloud :	These are medium clouds that are arranged in layers
4. Cirrocumulus Cloud :	These are high vertical clouds with round top

Which of the pairs given above are correctly matched?

(a) 1 and 2 only   (b) 3 and 4 only

(c) 1, 2, 3 and 4   (d) 1, 2 and 3 only

100. Which of the following landforms is/are **NOT** associated with glaciers or glaciation.

1. Drumlins
2. Bergschrund
3. Inselberg
4. Moraines

Select the correct answer using the code given below:

(a) 3 only   (b) 1, 2 and 4 only

(c) 1 and 4 only   (d) 2 and 4 only

ANSWER KEY

1. (b)	**2.** (c)	**3.** (d)	**4.** (b)	**5.** (d)	**6.** (d)	**7.** (d)	**8.** (b)	**9.** (d)	**10.** (d)
11. (c)	**12.** (b)	**13.** (b)	**14.** (c)	**15.** (d)	**16.** (a)	**17.** (b)	**18.** (d)	**19.** (c)	**20.** (d)
21. (b)	**22.** (a)	**23.** (c)	**24.** (b)	**25.** (c)	**26.** (d)	**27.** (d)	**28.** (b)	**29.** (d)	**30.** (b)
31. (b)	**32.** (d)	**33.** (b)	**34.** (c)	**35.** (c)	**36.** (b)	**37.** (b)	**38.** (b)	**39.** (d)	**40.** (c)
41. (a)	**42.** (b)	**43.** (d)	**44.** (d)	**45.** (a)	**46.** (a)	**47.** (b)	**48.** (d)	**49.** (a)	**50.** (b)
51. (b)	**52.** (c)	**53.** (d)	**54.** (a)	**55.** (c)	**56.** (a)	**57.** (b)	**58.** (b)	**59.** (c)	**60.** (b)
61. (a)	**62.** (c)	**63.** (a)	**64.** (c)	**65.** (a)	**66.** (d)	**67.** (b)	**68.** (a)	**69.** (d)	**70.** (a)
71. (d)	**72.** (c)	**73.** (c)	**74.** (c)	**75.** (d)	**76.** (c)	**77.** (b)	**78.** (a)	**79.** (a)	**80.** (c)
81. (d)	**82.** (c)	**83.** (d)	**84.** (b)	**85.** (d)	**86.** (a)	**87.** (d)	**88.** (a)	**89.** (d)	**90.** (d)
91. (c)	**92.** (c)	**93.** (d)	**94.** (b)	**95.** (b)	**96.** (d)	**97.** (d)	**98.** (b)	**99.** (a)	**100.** (a)

EXPLANATION

1. b
- **The first statement is incorrect and second statement is correct:** Cooperative Federalism means there should be a cooperative relation between centre and state and not confrontation.
- There should be harmony and not conflict in Indian.
- There are some constitutional mechanisms as also some extra constitutional mechanisms to foster the spirit of Cooperative federalism.
- It originated in Australia and not in Britain.

2. c
- **The first statement is incorrect:** Article 263 is about Interstate council and Zonal councils which is a statutory body (State Reorganisation Act 1956).
- **The second and third statements are correct:** The act divided the country into five zones (Northern, Central, Eastern, Western and Southern) and provided a zonal council for each zone. In addition to the above Zonal Councils, a North-Eastern Council was created by a separate Act of Parliament i.e. the North Eastern Council Act of 1971. It is considered separately.

3. d
- **All the statements are correct:** A major step towards decentralisation was taken in 1992. The Constitution was amended to make the third tier of democracy more powerful and effective.

- Now it is constitutionally mandatory to hold regular elections to local government bodies.
- Seats are reserved in the elected bodies and the executive heads of these institutions for the Scheduled Castes, Scheduled Tribes and Other Backward Classes.
- At least one-third of all positions are reserved for women.
- An independent institution called the State Election Commission has been created in each State to conduct panchayat and municipal elections.
- The State governments are required to share some powers and revenue with local government bodies. The nature of sharing varies from State to State.

4. b
- Some of them are available only to the citizens while others are available to all persons whether citizens, foreigners or legal persons like corporations or companies.
- They are not absolute but qualified. The state can impose reasonable restrictions on them.
- Most of them are available against the arbitrary action of the State, with a few exceptions like those against the State's action and against the action of private individuals.

- They are justiciable, allowing persons to move the courts for their enforcement, if and when they are violated.

5. d
- **The first statement is correct:** Dolphin distribution in Chilika is considered to be the highest single lagoon population. Recently, 146 endangered Irrawaddy dolphins are sighted in Chilika Lake. It is the highest single lagoon population of the aquatic mammal in the world. It is incidental to note that Chilika is Asia's largest and world's second largest lagoon. Irrawaddy dolphins are found in coastal areas in south and southeast Asia. They are also found in three rivers i.e., Irrawaddy (Myanmar), Mahakam (Indonesian Borneo) and Mekong (China). They are endangered as per IUCN Red List.
- **The second statement is also correct:** Chilika lake is considered as the largest wintering ground for migratory birds on the Indian sub-continent.
- **The third statement is also correct:** the Nalabana Island in Chilika Lake, covering about 16 sq.km, was declared a bird sanctuary. The first regional centre of the Bombay Natural History Society was established a few years ago. It would be engaged in identifying the air route of the foreign birds flocking the Chilika lake during winter.
- **The fourth statement is correct:** Kalijai Temple is located on an island in Chilika Lake. It is considered to be the abode of the Goddess Kalijai.

6. d
- **All the statements are correct:** The International Tropical Timber Organization (ITTO) is an intergovernmental organization promoting the sustainable management and conservation of tropical forests and the expansion and diversification of international trade in tropical timber from sustainably managed and legally harvested forests.
- It Develops internationally agreed policy guidelines and norms to encourage sustainable forest management (SFM) and sustainable tropical timber industries and trade.
- It promotes sustainable tropical timber supply chains.
- It helps develop capacity in tropical forestry.
- ITTO's membership represents about 90% of the global tropical timber trade and more than 80% of the world's tropical forests.
- India is a member of this Organisation.

7. d
- **The first statement is correct:** Polycrack is the world's very first patented heterogeneous catalytic process which can convert multiple feed stocks into hydrocarbon liquid fuels, gas, carbon and water. The waste generated will become the feeder material for the waste to energy plant. Gas generated in the process is re-used to provide energy to the system thereby making it self-reliant and also bring down the operating cost.
- **The second statement is correct:** All kinds of existing plastic, Petroleum sludge, un segregated municipal solid waste with moisture up to 50%, E-waste, Automobile fluff, Organic waste can be added as raw materials. The pre-segregation of waste is not required for processing in the plant. The waste as collected from the source, can be directly fed into the polycrack plant. The plant has high tolerance to moisture hence drying of the waste is not required. These are some of the advantages of the technology.

8. b
- **The first statement is correct:** Based on whether the nucleus of a cell is surrounded by a membrane or not, organisms are classified as- Prokaryotic- which lack cells with membrane bound nucleus, e.g. bacteria, blue- green algae, mycoplasma, etc.
- **The second statement is also correct:** Eukaryotic- which possess cells with membrane bound nucleus, e.g. protists, fungi, all other multicellular organisms
- **The third statement is incorrect:** being a prokaryotic or a eukaryotic organism is not related to having single or multi cells; yeast is a single celled fungi which is a eukaryote.

9. d
- **The first statement is correct:** Saline soils contain a larger proportion of sodium, potassium and magnesium, and thus, they are infertile, and do not support any vegetative growth. They lack in nitrogen and calcium.
- **The second statement is correct:** Excessive irrigation in areas of green revolution makes the fertile alluvial soils into saline. Excessive irrigation with dry climatic conditions promotes capillary action, which results in the deposition of salt on the top layer of the soil.
- **The third statement is correct:** Farmers are advised to add gypsum to the saline soil to solve the problem of salinity in the soil in areas of Punjab and Haryana.

10. d
- **The first statement is incorrect:** Chambal (a tributary of Yamuna), Betwa, Son emerges from peninsular uplands.
- **The second statement is correct:** The Ghaghara, the Gandak and the Kosi rises in the Nepal Himalayas.
- **The third statement is correct:** The Narmada and the Tapi are the only long rivers, which flow west and make estuaries.
- **The fourth statement is correct:** Son River of central India is the second largest of the Ganges' southern tributaries after Yamuna River.

11. c
- Ferrous minerals such as iron ore, manganese, chromite, etc., provide a strong base for the development of metallurgical industries.
- **The first statement is incorrect:** About 95 percent of total reserves of iron ore is located in the States of Odisha, Jharkhand, Chhattisgarh, Karnataka, Goa, Telangana, Andhra Pradesh and Tamil Nadu. Iron has great demand in international market due to its superior quality. The iron ore mines occur in close proximity to the coal fields in the northeastern plateau region of the country which adds to their advantage.
- **The second statement is incorrect:** Manganese is an important raw material form smelting of iron ore and also used for manufacturing ferrous alloys. Manganese deposits are found in almost all geological formations; however, it is mainly associated with Dharwar system.
- **The third statement is correct:** Over 97 percent of coal reserves occur in the valleys of Damodar, Sone, Mahanadi and Godavari.

12. b
- **The first statement is incorrect:** When the saturated air mass comes across a mountain, it is forced to ascend and as it rises, it expands; the temperature falls, and the moisture is condensed. The chief characteristic of this sort of rain is that the windward slopes receive greater rainfall.
- **The second statement is correct:** After giving rain on the windward side, when these winds reach the other slope, they descend, and their temperature rises. Then their capacity to take in moisture increases and hence, these leeward slopes remain. The area situated on the leeward side, which gets less rainfall is known as the rain-shadow area. It is also known as the relief rain.

13. b
- **The first statement is correct:** During the previous decade, the Consumer Price Index-based inflation came down to less than half of what it was a decade ago.
- **The second statement is incorrect:** It is clearly evident that sometimes CPI is higher and sometimes WPI. The basic reason is due to the weightages. CPI has got higher weightage for food and beverages. Moreover, services are not included in WPI.

14. c
- **The first and third statements are correct:** A Special Drawing Rights is essentially an artificial currency instrument used by the International Monetary Fund (IMF) and is built from a basket of important national currencies. The IMF uses SDRs for internal accounting purposes. It is held with the Government or central bank of the member countries. In India, it is with RBI's exchange reserve.
- **The second statement is incorrect:** Pound sterling is having lowest weightage in SDR basket of currencies.

15. d
- **The first statement is correct:** Operation Twist is an example of open market operations. Normally, through open market operations what RBI does is, whenever there is excess liquidity in the system, it sells bonds in the market and sucks excess liquidity. Similarly, when there is lack of liquidity in the financial markets, RBI purchases bonds and it increases liquidity. Recently, a peculiar situation arose, where asymmetric liquidity became a problem. The liquidity was abundant at the shorter end, but, not on the longer end. To correct this asymmetry, Operation Twist is simultaneous buying of long-term Government bonds and selling of short-term Government bonds. Hence, we can consider this as one type of open market operations.
- **The second statement is also correct:** It is expected to result in monetary transmission since the liquidity management is done by sucking at the shorter end and infusing at the longer end.
- **The third statement is correct:** Operation Twist first appeared in 1961 as a way to strengthen the U.S. dollar and stimulate cash flow into the economy.

16. a
- **The first statement is correct:** Increase in fiscal deficit, in general, indicates that the

Government is borrowing more. Under these circumstances, the domestic savings available for private sector investments are expected to come down. Hence, there is every possibility of crowding-out of the private investments.

- **The second statement is incorrect:** The increase in capital expenditure need not be commensurate with the increase in fiscal deficit. It all depends on revenue deficit. In the year 2019-20, as per the Revised Estimate, the fiscal deficit increased by 0.5% of GDP, but, if we look at the increase in capital expenditure, it is just 0.1%. Hence, 80% of the increased fiscal deficit has been used for revenue expenditure or non-asset forming expenditure.

17. b
- **The first statement is incorrect:** The domestication of animals started in the later Mesolithic period. The Neolithic people were acquainted to agriculture.

- **The second statement is incorrect:** Burzahom is an important Neolithic site 16 kms northwest of Kashmir.

- **The third statement is correct:** First human colonization of the Ganga plains was started in Mesolithic Period.

18. d
- Sravanabelagola is associated with Jainism. The famous statue of Bahubali is situated in Sravanabelagola.

- Kapilavastu, Vaisali and Gaya were associated with the life of Buddha. The kingdoms visited by Buddha are Kosala and Magadha. **Hence option (d) is correct.**

19. c
- **The first statement is correct:** Hampi is located in the Krishna- Tungabhadra basin which formed the nucleus of the Vijaynagara Empire, founded in 1336.

- **The second statement is incorrect:** The magnificent ruins at Hampi reveal a well-fortified city. No mortar or cementing agent was used in the construction of these walls and technique followed was to wedge them together by interlocking.

- **The third statement is correct:** The architecture of Hampi was distinctive. The buildings in the royal complex had splendid arches, domes and pillared halls with niches for holding sculptures. They also had well planned orchards and pleasure gardens with sculptural motifs such as the lotus and corbels.

- **The fourth statement is correct:** One of the unique features of temples at Hampi is the wide chariot streets flanked by the row of pillared mandapas.

20. d
- **First and second statements are correct:** The word Upanishad is derived from upa (nearby), and nishad (to sit-down), that is, — sitting down near. Groups of pupils sit near the Guru to learn from him in the Guru-shishya tradition. The Upanishads mark the culmination of Indian thought and are the final parts of the Vedas. As the Upanishads contain abstract and difficult discussions of ultimate philosophical problems, they were taught to the pupils at the end. That is why they are called the end of Vedas.

- **The third statement is also correct:** The Oldest Upanishads are Brhadaranyaka and Chandogya Upanishads which date as back as the first millennium BC. Latest were composed in the medieval and early modern period.

21. b
- It may be relevant to recall that the Alma-Ata declaration of the World Health Organization (1978) which outlined an integrated, local government-centric approach with simultaneous focus on access to water, sanitation, shelter and the like.

- The Fifteenth Finance Commission claims that it seeks to achieve the "desirable objective of evenly balancing the union and the states".

- It is not clear why there is no recognition of the third tier in this balancing act.

- Although the Fifteenth Finance Commission outlines nine guiding principles as the basis of its recommendation to local governments, there is no integrated approach (in contrast to the recommendations of the Thirteenth Finance Commission).

- It is forgotten that public finance is an integrated whole. That the tasks of the Union Finance Commission were broadened as part of the decentralisation reforms (280(3) (bb) and (c)) is a firm recognition of the organic link of public finance with the development process at all tiers of government.

22. a
To promote federalism: The creation of NITI Aayog, the establishment of the Goods and Services Tax Council, the restructuring of central schemes and accepting the Fifteenth Finance Commission's recommendations for greater devolution are clear examples of the Union Government viewing States as equal partners.

23. c
- Recently, India signed an agreement to build the Shahtoot dam near Kabul.
- Thus, its economic, strategic and security ties could be disrupted if the Taliban were to take over.
- The question India faces, like the other stakeholders, is how to help Afghanistan end the violence without a total capitulation to the Taliban.
- India joining the peace process could strengthen the hands of the Afghan government, which is negotiating from a position of weakness.

24. b
- The Budget division in the Department of Economic Affairs revised downwards the interest rates payable on small savings instruments for the April-June 2021 quarter, by 40 basis points (0.4%) to 110 basis points (1.1%).
- The return on the most popular PPF scheme was pegged at 6.4%, the lowest level in 46 years.
- The government had refrained from tweaking these rates for the last three quarters after effecting a similarly sharp cut in Q1 of 2020-21, when the PPF interest was pruned from 7.9% to 7.1%.

25. c
- The Preamble in the Constitution gives prominent importance to liberty of belief, faith and worship to all citizens, and the same is sought to be weakened and effectively nullified or severely damaged by the enactment of the Act of 1991 in its current format.
- The concepts of faith, belief and worship are the foundations of Articles 25 and 26 of the Constitution of India.
- Therefore, prohibiting citizens from approaching appropriate courts with respect to suit or any other proceedings to handover the land of any temple of certain essential significance (such as being the birthplace of Lord Rama in Ayodhya and Lord Krishna in Mathura or Lord Shiva sending his fiery Jyotirlinga in the Gyanvapi premises of Varanasi), is arbitrary, unreasonable and mala fide in the context of the fundamental rights to pray and perform religious practice as guaranteed by Articles 25 and 26 of the Constitution of India.

26. d
- **The first statement is correct:** The early atmosphere, with hydrogen and helium, is supposed to have been stripped off as a result of the solar winds. This happened not only in case of the earth, but also in all the terrestrial planets, which were supposed to have lost their primordial atmosphere through the impact of solar winds.
- **The second statement is also correct:** During the cooling of the earth, gases and water vapour were released from the interior solid earth. This started the evolution of the present atmosphere. The early atmosphere largely contained water vapour, nitrogen, carbon dioxide, methane, ammonia and very little of free oxygen. The process through which the gases were outpoured from the interior is called degassing.

27. d
- Energy Efficiency Services Limited (EESL) is a joint venture of four national Public-Sector Undertakings – NTPC Limited, Power Finance Corporation Limited, Rural Electrification Corporation Limited and POWERGRID Corporation of India Limited. As South Asia's first and foremost energy efficiency leader, EESL leads the market-related activities of the National Mission for Enhanced Energy Efficiency (NMEEE). **Hence option (d) is correct.**

28. b
- **The first statement is correct:** Optical communication is in which light is used to carry the signal to the remote end. Optical Fiber Communication (OFC) relies on optical fibers to carry signals to their destinations. Optical Fiber Communication (OFC) carry signal in from of light.
- **The second statement is incorrect:** Optical communication signal can be transferred through either Optical Fiber Communication (OFC) or by Light guided medium, Optical communication signal can 't guide through conventional electrical medium. For such purposes optical fibres have largely replaced copper wire communications in core networks to boost optical communication.

29. d
- **All the statements are correct:** Like other coronaviruses, SARS-CoV-2 particles are spherical and have proteins called spikes protruding from their surface. These spikes latch onto human cells, then undergo a structural change that allows the viral membrane to fuse with the cell membrane. The viral genes can then enter the host cell to be copied, producing more viruses.

- Recent work shows that, like the virus that caused the 2002 SARS outbreak, SARS-CoV-2 spikes bind to receptors on the human cell surface called angiotensin-converting enzyme 2 (ACE2).

- The researchers found that the SARS-CoV-2 spike was 10 to 20 times more likely to bind ACE2 on human cells than the spike from the SARS virus from 2002. This may enable SARS-CoV-2 to spread more easily from person to person than the earlier virus.

30. b • The members of state legislatures assembly participate in presidential elections.

- One third of members of legislative assembly are elected by the members of Legislative Assembly of the State from among the persons who are not members of the State Legislative Assembly. **Hence option (b) is correct.**

31. b • **The first statement is incorrect:** The 1977 Act does not provide for the requirement of 1/10th of the members of the total membership of the Lok Sabha to get recognition as Leader of the Opposition.

- **The second statement is correct:** Discretionary powers are given to the Speaker of Lok Sabha. The 1977 Act defines Leader of the Opposition as "the member of the House, who is the Leader in that House in Opposition to the Government having greatest numerical strength and recognized as such by the Speaker of the House of the People" and hence, the discretion lies with the Speaker of the Lok Sabha. There is no provision in the Constitution or even in Lok Sabha rules of procedure with regard to the Leader of the Opposition. The convention is to recognize the leader of the largest party in opposition as the Leader of the Opposition provided that the party has a strength enough to constitute the quorum for the sitting of the house i.e., 1/10th of the total membership of the House, which comes to 55 members.

32. d • **Both statements are incorrect:** Double jeopardy applies only to in the case of judicial body. It does not apply for the punishment given by a non-judicial body. Departments are non-judicial bodies, thus Double jeopardy is not applicable in any of these cases.

33. b • **The first statement is correct, and third statement is incorrect:** The Village Panchayat or Gram Panchayat is the executive committee of Gram Sabha. A Gram Sabha or Village Assembly consists of all the adults i.e. voters (persons above the age of 18 years) living in the area of a Gram Panchayat i.e., village or a group of small villages.

- **The second statement is correct:** The Gram Sabha has now been recognized as a legal body.

34. c • **Both statements are correct:** Wasteland - All lands affected by water erosion, wind erosion, floods, waterlogging, soil salinisation, and soil alkalisation, thereby rendered unfit for cultivation of most plants. Wastelands include Barren land, Degraded Forest, Waterlogged Area, Upland Without Scrub, Land With Scrub, Degraded pastures or grazing lands, Gullied Land, Ravinous Land, Salt Affected Land, Salt Encrustation, Shifting Cultivation area, Snow Covered Area, Steep Sloping Area, Coastal sand, Desertic sand, etc.

- Article 1 of the Ramsar Convention states that "wetlands are areas of marsh, fen, peatland or water, whether natural or artificial, permanent or temporary, with water that is static or flowing, fresh, brackish or salt, including areas of marine water the depth of which at low tide does not exceed six metres". Hence, as defined by the Convention, wetlands include a wide variety of inland habitats such as marshes, peat-lands, floodplains, rivers and lakes, and coastal areas such as saltmarshes, mangroves, intertidal mudflats and seagrass beds, and also coral reefs and other marine areas no deeper than six metres at low tide, as well as human-made wetlands such as dams, reservoirs, rice paddies and wastewater treatment ponds and lagoons.

35. c • **The first statement is correct:** Nicobar megapode, a bird species found only in the Nicobar Islands is in serious trouble. More than 70 per cent of the Nicobar megapode (Megapodius nicobariensis) — a large-footed bird that build nests on the ground – have disappeared over the last 12 years.

- **The second statement is incorrect:** The Sarus Crane is found in south-east Asia and Australia and is the tallest of the crane species. They have light grey wings and bodies. The IUCN lists this bird as 'Vulnerable' due to destruction of its environment, pesticides, and the hunting, and the collection of eggs and chicks for trade, food, and medicinal purposes.

- **The third statement is correct:** The Asiatic wild ass, locally known as ghudkhar has been classified as nearly threatened 'animal by the International Union for Conservation of Nature (IUCN). The animal found only in the Little Rann of Kutch in Gujarat in India, was earlier classified as 'endangered. 'The IUCN added that the population of the Asiatic wild ass has declined by an alarming 52% in the past 16 years.

- **The fourth statement is incorrect:** one-horned rhinoceros is native to the Indian subcontinent. It is listed as Vulnerable on the IUCN Red List. The Indian rhinoceros once ranged throughout the entire stretch of the Indo-Gangetic Plain, but excessive hunting and agricultural development reduced its range drastically to 11 sites in northern India and southern Nepal.

36. b
- **The first statement is correct:** Its purpose is to provide for the proper conservation of whale stocks, thus making possible the orderly development of the whaling industry. the International Whaling Commission is the primary organization to pursue the objectives of the Convention.

- **The second statement is incorrect:** The whaling regime under the Convention provides for three types of whaling: commercial whaling; aboriginal (indigenous whaling); and scientific whaling. This Convention does not give a generic definition to the term "whale" and merely lists out species under its protection. In practice, the Convention's object of regulation remains vague and difficult to determine.

- **The third statement is correct:** India is a member to the convention. The membership of IWC is given to any country in the world that adheres to the 1946 ICRW Convention.

37. b
- **The first statement is correct:** Maputo Bay is situated in Western Indian Ocean off the coast of Mozambique. Seagrass Restoration Project in Maputo and Inhambane bays directly benefit the communities and lead to more carbon sequestration and protection from coastal erosion, says United Nations Environment Programme (UNEP). The initiative is a project of the Nairobi Convention, part of UNEP's Regional Seas Programme. It is funded by Global Environment Facility.

- **The second statement is correct:** The bay is the northern termination of the series of lagoons which line the coast from Saint Lucia Bay.

- **The third statement is incorrect:** Seagrass has very high carbon storage potential. It can store carbon from the atmosphere at a rate 35 times greater than tropical rainforest. Hence, it is useful in tackling the climate change. Moreover, seagrass also provides habitat for many marine animals. Seagrasses are marine angiosperms widely distributed in both Tropical and Temperate coastal waters.

- **The fourth statement is correct:** Overfishing leads to destruction of the seagrass. Removal of fish disrupts important components of the food web. When large predators are removed, intermediate predators can become more abundant and subsequently, it results in decline of the smaller organisms that keep the blades of the seagrasses clean. This has been observed prominently in the Baltic sea. Destructive shellfish harvesting along with the flooding and sedimentation from rivers emptying into the bay are destroying the seagrass beds in Maputo Bay. Seagrass acts as a kind of oxygen battery for the ocean. It removes and prevents dangerous pathogens from polluting the water, making the sea safer and cleaner for fisheries.

38. b
- **The first statement is incorrect:** The arrival of Indian Monsoon is sudden and the withdrawal is gradual. Around the time of its arrival, the normal rainfall increases suddenly and continues constantly for several days. This is known as the 'burst' of the monsoon.

- The withdrawal of the monsoon begins in north-western States of India by early September. By mid-October, it withdraws completely from the northern half of the peninsula. The withdrawal from the southern half of the peninsula is fairly rapid.

- **The second statement is correct:** The islands of Arabian Sea receive the very first monsoon showers, progressively from South to North, from the first week of April to the first week of May. Kerala is the first Indian State to receive monsoon showers.

- **The third statement is correct:** Indian monsoon shows complete reversal of wind. In its ideal form there is a complete 180° reversal of wind. Thus, it is also called true monsoon.

39. d
- **The first statement is correct:** An urban heat island, or UHI, is a metropolitan area that's a lot warmer than the rural areas surrounding it. Heat is created by energy from all the people, cars, buses, and trains in big cities like New York, Paris, and London. Urban heat islands are created in areas like these places that have lots of activity and lots of people.
- **The second statement is correct:** Building materials are usually very good at insulating, or holding in heat. This insulation makes the areas around buildings warmer. People and their tools, such as cars and factories, are always burning off energy, whether they're jogging, driving, or just living their day-to- day lives. The energy people burn off usually escapes in the form of heat. And if there are a lot of people in one area, that's a lot of heat. Urban areas are densely populated, meaning there are a lot of people in a small space. Urban areas are also densely constructed; meaning buildings are constructed very close together. When there is no more room for an urban area to expand, engineers build upward, creating skyscrapers. All this construction means waste heat—and heat that escapes insulation has nowhere to go.
- **The third statement is correct:** Night-time temperatures in UHIs remain high. This is because buildings, sidewalks, and parking lots block heat coming from the ground from rising into the cold night sky. Because the heat is trapped on lower levels, the temperature is warmer.

40. c
- The Shola vegetation are tropical montane forests found in the Western Ghats separated by rolling grasslands at high altitudes above 2000 meters of sea- level.
- The shola forests form unique regions called —Sky Islands which occur only at higher elevations.
- The shola forests have high water retention capacity than any other soil. They are the source of water in rivers like Cauvery, Thamirabarani, Vaigaietc.
- The shola forest and grassland complex has been described as a climatic climax vegetation with forest regeneration and expansion restricted by climatic conditions such as frost or soil characteristics.
- The soil characteristics widely vary between the Shola forest and that of the grasslands surrounding it. The soil of the grasslands around is usually poor in nutrition and water retention and hence cannot support the shola species. While the soil of the shola forests are highly nutritive and they have high water retention capacity. The top layer of the soil is mainly made of peat and leaf debris which when removed is very difficult to form again. This adds to the vulnerability of these forests. **Hence option (c) is correct.**

41. a
- **The first statement is incorrect:** Delta is a low triangular area of alluvial deposits where a river divides before entering a larger body of water. Estuaries are transitional zones between the sea and rivers where freshwater streams or rivers merge with the ocean.
- **The second statement is correct:** Estuaries constitute a variety of fauna including worms, oysters, crabs and waterfowl. The estuarine animals show a number of adaptations to the unstable conditions of the environment. They have special ability to maintain salt and water balance in the presence of changing environment. They also have special adaptations to tidal and wave action.
- **The third statement is incorrect:** An Estuary is the region which has high tides and rift valley, whereas a delta is a region which has low tides and coastal plants.
- **The fourth statement is correct:** Estuaries form a transition zone (ecotone) between river environments and maritime environments.

42. b
- **The first statement is correct:** Purchasing Managers' Index (PMI) is released for both manufacturing and services.
- **The second statement is also correct:** It broadly indicates the health of the private sector companies.
- **The third statement is incorrect:** An index over 50 indicates expansion and figure below 50 shows contraction.
- **The fourth statement is correct:** The PMI is usually released at the start of every month. It is, therefore, considered a good leading indicator of economic activity.

43. d
- **The first statement is correct:** Gig Economy is the economy, where temporary/ flexible jobs become the norm. The workers of Flipkart, Swiggy, Zomato and Amazon are the examples of Gig Economy jobs.

- **The second statement is also correct:** Gig Economy becomes cheaper for the companies. Large number of people in a country like India is willing to work part-time, hence, Gig Economy becomes cheaper.

- **The third statement is also correct:** The existing regulatory framework in various countries is generally considered insufficient to regulate Gig Economy jobs. Across the world, several workers are approaching courts. The regulatory framework in various countries, including India, needs to be redefined to suit Gig Economy.

- **The fourth statement is correct:** An estimated 56% of new employment in India is being generated by the gig economy companies across both the blue-collar and white-collar workforce.

44. d
- **The first statement is correct:** The Reserve Bank of India (RBI) board recently finalized a three-year roadmap —Utkarsh 2022 to improve regulation and supervision, among other functions of the central bank.

- **The second statement is correct:** In line with the evolving macroeconomic environment, to achieve excellence in the performance of RBI's mandates and strengthening the trust of citizens and other institutions.

- **The third statement is correct:** A formal strategic management framework was launched in April 2015 to rearticulate the core purpose, values and vision statement of the Reserve Bank so as to delineate its strategic objectives in contemporary terms, to provide a framework and backdrop within and against which its policies would be formulated. The strategic framework contains, inter alia, the Bank's Mission, Core Purpose, Values and Vision Statements, reiterating the Bank's commitment to the Nation.

45. a
- **The first and second statements are correct:** The Board for Financial Supervision (BFS) was constituted in November 1994 as an autonomous body under the RBI. The Reserve Bank of India performs the supervisory function under the guidance of the Board for Financial Supervision (BFS). The primary objective of BFS is to undertake consolidated supervision of the financial sector comprising Scheduled Commercial and Co-operative Banks, All India Financial Institutions, Local Area Banks, Small Finance Banks, Payments Banks, Credit Information Companies, Non-Banking Finance Companies and Primary Dealers.

- **The third statement is incorrect:** The Board is constituted by co-opting four Directors from the Central Board as Members and is chaired by the Governor. One Deputy Governor, traditionally, the Deputy Governor in charge of supervision, is nominated as the Vice-Chairman of the Board.

46. a
- Pakistan's decision to suspend bilateral trade with India in August 2019 was a fallout of the constitutional changes in Jammu and Kashmir, which Pakistan said were "illegal".

- However, an underlying reason for suspending trade was the 200 per cent tariff imposed by New Delhi on Pakistani imports earlier that year after India revoked Pakistan's Most Favoured Nation (MFN) status in the aftermath of the Pulwama terrorist attack.

- Trade between the two countries suffered greatly – India's exports to Pakistan dropped nearly 60.5 per cent to $816.62 million, and its imports plummeting 97 per cent to $13.97 million in 2019-20.

- The Pakistani decision to lift the ban on cotton imports comes in the backdrop of a shortage in raw material for Pakistan's textile sector, which has reportedly suffered due to low domestic yields of cotton.

- Also, imports from countries like the US and Brazil are costlier and take longer to arrive

47. b
- In a notification, the Department of Economic Affairs announced that the inflation target for the quinquennium ending on March 31, 2026, will be 4%, with an upper tolerance level of 6% and a lower tolerance level of 2%.

- Economic Affairs Secretary Tarun Bajaj said that the framework's parameters would remain unchanged from what had prevailed in the five years that ended on March 31.

- The government's announcement is a welcome step in reiterating that inflation targeting remains the centre-piece of the monetary policy framework and signals that the fiscal and monetary authorities are in lockstep in ensuring the primacy of price stability as the bedrock for all macro-economic development.

48. d
- The corrective justice pertains to the righting of wrongs. Climate justice demands that every individual who is born on this earth has a right to development and dignified living.
- Commutative justice refers to agreements or commitments, and other kinds of social contracts. In the climate change discourse, it would refer to the honouring of past commitments in good faith.
- Distributive justice pertains to how resources should be distributed in terms of principles of equality, equity and merit. For climate change, the most important resource is the global carbon space.
- It is important to note that even though industrialisation in the developed countries is responsible for a large part of the build-up in greenhouse gases which causes climate change, people of the developing countries are suffering disproportionately more from its impacts.

49. a
- The right to education was initially mentioned in Article 45 as a part of the Directive Principles. It indicated that the state should provide free and compulsory education to children up to the age of 14 within a decade.
- RTE Act was amended in 2012 to mention that its provisions were subject to Articles 29 and 30 which protect the administrative rights of minority educational institutions.
- This was completely different from the way the court had envisaged the issue in its earlier judgments.
- When the RTE Act was subsequently enacted in 2009, it did not directly discriminate between students studying in minority and non-minority institutions.

50. b
- UNESCO's actions against racism through education, the sciences, culture, and communication offer an example of a way forward.
- UNESCO promotes the role of education in providing the space for young people to understand processes that sustain racism, to learn from the past, and to stand up for human rights.
- Through new approaches to inter-cultural dialogue and learning, youth and communities can be equipped with skills to eradicate harmful stereotypes and foster tolerance.
- UNESCO also offers master classes to empower students to become champions of anti-racism in their schools and communities.

51. b
- **The second statement is correct:** Ancient Buddhist texts like Anguttara Nikaya makes frequent reference to sixteen great kingdoms and republic which has evolved and flourished stretching from Gandhara in northwest to Anga in the eastern part.
- NBPW- an urban Iron Age Indian culture lasting from 700-200 BC. It succeeded Painted grey ware culture and black and red ware culture. The NBPW coincides with the emergence of 16 states or Mahajanapadas.
- **The first and third statements are incorrect:** Not all Mahajanapadas were monarchies. Two were gana-sanghas i.e. oligarchies. They were found on the periphery of the Indian kingdoms and tended to occupy Himalayan foothills. Example- Shakya Koll.

52. c
- After the arrest of Gandhi in 1922 a debate started among congressmen over the issue of next course of action during the passive phase of the movement.
- The congress was divided in two section Swarajist advocated entry into the legislative councils on the ground that upon entering into councils they could expose the basic weakness of these assemblies and use them for advancing political struggle.
- While on the hand, No Change: the school of thought led by C. Rajagopalachari, Sardar Patel, Rajendra Prasad and M.A. Ansari, opposed council entry and advocated for constructive work, continuation of boycott and non-cooperation. **(Thus only fourth statement is Incorrect).**
- The Swarajists proposal was defeated at the Gaya session of Congress (December 1922). Thereafter, CR Das and Motilal Nehru resigned from presidentship and secretary ship of the congress respectively and announced the formation of Congress-khilafat Swarajya party i.e Swarajist Party.

53. d
- **All statements are correct:** Kuchipudi is one of the Classical styles of Indian dance.
- Around the third and fourth decade of this century it emerged out of a long rich tradition of dance drama enacted by Brahmins in temples.

- It was traditionally a male preserve. Under the impact of Vaishnavism, the themes began to be based on the Bhagavat Purana.

- The dance is named after the village of its birth, Kuchelapuram or kuseclavapuriin Andhra Pradesh. The Kuseelavas (or Kuchigallu) were groups of actors going from village to village.

- Kuchipudi is the colloquial form of the Sanskrit term 'Keshavapur'. The Vijayanagara kings patronized the dance form as did the Golconda rulers after them.

- In Kuchipudi, one can witness acting and also another thing that keeps it apart from others is the occasional use of dialogues. Dialogues are something that no other classical dance form of India is based on.

- The "Tarangam", is another unique feature of Kuchipudi

- In this, a dancer dances on the edge of a brass plate matching to the rhythm of music. Sometimes, dancers also balance a pot of water on the head. Acrobatic dancing became part of the repertoire. The music that accompanies the dance is according to the classical school of carnatic music and is delightfully syncopatic.

- The accompanying musicians besides the vocalist area mridangam player to provide percussion music, a violin or veena player or both for providing instrumental melodic music, and a cymbal player who usually conducts the orchestra and recites the sollukattu (mnemonic rhythm syllables).

54. a
- **The first statement is correct:** The Harappan probably used the wooden ploughshare to plough the fields. We don't knows whether the plough was drawn by men or oxen. Stone sickles may have been used for harvesting the crops.

- **The second statement is also correct:** Cereals were received as taxes from peasants and stored in granaries for the payment of wages as well as for use during emergencies. This can be said on the analogy of Mesopotamian cities where wages were paid in barley.

- **The third statement is incorrect:** Evidence of the horse comes from a superficial level of Mohenjo-daro and from a doubtful terracotta figurine from lothal. The remains of the horse are reported from Surkotada, situated in west Gujarat, and belong to around 2000 B.C. but the identity is doubtful. In any case the Harappan culture was not horse-centered. Neither the bones of horse nor its representation appears in early and mature Harappan culture.

55. c
- **The first statement is incorrect:** To bring in standardization and for effective monitoring of rare diseases, it is essential to arrive at a definition of rare diseases which is best suited to India. Thus, National Registry for Rare Diseases was proposed to be created by the Indian Council of Medical Research and not by Indian Medical Association.

- **The second statement is incorrect:** The policy creates three categories of rare diseases:
  - Diseases requiring one-time curative treatment.
  - Diseases which need long term treatment, but cost is low.
  - Diseases that require lifelong treatment, but cost is high.

- **The third statement is correct:** Rare diseases are also called as orphan diseases. Rare diseases are a health condition of diseases having low prevalence affecting a small number of people as compared to other prevalent diseases in the general population. There is no universal definition that is available for the rare diseases and each country comes up with its own definition. WHO defines rare diseases as often debilitating lifelong disease or disorder condition with the prevalence of one or less per thousand persons.

- **The fourth statement is also correct:** The policy recommends crowd funding as a source to fund treatment of rare diseases and advices hospitals to report such cases on digital platforms to gather more funds.

56. a
- Scientists from the University of Minnesota, USA discovered the chemical element, Ruthenium (Ru) to have unique magnetic properties at the room temperature.

- So far only 3 periodic table elements Iron (Fe), Cobalt (Co), Nickel (Ni) are found to be ferromagnetic at room temperatures. **Hence option (a) is correct.**

57. b
- **The first statement is incorrect:** Small Satellite Launch Vehicle (SSLV) is intended to carry payload up to 500 kg. Payload is the carrying capacity of the Launch Vehicle. SSLV

is being developed by the Vikram Sarabhai Space Centre of ISRO.

- **The second statement is correct:** The mass production would be offered to the private industry and this is the dream project of ISRO Chief Dr. Sivan.

- **The third statement is correct:** It has three stage solid propulsion system, and like the PSLV and GSLV, can accommodate multiple satellites, albeit smaller ones.

58. b
- **The first statement is correct:** Bacteria turn nitrogen from the air into ammonia and subsequently into nitrates. Hence, fixing the element of nitrogen in a form, which plants can absorb, is facilitated by bacteria. Subsequently plants convert these nitrates into proteins. Bacteria also protect plants from pathogens by secreting antibiotics.

- **The second statement is also correct:** Bacteria play a primary role in the formation of colonies called "biofilms" on the surfaces of soil particles and this help trap water in the soil. Although fungi, algae, and protozoa are common inhabitants in formation of these colonies, the primary role is played by bacteria.

- **The third statement is incorrect:** Fungi play a key role in the networks of hyphae. Fungi which consist of long networks of hyphae often penetrate plant roots. This facilitates uptake of nutrients from the soil by these roots.

59. c
- Attorney General for India represents the Government of India in any reference made by the President to the Supreme Court under Article 143 of the constitution.

- Cognizance for criminal contempt could be taken by the Court by three methods, namely on its own motion, or on the motion of the Attorney-General or the Solicitor- General, or on the motion of any other person with the consent of the Attorney General.

60. b
- **The first statement is incorrect:** Article 87(1) in the Constitution of India -At the commencement of the first session after each general election to the House of the People and at the commencement of the first session of each year the President shall address both Houses of Parliament assembled together and inform Parliament of the causes of its summons.

- **The second statement is correct:** The President's election is held in accordance with the system of proportional representation by means of the single transferable vote and the voting is by secret ballot.

- **The third statement is correct:** The President of India is the part of Union Executive along with Vice-President, Prime Minister, Council of Ministers and Attorney-General of India.

61. a
- **The first statement is correct:** Article 244 of the Constitution provides for the establishment of Tribal Advisory Council in tribal areas.

- **The second statement is correct:** This Council should consist of not more than twenty members.

- **The third statement is incorrect:** Not less than three-fourth members of council shall be the representatives of the Scheduled Tribes in the Legislative Assembly of the State.

- Tribes Advisory Council has been constituted in the nine Scheduled Area States of Andhra Pradesh Chhattisgarh, Gujarat, Himachal Pradesh, Jharkhand, Madhya Pradesh, Maharashtra, Odisha and Rajasthan and two non-Scheduled Areas States of Tamil Nadu and West Bengal.

62. c
- **The first statement is correct:** The term 'federation' has nowhere been used in the Constitution. Instead, Article 1 of the Constitution describes India as a 'Union of States'.

- **The second statement is also correct:** The Parliament is empowered to legislate on any subject of the State List if Rajya Sabha passes a resolution to that effect in the national interest. This means that the legislative competence of the Parliament can be extended without amending the Constitution.

63. a
- **The first statement is incorrect:** In arid regions, animals adapt to lower their water consumption as low as possible. For example, kangaroo rats conserve water by concentrating their urine, sometimes even excreting solid urine and can live from birth to death without water.

- **The second statement is correct:** The freeze tolerant organisms can tolerate environmental temperatures below 0 degree Celsius by accumulating glycerol or antifreeze proteins that lower freezing point of their body fluids.

- **The third statement is correct:** Animals living in colder regions of the world have shorter limbs than those living in warmer regions as an adaptation to control the dissipation of heat. A smaller body surface area helps animals in colder regions stay warm by slowing down the loss of body heat.

64. c • **The first statement is incorrect:** The Sarus crane has three disjunct populations in the Indian sub-continent, south-east Asia and northern Australia with an estimated global population of 25,000-37,000 individuals. In the Indian subcontinent, it is found in northern and central India, Terai Nepal and Pakistan. It was once a common site in the paddy fields of Uttar Pradesh, Bihar, Rajasthan, West Bengal, Gujarat, Madhya Pradesh and Assam.

• **The second statement is incorrect:** It has been listed in Schedule IV of the Wildlife (Protection) Act 1972 and as Vulnerable on IUCN Red List.

• **The third statement is correct:** The Sarus Crane is the tallest flying bird in the world and was declared as the state bird of Uttar Pradesh (UP) in 2014.

65. a • **The first statement is correct:** Nearly 80% of the polyethylene terephthalate (PET) bottles, commonly used to package mineral water or juice, are collected, and recycled. India, in this case, has even beaten the world's most advanced countries like the US or even the European countries.

• **The second statement is incorrect:** This is not due to the strict implementation of Extended Producer Responsibility, but this was made possible due to the lakhs of informal rag-pickers in India.

66. d • **All statements are correct:** The United Nations Environment Assembly (UNEA) is the world's highest-level decision-making body on the environment.

• The Environment Assembly meets biennially to set priorities for global environmental policies and develop international environmental law.

• The United Nations Environment Assembly was created in June 2012, when world leaders called for UN Environment to be strengthened and upgraded during the United Nations Conference on Sustainable Development, also referred to as RIO+20.

• The Assembly is led by a Bureau and its President.

• The Assembly is the governing body of the UN Environment Programme (UN Environment) and the successor of its Governing Council, which was composed of 58 member States. It addresses the critical environmental challenges facing the world today.

67. b • **The first statement is correct:** According to Plate Tectonics, plates move horizontally over the asthenosphere as rigid units.

• **The second statement is incorrect:** These rates plate movement vary considerably. The Arctic Ridge has the slowest rate (less than 2.5 cm/yr), and the East Pacific Rise near Easter Island, in the South Pacific about 3,400 km west of Chile, has the fastest rate (more than 15 cm/yr).

• **The third statement is correct:** The mobile rock beneath the rigid plates is believed to be moving in a circular manner. The heated material rises to the surface, spreads and begins to cool, and then sinks back into deeper depths. This cycle is repeated over and over to generate what scientists call a convection cell or convective flow. Heat within the earth comes from two main sources: radioactive decay and residual heat.

68. a • **The first and second statements are correct:** Zero budget farming promises to end a reliance on loans and drastically cut production costs, ending the debt cycle for desperate farmers.

• The word budget refers to credit and expenses, thus the phrase Zero Budget means without using any credit, and without spending any money on purchased Inputs.

• The main aim of ZBNF Is eliminates use of chemical pesticides and uses biological pesticides and promote of good agronomic practices.

• Farmers use earthworms, cow dung, urine, plants, human excreta and such biological fertilizers for crop protection.

• **The third statement is incorrect:** It has attained wide success in southern India especially the southern Indian state of Karnataka where it first evolved. The movement in Karnataka state was born out of collaboration between Mr Subhash Palekar who put together the ZBNF practices, and the state farmers association Karnataka Rajya Raitha Sangha (KRRS).

69. d
- **The fourth statement is correct:** Tso Moriri lake is located to the southeast of Leh in eastern Ladakh and it is saline water lake.
- The lake is at an altitude of 4,522m (14,836ft). it is the largest of the high-altitude lakes entirely within India and entirely within Ladakh in Trans-Himalayan biogeographic region.
- **The first statement is correct:** Pangong Tso Lake is also a brackish water lake located on boundary of India and China and comes in the Ladakh region.
- **The second statement is incorrect:** Chandra Taal Lake is situated in the Lahaul and Spiti of Himachal Pradesh.
- **The third statement is correct:** The Tso-Kar Lake also known as White Lake is one of the three high altitude salt Water lakes In Ladakh. It is known as 'White Lake' because the white salt of the water deposits all over the lake shores. Tso-kar Lake is the smallest lake among the three important lakes in Ladakh. It is situated In Rupshu Valley about 250 km southeast from its principle town, Leh.

70. a
- **INDIRECT TAX:** Those taxes for which the tax-burden can be shifted or passed on to other persons later through business transactions of goods/ services. These taxes are indirect because the agent who bears the burden of the tax is not the one on whom it is normally levied. Indirect taxes include Customs Duties, Excise Duties, Service Tax, Sales Tax / Value Added Tax (VAT), Goods and Service Tax, Octroi etc.
- **DIRECT TAX:** Those taxes for which, the burden of the tax falls on the entity that is being taxed are known as direct taxes. Dividend Distribution Tax, Corporate Tax, Fringe Benefit Tax, Capital Gain Tax are examples of Indirect Taxes. **Hence option (a) is correct.**

71. d
- There are seven challenges in employment: creating productive jobs for seven to eight million per year; correcting the mismatch between demand and supply of labour (only 2.3% of India's workforce has formal skill training as compared to 96% in South Korea, 80% in Japan, and 52% in the United States; Structural change challenge (manufacturing should be the engine of growth).

72. c
- A pre-pack is the resolution of the debt of a distressed company through an agreement between secured creditors and investors instead of a public bidding process.
- This system of insolvency proceedings has become an increasingly popular mechanism for insolvency resolution in the UK and Europe over the past decade.
- Under the pre-pack system, financial creditors will agree to terms with a potential investor and seek approval of the resolution plan from the National Company Law Tribunal (NCLT).

73. c
- Saudi Arabia has consistently been the second-largest source of crude oil for India after Iraq was displaced by the United States in February.
- India imported 2.88 million tonnes of crude oil from Saudi Arabia in January according to data collated by the Directorate General of Commercial Intelligence and Statistics.
- A reduction in crude oil imports from Saudi Arabia would likely lead to increased imports from other gulf countries and the United States according to sources aware of developments.
- OPEC+, a group of 23 major oil-producing countries that had cut crude oil production levels during the peak of the Covid-19 pandemic as the price of Brent crude fell to below $20 per barrel, had decided to maintain lower production levels through April despite crude oil prices recovering to pre-pandemic levels.

74. c
- India will meet its Paris Agreement target for 2030, its per-capita emissions are a third of the global average, and it will in future remain within its share of ecological space.
- The pressure arises from the way the agenda has been set.
- Annual emissions make India the fourth largest emitter, even though climate is impacted by cumulative emissions, with India contributing a mere 3% compared with 26% for the United States and 13% for China.

75. d
- The Medical Termination of Pregnancy (Amendment) Act 2021 fails miserably on the main count while introducing few collateral progressive measures.
- First, the Act fails to recognise the absolute right of a woman over her body in taking decisions regarding abortions and reproductive health.
- Second, even though the limit has been pushed back from 20 to 24 weeks, this comes with the same state conditionalities as before.
- Third, 24 weeks is not rational given today's technology where abortions can be done safely up to full term.

- The right to seek termination is restricted to "such category of women as may be prescribed by rules".

76. c
- **The first and third statements are correct:** Exchange Traded Funds are mutual funds listed and traded on stock exchanges like shares. Usually, ETFs are passive funds where the fund manager doesn't select stocks on other's behalf. Instead, the ETF simply copies an index and endeavours to accurately reflect its performance. In an ETF, one can buy and sell units at prevailing market price on a real time basis during market hours.

- **The second statement is incorrect:** Government is focusing on Exchange Traded Funds (ETFs) route to disinvest its holdings in public sector companies rather than sell them on a piecemeal basis in the market. One such vehicle is the Bharat 22 ETF, a fund which houses 22 public sector companies. It allows the Government to park its holdings in selected PSUs in an ETF and raise disinvestment money from investors at one go. It tracks the specially made S&P BSE Bharat 22 Index, managed by Asia Index Private Limited. This index is made up of 22 PSU stocks and with a few private sector companies.

- **The fourth statement is correct:** ETF reflects the composition of an Index, like BSE Sensex. Its trading value is based on the Net Asset Value (NAV) of the underlying stocks (such as shares) that it represents.

77. b
- **The first statement is incorrect:** Bombay Stock Exchange (BSE) was established in 1883 as Asia's oldest stock exchange.

- **The second and third statements are correct:** National Stock Exchange was established in 1993 based on the recommendation of Pherwani committee. NIFTY which measures the price movement of 50 companies is index of NSE.

- Sensex which measures the price movement of 30 companies is index of BSE.

- **The fourth statement is incorrect:** It was the first exchange in India to provide fully computerized electronic trading. NSE is one of the pioneers in technology and innovation which ensured the high-end performance of its systems.

78. a
- **The first statement is correct:** Nationalisation aimed to provide stability to the banking system by preventing bank failures and speculative activities. Nationalised banks have helped India emerge as one of the largest developing economies, gain self-sufficiency in food grains production, and make significant strides in financial inclusion.

- **The second statement is correct:** Nationalisation was aimed to ensure the balanced flow of credit to all the productive sectors, across various regions and social groups of the country. 2019 marks the 50th anniversary of bank nationalisation, arguably the biggest structural reform introduced in the financial sector during the post-Independence period.

- **The third statement is incorrect:** Bank nationalization aimed to break the nexus between the banks and the big businesses who were disproportionately cornering bank finance for their narrow, selfish ends and rapidly expand the banking network to the unbanked regions, especially rural areas and deliver institutional credit to the farmers, small businesses and other weaker sections of society, many of whom were caught in a vicious trap of usury.

79. a
- **The first and second statements are correct, but third statement is incorrect:** The Zamindars held extensive personal lands termed milkiyat, meaning property. Milkiyat lands were cultivated for the private use of zamindars, often with the help of hired or servile labour. The zamindars could sell, bequeath or mortgage these lands at will. Zamindars also derived their power from the fact that they could often collect revenue on behalf of the state, a service for which they were compensated financially. Control over military resources was another source of power. Most zamindars had fortresses (qilachas) as well as an armed contingent comprising unit of cavalry, artillery and infantry.

80. c
- **Both statements are correct:** Swami Vivekananda was a Hindu monk and one of the most celebrated spiritual leaders of India. He was more than just a spiritual mind, he was a prolific thinker great orator and passionate patriot. He carried on the free-thinking philosophy of his guru, Ramakrishna Paramhansa forward into a new paradigm.

- He worked tirelessly towards betterment of the society, in servitude of the poor and needy dedicating his all for his country.

- He was responsible for the revival of Hindu spiritualism and established Hinduism as a revered religion on world stage.

- His message of universal brotherhood and self-awakening remains relevant especially in the current backdrop of widespread political turmoil around the world.

- The young monk and his teachings have been an inspiration to many, and his words have become goals of self-improvement especially for the youth of the country. For this very reason, his birthday January 12, is celebrated as the National Youth Day in India.

81. d • Mahmud Gawan, Peshwa of Bahmani kingdom, carried out many reforms. He divided kingdom into eight provinces (tarafs) and it was governed by tarafdar.

- Salaries and obligations of each noble were fixed and were paid in form of cash or jagir. Those who were paid in form of jagir were allowed expenses for the collection of land revenue.

- In every province, a tract of land or khalisa was set apart for the expenses of sultan. **Hence, all the statements are correct.**

82. c • **The first statement is correct:** In early March 1925, Gandhiji began his tour of Kerala and supported the movement.

- **The second statement is correct:** Many Savarna (or Higher caste hindus) organization like Nair Service Society, Nair Samajam and kerala Hindu Sabha, supported temple entry movement.

83. d • In several places, migrant workers travelling to their home states, or their belongings, were sprayed with a disinfectant, apparently to sanitise them.

- **The first statement is correct:** It is corrosive and is not recommended to be used on human beings, certainly not as a spray or shower.

- **The second statement is also correct:** Sodium hypochlorite is commonly used as a bleaching agent, and also to sanitise swimming pools.

- **The third statement is correct:** The diluted form of sodium hypochlorite is commonly used as an antacid to treat heartburn, indigestion, and upset stomach.

84. b • **The first statement is incorrect:** Nuclear DNA is inherited from both the parents, whereas Mitochondrial DNA is inherited only from the mother. DNA in a cell exists both in nucleus and mitochondria. Nuclear DNA is longer as compared to the Mitochondrial DNA. Other important aspect is Nuclear DNA contain around 20,000 to 25,000 genes, while mitochondrial DNA contains only 37 genes.

- **The second statement is also incorrect:** Nuclear DNA consists of 46 chromosomes, whereas Mitochondrial DNA consists of only 1 chromosome.

- **The third statement is correct:** The chromosomes in Nuclear DNA are responsible for genetic make-up of a human being, while the chromosome of the Mitochondrial DNA is responsible for the metabolic activities.

85. d • In recent times the prices of Palladium, Rhodium sky rocketed. Around 4/5th of global demand for Rhodium comes from the automotive industry. Rhodium along with Platinum, Palladium are used in catalytic converters, which convert toxic gases like carbon monoxide into less harmful substances before they leave the tailpipe. Due to the stricter emission regulations around the World, car makers are demanding more for these metals. **Hence option (d) is correct.**

86. a • **The first statement is correct:** The first-ever image of a black hole is captured by Event Horizon Telescope project. The Event Horizon Telescope team observed M87 and Sagittarius A*, the black hole at the centre of our Milky Way.

- **The second statement is incorrect:** light cannot escape from a black hole. The gravitational fields are so powerful that even light cannot escape. Students should have clarity about how the image is captured. To explain further, black holes are formed when giant stars explode at the end of their life cycle. This explosion is called a supernova. It results in the concentration of a huge amount of mass densely packed in an incredibly small area. This point of almost zero value and infinite density is called the "Singularity". The image is captured by capturing the charged particles around the black holes, as black holes themselves are invisible.

87. d • **All statements are correct:** The Ministers are responsible to the Parliament for all their acts

of omission and commission. The Parliament exercises control over the ministers through various devices like question hour, discussions, adjournment motion, no confidence motion, etc.

88. a • **The first statement is incorrect:** An amendment of the Constitution can be initiated only by the introduction of a bill for the purpose in either House of Parliament or not in the State Legislatures. The bill can be introduced either by a Minister or by a private member and does not require prior permission of the President.

• **The second statement is correct:** If the bill seeks to amend the federal provisions of the Constitution, it must also be ratified by the legislatures of half of the States by a simple majority, that is, a majority of the members of the House present and voting. After duly passed by both the Houses of Parliament and ratified by the State Legislatures, where necessary, the bill is presented to the President for assent.

89. d • **The first statement is incorrect:** Articles 233 and 234 vested the powers of recruitment and appointments to the lower judiciary to the State Public Service Commissions and the High Courts.

• **The second statement is also incorrect:** Parliament in 1970s, amended Article 312 to allow for the Rajya Sabha to pass a resolution by 2/3rd majority in order to start the process of creating AIJS for the recruitment of district judges. Once the resolution is passed by Rajya Sabha, Parliament can amend Articles 233 and 234 by a simple majority and this strip the States of their appointment powers. It paves the way for creation of AIJS. Hence, the Constitutional amendment under Article 368 with ratification by the State Legislatures is not mandatory.

90. d • **The first, second and fourth statements are correct, and third statement is incorrect:** Appellate Jurisdiction of The Supreme Court is the highest court of appeal.

• A person can appeal to the Supreme Court against the decisions of the High Court. However, High Court must certify that the case is fit for appeal that is to say that it involves a serious matter of Interpretation of law or Constitution. In addition, in criminal cases. Of the lower court has sentenced a person to death then an appeal can be made to the High Court or Supreme Court.

• Of course, the Supreme Court holds the powers to decide whether to admit appeals even when appeal is not allowed by the High Court. Appellate jurisdiction means that the Supreme Court will reconsider the case and the legal issues involved in it.

91. c • **All statements are correct:** The idea of 'Biosphere Reserves' was initiated by UNESCO in 1971 under its Man and the Biosphere (MAB) Programme, as "Conservation of natural areas and of the genetic material they contain".

• UNESCO's Man and the Biosphere Programme (MAB) is an Intergovernmental Scientific Programme that aims to establish a scientific basis for the improvement of relationships between people and their environments.

• MAB combines the natural and social sciences, economics and education to improve human livelihoods and the equitable sharing of benefits, and to safeguard natural and managed ecosystems, thus promoting innovative approaches to economic development that are socially and culturally appropriate, and environmentally sustainable.

• It study and compare the dynamic interrelationships between natural/near-natural ecosystems and socio-economic processes, in particular in the context of accelerated loss of biological and cultural diversity with unexpected consequences that impact the ability of ecosystems to continue to provide services critical for human well-being.

• The Indian National Man and Biosphere Committee constituted by the Central Govt. (Annexure-V) identify new sites, and it has guided and shaped the programme in India.

• In India, Department of Environment is nodal agency for Biosphere Reserve programmes.

92. c • **The first statement is incorrect:** The Multidisciplinary drifting Observatory for the Study of Arctic Climate (MOSAiC) was the first year-round expedition mission into the central Arctic to study the Arctic climate system and its impact on the rest of the world.

• **The second statement is also incorrect:** The mission will be spearheaded by the Alfred Wegener Institute in Germany. It is the largest ever Arctic expedition in history. Scientists from 17 nations will take part in the year-long mission.

- India's Vishnu Nandan will be the only Indian aboard the multidisciplinary drifting observatory for the Study of Arctic Climate (MOSAiC) expedition.
- The icebreaker R V Polarstern is a German Research Vessel which is mainly used for research in the Arctic and Antarctica.
- The project has been designed by an international consortium of leading polar research institutions, under the umbrella of the International Arctic Science Committee (IASC).

93. d
- **The first statement is correct:** India is the first country in the world to make corporate social responsibility (CSR) mandatory. Following an amendment to the Companies Act, 2013 in April 2014.
- The amendment notified in the Companies Act, 2013 requires companies with a net worth of INR 500 crore or more, or an annual turnover of INR 1000 crore or more, or net profit of INR 5 crore or more, to spend 2 percent of their average net profits of three years on CSR.
- **The second statement is correct:** The Finance Act, 2014 provides that any expenditure incurred by an assesses on the activities relating to corporate social responsibility referred to in section 135 of the Companies Act, 2013 shall not be deemed to be an expenditure incurred by the assessed for the purposes of the business or profession.
- **The third statement is correct:** While no specific tax exemption has been extended to expenditure incurred on CSR, spending on several activities like contributions to Prime Minister's Relief Fund, scientific research, rural development projects, skill development projects, agricultural extension projects, etc., which find place in Schedule VII, already enjoy exemptions under different sections of the Income Tax Act, 1961.
- **The fourth statement is correct:** Recently, Injeti Srinivas panel had been set up to study CSR expenditure.

94. b
- **The first statement is correct:** Champaran Satyagraha (1917)-First Civil Disobedience Movement - Gandhi was requested by Rajkumar Shukla to look into the problems of the Indigo planters, of Champaran in Bihar. The European planters had been forcing peasants to grow indigo on 3/20 of the total land (called tinkathia system).
- **The second statement is incorrect:** Towards the end of the 19th century German synthetic dyes replaced indigo European planters demanded high rents and illegal dues from the peasants in order to maximise their profits before the peasants could shift to other crops. Besides the peasants were forced to sell the produce at prices fixed by the Europeans.
- Gandhi reached Champaran to probe into the matter, defying the orders to leave. Finally, the authorities retreated and permitted Gandhi to make an enquiry. Government appointed a committee to look into the matter and nominated Gandhi as a member.
- **The third statement is correct:** Gandhi was able to convince the authorities that the tinkathia system should be abolished and the peasants should be compensated for the illegal dues extracted from them. The landlords under the British government were made to sign an agreement that granted the farmers more control over what they wanted to grow on their own lands, among other benefits. As a compromise with the planters, he agreed that only 25% of the money taken should be compensated. Within a decade, the planters left the area.

95. b After the death of Dev Raya II, a confusion raised in Vijayanagar Empire. There was a series of civil wars among various contenders to the throne, as rule of primogeniture was absent. Many feudatories assumed independence in the process. **Hence, option (a) is incorrect.**

After his rule, Saluva dynasty ruled the region but ended very soon and taken over by Tuluva dynasty which was founded by Krishna Deva Raya. In a series of battles, he compelled the rulers of Orissa to restore Vijayanagar all the territories up to the river Krishna. Itallian traveller, Domingo Paes spent a number of years in his court and wrote a glowing account on his personality. He was a great builder as well, as he built a new city near Vijaynagar and dug an enormous tank which was used for irrigation purpose. Barbosa also paid tribute to him for prevailing justice and equity in his empire. **Hence, option (b) is correct.**

Harihara I ruled Vijayanagar in the early years. Rama Raja was a later ruler of Vijayanagar who faced the famous battle of Talikota. **Hence, option (c) and (d) are also incorrect.**

96. d • **Both the statements are incorrect:** In May 1947, Mountbatten came up with a plan under which he proposed that the provinces be declared independent successor states and then be allowed to choose whether to join the constituent assembly or not. This plan was called the 'Dickie Bird Plan'. It was also called Plan Balkan as it would lead to balkanisation of the country.

• However, it was not the first to propose the separation of provinces. In March 1942, the Cripps Mission had laid the provision that any province not willing to join the Union can form a separate union.

• The Cabinet Mission had rejected the demand for a full-fledged Pakistan whereas the Balkan Plan included the principles of partition, autonomy, sovereignty to both nations, right to make their own constitution. British India was to be partitioned into two dominions – India and Pakistan.

97. d • **The first statement is incorrect:** The Centre for Augmenting WAR with COVID-19 Health Crisis (CAWACH) is an initiative by National Science & Technology Entrepreneurship Development Board (NSTEDB), Department of Science and Technology (DST), Government of India.

• **The second statement is correct:** It is mandated to extend timely support to potential start-ups by way of the requisite financial assistance targeting innovations that are deployable in the market within the next 6 months.

• **The third statement is correct:** Society for Innovation and Entrepreneurship (SINE) is the Implementing Agency of the CAWACH.

• CAWACH supports innovations in the areas of diagnostics, devices, informatics including bio-informatics & information management systems, any intervention for the control of COVID-19 and/or start-up ideas to address/mitigate various challenges faced by country / society due to severe impact of COVID-19.

98. b • **The first statement is incorrect:** The Rajya Sabha can pass a resolution by 2/3rd majority of its members for declaring a State List subject as a subject of national importance.

• **The second and third statements are correct:** Article 252 of The Indian Constitution mention that Power of Parliament to legislate for two or more States by consent and adoption of such legislation by any other State. **Hence, option (b) is correct.**

99. a • Cumulonimbus cloud is an overgrown cumulus cloud, extending for tremendous vertical height from a base of 2000-3000 feet. It takes variety of shapes. It is also referred to as thunder cloud that brings convectional rain.

• **Nimbostratus cloud:** This is a dark dull cloud, clearly layered and is also known as 'rain cloud'. It brings continuous rain, snow or sleet.

• **Cirrostratus cloud:** It is a high cloud that resembles a thin white sheet or veil.

• **Cirrocumulus cloud:** It is high cloud, that appears as white globular masses forming ripples in 'mackerel sky'. It is not Cirrocumulus, but the cumulus cloud that is vertical with round top.

100. a • Drumlin, oval or elongated hill believed to have been formed by the streamlined movement of glacial ice sheets across rock debris, or till.

• Bergschrund, a crevasse or series of crevasses often found near the head of a mountain glacier. The erosion of the rock beneath a bergschrund contributes to the formation of a cirque, or natural amphitheatre.

• Inselberg, isolated hill that stands above well-developed plains and appears not unlike an island rising from the sea. These are characterised by their steep slopes. These are typical of many desert and semi-arid landscapes.

• Moraines are accumulations of dirt and rocks that have fallen onto the glacier surface or have been pushed along by the glacier as it moves. The dirt and rocks composing moraines can range in size from powdery silt to large rocks and boulders. A receding glacier can leave behind moraines that are visible long after the glacier retreats. **Hence option (a) is correct.**

Mock Test 5
General Studies Paper I

1. Which of the following statements is/are correct regarding Rafale?
   1. It is 5th generation fighter with a wide range of weapons.
   2. It is a twin-engine omnirole with ground support aircraft.
   3. It was formally inducted into Air Force on 10th Sep 2020 at Ambala Air Force station.

   Select the correct answer using the code given below:
   (a) 1 only
   (b) 2 and 3 only
   (c) 1 and 2 only
   (d) 1, 2 and 3

2. Consider the following statements:
   1. A narrow coastal strip lies between Western Ghats and Arabian Sea.
   2. There is a broader coastal area between Eastern Ghats and Bay of Bengal.
   3. Nilgiri Hills is the extension of Western Ghats.

   Which of the statements given above is/are correct?
   (a) 3 only
   (b) 2 and 3 only
   (c) 1 and 2 only
   (d) 1, 2 and 3

3. Consider the following statements regarding geological structure of India:
   1. The present configuration of India is attributed to the collision of Indian plate with Eurasian plate.
   2. The Indo-Gangetic plains are mature in age having high fertility which consist alluvium deposited by the Himalayan Rivers flowing in plains.
   3. The Peninsular region is an inverted triangular in shape and considered as a storehouse of economic minerals for India.

   Which of the statements given above is/are correct?
   (a) 1 and 3 only
   (b) 2 only
   (c) 2 and 3 only
   (d) 1, 2 and 3

4. Which of the following are principle tributaries of Brahmaputra river?
   1. Puthimari
   2. Manas
   3. Pagaldiya
   4. Barak

   Select the correct answer using the code given below:
   (a) 1, 2 and 3 only
   (b) 2, 3 and 4 only
   (c) 3 and 4 only
   (d) 1, 2, 3 and 4

5. Consider the following statements:
   1. Crude birth rate measures birth rates when total number of live births in a year is divided by the total mid-year population and multiplied by 1000.
   2. It has reached 20.0 per 1000 population in India in 2020.

   Which of the statements given above is/are correct?
   (a) 1 only
   (b) 2 only
   (c) Both 1 and 2
   (d) Neither 1 nor 2

6. Consider the following statements regarding Solicitor General of India:
   1. He is government's chief legal advisor and primary lawyer in the Supreme Court of India.
   2. He is the secondary law officer of the country who assist Attorney-General of India.
   3. He gets appointed by an appointment committee of the Cabinet as per instructions given in Article 76.

   Which of the statements given above is/are correct?
   (a) 3 only
   (b) 1 and 2 only
   (c) 2 and 3 only
   (d) 1, 2 and 3

7. Consider the following statements regarding physical diversity of India:
   1. The maximum height of the hills of the plateau is around 1500 metres.
   2. The Eastern coast area is broader than its western counterpart.

   Which of the statements given above is/are correct?
   (a) 1 only
   (b) 2 only
   (c) Both 1 and 2
   (d) Neither 1 nor 2

8. Consider the following statements with respect to the Comptroller General of Accounts:

1. The procedure for his removal is similar to that of Supreme Court Judge.

2. His duties and powers are specified by the constitution.

Which of the statements given above is/are correct?

(a) 1 only
(b) 2 only
(c) Both 1 and 2
(d) Neither 1 nor 2

9. The provision for setting up an Inter-State Council (ISC) is mentioned in Article 263 of the Constitution. Consider the following statements with respect to the ISC:

1. It was based on the recommendation of the Punchhi Commission.

2. The Office of the Vice-Chairman is held by the Chief Minister by annual rotation.

3. It has been assigned duty to discuss and investigate subjects of common interest among states.

Which of the statements given above is/are correct?

(a) 1 only
(b) 2 and 3 only
(c) 1 and 3 only
(d) 3 only

10. Consider the following statements regarding the 'crops pricing policy' by the government:

1. Commission for 'Agricultural Costs and Prices' recommends the price for rabi crops, kharif crops and sugarcane only.

2. The pricing policy is rooted in the 'cost plus' approach.

Which of the statements given above is/are correct?

(a) 1 only
(b) 2 only
(c) Both 1 and 2
(d) Neither 1 nor 2

11. Which of the following statements are correct regarding the fisheries sector of the country?

1. India is the second largest fish producing nation in the world.

2. It can be classified as a sunrise sector.

3. Production from inland fisheries is more than that from marine fisheries in India.

4. Freshwater aquaculture accounts for more than two-third of the production by inland fisheries.

Select the correct answer using the code given below:

(a) 1 and 2 only
(b) 2 and 3 only
(c) 1 and 3 only
(d) 1, 2, 3 and 4

12. Which of the following statements are correct regarding the Members of Parliament Local Area Development Scheme?

1. It was launched by the Ministry of Statistics and Programme Implementation.

2. Funds are released in the form of grants-in-aid directly to the district authorities.

3. At present, the annual entitlement per MP/constituency is Rs. 5 crore.

Select the correct answer using the code given below:

(a) 1 and 2 only
(b) 2 and 3 only
(c) 1 and 3 only
(d) 1, 2 and 3

13. Consider the following statements regarding to India's Foreign Trade policies:

1. The Merchandise Exports from India Scheme (MEIS) for export of specified goods was introduced under the Foreign Trade Policy 2015-20.

2. Advance Authorization Scheme allows duty free import of inputs for manufacturing, excluding oil.

Which of the statements given above is/are correct?

(a) 1 only
(b) 2 only
(c) Both 1 and 2
(d) Neither 1 nor 2

14. Consider the following statements regarding the National Trade Facilitation Committee (NTFC):

1. It was constituted following India's ratification of the WTO Agreement on Trade Facilitation (TFA).

2. Under this, Export Data Processing and Monitoring System is developed by the RBI.

Which of the statements given above is/are correct?

(a) 1 only
(b) 2 only
(c) Both 1 and 2
(d) Neither 1 nor 2

15. Which of the following statements are correct regarding the 'tele density' in India?

1. Tele-density denotes the number of telephones per 1000 populations.

2. Amongst the service areas, Himachal Pradesh had the highest tele-density in 2019.

3. Rural tele density is less than half of the urban tele density.

Select the correct answer using the code given below:

(a) 1 and 2 only
(b) 2 and 3 only
(c) 1 and 3 only
(d) 1, 2 and 3

16. Which of the following statements is/are correct regarding the provisions related to 'cyber security'?

1. The National Cyber Security policy was put in place in 2013.
2. Indian Computer Emergency Response Team (CERT-In) has launched the Cyber Swachhta Kendra.
3. Cyber Regulations Appellate Tribunal was established under the provisions of Information Technology Act 2000.

Select the correct answer using the code given below:

(a) 1 only   (b) 2 and 3 only
(c) 1 and 3 only   (d) 1, 2 and 3

17. Which of the following priorities are aligned with the Foreign Trade Policy of India?

1. Goods and Services Tax
2. Digital India
3. Ease of Doing Business
4. Trade Facilitation

Select the correct answer using the code given below:

(a) 1, 2 and 3 only   (b) 2, 3 and 4 only
(c) 3 and 4 only   (d) 1, 2, 3 and 4

18. Employees of which of the following institutions are **NOT** covered under the Postal Life Insurance (PLI)?

1. Centre and State Public Sector Undertakings.
2. Nationalised Banks
3. Engineers
4. Government aided educational institutions.

Select the correct answer using the code given below:

(a) 1 and 2 only
(b) 2 and 3 only
(c) 1 and 3 only
(d) None of the above

19. Consider the following statements regarding initiatives for promoting philatelic activities in India:

1. SPARSH is a philately scholarship scheme for the students of class VI to XII.
2. A Philatelic Advisory Committee (PAC) advises the Government of India on the annual programme for issue of definitive stamps.

Which of the statements given above is/are correct?

(a) 1 only   (b) 2 only
(c) Both 1 and 2   (d) Neither 1 nor 2

20. Consider the following statements regarding the National Pension Scheme (NPS):

1. It is applicable only to the Indian residents.
2. Any resident in the age group of 18 to 55 can join NPS.

Which of the statements given above is/are correct?

(a) 1 only   (b) 2 only
(c) Both 1 and 2   (d) Neither 1 nor 2

21. Consider the following statements regarding India's contribution to UN Peacekeeping:

1. Indian army is the second largest troops contributor in various UN missions.
2. 'Centre for United Nations Peacekeeping' is established in Delhi for training personnel.

Whch of the statements given above is/are correct?

(a) 1 only
(b) 2 only
(c) Both 1 and 2
(d) Neither 1 nor 2

22. Which of the following statements is/are **incorrect** with respect to Sainik Schools?

1. These were established as a joint venture of the central and state government.
2. Every state has at least one Sainik School.
3. Only Boys are allowed admission in Sainik Schools.

Select the correct answer using the code given below:

(a) 1 only
(b) 2 only
(c) 1 and 3 only
(d) 1, 2 and 3

23. Consider the following statements regarding the operations by the defence forces of India:

1. Operation Madad was conducted to provide assistance to Kerala flood affected areas.
2. Sadbhavana initiative was taken by the Army to address grievances of naxalism affected people.

Which of the statements given above is/are correct?

(a) 1 only   (b) 2 only
(c) Both 1 and 2   (d) Neither 1 nor 2

24. Consider the following statements regarding the Hindustan Aeronautics Limited:

    1. It is a Defense Public Sector Understanding with the Navratna Status.

    2. It provides 100% fleet maintenance support to all the three services of defense.

    Which of the statements given above is/are correct?

    (a) 1 only   (b) 2 only

    (c) Both 1 and 2   (d) Neither 1 nor 2

25. Consider the following statements regarding the Kasturba Gandhi Balika Vidyalaya (KGBV):

    1. It provides residential primary school services for girls from SC, ST, OBC Muslim communities and BPL girls.

    2. It provides minimum reservation of 50 per cent seats for girls from SC/ST/OBC and minorities.

    Which of the statements given above is/are correct?

    (a) 1 only   (b) 2 only

    (c) Both 1 and 2   (d) Neither 1 nor 2

26. Which of the following is NOT a sub programme under Sarva Siksha Abhiyan?

    1. The Padhe Bharat Badhe Bharat

    2. The Rashtriya Aavishkar Abhiyan

    3. Vidyanjali

    4. ShaGun portal

    Select the correct answer using the code given below:

    (a) 1 only   (b) 2 only

    (c) 1 and 3 only   (d) None of the above

27. Consider the following pairs:

(Scheme)		(Objective of the scheme)
1. Ishan Uday	:	Academic Exposure for North Eastern Students
2. Ishan Vikas	:	Scholarship for students of North East region.
3. Pragati	:	Scholarship for girl students.
4. Yukti	:	Skill development in traditional crafts.

    Which of the pairs given above are correctly matched?

    (a) 1 and 2 only   (b) 3 and 4 only

    (c) 1, 2, 3 and 4   (d) 1, 2 and 3 only

28. The scheme of 'Tithi Bhojan' is related to -

    1. Promotion of local cuisine at prominent tourist destinations.

    2. Food distribution by religious and charitable organisations

    3. Public participation under Mid-Day Meal Programme.

    4. Subsidised meal for those belonging to BPL category

    Select the correct answer using the code given below:

    (a) 1, 2, 3 and 4   (b) 3 and 4 only

    (c) 4 only   (d) 1 and 2 only

29. Consider the following statements regarding the Rashtriya Madhyamik Shiksha Abhiyan:

    1. It aims to ensure Gross Enrolment Ratio of 100 per cent in secondary education by 2020.

    2. Shaala Siddhi is an initiative under RMSA for school evaluation.

    Which of the statements given above is/are correct?

    (a) 1 only   (b) 2 only

    (c) Both 1 and 2   (d) Neither 1 nor 2

30. Consider the following statements regarding the National Achievement Survey:

    1. It assesses the learning level of students from class 6th to 10th only.

    2. It releases the district and state learning reports after the assessment.

    Which of the statements given above is/are correct?

    (a) 1 only   (b) 2 only

    (c) Both 1 and 2   (d) Neither 1 nor 2

31. Which of the following statements is/are **NOT** the components under Deendayal Upadhyaya Gram Jyoti Yojana?

    1. Separate agriculture and non-agriculture feeders in rural areas.

    2. Augmenting the sub transmission infrastructure.

    3. Metering in rural areas.

    4. Providing electricity connection to all un-electrified households in rural areas.

    Select the correct answer using the code given below:

    (a) 3 only   (b) 4 only

    (c) 1 and 4 only   (d) 2 and 4 only

32. Consider the following statements regarding the Ujjwala Scheme:

1. It is a well-targeted scheme of subsidy delivery to LPG consumers.
2. The eligible families are identified through Socio-Economic Caste Census list.

Which of the statements given above is/are correct?

(a) 1 only   (b) 2 only
(c) Both 1 and 2   (d) Neither 1 nor 2

33. Consider the following statements regarding the pricing of the petroleum products:

1. The pricing of all the petroleum products is now market determined.
2. The pricing mechanism for petrol and diesel has been changed from import parity to trade parity.

Which of the statements given above is/are correct?

(a) 1 only   (b) 2 only
(c) Both 1 and 2   (d) Neither 1 nor 2

34. Consider the following statements regarding the India's energy sector:

1. The estimated renewable energy potential for wind energy is more than that of solar energy.
2. More than two-third of power generation capacity is based on coal.

Which of the statements given above is/are correct?

(a) 1 only   (b) 2 only
(c) Both 1 and 2   (d) Neither 1 nor 2

35. Which of the following is/are **NOT** covered under the functions of Zoological Survey of India?

1. Environmental Impact Assessment with regard to fauna.
2. Environmental Information System (ENVIS) on faunal diversity.
3. Custodian of the National Zoological Collections.

Select the correct answer using the code given below:

(a) 1 and 2 only   (b) 2 only
(c) 2 and 3 only   (d) None of the above

36. Consider the following statements regarding the Cartagena Protocol:

1. It was negotiated under the aegis of the Convention on Biological Diversity (CBD) and adopted in 2000.
2. It is aimed at fair and equitable sharing of benefits arising from the utilization of genetic resources.

Which of the statements given above is/are correct?

(a) 1 only   (b) 2 only
(c) Both 1 and 2   (d) Neither 1 nor 2

37. Consider the following statements regarding the Project Tiger:

1. Project Tiger covers all the 50 Tiger Reserves across 18 states of India.
2. It conducts country level assessment of tiger and its habitat once in every four years.

Which of the statements given above is/are correct?

(a) 1 only
(b) 2 only
(c) Both 1 and 2
(d) Neither 1 nor 2

38. Consider the following statements regarding the Solid Waste Management Rules, 2016:

1. The new rules now cover urban agglomerations, census towns and notified industrial townships.
2. The Rules mandate state governments to frame their bye-laws to impose 'User Fee'.

Which of the statements given above is/are correct?

(a) 1 only   (b) 2 only
(c) Both 1 and 2   (d) Neither 1 nor 2

39. Consider the following pairs:

(Convention)	**(Related object)**
1. Rotterdam Convention	Transboundary Movements of Hazardous Wastes
2. Stockholm convention	Persistant Organic Pollutants
3. Basel Convention	Prior Informed consent procedure for Hazardous Chemicals
4. Minamata Convention	Mercury

Which of the pairs given above are correctly matched?

(a) 1, 2 and 3 only
(b) 1 and 2 only
(c) 2 and 4 only
(d) 1, 2, 3 and 4

40. Which of the following is/are included among the functions of the Wildlife Crime Control Bureau (WCCB)?
    1. Collect intelligence related to organized wildlife crime activities.
    2. Assist foreign authorities for wildlife crime control.
    3. To establish a centralized wildlife crime data bank.

    Select the correct answer using the code given below:

    (a) 1 and 2 only   (b) 1 and 3 only
    (c) 2 and 3 only   (d) 1, 2 and 3

41. Consider the following statements regarding the Financial Stability Board (FSB):
    1. It was established in 2009 by the Government of India.
    2. It's main objective is to enhance inter-regulatory coordination for financial inclusion.

    Which of the statements given above is/are correct?

    (a) 1 only   (b) 2 only
    (c) Both 1 and 2   (d) Neither 1 nor 2

42. Consider the following statements regarding the International Finance Corporation (IFC):
    1. It focuses exclusively on investing in the private sector in developing countries.
    2. India is among the founding members of the IFC.

    Which of the statements given above is/are correct?

    (a) 1 only   (b) 2 only
    (c) Both 1 and 2   (d) Neither 1 nor 2

43. Consider the following statements regarding the Financial Intelligence Unit-India:
    1. It is an independent body reporting to the Economic Intelligence Council (EIC).
    2. It has been conferred investigative powers in money laundering-related cases.

    Which of the statements given above is/are correct?

    (a) 1 only   (b) 2 only
    (c) Both 1 and 2   (d) Neither 1 nor 2

44. Which of the following institutions does not come under the provisions of the Company's Act?
    1. National Company Law Tribunal (NCLT)
    2. The Competition Commission of India (CCI)
    3. The Serious Fraud Investigation Office (SFIO)
    4. Investor Education and Protection Fund

Select the correct answer using the code given below:

(a) 3 and 4 only   (b) 2 and 3 only
(c) 1 and 4 only   (d) None of the above

45. Consider the following statements regarding the National Company Law Appellate Tribunal (NCLAT):
    1. NCLAT was formed after the dissolution of Competition Appellate Tribunal.
    2. It also hears appeals from orders issued by the Insolvency and Bankruptcy Board of India.

    Which of the statements given above is/are correct?

    (a) 1 only   (b) 2 only
    (c) Both 1 and 2   (d) Neither 1 nor 2

46. Which of the following statements is/are correct regarding the International Grains Council (IGC)?
    1. It is an inter-governmental forum of countries trading in wheat and coarse grain.
    2. India has been included in the IGC in the category of importing member.
    3. The IGC Secretariat is based in Geneva, Switzerland.

    Select the correct answer using the code given below:

    (a) 1 only   (b) 2 and 3 only
    (c) 1 and 3 only   (d) 3 only

47. Consider the following statements regarding the food processing sector in India:
    1. 'Nivesh Bandhu' is a dedicated portal to aid and assist potential investors in the food processing sector.
    2. 75% FDI is permitted under automatic route in this sector.

    Which of the statements given above is/are correct?

    (a) 1 only   (b) 2 only
    (c) Both 1 and 2   (d) Neither 1 nor 2

48. Consider the following statements regarding the Warehousing sector for agricultural commodities:
    1. The government constituted the Warehousing Development and Regulatory Authority (WDRA) in 2007 for regulating the warehousing sector.
    2. Warehouses need to be registered with the WDRA for issuing Negotiable Warehouse Receipts.

Which of the statements given above is/are correct?

(a) 1 only   (b) 2 only

(c) Both 1 and 2   (d) Neither 1 nor 2

49. Consider the following statements with respect to the Kisan Sampada Yojana:

1. It is a Centrally Sponsored Scheme for development of Agro-processing clusters.

2. Its implementation period is coterminous with the 14th Finance Commission cycle.

Which of the statements given above is/are correct?

(a) 1 only   (b) 2 only

(c) Both 1 and 2   (d) Neither 1 nor 2

50. Consider the following statements regarding the Mera Aspataal (My Hospital) application:

1. It is developed to track information regarding doctor's appointments in a hospital.

2. It covers both in-patients and outpatients.

Which of the statements given above is/are correct?

(a) 1 only   (b) 2 only

(c) Both 1 and 2   (d) Neither 1 nor 2

51. Consider the following statements regarding the SUGAM initiative:

1. It facilitates inventory management and distribution of various drugs and surgical items.

2. It is implemented by the Central Drugs Standards Control Organisation (CDSCO).

Which of the statements given above is/are correct?

(a) 1 only   (b) 2 only

(c) Both 1 and 2   (d) Neither 1 nor 2

52. Consider the following statements regarding the Pradhan Mantri Surakshit Matritva Abhiyan:

1. It covers quality ante-natal and post-natal care of pregnant and lactating women.

2. It entails the mandatory engagement with private sector.

Which of the statements given above is/are correct?

(a) 1 only   (b) 2 only

(c) Both 1 and 2   (d) Neither 1 nor 2

53. The 'Test and Treat policy' is launched under which of the following programme?

(a) National Mental Health Programme

(b) National AIDS Control Programme

(c) Revised Tuberculosis Control Programme

(d) National Leprosy Eradication Programme

54. Consider the following statements regarding the Central Council of Indian Medicine (CCIM):

1. It is a statutory body constituted under the Indian Medicine Central Council Act, 1970.

2. It prescribes the educational courses for Ayurveda, Siddha and Homeopathy systems of medicine.

Which of the statements given above is/are correct?

(a) 1 only   (b) 2 only

(c) Both 1 and 2   (d) Neither 1 nor 2

55. Consider the following statements regarding the International Solar Alliance:

1. It is the first UN-affiliated inter-governmental organization to be headquartered in India.

2. ISA's inauguration in Delhi coincided with the first Global Re-invest Meet.

Which of the statements given above is/are correct?

(a) 1 only   (b) 2 only

(c) Both 1 and 2   (d) Neither 1 nor 2

56. India has recently been elected or re-elected to which of the following UN bodies?

1. UN Human Rights Council (HRC)

2. Commission on Crime Prevention and Criminal Justice (CCPCJ)

3. UN-Women

4. Commission for Social Development

Select the correct answer using the code given below:

(a) 1 and 4 only   (b) 2 and 3 only

(c) 1 and 3 only   (d) 1, 2, 3 and 4

57. Consider the following statements regarding the 'States Division':

1. It was established to foster closer links between Indian missions and posts abroad and states/union territories.

2. It is created under the Ministry of Home Affairs.

Which of the statements given above is/are correct?

(a) 1 only   (b) 2 only

(c) Both 1 and 2   (d) Neither 1 nor 2

58. Consider the following statements regarding 'Invest India':

1. It was set up as a joint venture between Department of Industrial Policy and Promotion and industrial associations.

2. It provides assistance to investors in both pre and post investment phase.

Which of the statements given above is/are correct?

(a) 1 only   (b) 2 only

(c) Both 1 and 2   (d) Neither 1 nor 2

59. Consider the following statements regarding the Powerloom Sector:

1. Powerlooms produce more than 50 percent of the total cloth in the country.

2. e-Dhaaga app is developed to provide quality input to powerlooms.

Which of the statements given above is/are correct?

(a) 1 only   (b) 2 only

(c) Both 1 and 2   (d) Neither 1 nor 2

60. Consider the following statements regarding Public Procurement:

1. The Public Procurement Order was issued in accordance with the General Financial Rules 2017.

2. It is applicable to the procurement of both goods and services.

Which of the statements given above is/are correct?

(a) 1 only   (b) 2 only

(c) Both 1 and 2   (d) Neither 1 nor 2

61. Consider the following pairs:

(Security Force)		(Function)
1. National Security	:	Federal contingency Guard force
2. Rapid Action Force	:	To deal with communally tensed situation.
3. Central Industrial	:	Security to industrial Security Force units
4. Commando Battalion for Resolute Action	:	Striking at naxal affected areas

Which of the pairs given above are correctly matched?

(a) 1 and 2 only   (b) 1, 3 and 4 only

(c) 1, 2 and 4   (d) 1, 2, 3 and 4

62. Consider the following statements regarding the "Access to Justice for the Marginalised" Programme:

1. It was started by the Department of Justice in partnership with UNESCO.

2. It extends to all the States and Union Territories of India.

Which of the statements given above is/are correct?

(a) 1 only   (b) 2 only

(c) Both 1 and 2   (d) Neither 1 nor 2

63. Consider the following statements regarding e-Courts Integrated Mission Mode Project:

1. It is being implemented in High Courts and district/subordinate courts of the country.

2. It was conceptualised under the National Mission for Justice Delivery and Legal Reforms.

Which of the statements given above is/are correct?

(a) 1 only   (b) 2 only

(c) Both 1 and 2   (d) Neither 1 nor 2

64. Consider the following statements regarding the United News of India (UNI):

1. It is established as a society under the Society Registration Act, 1860.

2. UNIVARTA is the full-fledged Hindi wire service provided by UNI.

Which of the statements given above is/are correct?

(a) 1 only   (b) 2 only

(c) Both 1 and 2   (d) Neither 1 nor 2

65. Which of the following statements is/are correct with respect to Shram Yogi Maan-dhan (PM-SYM).

1. The person must belong to the age group of 18-40 years to be eligible for the scheme.

2. It is voluntary and contributary pension scheme.

3. Subscriber's contribution is fixed at Rupees 100 per month.

4. It is implemented through both LIC and Common Services Centres-SPV.

Select the correct answer using the code given below:

(a) 1 and 3 only   (b) 2 and 3 only

(c) 1, 2 and 3 only   (d) 1, 2 and 4 Only

66. Consider the following statements regarding the National Child Labour Project (NCLP) Scheme:

1. The scheme aims to rehabilitate children rescued from child labour.

2. The NCLP schools also serve as the training centres as per the Right to Education Act.

Which of the statements given above is/are correct?

(a) 1 only

(b) 2 only

(c) Both 1 and 2

(d) Neither 1 nor 2

67. Consider the following pairs:

(Awards given to		(Area of excellence) employees or workers)
1.	Prime Minister's Shram Awards	: performance of PSU workers.
2.	Vishwakrama Rashtriya Puruskar	: Outstanding suggestions of individuals
3.	National Safety Awards	: Safety performance of industries.

Which of the pairs given above is/are correctly matched?

(a) 1 and 2 only   (b) 3 only

(c) 1 only   (d) 1, 2 and 3

68. Consider the following statements regarding the Press Trust of India:

1. It is a non-profit sharing cooperative owned by the country's newspapers.

2. 'Bhasha' is the Hindi language news service of the agency.

Which of the statements given above is/are correct?

(a) 1 only   (b) 2 only

(c) Both 1 and 2   (d) Neither 1 nor 2

69. Consider the following statements regarding the National Skill Development Mission (NSDM):

1. It was launched in 2015 to create convergence among skilling activities.

2. National Policy on Skill Development (NPSD) was notified in pursuant of the NSDM.

Which of the statements given above is/are correct?

(a) 1 only   (b) 2 only

(c) Both 1 and 2   (d) Neither 1 nor 2

70. Which of the following statements is/are correct regarding the Five Year Plans of India?

1. The 'Annual Plan' period was preceded by the Indo-Pakistan conflict of 1965.

2. Jawahar Rojgar Yojana was launched during the Fifth Five Year Plan.

3. Ninth Five Year Plan laid emphasis on the seven identified Basic Minimum Services.

4. The Tenth Five Year Plan envisaged, for the first time, rapid growth in labour force.

Select the correct answer using the code given below:

(a) 1 and 3 only   (b) 2 and 3 only

(c) 1, 3 and 4 only   (d) 1, 2 and 4 only

71. Which of the following is an initiative under the Atal Innovation Mission?

1. The Mentor India programme

2. Atal New India Challenge

3. Atal Incubation Centres

Select the correct answer using the code given below:

(a) 1 and 3 only

(b) 2 and 3 only

(c) 1 and 3 only

(d) 1, 2 and 3

72. Consider the following statements regarding to Deen Dayal Upadhyaya Grameen Kaushal Yojana (DDU-GKY):

1. It is the flagship placement linked skill-training programme under the Ministry of Skill Development and Entrepreneurship.

2. It is the first such scheme to introduce IT solutions for skilling.

Which of the statements given above is/are correct?

(a) 1 only   (b) 2 only

(c) Both 1 and 2   (d) Neither 1 nor 2

73. Consider the following statements regarding constitutional mandate regarding the Panchayati Raj:

1. The Constitution of India stipulates direct elections of all members of panchayats.

2. It is compulsory for states to constitute a State Finance Commission (SFC) every fifth year.

Which of the statements given above is/are correct?

(a) 1 only   (b) 2 only

(c) Both 1 and 2   (d) Neither 1 nor 2

74. Which of the following is/are component of Deendayal Antyodaya Yojana—National Rural Livelihoods Mission (DAY-NRLM).

1. Sensitive Support Structures.

2. Mahila Kisan Sashaktikaran Pariyojana

3. Ajeevika Grameen Express Yojana

4. Infrastructure Creation and Marketing Support

Select the correct answer using the code given below:

(a) 1 and 3 only

(b) 1, 2 and 3 only

(c) 2, 3 and 4 only

(d) 1, 2 3, and 4

75. Consider the following statements regarding the Ganga Gram initiative:

1. It is an inter-ministry project between Swachh Bharat Mission and the Namami Gange Programme.

2. Ministry of Rural Development is coordinating this project.

Which of the statements given above is/are correct?

(a) 1 only
(b) 2 only
(c) Both 1 and 2
(d) Neither 1 nor 2

76. Consider the following statements with respect to 'Innovation in science pursuit for inspired research' (INSPIRE):

1. Inspire awards are provided to graduates from technical background to attract talent for science.

2. It also provides interactive sessions for the students with the science icons from India.

Which of the statements given above is/are correct?

(a) 1 only
(b) 2 only
(c) Both 1 and 2
(d) Neither 1 nor 2

77. Which of the following statements is/are correct regarding the Survey of India (SOI)?

1. It functions as the National Principal Mapping Agency of India.

2. It also provides support to other countries in the field of mapping.

3. It also meets the needs of specific users by providing specialised thematic maps.

Select the correct answer using the code given below:

(a) 1 only
(b) 2 and 3 only
(c) 1 and 3 only
(d) 1 and 2 only

78. Consider the following statements regarding The Indian Nuclear Power Programme Stage:

1. The Fast Breeder Test Reactor (FBTR), operating at Kalpakkam forms the second stage of the programme.

2. Nuclear power employing closed fuel cycle is the third and final stage.

Select the correct answer using the code given below:

(a) 1 only
(b) 2 only
(c) Both 1 and 2
(d) Neither 1 nor 2

79. Consider the following statements with respect to the The Earth System Science Organization (ESSO):

1. ESSO is a statutory body under the Ministry of Earth Sciences.

2. National Centre for Medium Range Weather Forecasting is one of the centres of the ESSO.

Select the correct answer using the code given below:

(a) 1 only
(b) 2 only
(c) Both 1 and 2
(d) Nether 1 or 2

80. Consider the following statements regarding Polar and Cryosphere Research (PACER):

1. National Centre for Antarctic and Ocean Research (NCAOR) of India is located at Chennai.

2. The NCAOR has established high altitude research station in Himalaya called Himansh in Leh.

Which of the statements given above is/are correct?

(a) 1 only
(b) 2 only
(c) Both 1 and 2
(d) Neither 1 nor 2

81. Which of the following statements is/are correct regarding the Bharatmala Pariyojana?

1. Its main objective is the development of economic corridors for carrying freight traffic.

2. The 'principle of shortest distance' is followed for connecting important economic centres.

3. It also envisages replacement of level crossing on national highways by Road Over Bridges.

Select the correct answer using the code given below:

(a) 1 and 2 only

(b) 2 and 3 only

(c) 1 and 3 only

(d) 1, 2 and 3

82. Consider the following statements regarding the National Dope Testing Laboratory (NDTL):

1. It is an executive body under the Ministry of Youth Affairs and Sports.

2. NDTL is one of the 33 laboratories in the world which are accredited by World Anti-Doping Agency (WADA).

Which of the statements given above is/are correct?

(a) 1 only
(b) 2 only
(c) Both 1 and 2
(d) Neither 1 nor 2

83. Consider the following statements regarding The Tribal Cooperative Marketing Development Federation of India Limited (TRIFED):

1. It was set up under the Multi State Cooperative Societies Act, 1984.

2. It is the procurement agency for the Minor Forest Produce from the tribals.

Which of the statements given above is/are correct?

(a) 1 only   (b) 2 only

(c) Both 1 and 2   (d) Neither 1 nor 2

84. Which of the following is/are the functions of the Central Water Commission (CWC)?

1. Hydro-meteorological observation

2. Water quality monitoring.

3. Flood forecasting

Select the correct answer using the code given below:

(a) 1 and 2 only

(b) 1 and 3 only

(c) 1 only

(d) 1, 2 and 3

85. Consider the following statements regarding Rajiv Gandhi National Fellowship for SC Students:

1. It provides financial assistance to scheduled caste students for pursuing research studies.

2. University Grants Commission (UGC) is the nodal agency for implementing the Scheme.

Which of the statements given above is/are correct?

(a) 1 only

(b) 2 only

(c) Both 1 and 2

(d) Neither 1 nor 2

86. Consider the following statements regarding the Scheduling and De-Scheduling of Tribes:

1. Scheduled Tribes are notified by the Presidential order after consultation with state governments.

2. The criteria to specify schedule tribe is not mentioned in the constitution.

Which of the statements given above is/are correct?

(a) 1 only

(b) 2 only

(c) Both 1 and 2

(d) Neither 1 nor 2

87. Consider the following pairs:

(Schemes for welfare of minorities)		**(About the scheme)**
1. Naya Sawera	:	Financial assistance to students clearing prelims of UPSC
2. Nayi Udan	:	Free coaching services
3. Nayi Roshni	:	leadership among women
4. Padho Pardes	:	Interest subsidy for higher education abroad.

Which of the pairs given above are correctly matched?

(a) 1, 2 and 3 only   (b) 3 and 4 only

(c) 1, 2, 3 and 4   (d) 1 and 2 only

88. Consider the following statements regarding Command Area Development and Water Management (CAD&WM) Programme:

1. It is being implemented as a component of Pradhan Mantri Krishi Sinchai Yojana.

2. The activities covered under CAD is limited to non-structural interventions.

Which of the statements given above is/are correct?

(a) 1 only   (b) 2 only

(c) Both 1 and 2   (d) Neither 1 nor 2

89. Consider the following statements regarding Gender Budgeting:

1. Ministry of Women and Child Development has mandated 'Gender Budgeting Cell' in all the Ministries.

2. Ministry of Finance is the nodal agency for gender budgeting.

Which of the statements given above is/are correct?

(a) 1 only   (b) 2 only

(c) Both 1 and 2   (d) Neither 1 nor 2

90. Consider the following statements regarding the National Scheduled Tribes Finance and Development Corporation:

1. It was set up as a statutory body under the Ministry of Tribal Affairs.

2. It provides financial assistance for procurement and marketing minor forest produce.

Which of the statements given above is/are correct?

(a) 1 only   (b) 2 only

(c) Both 1 and 2   (d) Neither 1 nor 2

91. Consider the following statements regarding Water Resource Information System:

1. It was developed jointly by the Central Water Commission and National Water Academy.
2. It publishes all the unclassified data of Central Water Commission stations on it's website.

Which of the statements given above is/are correct?

(a) 1 only   (b) 2 only
(c) Both 1 and 2   (d) Neither 1 nor 2

92. Consider the following statements regarding the Global Environment Facility (GEF):

1. India is one of the founding members of the Global Environment Facility.
2. The GEF grants are available only under the areas of climate change and biodiversity.

Which of the statements given above is/are correct?

(a) 1 only   (b) 2 only
(c) Both 1 and 2   (d) Neither 1 nor 2

93. Consider the following statements regarding POSHAN Abhiyan:

1. It is a flagship programme of Government of India to improve nutritional outcomes for children, pregnant women and lactating mothers.
2. It directs attention of the country towards the problem of malnutrition and addresses it in a mission mode.
3. People's movement is one of the pillars of the scheme.

Which of the statements given above is/are correct?

(a) 1 and 2 only   (b) 3 only
(c) 2 and 3 only   (d) 1, 2 and 3

94. Which of the following is/are the aims of CAWACH for Covid-19?

1. Start-ups in the areas of diagnostics and drugs
2. Innovation to create disinfectants and sanitizers
3. PPEs and informatics to address Covid-19 challenges

Select the correct answer using the code given below:

(a) 1 only   (b) 2 and 3 only
(c) 1 and 2 only   (d) 1, 2 and 3

95. Which of the following are objectives of National Water Mission?

1. Comprehensive water database in public domain
2. Assessment of impact of climate change on water resources
3. Promotion of action for water conservation, augmentation and preservation
4. Water use efficiency to be increased by 20 per cent

Select the correct answer using the code given below:

(a) 1 and 2 only   (b) 2 and 3 only
(c) 3 and 4 only   (d) 1, 2, 3 and 4

96. Consider the following statements:

1. Gender budgeting is a tool for achieving gender mainstreaming to ensure benefits if development reach women as much as men.
2. Gender Budgeting Cells in all ministries was mandated by the Ministry of women and child development.

Which of the statements given above is/are correct?

(a) 1 only   (b) 2 only
(c) Both 1 and 2   (d) Neither 1 nor 2

97. Consider the following statements:

1. Agriculture and allied sectors support more than 60 per cent of population in Andhra Pradesh.
2. Rice and wheat are staple food crop contributing a large chunk of the foodgrain production.
3. The third advance estimates for the year 2019-20 has shown an increase in the area and production of foodgrains over the previous years.

Which of the statements given above is/are correct?

(a) 2 only   (b) 1 and 3 only
(c) 2 and 3 only   (d) 1, 2 and 3

98. Andhra Pradesh is globally known as Ratna Garbha due to which of the following reason?

(a) Due to existence of plenty of gold mines
(b) State is the biggest exporter of gold
(c) Variety of rocks and minerals
(d) None of the above

99. Which of the following state is known as 'Land of Red River and Blue Hills'?

(a) Assam   (b) Meghalaya
(c) Manipur   (d) Nagaland

100. Consider the following pairs:

(Tributaries)		(River)
1. Jhelum	:	Indus
2. Mahananda	:	Ganga
3. Puthimari	:	Brahmaputra
4. Makku	:	Barak

Which of the pairs given above are correctly matched?

(a) 1, 2 and 3 only   (b) 3 and 4 only
(c) 1, 2, 3 and 4   (d) 1 and 2 only

ANSWER KEY

1. (b)	**2.** (c)	**3.** (a)	**4.** (a)	**5.** (a)	**6.** (b)	**7.** (b)	**8.** (a)	**9.** (d)	**10.** (d)
11. (d)	**12.** (b)	**13.** (a)	**14.** (c)	**15.** (b)	**16.** (d)	**17.** (d)	**18.** (d)	**19.** (d)	**20.** (b)
21. (c)	**22.** (a)	**23.** (a)	**24.** (a)	**25.** (d)	**26.** (d)	**27.** (b)	**28.** (b)	**29.** (c)	**30.** (b)
31. (b)	**32.** (b)	**33.** (b)	**34.** (b)	**35.** (d)	**36.** (a)	**37.** (c)	**38.** (a)	**39.** (c)	**40.** (d)
41. (d)	**42.** (c)	**43.** (a)	**44.** (d)	**45.** (c)	**46.** (a)	**47.** (a)	**48.** (b)	**49.** (b)	**50.** (b)
51. (b)	**52.** (d)	**53.** (b)	**54.** (a)	**55.** (a)	**56.** (d)	**57.** (a)	**58.** (c)	**59.** (a)	**60.** (c)
61. (d)	**62.** (d)	**63.** (a)	**64.** (b)	**65.** (d)	**66.** (c)	**67.** (d)	**68.** (c)	**69.** (a)	**70.** (c)
71. (d)	**72.** (b)	**73.** (c)	**74.** (d)	**75.** (a)	**76.** (b)	**77.** (d)	**78.** (c)	**79.** (b)	**80.** (d)
81. (a)	**82.** (b)	**83.** (a)	**84.** (d)	**85.** (c)	**86.** (c)	**87.** (b)	**88.** (a)	**89.** (d)	**90.** (b)
91. (b)	**92.** (a)	**93.** (d)	**94.** (d)	**95.** (d)	**96.** (c)	**97.** (b)	**98.** (c)	**99.** (a)	**100.** (c)

EXPLANATION

1. b Rafale is a 4.5 generation, twin-engine omnirole, air supremacy, interdiction, aerial reconnaissance, ground support, in-depth strike, anti-ship and nuclear deterrence fighter aircraft, equipped with a wide range of weapons. The rafale aircraft was formally inducted into Indian Air Force on 10th September 2020 at a formal function at Air Force station, Ambala.

2. c Between Western Ghats and the Arabian Sea lies a narrow coastal strip, while between Eastern Ghats and the Bay of Bengal, there is a broader coastal area. The Southern point of the plateau is formed by the Nilgiri Hills where the Eastern and the Western Ghats meet. The Cardamon Hills lying beyond may be regarded as a continuation of the Western Ghats.

3. a The Indian sub-continent can be divided in three regions: (i) Extra peninsular regions (Himalayas), (ii) Indo-Gangetic plains, (iii) Peninsular regions. The present configuration of India is attributed t the collision of Indian plate with the Eurasian plate around 4-5 crore years ago. In the south of Himalayas, the foreland basin is called Indo-Gangetic plains which is youngest in age, highly fertile in nature and mainly consist of alluvium deposited by the rivers draining from the Himalayas and the Peninsular regions. The Peninsular region is shaped like an inverted triangle and considered a storehouse of economic minerals in India.

4. a The Principal tributaries of Brahmaputra in India are the Subansiri, Jia Bhareli, Dhansiri, Puthimari, Pagaldiya and the Manas. The Brahmaputra in Bangladesh fed by Teesta, etc. and finally falls into the Ganga. The Barak river, the head stream of Meghana, rises in the hills of Manipur.

5. a The Crude Birth Rate is a measure of birth rates and is defined as the total number if live births in a years divided by the total mid-year population and multiplied by 1,000 to express it per 1,000 population. It has reached 20.0 per 1,000 population in 2018.

6. b The Solicitor General of India is the Government's chief legal advisor, and it is primary lawyer on the Supreme Court of India. The Solicitor General of India is the secondary law officer of the country, assists the Attorney-General and is himself assisted by several Additional Solictore General of India. Unlike the post of Attorney General for India, which is a Constitutional post under Article 76, the post of Solicitor General and Additional Solicitor Generals are statutory. They get appointed by an Appointment Committee of the Cabinet.

7. b • **The first statement is incorrect:** The Peninsular Plateau is marked off from the plains of the Ganga and the Indus by a mass of mountain and hill ranges varying from 460 to 1,220 metres in height. Prominent among these are the Aravali, Vindhya, Satpura, Maikala and Ajanta.

- The Peninsula is flanked on the one side by the Eastern Ghats where average elevation is about 610 metres and on the other by the Western Ghats where it is generally from 915 to 1,220 metres, rising in places to over 2,440 metres.

- **The second statement is correct:** Between the Western Ghats and the Arabian Sea lies a narrow coastal strip, while between Eastern Ghats and the Bay of Bengal, there is a broader coastal area. The southern point of the plateau is formed by the Nilgiri Hills where the Eastern and the Western Ghats meet. The Cardamom Hills lying beyond may be regarded as a continuation of the Western Ghats.

8. a
- **The first statement is correct:** The Comptroller and Auditor General (CAG) of India is appointed by the President. The procedure and the grounds for his removal from office are the same as for a Supreme Court judge. He is not eligible for further office under the union or a state government after he ceases to hold his office.

- The accounts of the Union and of the states shall be kept in such form as the President may, on the advice of the CAG. The reports of the CAG of India, relating to the accounts of the union shall be submitted to the President, who shall cause them to be laid before each House of Parliament.

- **The second statement is incorrect:** The duties, powers and conditions of service of the CAG have been specified by the Comptroller and Auditor General's (Duties, Powers and Conditions of Service) Act, 1971.

9. d
- **The first statement is incorrect:** The provision for setting up an Inter-State Council is mentioned in Article 263 of the Constitution. In pursuance of the recommendation made by the Sarkaria Commission on Centre-State Relations, the Inter-State Council was set up in 1990.

- **The second statement is incorrect:** It is in the case of Zonal Council (not ISC) where the Office of the Vice-Chairman is held by the Chief Minister of the Member State of the respective zonal council by annual rotation, each holding office for a period of one year at a time.

- **The third statement is correct:** The Inter-State Council (ISC) is a recommendatory body and has been assigned the duties of

investigating and discussing such subjects, in which some or all of the states or the union territories and one or more of the states have a common interest, for better coordination of policy and action with respect to that subject. It also deliberates upon such other matters of general interests to the states as may be referred by the Chairman to the Council.

10. d
- **Both the statements are incorrect:** Commission for 'Agricultural Costs and Prices' (CACP), set up with a view to evolve a balanced and integrated price structure, is mandated to advice on the price policy (MSP) of 23 crops.

- CACP submits its recommendations in the form of Price Policy Reports every year, separately for five groups of commodities namely kharif crops, rabi crops, sugarcane, raw jute and copra.

- Cost of production (CoP) is one of the important factors in the determination of MSP of mandated crops. Besides cost, the Commission considers other important factors such as demand and supply, price trend in the domestic and international markets, inter-crop price parity, terms of trade between agricultural and non-agricultural sectors and the likely impact of MSPs on consumers, in addition to ensuring rational utilization of natural resources like land and water. Thus, pricing policy is rooted not in 'cost plus' approach, though cost is an important determinant of MSP.

11. d
- **All the statements are correct:** Presently India is the second largest fish producing and second largest aquaculture nation in the world. India is also a major producer of fish through aquaculture and ranks second in the world after China.

- The total fish production during 2017-18 (provisional) stood at 12.61 million metric tonne (MMT) with a contribution of 8.92 MMT from inland sector and 3.69 MMT from marine sector.

- Fisheries is a sunrise sector with varied resources and potential, engaging over 14.50 million people at the primary level and many more along the value chain. Transformation of the fisheries sector from traditional to commercial scale has led to an increase in fish production.

- The total fish production during 2017-18 (provisional) stood at 12.61 million metric tonne (MMT) with a contribution of 8.92 MMT from inland sector and 3.69 MMT from marine sector.

- Within inland fisheries there is a shift from capture fisheries to aquaculture during the last two and a half decade. Freshwater aquaculture with a share of 34 per cent in inland fisheries in mid-1980s has increased to about 80 per cent in recent years. It has emerged as a major fish producing system.

12. b • **The first statement is incorrect:** The Members of Parliament Local Area Development Scheme (MPLADS) was launched in 1993. Initially, Ministry of Rural Development was the Nodal Ministry for this scheme. In October, 1994 this scheme was transferred to the Ministry of Statistics and Programme Implementation. The objective of MPLAD Scheme is to enable MPs to recommend works of developmental nature with emphasizes on creation of durable community assets in the areas of national priorities

- **The second statement is correct:** The Scheme is fully funded by the Government of India under which funds are released in the form of grants-in-aid directly to the district authorities.

- **The third statement is correct:** The funds released under the Scheme are non-lapsable, i.e., the entitlement of funds not released in a particular year is carried forward to the subsequent years, subject to eligibility. At present, the annual entitlement per MP/constituency is [1] 5 crore.

- The elected Lok Sabha Members can recommend works in their respective constituencies. The elected members of the Rajya Sabha can recommend works anywhere in the state from which they are elected. Nominated Members of the Parliament can recommend works for implementation, anywhere in the country.

13. a • **The first statement is correct:** The Five-year Foreign Trade Policy (FTP) 2015-20 provides a framework for increasing exports of goods and services. The FTP introduces two new schemes, namely Merchandise Exports from India Scheme (MEIS) for export of specified goods to specified markets and Service Exports from India Scheme (SEIS) for increasing exports of notified services.

- **The second statement is incorrect:** Advance Authorization Scheme allows duty free import of inputs, along with fuel, oil, catalyst, etc., required for manufacturing the export product. Inputs are allowed either as per Standard Input Output Norms (SION) or on adhoc norms basis under actual user condition.

- Norms are fixed by Technical Committee or Norms Committee. This facility is available for physical exports (also including supplies to SEZ units and SEZ Developers) and deemed exports including intermediate supplies.

- Minimum value addition prescribed is 15 per cent except for certain items. Exporter has to fulfil the export obligation over a specified time period, both quantity and value wise.

14. c • **Both the statements are correct:** National Trade Facilitation Committee (NTFC) was set up following ratification by India of the Trade Facilitation Agreement (TFA). Four working groups have been set up to focus on (i) infrastructure, (ii) legal issues, (iii) outreach and (iv) time release study. Further, the National Trade Facilitation Action Plan (NTFAP) drawn out in consultation with the stakeholders, identifying 76 trade facilitation measures with implementation timelines of which 51 are TFA-plus activities.

- Comprehensive IT-based system called Export Data Processing and Monitoring System (EDPMS) for monitoring of export of goods and software and facilitating authorised dealer banks to report various returns through a single platform developed by RBI. 24x7 Customs clearance facility has been extended to all Bills of Entry at 19 sea ports and 17 air cargo complexes.

15. b • **The first statement is incorrect:** Tele-density, which denotes the number of telephones per 100 populations, is an important indicator of telecom penetration. Overall tele-density in the country was 90.10 per cent at the end of March 2019.

- **The second statement is correct:** Amongst the service areas, Himachal Pradesh (146.37 per cent) had the highest tele-density followed by Kerala (126.15 per cent), Punjab (125.35 per cent), Tamil Nadu (116.94 per cent) and Karnataka (110.04 per cent). On the other hand, tele-density is comparatively low in service areas such as Bihar (59.95 per cent), Uttar Pradesh (69.63 per cent), Assam (68.81 per cent), Madhya Pradesh (70.11 per cent), West Bengal (71.39 per cent) and Odisha (75.74 per cent). Amongst the metros, Delhi tops in tele-density with 238.57 per cent, followed by Mumbai (165.62 per cent) and Kolkata (165.51 per cent).

- **The third statement is correct:** The rural tele-density was 57.50 per cent while that in urban areas it was 159.66 per cent.

16. d
- **All the statements are correct:** Considering its vital importance, a National Cyber Security Policy, 2013 was put in place. It is aimed at building a secure and resilient cyber space for citizens, businesses and government, by way of actions to protect information and information infrastructure in cyber space, build capabilities to prevent and respond to cyber threats, reduce vulnerabilities and minimize damage from cyber incidents through a combination of institutional structures, people, processes, technology and cooperation.

- Indian Computer Emergency Response Team (CERT-In) has launched a Cyber Swachhta Kendra (Botnet Cleaning and Malware Analysis Centre). This centre is providing detection of malicious programmes and free tools to remove the same for banks as well as common users.

- In accordance with the provision contained under Section 48(1) of the IT Act 2000, the Cyber Regulations Appellate Tribunal (CRAT) was established in 2006. As per the IT Act, any person aggrieved by an order made by the Controller of Certifying Authorities or by an Adjudicating Officer under the Act can appeal before the Cyber Appellate Tribunal (CAT).

17. d The FTP is aligned with the broader priorities of the Government of India such as the implementation of 'Goods and Services Tax', Digital India, Skill India, Startup India, Ease of Doing Business and Trade Facilitation initiatives. Because of pandemic the FTP 2015-20 has been extended by one year i.e. up to March 31, 2021.

18. d
- Employees all the given institutions are covered under the PLI. Postal Life Insurance (PLI) was introduced on 1st February 1884, as a welfare scheme for the benefit of postal employees and later extended to the employees of telegraph department in 1888. It now covers employees of central and state governments, central and state public sector undertakings, universities, government aided educational institutions, nationalized banks and local bodies.

- PLI also extends the facility of insurance to defence services and para-military forces. Life cover through Postal Life Insurance has been extended to employees of scheduled commercial banks, credit co-operative societies, joint ventures having a minimum 10 per cent stake of central/state govt/PSUs/banks etc., universities/educational institutions affiliated to University Grants Commission/Central Board of Secondary Education/All India Council of Technical Education/Medical Council of India.

- Benefits of PLI are now available to professionals such as Doctors, Engineers, Management Consultants, Charted Accountants, Architects, Lawyers, Bankers etc. and to employees of listed companies of NSE (National Stock Exchange) and BSE (Bombay Stock Exchange)

19. d
- **Both the statements are incorrect:** A philately scholarship scheme called Deen Dayal SPARSH (Scholarship for Promotion of Aptitude and Research in Stamps as a Hobby) Yojana was introduced in 2017-18 to promote philately among children at a young age in a sustainable manner that can reinforce and supplement the academic curriculum in addition to providing a hobby that can help them relax and de-stress.

- Under this scheme, 920 scholarships are awarded throughout the country to students from Classes VI, VII, VIII and IX every year.

- In keeping with their dual character as a 'Token of Postage' and as 'Cultural Ambassador', there are two categories of stamps viz., definitive and commemorative postage stamps. The definitive postage stamps are meant for day-to-day use as a token of payment of postage on mail articles.

- On the other hand the commemorative postage stamps are designed and printed with greater aesthetic inputs. These are manufactured in limited quantities and generate great interest among philatelists and collectors.

- A Philatelic Advisory Committee (PAC) advises the Government of India on the annual programme for issue of commemorative stamps.

20. b

- **The first statement is incorrect:** National pension scheme, earlier known as New Pension System (NPS), for common citizens was introduced by government in 2009. India Post is a point of presence for the national pension system.

- It is open to all the Indian Citizens.

- **The second statement is correct:** Subscribers (any Indian citizen) in the age group of 18 to 55 can join NPS and contribute till the age of 60. These pension contributions are invested in various schemes of different pension fund managers appointed by Pension Fund Regulatory and Development Authority (PFRDA).

21. c

- **Both the statements are correct:** Despite operational and internal security commitments, the Indian Army has been significantly contributing to United Nations Peacekeeping Missions and is the second largest troops contributor in various UN missions. Currently, four UN Peace Keeping missions' contingents of India are deployed around the world.

- Since 1950, Indian Army has participated in 51 UN missions out of the total of 71 UN missions, across the globe. It has contributed more than 2,34,000 Indian troops in various UN missions. The most significant contribution of the Indian Army has been to ensure peace and stability in Africa and parts of Asia.

- India has a well-established training institute in 'Centre for United Nations Peacekeeping' in Delhi, which was established in 2000, training both personnel from India and abroad on UN peacekeeping.

- Seven international courses are conducted for international participants to include, UN Military Observers Course, UN Female Military Officers Course and UN Contingent Commanders Course.

22. a

- **The first statement is correct:** The Sainik Schools were established as a joint venture of the central and state government. These are under the overall governance of Sainik Schools Society.

- **The second statement is incorrect:** At present, there are 26 Sainik Schools located in various parts of the country. The objectives of Sainik Schools include bringing quality public school education within the reach of the common man, all round development of a child's personality and to remove regional imbalance in the officer's cadre of the Armed Forces.

- The Sainik Schools have shown an upward trend in the number of cadets joining the National Defence Academy in keeping with the primary aim of establishing of Sainik Schools to prepare boys academically, physically and mentally for entry into the National Defence Academy.

- **The third statement is incorrect:** Defence Minister Rajnath Singh has approved the proposal for the admission of female candidates into Sainik Schools from 2021-22 academic sessions onwards. The admissions will be conducted in phases as per the official statement. The decision to admit female students to Sainik schools was taken following the successful pilot project which was started by the Defence Ministry for the admissions of girls to Sainik School in Chhingchhip Mizoram two years ago.

23. a

- **The first statement is correct:** 'Op Madad' was conducted to provide SAR and relief assistance in the flood affected areas of Kerala. IN also contributed 8.92 crore towards Kerala CM Relief Fund.

- **The second statement is incorrect:** The Army undertakes a unique human initiative in Jammu and Kashmir and Ladakh to address the aspirations of people affected by terrorism. Operation Sadbhavna has provided succour to a large section of population. Launched in an extremely challenging operation environment, the Operation is a part of the Counter Terrorist strategy to wrest the initiative and re-integrate the 'Awaam' with the national mainstream.

- The aim of Operation Sadbhavna is also to supplement the efforts of the government in restoring public services, rebuilding infrastructure and creating a conducive environment for development by restoring public services, rebuilding infrastructure and creating a conducive environment for development in the region.

24. a

- **The first statement is correct:** Hindustan Aeronautics Limited: Hindustan Aeronautics Limited (HAL), established in 1940, is a premier aeronautical Company of Asia. HAL, a Navratna DPSU with 20 production Divisions and 11 R&D centers spread across the country in nine geographical locations. HAL's expertise encompasses Design and Development, production, repair, overhaul and upgrade of Aircraft, Helicopters, Aero-engines, Accessories, Avionics and Systems.

- **The second statement is incorrect:** HAL's maintenance support to Indian Army and to Coast Guard is 100 per cent of their fleet and in respect of Indian Air Force and Indian Navy it is 75 per cent and 61 per cent.

- HAL has positioned itself as a comprehensive solution provider to the Indian Defence Services for aviation requirements that include trainer, fighter, transport aircraft and light helicopters.

25. d • **Both the statements are incorrect:** Kasturba Gandhi Balika Vidyalaya (KGBV): KGBV are residential *upper primary schools* for girls from SC, ST, OBC Muslim communities and BPL girls. KGBVs are set up in educational backward blocks where schools are at great distances and are a challenge to their security of girls.

- KGBVs reach out to adolescent girls who are unable to go to regular schools to out of school girls in the 10+ age group who are unable to complete primary school and younger girls of migratory populations in difficult areas of scattered habitations that do not qualify for primary/upper primary schools.

- KGBVs provide for a minimum reservation of *75 per cent seats* for girls from SC/ST/OBC and minorities and 25 per cent to girls from families that live below the poverty line. 3,600 KGBVs are functional in the states and 3,66,756 girls are enrolled in them.

26. d • The Padhe Bharat Badhe Bharat (PBBB), a sub-programme of the SSA, in classes I and II is focusing on foundational learning in early grades with an emphasis on reading, writing and comprehension and mathematics. States and UTs have been implementing specific interventions like ABL in Tamil Nadu, Nalli Kali in Karnataka, Pragya in Gujarat; steps have been taken to develop specific teacher training modules for teachers teaching students in classes 1 and II.

- The Rashtriya Aavishkar Abhiyan (RAA), also under the SSA, aims to motivate and engage children of the age group 6-18 years, in science, mathematics and technology by observation, experimentation, inference drawing and model building, through both inside and outside classroom activities. Schools have been adopted for mentoring by institutions of higher education like IIT's, IISER's and NIT's.

- Vidyanjali, another sub-programme under SSA, was launched to enhance community and private sector involvement in Government run elementary schools across the country. The aim of the programme is to strengthen implementation of co-scholastic activities in government schools through services of volunteers.

- ShaGun portal - an Initiative to monitor the implementation of SSA: MHRD has developed a web portal called ShaGun. It aims to capture and showcase innovations and progress in elementary education sector by continuous monitoring. ShaGun will help monitor progress by assessing performance of states and UTs on key parameters and thereby serve as a platform for the central government for effective planning and deliver on the promise of providing quality education to all. ShaGun, which has been coined from the words 'Shala' meaning schools and 'Gunvatta' meaning quality, has been developed with a twin track approach.

27. b • **Yukti - Yogya Kalakriti ki Takneek:** Yukti aims at skill development and upgradation of design and technologies enhancing the economic prospects of those engaged in traditional crafts and arts as a means of livelihood. It aims at introducing appropriate designs and technology for innovation and pedagogical methods for introducing skills for upgradation.

- **Ishan Uday-for Students of North East Region:** The UGC launched a special scholarship scheme for students of north east region, Ishan Uday from the academic session 2014-15. The Scheme envisages grant of 10,000 scholarships to students from the region whose parental income is below [1] 4.5 lakh per annum and would be provided scholarship ranging from [1] 3,500 to [1] 5,000 per month for studying at undergraduate level in colleges/ universities.

- **Ishan Vikas - Academic Exposure for North Eastern Students:** The programme has been launched with a plan to bring selected college and school students from the north eastern states into close contact with IITs, NITs and IISERs during their vacation periods for academic exposure.

- Pragati (scholarship for girl students) - is a scheme of AICTE aimed at providing assistance for advancement of girls participation in technical education. Education is one of the most important means of empowering women with the knowledge, skill and self-confidence necessary to participate fully in the development process.

28. b
- "Tithi Bhojan" is a concept designed to ensure greater public participation under the Mid-Day Meal Programme being followed in Gujarat. In order to bring in greater community participation, local communities are encouraged to celebrate important family events viz., birth of a child, success in exam, inauguration of new house, etc., by contributing to the mid-day meal served in the local schools.

- It is voluntarily served by the community/family among school children in several forms like sweets and namkeen along with regular MDM, full meals, supplementary nutritive items like sprouted beans, contribution in kind such as cooking ware, utensils, dinner sets or glasses for drinking water. All the states/UTs have been requested to consider adopting the practice of Tithi Bhojan with this nomenclature or any nomenclature suitable to the state/ UT governments.

- The concept has been adopted by different states with local nomenclatures like 'Sampriti Bhojan' in Assam, 'Dham' in Himachal Pradesh, 'Sneh Bhojan' in Maharashtra, 'Shalegagi Naavu Neevu' in Karnataka, 'Anna Dhanam' in Puducherry, 'Priti Bhoj' in Punjab and 'Utsav Bhoj' in Rajasthan. **Hence option (b) is correct.**

29. c
- **Both the statements are correct:** Rashtriya Madhyamik Shiksha Abhiyan (RMSA was launched in 2009 with the objective to enhance access to secondary education and improve its quality.

- The schemes envisages to enhance the enrolment at secondary stage by providing a secondary school with a reasonable distance of habitation, with an aim to ensure GER of 100 per cent and universal retention by 2020.

- The other objectives include improving quality of education imparted at secondary level through making all secondary schools conform to prescribed norms, removing gender, socio-economic and disability barriers, etc.

- **Shaala Siddhi:** School Standards and Evaluation Framework and its web portal was launched in 2015 under RMSA. It is a comprehensive instrument for school evaluation leading to school improvement.

- Developed by the National University of Educational Planning and Administration (NUEPA), it aims to enable schools to evaluate their performance in a more focused and strategic manner and facilitate them to make professional judgments for improvement.

- The programme's objective is to establish an agreed set of standards and benchmarks for each school, by focussing on key performance domains and their core standards.

30. b
- **The first statement is incorrect:** National Achievement Survey (NAS) assessed the learning levels of the students in classes 3, 5, 8 and 10.

- **The second statement is correct:** Initially the district report cards were released and later the state learning reports were made available on the website for classes 3, 5 and 8 in May, 2018 and for Class 10 in November, 2018.

- The Post NAS Interventions (2018-19) were initiated to reach out to all the districts in the different states. The learning gaps identified were used to provide feedback to the districts. A framework of intervention to improve the quality of learning in the schools is being suggested. The designing and implementation of the interventions include in its ambit the school leaders, teachers and the whole network of officials at clusters, blocks, DIETs, SCERT and the Directorates of education, in the different states/UTs.

31. b
- Government of India launched a new scheme namely Deendayal Upadhyaya Gram Jyoti Yojana (DDUGJY) with the following objectives (a) to separate agriculture and non-agriculture feeders for judicious rostering of supply to agricultural and non-agricultural consumers in rural areas; (b) strengthening and augmentation of sub transmission and distribution infrastructure in rural areas; (c) metering in rural areas (feders, distribution transformers and consumers).

- The erstwhile rural electrification scheme was subsumed in DDUGJY as a separate rural electrification component and the approved outlay of the erstwhile scheme has been carried forward to the DDUGJY.

- To achieve universal *household electrification* in the country by March, 2019, Government launched *Saubhagya scheme* with total cost of Rs. 16,320 crore including gross budgetary support of Rs. 12,320 crore during the entire implementation period. The scope of the Scheme includes: *providing electricity connections to all un-electrified households in rural areas.* **Hence option (b) is correct.**

32. b

- **The first statement is incorrect:** Government, as a measure of Good Governance introduced well targeted systems of subsidy delivery to LPG consumers through *PAHAL* (not Ujjwala). This initiative was aimed at rationalizing subsidies based on approach to cut subsidy leakages, but not subsidies per se. Applicable subsidy is directly transferred into the bank account of the beneficiaries. So far, more than 22.40 crore LPG consumers have joined the Scheme.

- In order to provide clean cooking fuel to poor households especially in rural areas, the Government had launched Pradhan Mantri Ujjwala Yojana to provide deposit free LPG connections to 8 crore women belonging to the Below Poverty Line (BPL) households.

- The primary objective is to provide access to clean cooking fuel LPG to BPL households thereby protecting their health by reducing the serious health hazards associated with use of conventional cooking fuels such as firewood, coal, cowdung, etc., which causes servere indoor household air pollution.

- **The second statement is correct:** The eligible families are identified through Socio-Economic Caste Census list and in case, name is not found in SECC list , from seven categories i.e., beneficiaries of Pradhan Mantri Awas Yojana (PMAY-Gramin), beneficiaries of Antyodaya Anna Yojana, SC/ST households, most backward classes, forest dwellers, tea/ex-tea garden tribes and residents of islands/river islands subject to fulfilling other terms and conditions of the Scheme.

33. b

- **The first statement is incorrect:** The Administered Pricing Mechanism (APM) or cost plus pricing for petroleum products which was introduced in 1976 was abolished from 2002, consequent to the de-regulation of the oil sector in India.

- The Government notified that pricing of all petroleum products *except PDS kerosene and domestic LPG*, would be market determined.

- **The second statement is correct:** In 2006, based on the recommendations of the Rangarajan Committee, the government changed the pricing mechanism for petrol and diesel from import parity to trade parity (trade parity being the weighted average of import parity and export parity prices in the ratio of 80:20) while the pricing of PDS kerosene and domestic LPG continues on import parity basis.

34. b

- **The first statement is incorrect:** India has an estimated renewable energy potential of about 900 GW from commercially exploitable sources viz. Wind - 102 GW (at 80 metre mast height); small hydro - 20 GW; bioenergy - 25 GW; and 750 GW solar power, assuming 3% wasteland is made available.

- The Ministry had taken up a new initiative in 2014 for implementation of wind resource assessment in uncovered / new areas with an aim to assess the realistic potential at 100 m level in 500 new stations across the country under the National Clean Energy Fund (NCEF).

- **The second statement is correct:** At present around 69.5 per cent of India's power generation capacity is based on coal. In addition, there is an increasing dependence on imported oil, which is leading to imports of around 33 per cent of India's total energy needs.

- Despite increase in installed capacity by more than 113 times, India is still not in a position to meet its peak electricity demand as well as energy requirement.

35. d

- **The functions of the ZSI entail all the given options:** The Zoological Survey of India (ZSI), a premier research institution under the Ministry has completed 100 years of services to the Nation, undertaking survey, exploration and research leading to the advancement of our knowledge on the exceptionally rich faunal diversity of the country since its inception in 1916.

- Over the successive plan periods functions of ZSI have also expanded gradually encompassing areas like the Environmental Impact Assessment with regard to fauna; survey of conservation areas; status survey of endangered species; computerization of digitization of data on faunal resources; Environmental Information System (ENVIS) on faunal diversity; identification and advisory services; National Designated Repository of type and voucher specimens; supporting enforcement of Wildlife (Protection) Act, 1972; establishment of marine aquaria and Museum for awareness on conservation etc., and acts as a custodian of the National Zoological Collections.

- Headquarters are at Kolkata and 16 Regional centres are located at different parts of the country. **Hence option (d) is correct.**

36. a
- **The first statement is correct:** Cartagena Biosafety Protocol (CPB) negotiated under the aegis of the Convention on Biological Diversity (CBD) and adopted in 2000. India is a party to the Protocol.

- The main objective of the Protocol is to ensure safe transfer, handling and use of living modified organisms (LMOs) resulting from modern biotechnology that may have adverse effect on the conservation and sustainable use biological diversity, taking into account risk to human health.

- **The second statement is incorrect:** It is the Nagoya Protocol on access and benefit sharing (ABS) adopted under the aegis of CBD in 2010 (not Cartagena Protocol) that is aimed at fair and equitable sharing of benefits arising from the utilization of genetic resources.

37. c
- **Both the statements are correct:** Project Tiger was launched in 1973 for conserving the tiger. From 9 tiger reserves since its formative years, the Project Tiger coverage has increased to 50, spread out in 18 of tiger range states. These reserves are constituted on a core / buffer strategy.

- The core areas have the legal status of a national park or a sanctuary, whereas the buffer or peripheral areas are a mix of forest and non-forest land, managed as a multiple use area. It is an ongoing scheme of this Ministry providing central assistance to the tiger states for conservation.

- The NTCA / Project Tiger also conducts the country level assessment of the status of tiger, co-predators, prey and habitat once in four years, using the refined methodology, as approved by the Tiger Task Force.

- Due to the concerted efforts under the Project, India has the distinction of having the maximum number of tigers in the world - 2,967 - to be precise, as per the results of the 4th cycle of the All India Tiger Estimation. The tiger corridors for gene flow have been mapped in the GIS domain.

- International Tiger's Day is held every year on 29th July to raise public awareness and support regarding several issues related to tiger conservation. The idea behind such an event came up at the St. Petersburg Tiger Summit in 2010.

- It was also decided that 29th July would be known as Global Tiger Day. During the summit, a panel of experts declared a goal towards tiger conservation, which was to double its population by 2022.

38. a
- **The first statement is correct:** The Ministry revised the rules for management of solid waste in the municipal areas after 16 years. The new rules are now applicable beyond municipal areas and extend to urban agglomerations, census towns, notified industrial townships, areas under the control of Indian Railways, airports, airbase, port and harbour, defence establishments, special economic zones, state and central government organizations, places of pilgrimage, religious and historical importance.

- The segregation of waste at source has been mandated. Responsibilities of generators have been fixed for segregation of waste in to three streams, wet (biodegradable), dry (plastic, paper, metal, wood, etc.) and domestic hazardous wastes (diapers, napkins, empty containers of cleaning agents, mosquito repellents, etc.)

- **The second statement is incorrect:** The Rules provide ways for integration of waste pickers/ rag pickers. The Rules *mandate local bodies* to frame their bye-laws to impose 'User Fee', to be paid by the generator to waste collector and for 'Spot Fine' for littering and non-segregation.

39. c • The Basel Convention on the Control of Transboundary Movements of Hazardous Wastes and their Disposal was adopted in 1989 in Basel, Switzerland. The overarching objective of the Basel Convention is to protect human health and the environment against the adverse effects of hazardous wastes.

 • The Rotterdam Convention on the prior informed consent procedure for certain Hazardous Chemicals and Pesticides in International Trade came into force in 2004. India acceded to the convention a year later. The Designated National authorities (DNAs) for India are in Ministry of Agriculture and Cooperation.

 • The Stockholm Convention on persistent Organic Pollutants (POPs) is a global treaty to protect human health and the environment from POPs. The Convention sought initially 12 chemicals, for restriction or elimination of the production and release. Now, the Convention covers 23 chemicals. The Convention came into force in 2004. India ratified the Convention in 2006.

 • In February 2009, the Governing Council of UNEP adopted Decision 25/5 on the development of a global legally binding instrument on mercury. At the Conference of Plenipotentiaries held in 2013 in Minamata and Kumamoto, Japan, the "Minamata Convention on Mercury", a global treaty to protect human health and the environment from the adverse effects of mercury, was formally adopted. **Hence option (c) is correct.**

40. d • Wildlife Crime Control Bureau (WCCB) is a statutory multi-disciplinary body established under the Ministry, to combat organized wildlife crime in the country. The Bureau has its headquarters in New Delhi and five regional offices at Delhi, Kolkata, Mumbai, Chennai and Jabalpur; three sub-regional offices at Guwahati, Amritsar and Cochin; and five border units at Ramanathapuram, Gorakhpur, Motihari, Nathula and Moreh.

 • It is mandated to collect and collate intelligence related to organized wildlife crime activities and to disseminate the same to state and other enforcement agencies for immediate action so as to apprehend the criminals; to establish a centralized wildlife crime data bank; coordinate actions by various agencies in connection with the enforcement of the provisions of the Act; assist foreign authorities and international organization concerned to facilitate co-ordination and universal action for wildlife crime control; capacity building of the wildlife crime enforcement agencies for scientific and professional investigation into wildlife crime and assist state governments to ensure success in prosecutions related to wildlife crimes; and advise the Government of India on issues relating to wildlife crimes having national and international ramifications, relevant policy and laws.

 • The Wildlife Crime Control Bureau was constituted in 2007.

41. d • **Both the statements are incorrect:** Financial Stability Board (FSB) was established in 2009 under the aegis of G20 by bringing together the national authorities, standard setting bodies and international financial institutions for addressing vulnerabilities and developing and implementing strong regulatory, supervisory and other policies in the interest of financial stability. India is an active member of the FSB having three seats in its Plenary.

 • Financial Stability and Development Council (FSDC) was set up as the apex level forum in 2010 for maintaining financial stability, enhancing inter-regulatory coordination and promoting financial sector development.

42. c • **Both the statements are correct:** International Finance Corporation (IFC), a member of the World Bank Group, focuses exclusively on investing in the private sector in developing countries. Established in 1956, IFC has 184 members.

 • India is founding member of IFC. It is an important development partner for India with its operations of financing and advising the private sector in the country. India represents IFC's largest portfolio exposure globally.

 • The IFC's investments in India are spread across important sectors like infrastructure, manufacturing, financial markets, agribusiness, SMEs and renewable energy.

 • Keeping in alignment with the Country Partnership Strategy (CPS) of the World Bank Group in India, IFC focuses on low-income states in India.

43. a
- **The first statement is correct:** Financial Intelligence Unit-India (FIU-IND) is the central national agency for receiving, processing, analyzing and disseminating information relating to suspect financial transactions.
- FIU-IND was established by the Government of India in 2004 for coordinating and strengthening collection and sharing of financial intelligence through an effective national, regional and global network to combat money laundering, related crimes and terrorist financing.
- It is an independent body reporting to the Economic Intelligence Council (EIC) headed by the Finance Minister. For administrative purposes, FIU-IND is under the Department of Revenue, Ministry of Finance.
- **The second statement is incorrect:** FIU-IND does not investigate cases. The main functions of FIU-IND include domestic co-operation, international co-operation, outreach, compliance and administration of an Information Technology based platform(FINnet) providing end-to-end solution for filing, analysis and dissemination of information, including making request and submission of feedback.

44. d
- National Company Law Tribunal (NCLT) has been constituted under Section 408 in 2016. These bodies have been constituted for faster resolution of corporate disputes and reducing the multiplicity of agencies thereby promoting 'ease of doing business' in the country.
- The Competition Commission of India (CCI) was established in 2003 under the Competition Act, 2002, with the objective of eliminating practices having an adverse effect on competition, promoting and sustaining competition, protecting the interest of consumers and ensuring freedom of trade in India.
- The Serious Fraud Investigation Office (SFIO) was set up in 2003. The Companies Act, 2013, interalia, has accorded statutory status to SFIO and its functions and powers have been enhanced substantially with number of enabling provisions in the Act and it was established under Section 211 of the Companies Act, 2013.

- The Companies Act provides for establishment of Investor Education and Protection Fund (IEPF) for promoting Investor Awareness and protecting their interests. Section 125 of Companies Act, 2013 allows refund of unpaid amounts transferred to IEPF. Such refunds are to be made by the Investor Education and Protection Fund Authority under Section 125 of the Act. **Hence option (d) is correct.**

45. c
- **Both the statements are correct:** The constitution of National Company Law Tribunal (NCLT) and National Company Law Appellate Tribunal (NCLAT) was done in 2016. These bodies have been constituted for faster resolution of corporate disputes and reducing the multiplicity of agencies thereby promoting 'ease of doing business' in the country.
- With the constitution of National Company Law Tribunal (NCLT), the Company Law Board (CLB) stands dissolved and cases pending with CLB were transferred to NCLT.
- The Competition Appellate Tribunal under the provisions of Competition Act was dissolved in 2017 and merged with NCLAT. The appeal against the orders of Competition Commission of India is now with NCLAT.
- The tribunal also hears appeals from orders issued by the Insolvency and Bankruptcy Board of India under Section 202 and Section 211 of IBC. It also hears appeals from any direction issued, decision made, or order passed by the Competition Commission of India (CCI).

46. a
- **The first statement is correct:** International Grains Council (IGC) is an inter-governmental forum of exporting and importing countries for cooperation in wheat and coarse grain matters which was previously known as International Wheat Council upto 1995. It administers the Grains Trade Convention, 1995.
- **The second statement is incorrect:** India is a signatory to the International Grains Agreement (IGA), 1995 and its Grain Trade Convention (GTC), 1995 which is effective from 1995. IGC has two types of members— importing and exporting members. India has been included in the category of exporting member in July, 2003 and represented in the meetings/sessions of the Council held from time to time.

- **The third statement is incorrect:** The IGC Secretariat, based in London since 1949, also services the Food Aid Committee, established under the Food Aid Convention. International Grains Agreement comprises Grains Trade Convention (GTC) and Food Aid Convention (FAC).

47. a

- **The first statement is correct:** A dedicated investors's portal called 'Nivesh Bandhu' was launched in 2017 to aid and assist potential investors in the food processing sector in taking informed decision. This portal is a 'one stop information source' on central and state government policies, incentives offered, AgriResources and infrastructure facilities across the country.
- An investor friendly Mobile APP- 'Nivesh Bandhu' was developed and launched to enable the investor to have access to relevant information very conveniently and from any destination from their mobile proving to be game changers for the investors in taking informed investment decisions.
- **The second statement is incorrect:** Cent per cent FDI is permitted under the automatic route in food processing industries- manufacturing sector. FDI is allowed through approval route for trading, including through e-commerce in respect of food products manufactured and/or produced in India.

48. b

- **The first statement is incorrect:** For the growth and development of warehousing sector, to bring reforms in the agricultural marketing and to increase credit flow in the farm sector, the government introduced a negotiable warehouse receipt system in the country by enacting the Warehousing (Development and Regulation) Act, 2007 which is in place since 2010.
- The government constituted the *Warehousing Development and Regulatory Authority (WDRA) in 2010* for implementation of the provisions of the Act.
- **The second statement is correct:** The Negotiable Warehouse Receipts (NWRs) issued against stocks of farm produces deposited by the farmers in warehouses would help the farmers in seeking loan from banks.
- It would help overcoming the situation of distress sale of agricultural commodities by the farmers during peak harvest season. Warehouses need to be registered with the WDRA for issuing NWRs.
- The warehouses are inspected by the empanelled inspection agencies prior to grant of registration to ensure that basic requirements of scientific and safe storage of agricultural and other commodities are fully met by the warehouses.

49. b

- **The first statement is incorrect:** Government of India approved a new central sector scheme - Kisan Sampada Yojana - (Scheme for Agro-Marine Processing and Development of Agro-Processing Clusters) in 2017 with an outlay of Rs. 6,000 crore.
- **The second statement is correct:** The implementation period is coterminous with the 14th Finance Commission cycle.
- It is a comprehensive package which will result in creation of modern infrastructure with efficient supply chain management from farm gate to retail outlet. It will not only provide a big boost to the growth of food processing sector in the country but also help in providing better prices to farmers and is considered a big step towards doubling of farmers income, creating huge employment opportunities especially in the rural areas, reducing wastage of agricultural produce, increasing the processing level and enhancing the export of the processed foods.

50. b

- **The first statement is incorrect:** Mera Aspataal (My Hospital) application is an IT based feedback system to collect information on patients' level of satisfaction using a multi-channel approach viz. short message service (SMS), outbound dialing (OBD), web portal, and mobile application.
- **The second statement is correct:** The application automatically contacts the patient (outpatient after the closure of the OPD and the inpatient at the time of discharge) using the above tools to collect information on patients' level of satisfaction.

51. b

- **The first statement is incorrect:** SUGAM enables online submission of applications, their tracking, processing & grant of approvals online mainly for drugs, clinical trials, ethics committee, medical devices, vaccines and cosmetics. Provides a single window for

- multiple stakeholders (Pharma Industry, Regulators, Citizens) involved in the processes of CDSCO.

- Drugs and Vaccine Distribution Management System (DVDMS) (eAushidhi) deals with purchase, inventory management and distribution of various drugs, sutures and surgical items to various district drug warehouse of state/UT, district hospitals, their sub-stores, etc., by automating the workflow of procurement, supply chain, quality control and finance department in state/UT level.

- **The second statement is correct:** It is implemented by the Central Drugs Standards Control Organisation (CDSCO).

52. d
- **Both the statements are incorrect:** The programme aims to provide assured, comprehensive and *quality antenatal care*, free of cost, universally to all pregnant women on the 9th of every month.

- PMSMA guarantees a minimum package of antenatal care services to women in their *2nd/ 3rd trimesters of pregnancy* at designated government health facilities.

- The programme follows a systematic approach for engagement with private sector which includes motivating private practitioners to volunteer for the campaign; developing strategies for generating awareness and appealing to the private sector to participate in the Abhiyan at government health facilities

53. b
- National AIDS Control Programme is a 100 per cent central sector scheme. More than 10 lakh people living with HIV are on ART; one lakh additional patients brought under the ambit of Anti Retro Viral (ARV) treatment in line with 'Test and Treat' Policy launched for covering all patients with ART cover irrespective of CD count or clinical stage.

- The goal of Revised National Tuberculosis Control Programme (RNTCP) is to decrease mortality and morbidity due to TB and cut transmission of infection until TB ceases to be a major public health problem in India. Under Revised National Tuberculosis Control Programme (RNTCP), the government provides support to the state /UT governments for human resource, drugs, diagnostics and consumables.

- National Leprosy Eradication Programme: Its objective is to reduce leprosy burden in the country by providing quality leprosy services through general health care - to achieve elimination of leprosy as a public health problem in all states and districts i.e., reduce annual new case detection Ratio to < 1 per 100,000 populations at national level.

- National Mental Health Programme (NMHP) is being implemented to improve coverage and accessibility of mental health care in the country. Under it there is provision of regular psychiatric OPD and IPD services at district hospital, free supply of psychotropic drugs, ambulatory support for psychiatric patients, awareness generation .

54. a
- **The first statement is correct:** The Central Council of Indian Medicine is a statutory body constituted under the Indian Medicine Central Council Act, 1970. The main objectives of the Central Council include: (i) to prescribe the minimum standards of education in *Indian Systems of Medicine viz., Ayurveda, Siddha, Unani Tib and Sowa Rigpa.*; (ii) to advise central government in matters relating to recognition (inclusion/withdrawal) of medical qualification in/from Second Schedule to Indian Medicine Central Council Act, 1970.; (iii) to maintain a Central Register of Indian Medicine and revise the Register from time to time.; and (iv) to prescribe standards of professional conduct, etiquette and code of ethics to be observed by the practitioners.

- **The second statement is incorrect:** The Central Council of Indian Medicine has prescribed Regulations for Under-graduate and Post-graduate courses of Ayurveda, Siddha, Unani Tib and Sowa Rigpa considering that after completion of education, they would become profound scholars having deep basis of Ayurveda, Siddha, Unani and Sowa Rigpa with scientific knowledge in the fundamentals respective systems.

- *Central Council of Homoeopathy* has been constituted by the central government under the provisions of the Homoeopathy Central Council Act, 1973 for the maintenance of a Central Register of Homoeopathy and for other matters connected therewith.

- Besides the maintenance of the Central Register, Homoeopathy Central Council Act, 1973 (as amended) empowers the Central Council *to prescribe minimum standards of education in Homoeopathy to be followed by universities and medical institutions.*

55. a
- **The first statement is correct:** The ISA is the first UN-affiliated inter-governmental organization to be headquartered in India.

- The **International Solar Alliance (ISA)** is an alliance of more than 122 countries initiated by India, most of them being **sunshine countries**, which lie either completely or partly between the Tropic of Cancer and the Tropic of Capricorn, now extended to all members of UN.

- **The second statement is incorrect:** The General Assembly of the International Solar Alliance (ISA) was inaugurated in Delhi, along with the *2nd IORA Renewable Energy Ministerial Meeting and 2nd Global Re-invest Meet.*

56. d
- India was elected to the UN Human Rights Council (HRC) for the term 2019-2021, securing the highest number of votes (188 out of 193) among all the 18 candidate countries.

- India was re-elected to the Committee on Non-Governmental Organisations (CNGO) for the term 2019-2022.

- **India was also elected to five UN Bodies:** Commission on Crime Prevention and Criminal Justice (CCPCJ) for the term 2019-21; Executive Board of UNDP/UNFPA/UNOPS for the term 2019-2021; UN-Women (Executive Board of UN-WOMEN) for the term 2019-2021; CPD (Commission on Population and Development) from 2018 to 2021; and CSoCD (Commission for Social Development) from 2018 to 2021.

- India was re-elected as a member of the International Telecommunications Union Council (ITU) for 2019-2022 term.

57. a
- **The first statement is correct:** States Division, established in 2014, to foster closer links between Indian missions and posts abroad and states/union territories.

- The Division successfully endeavoured in promoting external outreach of states through provisional and regional cooperation in the domain of bilateral relations. It facilitates the signing of various Sister City/Sister States and other MoUs between state/union territory governments and foreign entities.

- **The second statement is incorrect:** It was created under the Ministry of External Affairs. In order to enhance external outreach of states/union territories, it represented MEA at various events in the states, including global investor meets and significant cultural events of states that generate significant international exposure for the states of India. This Division rendered assistance to foreigners in distress and eliminate any negative fallout from these events abroad.

58. c
- **Both the statements are correct:** Invest India has been set up as a joint venture (not for profit) company between Department of Industrial Policy and Promotion, Federation of Indian Chambers of Commerce & Industry (FICCI), CII, NASSCOM and various state governments.

- Invest India is the National Investment Promotion and Facilitation Agency of India and acts as the first point of reference for investors. It is transforming the country's investment climate by simplifying the business environment for investors.

- Its experts, specializing across different countries, states and sectors, handhold investors through their investment lifecycle – from pre-investment to after-care.

- This venture provides multiple forms of support such as market entry strategies, deep dive industry analysis, partner search and location assessment policy advocacy with decision makers.

59. a
- **The first statement is correct:** The powerloom sector is predominantly an unorganised sector and has many micro and small units - with 24.86 lakh powerlooms producing 57 percent of the total cloth in the country.

- With a view to enhance quality and productivity of the powerloom, the Government launched IN SITU upgradation of plain powerlooms as part of PowerTex India under which plain powerlooms are attached with process control equipment leading to higher productivity, better quality and more than 50 per cent additional value realisation.

- **The second statement is incorrect:** e-Dhaga App: Govt of India launched Enterprise Resource Planning System (ERP) and e-Dhaga mobile App in 2016 to bring efficiency in service delivery to the handloom weavers and help them to access information on 24x7 basis.

- The App is available in 10 languages-Hindi, English, Assamese, Odiya, Kannada, Tamil, Telugu, Malayalam, Urdu and Bangla.

60. c
- **Both the statements are correct:** The Public Procurement (Preference to Make in India) Order 2017 (PPP-MII Order) was issued in 2017 pursuant to Rule 153 (iii) of the General Financial Rules 2017 as an enabling provision to promote domestic value addition in public procurement.

- This Order is applicable for procurement of goods , services and works (including turnkey works) by a central ministry/department, their attached/subordinate offices, autonomous bodies controlled by the Government of India and government companies as defined in the Companies Act.

- Under the PPP-MII Order, a Standing Committee, DPIIT has been constituted to review the implementation of order. A Public Procurement Cell has been created in the Department to monitor the grievances received for violation of PPPMII Order.

- 19 nodal departments have been designated for notifying minimum local content for the relevant product categories.

61. d
- **All the pairs are correctly matched:** National Security Guard (NSG) was conceptualised and created after studying and analysing Special Force like SAS in the United Kingdom, GIGN in France, GSG-9 in Germany, Shar-et-matkal in Israel and Delta Force in the USA. Accordingly, NSG was raised in October, 1985 as a Federal Contingency Force under the MHA.

- It consists of selected and highly motivated personnel from the army as well as the central armed police. 53 per cent of the personnel are drawn from the army while the central armed police like BSF, CRPF and ITBP contribute 47 per cent.

- The personnel in RAF are trained and equipped to be an effective strike Force in communal riots and similar situations. These Battalions are located at 10 communally sensitive locations across the country to facilitate quick response in case of any such incident. All these Battalions are organized on an unattached pattern and are working under the supervision of an Inspector General.

- Raised in 1969, Central Industrial Security Force (CISF) is providing security cover to 303 units including 59 domestic and international airports and fire protection cover to 87 industrial undertakings.

- In order to effectively tackle the Maoists, the need for a Special Force, capable of striking at the core of naxal heartland was felt. With this idea, ten CoBRA (Commando Battalion for Resolute Action) battalions were raised between 2008 and 2011.

- The selected personnel are put through specialized training regimen to prepare physically and mentally to survive the rigours of the treacherous and inhospitable terrains and fight the guerillas like the guerillas. Out of the ten CoBRA battalions, nine are deployed in LWE (Left Wing Extremism, i.e. Maoists infested areas) and one in Assam.

62. d
- **Both the statements are incorrect:** In partnership with the United Nations Development Programme (UNDP), the Department of Justice (DoJ), Ministry of Law and Justice, is implementing a decade long programme on Access to Justice for Marginalised People (2008- 2017).

- The project extends to the eight UNDAF states of Bihar, Chattisgarh, Jharkhand, Madhya Pradesh, Rajasthan, Uttar Pradesh, Maharashtra and Odisha.

- This project focuses on strengthening access to justice for the marginalised people by developing strategies that address barriers to accessing justice in legal, social and economic domains. The project is presently in the second phase of implementation.

63. a
- **The first statement is correct:** The e-Courts Integrated Mission Mode Project is one of the e-Governance projects being implemented in High Courts and district/subordinate courts of the country.

- **The second statement is incorrect:** The project has been conceptualized on the basis of the "National Policy and Action Plan for Implementation of Information and Communication Technology in the Indian Judiciary-2005" by the e-Committee of the Supreme Court of India. The *e-Committee was formed in 2004* to draw up an action plan for the ICT enablement of the Judiciary with the

Patron in Chief-cum-Adhoc Chairman as the Chief Justice of India.

- *National Mission for Justice Delivery and Legal Reforms, on the other hand, was set up in 2011 with the twin objectives of increasing access by reducing delays and arrears in the system and enhancing accountability through structural changes and by setting performance standards and capacities.*

64. b
- **The first statement is incorrect:** United News of India (UNI) was incorporated under the Companies Act, 1956 in December, 1959 and started functioning effectively from 1961.

- In the past five decades, UNI has grown into a major news organisation in India and, with its vibrant presence, provided the much-needed spirit of competition in the vital areas of news gathering and dissemination.

- **The second statement is correct:** It also has a full-fledged Hindi wire service 'UNIVARTA' since 1982 and a Photo Service and a Graphics Service in the same decade. In June 1992, it launched the first ever wire service in Urdu. UNI's Photo Service distributes about 200 pictures every day, including sixty international photographs from EPA, the European Pressphoto Agency and Reuters. Its Graphics Service distributes five or six graphics every day.

65. d
- Govenment of India introduced a pension scheme for unorganised workers under Pradhan Mantri Shram Yogi Maan-dhan (PM-SYM) to ensure old age protection for unorganised workers. Enrollment under the scheme has started since February, 2019.

- **The first statement is correct:** The unorganised workers mostly engaged as home based workers, street vendors, mid-day meal workers, head loaders, brick kiln workers, cobblers, rag pickers, domestic workers, washermen, rickshaw pullers, landless labourers, own account workers, agricultural workers, construction workers, beedi workers, handloom workers, leather workers, audio-visual workers and those engaged in similar other occupations, whose monthly income is [1] 15,000/ per month or less are eligible to enroll under PY-SYM subject to these conditions:

- These should belong to the entry age group of 18-40 years; should not be covered under New Pennsion Scheme (NPS); Employees' State Insurance Corporation (ESIC) scheme or Employees' Provident Fund Organisation (EPFO); should not be an income tax payee.

- **The second statement is correct:** PM-SYM is a voluntary and contributory pension scheme on a 50:50 basis

- **The third statement is incorrect:** Age-specific contribution is made by the beneficiary and the matching contribution by the central government as per the scheme guidelines. The subscriber's contributions to PM-SYM is through 'auto-debit' facility from his/ her savings bank account/Jan- Dhan account and it ranges from Rs. 55 /- to Rs. 200/- per month depending at the entry age of the subscriber.

- **The fourth statement is correct:** The Scheme is being implemented through LIC and Common Services Centres-SPV. LIC is the Pension Fund Manager and responsible for Pension pay out, CSC-SPV is responsible for enrolling the beneficiaries through its approx. 3 lakh CSCs across the country. Under the scheme, contribution amount for the first month is being paid in cash.

66. c
- **Both the statements are correct:** In pursuance of National Child Labour Policy, the National Child Labour Project (NCLP) Scheme was started in 1988 to rehabilitate children rescued from child labour. It is an ongoing Central Sector Scheme and at present sanctioned in 270 districts in the country.

- Under the Scheme, working children are identified through child labour survey, withdrawn from work and put into the special training centres so as to provide them with an environment to subsequently join mainstream education system.

- With the enactment of Right to Education (RTE) Act, 2009, there was a need for realignment of the NCLP Scheme with the provisions of RTE Act, 2009.

- The NCLP Schools could now serve as special training centres for un-enrolled and out of school children in accordance with the provisions of Section 4 of the RTE Act and Rule 5 of the Right of Children for free and compulsory education (RTE) Rules, 2010.

67. d
- **All the pairs are correctly matched:** The Prime Minister's Shram Awards are given to the workers employed in department/public sector

undertakings of the Central and state governments and the manufacturing units employing 500 or more workers in the private sector in recognition of their performance, devotion to duty, etc.

- The Vishwakarma Rashtriya Puraskars (VRPs) are given to individual workers or group of workers for their outstanding suggestions leading to improvement in productivity, safety and health as well as the import substitution resulting in the savings of foreign currency.

- The National Safety Awards (NSAs) are given in recognition of good safety performance on the part of the industrial establishments covered under the Factories Act, 1948, the employers covered under the Dock Workers (Safety, Health and Welfare) Act, 1986 and Building and other Construction Workers (Regulation of Employment and Conditions of Service) Act, 1996.

- The National Safety Award (Mines) are given at the national level in recognition of outstanding safety performance in mines covered under the Mines Act, 1952.

68. c
- **Both the statements are correct:** India's largest news agency, Press Trust of India (PTI) is a non-profit sharing cooperative owned by the country's newspapers with a mandate to provide efficient and unbiased news to all subscribers.

- Founded in August, 1947, PTI began functioning from 1949. It offers its news services in English and Hindi languages. Bhasha is the Hindi language news service of the agency. PTI subscribers include 500 newspapers in India and scores abroad.

- All major TV and radio channels in India and several abroad, including BBC in London, receive its services. PTI now has its own satellite delivery system through a transponder on an INSAT satellite for reaching its services directly to subscribers anywhere in the country. Increasingly more and more subscribers are opting for satellite reception. Photo service is delivered by satellite as well as accessed by dial up.

69. a
- **The first statement is correct:** The National Skill Development Mission was launched in 2015 on the occasion of World Youth Skills Day. It aims to create convergence and expedite cross-sectoral decisions through a high-powered decision-making framework.

- It is expected to converge, coordinate, implement and monitor skilling activities on a pan-India basis. The Mission aims to create convergence and expedite cross-sectoral decisions through a high-powered decision-making framework.

- At the outset, seven sub-missions have been proposed in the following areas: (i) Institutional Training, (ii) Infrastructure, (iii) Convergence, (iv) Trainers, (v) Overseas Employment, (vi) Sustainable Livelihoods, (vii) Leveraging Public Infrastructure.

- **The second statement is incorrect:** The first National Policy on Skill Development (NPSD) was notified in 2009. The 2009 policy itself provided for review every five years to align the policy framework with the emerging trends in the national and international milieu. Accordingly, the new National Policy on Skill Development and Entrepreneurship was notified 2015 which replaces the policy of 2009.

70. c
- **The first statement is correct:** The situation created by the Indo-Pakistan conflict in 1965, two successive years of severe drought, devaluation of the currency, general rise in prices and erosion of resources available for Plan purposes delayed the finalization of the Fourth Five Year Plan. Instead, between 1966 and 1969, three Annual Plans were formulated within the framework of the draft outline of the Fourth Plan.

- **The second statement is incorrect:** It was during *the Seventh Five Year Plan* when to reduce unemployment and consequently, the incidence of poverty, special programmes like Jawahar Rozgar Yojana were launched in addition to the existing programmes.

- **The third statement is correct:** The Ninth Plan (1997-2002) was launched in the fiftieth year of India's Independence. The Plan aimed at achieving a targeted GDP growth rate of seven per cent per annum and there was emphasis on the seven identified Basic Minimum Services (BMS) with additional Central Assistance earmarked for these services with a view to obtaining a complete coverage of the population in a time-bound manner.

- **The fourth statement is correct:** The Tenth Plan had a number of new features that include the recognition for the rapid growth in the labour force. At current rate of growth and labour intensity in production, India faces the possibility of rising unemployment, which could lead to social unrest. The Tenth Plan therefore aims at creating 50 million job opportunities during the period, by placing special emphasis on employment intensive sectors of agriculture, irrigation, agro-forestry, small and medium enterprises, information and communication technology and other services.

71. d
- The Atal Innovation Mission (AIM) is a flagship initiative of the Central Government, set up by NITI Aayog to promote innovation and entrepreneurship across the length and breadth of the country. AIM is also envisaged as an umbrella innovation organization that would play an instrumental role in alignment of innovation policies between central, state and sectoral innovation schemes incentivizing establishment of an ecosystem of innovation and entrepreneurship at various levels higher secondary schools, science, engineering and higher academic institutions, and SME industry / corporate levels. AIM is setting up Atal Tinkering Labs (ATL) in schools across all 700+ districts across the country.
- The Mentor India programme launched by AIM is a path-breaking initiative to catalyse the academia– industry partnerships. Under it, more than 3,200 mentors from all over the country belonging to various industry sectors have been assigned to work with 1800+ ATLs on a continuous basis.
- Atal Incubation Centres (AICs) and Established Incubation Centres are incubation spaces intended to provide incubation facilities to innovative start-ups like capital equipment and operating facilities along with sectoral experts.
- Atal New India Challenge (ANIC), which is an initiative by Atal Innovation Mission aimed at supporting innovators to create products/ solutions based on advanced technologies in areas of national importance and social relevance through a grant-based mechanism.

72. b
- **The first statement is incorrect:** Deen Dayal Upadhyaya Grameen Kaushalya Yojana (DDU-GKY) is the flagship placement linked skill-training programme under the *Ministry of Rural Development (MoRD).*
- Announced in 2014, DDU-GKY is a critical component of the National Skill Development Policy, and has an ambitious agenda, to benchmark wage placement-linked skill programmes to global standards and requirements.
- **The second statement is correct:** The scheme is a pioneer in standards-led delivery of skilling, the first to notify standard operating procedures for training, and the first to introduce IT solutions for skilling, including mandatory tablets for trainees, Aadhar-linked biometric information on attendance, and geo-tagged time-stamped record of training centres and classes.
- DDU-GKY has its roots in the Swarnjayanti Gram Swarozgar Yojana (SGSY). SGSY was formed by the restructuring of the Integrated Rural Development Programme (IRDP) in 1999, with a 15 per cent allocation for special projects.

73. c
- **Both the statements are correct:** The Constitution of India also stipulates direct elections of all members of panchayats. For conducting these elections, all states are mandated to constitute a State Election Commission.
- Also, it is compulsory for states to constitute a State Election Commission. Also, it is compulsory for states to constitute a State Finance Commission (SFC) every fifth year for recommending principles for division of financial resources between state and local governments (both urban and rural).
- SFCs are to make re commendations to the Governor regarding the distribution between the state and panchayats of the net proceeds to taxes, duties, toll and fees, etc. the determination of taxes, duties, tolls and fees which may be assigned to, or appropriated by, the panchayats, and grants-in-aid to the panchayats from the Consolidated Fund of the State, as well as measures needed to improve the financial position of panchayats.

74. d
- **All statements are correct:** National Rural Livelihoods Mission renamed as Deendayal Antyodaya Yojana—National Rural Livelihoods Mission (DAY-NRLM) was launched in 2011. It seeks to reach out to 8-9 crore rural poor households and organize one-woman member from each household into affinity based women SHGs and federations at village level and at higher levels.

- Infrastructure Creation and Marketing Support: DAY-NRLM ensures that infrastructure needs for major livelihoods activities of poor are met with. It also provides support for marketing to institutions of poor. The range of activities in marketing support include market research, market intelligence, technology extension, developing backward and forward linkages, building livelihoods collectives and supporting their business plans.

- Sensitive Support Structures: DAY-NRLM has set up sensitive and dedicated support structures at the national, state, district and sub-district levels. These support structures are staffed with dedicated professionals

- Mahila Kisan Sashaktikaran Pariyojana (MKSP): MKSP is a sub-component of NRLM to meet the specific needs of women farmers and achieve socio-economic and technical empowerment of the rural women farmers, predominantly small and marginal farmers.

- Aajeevika Grameen Express Yojana: The Government of India has introduced a new sub-scheme under Deendayal Antyodaya Yojana-National Rural Livelihoods Mission (DAY-NRLM) entitled "Aajeevika Grameen Express Yojana" (AGEY) from the financial year 2017-18. The main objectives of AGEY are: to provide an alternative source of livelihoods to members of SHGs under DAY-NRLM by facilitating them to operate public transport services in backward rural areas.

75. a
- **The first statement is correct:** Ganga Gram is another inter-ministry project between SBM and the Namami Gange Programme. The Project is focused on better cleanliness and infrastructure facilities, through convergence with other departments.

- **The second statement is incorrect:** Ministry of Jal Shakti which is responsible for sanitation in villages on the banks of river Ganga, is also coordinating the Ganga Gram Project. Ganga Gram Project was unveiled in 2017 at a grand sammelan of sarpanches where all 4,475 Ganga Grams were declared Open Defecation Free (ODF).

- Later, state governments identified 24 Ganga villages to be taken up as pilot project to transform them into Ganga Grams which encompasses Open Defecation Free (ODF),

renovation of ponds and water sources, promotion of sprinkler irrigation, promotion of tourism, modern crematorium infrastructure, convergence of central and state schemes.

76. b
- **The first statement is incorrect:** Innovation in science pursuit for inspired research (INSPIRE) is an ongoing initiative for attracting talent for science and research.

- About 3.67 lakh students in the age group of 10-15 have been provided INSPIRE awards during the last 3 years.

- **The second statement is correct:** Science camps are organised to provide opportunity to class XI students pursuing science to interact with the science icons from India and abroad including Nobel Laureates to experience the joy of innovations. Around 40,000 students have been awarded scholarship for higher education during last three years.

- INSPIRE faculty awards are provided to post-doctoral researchers in the age group of 27-32 years through contractual and tenure positions for 5 years in basic and applied sciences. Faculty awards have been given to over 700 candidates awarded in the last four years.

77. d
- **The first statement is correct:** Survey of India (SOI), the national survey and mapping organisation under the Ministry of Science and Technology, was set up in 1767. In its assigned role as the National Principal Mapping Agency, Survey of India bears a special responsibility to ensure that the country's domain is explored and mapped suitably to provide base maps for expeditious and integrated development and ensure that all resources contribute their full measure to the progress, prosperity and security of the country.

- **The second statement is correct:** The Survey of India also provides support to other countries e.g., Nigeria, Afghanistan, Kenya, Iraq, Nepal, Sri Lanka, Zimbabwe, Indonesia, Bhutan, Mauritius, etc., in the field of mapping, survey education, transfer of technology, and various other surveying technologies under bilateral arrangements. Under UN mandate, Survey of India also provides support to countries in Asia-Pacific region for capacity building in spatial data infrastructures.

- **The third statement is incorrect:** While Survey of India meets the national needs in cartography, some specialised thematic maps required to meet the needs of the specific users are taken care of by the National Atlas and Thematic Mapping Organisation (NATMO) operating under the Department.

- It also concentrates in a number of areas to integrate resource maps with other relevant socio-economic data and represent them in spatial forms, useful for developmental planning.

78. c • **Both the statements are correct:** Fast Breeder Reactors: For the second stage of the Nuclear Power Generation Programme, the Indira Gandhi Centre for Atomic Research (IGCAR) is pursuing development of sodium cooled fast breeder reactors and associated fuel cycle technologies. Breeder reactors produce more fuel than they consume.

- The fast reactor programme of IGCAR is supported by its research and development endeavour in a range of disciplines such as reactor engineering, metallurgy, materials science, instrumentation, safety, etc. The Fast Breeder Test Reactor (FBTR), operating at Kalpakkam for over 25 years, also caters to technology development related to fast reactors.

- Thorium Based Reactors: Nuclear power employing closed fuel cycle is the only sustainable option for meeting a major part of the world energy demand.

- World resources of thorium are larger than those of uranium. Thorium, therefore, is, widely viewed as the 'fuel of the future'.

- The Indian Nuclear Power Programme Stage-3 aims at using thorium as fuel for power generation on a commercial scale. In the thorium fuel cycle, thorium 232 is transmuted into the fissile isotope uranium 233 which is a nuclear fuel.

79. b • **The first statement is incorrect:** The Earth System Science Organization (ESSO) operates as an executive arm of the MoES for its policies and programmes. It provides overall direction for the centres/units and reviews the implementation of the programmes.

- The ESSO was established in 2007 as a virtual organization, bringing all meteorological and ocean development activities under one umbrella, recognizing the importance of strong coupling among various components of the earth viz., atmosphere, oceans, cryo-sphere and geo-sphere.

- It has four major branches of earth sciences, viz.: (i) ocean science and technology (ii) atmospheric and climate science (iii) geo-science and technology and (iv) polar science and cryo-sphere.

- **The second statement is also correct:** ESSO functions through its following centres: Centre for Marine Living Resources and Ecology (CMLRE); National Centre of Coastal Research (NCCR); National Centre for Seismology (NCS); National Centre for Medium Range Weather Forecasting (NCMRWF); India Meteorological Department (IMD); National Institute of Ocean Technology (NIOT); Indian National Centre for Ocean Information Services (INCOIS); National Centre for Polar and Ocean Research (NCPOR); Indian Institute of Tropical Meteorology (IITM); and National Centre for Earth Science Studies(NCESS).

80. d • **Both the statements are incorrect:** National Centre for Antarctic and Ocean Research (NCAOR), Goa established a high altitude research station in Himalaya called Himansh (literally meaning, a slice of ice), situated above 13,500 ft (>4000 m) at a remote region in Spiti Himachal Pradesh.

- This station is equipped with instruments such as, automatic station, water level recorder, steam drill, snow ice corer, ground penetrating radar, differential global positioning system, snow fork, flow tracker, thermister string, radiometer, etc.

- Water level recorders were installed at five locations along the stretch of 130 km of Chandra river in western Himalaya for hydrological balance/modeling. Glaciers were monitored for mass balance, dynamics, energy balance and hydrology.

81. a • **The first statement is correct:** The Bharatmala Pariyojana envisages development of about 26,000 km length of economic corridors, which along with Golden Quadrilateral (GQ) and North-South and East-West (NS-EW) Corridors are expected to carry majority of the freight traffic on roads.

- Further, about 8,000 km of inter corridors and about 7,500 km of feeder routes have been identified for improving effectiveness of economic corridors, GQ and NS-EW Corridors. The programme envisages development of Ring Roads / bypasses and elevated corridors to decongest the traffic passing through cities.

- **The second statement is correct:** The principle of shortest distance has been followed in identification and determination of green-field alignments for connecting important economic centres to reduce the overall costs as compared to upgradation of the brown-field/existing alignments, as the shorter green-field alignments enable significant reduction both in capital cost and vehicle operating cost over time.

- **The third statement is incorrect:** It is the Setu Bharatam scheme that envisages replacement of level crossing on national highways by Road Over Bridges (ROBs)/Road Under Bridges (RUBs).

82. b - **The first statement is incorrect:** The National Dope Testing Laboratory (NDTL) is an autonomous body under the Ministry. It is accredited by National Accreditation Board for Testing and Calibration Laboratories (NABL) and World Anti- Doping Agency (WADA) (September, 2008) for testing of urine and blood samples from human sports.

- National Anti Doping Agency (NADA), set up in 2009, is the national organization responsible for promoting, coordinating, and monitoring the doping control programme in sports in the country. The Anti Doping rules of NADA are compliant with the Anti Doping Code of WADA.

- **The second statement is correct:** NDTL is one of the 33 WADA accredited laboratories in the world and one among seven in Asia. It has state-of-the-art facilities for both routine and research activities. NDTL was registered in 2008 under Registration of Society Act, 1860. Apart from human dope testing, NDTL has diversified in the area of horse dope testing and proficiency testing programme.

83. a - **The first statement is correct:** The Tribal Cooperative Marketing Development Federation of India Limited (TRIFED), was set up in 1987 as a national level apex body under the Multi State Cooperative Societies Act, 1984 (MSCS Act, 1984)

- After the enactment of the Multi-State Cooperative Societies Act, 2002 (MSCS Act, 2002) TRIFED is deemed to be registered under the latter Act and is also listed in the Second Schedule to the Act as a National Cooperative Society.

- **The second statement is incorrect:** The bye-laws of TRIFED were revised in April, 2003 in tune with the new Multi State Cooperative Societies Act, 2002 read with the Multi State Cooperative Societies Rules, 2002.

- Under its revised mandate TRIFED has *stopped bulk procurement in Minor Forest Produce (MFP) and surplus Agricultural Produce (SAP)* from tribals. TRIFED now functions as a 'market developer' for tribal products and as 'service provider' to its member federations.

84. d - CWC is charged with the general responsibility of initiating, coordinating and furthering in consultation with the state governments concerned, schemes for control, conservation and utilization of water resources in the respective state for the purpose of flood management, irrigation, drinking water supply and water power generation. The Commission, if so required, can undertake the construction and execution of any such scheme.

- Central Water Commission is operating a network of 878 hydro-meteorological observation stations throughout the country on all major river basins to observe (i) water level (gauge), (ii) discharge, (iii) water quality, (iv) silt (v) selected meteorological parameters including snow observations at key stations.

- Central Water Commission is monitoring water quality at 429 key locations covering all the major river basins of India. It is maintaining a three tier laboratory system for analysis of the physio-chemical parameters of the water.

- CWC has been making continuous endeavour for modernization and expansion of its flood forecasting network in order to have desired automatic system of data collection and real time data transmission. So far, 510 data collection stations have been modernized, three earth receiving stations have been set up at New Delhi, Jaipur and Burla, 21 Modelling Centres have been equipped with latest computer systems for analysis of data, flood forecast formulation and its dissemination

85. c • **Both the statements are correct:** The Scheme provides financial assistance to scheduled caste students for pursuing research studies leading to M. Phil, Ph.D, and equivalent research degree in universities, research institutions and scientific institutions.

• University Grants Commission (UGC) is the nodal agency for implementing the Scheme. About 2000 Junior Research Fellowships (JRF) per year are awarded to scheduled caste students. Number of fellowships were increased from 1333 in 2010 to 2000 in 2011.

• In case of non-availability of adequate number of scheduled caste candidates, the number of fellowships not availed during a year will be carried forward to the next academic session.

• In case, the number of candidates exceeds the number of available awards, the UGC selects the candidates based on the percentage of marks obtained by the candidates in their post graduation examination. There is no income ceiling prescribed under the Scheme.

86. c • **Both the statements are correct:** The first specification of scheduled tribes in relation to a particular state/ union territory is by a notified order of the President, after consultation with the state governments concerned.

• The criteria generally adopted for specification of a community as a scheduled tribe are : (a) indications of primitive traits; (b)distinctive culture; (c) shyness of contact with the community at large; and (d) geographical isolation i.e., backwardness.

• These are not spelt out in the Constitution but have become well established. They take into account the definitions in the 1931 Census, the reports of the first Backward Classes Commission (Kalelkar Committee), 1955, the Advisory Committee on Revision of SC/ ST lists (Lokur Committee), 1965 and the Joint Committee of Parliament on the Scheduled Castes and Scheduled Tribes Orders (Amendment) Bill, 1967 (Chanda Committee), 1969.

• There are over 700 tribes (with many of them overlapping in more than one state) as notified under Article 342 of the Constitution of India, spread over different states and union territories of the country. It is worth noting that no community has been specified as a scheduled tribe in relation to the states of Haryana and Punjab and the union territories of Chandigarh, Delhi and Puducherry.

87. b • Naya Savera - Free Coaching and Allied Scheme. The "Free Coaching and Allied Scheme for the candidates belonging to miniority communities was launched in 2007 by this Ministry.

• Nai Udaan: The objective of the Scheme is to provide financial support to the minority candidates clearing prelims conducted by Union Public Service Commission, Staff Selection Commission and State Public Service Commissions.

• **Padho Pardes:** The objective of the Scheme is to award interest subsidy to meritorious students belonging to economically weaker sections of notified minority communities so as to provide them better opportunities for higher education abroad and enhance their employability. The interest subsidy under the Scheme shall be available to the eligible students only once, either for masters or Ph.D levels.

• **Nai Roshni:** This Ministry implements an exclusive scheme 'Nai Roshni' for leadership development of minority women with an aim to empower and instill confidence in them by providing knowledge, tools and techniques for interacting with government systems, banks and intermediaries at all levels. It is implemented through empanelled non-governmental organizations.

88. a • **The first statement is correct:** The Programme was restructured and renamed as Command Area Development and Water Management(CAD&WM) Programme in 2004. The programme is under implementation as a sub-component of Har Khet Ko Pani (HKKP) component of Pradhan Mantri Krishi Sinchai Yojana (PMKSY) - from 2015-16 onwards.

• **The second statement is incorrect:** The ongoing CADWM programme has been restricted to the implementation of CAD works of 99 prioritized AIBP projects from 2016-17 onwards.

• The activities covered under CAD component are broadly categorized as 'Structural' and 'Non-Structural' interventions.

• **Structural intervention:** includes survey, planning, design and execution of: (i) on-farm

Development (OFD) works; (ii) construction of field, intermediate and link drains; (iii) correction of system deficiencies; and (iv) reclamation of waterlogged areas.

- **Non-structural intervention:** includes activities directed at strengthening of Participatory Irrigation Management (PIM): (i) one time functional grant to the registered water users' associations (WUAs); (ii) one time Infrastructure Grant to the registered WUAs; (iii)trainings, demonstration, and adaptive trials with respect to water use efficiency, increased productivity, and sustainable irrigation participatory environment.

89. d
- **Both the statements are incorrect:** Gender Budgeting (GB) is a powerful tool for achieving gender mainstreaming so as to ensure that benefits of development reach women as much as men. It is not an accounting exercise alone but an ongoing process of keeping a gender perspective at various steps of budget planning, allocation, implementation, impact/outcome assessment, review and audit.

- To institutionalize such budgeting in the country, the setting up of Gender Budgeting Cells (GBCs) in all ministries/departments was mandated by the Ministry of Finance in 2007.

- The MWCD as the nodal agency for gender budgeting is undertaking several initiatives for taking it forward at the national and state levels.

- 57 central ministries and departments have set up GBCs which are expected to serve as a focal point for coordinating gender budgeting initiatives, both intra and inter-ministerial. 21 states and union territories have designated Gender Budgeting nodal centres.

90. b
- **The first statement is incorrect:** National Scheduled Tribes Finance and Development Corporation (NSTFDC) was set up in 2001 under the Ministry of Tribal Affairs. The NSTFDC has been granted license under Section 25 of the Companies Act (A Company not for profit). In order to achieve the mandate set for the NSTFDC, (for undertaking self-employment ventures/activities) financial assistance is extended by NSTFDC to the scheduled tribes, who are having annual family income upto double the poverty line. NSTFDC also provides financial assistance as grant for skill and entrepreneurial development of the target group.

- The financial assistance is channelized through government owned agencies nominated by the respective ministries/state governments and union territory administrations.

- **The second statement is correct:** NSTFDC also provides financial assistance for procurement and marketing minor forest produce so as to avoid the distress sale of produce/ products by the scheduled tribes.

91. b
- **The first statement is incorrect:** CWC and ISRO jointly developed Water Resources Information System (India-WRIS) in 2010. Subsequently, four versions of the website of India-WRIS have been launched.

- The version 4.1 was launched in 2015 and is available in public domain at 1:250000 scale. The information system contains several GIS layers on water resources projects, thematic layers like major water bodies, land use/land cover, wastelands, land degradation, etc., environmental layers as well as infrastructure and other administrative layers.

- The information system has all the basic map viewing and navigation capabilities like zoom, overview, bookmark, table of contents, etc.

- **The second statement is correct:** As per provision of Hydro-Meteorological Data Dissemination Policy 2013 (MoWR), all unclassified data of CWC G&D stations has been made available on this website.

92. a
- **The first statement is correct:** India is a founder member of Global Environment Facility (GEF). Set up in 1991, GEF is the designated multilateral funding mechanism of 183 countries to provide incremental finance for addressing global environmental benefits which are also identified national priorities.

- The GEF mandate is decided as per the guidance provided by the Conference of the parties of the multilateral environmental conventions namely Convention on Biological Diversity (CBD), United Nations Framework Convention on Climate Change (UNFCCC), United Nations Convention to Combat Desertification (UNCCD), Stockholm Convention on PoPs and Minamata Convention on Mercury.

- **The second statement is incorrect:** The GEF grants are available under five focal areas namely, biodiversity, climate change, land degradation, international waters and chemicals and waste.

93. d POSHAN Abhiyan or National Nutrition Mission is a Government of India's flagship programme to improve nutritional outcomes for children, pregnant women and lactating mothers. It was launched in 2018 which directs the attention of the country towards the problem of malnutrition and addresses it in a mission-mode. For its implementation, the four-point strategy/pillars of the mission are:

i. Inter-sectorla convergence for better service delivery

ii. Use of technology (ICT) for real-time growth monitoring and tracking of women and children

iii. Intensified health and nutrition services for the first 1,000 days

iv. Jan Andolan or people's movement

94. d The financial year 2019-20 at its closure saw severe disruption due to SARS-COV-2 related pandemic. Visualizing the gravity of the situation and the necessity for an early outcome to combat the pandemic, DST launched a funding initiative-Centre for Augmenting WAR with Covid-19 Health Crisis (CAWACH) in March 2020. The aim was to nationally scout and support the innovation and start-ups in the areas of diagnostics and drugs, disinfectants and sanitizers, ventilators and medical equipment, PPEs and informatics to address Covid-19 challenges by scaling up efforts at the national level.

95. d National Water Mission was set up as the National Action Plan on Climate Change (NAPCC). The main objective of the mission are –

a. Comprehensive water database in public domain and assessment of impact of climate change on water resources

b. Promotion of citizen and state action for water conservation, augmentation and preservation

c. Focused attention to vulnerable areas including over-exploited areas

d. Increasing water use efficiency by 20 %

e. Promotion of basin level integrated water resources management

96. c Gender Budgeting Tool is a powerful tool for achieving gender mainstreaming so as to ensure that benefits of development reach women as much as men. It is not an accounting exercise alone but an ongoing process of keeping a gender perspective at various steps of budget planning, allocation, implementation, impact/outcome assessment, review and audit. To institutionalise such budgeting in the country, the setting up of Gender Budgeting Cells in all ministries/departments was mandated by the Ministry of Finance.

97. b Agriculture and allied sectors support more than 60 per cent of population in the state. Rice is a major food crop and staple food contributing a large chunk of the foodgrain production. Other important crops are jowar, maize, ragi, small millets, pulses, castor, tobacco, cotton and sugarcane. As per the third advance estimates for the year 2019-20, the area and production of foodgrains gas increased over the previous years.

98. c Andhra Pradesh is well-known globally for variety of rocks and minerals and is called Ratna Garbha. Minerals form a major contributor to the economic growth of the state. Minerals like crude oil and natural gas, barytes, bauxite, copper ore, asbestos, manganese, mica, coal, limestone, black and color granites are found in the state.

99. a Assam is also known as a "Land of Red River and Blue Hills" is one of the most attractive and beautiful states of the country. The mighty river Brahmaputra flows through it, serving as a lifeline for its people settled on both sides of its banks.

100. c • **All the pairs are correctly matched:** The Indus, which is one of the great rivers of the world, rises near Mansarovar in Tibet and flows through India and thereafter through Pakistan and finally falls into the Arabian sea near Karachi. Its important tributaries flowing in Indian territory are the Sutlej (originating in Tibet), the Beas, the Ravi, the Chenab and the Jhelum.

• The Yamuna, the Ramganga, the Ghaghra, the Gandak, the Kosi, the Mahananda and the Sone are the important tributaries of the Ganga. Rivers Chambal and Betwa are the important sub-tributaries, which join the Yamuna before it meets the Ganga. The Padma and the Brahmaputra join at Bangladesh and continue to flow as the Padma or Ganga.

• The principal tributaries of Brahmaputra in India are the Subansiri, Jia Bhareli, Dhansiri, Puthimari, Pagladiya and the Manas. The Brahmaputra in Bangladesh fed by Teesta, etc. finally falls into the Ganga.

• The Barak river, the head stream of Meghna, rises in the hills in Manipur. The important tributaries of the river are Makku, Trang, Tuivai, Jiri, Sonai, Rukni, Katakhal, Dhaleswari, Langachini, Maduva and Jatinga. Barak continues in Bangladesh till the combined Ganga-Brahmaputra join it near Bhairab Bazar.

Printed by Libri Plureos GmbH in Hamburg,
Germany